AF855503

Microsoft Official Academic Course

# Microsoft Office 2013

Custom Edition

Columbia Southern University
Personal Computer Fundamentals
ITC 3001

Wiley Custom Learning Solutions

To order books or for customer service, please call 1(800)-CALL-WILEY (225-5945).

Printed in the United States of America.

ISBN 978-1-119-10222-9
Printed and bound by Strategic Content Imaging.

# CONTENTS

## Microsoft® Official Academic Course

# Microsoft Office: 2013 Edition

WILEY

| | |
|---|---|
| EDITOR | Bryan Gambrel |
| PUBLISHER | Don Fowley |
| DIRECTOR OF SALES | Mitchell Beaton |
| EXECUTIVE MARKETING MANAGER | Chris Ruel |
| ASSISTANT MARKETING MANAGER | Debbie Martin |
| MICROSOFT STRATEGIC RELATIONSHIPS MANAGER | Gene Longo of Microsoft Learning eXperience |
| EDITORIAL PROGRAM ASSISTANT | Allison Winkle |
| SENIOR CONTENT MANAGER | Kevin Holm |
| SENIOR PRODUCTION EDITOR | Jill Spikereit |
| CREATIVE DIRECTOR | Harry Nolan |
| COVER DESIGNER | Tom Nery |
| TECHNOLOGY AND MEDIA | Wendy Ashenberg; Jennifer Welter |
| WRITERS | Walter Holland; Jennifer Smith, Microsoft MVP |
| EDITOR | Christopher Smith |
| TECHNICAL EDITORS | Lauren Mickol; Cathy Auclair |
| PROJECT MANAGER | Cheri White |
| PRODUCTION | American Graphics Institute; Avlade |

This book was set in Adobe Garamond Pro and printed and bound by Courier/Kendallville. The covers were printed by Courier/Kendallville.



ISBN 978-0-470-13306-4

Printed in the United States of America

## Foreword from the Publisher

Wiley's publishing vision for the Microsoft Official Academic Course series is to provide students and instructors with the skills and knowledge they need to use Microsoft technology effectively in all aspects of their personal and professional lives. Quality instruction is required to help both educators and students get the most from Microsoft's software tools and to become more productive. Thus our mission is to make our instructional programs trusted educational companions for life.

To accomplish this mission, Wiley and Microsoft have partnered to develop the highest quality educational programs for Information Workers, IT Professionals, and Developers. Materials created by this partnership carry the brand name "Microsoft Official Academic Course," assuring instructors and students alike that the content of these textbooks is fully endorsed by Microsoft, and that they provide the highest quality information and instruction on Microsoft products. The Microsoft Official Academic Course textbooks are "Official" in still one more way—they are the officially sanctioned courseware for Microsoft IT Academy members.

The Microsoft Official Academic Course series focuses on workforce development. These programs are aimed at those students seeking to enter the workforce, change jobs, or embark on new careers as information workers, IT professionals, and developers. Microsoft Official Academic Course programs address their needs by emphasizing authentic workplace scenarios with an abundance of projects, exercises, cases, and assessments.

The Microsoft Official Academic Courses are mapped to Microsoft's extensive research and job-task analysis, the same research and analysis used to create the Microsoft Office Specialist (MOS) exams. The textbooks focus on real skills for real jobs. As students work through the projects and exercises in the textbooks they enhance their level of knowledge and their ability to apply the latest Microsoft technology to everyday tasks. These students also gain resume-building credentials that can assist them in finding a job, keeping their current job, or in furthering their education.

The concept of life-long learning is today an utmost necessity. Job roles, and even whole job categories, are changing so quickly that none of us can stay competitive and productive without continuously updating our skills and capabilities. The Microsoft Official Academic Course offerings, and their focus on Microsoft certification exam preparation, provide a means for people to acquire and effectively update their skills and knowledge. Wiley supports students in this endeavor through the development and distribution of these courses as Microsoft's official academic publisher.

*Joe Heider*
General Manager and Senior Vice President

# Preface

Welcome to the Microsoft Official Academic Course (MOAC) program for Microsoft Office 2013. MOAC represents the collaboration between Microsoft Learning and John Wiley & Sons, Inc. publishing company. Microsoft and Wiley teamed up to produce a series of textbooks that deliver compelling and innovative teaching solutions to instructors and superior learning experiences for students. Infused and informed by in-depth knowledge from the creators of Microsoft Office and Windows, and crafted by a publisher known worldwide for the pedagogical quality of its products, these textbooks maximize skills transfer in minimum time. Students are challenged to reach their potential by using their new technical skills as highly productive members of the workforce.

Because this knowledgebase comes directly from Microsoft, architect of the Office 2013 system and creator of the Microsoft Office Specialist (MOS) exams (www.microsoft.com/learning/mcp/mcts), you are sure to receive the topical coverage that is most relevant to students' personal and professional success. Microsoft's direct participation not only assures you that MOAC textbook content is accurate and current; it also means that students will receive the best instruction possible to enable their success on certification exams and in the workplace.

## THE MICROSOFT OFFICIAL ACADEMIC COURSE PROGRAM

The *Microsoft Official Academic Course* series is a complete program for instructors and institutions to prepare and deliver great courses on Microsoft software technologies. With MOAC, we recognize that, because of the rapid pace of change in the technology and curriculum developed by Microsoft, there is an ongoing set of needs beyond classroom instruction tools for an instructor to be ready to teach the course. The MOAC program endeavors to provide solutions for all these needs in a systematic manner in order to ensure a successful and rewarding course experience for both instructor and student—technical and curriculum training for instructor readiness with new software releases; the software itself for student use at home for building hands-on skills, assessment, and validation of skill development; and a great set of tools for delivering instruction in the classroom and lab. All are important to the smooth delivery of an interesting course on Microsoft software, and all are provided with the MOAC program. We think about the model below as a gauge for ensuring that we completely support you in your goal of teaching a great course. As you evaluate your instructional materials options, you may wish to use the model for comparison purposes with available products.

## Illustrated Book Tour

### PEDAGOGICAL FEATURES

The MOAC courseware for Microsoft Office 2013 system are designed to cover all the learning objectives. Many pedagogical features have been developed specifically for Microsoft Official Academic Course programs. Unique features of our task-based approach include a Lesson Skills Matrix that correlates skills taught in each lesson to real-world business application, business case scenarios, and three levels of increasingly rigorous lesson-ending activities: Competency, Proficiency, and Mastery Assessment.

Presenting the extensive procedural information and technical concepts woven throughout the textbook raises challenges for the student and instructor alike. The Illustrated Book Tour that follows provides a guide to the rich features contributing to Microsoft Official Academic Course program's pedagogical plan. Following is a list of key features in each lesson designed to prepare students for success on the certification exams and in the workplace:

- Each lesson begins with a **Lesson Skill Matrix**. More than a standard list of learning objectives, the skill matrix correlates each software skill covered in the lesson to real-world application.
- Each lesson features a real-world **Business Case** scenario that places the software skills and knowledge to be acquired in a real-world setting.
- Every lesson opens with a **Software Orientation**. This feature provides an overview of the software features students will be working with in the lesson. The orientation will detail the general properties of the software or specific features, such as a ribbon or dialog box; and it includes a large, labeled screen image.
- Concise and frequent **Step-by-Step** instructions teach students new features and provide an opportunity for hands-on practice. Numbered steps give detailed, step-by-step instructions to help students learn software skills. The steps also show results and screen images to match what students should see on their computer screens.
- Illustrations: Screen images provide visual feedback as students work through the exercises. The images reinforce key concepts, provide visual clues about the steps, and allow students to check their progress.
- Key **Terms:** Important technical vocabulary is listed at the beginning of the lesson. When these terms are used later in the lesson, they appear in bold italic type with yellow highlighter and are defined. The Glossary contains all of the key terms and their definitions.
- Engaging point-of-use **Reader aids**, located throughout the lessons, tell students why this topic is relevant (*The Bottom Line*), provide students with helpful hints (*Take Note*), or show alternate ways to accomplish tasks (*Another Way*), or point out things to watch out for or avoid (*Troubleshooting*). Reader aids also provide additional relevant or background information that adds value to the lesson.
- **Workplace Ready.** These new features preview how the Microsoft Office 2013 system applications are used in real-world situations.
- Each lesson ends with a **Skill Summary** recapping the topics covered in the lesson.

- Knowledge **Assessment:** Provides a total of 20 questions from a mix of True/False, Fill-in-the-Blank, Matching or Multiple Choice testing students on concepts learned in the lesson.

- Competency, **Proficiency, and Mastery Assessment:** provide three progressively more challenging lesson-ending activities.

Online files: The student companion website contains the data files needed for each lesson. These files are indicated by the file download icon in the margin of the textbook.

# LESSON FEATURES

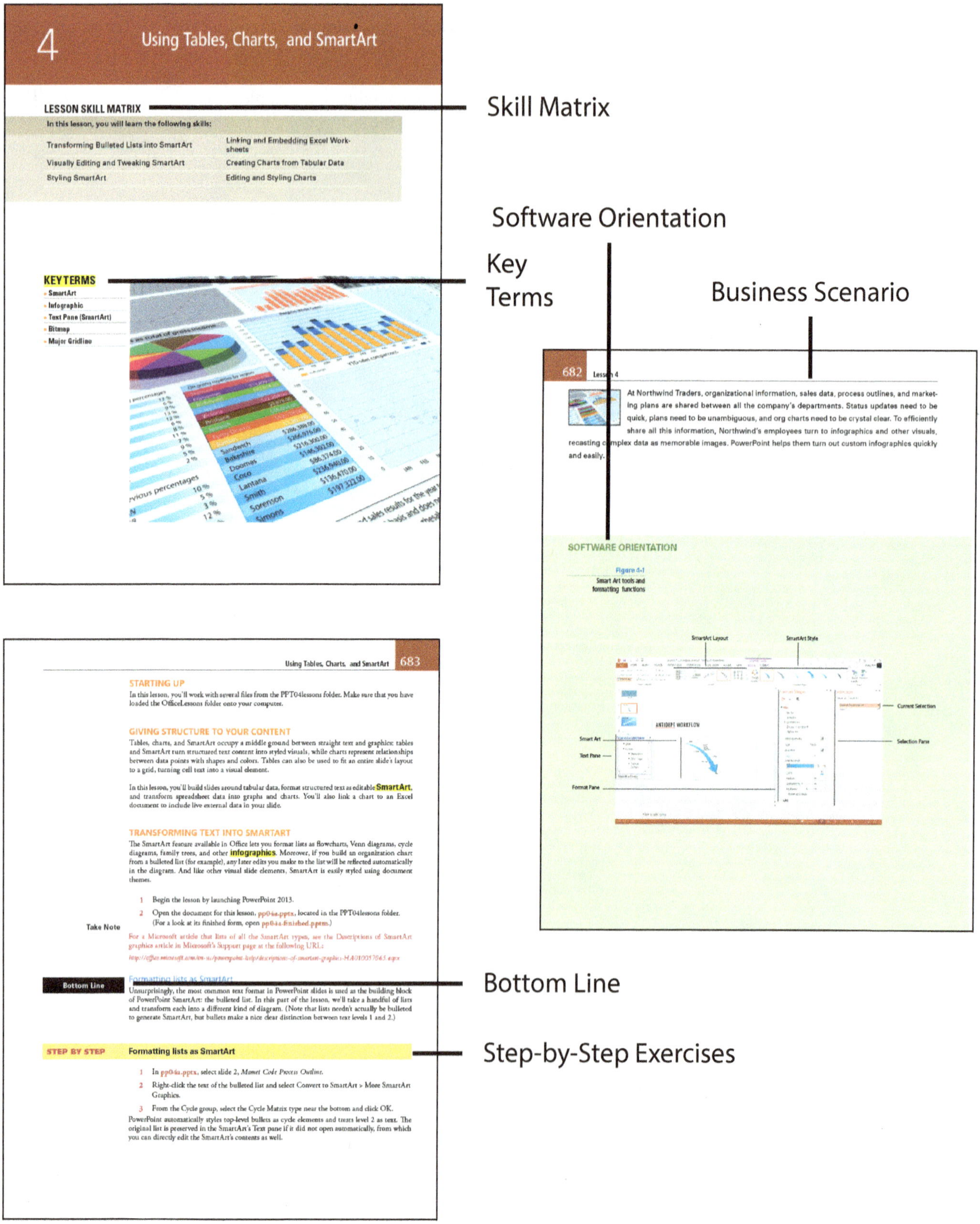

Easy-to-Read tables

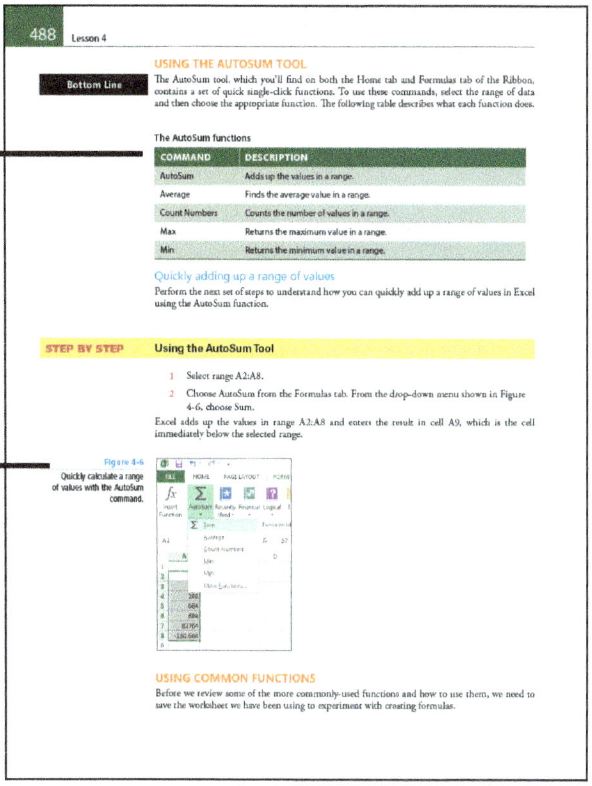
488 Lesson 4

Bottom Line

USING THE AUTOSUM TOOL

The AutoSum tool, which you'll find on both the Home tab and Formulas tab of the Ribbon, contains a set of quick single-click functions. To use these commands, select the range of data and then choose the appropriate function. The following table describes what each function does.

The AutoSum functions

| COMMAND | DESCRIPTION |
|---|---|
| AutoSum | Adds up the values in a range. |
| Average | Finds the average value in a range. |
| Count Numbers | Counts the number of values in a range. |
| Max | Returns the maximum value in a range. |
| Min | Returns the minimum value in a range. |

Quickly adding up a range of values

Perform the next set of steps to understand how you can quickly add up a range of values in Excel using the AutoSum function.

STEP BY STEP Using the AutoSum Tool

1 Select range A2:A8.

2 Choose AutoSum from the Formulas tab. From the drop-down menu shown in Figure 4-6, choose Sum.

Excel adds up the values in range A2:A8 and enters the result in cell A9, which is the cell immediately below the selected range.

Figure 4-6 Quickly calculate a range of values with the AutoSum command.

USING COMMON FUNCTIONS

Before we review some of the more commonly-used functions and how to use them, we need to save the worksheet we have been using to experiment with creating formulas.

Screen Images with Callouts

Workplace Ready

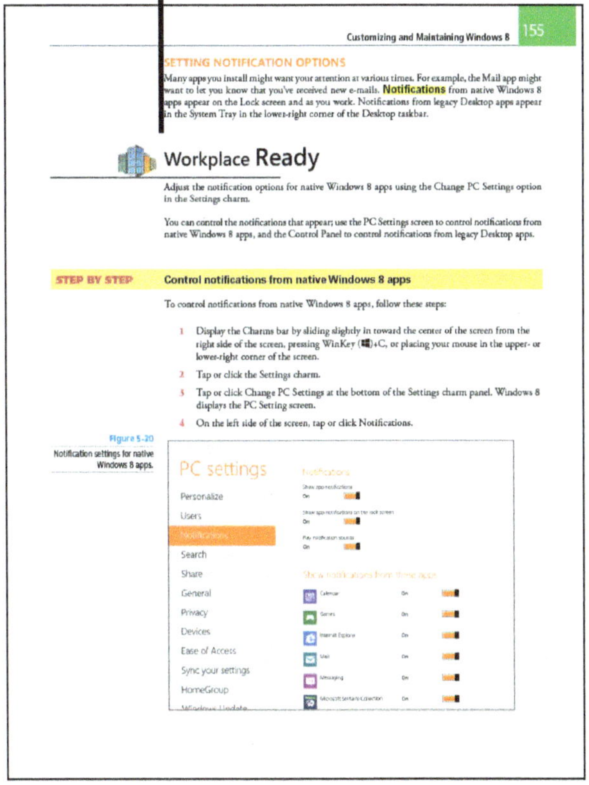
Customizing and Maintaining Windows 8 155

SETTING NOTIFICATION OPTIONS

Many apps you install might want your attention at various times. For example, the Mail app might want to let you know that you've received new e-mails. Notifications from native Windows 8 apps appear on the Lock screen and as you work. Notifications from legacy Desktop apps appear in the System Tray in the lower-right corner of the Desktop taskbar.

Workplace Ready

Adjust the notification options for native Windows 8 apps using the Change PC Settings option in the Settings charm.

You can control the notifications that appear; use the PC Settings screen to control notifications from native Windows 8 apps, and the Control Panel to control notifications from legacy Desktop apps.

STEP BY STEP Control notifications from native Windows 8 apps

To control notifications from native Windows 8 apps, follow these steps:

1 Display the Charms bar by sliding slightly in toward the center of the screen from the right side of the screen, pressing WinKey (⊞)+C, or placing your mouse in the upper- or lower-right corner of the screen.

2 Tap or click the Settings charm.

3 Tap or click Change PC Settings at the bottom of the Settings charm panel. Windows 8 displays the PC Setting screen.

4 On the left side of the screen, tap or click Notifications.

Figure 5-20 Notification settings for native Windows 8 apps.

Skill Summary

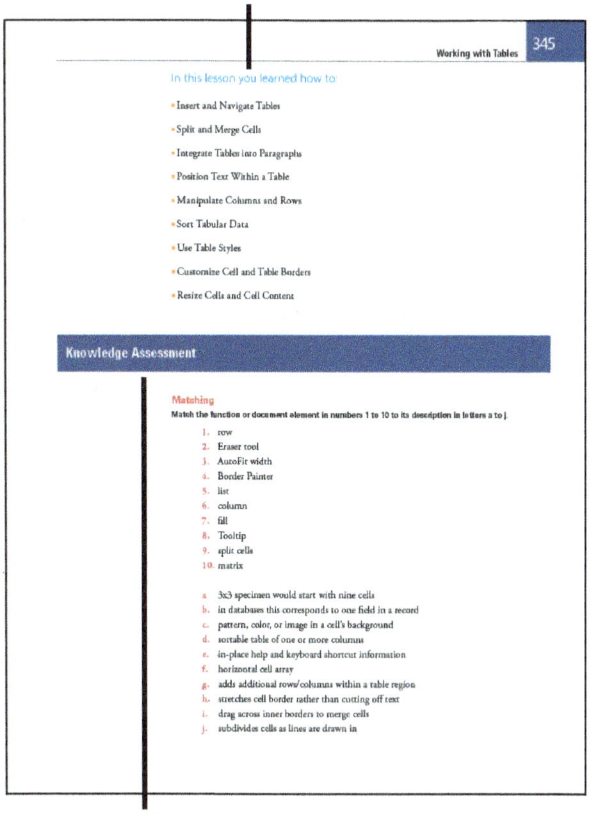
Working with Tables 345

In this lesson you learned how to:

- Insert and Navigate Tables
- Split and Merge Cells
- Integrate Tables into Paragraphs
- Position Text Within a Table
- Manipulate Columns and Rows
- Sort Tabular Data
- Use Table Styles
- Customize Cell and Table Borders
- Resize Cells and Cell Content

Knowledge Assessment

Matching

Match the function or document element in numbers 1 to 10 to its description in letters a to j.

1. row
2. Eraser tool
3. AutoFit width
4. Border Painter
5. list
6. column
7. fill
8. Tooltip
9. split cells
10. matrix

a. 3x3 specimen would start with nine cells
b. in databases this corresponds to one field in a record
c. pattern, color, or image in a cell's background
d. sortable table of one or more columns
e. in-place help and keyboard shortcut information
f. horizontal cell array
g. adds additional rows/columns within a table region
h. stretches cell border rather than cutting off text
i. drag across inner borders to merge cells
j. subdivides cells as lines are drawn in

Knowledge Assessment Questions

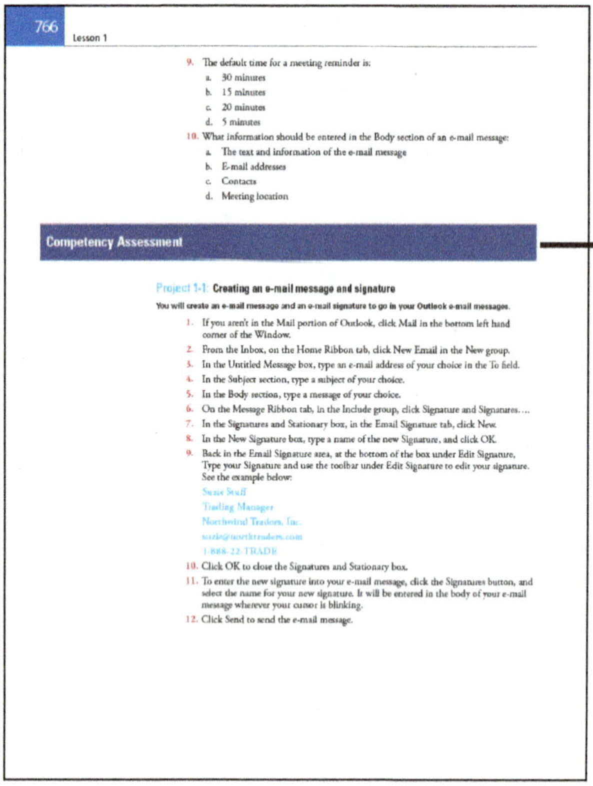



9. The default time for a meeting reminder is:
   a. 30 minutes
   b. 15 minutes
   c. 20 minutes
   d. 5 minutes
10. What information should be entered in the Body section of an e-mail message:
   a. The text and information of the e-mail message
   b. E-mail addresses
   c. Contacts
   d. Meeting location

## Competency Assessment

### Project 1-1: Creating an e-mail message and signature

**You will create an e-mail message and an e-mail signature to go in your Outlook e-mail messages.**

1. If you aren't in the Mail portion of Outlook, click Mail in the bottom left hand corner of the Window.
2. From the Inbox, on the Home Ribbon tab, click New Email in the New group.
3. In the Untitled Message box, type an e-mail address of your choice in the To field.
4. In the Subject section, type a subject of your choice.
5. In the Body section, type a message of your choice.
6. On the Message Ribbon tab, in the Include group, click Signature and Signatures....
7. In the Signatures and Stationary box, in the Email Signature tab, click New.
8. In the New Signature box, type a name of the new Signature, and click OK.
9. Back in the Email Signature area, at the bottom of the box under Edit Signature, Type your Signature and use the toolbar under Edit Signature to edit your signature. See the example below:
   Susie Stuff
   Trading Manager
   Northwind Traders, Inc.
   suzie@northtraders.com
   1-888-22-TRADE
10. Click OK to close the Signatures and Stationary box.
11. To enter the new signature into your e-mail message, click the Signatures button, and select the name for your new signature. It will be entered in the body of your e-mail message wherever your cursor is blinking.
12. Click Send to send the e-mail message.

Compentency Assessment Projects

Proficiency Assessment Projects

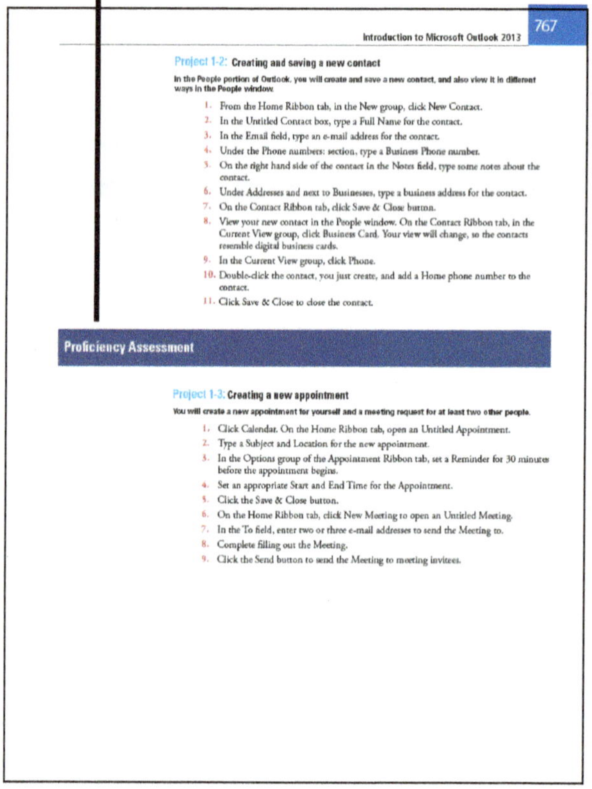



### Project 1-2: Creating and saving a new contact

**In the People portion of Outlook, you will create and save a new contact, and also view it in different ways in the People window.**

1. From the Home Ribbon tab, in the New group, click New Contact.
2. In the Untitled Contact box, type a Full Name for the contact.
3. In the Email field, type an e-mail address for the contact.
4. Under the Phone numbers: section, type a Business Phone number.
5. On the right hand side of the contact in the Notes field, type some notes about the contact.
6. Under Addresses and next to Businesses, type a business address for the contact.
7. On the Contact Ribbon tab, click Save & Close button.
8. View your new contact in the People window. On the Contact Ribbon tab, in the Current View group, click Business Card. Your view will change, so the contacts resemble digital business cards.
9. In the Current View group, click Phone.
10. Double-click the contact, you just create, and add a Home phone number to the contact.
11. Click Save & Close to close the contact.

## Proficiency Assessment

### Project 1-3: Creating a new appointment

**You will create a new appointment for yourself and a meeting request for at least two other people.**

1. Click Calendar. On the Home Ribbon tab, open an Untitled Appointment.
2. Type a Subject and Location for the new appointment.
3. In the Options group of the Appointment Ribbon tab, set a Reminder for 30 minutes before the appointment begins.
4. Set an appropriate Start and End Time for the Appointment.
5. Click the Save & Close button.
6. On the Home Ribbon tab, click New Meeting to open an Untitled Meeting.
7. In the To field, enter two or three e-mail addresses to send the Meeting to.
8. Complete filling out the Meeting.
9. Click the Send button to send the Meeting to meeting invitees.

Mastery Assessment Projects

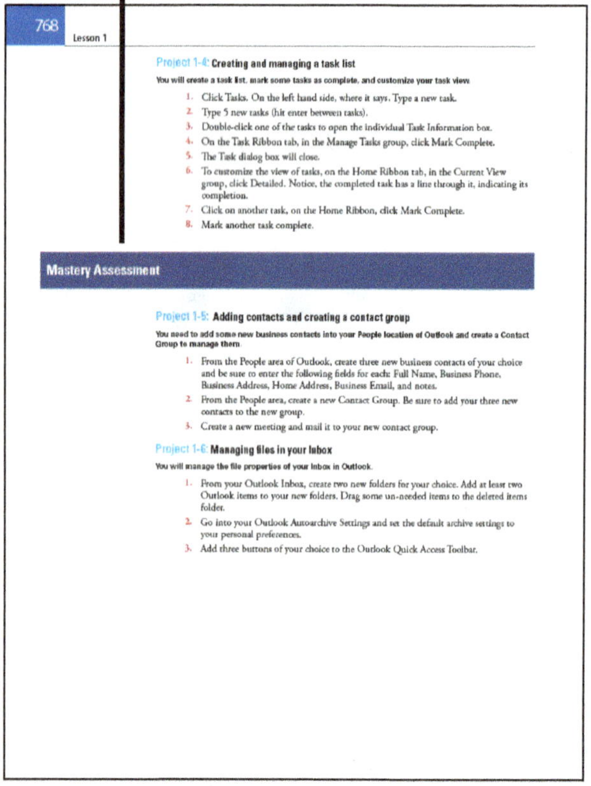



### Project 1-4: Creating and managing a task list

**You will create a task list, mark some tasks as complete, and customize your task view.**

1. Click Tasks. On the left hand side, where it says, Type a new task.
2. Type 5 new tasks (hit enter between tasks).
3. Double-click one of the tasks to open the individual Task Information box.
4. On the Task Ribbon tab, in the Manage Tasks group, click Mark Complete.
5. The Task dialog box will close.
6. To customize the view of tasks, on the Home Ribbon tab, in the Current View group, click Detailed. Notice, the completed task has a line through it, indicating its completion.
7. Click on another task, on the Home Ribbon, click Mark Complete.
8. Mark another task complete.

## Mastery Assessment

### Project 1-5: Adding contacts and creating a contact group

**You need to add some new business contacts into your People location of Outlook and create a Contact Group to manage them.**

1. From the People area of Outlook, create three new business contacts of your choice and be sure to enter the following fields for each: Full Name, Business Phone, Business Address, Home Address, Business Email, and notes.
2. From the People area, create a new Contact Group. Be sure to add your three new contacts to the new group.
3. Create a new meeting and mail it to your new contact group.

### Project 1-6: Managing files in your Inbox

**You will manage the file properties of your Inbox in Outlook.**

1. From your Outlook Inbox, create two new folders for your choice. Add at least two Outlook items to your new folders. Drag some un-needed items to the deleted items folder.
2. Go into your Outlook Autoarchive Settings and set the default archive settings to your personal preferences.
3. Add three buttons of your choice to the Outlook Quick Access Toolbar.

# Conventions and Features Used in This Book

This book uses particular fonts, symbols, and heading conventions to highlight important information or to call your attention to special steps. For more information about the features in each lesson, refer to the Illustrated Book Tour section.

| | |
|---|---|
| **Bottom Line** | This feature provides a brief summary of the material to be covered in the section that follows. |
| **Take Note** | Reader aids appear in shaded boxes found in your text. Take Note provides helpful hints related to particular tasks or topics. |
| **ALT+TAB** | A plus sign (+) between two key names means that you must press both keys at the same time. Keys that you are instructed to press in an exercise will appear in the font shown here. |
| **Key Term** | Key terms appear in bold italic. |
| Type **My Name is** | Any text you are asked to key appears in color. |
| Click **OK** | Any button on the screen you are supposed to click on or select will also appear in color. |
| **BudgetWorksheet1** | The names of data files will appear in bold and red for easy identification. These data files are available for download from the Student Companion Site (www.Wiley.com/college/Microsoft) |

## Instructor Support Program

The *Microsoft Official Academic Course* programs are accompanied by a rich array of resources that incorporate the extensive textbook visuals to form a pedagogically cohesive package. These resources provide all the materials instructors need to deploy and deliver their courses. Resources available online for download include:

- The **Instructor's Guide** contains Solutions to all the textbook exercises as well as chapter summaries and lecture notes. The Instructor's Guide and Syllabi for various term lengths are available from the Instructor's Book Companion site (www.wiley.com/college/microsoft).

- The **Solution Files** for all the projects in the book are available online from our Instructor's Book Companion site (www.wiley.com/college/microsoft).

- The **Test Bank** contains hundreds of questions organized by lesson in multiple-choice, true-false, short answer, and essay formats and is available to download from the Instructor's Book Companion site (www.wiley.com/college/microsoft). A complete answer key is provided.

- This title's test bank is available for use in Respondus' easy-to-use software. You can download the test bank for free using your Respondus, Respondus LE, or StudyMate Author software.

- Respondus is a powerful tool for creating and managing exams that can be printed to paper or published directly to Blackboard, WebCT, Desire2Learn, eCollege, ANGEL and other eLearning systems.

- PowerPoint **Presentations and Images**. A complete set of PowerPoint presentations is available on the Instructor's Book Companion site (www.wiley.com/college/microsoft) to enhance classroom presentations. Tailored to the text's topical coverage and Skills Matrix, these presentations are designed to convey key Microsoft Office concepts addressed in the text.

- All figures from the text are on the Instructor's Book Companion site (www.wiley.com/ college/ microsoft). You can incorporate them into your PowerPoint presentations, or create your own overhead transparencies and handouts.

- By using these visuals in class discussions, you can help focus students' attention on key elements of Microsoft Office and help them understand how to use it effectively in the workplace.

- **Wiley OfficeGrader** automated grading system allows you to easily grade student data files in Word, Excel, PowerPoint or Access format, against solution files. Save tens or hundreds of hours each semester with automated grading. More information on Wiley OfficeGrader is available from the Instructor's Book Companion site (www.wiley.com/college/microsoft).

- The **Student Data Files** are available online on both the Instructor's Book Companion Site and for students on the Student Book Companion Site.

- **Wiley Faculty Network:** When it comes to improving the classroom experience, there is no better source of ideas and inspiration than your fellow colleagues. The Wiley Faculty Network connects teachers with technology, facilitates the exchange of best practices, and helps to enhance instructional efficiency and effectiveness. Faculty Network activities include technology training and tutorials, virtual seminars, peer-to-peer exchanges of experiences and ideas, personal consulting, and sharing of resources. For details visit www.WhereFacultyConnect.com.

## DREAMSPARK PREMIUM

### FREE 3-YEAR MEMBERSHIP AVAILABLE TO QUALIFIED ADOPTERS!

DreamSpark Premium is designed to provide the easiest and most inexpensive way for schools to make the latest Microsoft developer tools, products, and technologies available in labs, classrooms, and on student PCs. DreamSpark Premium is an annual membership program for departments teaching Science, Technology, Engineering, and Mathematics (STEM) courses. The membership provides a complete solution to keep academic labs, faculty, and students on the leading edge of technology.

Software available through the DreamSpark Premium program is provided at no charge to adopting departments through the Wiley and Microsoft publishing partnership.

Contact your Wiley rep for details.

For more information about the DreamSpark Premium program, go to Microsoft's DreamSpark website

## IMPORTANT WEB ADDRESSES AND PHONE NUMBERS

To locate the Wiley Higher Education Rep in your area, go to the following Web address and click on the "Contact Us " link at the top of the page.

www.wiley.com/college

Or Call the MOAC Toll Free Number: 1 + (888) 764-7001 (U.S. & Canada only).

To learn more about becoming a Microsoft Certified Professional and exam availability, visit www.microsoft.com/learning/mcp.

# Student Support Program

## STUDENT DATA FILES

All of the practice files that you will use as you perform the exercises in the book are available for download on our student companion site. By using the practice files, you will not waste time creating the samples used in the lessons, and you can concentrate on learning how to use Microsoft Office 2013. With the files and the step-by-step instructions in the lessons, you will learn by doing, which is an easy and effective way to acquire and remember new skills.

## COPYING THE PRACTICE FILES

Your instructor might already have copied the practice files before you arrive in class. However, your instructor might ask you to copy the practice files on your own at the start of class. Also, if you want to work through any of the exercises in this book on your own at home or at your place of business after class, you may want to copy the practice files.

**STEP BY STEP** **Copying the Practice Files**

**OPEN Internet Explorer.**

1. In Internet Explorer, go to the student companion site: www.wiley.com
2. Search for your book title in the upper right hand corner.
3. On the Search Results page, locate your book and click on the Visit the Companion Sites link.
4. Select Student Companion Site from the pop-up box.
5. From the menu, select the arrow next to Browse By Resource and select Student Data Files from the menu.
6. A new screen will appear.
7. On the File Download dialog box, select Save As to save the data files to your external drive (often called a ZIP drive or a USB drive or a thumb drive) or a local drive.
8. In the Save As dialog box, select a local drive in the left-hand panel that you'd like to save your files to; again, this should be an external drive or a local drive. Remember the drive name that you saved it to.

## Acknowledgments

We'd like to thank the many instructors and reviewers who pored over the Microsoft Official Academic Course series design, outlines and manuscript, providing invaluable feedback in the service of quality instructional materials.

Erik Amerikaner, Oak Park Unified

Sue Bajt, Harper College

Gregory Ballinger, Miami-Dade College

Catherine Bradfield, DeVry University

DeAnnia Clements, Wiregrass Georgia Technical College

Mary Corcoran, Bellevue College

Andrea Cluff, Freemont High School

Caroline de Gruchy, Conestoga College

Janis DeHaven, Central Community College

Rob Durrance, East Lee County High School

Janet Flusche, Frenship High School

Greg Gardiner, SIAST

Debi Griggs, Bellevue College

Phil Hanney, Orem Junior High School

Dee Hobson, Richland College

Terri Holly, Indian River State College

Kim Hopkins, Weatherford College

Sandra Jolley, Tarrant County College

Joe LaMontagne, Davenport University

Tanya MacNeil, American InterContinental University

Donna Madsen, Kirkwood Community College

Lynn Mancini, Delaware Technical Community College

Edward Martin, Kingsborough Community College-City University of New York

Lisa Mears, Palm Beach State College

Denise Merrell, Jefferson Community and Technical College

Diane Mickey, Northern Virginia Community College

Robert Mike, Alaska Career College

Cynthia Miller, Harper College

Sandra Miller, Wenatchee Valley College

Mustafa Muflehi, The Sheffield College

Aditi Mukherjee, University of Florida—Gainesville

Linda Nutter, Peninsula College

Diana Pack, Big Sandy Community & Technical College

Bettye Parham, Daytona State College

Tatyana Pashnyak, Bainbridge State College

Kari Phillips, Davis Applied Technical College

Michelle Poertner, Northwestern Michigan College

Barbara Purvis, Centura College

Dave Rotherham, Sheffield Hallam University

Theresa Savarese, San Diego City College

Janet Sebesy, Cuyahoga Community College-Western

Lourdes Sevilla, Southwestern College

Elizabeth Snow, Southwest Florida College

Amy Stolte, Lincoln Land Community College

Dorothy Weiner, Manchester Community College

We would also like to thank the team at Microsoft Learning Xperiences (LeX), including Alison Cunard, Tim Sneath, Zubair Murtaza, Keith Loeber, Rob Linsky, Anne Hamilton, Wendy Johnson, Gene Longo, Julia Stasio, and Josh Barnhill for their encouragement and support in making the Microsoft Official Academic Course programs the finest academic materials for mastering the newest Microsoft technologies for both students and instructors.

# Author Credits

## JENNIFER SMITH

Thanks to James Senior, Chris Mayo, and the many Windows product managers for their useful assistance in gathering the information required for the Windows 8 section of this book. Thanks also to the teams at Avlade and at American Graphics Institute for their many contributions to this book.

# Microsoft Windows 8

# Getting Started with Windows 8 1

## LESSON SKILL MATRIX

| In this lesson, you will learn the following skills: |
| --- |
| How to sign into Windows |
| About Microsoft accounts and local accounts |
| How to use Windows 8 with a Mouse and Keyboard |
| How to find help when troubleshooting |
| How to shut down Windows 8 |

## KEY TERMS

- **Lock Screen**
- **Sign in screen**
- **Start Screen**
- **Local accounts**
- **Hotspots**
- **WinKey**
- **Charms bar**
- **Desktop app**
- **Quick Link menu**
- **Sleep mode**
- **Hibernate mode**
- **Restart command**
- **Shut Down**

©webphotographeer/iStockPhoto

©webphotographeer/ iStockPhoto

Elaine recently purchased a new laptop running Windows 8. She needs to learn how to sign into a new account on her laptop and use the mouse and keyboard on the new operating system before she starts a new accounting position at Fabrikam.

## SOFTWARE ORIENTATION

To use your Windows personal computer or tablet, you must be able to use Windows 8. Windows 8 is an operating system, which controls the way in which applications, also known as apps, interact with you, the user, and with other parts of the computer such as the display and keyboard, and with other connected devices, such as printers. After you log-in to Windows 8, you can access and manage your device.

**Figure 1-1**

Windows 8 Charms

## SIGNING IN TO WINDOWS

When you start Windows 8, the default appearance is for it to display a **lock screen**. You'll need to sign-in to Windows in order to perform any tasks such as checking email or writing a document.

The sign-in process involves moving past the lock screen, selecting an account to use, and entering the password for that account.

**Take Note** While it's possible to avoid the sign-in process and jump directly to the Start screen if you set up a local account, this option is not advisable for most users. The sign-in process requires you to enter your password, and keeps unauthorized users from accessing your account. For this reason, it's advisable to always use the sign-in process.

**Figure 1-2**

The Windows Lock screen appears when you first start your computer.

*Image used with permission of Microsoft*

To sign-in to your computer and start using Windows 8, do any of the following from the Lock screen.

- **Use** your finger to swipe up the screen.
- **Click** your mouse anywhere on the screen.
- **Press** any key on your keyboard.

The **Sign In screen** appears; it will look like the one below and display an e-mail address below your name if you are signing in using a Microsoft account.

**Figure 1-3**

The Windows 8 sign in screen.

*Image used with permission of Microsoft*

Type your password and tap or click the arrow beside the password box to display the Windows 8 Start screen.

**Take Note** If you're using a touch device, the on-screen touch keypad automatically appears so that you can type your password

## UNDERSTANDING MICROSOFT ACCOUNTS AND LOCAL ACCOUNTS

Your account contains information about how you prefer your computer to operate, its appearance, along with the documents and applications you use. There are two types of accounts available with Windows 8. One option allows you to have your information shared between various computers you use with data backed-up over the Internet, the other is suitable if you only use computer and don't wish to have your data stored for you.

### Microsoft accounts

**Workplace Ready**

Use a Microsoft account to share your settings and important files in the cloud when you work on multiple devices.

Use a Microsoft account to share your settings and important files in the cloud when you work on multiple devices. Microsoft accounts are made up of an e-mail address registered with Microsoft and a required password. Microsoft accounts don't need to be from a Microsoft operated service. You can use your company email address or a personal email address from any provider. Yet all *hotmail.com*, *live.com*, and *outlook.com* e-mail addresses are automatically Microsoft accounts because Microsoft owns and manages these domains and e-mail addresses.

**Take Note** You don't need a *hotmail.com*, *live.com*, or *outlook.com* e-mail address to have a Microsoft account. You can register any e-mail address as a Microsoft account.

When you sign in to Windows 8 using a Microsoft account, you are connecting your computer to Microsoft's computers in *the cloud*. These computers are operated by Microsoft for the purpose of backing up your data and sharing your data between different computers you might own. If you sign into Windows 8 on your desktop PC, Windows automatically synchronizes some settings, such as your picture, backgrounds, Internet Explorer history and favorites to and from the cloud. If you sign in to Windows 8 on another device, such as a tablet PC, using the same Microsoft account, the synchronized settings from your desktop computer appear on your tablet PC. Many Windows 8 native apps require that you sign in to Windows using a Microsoft account.

### Local accounts

**Local accounts** are made up of a name rather than an e-mail address and a password, which is optional. There are two types of local accounts: administrator and standard. As you start working with Windows 8, the key concept for you to understand is that when you sign in to Windows 8 using a local account, you are signing in to just your PC, not the cloud. No synchronization happens when you sign in using a local account. Windows 8 remembers your computer's settings just like previous versions of Windows did, and these settings are connected to one specific computer.

If you use multiple Windows 8 devices and want your settings to travel with you between devices and you also want to use the Windows 8 native apps, use a Microsoft account.

**Take Note** You can control the settings that Windows 8 synchronizes when you sign in using a Microsoft account.

## STEP BY STEP Registering an existing e-mail address as a Microsoft account

If you have a **hotmail.com, live.com**, or **outlook.com** e-mail address, you already have a registered Microsoft account and can jump ahead to the next section. If you don't have one of these e-mail addresses and you will want to register an existing e-mail address as a Microsoft account using the following steps:

1. Open a web browser such as Internet Explorer. Right-click or swipe up or down the page to make the address bar visible.
2. Type **signup.live.com** in the address bar and press **Enter** to display the Microsoft account signup form.

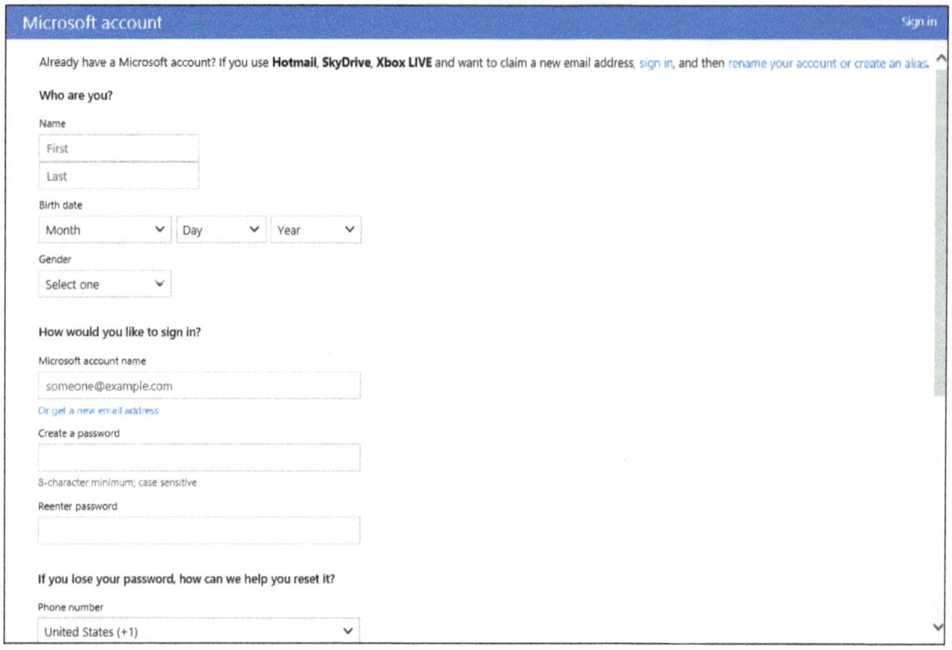


**Figure 1-4**

The form you complete to register an e-mail address as a Microsoft account.

3 Complete the form, supplying the e-mail address you want to use as your Microsoft account in the Microsoft account name text field.

**Take Note** Do not supply the password associated with the e-mail address; instead, make up a new password that you want to use to sign in to Windows 8 or any website where you will use your Microsoft account.

4 At the bottom of the form, tap or click the **I accept** button.

## USING WINDOWS 8 WITH A MOUSE AND KEYBOARD

Windows 8 works well, regardless of whether you are using a touchscreen device or traditional keyboard, mouse or trackpad.

If you are using Windows 8 with a traditional mouse and keyboard, there are hundreds of mouse and keyboard shortcuts that can help you work more efficiently; you can find a complete list at *http://windows.microsoft.com/en-US/windows-8/keyboard-shortcuts.*

## Workplace Ready

Use keyboard shortcuts to help you work more efficiently with tasks you perform the most often.

In this section, you'll learn about the shortcuts you are likely to use most often.

### Understanding Corner Navigation

Microsoft has built "hotspots" into each of the corners of the Windows 8 Start screen that aid both mouse and touch users. To take advantage of the corner **"hotspots,"** you need to move the mouse to the corner of the screen, so the mouse pointer appears almost outside the screen edge. A portion of the pointer may disappear.

## Getting back to the Start screen

To get back to the Start screen, open any app—from the Windows 8 Start screen. After you open an app, you can redisplay the Start screen by:

- Pressing the Windows logo key (⊞), also known as the **WinKey**.
- Pointing the mouse at the lower-left corner of the screen until a small image of the Start screen appears, and then click it.

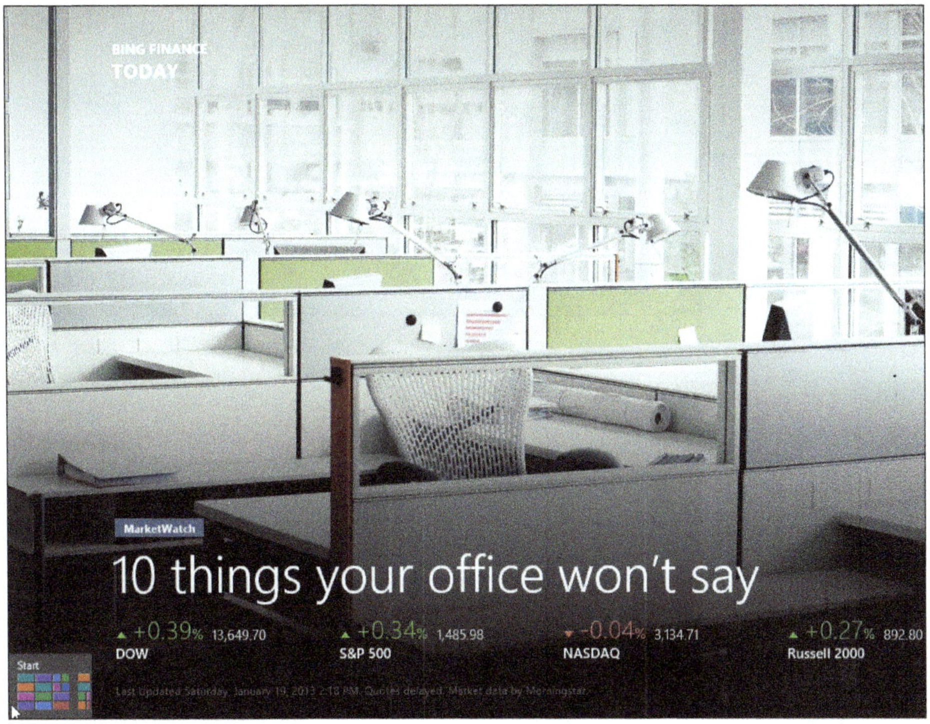


**Figure 1-5**

Click the image of the Start screen in the lower-left corner of your monitor to redisplay the Start screen.

*Image used with permission of Microsoft*

You also can display the Start screen from the Charms bar which appears along the right side of your display. You can display the Charms bar along the right side of the screen by dragging your mouse down or swiping across the right edge of the screen then click Start to return to the Start screen.

**Take Note** If you are viewing the Start screen when you use any of these shortcuts, you can switch back to the last app you were viewing. Pressing the WinKey (⊞) switches you back and forth between the Start screen and the last app you viewed.

Your touch device may also have a Windows logo key (⊞) that you can press to redisplay the Start screen.

## Displaying the Charms bar

You can use the Charms bar to perform a search on your computer, to share information between Windows 8 native apps, to display the Start screen, to connect hardware on your computer to Windows 8 native apps, or to display settings available for Windows 8 native apps or settings available for Desktop apps.

To display the **Charms bar**, shown in the figure, do one of the following:

**Figure 1-6**

The Charms bar appears on the right side of your screen.

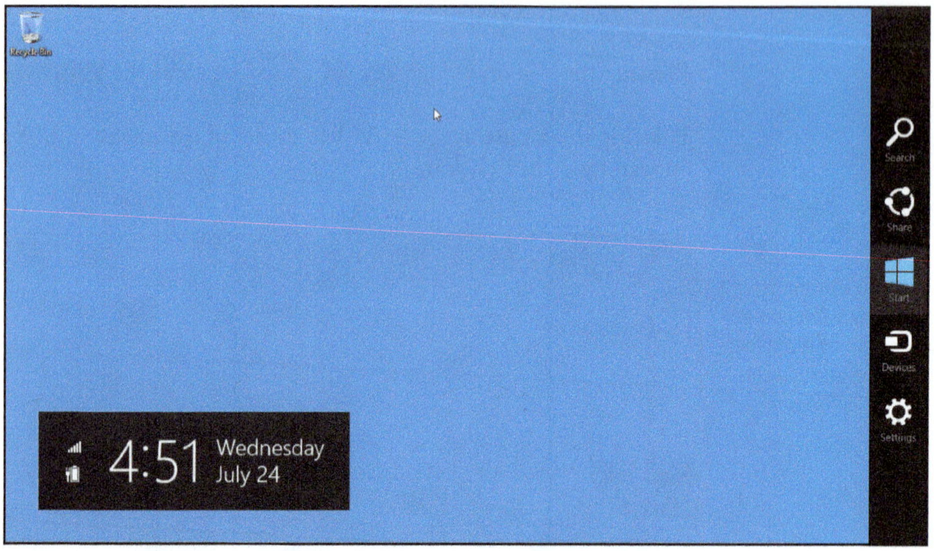


- Press WinKey (⊞)+C
- Point the mouse in the lower-right or upper-right corner of the screen. Remember that you need to move the mouse to the corner of the screen, so the mouse pointer appears outside the screen edge.

You can then point the mouse at each charm on the Charms bar and click to select the appropriate charm.

You also can use the following keyboard shortcuts to directly open a Charm:

## Workplace Ready

Use shortcuts to efficiently access useful functionality in Windows 8, which you can use to change settings, connect devices, share information, or search.

- WinKey (⊞)+I opens the Settings charm
- WinKey (⊞)+K opens the Devices charm
- WinKey (⊞)+H opens the Share charm
- WinKey (⊞)+Q opens the Search pane

## SWITCHING AMONG OPEN APPS

### The Desktop is an app

In earlier editions of Windows, the Desktop represented the operating system, and users did all their work from the Desktop. All programs (apps) required the Desktop to function.

Windows 8 introduces a new kind of app that doesn't need the Desktop to run. These Windows 8 native apps function in much the same way other computer programs function, each with their own set of commands you use to accomplish what you want. The Windows 8 native apps don't need the traditional Desktop you used in earlier editions of Windows.

Once you understand that Windows 8 supports two kinds of apps (those that need the Desktop and those that don't), you'll find it easy to visualize the Desktop as an app, with its own set of commands that you use to control it. The Desktop has the distinction of being the only app that can run other apps. You can open multiple programs on the Desktop, just as users have done in earlier editions of Windows. But, because the Desktop is an app, you must use the Desktop techniques described in Lesson 3, "Working with Desktop Apps" to switch among open Desktop apps. You cannot use the techniques described in this section. When you switch among open apps as described in this section, the Desktop is a single app that you can display, even if multiple Desktop programs are running.

To switch among open Windows 8 apps, including the **Desktop app** , do one of the following from any running app:

- Press WinKey (⊞)+Tab
- Slide the mouse pointer to the upper-left corner of the screen; the last app you viewed appears. Slide the mouse down the left side of the screen to display the Running Apps bar.

**Take Note** No official name seems to exist for the bar that appears down the left side of your screen when you perform any of the actions listed above. Since it displays a list of apps currently running on your computer, in this lesson, we'll refer to it as the Running Apps bar.

Once the Running Apps bar appears, click the app you want to display.

**Figure 1-7**

The Running Apps bar appears on the left side of the screen.

*Photos used with permission from Microsoft Images and clip art used with permission of Microsoft.*

**Take Note** Alt+Tab works as it did in earlier editions of Windows. You can press and hold Alt as you press Tab to cycle through all the running apps. Release Alt when you see the app you want to switch to.

**STEP BY STEP** **Displaying the Quick Link menu**

The **Quick Link menu** displays a wide range of useful commands, especially for power users. With it, you can switch to the Desktop or open Desktop apps such as the Device Manager, Control Panel, Disk Manager, Computer Management Console, Task Manager, File Explorer, etc.

## Workplace Ready

Quickly switch to the Desktop or Desktop apps that you can use to manage your computer or explore files on your hard drive.

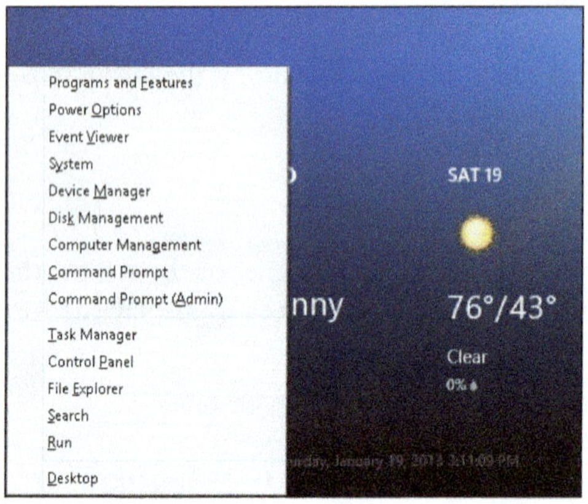


**Figure 1-8**
A useful context menu to help you quickly navigate to commonly used applications.

You can easily display the Quick Link menu by pressing WinKey (⊞)+X. To display it using your mouse, follow these steps:

1. From any app or on the Start screen, slide the mouse to the lower-left corner of your screen.
2. When the image of the last app you used appears, right-click it.

### Closing an app

Closing a Windows 8 native app is not as obvious as closing a program that runs on the Desktop. You won't find a red X in the upper-right corner of Windows 8 native apps. While you don't have to close Windows 8 native apps most users, through force of habit, want to close them. These apps run in the background on your computer and don't take up as much memory as legacy programs do. You can do any of the following to close an app:

- On your keyboard, press Alt+F4.
- Using your mouse, do one of the following:
- Display the Running Apps bar on the Start screen as described in the section "Switching among open apps," then tap and hold, right-click a tile and tap, or click Close.

**Figure 1-9**

Display the Running Apps bar and tap and hold or right-click an app to close it.

*Photos used with permission from Microsoft*
*Images and clip art used with permission of Microsoft.*

- While viewing the app, move the mouse pointer to the top of the screen until it changes to a hand. Then, click and drag down to the bottom of your screen. The app will minimize as you drag; when you drag it off the bottom of screen, the app closes.

**Figure 1-10**

Drag from the top of the app to the bottom to close it.

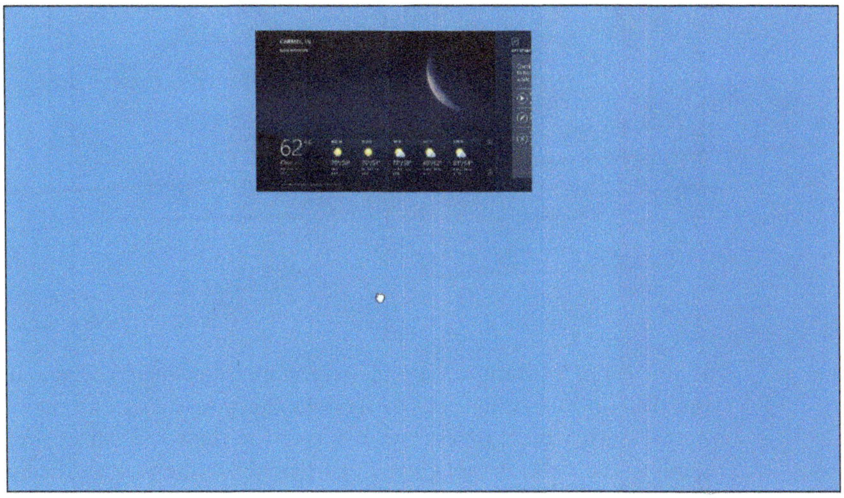

*Photos used with permission from Microsoft*

**Take Note** As mentioned previously, the Desktop app is in a category of its own. You can use either mouse technique to close the Desktop app, but the keyboard shortcut prompts you to shut down your computer. You will learn about shutting down your computer later in this lesson.

## Displaying the Desktop

While the Windows 8 Desktop app is different from the desktop in earlier editions of Windows, the Windows 8 Desktop will be more familiar to Windows users than the Start Screen.

To display the Desktop app, you can:

- Press WinKey (⊞)+D.
- Click the Desktop tile on the Start screen.

## Locking your computer

If you want to walk away from your computer, yet you don't want to shut it down, you can lock it. Locking the computer displays the lock screen shown at the beginning of this lesson and leads you to the sign in screen, where you must re-enter your password to sign in to your computer. You can lock your computer using either of the following methods:

- Press WinKey (⊞)+L.
- Click your name or picture on the Start screen and then click Lock.

**Figure 1-11**

Click your name or picture to view this menu, where you can lock your computer.

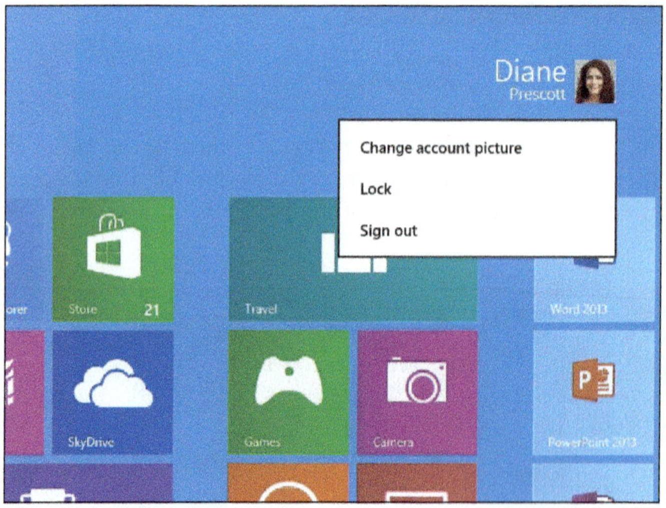


*Photos used with permission from Microsoft*

## Zooming the Start screen

If you're not working on a wide-screen monitor, or if you are and you have lots of programs installed on your computer, you'll notice that you can't see all the tiles representing your programs on the Start screen, unless you swipe or use the scroll bar at the bottom of the Start screen to scroll to the right. Although you can reorganize the tiles on the Start screen, reorganizing might not solve the problem of viewing the tile you need. When you zoom out, the Start screen displays many small tiles. You can click an area of the screen to zoom in to that area so that you can click a tile and launch an app.

**Figure 1-12**

The Start screen when zoomed out.

You can zoom out or in the Start screen using any of the following techniques:

- Press Ctrl+minus (-) to zoom out and view a larger number of smaller tiles or Ctrl+plus (+) to view a smaller number of larger tiles.
- Press and hold Ctrl as you use the scroll wheel on your mouse.
- Click the Zoom button in the lower-right corner of the Start screen.

**Figure 1-13**

You can click the Zoom button to zoom out and view many small tiles on the Windows Start screen.

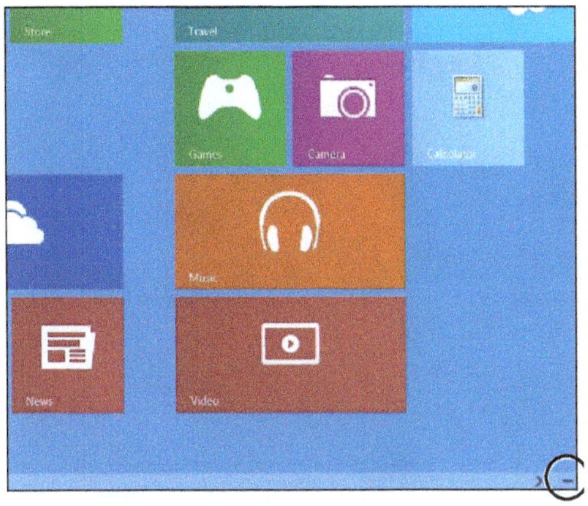

## STEP BY STEP Getting Help

If you run into a problem using Windows 8, you can use web-based help or you can search the Desktop Windows Help and Support app using a search word or phrase to view a list of links to related Help articles.

To use web-based support:

1. Display the Charms bar.
2. Choose the **Settings** charm.
3. At the top of the pane, choose **Help**.

4 Select a topic, and the Windows 8 native app for Internet Explorer opens the Help page.

**Figure 1-14**

Web-based topics you can read using Windows 8 native help.

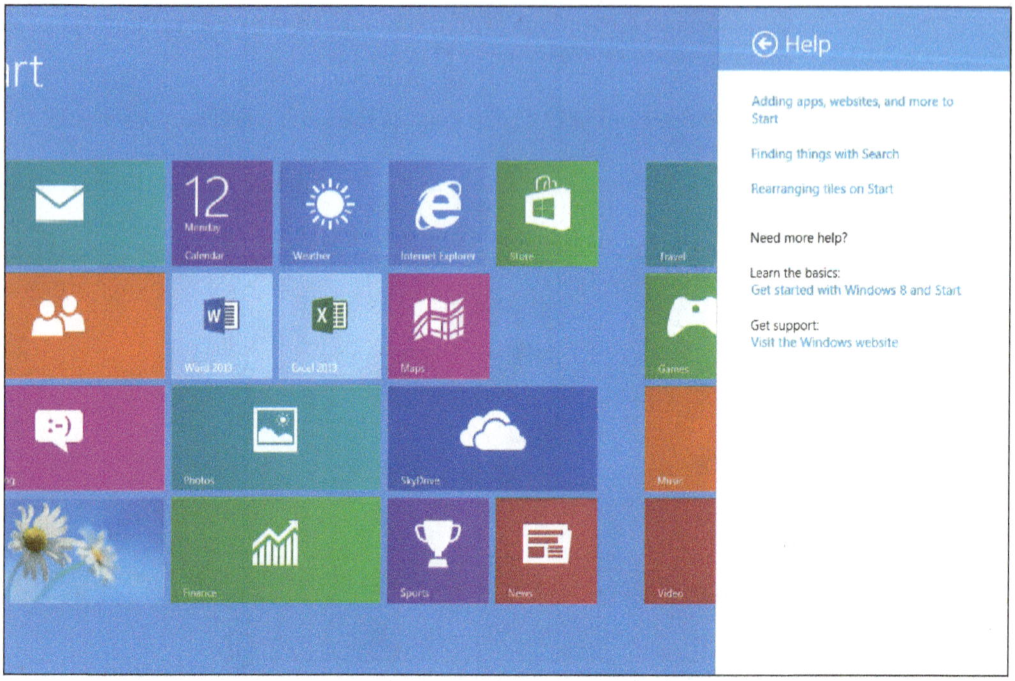


*Images and clip art used with permission of Microsoft.*

Using the Desktop Windows Help and Support app, you can control the search by supplying a search keyword or phrase. For example, you can search for help in using the built-in Windows word processing program, WordPad.

**Take Note** The fewer words you supply as your search criteria, the more results Help and Support will display.

## STEP BY STEP Getting Help and Support

The Windows Help and Support app runs as a Desktop program, but you launch it from the Start screen:

1 Display the Start screen.

2 Type **Help** to display a list of help sources.

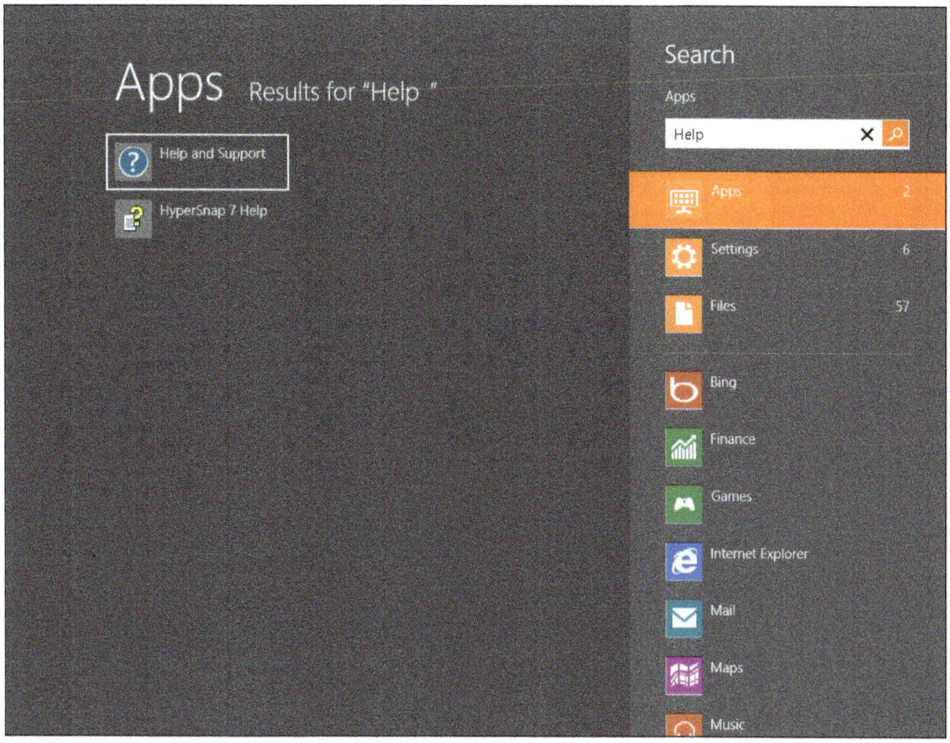


**Figure 1-15**

Any apps, settings, or file names containing the word "help" appear in a list.

3 Tap or click **Help and Support**.

4 Type **word processing**, in the text field at the top of the window and press **Enter**, or tap or click the **magnifying glass** button Windows Help and Support displays a list of links to articles that relate to the phrase you typed.

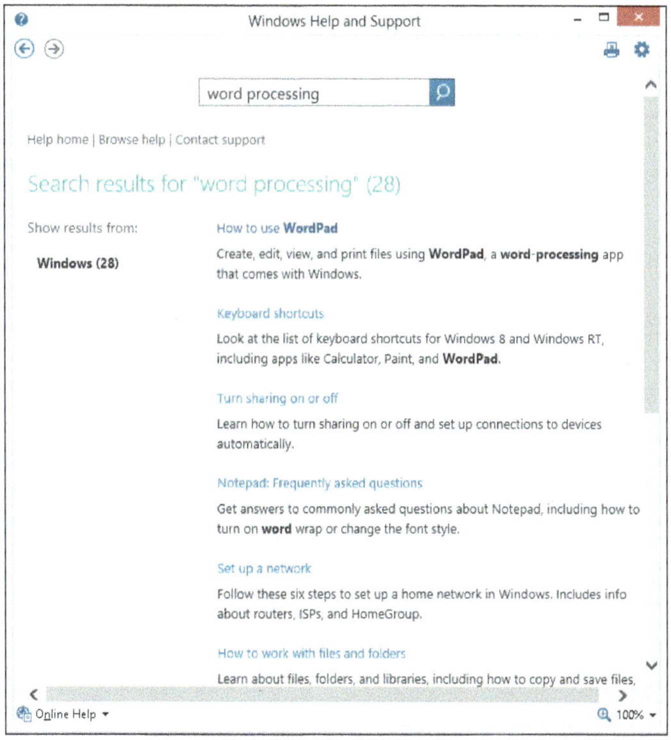


**Figure 1-16**

Type a keyword or phrase for which you want to search in the text field at the top of the Help and Support window.

1 Click or tap a link that seems relevant to display the article.

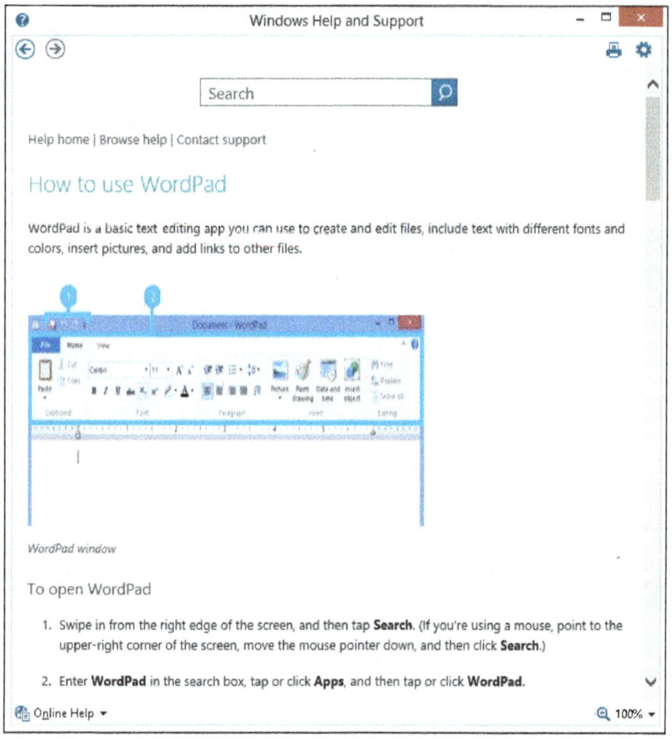


**Figure 1-17**

A typical article in the Windows Help and Support app.

**Take Note** You can also browse Help topics without searching. Tap or click the Browse Help link just below the Search text field to display the Help table of contents, which contains a series of topic links. Tap or click a link to see additional links related to that topic. As you click each link, your search narrows. Eventually, Windows Help and Support displays an article.

Keep in mind that if you are using Windows 8.1 you can access Help directly from the Search Charm.

## SHUTTING DOWN WINDOWS 8

Windows 8's default shut down and start up processes are different from those of all previous editions of Windows.

When you shut down a desktop computer, you'll see three choices:

- Sleep
- Shut Down
- Restart

Laptop and tablet computers may also display a "hibernate" option.

## What's the difference between sleep, hibernate, restart, and shut down?

**Sleep mode** is a power-saving state. In Sleep mode, also called Standby mode, power is withheld from non-essential components. A computer can quickly resume operation, typically in seconds, when you wake it from Sleep mode, usually by moving your mouse or possibly by touching the power button on the computer. Once it awakens, you'll find everything exactly as it was when you put the computer to sleep—all open programs and running apps will be just where they were. You can think of a computer in Sleep mode in the same way you think of a DVD player that you have paused: both devices immediately stop what they are doing and start almost immediately when you tell them to start. The one danger you face from using Sleep mode on your computer comes from the potential for an external power failure. If power is cut off from your computer, the sleep state is lost. You won't be able to wake your computer; instead, you'll need to restart it. Because of the potential for power failure, you should save data in open programs before you put your computer to sleep. That way, you won't lose any information due to a power failure.

**Hibernate mode** is also a power-saving state, designed primarily for laptop computers. Sleep mode puts your computer's state (open programs, settings, etc.) in memory, while Hibernate mode saves your computer's state to a file on your hard disk, and then turns off your computer. Hibernate mode uses less power than sleep mode and restores your computer to an awake state fairly quickly, typically when you touch the Power button on the computer; when your computer wakes up, things will be just the way they were when you put the computer in Hibernate mode.

The **Restart command** does not attempt to save your computer's state; instead, it closes all open programs then temporarily powers off the machine and immediately powers it on again. The Restart process essentially clears everything out of your computer's memory and does not attempt to save your computer's state to your hard drive. Restarting your computer can be a useful problem-solving technique if your computer starts misbehaving

When you use the **Shut Down command**, you essentially turn off the computer so that it uses no electricity. Windows does not try to retain any record of open programs or files in memory or on your hard drive. Instead, Windows assumes that you will close all your programs and save all your work before you shut down the computer. If you don't, the Shut Down command closes your programs for you, without saving your work. Since shutting down a computer essentially eliminates the computer's use of power, a power failure has no effect on the computer, and you won't lose any work. At the same time, when you turn your computer back on, it will need to go through its startup process, which takes more time than awakening a computer from either Sleep or Hibernate mode.

Windows 8's Shut Down command performs the same function that hibernating performed in previous editions. Windows Help and Support refers to this behavior as "fast startup" and describes fast startup as follows:

"Fast startup is a setting that helps your PC start up faster after shutdown. Windows does this by saving system info to a file upon shutdown. When you start your PC again, Windows uses that system info to resume your PC instead of restarting it."

Essentially, when you shut down a Windows 8 computer, the operating system performs a hybrid shutdown, closing all user sessions, then copying anything that is still running in RAM (primarily, the core of the operating system) onto the hard drive, and finally turning off the system hardware. When Windows 8 starts up after a hybrid shutdown, it performs an abbreviated startup. After starting the computer's hardware, Windows 8 reloads its core from the hard drive, picking up right from where it left off. Starting a powered-off computer that uses Windows 8 is typically much faster than starting a powered-off computer using earlier editions of Windows.

**Take Note** Since Windows 8 uses the Shut Down command differently than earlier editions of Windows, you might run into trouble trying to get into your computer's BIOS using traditional techniques such as tapping F2 while the computer starts up. You might need to contact your computer's manufacturer to find out how to bypass the Windows 8 startup process to get into the BIOS.

To shut down or restart your computer, or to put it to sleep, you can start the Desktop app and then press Alt+F4 to display this dialog box and choose an option from the list.

**Figure 1-18**

Select an option to shut down or restart your computer or put it to sleep.

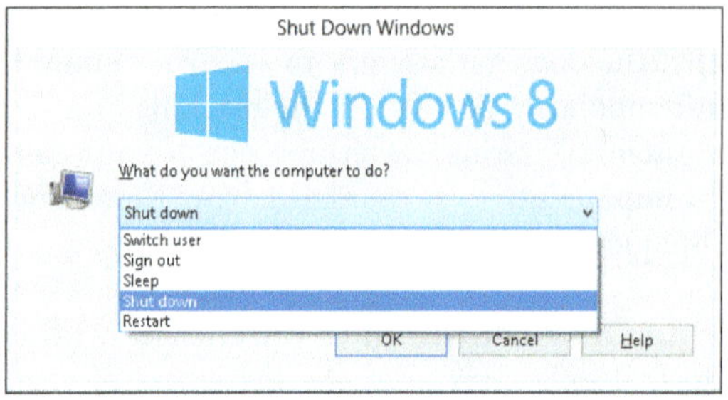


## STEP BY STEP Shut down, restart, or put your computer to sleep

Follow these step to shut down, restart, or put your computer to sleep:

1 Press **WinKey** (⊞)**+C** to display the Charms bar.

2 Click or use the arrows keys on the keyboard to highlight and then select the **Settings** charm.

**Take Note** To directly display the Settings charm, press WinKey (⊞)+I.

3 Click the **Power** button.

4 Click a choice.

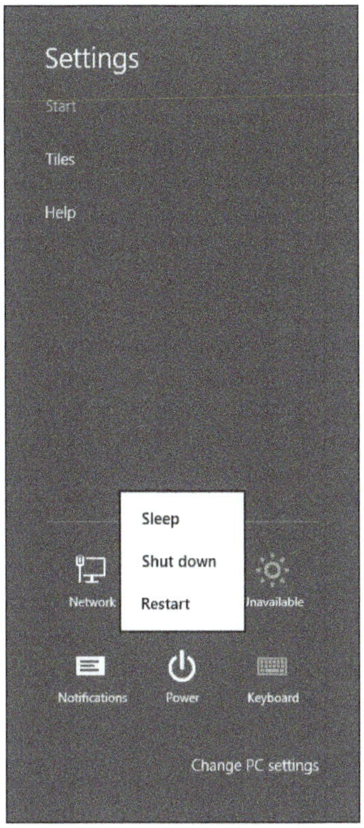


**Figure 1-19**

Select an option from the Power button, available on the Settings charm.

## What you learned in this lesson

- How to sign into Windows
- About Microsoft accounts and local accounts
- How to use Windows 8 with a Mouse and Keyboard
- How to find help when troubleshooting
- How to shut down Windows 8

**Bottom Line**

This chapter showed you how to set up accounts, lock and shut down your computer, and access fundamental controls such as settings, help, and use connected devices.

# Knowledge Assessment

## True / False

**Circle T if the statement is true or F if the statement is false.**

T F 1. You need to have a Microsoft operated email account to register a new account with Windows 8

T F 2. A Microsoft account lets you sync your files and settings between devices.

T F 3. A Local account can be shared between devices, as long as you use the same username and password combination.

T F 4. A desktop app and a native app are functionally the same.

T F 5. You can use the Quick Link menu to open Desktop apps.

T F 6. You need to close native apps because they consume too much memory.

T F 7. You cannot zoom the Start screen in or out, you can only scroll left and right.

T F 8. There is no difference between putting your computer into sleep and hibernate mode, sleep mode is for a desktop and hibernate is for a laptop.

T F 9. Locking your computer powers your computer off so no one else can use it.

T F 10. You can shut down your computer from the Charms bar.

## Multiple Choice

**Select the best response for the following statements.**

1. What are the two kinds of apps that Windows 8 can run?
   a. Desktop apps and Charm apps.
   b. Native apps and Desktop apps.
   c. Native apps and Windows apps.
2. What is a unique feature of the desktop app?
   a. The desktop is the only app that can run other apps.
   b. The desktop app can only run native apps.
   c. The desktop app can only run desktop apps.
   d. The desktop is the only location where you can access Clippy, a virtual assistant.
3. How do you display the Charms bar?
   a. Point the mouse in the lower-left corner of the screen.
   b. Press WinKey+B
   c. Press WinKey+C
4. Name two of the Charms on the Charms bar.
   a. Settings and Devices
   b. Share and Save
   c. Search and Launch
   d. Save and Search
5. Name one way to cycle through Windows 8 apps.
   a. Press WinKey+Spacebar
   b. Press Alt+Tab
   c. Press WinKey+Shift
   d. Slide the mouse pointer to the lower-left corner of the screen.

6. How do you display the Start screen only using the keyboard?
    a. Press Ctrl+W
    b. Press WinKey+Shift
    c. Press WinKey
7. How can you display the Quick Link menu using your mouse or a shortcut?
    a. WinKey+Q
    b. Slide the mouse to the lower-right corner of your screen and right-click the image of the app
    c. WinKey+X
    d. Slide the mouse to the center of the screen, and click WinKey+Q
8. How can you close an app using the keyboard?
    a. Press Ctrl+F2
    b. Press Alt+F4
    c. Press WinKey+C
9. How do you lock your computer?
    a. Press WinKey+M
    b. Click your name or picture on the Start screen and click Lock.
    c. Hold the WinKey and right-click, then click the Lock icon.
10. How do you launch the Help and Support application?
    a. Return to the desktop and press WinKey+C to launch Clippy, a virtual assistant.
    b. From the Start Screen, type Help and choose Help and Support then enter a query.
    c. From the Charms bar, select the Help icon and then enter a query.

## Competency Assessment

### Project 1-1: Help and Support

1. Access the Start screen, and then type **Help and choose Help and Support**.
2. Search for Help on Signing In.
3. Search for or locate information on creating a strong password.

### Project 1-2: Hibernate Mode

1. Open the desktop app.
2. Press **Alt+F4** to display the Shut Down options dialog box.
3. Sleep or Hibernate your computer.
4. After your computer is in sleep or hibernate mode, wake your computer and log in.

## Proficiency Assessment

### Project 1-3: Changing the Password

1. Change the password of your main user account.
2. Lock your computer, and then sign in using your new password.

### Project 1-4: Switch between running apps

1. Switch between running apps in two different ways: Use WinKey+Tab to access and then switch to another running app.
2. After you have switched apps, use Alt+Tab to cycle through your other running apps.

## Mastery Assessment

### Project 1-5: Access Quick Link

1. Access the Quick Link menu and open the Control Panel.
2. Change your desktop background to an image, and change your screen resolution.

### Project 1-6: Create more then one user

1. Create a second and third user account on your computer; one that is a local account and a second that is a Microsoft account with admin privileges.
2. Logout and then sign as each user
3. Sign into your main user account again.

# Navigating and Customizing the Start Screen 2

## LESSON SKILL MATRIX

| In this lesson, you will learn the following skills: |
| --- |
| Navigate on the Start screen |
| Work with tiles |
| Search your computer |
| Reorganize the Start Screen |
| Work with the Charms bar |

## KEY TERMS

- Panning
- Hot spots
- Tiles
- Live tiles
- Windows legacy apps
- Pinning
- Unpinning

©Livingpix/iStockPhoto

Simon recently upgraded his laptop to Windows 8, while working on a major project at Fabrikam, Inc., a real estate agency. He needs to learn how to search his computer to locate all of his existing project files, and reorganize the Start Screen so he can manage the project efficiently.

## SOFTWARE ORIENTATION

The Windows 8 start screen is your starting point for working with apps and your device.

**Figure 2-1**
Windows 8 Start Screen

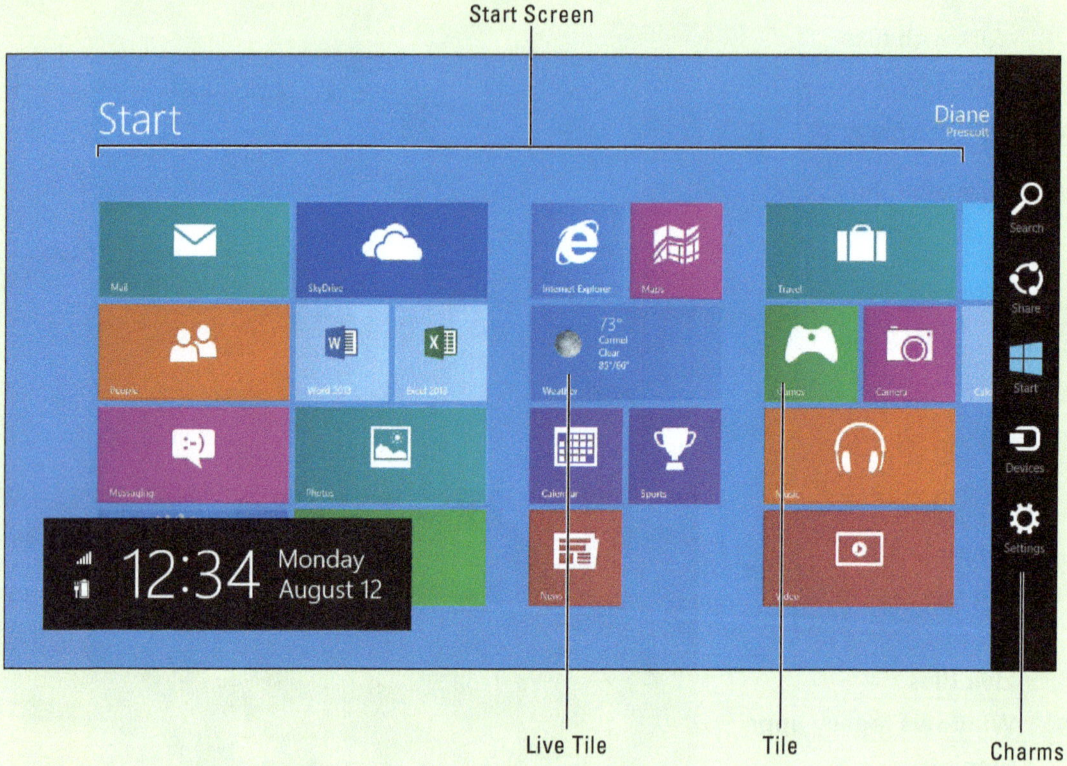


*Photos used with permission from Microsoft*

## STARTING UP

You will not need to work with any files for this lesson.

## REVIEWING NAVIGATION

The Start screen was designed to accommodate users of touch devices, but those who are using a mouse and keyboard can still find their way around the Start screen. For common mouse and keyboard shortcuts you can use with Windows 8, refer to Lesson 1, "Getting Started with Windows 8."

In this lesson, we'll begin with a short review of navigation techniques. The following table lists some common actions you'll take while using Windows 8, along with their mouse, keyboard, and touch equivalents.

Take Note

Blank boxes in the table below indicate that an equivalent action could not be found.

| Action | Mouse | Keyboard | Touch |
|---|---|---|---|
| Choosing | Click | Press Enter | Tap when using the Start screen or a Windows 8 native app; double-tap when using the Desktop app |
| Open any app (including the Desktop) | From the Windows Start screen, click the app | | From the Windows Start screen, tap the app |
| Display the App bar, which contains commands and options for a Windows 8 native app | Right-click anywhere on the screen | Press WinKey (■)+Z | Drag up slightly from the bottom of the screen |
| Display the Start screen while working in an app (including the Desktop app) | Slide the mouse into the upper- or lower-right corner to display the Charms bar, and then click Start | Press WinKey (■) | From the right edge of the screen, swipe to the left slightly to display the Charms bar; then tap the Start button |
| Display a list of all apps installed on the computer | From the Start screen, right-click to display the Apps bar at the bottom of the screen; then click All Apps | From the Start screen, press WinKey (■)+Z and then press Enter | Drag up slightly from the bottom of the screen and then tap All Apps |
| Scroll horizontally (also called **panning**) from one side of the Start screen to the other | Use your mouse's scroll wheel | Click the arrow keys or drag the scroll box at the bottom of the screen | Slide your finger from left to right or from right to left |
| Scroll vertically in legacy apps | Use your mouse's scroll wheel | Use the arrow keys to scroll one line at a time or the Page Up or Page Down keys to scroll one screen at a time | Slide your finger up the page to scroll down and down the page to scroll up |
| Display the Charms bar | Slide your mouse to the top- or bottom-right corner of your screen | Press WinKey (■)+C | Swipe in from the right edge of the screen |
| Switch apps | Slide the mouse pointer to the upper-left corner of the screen. When the last app you viewed appears, slide the mouse down the left side of the screen to display the Running Apps bar shown in the figure | Press WinKey (■)+Tab | From the left edge of the screen, swipe your finger to the right slightly and then back again to the edge to display the Running Apps bar, making a loop with your finger |

| Action | Mouse | Keyboard | Touch |
|---|---|---|---|
| Zoom the Start screen | Click the Zoom box in the lower-right corner of the Start screen | Press Ctrl+Plus sign to zoom in, or Ctrl+Minus sign to zoom out | Pinch your fingers together to zoom out; pinch them out to zoom in |
| Display the Quick Link menu | From any app or on the Start screen, slide the mouse to the lower left corner of your screen. When the image of the last app you used appears, right-click | Press WinKey (⊞)+X | |
| Using the Desktop app or a legacy program, display a shortcut menu | Right-click | Press Shift+F10 | Tap and hold |
| Close a Windows 8 native app | Drag the mouse pointer down from the top of the screen to the bottom | Press Alt+F4* | Drag your finger down from the top of the screen to the bottom |
| Shut down your computer | Place the mouse pointer in the upper- or lower-right corner of the screen to display the Charms bar. Click the Settings charm, click the Power button, and then click an option | Display the Desktop App Using Alt+D. Then, Press Alt+F4 while viewing the Desktop App. From the Start Screen, press the Windows Logo Key (Windows Key Image)+I to display the Settings Charm; then press tab and the Arrow Keys until you highlight power. Then, press Enter to choose an option | Swipe in from the right edge of the screen to display the Charms bar. Tap the Settings charm, tap the Power button, and then tap an option |

* The keyboard shortcut works for all apps, except the Desktop app; if you use the keyboard shortcut Alt+F4 while viewing the Desktop app, Windows 8 will prompt you to shut down your computer.

**Take Note** Microsoft has encouraged hardware manufacturers to introduce their own touch gestures; to find out whether your device supports additional gestures, go to your device manufacturer's website.

## Corner navigation

The Windows 8 Start screen uses the corners of the display as "**hot spots**" for your finger or your mouse, with keyboard shortcuts available for each corner. Each corner has a function; remembering the function will help you immeasurably when navigating in Windows 8.

- The upper- or lower-right corner displays the Charms bar.
- The upper-left corner controls the display of the Running Apps bar.
- The lower-left corner controls the display of a handy context menu.

**Take Note** Be aware that the corner hot spots are very close to the edge of your screen. To access a hot spot with your mouse, you might need to move the pointer almost outside the screen.

## Redisplaying the Start screen

Although we explained how to redisplay the Start screen in the table shown in the preceding section, it bears repeating, since you tend to start everything from the Start screen. If you're using a keyboard and mouse to navigate Windows 8, you can most quickly redisplay the Start screen by pressing the WinKey (⊞) on the keyboard. If you're using a touch device, swipe left from the right edge of the screen to display the Charms bar, then tap the Start button.

**Take Note** Repeatedly pressing WinKey (⊞) cycles between the Start screen and the last app you were viewing.

## SEARCHING

You can easily perform searches on your computer in Windows 8 in a couple of different ways. First, you can start typing while viewing the Start screen. For example, if you've installed Microsoft Office and you would like to run Microsoft Excel. While viewing the Start screen, start typing **Excel**. As you type, Windows displays the Search bar on the right side of the screen, and programs that match your search criteria on the left side of the screen. To run a program that appears in the search results list, tap, click it, or use the arrow keys on the keyboard to highlight it and press Enter.

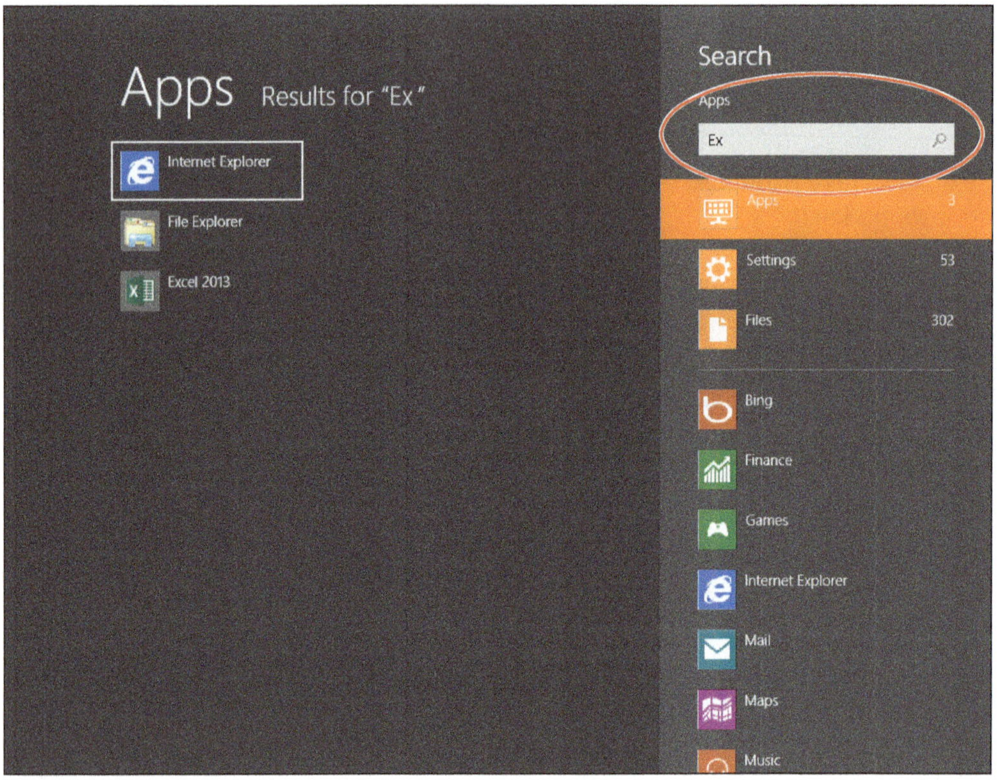


**Figure 2-2**
To find a program you want to run, start typing its name while viewing the Start screen.

By default, when you type on the Start screen, Windows searches for apps. But the Search charm helps you narrow your search by enabling you to search for apps, settings, or files. These choices appear in the Search charm's Search bar on the right side of the screen. You can start typing, let Windows 8 search for an app, and when the Search bar appears, click Settings or Files to change the type of search.

Figure 2-3

Using the Search bar, you can narrow your search.

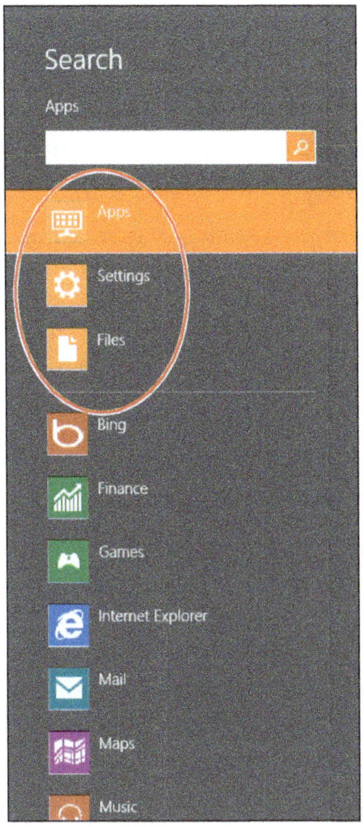


Using touch gestures or a mouse, you can select a search category if you display the Charms bar and select the Search charm, then select the search category from the Search bar. You can also use any of the following three keyboard shortcuts to specify a search category:

- WinKey (⊞)+Q searches for apps
- WinKey (⊞)+W searches for settings
- WinKey (⊞)+F searches for files

## STEP BY STEP To use the Search charm and search for files

1. Display the Search bar for files by pressing **WinKey (⊞)+F** or by selecting the **Search** charm from the Charms bar and then tapping or clicking **Files** at the top of the Search bar.
2. In the Search box at the top of the Search bar, type the first few letters of the file for which you want to search. Possible files appear below the search box.
3. If the file you want to open doesn't appear in the list, type a few more letters.
4. When the file appears, tap or click it to open it.

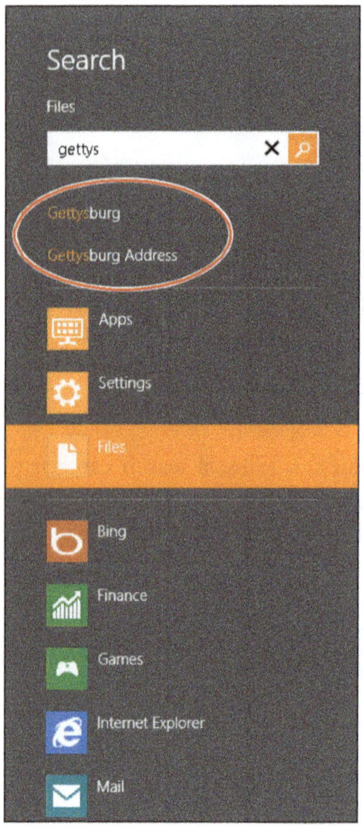


**Figure 2-4**

Using the File search charm, search results appear below the Search box.

**STEP BY STEP** **Typing on the Start screen**

Do you have to specify the type of search you want if you are searching for something other than an app? Well, yes and no. Although Windows searches for apps by default, you can type on the Start screen and then change the type of search after Windows displays the Search bar.

1. While viewing the Start screen, type a couple letters of the file name (such as "**Ge**" of Gettysburg Address, in this example).
2. When the Search bar appears, select the type of search you really meant—**Settings** or **Files**. Windows 8 searches again, this time showing names that contain the letters you typed and match the type of search you selected.
3. If the file doesn't appear, type a few more letters.
4. Results appear on the left side of the screen. Tap or click one to open it.

**Figure 2-5**

You can type a search string on the Start screen and then specify the type of search without using the Charms bar.

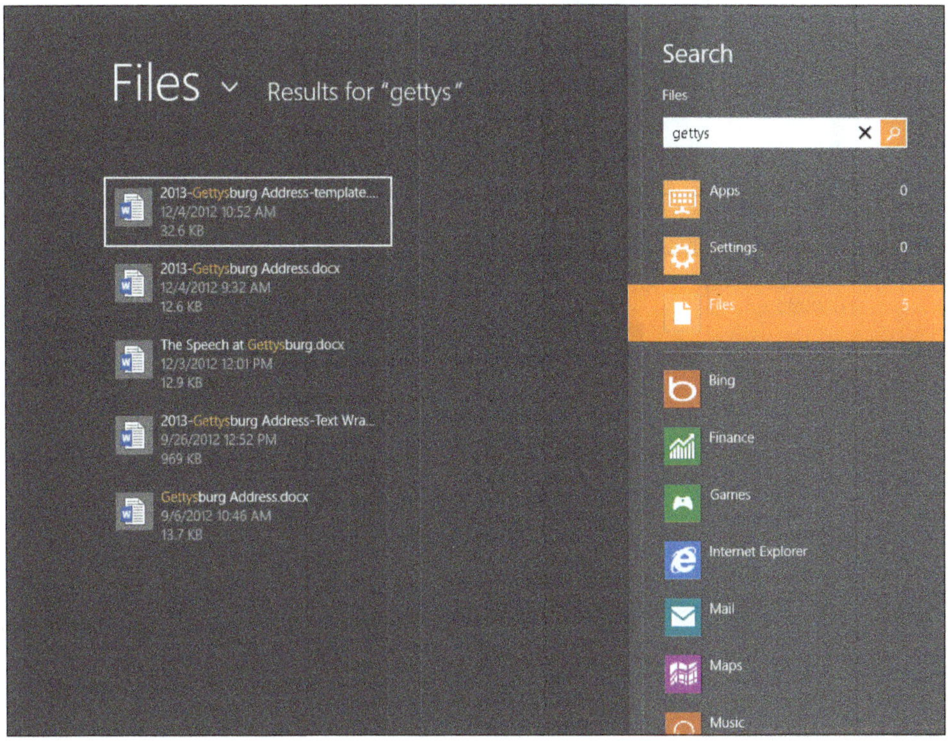

If you are using Windows 8.1 you have additional search options. You can select the type of file you are looking for directly beneath the Search heading, as well as the ability to click on the magnifying glass icon to see a full search result page.

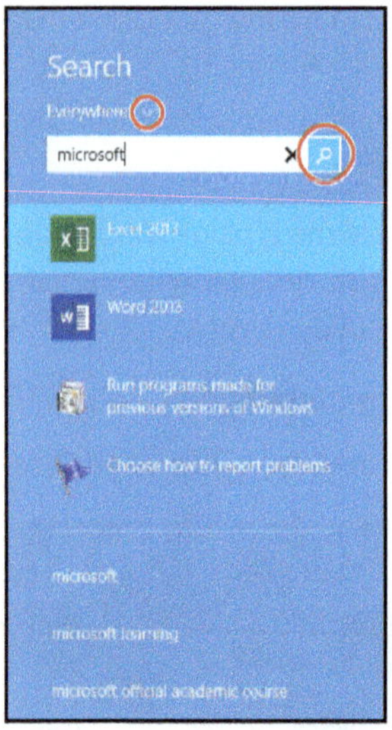


**Figure 2-6**

In Windows 8.1 you have additional search options.

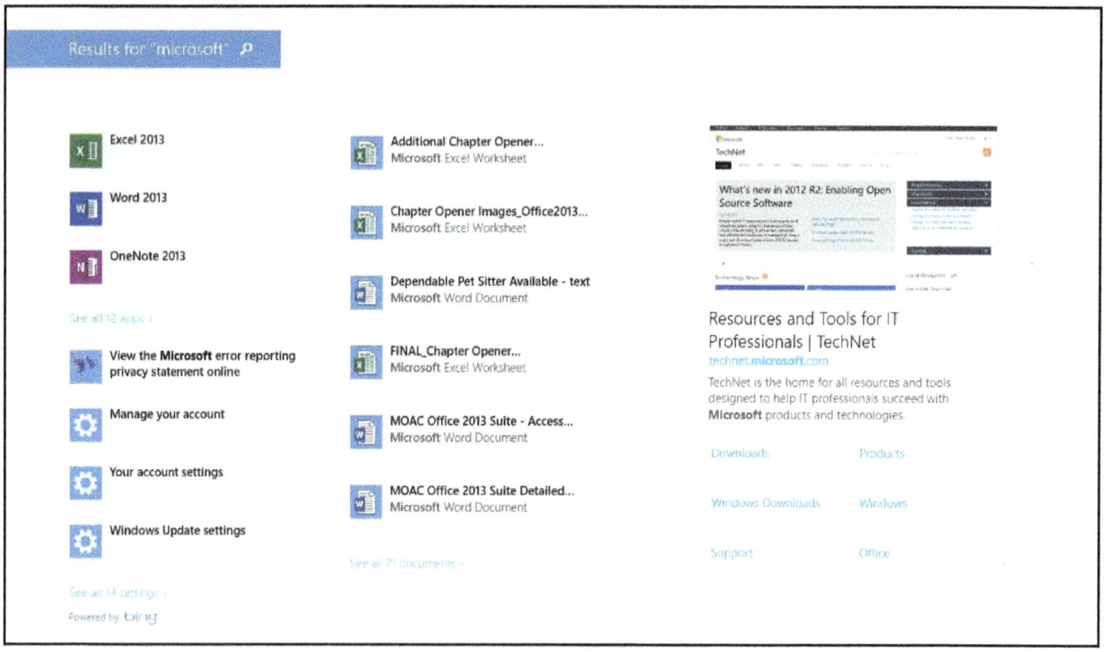


**Figure 2-7**

Click on the Magnifying Glass to see a full result page in Windows 8.1

## WORKING WITH TILES

The Start screen contains **tiles** that represent the apps you run. You can think of tiles as the desktop icons you used in earlier editions of Windows to run programs. If you were concerned with icon organization in earlier editions of Windows, you could drag your icons around to place them where you wanted, pin them to the Windows task bar or the top of the Start menu, and even place them in folders on the Windows Start menu.

In Windows 8, you can also control and organize tiles. The tiles that represent Windows 8 native apps also display updated information on the Start screen—a phenomenon called **live tile**. Now, you have several ways that you can control tile behavior and the appearance of the Windows 8 Start screen to make it reflect the way you work.

Customize how your Start Screen looks in order to work most efficiently. Organize the apps you use the most at the center of the screen, and move apps you use less frequently off to the side.

### Setting tile options

Change options for tiles you use the most and least. Unpin apps you rarely use, and make pins you use frequently a larger size.

To set the options for a tile, display the options by right-clicking the tile or, on touch devices, you can display a tile's options by dragging the tile down slightly until a checkmark appears above the upper-right corner of the tile, then release the tile. The options appear at the bottom of the Start screen, and a checkmark appears in the tile you selected. In addition, the options you see depend on whether you select a Windows 8 native app tile or a legacy program tile.

**Take Note** You can hide tile options by right-clicking the tile or dragging the tile down slightly (swiping) so that the checkmark disappears and then release the app.

For Windows 8 native apps, you can select any of the options shown in the following list.

| Option | Function |
|---|---|
| Unpin from the Start screen | The app remains on your computer and you can still run it; you simply won't see a tile for it on the Start screen. For details on running an app that doesn't appear on the Start screen, see the next section. |
| Uninstall the app | This option removes the app from your computer and from the Start screen. |
| Control the size of the tile on the Start screen | This option allows you to resize your apps depending on organization or importance. |
| Tap or click the Turn Live Tile Off option | For tiles that can display updated information, this option makes the tile stop displaying that information. |

## Workplace Ready

Turn off Live Tiles that could contain sensitive information that you do not want your co-workers to see, particularly if you regularly share your screen. Live tiles can display images from your connected accounts, such as photos and the contents of Facebook messages.

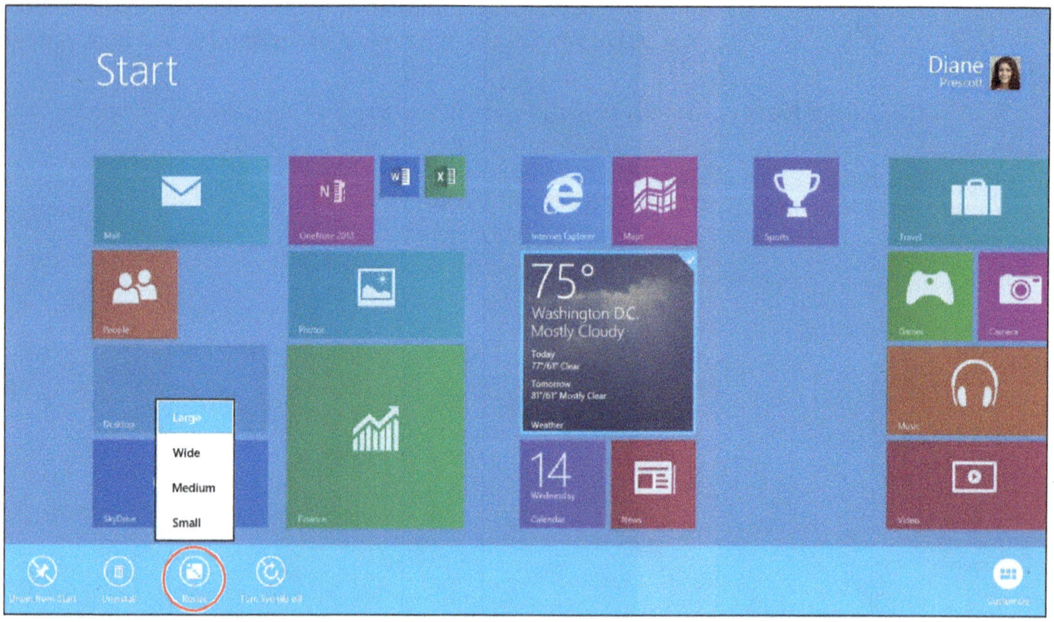


**Figure 2-8**

The options you can set for a Windows 8 native app. This Start screen shows some of the new tile size options available for Windows 8.1

*Photos used with permission from Microsoft*

For legacy apps, the ones that run on the Desktop app, you can select any of the options listed in the following table.

| Option | Function |
|---|---|
| Unpin from Start | The app remains on your computer and you can still run it; you simply won't see a tile for it on the Start screen. For details on running an app that doesn't appear on the Start screen, see the next section. |
| Pin to taskbar | Pin an icon for this app to the Desktop taskbar so that you can run the app directly from the Desktop. |
| Open a new window | This option enables you to run a second instance of a program that's already running. |
| Run as administrator | This option enables a user logged in using a standard local account to run a program using administrator level privileges. |
| Open file location | This option switches to the Desktop and launches File Explorer, displaying the folder containing the file used to run the program. |

## Workplace Ready

Some application functionality, such as installing a new app, may require you to run the program as an administrator.

**Figure 2-9**

The tile options available for a legacy app.

*Photos used with permission from Microsoft Images and clip art used with permission of Microsoft.*

**Take Note** If you change your mind and don't want to change an app's options, drag up slightly from the bottom of the screen or right-click the bar displaying the options.

## Displaying tiles in list format

By default, when you first install Windows, the only apps that appear on the Windows 8 Start screen are the Windows 8 native apps. **Windows legacy apps**, such as WordPad, the Calculator, and Paint are installed, but are not pinned to the Start screen.

**Take Note** If you bought Windows 8 pre-installed on a computer, the manufacturer may have added apps to the Start screen, including some of the legacy apps.

You can quickly and easily display all the apps installed on your computer in list format by dragging your finger up slightly from the bottom of the screen or by right-clicking anywhere on the Start screen. When a bar appears at the bottom of the Start screen, tap or click All Apps at the right edge of the bar.

**Figure 2-10**

Display apps in list format on the Start screen.

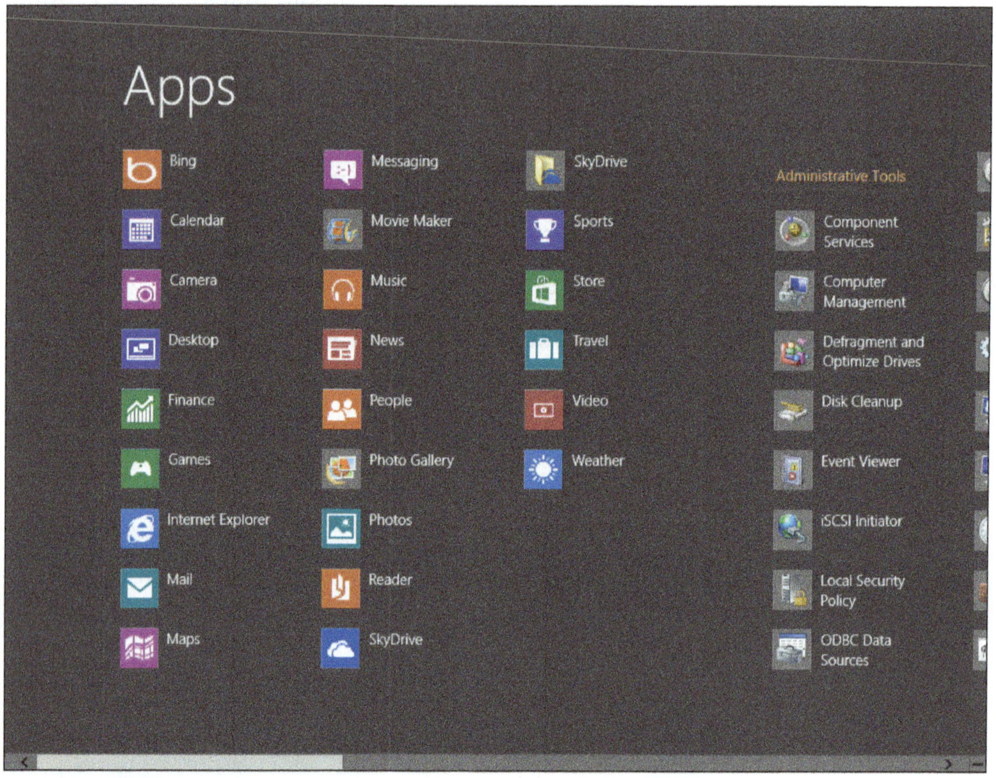


The Windows 8 native apps appear, by default, at the beginning of the list, and as you scroll to the right, legacy apps appear. You can think of the groups in which the legacy apps appear as the folders that appeared on the Start menu in earlier editions of Windows.

**Figure 2-11**

Legacy apps are organized into groups.

In Windows 8.1 you can see your app list by clicking on the arrow in the lower-left corner of the Start Screen.

**Figure 2-12**

Click on the arrow in the lower-left of the Start screen in Windows 8.1 to quickly show all applicationss.

*Photos used with permission from Microsoft*

## Pinning and unpinning tiles

Most programs you install automatically create tiles for themselves on the Windows 8 Start screen. In addition, most of them place tiles into groups on the Start screen. But you can control the programs that appear on the Start screen.

## STEP BY STEP Pinning to the Start screen

For example, if you want tiles for certain Windows Accessories to appear on the Start screen, you can easily add tiles for these apps to the Start screen by **pinning**:

**Take Note** Pinning is the term used to describe adding a tile to the Start screen or the Desktop task bar; **unpinning** is the term used to describe removing a tile from either location. Note that unpinning is not the same as uninstalling, which completely removes the app from your computer.

1. Drag your finger up slightly from the bottom of the screen or right-click anywhere on the Start screen to display the options bar at the bottom of the screen.
2. Choose **All Apps**.
3. Find the app for which you want to create a tile on the Start screen.
4. Right-click the app or drag the app down slightly. When a checkmark appears above the upper-right corner of the app, release it to display the bar at the bottom of the Start screen.

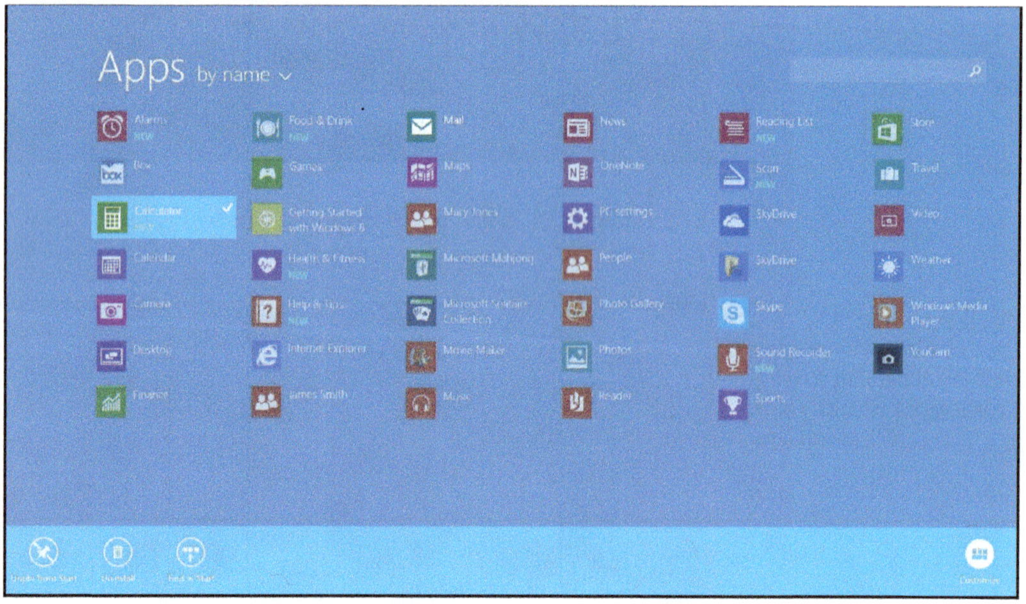


**Figure 2-13**
Display the options for the app.

5. Tap or click **Pin to Start**.

When you redisplay the Start screen in its default view and you scroll to the right, you'll find a tile for the app you selected at the end of the Start screen.

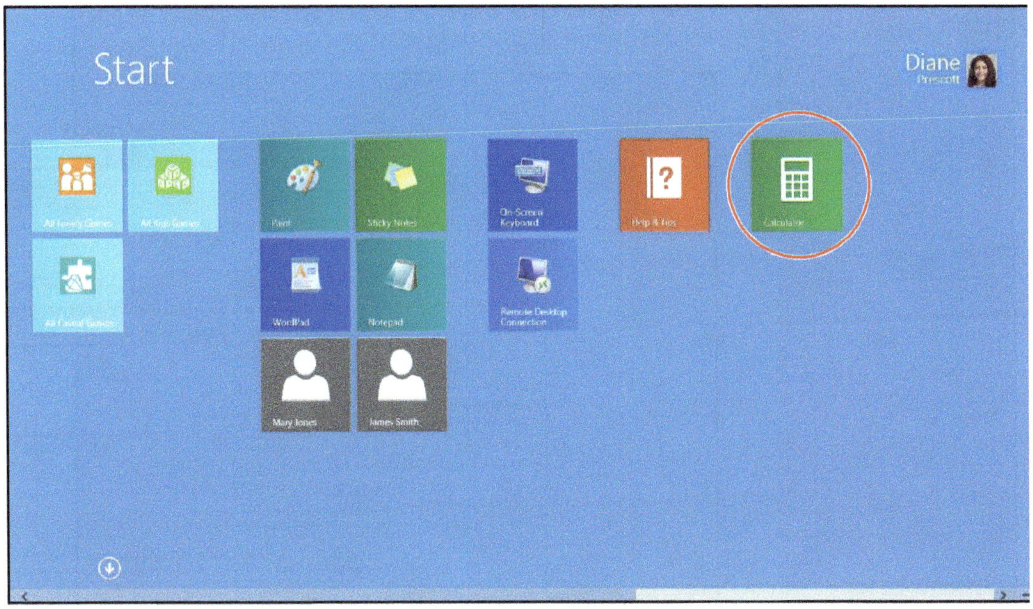


**Figure 2-14**

A tile for the app now appears on the Start screen.

To remove a tile from the Start screen, repeat the steps, choosing Unpin from Start in Step 4. Remember, unpinning is not the same as uninstalling. Even though no tile appears for the app on the Start screen, you can still run it by tapping or clicking it while viewing all apps.

## STEP BY STEP Pin web pages to the Start screen

### Workplace Ready

Pin the pages you visit every day to the Start screen to quickly access them while you work. For example, you might pin your company's intranet dashboard to your Start screen.

You can also pin web pages to the Start screen; if you visit a site frequently, you might find pinning it to the Start screen useful. The following example uses the legacy Internet Explorer on the Desktop to find a website and then pin it to the Start screen. After the steps, you'll find a tip that tells you how to use the Windows 8 native Internet Explorer to pin a page to the Start screen.

1. Display the page in Internet Explorer.

2 Tap or click the **Gear** tool in the upper-right corner of the window.

**Figure 2-15**

Adding a website to the Start screen.

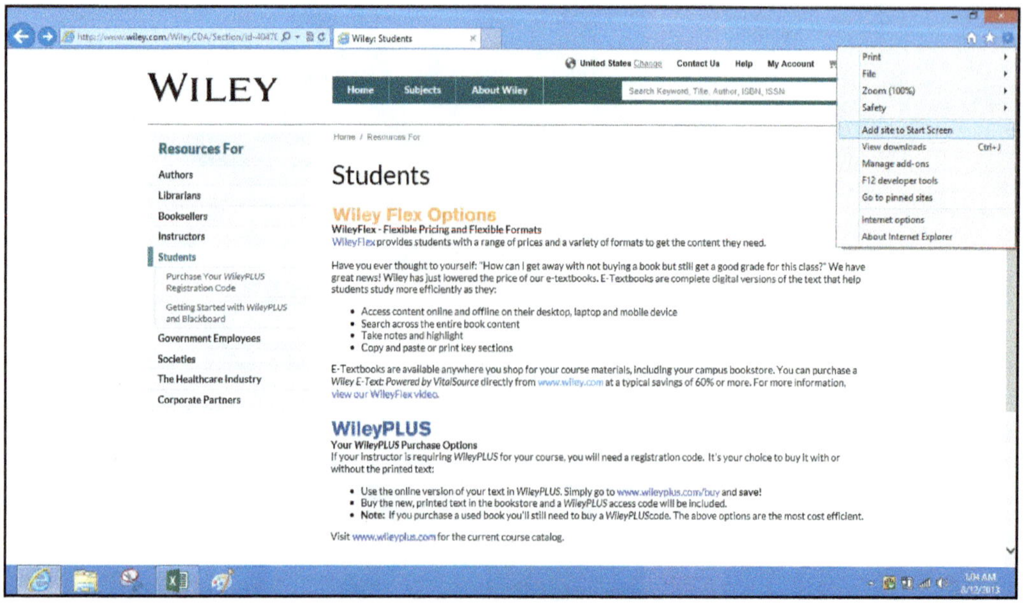


3 Choose **Add Site to Start Screen**. Internet Explorer displays a dialog box showing the web site title and address.

4 Tap or click **Add**. Windows adds a tile for the website to the end of the Start screen.

**Take Note** The steps above work in both the legacy version and the Windows 8 native version of Internet Explorer. In the native version, for Step 2, tap or click the Pin icon at the bottom of the window and then tap or click Pin to Start. In the window that appears—the equivalent of Step 3 above—tap or click Pin to Start again.

## Rearranging tiles

By now, you've noticed that you can easily launch programs that have tiles on the left side of the Start screen, but it's not quite as easy to launch a program that has a tile on the right side of the screen. You have to scroll to find it, or you need to type a few letters of its name.

The default order of the Start screen is not set in stone, you can move tiles around to suit your needs. For example, if you don't use a Windows native app, move it to the right or unpin it from the Start screen. If you use a legacy app regularly, move it to the left side of the screen.

How do you move a tile? Tap and hold the tile, then move it either up or down, and then drag it to a new position. Using a mouse, drag the tile in any direction to the new position.

To quickly move a tile a long distance, i.e., from one end of the Start screen to the other, drag the tile down to the bottom of the screen. Windows 8 zooms the Start screen to display all the tiles at once. You can then drag and drop the tile where you want it.

**Figure 2-16**

Moving a tile a long distance.

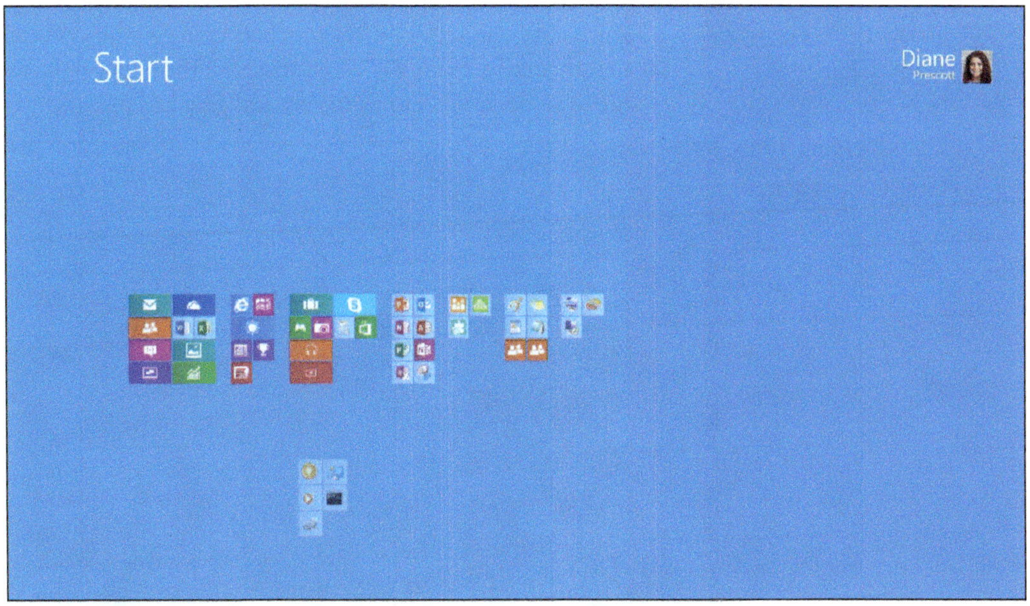


*Photos used with permission from Microsoft*

Before you dive into moving all your tiles around, consider creating groups for them and then move the entire group at once.

**STEP BY STEP** **Creating and managing tile groups**

## Workplace Ready

Group apps that you use daily for your work into a single group to work more efficiently. If you use a lot of apps each day, group apps that you use for particular tasks into task-related groups such as a group for Scheduling and another for Communication.

For an even cleaner Start screen, you can organize tiles into groups. For example, if you added Movie Maker and Photo Gallery to your computer from the available Windows Essentials tools (formerly called Windows Live tools) along with some of the standard accessories that you use frequently, such as the Calculator, Notepad, and the Snipping tool. Storing these apps in a group and naming it "My Windows Tools" will enable you to use that screen space for other essential apps. You can begin by creating a new group.

1. Use the mouse to drag one of the tiles that should be part of the group to an open space until you see a vertical gray bar. Using a touch device, you can drag the tile down slightly until a checkmark appears above the upper-right corner of the tile, then drag the tile to an open space until the vertical gray bar appears.

**Figure 2-17**

Creating a new group.

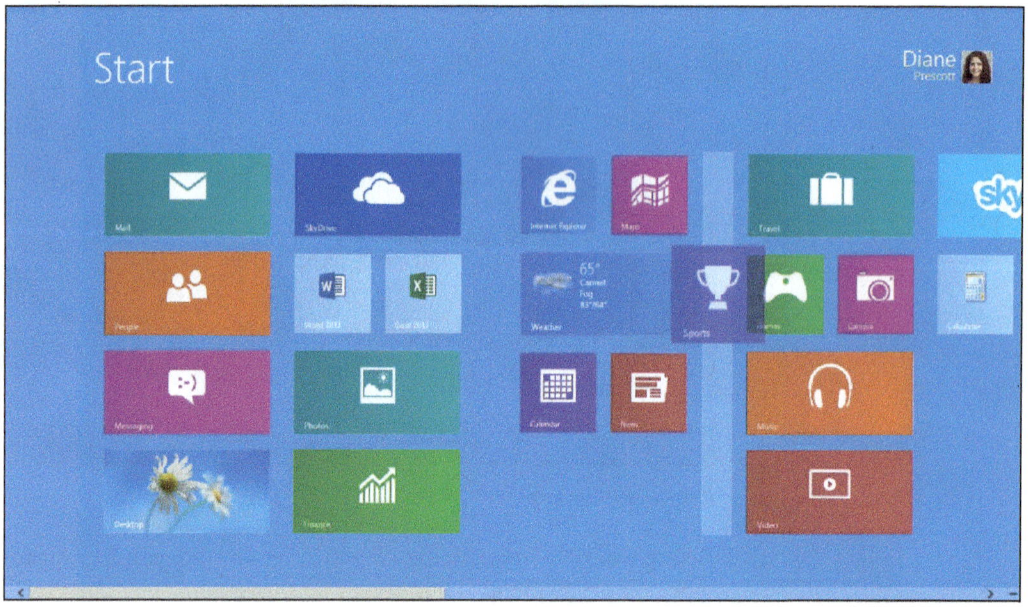


*Images and clip art used with permission of Microsoft.*

2 Release the tile. Windows 8 creates a new group and places the tile in that group.

**Figure 2-18**

The tile appears in the new group.

*Images and clip art used with permission of Microsoft.*

3 Using the technique described in Step 1, drag more tiles next to the first tile.

4 Repeat Step 3 until all appropriate tiles appear in the group.

## STEP BY STEP Naming tile groups in Windows 8

Naming groups helps you organize your start screen and make apps easier to locate efficiently.

To name the group in Windows 8, follow these steps:

1 View all the tiles, or zoom out, by pinching your fingers together on the Start screen or clicking the Zoom button in the lower-right corner of the Start screen.

2 Select the group you want to name. Using a mouse, you can right-click the group to select it and display a bar at the bottom of the screen. To select a group on a touch device, drag the group down slightly until a checkmark appears. When you release the group, Windows displays the bar at the bottom of the screen.

**Figure 2-19**

A. Name group button.
B. Name group dialog box.
C. Selected group.

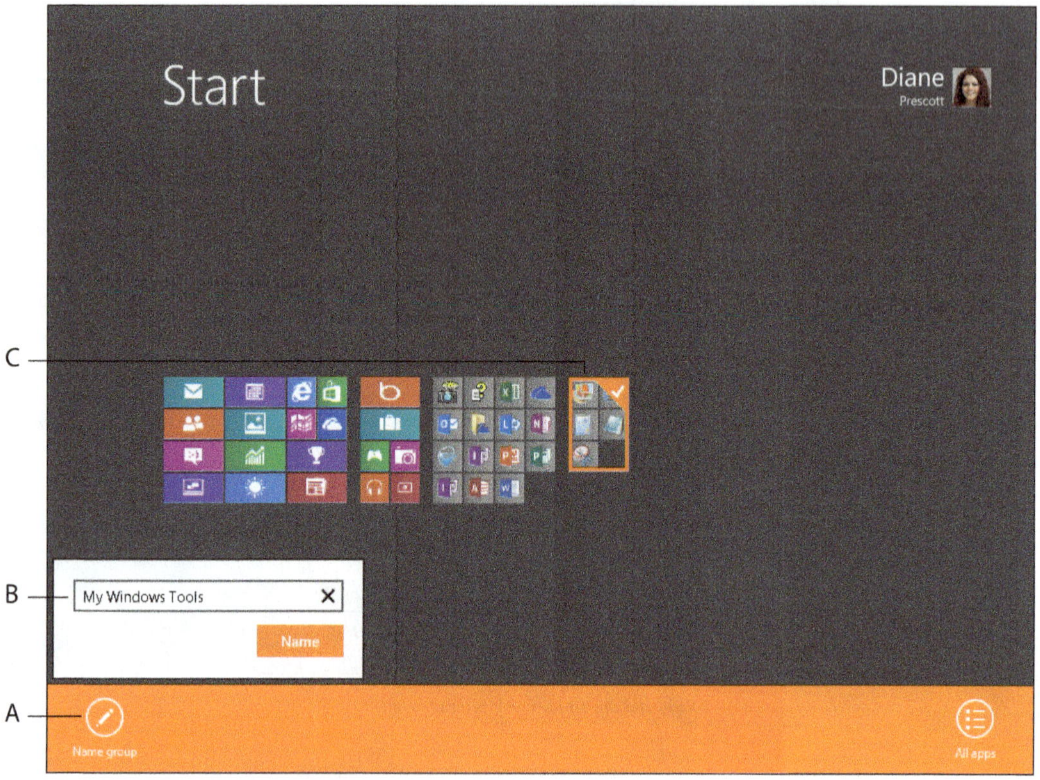


*Photos used with permission from Microsoft*

3 Tap or click the **Name** group from the bar at the bottom of the screen.

4 Enter **My Windows Tools**.

5 Tap or click **Name**. When you redisplay the Start screen in its default form, the group name you assigned appears above the group.

**Figure 2-20**

A named group on the Start screen.

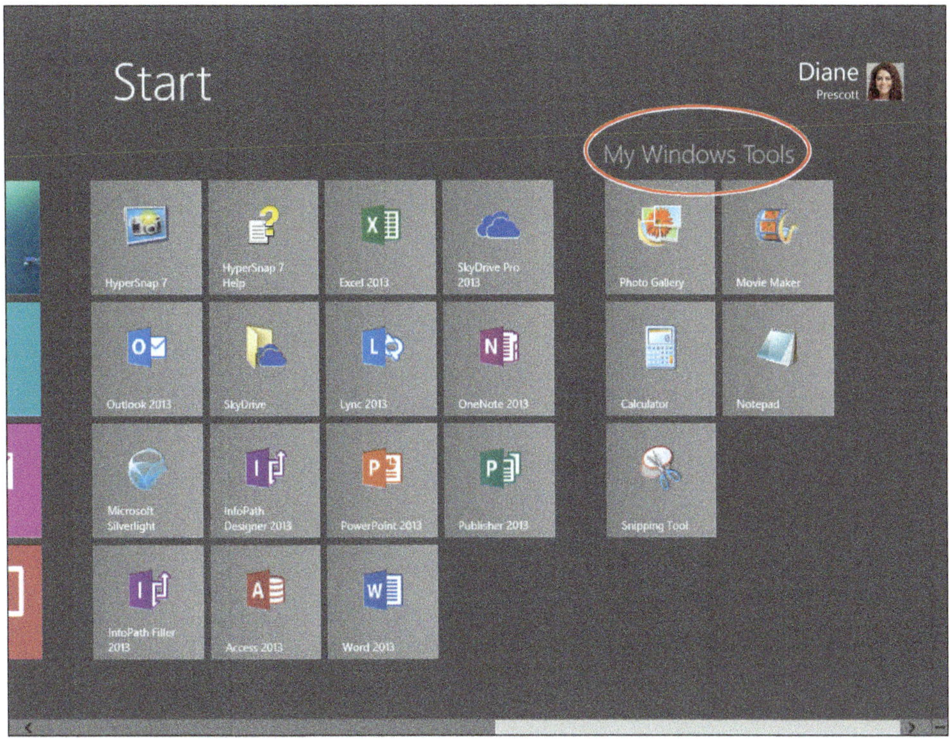


*Photos used with permission from Microsoft*

**Take Note** You can move an entire group to a new position on the Start screen: complete Step 1 above; then select the group (if you select using touch techniques, don't release the group) and drag it to its new position on the Start screen.

To name your group in Windows 8.1 do the following

**STEP BY STEP** **Naming a group in Windows 8.1**

1. Right-click, or swipe down on any tile within a group.
2. Click inside the group name that is displayed above the group.

3 Press **Enter** when you have entered a group name.

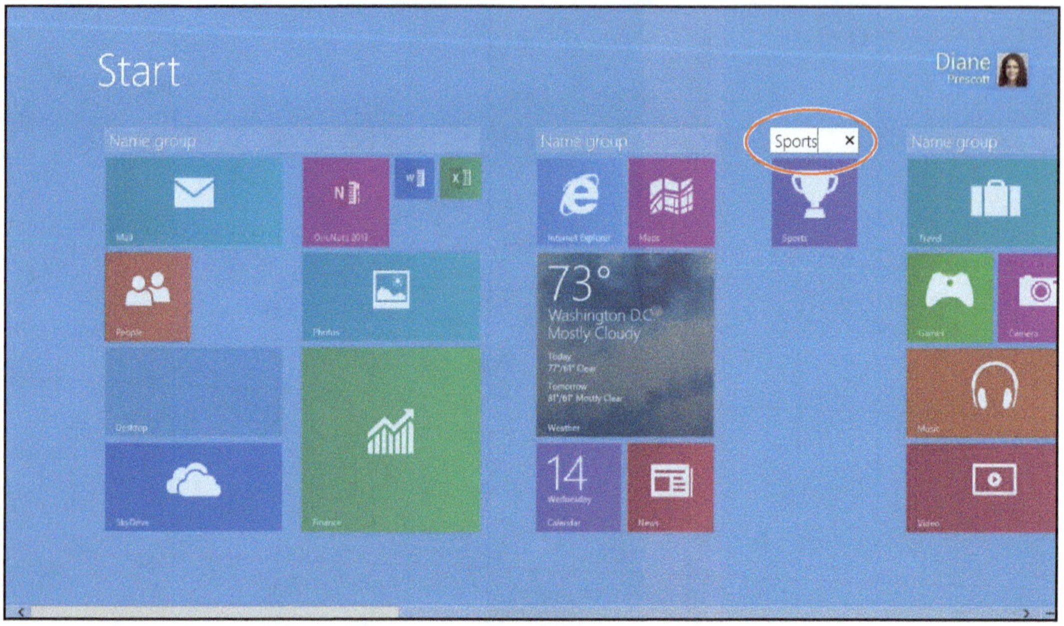


**Figure 2-21**

In Windows 8.1 you can name the group after swiping any tile the Start screen.

*Photos used with permission from Microsoft*

## WORKING WITH THE CHARMS BAR

The Charms bar is a multi-purpose bar that appears on the right side of the screen. If you display it from the Start screen, it can help you to:

- Perform searches on your computer
- Share information between Windows 8 native apps
- Display the Start screen or the last app you viewed
- Connect hardware on your computer to Windows 8 native apps
- Display settings available for Windows 8 native apps

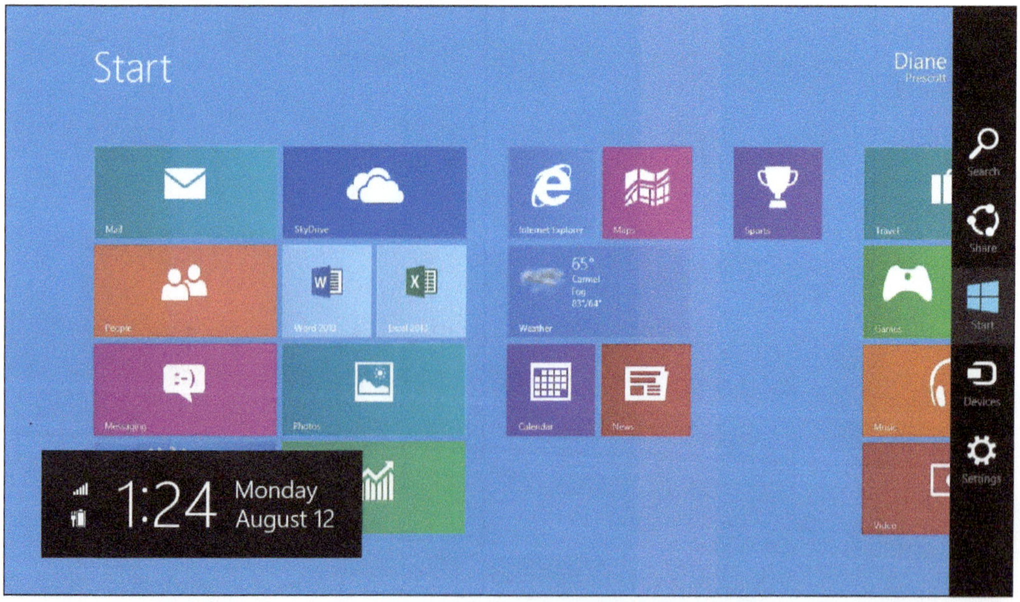


**Figure 2-22**

The Charms bar appears on the right side of your screen.

*Photos used with permission from Microsoft*

Be aware that things look a little different if you display the Charms bar from the Desktop app. The Share and Devices charms function only for Windows 8 native apps; on the Desktop app, you won't see any available options for these two charms. You will, however, see options for the Settings charm that are specific to Desktop apps.

To display the Charms bar, do one of the following:

- Press WinKey (⊞)+C
- Point the mouse in the lower-right or upper-right corner of the screen
- Swipe in from the right side of the screen

Using keyboard shortcuts, you can open a Charm directly, as indicated in the following table.

| Shortcut key combination | Result |
|---|---|
| WinKey (⊞)+Q | Opens the Search pane to search for apps |
| WinKey (⊞)+F | Opens the Search pane to search for files |
| WinKey (⊞)+W | Opens the Search pane to search for settings |
| WinKey (⊞) | Displays the Start screen or the last app you viewed |
| WinKey (⊞)+I | Opens the Settings charm |
| WinKey (⊞)+K | Opens the Devices charm |
| WinKey (⊞)+H | Opens the Share charm |

We covered the Search charm and its associated pane earlier in this lesson. The Start charm simply displays the Start screen if you're viewing an app. If you're viewing the Start screen and select the Start charm, Windows 8 displays the last app you viewed. When using a keyboard and mouse, you can bypass the Start charm and press WinKey (⊞) to display the Start screen or toggle between the Start screen and the last app you viewed.

**STEP BY STEP**

## Working with the Charms Bar

In this example, you will use the Devices charm while working in a Windows 8 native app to print a web page from the Windows 8 native version of Internet Explorer.

1. Open Internet Explorer from the Start screen and navigate to a web page.

2 Open the Charms bar and tap or click the **Devices** option. The Devices charm lists all devices—both wired and wireless—attached to your computer.

**Figure 2-23**

The Devices charm and the Windows 8 native app for Internet Explorer.

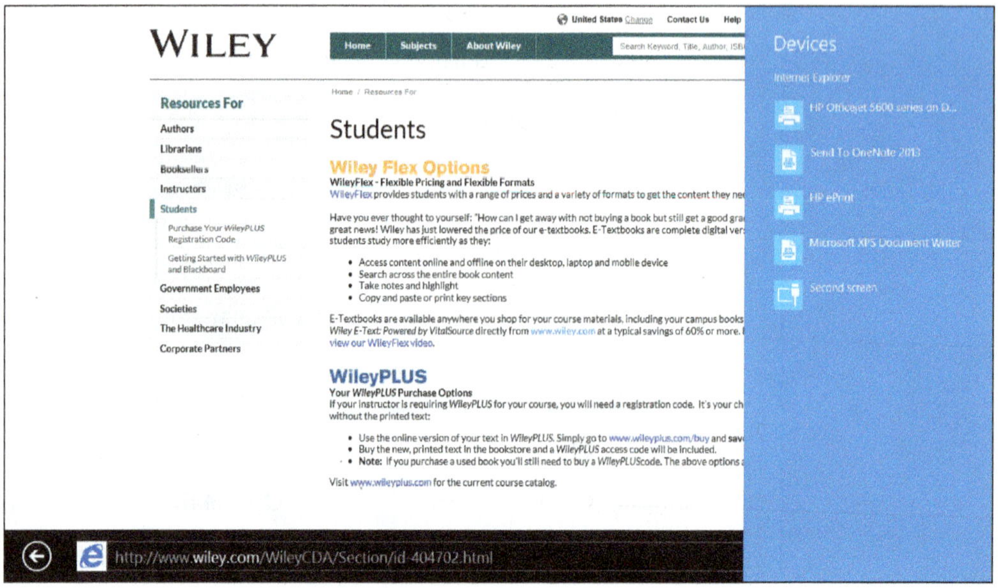


3 Choose a printer to use to print the page.

The Share charm is the Windows 8 native app equivalent to the Windows legacy app, Clipboard, that runs in the Desktop app. The Windows Clipboard is used to share information between legacy apps on the Desktop. The Share charm enables you to share information between Windows 8 native apps.

Quickly move information between native apps using the Share charm. When you have a file open, activate the charm to send the information to another app and continue your work.

**STEP BY STEP**

## Attaching a picture to an e-mail

In this example, you will attach a picture to an e-mail.

1 From the Start screen, choose the **Photos** app. From the library options, tap or click one of the options: Pictures, SkyDrive, Flickr, Facebook, or an external device. You must have at least one photo in one of the libraries for this example.

2 Choose a photo from your chosen library.

3 Open the Charms bar, and tap or click the **Share** option. Windows 8 displays a list of native apps with which you can share the picture.

**Figure 2-24**

Display the Share charm while working in a Windows 8 native app, and you'll see other native apps with which you can share information.

*Images and clip art used with permission of Microsoft.*

4 From the list, select the **Mail** app. The Windows 8 native Mail app opens and an e-mail message is started for you with the photo embedded.

**Figure 2-25**

Sharing information between two Windows 8 native apps.

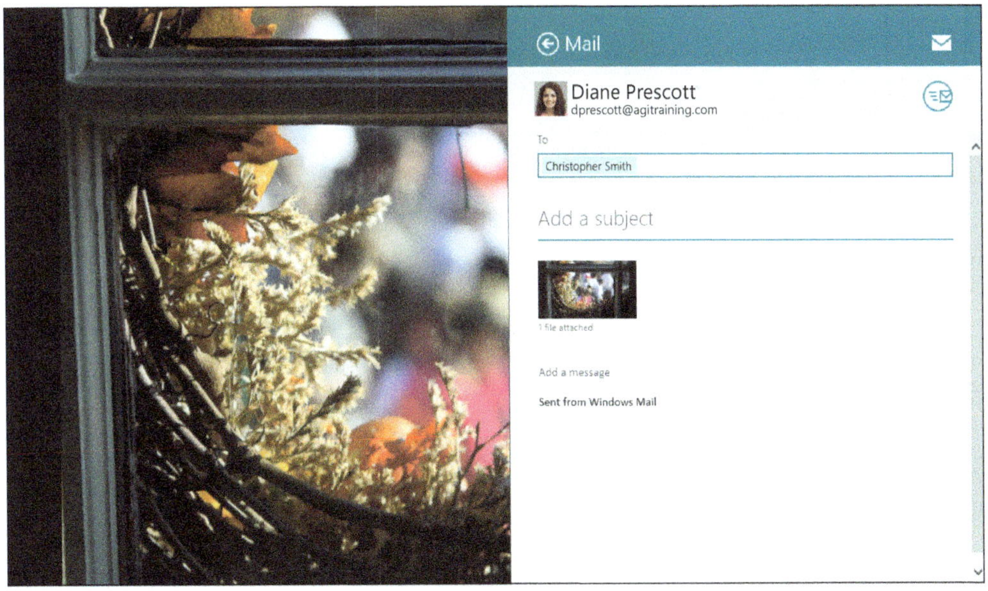


*Images and clip art used with permission of Microsoft.*

From the Start screen, you can control settings for tiles and also get Help. You can also access settings for your network, speaker volume, display brightness, display notifications, and change PC settings; shut down your computer, enable Sleep mode, or restart. From a touch device, you can display the on-screen keyboard.

**Figure 2-26**

The Settings charm as it appears from the Start screen.

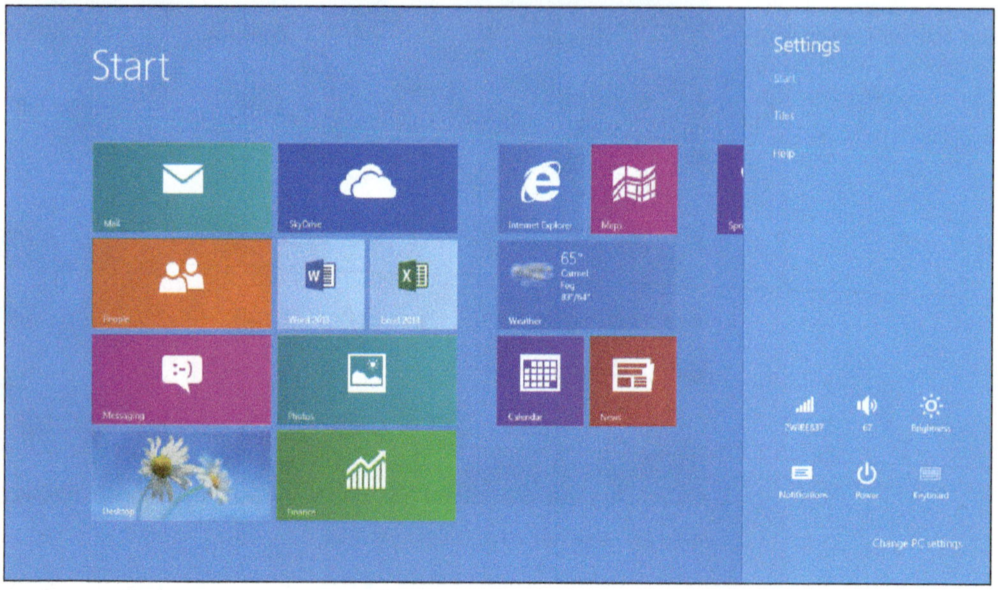


*Images and clip art used with permission of Microsoft.*

**Take Note** If you open the Settings charm while working in a Windows 8 native app, options you can use to control the settings of that app are displayed.

There are different options available when you display the Settings charm from the Desktop. The options at the bottom of the Settings charm pane are the same as the ones you see when you display the Settings charm from the Start screen. But at the top of the Settings charm pane, you find options to display the Desktop Control Panel, the Desktop Personalization window, your PC's information, and the Desktop Windows Help and Support app.

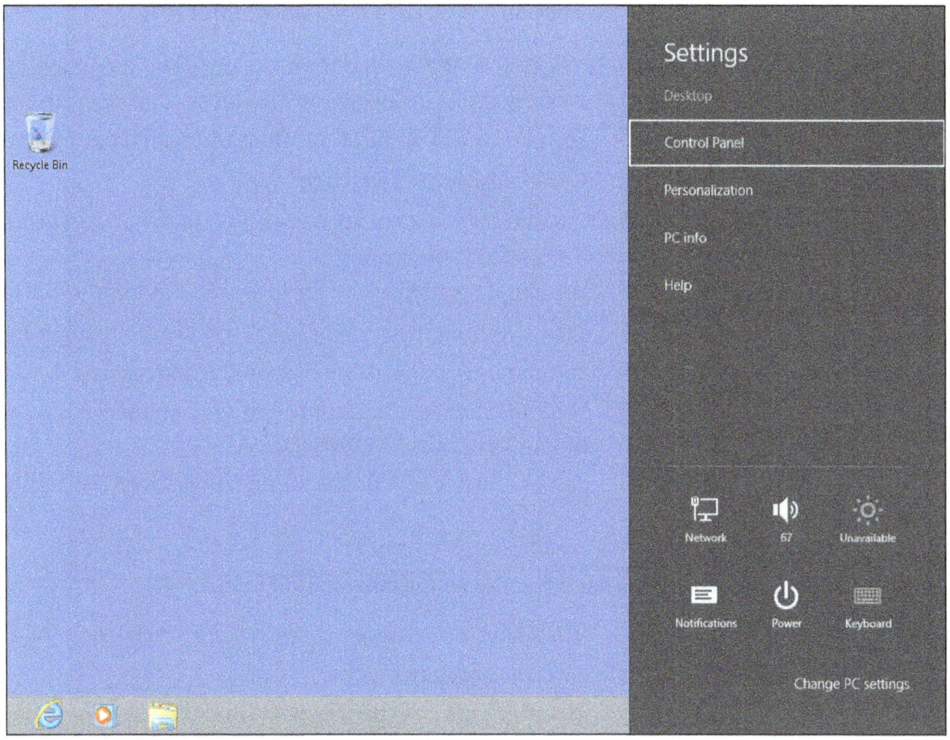


**Figure 2-27**

The Settings charm as it appears while using the Desktop app.

## In this lesson you learned how to:

- Navigate on the Start screen
- Work with tiles
- Search your computer
- Reorganize the Start Screen
- Work with the Charms bar

**Bottom Line**

This chapter shows you how to organize the Start Screen in order to quickly and easily locate the apps you work with on a daily basis. You also learn how to use the Charms bar to share files and access your hardware devices.

# Knowledge Assessment

## True/False

**Circle T if the statement is true or F if the statement is false.**

T F 1. The corners of the display can be used to navigate to special functionality.

T F 2. Pressing the WinKey repeatedly can be used to cycle between open documents.

T F 3. You can launch applications from the Search bar.

T F 4. Use WinKey+A to search for apps.

T F 5. You can only change the size of tiles on the Start screen by zooming in and out from the Start screen.

T F 6. You can display tiles in a list format in addition to tile format.

T F 7. When you unpin an application, you are removing it from your computer.

T F 8. You can only move single tiles on the Start Screen.

T F 9. You can enter an email address to send an image to using the Share charm, but you cannot customize the message.

T F 10. You can enable and disable notifications from the Settings charm.

## Multiple Choice

**Select the best response for the following statements.**

1. What happens when you press Alt+F4 when using the Desktop app?
   a. The computer locks.
   b. You open the Settings window.
   c. The computer shuts down.
   d. You start a new search.
2. What is one way to open tile settings?
   a. Right-click the tile.
   b. Option-click the tile.
   c. Ctrl-click the tile.
   d. Press WinKey+S, and choose Settings.
3. What are two tile settings you can change by right-clicking the tile?
   a. Uninstall the application.
   b. Unpin the application from the Start screen.
   c. Stop displaying updated information.
   d. B and C
   e. All of the above.
4. What are some of the additional settings you can control for legacy applications (ones that run on the Desktop app)?
   a. Stop the app from running.
   b. Open a new window.
   c. Open file location
   d. B and C.
   e. All of the above.

5. How do you show all installed applications on the Start Screen?
   a. Right-click and choose All apps from the right-edge of the bar that appears.
   b. Right-click and choose All apps from a context menu.
   c. Ctrl-click and choose All apps from the right-edge of the bar that appears.
   d. Move the mouse to the bottom of the screen, and choose All apps from the Charms bar.
6. What does pinning an app refer to?
   a. Installing an application onto the Start Screen.
   b. Launching a pinned application.
   c. Opening the app from the Start screen.
   d. Adding a tile to the Start screen or Desktop task bar that represents an application.
7. What is one way to create a tile group?
   a. Right-click a tile and select New Group option at the bottom of the screen and then be drag more tiles to the first tile.
   b. Select the New Group charm, and drop apps on a grey bar that appears.
   c. Drag a tile to an open space, and drop it on a grey bar that appears and then drag more tiles to the first tile.
   d. B and C.
8. How do you move a group of tiles to a new location on the Start Screen?
   a. Select the group, and while pressing WinKey+M drag it to a new position.
   b. Select the group, press WinKey+M, and then click a new location on the Start Screen.
   c. Drag or swipe around the group of tiles and then click a new location on the Start screen.
   d. Select the group and drag it to a new position.
9. What option or device would you use to share a picture from an external hard drive?
   a. Select the image file and choose WinKey+S.
   b. Bluetooth.
   c. The Share charm.
   d. None of the above.
10. How do you name a group of tiles in Windows 8.0?
    a. With all tiles visible, right-click a tile group and enter the new name into the box that appears in the Charms bar.
    b. With all tiles visible, right-click the tile group and enter a new name into the bar at the bottom of the screen.
    c. Shift-click on all tiles in a group and then press Ctrl+G and enter the group name into the Group dialog box.
    d. Swipe down on the group name. When the Group Name text field becomes active, enter a new name for the group.

## Competency Assessment

### Project 2-1: Pin web pages to your start screen

1. Open the page in Internet Explorer
2. Tap the **Gear**, tool in the upper-right corner of the window, and select **Add Site to Start Screen**.
3. Click the **Add** button to add a tile to the Start screen representing that web page.

### Project 2-2: Print an email

1. Open an email message.
2. Open the Charms bar and click the **Devices** option.
3. Choose a printer to print the email message.

## Proficiency Assessment

### Project 2-3: Organize your Start Screen

1. Group your apps into at least three groups: Tools, Workplace apps, and Web/Sharing.
2. Name each of the groups to accurately represent your apps.

### Project 2-4: Use the Charms bar.

1. Use Charms in the Charms bar to copy a picture from a web page into an email.
2. Print the message.

## Mastery Assessment

### Project 2-5: Pin to the Start page

1. Find five apps that are installed on your computer but not pinned to your Start page.
2. Pin them to your Start page, and then group them into a tile group.
3. Install one new app, and group it with that new tile group.
4. After you have grouped the six apps, name the tile group and finally display all tiles in list format.

### Project 2-6: Pin a Legacy app to your taskbar

1. Pin a legacy app to your taskbar, and run the app as administrator.
2. After the app is running, open it in a new window so two instances of the program are running.

# Microsoft Word 2013

# 1 Microsoft Word 2013 Jumpstart

## LESSON SKILL MATRIX

**In this lesson, you will learn the following skills:**

| | |
|---|---|
| Interface Conventions | Document Viewing Modes |
| Working with Text and Fields | Working with Document Windows |
| Applying Styles to Text | Tracked Changes and Comment Threads |
| Working with Themes, Style Sets, Color Schemes | |
| Working with Images and Video | |
| Styling Images | |
| Using Online Images and Videos | |

## KEY TERMS

- **Launch Screen**
- **Placeholder Text**
- **Backstage Area**
- **Field**
- **Text Style**
- **Design Tab**
- **Theme Colors**
- **Word-wrap**
- **Gallery**
- **Heading**
- **Read Mode**
- **Print Layout**
- **Web Layout**
- **Draft View**
- **Markup**

*©jldeines/iStockPhoto*

©jldeines/iStockPhoto

The annual Northwind Traders Catalog is a large-scale, two-month print design job calling for a heavyweight layout program, but Northwind's sales flyers, which go out several times a week, are produced in-house using Word 2013. Word's large library of templates, reusable themes, and parallel digital/print outputs let the sales team try out a variety of designs for their weekly content without fiddling with layout at the pixel level, trading a little power for a huge efficiency boost.

## SOFTWARE ORIENTATION

The Microsoft Word 2013 workspace provides access to powerful tools for creating, editing, managing, and sharing documents. Many of the tools you use while working in Word are located on the ribbon, running across the top of the window. The ribbon is organized into task-oriented command tabs. Each tab is divided into task-specific command groups appropriate for the type of work you may need to perform. Because you can customize the ribbon, the tabs and display may include different options than shown in Figure 1-1.

**Figure 1-1**

Microsoft Word 2013 workspace

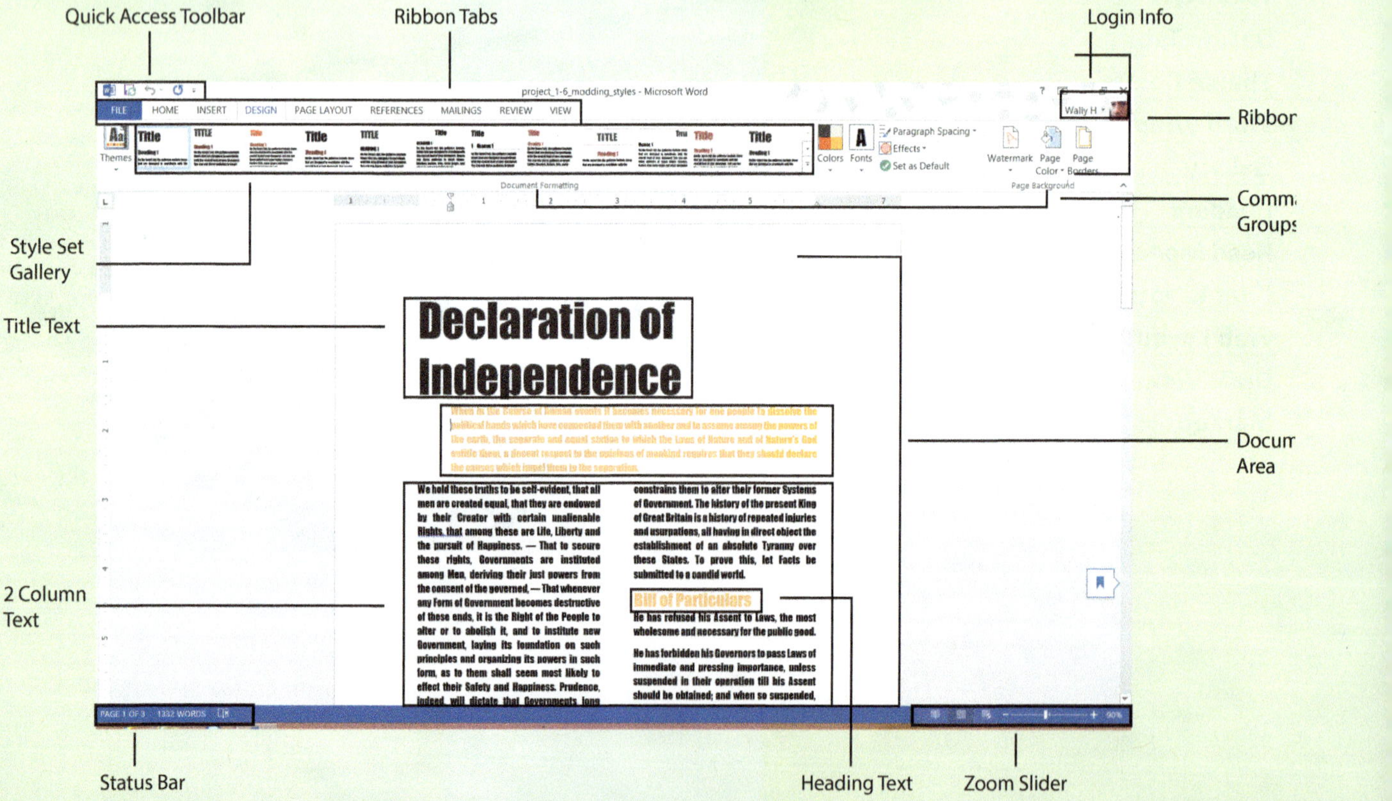

## STARTING UP

In this lesson, you'll work with several files from the Word01lessons folder along with the ready-made templates available for Word 2013 from Microsoft. Make sure that you have loaded the OfficeLessons folder onto your computer. Keep in mind that Microsoft might alter the default online Word 2013 templates, and they may appear to be different from the ones used in this book. if you find that to be the case, choose a comparable Word document to follow along.

### The project

**Bottom Line**

You'll begin this lesson by opening a document that shows several key features of Word 2013; you will then edit the document's content and layout. Note that this lesson requires you to be connected to the Internet.

## STEP BY STEP Opening a document

1 Launch Word 2013. Note that the new **launch screen** (see Figure 1-2) looks much like the File tab in Word 2013; file-management operations are handled in this separate area of the application, rather than in dialog boxes and pop-up menus.

**Figure 1-2**

Word displays a simplified version of Backstage view upon launch.

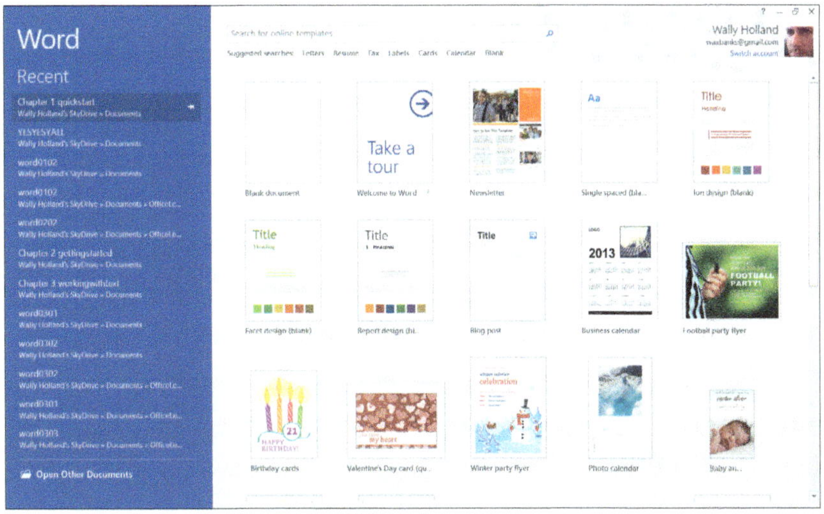


*Images and templates used with permission of Microsoft*

2 At the launch screen, a gallery of templates provided by Microsoft will appear. The gallery is initially populated with templates stored on your hard drive. In the search box, type **hip newsletter** and press **Enter** to search for one of Microsoft's online templates. Click the **icon** that appears in the list. A preview pane (see Figure 1-3) will appear with information about the template. Click **Create** to create a new newsletter document.

The resulting document contains **placeholder text** that serves as a useful introduction to the formatting, style, and layout tools available in Word 2013. We highly recommend that you read it.

**Figure 1-3**

The template you select will automatically download from office.com.

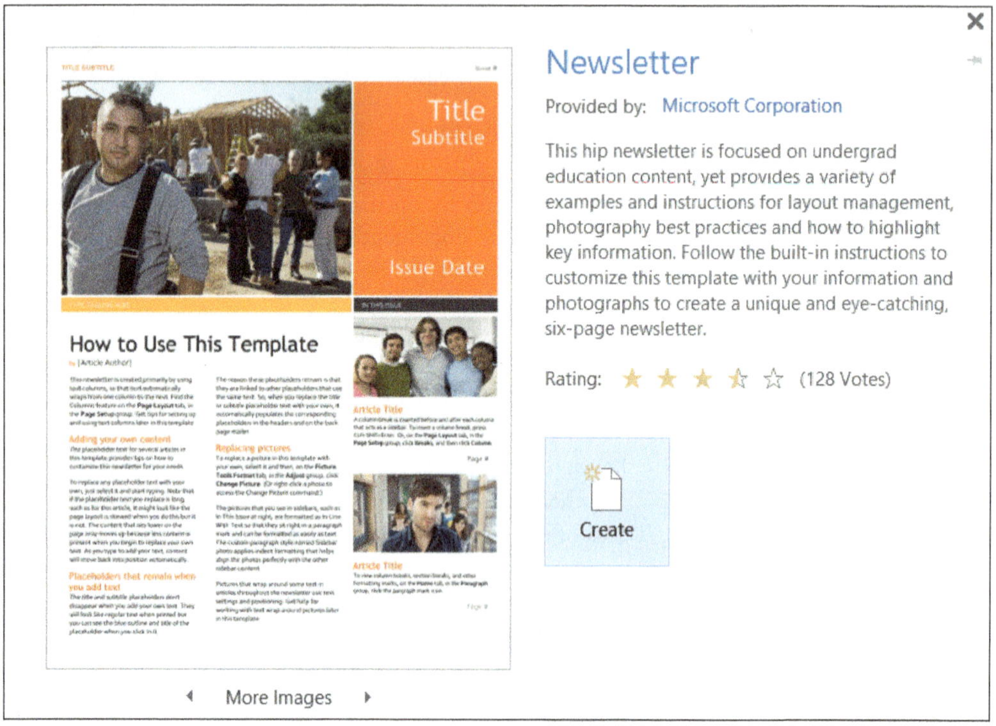


*© Hill Street Studios/Blend Images/Getty Images; © Image Source/Getty Images; © Westend61/Getty Images*

## Interface conventions

Instead of drop-down menus, Office features task-specific toolbars in its Ribbon; click any menu item (or tab), except File, to see the tools available in Word 2013. The File tab works differently: it now brings up Word's **Backstage area** screen.

### STEP BY STEP Interface Conventions

1 In the upper left corner of the screen is the Quick Access Toolbar, a customizable dock for frequently-used commands. By default, it contains icons for the Save, Undo, and Redo commands, as well as the application menu and a drop-down menu for customizing the toolbar.

2 Click the image of the student at the top left of the newsletter. Note that a small icon of text wrapping around an image appears to the right of the image, as in Figure 1-4. You can click this handle for quick access to the image layout tools.

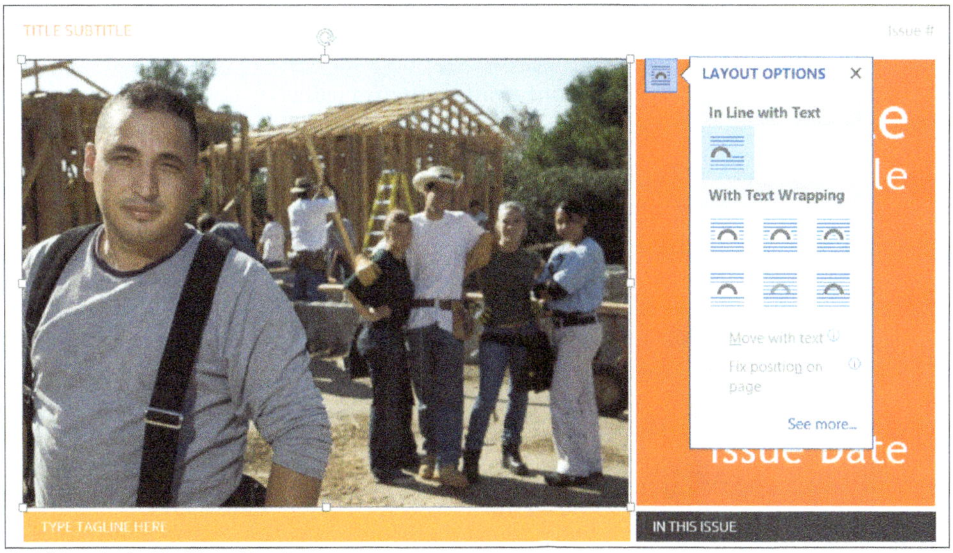


**Figure 1-4**
Click the Layout Options button to choose from common word-wrap settings.

*© Hill Street Studios/Blend Images/Getty Images*

Note that three new **context tabs** appear above the ribbon: Design and Layout (under the heading Table Tools), and Format (under the heading Picture Tools). The tools for adjusting, styling, and laying out images and tables reside in these tabs.

3 Click the **Layout** tab and select **View Gridlines** from the Table group (at the left side of the ribbon). Doing so reveals that the image and surrounding colored panes are laid out as a table with six cells in two columns; the right-hand column is four cells high.

4 Now right-click the image. Note that the context menu includes commands to style and lay out the image, but does *not* provide any table-layout commands.

## Working with words

Fields are like placeholder codes, which get replaced by the information they point to. Word handles fields a little differently from regular text; using fields to keep text flexible and up-to-date is a crucial step from beginner to intermediate Office user.

**STEP BY STEP** **Text and Fields**

1 Click the word **Title** in the large orange cell on the upper-right area of the first page and replace it with the word **Frustrum**. Note the handle that appears above the text, it's labeled Title: this indicates that you're editing the content of the document's Title field. **Fields** allow you to reuse data throughout your document.

2 Click anywhere else in the document and observe that the header on each page updates to reflect the changed newsletter title.

You can change the newsletter's subtitle and tagline in the same manner: select and replace the field you want to change, and then deselect the text to see the updated subtitle in the header (and anywhere else that the Subtitle field appears in the document). Note that when you edit the Subtitle text, you're changing the stored value of the Subtitle field, but if you select the handle instead, you're able to delete the field placeholder itself.

3 Select the word **Frustrum** (either by double-clicking it or by clicking-and-dragging) and note that Word 2013 immediately offers a pop-up menu with oft-used commands for text editing: font (see Figure 1-5), size, emphasis, bullet level, and so forth.

**Figure 1-5**

Choosing a font in the formatting minibar.

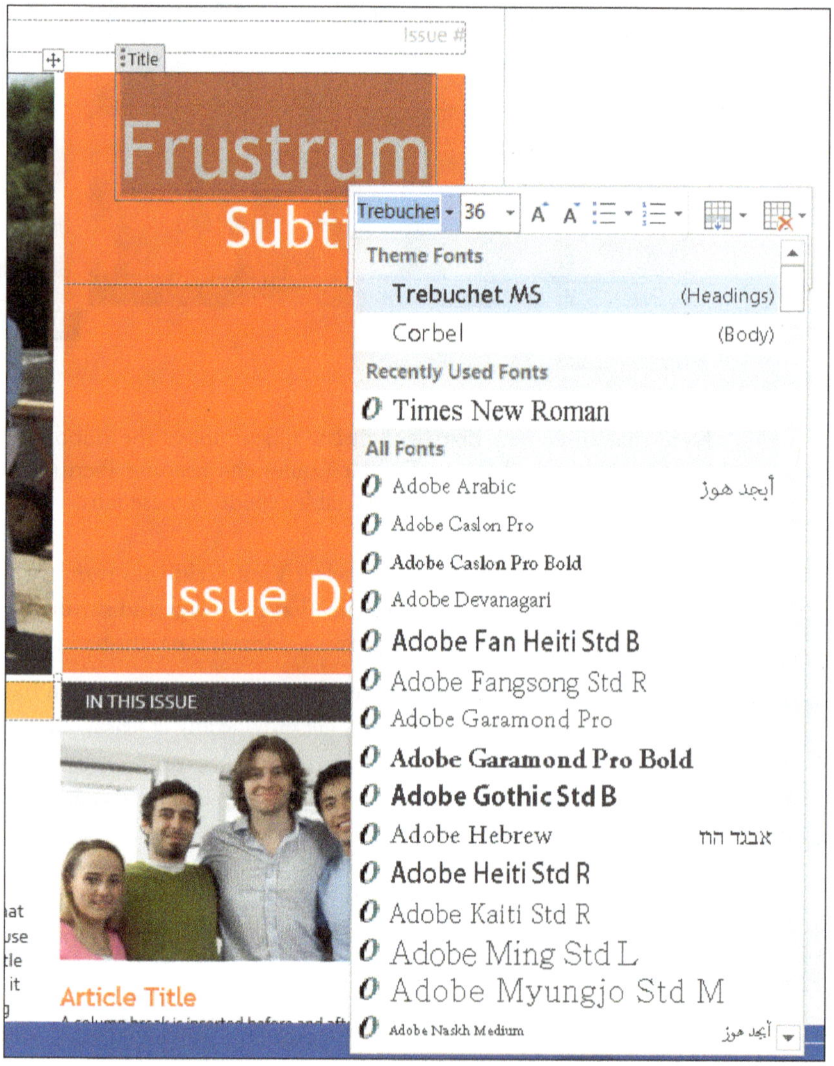


© Hill Street Studios/Blend Images/Getty Images; © Image Source/Getty Images

## Applying styles to text

**Bottom Line**

**Text Styles** in Word 2013 serve two purposes: they let you control the appearance of your text, and they help Word structure your document. We'll focus on visuals in this chapter; document structure is the focus of Lesson 4, "Structuring Complex Documents." First, we'll style some text and use the Live Preview feature of Word 2013.

**STEP BY STEP** **Styling text**

1 Triple-click the **How to Use This Template** headline—the text itself, not the field handle. Triple-clicking selects an entire paragraph; in this case, this is just a single line.

2 Open the Home tab; in the Styles group, note that the Heading 1 style is highlighted, indicating the current style of the selected text.

3 Mouse over the other styles in the Styles group without selecting one. Note that the text changes appearance as you do so; when you move the mouse away from the Styles group without selecting a new style, your text reverts to its original appearance. This feature is called Live Preview.

4 Select the **Subtitle** style to restyle the headline.

As you can see, the headline is now invisible (white on white) and right-justified rather than left-justified. You can change the color and alignment of a single piece of text to make the headline visible again, but it's also easy to modify the styles themselves.

5 Without deselecting the headline text, click **Home > Font > Font Color**. The text of the How to Use This Template headline turns red.

6 Right-click **Home > Styles > Subtitle**. Select **Update Subtitle to Match Selection** from the context menu.

When you update the Subtitle style in this fashion, any text that uses the Subtitle style in the current document changes to reflect the new style: in this case, the actual newsletter subtitle, next to the front page image of the student, turns red.

7 Finally, double-click the headline below the image of the student, and then click **Home > Paragraph > Align Left** (or press **Ctrl+L**). The headline should be flush against the left margin again.

Note that your new color selection is applied to all the text that uses the Subtitle style, but the alignment change is restricted to just the currently selected text. Reformatting a single piece of text doesn't affect the definition of the Subtitle style itself.

## YOUR DOCUMENT'S LOOK AND FEEL

### Working with themes, style sets, and color schemes

**Bottom Line**

Word 2013 gives you a variety of tools for altering the overall look and feel of your document. To see these tools, click the **Design tab**, newly designed for Word 2013. In the Design tab, you'll find a drop-down menu containing the built-in Themes available for Word 2013, a gallery of Style Sets, drop-down menus for selecting color and font schemes, and a handful of other document-level tools.

Now you'll make some changes to your document and start to see how Themes, Styles, and Colors interact. A Theme is basically a bundle of Colors, Fonts, and Effects; something like a visual identity for a set of documents. A Style Set is a collection of styles meant to work well together on the page or on the screen. Style Sets may or may not specify colors and fonts. The document's color scheme and font set can be switched without changing the Theme or Style definitions.

## STEP BY STEP Working with themes, style sets, and color schemes

Let's make some changes to show how these design tools work. In particular, we'll change various aspects of this elegant pre-built template, rendering it an unreadable mess, to see how different features of a document depend on one another.

1. In the Design tab, click the **Themes** drop-down menu. Note the option to Reset to Theme from Newsletter Template, indicating that the document template itself includes a built-in theme.
2. Mouse over several themes. Note which aspects of the document change and which do not; for instance, the colored panes at the top of the newsletter switch to the new **Theme Colors**, but the background color for the In This Issue column remains unchanged, indicating that its background color is defined in absolute terms.

Restricting your color choices to your current Theme Colors is a good way to maintain a consistent look-and-feel for your document, and it ensures that, if you change themes, you won't leave orphaned colors, as in the In This Issue sidebar.

**Figure 1-6**

Switching the theme sets font, color, style, layout, and effects options with a single click.

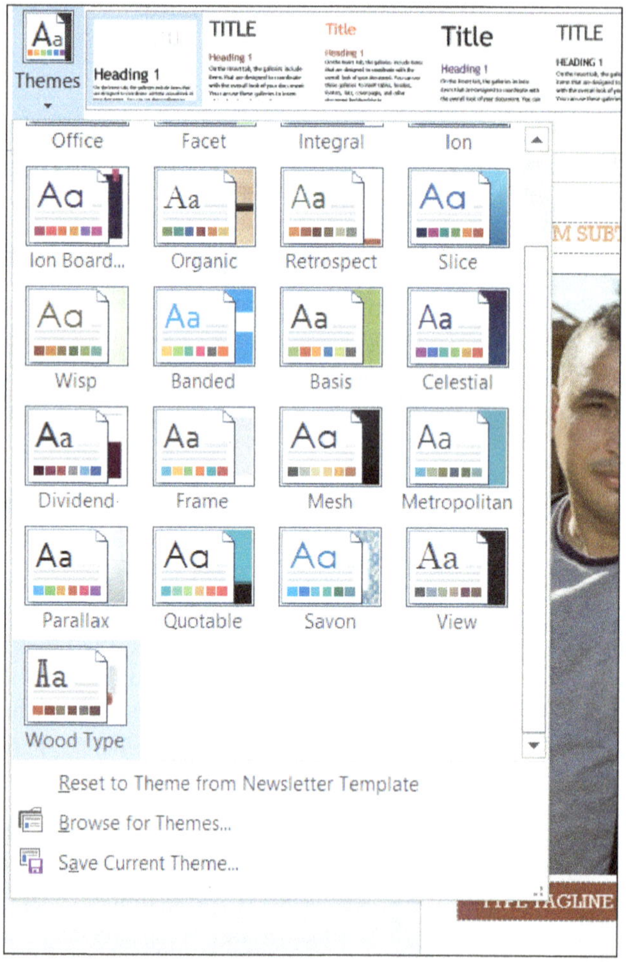


© Hill Street Studios/Blend Images/Getty Images

3. Choose the **Wood Type** theme (see Figure 1-6.) Scroll down through your document to see the changes this new theme has made.

As you can see, the careful multiple-column format is now broken: the tight fit of the text came from matching each article's length, layout, and font choice, and the new mix of styles and fonts breaks that arrangement.

Changing the document theme also reveals the difference between absolute and relative placement of images. Several images in the document retain their absolute positioning on the page and can be orphaned when you change the text; but the smaller single-column images are all placed in line with the paragraphs and have avoided being similarly orphaned. When laying out a document in Word, it's important to keep in mind the relationship between images and the text that surrounds them.

Now let's see how Themes, Style Sets, and Color Schemes relate.

4 Choose another theme and keep an eye on the Document Formatting group of the Design tab. Note that when you change themes, the gallery refreshes: the fonts and colors of each Style Set change.

Themes give overall visual guidelines; Style Sets define the relationships between styles within those guidelines.

5 Finally, choose another theme and note that the Color Scheme changes. Remember that you can still choose from all available color schemes, shown in Figure 1-7.

**Figure 1-7**

Color Schemes let you choose an overall palette without having to carefully match individual shades.

Feel free to experiment with changing colors, styles, or the document theme, noting the way changes propagate from one part of the document to another. Go ahead and edit any text you want in the document; text entry is very basic functionality, so we won't spend time on it in this Quick Start lesson. You can also experiment with changing the column layout of the article text; in particular, take note of the way the template's author makes use of hard column breaks to lay out sidebars, thus avoiding the use of floating text boxes.

## Working with images and video

**Bottom Line**

Like the new Windows 8 and Windows RT operating systems, Office 2013 is designed to take advantage of touch interfaces, such as the Microsoft Surface; Office 2013 also treats always-on

Internet and online (vs. local hard drive) storage as standard. The way Word 2013 handles visual media reflects these assumptions. Now we'll make some changes to the visuals in our newsletter to illustrate how Word 2013 handles images and video.

**STEP BY STEP**

## Styling an image

First we'll tour Word's layout, format, and retouching tools. Feel free to make drastic changes to the image in this section; you'll replace it afterward.

1. Click the image of the five smiling interns in the right-hand column of page 1. A horseshoe-shaped handle appears to the side; click it. The image-layout menu in Word 2013 appears. Experiment with changing the **word-wrap** mode to see how text flows around, behind, and in front of the image.
2. Make sure the image is still selected so the Format tab is available. Open the Format tab. Experiment with choosing different Picture Styles from the visual gallery in the Format tab. Note that the Picture Styles change the image's size, framing, and orientation, but leave its content unchanged.
3. Finally, use the Format > Adjust > Color, Corrections, and Artistic Effects **galleries** to make changes to the content of the image.

Note the way the image-related tools of Word 2013 are organized. The image layout context menu contains the most-used commands for placing and wrapping an image; these same tools are available from the Format > Arrange group. Image editing tools are found in the Format > Adjust group. The image's border is edited with tools in the Picture Styles group.

Word 2013 isn't really a full-featured image editor, but it does provide some tools for basic image manipulation, for example, Format > Remove Background.

### Working with online images and videos

**Bottom Line**

Office 2013 blurs the line between online and local media. In Word, you can still embed local images, and you can drop in pictures and videos you find on the Internet, without ever switching applications.

**STEP BY STEP**

## Inserting online images and video

Now let's get rid of the interns and find a replacement image online.

1. Right-click the image and choose **Change Picture** from the context menu. (In Windows RT, tap and hold to bring up the context menu.) An Insert Pictures dialog box appears.
2. In the Bing Image Search box, type the search term **happy toad**, and choose a replacement image from the gallery. Note that all the images in the gallery, shown in Figure 1-8. carry a Creative Commons license. When you find the one you like, click Insert.

**Take Note** In general, images with a Creative Commons license (there are several different CC licenses) can be reused for noncommercial purposes, as long as you credit their creators. For the purposes of this lesson, we don't need to worry about sourcing the images.

The same dialog box lets you search for local files and royalty free clip-art from Microsoft; we'll explore this tool more in a later lesson.

**Figure 1-8**

The image you select from your Bing Image Search will embed in your Word document, just like a local image would.

*Images and templates used with permission of Microsoft*

Any changes you make to an image using the Adjustments tools are lost when you replace the image, but the picture style and arrangement are preserved.

Now let's embed some online video into our otherwise conventionally static document.

3 Scroll to the bottom of your document and place your cursor. Click **Insert > Online Video**.

4 In the Search YouTube box, type **cute toddler**. Select a video from the gallery and click **Insert**.

A video object will insert into your document; Word 2013 handles online videos exactly like still images, except that you can click an embedded video to launch a built-in video player.

5 Select the video object, and then click **Format > Adjust > Color** or **Artistic Effects** to change the look of the embedded video.

Note that the Format tools affect the way the video appears on the page (the preview image) but leave the video itself untouched. If you print a Word 2013 document with an embedded video, only the (modified) preview image makes it to the printed page, but exporting the document as a PDF preserves the video link as a hyperlinked image.

## DIFFERENT VIEWS OF YOUR DOCUMENT

**Bottom Line**

Word 2013 provides several tools and editing modes to let you work more efficiently with your document, without unnecessary visual clutter and distraction. When you're comfortable with these tools, you'll spend less time trying to figure out Word 2013's interface, and more time improving your work.

### Collapsing document sections

Word treats headings as document divisions, and lets you collapse whole sections of your document into a **heading**; cleaning up your workspace with a single click.

**STEP BY STEP** **Collapsing document sections**

1 Change the newsletter's front page sidebar headlines, located just below the images on the bottom-right half the of the page, from Article Title to **Column Break** and **View Formatting Breaks**, respectively. In the Home > Styles gallery, note that these headlines have the Sidebar Heading style.

2 Change the top sidebar headline's style to **Heading 1**, and the bottom headline's style to **Heading 2**.

3 Now mouse over the top sidebar headline. A triangular button appears to the left of the headline. Click it; the contents of the sidebar disappear, leaving only the top headline. Click the button again to reveal the rest of the sidebar again.

This triangular button is a useful workflow tool that collapses and expands a section of the document, much like in the old Outline View. Word thinks of each document section as beginning with a Heading, and it hides and reveals the text based on the level of the Heading you're folding into. Perform the next step to see how this works.

4 Change the style of the second sidebar headline to **Heading 1**. Both sidebar headlines have the same style (Heading 1). Now collapse the *first* headline.

Note that the second headline is still visible: if you collapse a top-level heading (Heading 1), Word will treat lower-level headings (Heading 2, Heading 3, etc.) as subsections and assume you're not currently working with them. Word will then hide text and images until it reaches the next Heading 1 text. When working with complex documents, you're encouraged to use the built-in heading styles to take advantage of Word's document-structure features. We'll cover document structure in detail in Word Lesson 4, "Structuring Complex Documents."

## Working with Word's windows

**Bottom Line**

Word 2013 includes a number of features, old and new, to grant you multiple perspectives on a document and foreground your work rather than your workspace. You'll customize your work environment in later lessons; in this Quick Start you'll just survey the basic tools.

**STEP BY STEP** **Working with Word's views**

1 Click the **View > Views > Read Mode** icon to view your document without any onscreen editing interface. Use the arrow keys to scroll through the document; press **Escape** to return to your editing window.

Read Mode is optimized for touch; in Windows RT, you can swipe left and right to move through the document. Remember that it's just a quick overview of the flow and proportions of the document, not a preview of the final print/Web output.

2 Switch between **Print Layout** (**View > Views > Print Layout**) and **Web Layout** to see the different print/Web outputs of the same document. In particular, note that multi-column layouts are preserved in the source file, but will not render properly when you translate your document to HTML.

3 Switch to **Draft** view to see only the text in your document; note that headers, footers, images, and multi-column layouts do not display in Draft view.

4 Collapse the Ribbon by clicking the **caret** (^) at its bottom-right corner. To reveal again, open one of the Tabs at the top of the screen. To make the Ribbon permanently visible, click the **push pin** icon at the far right, where the caret was.

5 Finally, click **View > Window > Split** to look at two sections of your document simultaneously. Spend a few moments becoming familiar with the screen layout. Click **Remove Split** to switch back to one-window mode.

A split screen is helpful when you need to move content between parts of your document, or to see one section while you edit another.

## Collaboration and tracking changes

Word 2013 includes a variety of collaboration and simple version control features in the Review tab. These tools let you track a document's state through multiple rounds of revision and editing, and let you communicate with collaborators inside the Word document itself.

**STEP BY STEP** **Tracking changes**

1 Click **Review > Tracking > Track Changes**. The icon turns blue. Word 2013 will now preserve your edits, allowing you to make changes without losing track of your original data.

2 Select **Tracking > All Markup** from the uppermost drop-down menu.

3 Now make some edits to your document; delete and insert text, tables, and images, or restyle document elements.

Word indicates each edit with a subtle colored bar down the left margin of the document, thus marking its location, and either an information bubble (for formatting changes) or inline markings (for text insertions/deletions).

Note that if you delete an image with All Markup selected, the image will seem to stubbornly remain in the document. That's not the case; Word is simply indicating where the image was, but it's not actually in the layout anymore, as the next step reveals.

4 Select **Tracking > Simple Markup** from the uppermost drop-down menu. This is a new feature in Word 2013. Note that the colored bars that indicate the presence of edits remain, but Word hides the details.

5 Re-select **All Markup** and experiment with the options under Tracking > Show Markup.

At each stage of document revision, tailor these Markup options to your needs; for instance, if you add a large piece of new text late in a project, considering unmarking Insertions/Deletions to keep your editing window orderly.

**Bottom Line**

## Communicating with colleagues in comments

Word also lets you embed comments in a document, and preserve conversations with collaborators using the comments feature.

**STEP BY STEP** **Communicating with collegues in comments**

1 Make sure Review > Comments > Show Comments (or Tracking > All Markup) is enabled. Select a piece of text and click **Review > Comments > New Comment**. In the speech bubble that appears, type **Could you suggest better wording here?** and press **Escape** to return the cursor to the document window.

2 Now mouse over your comment and click the **Reply** icon that appears in the bubble. Type **Sure, get back to you shortly** and press **Escape** to return to editing your document. Note in Figure 1-9 the way Word displays inline conversations between document editors (they're just like threaded blog comments).

**Figure 1-9**

Threaded comments help clarify your document's editing history.

*Images and template used with permission of Microsoft*

3 Enable Simple Markup and deselect **Comments > Show Comments**. Word collapses each conversation into a comic book-style speech bubble.

4 Finally, select your second comment and click **Comments > Delete**. Note that the response is deleted but the conversation remains.

If you delete the first comment in a thread, the entire thread is deleted along with it.

Word 2013 is also built to support real-time and distributed collaboration: the File > Share group includes tools to post a copy of your document online, inviting colleagues to view or edit the file, or even turn your .docx file into a live presentation that distant users can view using a web browser.

## Save always

To complete this Word 2013 Quick Start lesson, save your newsletter to your SkyDrive folder.

**STEP BY STEP** **Saving and closing a document**

1 Click **File > Save As**.

2 In the Backstage view, select your SkyDrive folder; in the Save box, type **My Hip Newsletter**, and then click **Save**.

Note that while you initially opened the newsletter's template file (.dotx) rather than a document file (.docx), Word 2013 knows to save your document as a .docx, unless you specify otherwise. That said, when you work from a template, double-check to make sure you're saving a new Word document rather than editing the template itself.

3 Close your document (press **Ctrl+W** or click **File > Close**) and click **File > Open** (or press **Ctrl+O**).

Your newsletter will appear in the list of Recent Documents. Meanwhile, the Office Upload Center will try to upload your document to the cloud; if you're working offline, the Upload Center will upload your changes as soon as it detects an Internet connection; ideally, you'll never even notice.

## What you learned in this lesson:

- Interface Conventions
- Document Viewing Modes
- Working with Text and Fields
- Working with Document Windows
- Applying Styles to Text
- Tracked Changes and Comment Threads
- Working with Themes, Style Sets, Color Schemes
- Working with Images and Video
- Styling Images
- Using Online Images and Videos

# Knowledge Assessment

### True/False

**Circle T if the statement is true or F if the statement is false.**

T F 1. Word 2013 opens, by default, on a blank document.

T F 2. Selecting a field's handle and pressing Delete clears out the data the field refers to.

T F 3. A Text Style can specify font, size, color, alignment, and spacing.

T F 4. Text alignment options include right justification, left justification, center, and full justification.

T F 5. A Style Set defines the visual look of a single kind of text (e.g., Heading 1).

T F 6. To see how a Theme will affect the look of a document you must select it from the Themes Gallery.

T F 7. Theme Colors restrict the available colors in a template.

T F 8. It's not possible to edit your document in Read Mode.

T F 9. When you select an image, contextual tabs appear at the far left of the Ribbon.

T F 10. Document-wide formatting and style tools are found in the Design tab.

## Fill in the Blanks

**Complete the following sentences by writing the correct word or words in the blanks provided.**

1. Each image comes with a _____ pop-out menu attached, which opens a pane of formatting tools.
2. The title of a newsletter can be stored for reuse in a _____.
3. The Insert Pictures dialog lets you search Microsoft's clip art library, or do an image search on _____.
4. When you use Word's built-in heading styles, you can _____ sections of your document text into the headings to clear screen space.
5. The highest-level built-in heading style is _____.
6. When you print a document containing an embedded video, only the _____ will print in its place.
7. Color correction tools for images are found in the _____ tab.
8. You can set a default Theme, Style Set, and color scheme by saving a document as a _____.
9. In place of the old File menu, clicking the File tab takes you to Office's _____.
10. You can customize a pre-formatted calendar by searching the _____ for "calendar."

# Competency Assessment

### Project 1-1: Creating New Documents from Templates

**In this exercise you'll create a new file using the Template Gallery.**

1. Launch Word and browse the template gallery. Open a variety of templates to see the range of built-in document types Word offers.
2. Search Microsoft's online template collection for **calendar** and select a monthly calendar template. Try editing the template and saving it as a .docx file, then as a new .dotx (template) file.
3. Select **File > New** (rather than pressing Ctrl+N) and find the calendar template you selected near the top of the template gallery. Click the **pin** icon to keep it permanently in the gallery.
4. Close any open files and leave Word open for the next exercise.

### Project 1-2: Formatting Text

**In this exercise you'll work with character- and paragraph-level formatting tools.**

1. Open the project file **declaration_text** and save it in your working directory as **project_1-2_formatting**.
2. Click once on the word **events** in the first line and press **Ctrl+I** to apply italic formatting.

   Word will italicize the entire word, assuming from context that you didn't mean to insert italicized characters in the middle of a non-italicized word.
3. Double-click the word *events* to select the whole word, then click the italics symbol in the formatting popup to remove italic formatting from the word.
4. Triple-click **events** to select the entire line (paragraph) and apply italic formatting again. Then repeat the action.
5. Click in the final paragraph on pages 3-4 and select the **Intense Quote** style.
6. Add the line **Declaration of Independence** to the top of the document, formatted with the Title style.

7. Select everything except the title, first paragraph, and final paragraph, and format it as two-column text (Page Layout > Columns > Two).
8. Save and close your document.

## Proficiency Assessment

### Project 1-3: Headings

**In this exercise you'll add headings to your document.**

1. Open the project file 1-3-source and save it as project_1-3_headings.
2. Insert the line Bill of Particulars before the line "He has refused his Assent to Laws..." on page 1. Format the new line with the Heading 2 style.
3. Insert a Heading 2 line, Legal Affronts, before the "For quartering large bodies..." line on page 2.
4. Insert the Heading 2 line, Good Faith, before the "In every stage..." paragraph on page 3.
5. Collapse the three new headings by mousing over them and clicking the folding arrows that appear.

   (It is most convenient to carry out this step in order from first heading to last.)
6. Save and close your document.

### Project 1-4: Style Sets and Color Schemes

**In this exercise you'll work with Style Sets and alter a file's color scheme.**

1. Open the project file 1-4-source and save it as project_1-4_style_color.
2. Open the Design tab.
3. Select the Lines (Distinctive) Style Set.
4. Select the Violet II color scheme.
5. Save and close your document.

## Mastery Assessment

### Project 1-5: Working with Themes

**In this exercise you will assign an existing file a new theme and color scheme.**

1. Open the project file 1-5-source and save it as project_1-5_theme.
2. In the Design tab, experiment with various themes.

   Note that changing the theme overrides your choice of color scheme, though not document/character formatting like columns and italics.
3. Assign the Main Event theme with the Red Orange color scheme and Lines (Stylish) Style Set.
4. Assign the List Paragraph style to the first paragraph ("When in the course of...").

   Note that the italics are overridden by the new style assignment.
5. Save and close your document.

## Project 1-6: Modifying Styles

**In this exercise you'll modify styles to an existing file.**

1. Open the project file **1-6-source** and save it as **project_1-6_modding_styles**.
2. Select the first paragraph, *When in the course…* and assign it the same color as the *Bill of Particulars* heading has.
3. Select the paragraph again and update the List Paragraph style to reflect the new formatting.
4. Apply the **List Paragraph** style to the closing paragraph.
5. Alter all body text (Normal style) in the document to **Justified** rather than Align Left, by updating the style itself.

   Note that the Title style will also switch to full justification – it's a modification of the Normal style.
6. Fix the Title style by updating it to **Align Left**.
7. Save your work and close Word.

# 2 Getting Started with Word 2013

## LESSON SKILL MATRIX

**In this lesson, you will learn the following skills:**

| | |
|---|---|
| Navigating the Launch Screen and Template Gallery | Word's Different Viewing Modes |
| Opening a Document | Laying Out the Page |
| Using and Customizing the Ribbon | Adding Headers and Footers |
| Customizing the Quick Access Toolbar | Splitting Your Document View |
| Using the Navigation Pane | |

## KEY TERMS

- **pane**
- **Save**
- **Save As**
- **SkyDrive**
- **SharePoint**
- **keyboard shortcuts**
- **Quick Access Toolbar**
- **Navigation pane**
- **Heading style**
- **margins**
- **Portrait Orientation**
- **Landscape Orientation**
- **header**
- **footer**
- **float**
- **Synchronous Scrolling**

*©a-wrangler/iStockPhoto*

Temporary office workers at Northwind Traders need to jump right into creating, editing, and formatting documents to keep up with the heavy flow of research data through the office. Maintaining an efficient digital workspace is essential to doing well in that fast-paced environment. With document views, panes, and information displays, Word 2013 suggests (without strictly enforcing) a streamlined workflow. The more quickly Northwind's project workers learn their tools, the more useful they are to the company – and its thousand impatient clients.

## SOFTWARE ORIENTATION

This lesson provides you with additional foundation information to help you efficiently create and edit documents using Microsoft Word. The Home tab is an important starting point for controlling styles, navigating, and locating content within your documents.

**Figure 2-1**

The Home tab contains many commonly used controls for text editing.

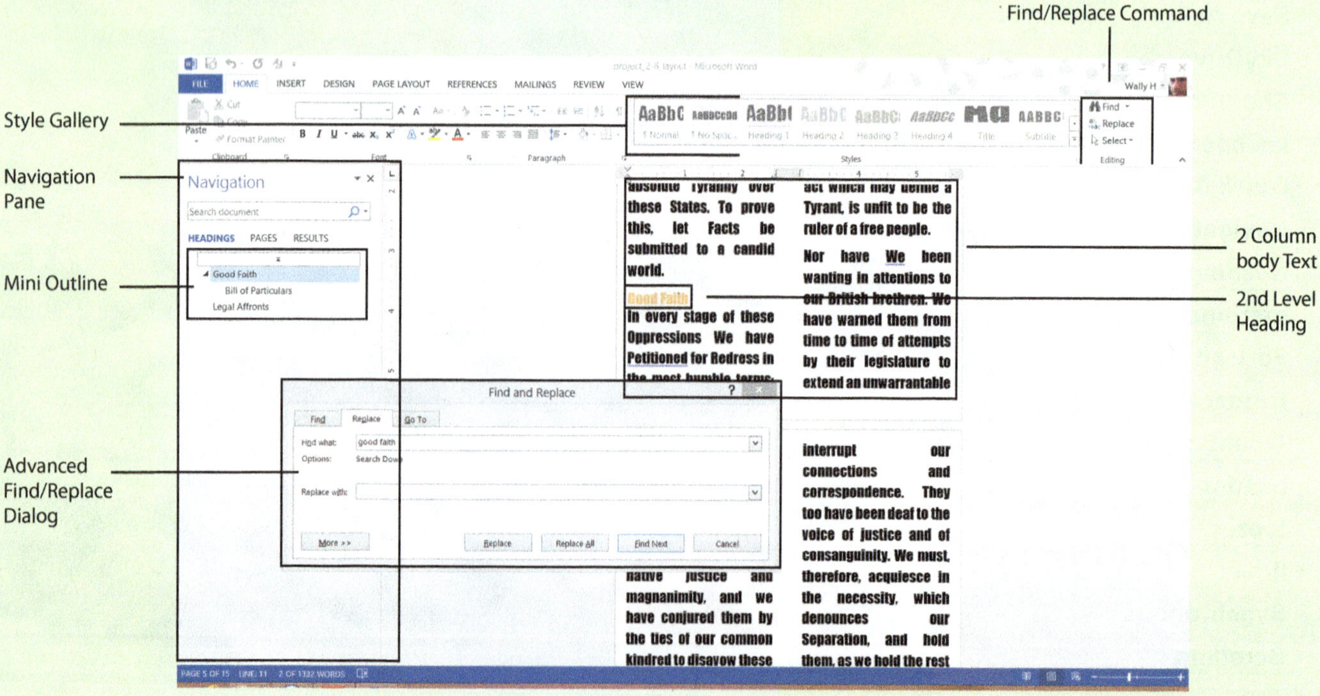

## STARTING UP

In this lesson, you'll work with several files from the Word02lessons folder. Make sure that you have loaded the OfficeLessons folder onto your computer.

### The Word 2013 interface

**Bottom Line**

Microsoft Word is a mature product; the first version of Word for Windows, in 1983, offered many computer users their first experience with a mouse. As you'd expect, Word 2013 is an incremental update rather than a revolutionary one. If you're familiar with Word 2007, 2010, or 2011, you won't find many surprises in this lesson. But Windows 8 and Windows RT, the operating systems on which Word 2013 runs, have several new features; and Word 2013 inherits its main interface features from Windows itself.

Many features of the Word 2013 work environment are common to all the apps in the Office 2013 application suite; we'll note these as we go and cover them with less detail than the unique features now available for Word.

### The Start screen and template gallery

**Bottom Line**

When you launch Word 2013, instead of a blank document, you're greeted with a new start screen, similar to the Backstage view (which replaced the File menu). In the left-hand **pane**, a list of recent documents appears; a gallery to the right offers a collection of document templates. Note that in the Start Screen there's no obvious distinction between documents stored on your hard drive and those stored in the cloud; in fact, many of the items in the template gallery are just links to templates hosted on Microsoft's own servers.

**STEP BY STEP** **The start screen and template gallery**

In the search box at the top of the gallery pane, you can search Microsoft's extensive online template database.

1 Type **cookbook** in the search box and press **Enter**.

As of this writing, Microsoft doesn't actually offer a cookbook template, but this empty results screen does offer something useful: at the bottom of the screen is a new gallery, Search results from your other applications. If you have Publisher, Excel, and PowerPoint installed on your computer, you'll see links to templates for those programs, which you can launch directly from the Start Screen in Word 2013.

Click the back arrow in the upper-left corner. In the Recent pane, you'll see a listing of recent documents, including the hip newsletter you worked with if you completed Lesson 1. Below that list is a link to Open Other Documents, which brings up the Backstage view itself; the same as if had you clicked File > Open (or pressed Ctrl+O).

2 At the lower left of the screen, click **Open Other Documents**.

## Opening a document

**Bottom Line**

Clicking File > Open brings up a three-paned window as shown in Figure 2-2. The left-hand pane should be familiar: it's the old File menu, complete with New, Open, **Save/Save As**, Print, and a handful of other commands, most of them unavailable when you launch Word 2013, because there's no document currently open. To the right of that pane is a list of Places: a customizable list of local and online storage locations. As you click each in turn, the right-hand pane provides a list of available documents in that location.

**STEP BY STEP**

## Opening a document

By clicking the Add a Place button, you can add **SkyDrive** and **SharePoint** links to the Places list.

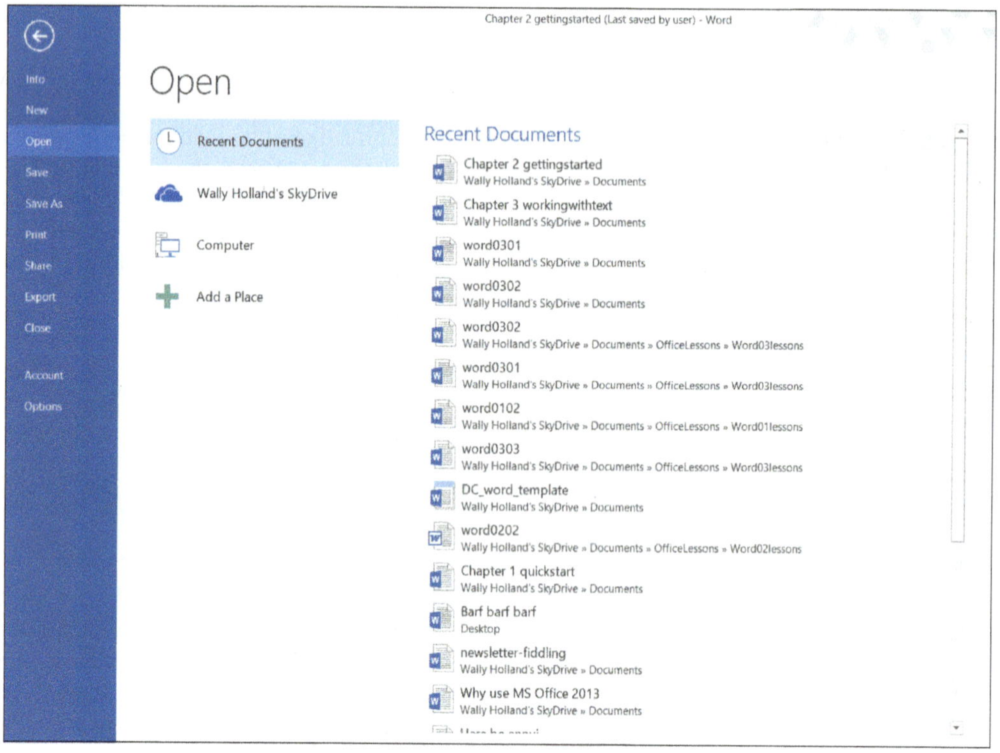


**Figure 2-2**

The Open command in Backstage View.

1 Choose **Computer** from the list and navigate to the Word02lessons folder you saved to your hard drive. Open the the file **word02a.docx**.

2 Choose **File > Save As** and save this document as **word02a_work**.

## The Ribbon

The main visual feature of the Word 2013 workspace is the **Ribbon**, which arrived in Microsoft Office in 2007 and has spread to a variety of Windows applications. The Ribbon replaced the 20-year-old system of drop-down menus (File, Edit, and so on) with clusters of graphical icons, each located on a tab (formerly a menu) within a group (submenu). The basic idea behind the Ribbon is this: the formatting options most users need most often are in the Home tab, while context-dependent actions (such as reformatting a table, changing the dimensions of a document, or styling an image) reside in other tabs.

**Take Note** For most Word tasks, **keyboard shortcuts** are faster and more precise than mouse movements. They're also easily discoverable. If you press just the Alt key in an Office application, a keyboard shortcut will appear for each tab; type one of them, and you'll get the same information for every icon within that tab. Shortcuts such as Ctrl-P (for Print) are also available for nearly every command. We've made an effort to include the most common shortcuts in the text. Of course, if you ever need help in Word (or nearly any other Windows productivity application), press F1.

Because of its size and prominence, the Ribbon sometimes gets in the way; for instance, when taking in an entire document, or drafting text with no formatting or layout. At those times, you can collapse the Ribbon into the tab bar, and only pin it back in place when necessary.

### STEP BY STEP Expanding and collapsing the Ribbon

1 To collapse the Ribbon, click the caret (^) on the document's far right side as displayed in Figure 2-3. Only the tab bar will remain visible at the top of the screen.

**Figure 2-3**

Click the caret to collapse the Ribbon

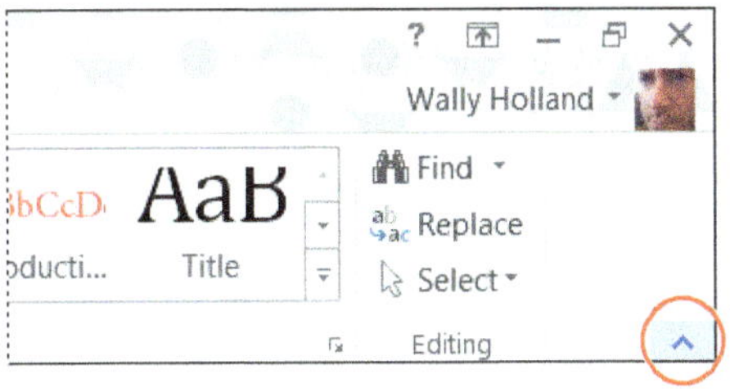


2 To expand the Ribbon, click one of the tabs. A push pin icon appears on the far right of the Ribbon as shown in Figure 2-4. To keep the Ribbon permanently visible (to pin it), click the **push pin** icon, which then changes back to a caret.

**Figure 2-4**

Click the push pin icon to expand the Ribbon.

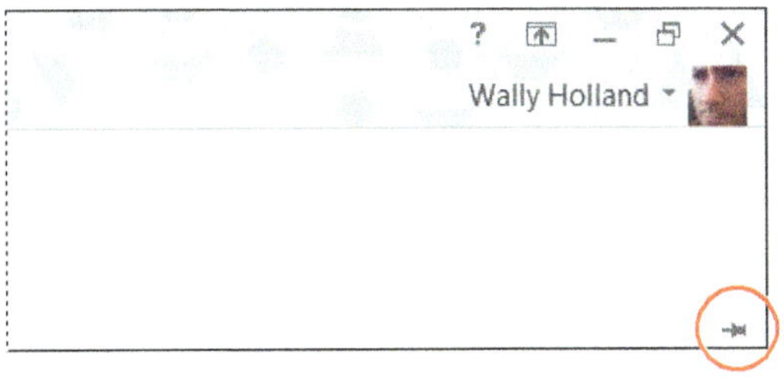


3 Alternatively, press **Ctrl-F1** to toggle Ribbon visibility.

Just as in old versions of Word, the Ribbon's commands can also be invoked with keyboard shortcuts. Alt+F works the same as clicking File; Alt+R is the equivalent to clicking Review, and so forth. Pressing the Alt key displays the keyboard equivalents for each tab (pressing Alt and then M *separately* accomplishes the same as Alt+M) and displays the Mailings tab with keyboard shortcuts for all its icons. Learning the key equivalents for your most-used tasks will increase your productivity with Word 2013 immensely.

## Customizing the Ribbon

**Bottom Line**

Because it's so central to the user experience in Word 2013, the Ribbon can be customized in several ways. You can hide, rename, and rearrange tabs, and do the same with the groups inside them; you can even create custom tabs and groups. The latter option can streamline your workflow when performing repetitive tasks. For instance, if you are working with a table-filled document, inserting footnotes and hyperlinks into a large number of cells, and changing table formatting, you might create a temporary Ribbon tab to group together the tools you need.

**STEP BY STEP** **Customizing the Ribbon**

1. Click **File > Options > Customize Ribbon** (or press **Alt+F+T**, and then click **Customize Ribbon**).
2. Click **New Tab**, then select your **New Tab (Custom)** and click **Rename**. For the name of your custom tab, type **TAAABLES**.
3. Use the arrow buttons at the right of the list (Customize the Ribbon) to move your new tab, which Word has marked Custom, to a spot between the Home and Insert tabs.
4. Click **New Group** found underneath the TAAABLES tab, then **Rename**. For the name of your custom group, type **GRUNT WORK**.
5. Make sure your GRUNT WORK group is selected in the right-hand list. From the list of Popular Commands at left, click **Hyperlink**, and then the **Add** button. Do the same with the Insert Footnote command.
6. Now select **All Tabs** from the top-left drop-down menu. The list of available commands changes to include one of the ribbon icons available in Word 2013, grouped by tab. Click through to select **Table Tools > Design > Borders > Borders and Shading**, and then click the **Add** button.
7. Finally, click **OK**.

Your Ribbon will update to include your custom tab and group (see Figure 2-5), which you can leave open for easy access while you work. Removing the tab works the same way.

**Figure 2-5**

Adding a custom group to the Ribbon.

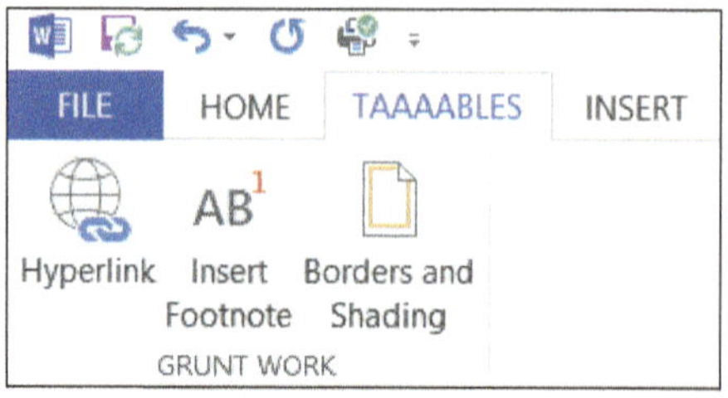


8. Click **File > Options > Customize Ribbon**.
9. On the right-hand list, right-click your custom group and choose **Remove**. Click **OK**.

You can actually hide any of the tabs and groups in Word 2013 from the same window: simply unclick the check box next to an entry in the right-hand list to render it invisible, and then click the box again to restore the tab or group.

## The Quick Access toolbar

Word 2013 also provides an always-on cluster of icons in the upper left corner of the screen called the Quick Access Toolbar. By default, this cluster of icons contains buttons to Save, Undo, and Redo, which come from the old File and Edit menus. If you click the rightmost icon in the toolbar, which resembles a tiny upside-down eject button, a drop-down menu appears with a list of available commands for the toolbar (Figure 2-6).

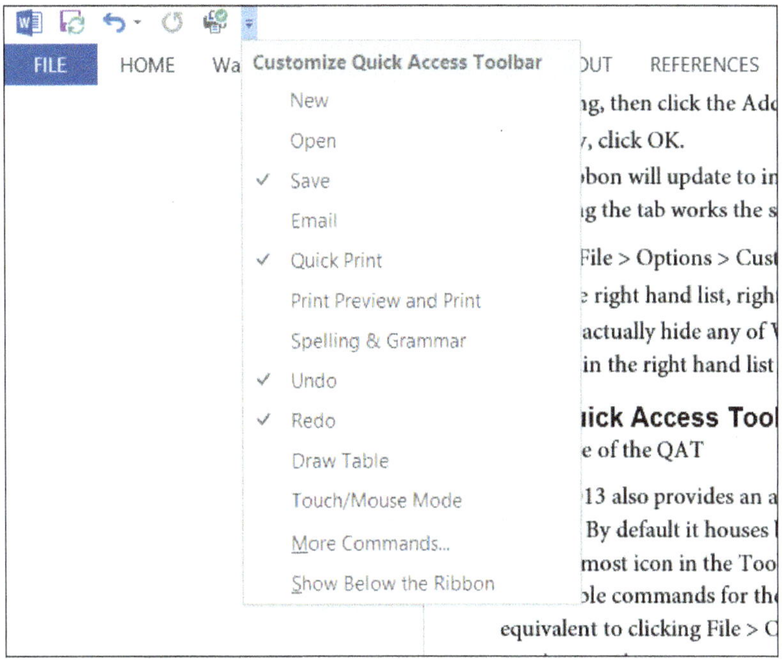


**Figure 2-6**

The Quick Access Toolbar is a customizable collection of frequently-used commands.

Choosing More Commands from this menu takes you to an options screen, equivalent to clicking File > Options > Quick Access Toolbar, which works just as the Customize Ribbon screen from the previous section.

You can stock your Quick Access Toolbar with the commands that you want available at all times: the Quick Print command, which was once prominent in Word's toolbar, is a popular choice; the E-mail command is also a handy option.

**Take Note** Clicking File > Print (or pressing Ctrl+P) brings up the Backstage View and lets you specify a printer or digital destination, alter some document properties, and so forth. The Quick Print command bypasses that screen, and simply prints according to your default preferences. It's not available in the Ribbon by default, which is why it's in the list of recommended commands for the Quick Access Toolbar.

## The Status bar

At the bottom of your Word 2013 document there is a slim status bar that doubles as an always-on info readout and a collection of buttons and toggles as shown in Figure 2-7. By default, it includes a minimal set of useful tools: the current page number, word count, a spellcheck button, zoom slider and percentage entry, and buttons to switch your document view. Clicking the page number brings up the Navigation pane; clicking the word count brings up a window with information such as character and line counts; and so forth.

**Figure 2-7**
The Status Bar.

You can customize the Status Bar by right-clicking anywhere along its length. The context menu lists the various options you can include on the bar. When you're finished customizing the display, press Escape to return to your document.

## The Navigation pane

The Find command has undergone some changes over the last few iterations of Microsoft Word. Like as Google search, Find has gotten *fuzzier* over time: once upon a time its main use was to grab a specific piece of text; now it's to move you *near* that text. It's now part of a handy tool called the **Navigation pane**, which combines the functionality of an outline, page-thumbnail view, and the old Find command.

### STEP BY STEP Using the Navigation pane

1 Press **Ctrl+F** or click the page count display in the Status Bar to bring up the Navigation pane.

The Navigation pane lets you move quickly through your document. Let's tour the file.

2 In the Search document field, type **chinatown**.

3 Click **Headings** in the Navigation pane.

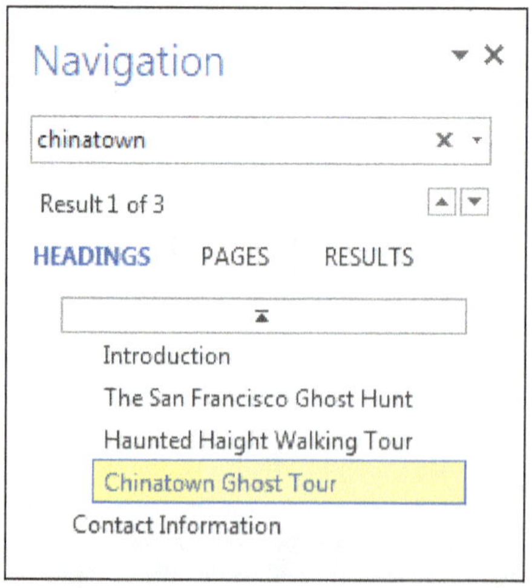


**Figure 2-8**
Listing Headings in the Navigation pane.

The Navigation pane, as shown in Figure 2-8 shows a simplified outline of the document with each level of the outline corresponding to a **Heading style** in the text: Heading 1 at the top level, and the various Heading 2 sections below. The final Heading 1 entry (Chinatown Ghost Tour) should be highlighted, indicating that the text you searched for is found within that section.

4 Click **Results**.

The Navigation pane shows three hits for the word *chinatown*, all in the same section of the document. You can click each result in turn to highlight its location in the editing window.

5 Click the first result in the Navigation pane, **Chinatown Ghost Tour**, and close the pane. You'll return to the main editing window with your cursor in the right place, ready to edit.

6 Type **San Francisco Chinatown**, press **Ctrl+F** to switch focus back to the Navigation pane, and then click **Headings**.

The outline dynamically updates to reflect the edit you just made; clicking any heading will place the cursor at that spot in the editing window.

**Take Note** Old Fashioned outline? Word 2013 still supports the old Outline view: click View > Outline (or press Alt+W+U) to get the old bullet points and Roman numerals. The Ribbon will update to reveal the Outlining tab. To return to Print Layout view, click the Print Layout button or press Alt+W+P.

## Different viewing modes

**Bottom Line**

There are several ways to view your document in Word 2013, all available in the View tab. Each offers a different perspective on your document, and is most useful at specific points in your workflow.

**Print Layout** is just what it sounds like: a WYSIWYG (What You See Is What You Get) preview of the document's final appearance on the page, with or without markup. This is the view most Word users prefer.

**Web Layout** is subtly different: it shows what Word will produce if you convert your document to HTML. (Switching to Web Layout mode doesn't actually do the conversion, though; you have to Save As an HTML document for that.)

**Outline View** is most useful early in the writing process: you build an outline for your document, and Word 2013 automatically generates the appropriate headings, providing a skeleton that you can fill in with prose, graphics, tables, and so on.

**Draft View** shows a pure-text view of your document, typewriter-style: no specialized fonts, no careful layout; just words on the page. Outline and Draft views let you work directly with text without worrying about layout.

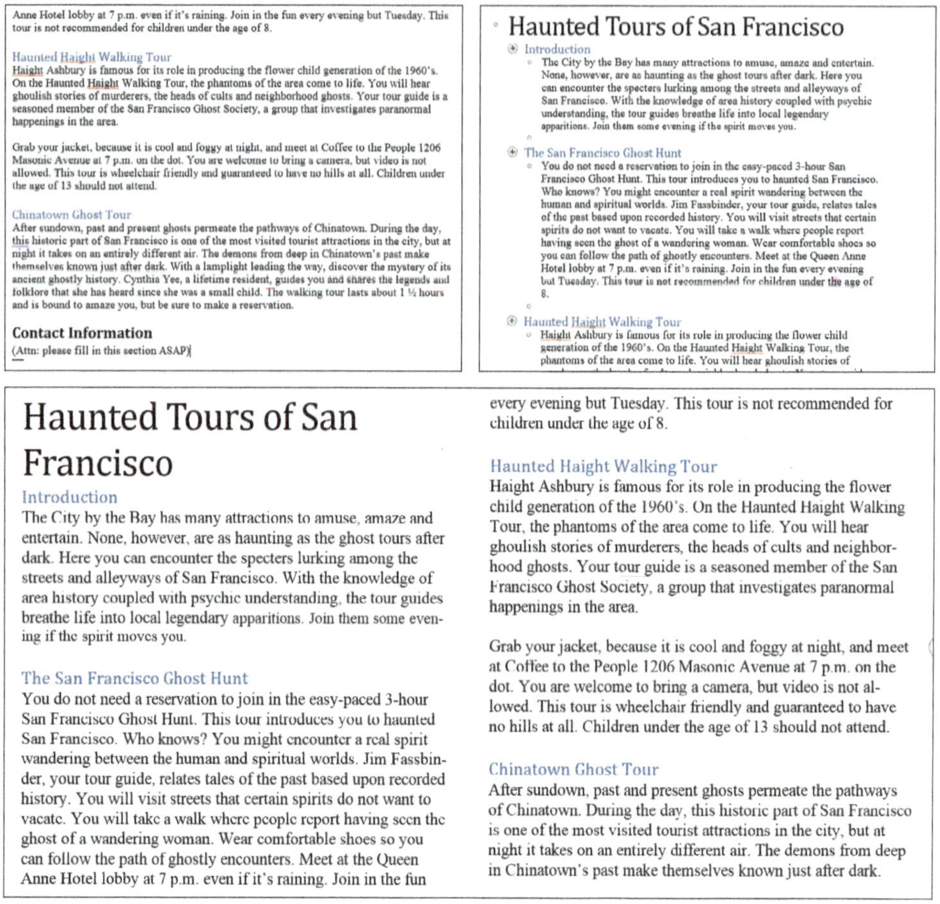

Anne Hotel lobby at 7 p.m. even if it's raining. Join in the fun every evening but Tuesday. This tour is not recommended for children under the age of 8.

Haunted Haight Walking Tour

Haight Ashbury is famous for its role in producing the flower child generation of the 1960's. On the Haunted Haight Walking Tour, the phantoms of the area come to life. You will hear ghoulish stories of murderers, the heads of cults and neighborhood ghosts. Your tour guide is a seasoned member of the San Francisco Ghost Society, a group that investigates paranormal happenings in the area.

Grab your jacket, because it is cool and foggy at night, and meet at Coffee to the People 1206 Masonic Avenue at 7 p.m. on the dot. You are welcome to bring a camera, but video is not allowed. This tour is wheelchair friendly and guaranteed to have no hills at all. Children under the age of 13 should not attend.

Chinatown Ghost Tour

After sundown, past and present ghosts permeate the pathways of Chinatown. During the day, this historic part of San Francisco is one of the most visited tourist attractions in the city, but at night it takes on an entirely different air. The demons from deep in Chinatown's past make themselves known just after dark. With a lamplight leading the way, discover the mystery of its ancient ghostly history. Cynthia Yee, a lifetime resident, guides you and shares the legends and folklore that she has heard since she was a small child. The walking tour lasts about 1 ½ hours and is bound to amaze you, but be sure to make a reservation.

**Contact Information**

(Attn: please fill in this section ASAP)

Haunted Tours of San Francisco

Introduction

- The City by the Bay has many attractions to amuse, amaze and entertain. None, however, are as haunting as the ghost tours after dark. Here you can encounter the specters lurking among the streets and alleyways of San Francisco. With the knowledge of area history coupled with psychic understanding, the tour guides breathe life into local legendary apparitions. Join them some evening if the spirit moves you.

The San Francisco Ghost Hunt

- You do not need a reservation to join in the easy-paced 3-hour San Francisco Ghost Hunt. This tour introduces you to haunted San Francisco. Who knows? You might encounter a real spirit wandering between the human and spiritual worlds. Jim Fassbinder, your tour guide, relates tales of the past based upon recorded history. You will visit streets that certain spirits do not want to vacate. You will take a walk where people report having seen the ghost of a wandering woman. Wear comfortable shoes so you can follow the path of ghostly encounters. Meet at the Queen Anne Hotel lobby at 7 p.m. even if it's raining. Join in the fun every evening but Tuesday. This tour is not recommended for children under the age of 8.

Haunted Haight Walking Tour

- Haight Ashbury is famous for its role in producing the flower child generation of the 1960's. On the Haunted Haight Walking Tour, the phantoms of the area come to life. You will hear ghoulish stories of

Haunted Tours of San Francisco

Introduction

The City by the Bay has many attractions to amuse, amaze and entertain. None, however, are as haunting as the ghost tours after dark. Here you can encounter the specters lurking among the streets and alleyways of San Francisco. With the knowledge of area history coupled with psychic understanding, the tour guides breathe life into local legendary apparitions. Join them some evening if the spirit moves you.

The San Francisco Ghost Hunt

You do not need a reservation to join in the easy-paced 3-hour San Francisco Ghost Hunt. This tour introduces you to haunted San Francisco. Who knows? You might encounter a real spirit wandering between the human and spiritual worlds. Jim Fassbinder, your tour guide, relates tales of the past based upon recorded history. You will visit streets that certain spirits do not want to vacate. You will take a walk where people report having seen the ghost of a wandering woman. Wear comfortable shoes so you can follow the path of ghostly encounters. Meet at the Queen Anne Hotel lobby at 7 p.m. even if it's raining. Join in the fun every evening but Tuesday. This tour is not recommended for children under the age of 8.

Haunted Haight Walking Tour

Haight Ashbury is famous for its role in producing the flower child generation of the 1960's. On the Haunted Haight Walking Tour, the phantoms of the area come to life. You will hear ghoulish stories of murderers, the heads of cults and neighborhood ghosts. Your tour guide is a seasoned member of the San Francisco Ghost Society, a group that investigates paranormal happenings in the area.

Grab your jacket, because it is cool and foggy at night, and meet at Coffee to the People 1206 Masonic Avenue at 7 p.m. on the dot. You are welcome to bring a camera, but video is not allowed. This tour is wheelchair friendly and guaranteed to have no hills at all. Children under the age of 13 should not attend.

Chinatown Ghost Tour

After sundown, past and present ghosts permeate the pathways of Chinatown. During the day, this historic part of San Francisco is one of the most visited tourist attractions in the city, but at night it takes on an entirely different air. The demons from deep in Chinatown's past make themselves known just after dark.

**Figure 2-9**

The same document in Draft, Outline, and Read modes.

The four viewing modes listed previously are holdovers from previous versions of Word. Word 2013 adds a new document view: Read Mode (Shown in Figure 2-9). Designed for tablets and touchscreens, Read Mode displays your document with no visual clutter: no Ribbon, no tool palettes, just a handful of commands. Crucially, you can't *edit* the document in Read Mode; you move through the document a page at a time, as if shuffling pieces of paper.

Read Mode is useful at the reviewing, revising, and editing stages, and when sharing documents. To switch to Read Mode, click View > Views > Read Mode, or press Alt+W+F; to return to editing, press Escape or click View > Edit Document.

## LAYING OUT THE PAGE

**Bottom Line**

Our info sheet uses a slightly nonstandard page layout: U.S. letter paper, as usual, but with narrow 0.5″ **margins** all around. (The default for U.S. users is a 1″ margin.) Click Page Layout > Page Setup > Margins to see the standard options. For inter-office memos and book reports, it's not worth worrying about page layout, but if design matters to your document, you'll start by thinking about the size and quality of the paper (or screen) where your work will appear.

### Page size, margins, and marginalia

Assume that we've laid out our flyer haphazardly for letter paper with thin margins and no page numbers. We are then told that our flyer will be included in a book of local event listings, and we need to bring our layout in line with some new artistic visual standards. Our task is to alter everything but the content of our flyer, from page size through document theme.

**STEP BY STEP** **Changing the page size, margins, and orientation**

1. If it's not still open from the previous exercise, open **word02a_work.docx**.
2. Click **Page Layout > Page Setup > Size > More Paper Sizes** (**Alt+P, SZ, A**).
3. Set the page width to 6″ and its height to 9″ (the dimensions of a trade paperback book) and click **OK**.

Word automatically lays out the text to fit the new page size, still in **portrait** (tall and narrow) orientation, with the same 0.5″ margins. Let's change those parameters as well.

4. Select **Orientation > Landscape**, and then **Margins > Wide** (both in the Page Layout tab).

Our new layout provides tons of left and right margin space, less at the top and bottom of the page. We'll take advantage of the roomy margins and place our page numbers at left, instead of in the usual header and footer.

**Take Note** The Margins > Mirrored setting sets the Inside and Outside margins, rather than Left and Right; referring directly to *print* output, in which page 1 sits alone on the right, then a spread of pages 2 (left) and 3 (right), and alternating from there. If your long document is destined for print rather than PDF or HTML, consider working with some variant of the Mirrored layout, with a generous inner margin to account for book binding; e-books don't need asymmetric layouts, nor do short documents destined for stapling.

5. Select **Insert > Header & Footer > Page Number > Page Margins > Circle Left**. Double-click the main document area to close the Header/Footer menu. The page number float fades, visually indicating that it's a page element unaffected by normal text entry.

**Take Note** Word opens the Header/Footer design tab when you insert a page number in the margin, even though marginal page numbers are floating text boxes that have nothing to do with headers or footers; this is one area where Word's do what I mean, not what I say approach is mildly confusing. If you click directly on the marginal page number, Word offers the correct tools to format floating text boxes. We'll discuss floats in great detail in later lessons.

## Headers and footers

**Bottom Line**

Broadly speaking, a page in Word 2013 can be separated into a **header**, **footer**, and margins (generally the same from page to page); text blocks (the main text area, different on every page); background elements such as textures and watermarks; and **floats**, which jostle for space with everything else. Most documents have empty right and left margins, but headers and footers are widely used in Office documents.

Compared to applications such as InDesign and Quark Express, Word can't easily handle complex page layout, but even its basic header/footer tools provide surprising flexibility for medium-size desktop publishing projects.

The most common use for headers and footers is to print page numbers, author info, or title and date info on every page of a document. Our paranormal event listing will be included in a Coming Events guide; after setting the right Theme and Style Set, we'll insert the guide's title into our footer on alternate pages.

## STEP BY STEP Headers and footers

1 Select **Design > Themes > Organic**, and then select the **Lines (Distinctive)** Style Set.

2 Scroll to the first page of the document. Click **Insert > Footer > Filigree**. Place the cursor to the left of the filigree symbol and type **Fun Francisco**. Then place the cursor to the right of the filigree and type **Thrillafornia**.

3 Select **Options > Different Odd & Even Pages**, and then click **Navigation > Next** to move to the page 2 footer.

4 Double-click the center of the page 2 footer (the cursor should change to centered text) as shown in Figure 2-10.

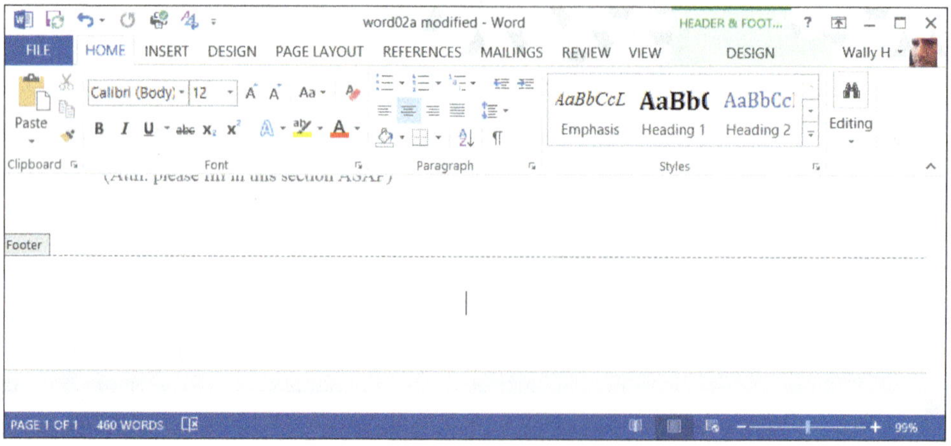


**Figure 2-10**

Word 2013 correctly assumes that text placed at the center of the footer is center-aligned.

5 Type **2013 Spooktacular**. Finally, double-click the main text area to close the header/footer tools.

## Windows and panes: splitting your document view

**Bottom Line**

At times, you may need to have more than one section of your document open at once; for instance, when paraphrasing one passage elsewhere in the document, or avoiding doing so. The Window Group in Word 2013 offers some tools to help you visually manage different parts of a document; we'll use the split-screen functionality to make some edits to our flyer.

## STEP BY STEP Changing the document view

1 Click **View > Window > Split** to divide the screen in half vertically. You can now scroll independently in each pane.

2 Click **New Window** to open another window on the current document.

3 Now click **View Side by Side** to reveal three angles on the document at once as displayed in Figure 2-11.

4 If it's not already selected, click **Synchronous Scrolling**.

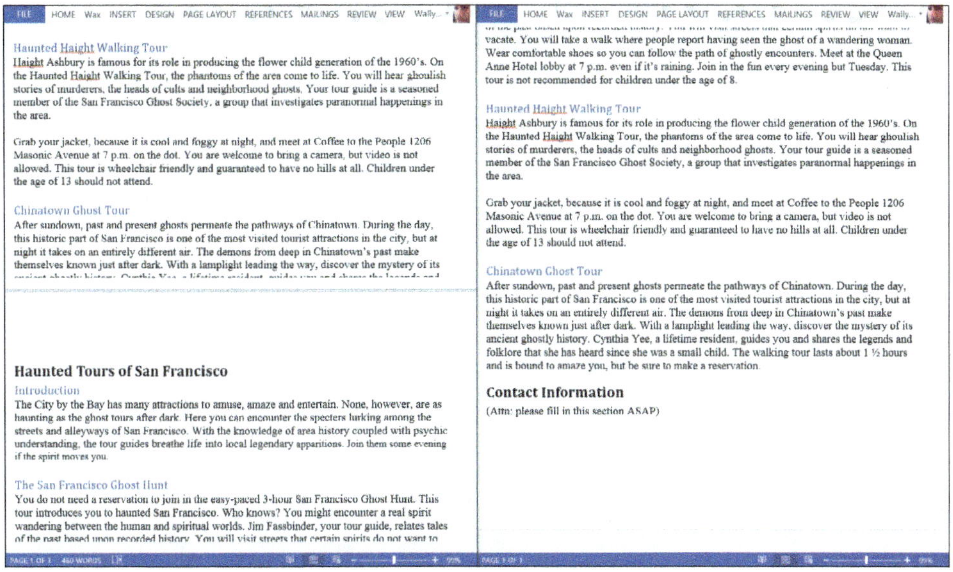


**Figure 2-11** One image, three views: Split Window and New Window.

Now scroll to the very bottom of the document in one of the short windows; the tall window scrolls along with it. This feature is most useful when comparing different documents; we don't need it now.

5 Close the tall window. In one of the half-height panes, scroll to the top of the document; in the other pane, scroll to the very bottom. To switch focus between panes, just click to place the cursor as normal.

To switch focus and move the cursor between the two open panes, press F6; note that this command actually switches between the open document panes, status bar, ribbon, and Navigation pane, if open. To switch between windows within Word, press Ctrl+F6.

6 Scroll down from the top of the document to gather the names of the various tour guides. At the end of the flyer, replace the placeholder text with their contact information, styled so as to draw attention (boldface, right justified):

**Jim Fassbinder (253) 555-2294**

**San Francisco Ghost Society (617) 22-SPOOKY**

**Cynthia Yee (503) 555-4YEE**

7 Click **View > Window > Remove Split** to return to a single editing window.

8 Choose **File > Save** and then **File > Close**.

# Knowledge Assessment

## Fill in the Blanks

**Complete the following sentences by writing the correct word or words in the blanks provided.**

1. To see the keyboard shortcut for a command, _____ its icon in the Ribbon.
2. Results of the Find command are displayed in the _____.
3. The simplest view of your document, stripped of images and formatting and niceties, is the _____ View.
4. To print the page number at the bottom of every page, insert it in the _____.
5. On the third page of a document designed for print, the left margin is also known as the _____ margin.
6. Tall thin documents are laid out in _____ orientation.
7. To display two views of a document in separate windows, use the _____ command.
8. The running word count display can be added to the _____.
9. To print a document without clicking the File tab, press the _____ keyboard shortcut.
10. The Replace command appears in a Navigation Pane dropdown or the _____ tab, and can be invoked directly with the _____ shortcut.

## Matching

**Match the action to its associated keyboard shortcut.**

1. Save As
2. Print Layout
3. Open Styles Pane
4. Italicize
5. Open File
6. Quit
7. Switch windows
8. Find/Replace
9. Close Document
10. Boldface

a. Alt+Ctrl+Shift+S
b. Ctrl+H
c. Ctrl+O
d. Ctrl+B
e. Ctrl+I
f. Ctrl+F6
g. Alt+F+A
h. Ctrl+W
i. Alt+W+P
j. Alt+F4

## Competency Assessment

### Project 2-1: Working with the Quick Access Toolbar

**In this exercise you'll customize the Quick Access Toolbar.**

1. Launch Word and create a new document.
2. Click the **dropdown** button on the Quick Access Toolbar and select **Email**.
3. Type some text in the main edit window, and then select the **Email** command from the Quick Access Toolbar.
4. Right click the **Email** command and choose **Remove**.
5. Select **More Commands...** from the dropdown. In the left hand pane, scroll down and select **Styles...**
6. Click the new **Styles...** command or press **Alt+Ctrl+Shift+S** to bring up the Styles task pane.

   Note the difference between this task pane and Apply Style (Ctrl+Shift+S) pane.
7. Close the pane and leave Word open for the next exercise.

### Project 2-2: Customizing the Status Bar

**In this exercise you'll tailor the Status Bar to your preferences.**

1. Right-click in the Status Bar and select **Page Number**.
2. Deselect **Zoom** while leaving **Zoom Slider** selected.

   You can choose to re-enable the direct-entry zoom tool later if you'd like.
3. Dismiss the menu and click the **"Page X of Y"** display on the Status Bar. Dismiss the Pane.
4. Experiment with adding other Status Bar elements and finding out what commands they enact when clicked.
5. Dismiss the Customize Status Bar menu.
6. Leave Word open for the next exercise.

## Proficiency Assessment

### Project 2-3: Using the Navigation Pane

**In this exercise you'll put the Navigation Pane to use for browsing and editing a file.**

1. Open the project file called **2-3-source** and save your document as **project_2-3_headings**.
2. Open the Navigation Pane.
3. Search for **king** in the document and click to view all results. Click on the two results in the Navigation Pane's Results tab.

   Note that "king" is a substring – the search hits both "king" and "taking."
4. With the second search result selected, switch to the Navigation Pane's Headings tab.
5. Drag the **Good Faith** entry in the Headings tab to the top of the mini outline.
6. Click the **Bill of Particulars** heading in the Pane to switch to its page.
7. Right-click the same entry in the outline list, and select **Demote**.

   Note the changes to both the outline and the newly-restyled heading itself.
8. Save and close your document.

### Project 2-4: Using Find/Replace

**In this exercise you'll test out Word's Find/Replace tool.**

1. Open the project file **2-4-source** and save it as **project_2-4_find**.
2. Press **Ctrl+F**. Open the Results tab in the Navigation Pane.
3. Type **our** in the search box, but don't press Return yet.

   Word displays search results as you type.
4. Complete the search term **ouring** and press **Return**.
5. Click the drop-down arrow on the search entry box itself and select **Replace…**
6. Replace ouring with **oring**. If prompted, continue the search from the beginning of the document, and click **OK** when all results are in.
7. Experiment with case-sensitive and case-insensitive searches in the Advanced Find dialog box, e.g., by searching for **for** with and without case-sensitive searching enabled.
8. Save and close your document.

## Mastery Assessment

### Project 2-5: Outline Mode

**In this exercise you'll add headings and notes to a file and make use of Outline View.**

1. Open the project file **2-5-source** and save it as **project_2-5_outline**.
2. Experiment with inserting a variety of headings – **Opening** and **Closing**, for instance, or a **Specific Complaints** top-level heading that includes both the Bill of Particulars and the Legal Affronts.
3. Use the Navigation Pane to quickly browse the file, using the new headings as a guide.
4. Switch to Outline View and experiment with moving and collapsing entire sections of the document.
5. Write a short note, **heading not in original**, and use Outline View to add it, as quickly as you can, to the beginning of every section of your reordered Declaration.
6. Save and close your document.

### Project 2-6: Laying Out the Page

**This exercise challenges you to create a page layout from scratch.**

1. Open the project file **2-6-source** and save it as **project_2-6_layout**.
2. Create a new page layout for the document according to the following specifications:
   - **6"** square page, **0.2"** margins on all four edges (ignore error message)
   - **40pt** title text, title alone on front page (add a Page Break)
   - **18pt** Normal text (note that Title is resized based on Normal…)
   - Page break after opening paragraph ("When in the course…")
3. Save your work and close Word.

# 3 Beginning Text and Layout Operations

## LESSON SKILL MATRIX

**In this lesson, you will learn the following skills:**

| | |
|---|---|
| Paragraph and Character Formatting | Using the Format Painter |
| Line and Paragraph Spacing | Formatting Multi-Column Text |
| Styles, Themes, and Live Preview | Adding Text Boxes and Images |
| Cut, Copy, and Paste | |

## KEY TERMS

- Character
- Alignment
- Justification
- Tab Stop
- Points
- Paste Options
- Format Painter
- Absolute Placement
- Text Box
- Rotation Handle
- Grouping
- In Line with Text (object layout)

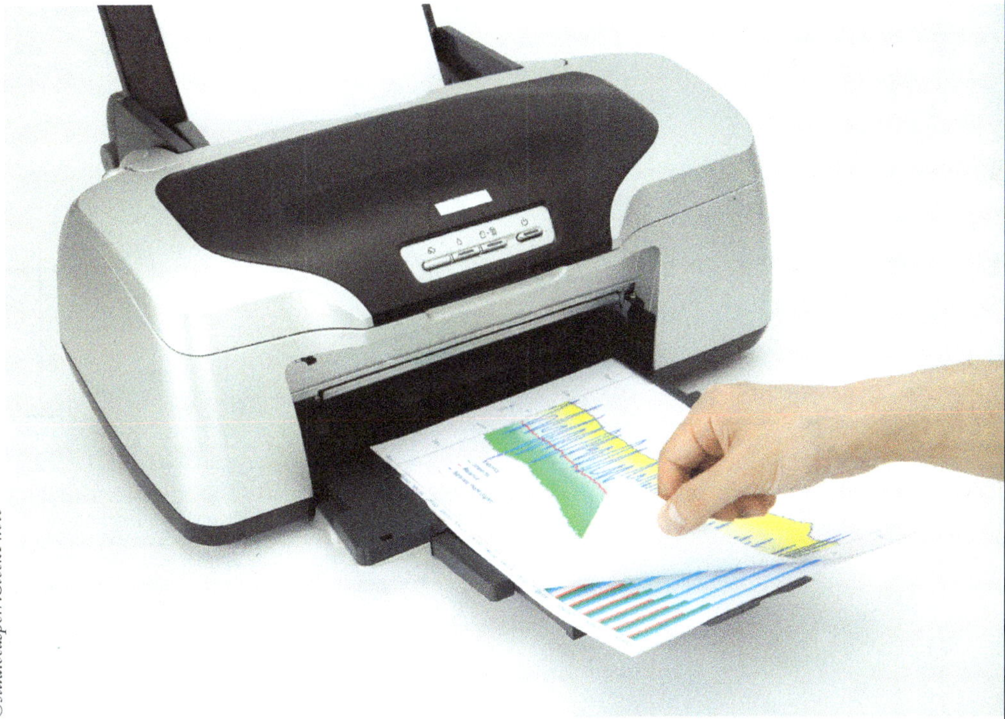

©studiocasper/iStockPhoto

Fabrikam's clients can submit Archival Research requests through Fabrikam's website; for auditing purposes, the plain text output of these requests is reformatted as Word documents for print. Fortunately, prettying up the plain text website data dumps is easy – Word's Style system and robust options for pasting and reformatting data give Fabrikam's documentation team a set of streamlined tools for radically transforming the look of a document while keeping its information intact.

## SOFTWARE ORIENTATION

Microsoft Word provides many options for controlling the appearance and position of text and objects on screen. In this lesson you'll be introduced to document formatting controls.

**Figure 3-1**

Formatting tools and controls

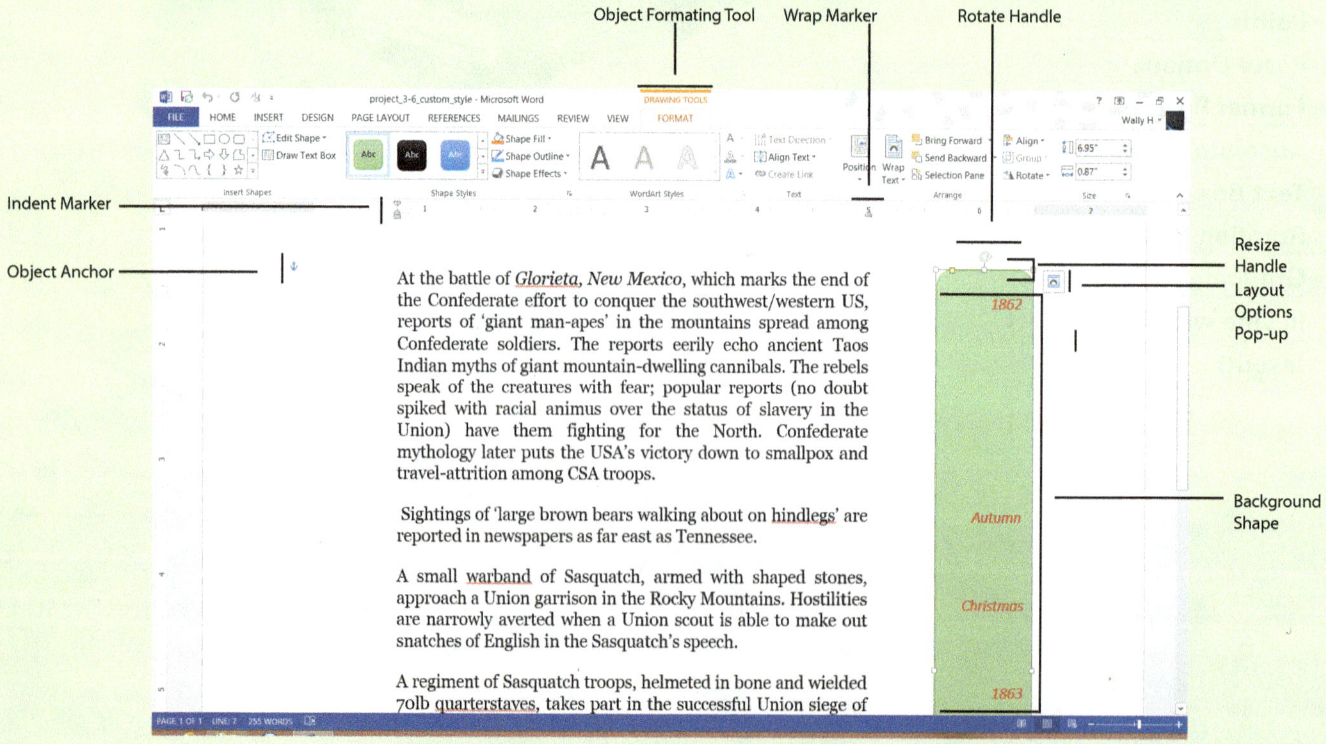

## STARTING UP

In this lesson, you'll work with several files from the Word03lessons folder. Make sure that you have loaded the OfficeLessons folder onto your computer.

## WORKING WITH TEXT IN WORD

Over the decades, MS Word has grown into a complex desktop publishing tool. Most of what you'll do with Word 2013 is just entering and editing text. But in a graphical application such as Word, text is as much a visual element as any image – so this lesson moves right from basic text entry and formatting to working with visual page elements.

To begin, open two files in your Word03lessons folder and look over them: **word03a.docx** and **word03b.docx**. The first is a draft info sheet on pandas; the second includes revised text from a colleague to be inserted into the info sheet. In this lesson, we'll tighten the prose in the info sheet, experiment with some layout changes, and better integrate the image and caption into the flow of the text.

### Paragraph and character formatting

**Bottom Line**

In Word 2013, a piece of text consists of a series of **characters** (letters, numbers, symbols) that are formatted one way or another. You control every aspect of the text's appearance: font (typeface), size, spacing, emphasis (italics, bold, underline), vertical and horizontal **alignment**, **justification** (i.e., how smooth is the edge of a block of text), indentation, and more.

You can alter the formatting of an individual character, word, or line. When you select one word from a line and press Ctrl+I, you change it to italic type. The rest of the line remains as it was. In contrast, you can't double-space a single word without doing the same to its entire paragraph. Word 2013 treats italics and line spacing differently; the former is one variety of character formatting, and is handled by the controls in the Home > Font group; the latter is paragraph formatting, found in Home > Paragraph. Both sets of controls are shown in Figure 3-2.

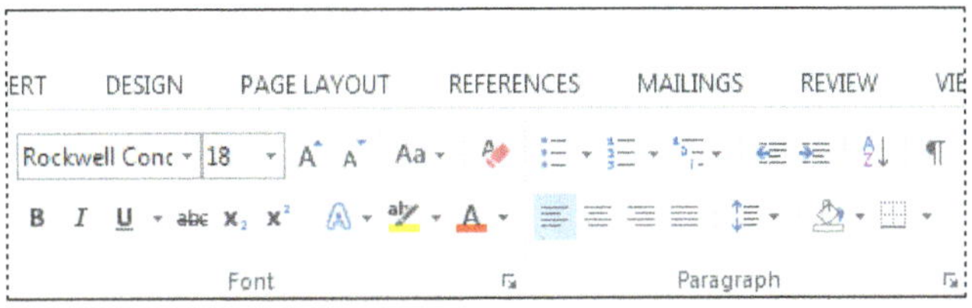


**Figure 3-2**

Word's basic formatting palette.

**STEP BY STEP** **Paragraph and character formatting**

Crucially, Word 2013 treats character and paragraph formatting commands differently in the Edit window. Let's see how:

1. Switch to **word03b.docx**. Open the Home tab.
2. Move your cursor just to the left of the word Edits, but don't select any text.
3. Click **Home > Font > Underline** (or press **Ctrl+U**).

The Underline icon is selected, but nothing happens to the text that's already on the page. You've told Word to switch to Underline text, but there's nothing selected, so the Underline command will only be applied to the text you type next.

4 Type **Important** and press the **spacebar**.

This is an important lesson for later: a blank space is a character just like a number, letter, punctuation mark, or symbol, and Word knows to underline blank spaces just the same. It does look foolish, but you can fix it by highlighting this space and deselecting Underline.

5 Click **Home > Paragraph > Align Right** (**Ctrl+R**). Move the cursor to the end of the line and type **—please update**.

6 Triple-click the word ***Edits*** and click **Center** (**Ctrl+E**).

Word applies paragraph formatting to the entire paragraph, whether you click somewhere in the line or select one or more words in it. The same applies to the rest of the formatting commands.

## Indendation and Tab Stops

The ruler at the top of the main document area is toggled with the View > Show > Ruler checkbox. It both shows you the position of a page element in units of physical distance (not just points), and allows you to set the placement of text with some precision by customizing indentation and tab stops.

The hourglass symbol at the left of the ruler is actually three parts, as indicated in <<figure 3-whatever>>: the first-line indent point, the indent point for subsequent (wrapped) lines in the paragraph, and a handle to drag both indent points at once. Each indent point indicates where a line of text will begin filling in. Practice changing indent settings to see what paragraph layouts they can generate.

A fourth handle, at the far right of the ruler, indicates the rightmost border of the text block – the wrap point. Any paragraph that runs past that point will instead be wrapped to the next line.

The pictured ruler also contains several tab stops. If you don't manually add tab stops, each time you press Tab, you'll insert blank space between the current cursor position and the next 0.5" increment. (You can set the default Tab increment in Options.) Tab stops let you specify alternate destinations. In the image, you can see a center tab stop and a right-justified tab stop – tabbing to the first will insert center-justified text at that spot, and tabbing to the next will let you insert right-justified text there.

A combination of left- and right-justified tab stops lets you simulate a multi-column or tabular layout. You can add tab stops by picking the variety you want using the tab selector (left of the ruler), then clicking in the ruler itself to place it. To remove a tab stop, just drag it out of the ruler.

Feel free to experiment with adding tab stops and changing the indentation of some text.

## Spacing

**Bottom Line**

Word's standard text spacing is meant to be readable on-screen and in print, but if you need to adjust the amount of whitespace between lines of text, the Home > Paragraph > Line Spacing command offers a plethora of options. Clicking the icon reveals a drop-down menu; selecting Line Spacing Options from the menu brings up the Indents and Spacing tab of the Paragraph Formatting dialog box seen in Figure 3-3. The numbers in the Spacing group refer to the space between lines of a paragraph; the larger the number, the more room Word leaves between lines in a paragraph. You can mouse over the options in the menu for a Live Preview of the different settings.

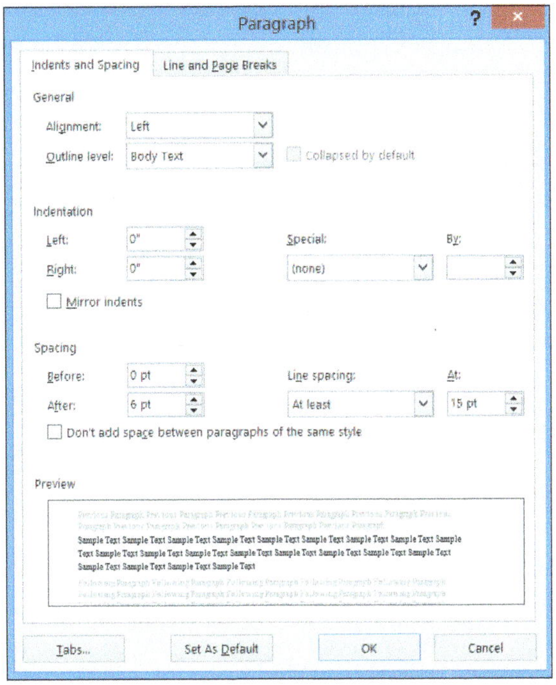


**Figure 3-3**

Fine-tune text block formatting in the Paragraph Settings dialog.

**Take Note** The default line spacing of Normal body text is 1.0; it seems logical that double-spaced text would have a line spacing of 2.0. But that setting leaves a vast empty space between lines. For a double-spaced report or memo, use the 1.5 or even 1.15 spacing options.

Spacing between paragraphs is set with the Page Layout > Paragraph commands. The spacing is measured in **points**, just like font size; 12 point (pt.) of space atop a paragraph leaves about as much room as a line of normal text. You can also control pre and post-paragraph spacing with the Line Spacing Option screen.

The Line and Paragraph Spacing command affects a single paragraph, or every paragraph in that Style; if you want to set spacing defaults for your entire document at once, use the Design > Document Formatting > Paragraph Spacing tool.

## Styles, themes, and live preview

Now take a look at **word03a.docx**. It contains several headings (Habitat, Diet, Status, and more) formatted in a different font, size, and color from the body text. Individually reformatting each heading would be a hassle; it's much easier to tell your word processor that the current text is a heading and to format this like the other headings. This is accomplished through the use of Styles—one of the most important features of Word 2013.

## STEP BY STEP Styles, themes and live preview

1. Open the Home tab. A gallery of Styles appears.
2. Click several different pieces of text in your document, and their various Styles will be highlighted in the gallery: Heading 1 and Heading 2 for the top line and paragraph headings, respectively; Caption for the Figure 1 caption; Normal for the body text.
3. Open the Design tab. Click **Design > Themes** to see that Wood Type is selected—that's the current document Theme, which sets colors, fonts, and more.
4. Under the Document Formatting options, you can see that Lines (Simple) is selected (See Figure 3-4.). That's the current Style Set for your document—a collection of styles chosen to work well together visually.

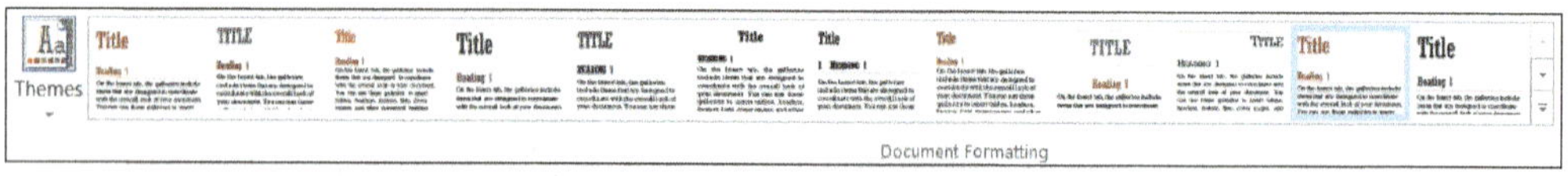


**Figure 3-4**
A gallery of Style Sets for the current theme.

To see how to work efficiently with Styles, let's make some changes to the look of our document—both line-by-line and globally. We'll begin by drawing a little more attention to the headings in our document.

## STEP BY STEP Working with Styles

1. Mouse over the style sets in the Design > Document Formatting gallery to see the names of each style set.

Note that when you mouse over an entry in the Style Set gallery, the appearance of your document changes to show the new style; this is Word's Live Preview feature at work. The new style set isn't applied until you click a gallery entry.

2. Click the paragraph heading, **Habitat**, and then select **Home > Paragraph > Align Right** (or press **Ctrl+R**). The heading is now flush with the right margin; Word treats the heading as a paragraph consisting of a single word, and then reformats the entire paragraph.
3. Double or triple-click the same heading. A mini toolbar, shown in Figure 3-5, will appear with commonly used character and paragraph-formatting commands.

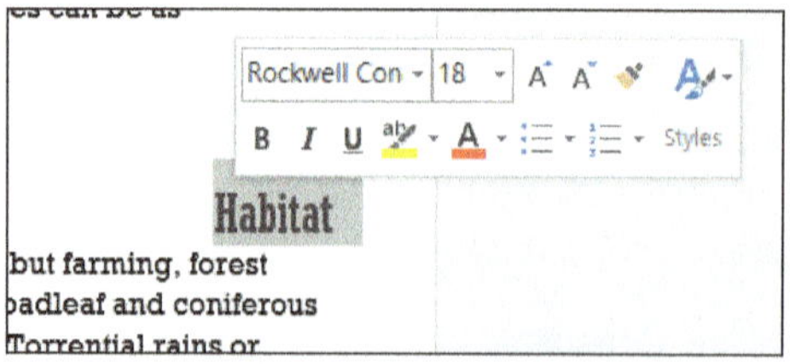


**Figure 3-5**
The mini formatting toolbar appears by default when you select a text block

**Take Note** Double-clicking selects a single word; triple-clicking selects an entire paragraph. From Word 2013's perspective, each paragraph is really a single line of characters, wrapped to fit in a single column; if your text were small enough or your page wide enough, every paragraph would fit onto its own line. But Word's formatting tools refer to paragraphs, not lines. This human-centered terminology is there to help you think about your document from a reader's perspective. Note that the word/line count in the Status Bar refers to lines in the reader sense, i.e., it counts lines on the page, not paragraphs.

4 Use the font size drop-down in the mini toolbar to set the Habitat heading to **18 pt.** type.

5 Right-click the **Heading 2** entry in the Home > Styles gallery and select **Update Heading 2 to Match Selection**.

First, we modified the heading style for one paragraph heading from Lines (Simple) Heading 2 (which sets font, color, size, and so on) to Lines (Simple) Heading 2 + right-justify + 18pt. We then instructed Word to make the same changes everywhere it finds the Heading 2 style, tweaking alignment and size, but leaving font and color the same.

To ensure that our top-level heading stands out from the paragraph headings, we'll make one more change to Heading 2 using the Modify Style tool.

6 Right-click the **Heading 2** entry in the Styles gallery and chose **Modify**. A dialog box will appear, as in Figure 3-6.

**Figure 3-6**

Modify Style dialog box.

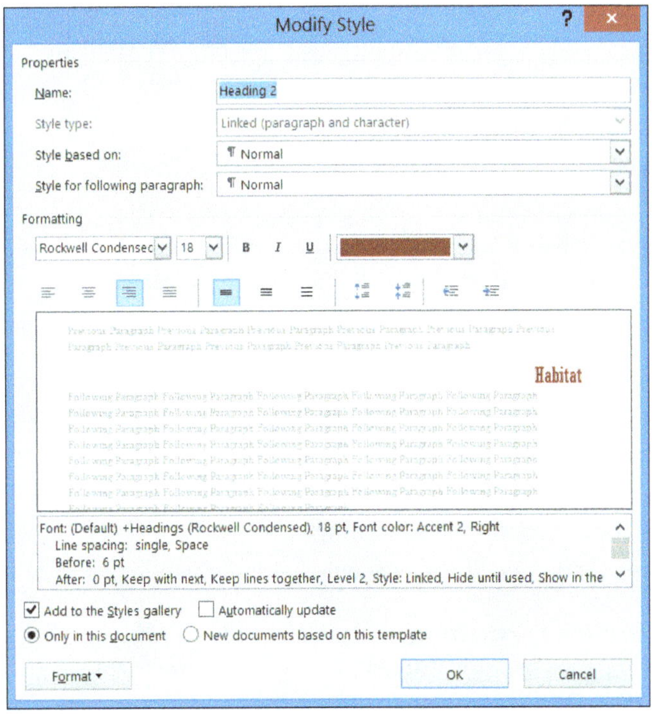


7 In the drop-down color menu, select **Gray-50%-Text 2** (top row, fourth from the left), and check **Automatically update**. Click **OK**.

8 Choose **File > Save As**. Navigate to the Word03lessons folder, and save the file as **word03a_work**.

Selecting Automatically update makes a change to all Heading 2 text in this document only. Yes, the right-justified headings look terrible atop short, wide text blocks; we'll switch to a compact two-column layout later in the lesson to make the headings more readable.

Styles in Word can be put to a wide array of uses; in Lesson 4, "Structuring Complex Documents," you'll take advantage of Word's heading styles to structure a document with many sections. In the meantime, go ahead and experiment with modifying Styles to tweak the look of your document.

## Cut, copy, and paste

### Workplace Ready

The most frequently used commands in Word are Cut, Copy, and Paste. In theory, they're very simple: select some text, duplicate it or remove it to memory, and then insert the stored text somewhere else. But remember, Word can format text at the character and paragraph levels, and when you paste Heading 3 + non-theme color text into the middle of a Caption + italics line, you have to work with the application to decide exactly how that Paste action should work.

What happens when your clipboard contains, not a string of text from a Word document, but an entire Excel spreadsheet? Or an image with a caption in a font that's not installed on your computer? In this section, we'll look at options built into Word to cover most cut/copy/paste situations.

### Paste options

We can take advantage of Live Preview to see how Word's Paste Options work.

**STEP BY STEP** **Paste options**

1. Switch over to **word03b.docx** and select the text from the word Habitat through the end of the file. Press **Ctrl+C** to copy the selected text.
2. Switch to **word03a_work.docx**. Select the Habitat heading and paragraph.
3. Click **Home > Clipboard > Paste** (or press **Ctrl+V**). The replacement text will overwrite the original, and a mini toolbar will appear with a clipboard icon. Click the mini toolbar to bring up Paste Options.
4. Mouse over each **Paste Option** in turn. Live Preview will show the available options for pasting the replacement text.

The Paste Options toolbar offers four choices for handling a Paste action:

**Keep Source Formatting** inserts the pasted text into your document as-is, preserving its character and paragraph formatting. In this situation, where consistent look and feel is important, this is obviously the wrong choice.

**Merge Formatting** will apply the style of the destination text to the pasted text; in this case, it chooses Heading 2 (the first style in the selected text from the info sheet) and applies that to the entire pasted selection. That makes sense for simple pastes, but not for pasting in a heading and paragraph, as we're doing.

**Use Destination Styles** is the default behavior for Word 2013 when pasting text from a Word document. All our source text uses the Normal style, so Word simply applies the formatting that the Normal style has in the Style Set Lines (Stylish).

**Keep Text Only** is useful for tasks such as converting a table to straight text. It eliminates all formatting from the source text: italics, centering, bullets, and more. In the present instance, Keep Text Only produces the same output as Merge Formatting, but that won't always be the case.

As you can see, Word has no way of knowing that our first line is a paragraph heading unless we use a heading style; the application treats our Paste as two paragraphs of Normal text. The default Paste behavior is fine; we can manually fix the heading style.

5 Press **Ctrl**, then **S** to accept Use Destination Styles paste option, then press **Escape** to dismiss the Paste Options minibar. Then select the lone word ***Habitat*** and switch its style to **Heading 2**.

## Copying a look: Format Painter

**Bottom Line**

Sometimes you want to grab, not the content of a text selection, but its formatting. This happens often enough that Word has a ready-made command for it: Home > Clipboard > **Format Painter**. To use it, select the text whose format you're grabbing, click Format Painter (or press Ctrl+Shift+C), and then click the text to which you want to apply the format (or press Ctrl+Shift+V).

Format Painter is especially valuable when you want to match to colored/resized text, but don't want to manually tweak multiple formatting options. It does not copy over the Style of the source text, just its look (so you can Paint a single sidebar to appear as a header without botching your document outline).

Word 2013 offers you refined control over the behavior of the Paste command.

**STEP BY STEP** **Setting additional paste options**

1 Click Home > Clipboard > Paste > Set Default Paste.

2 In the Options screen, shown in Figure 3-7, scroll to Cut, copy, and paste.

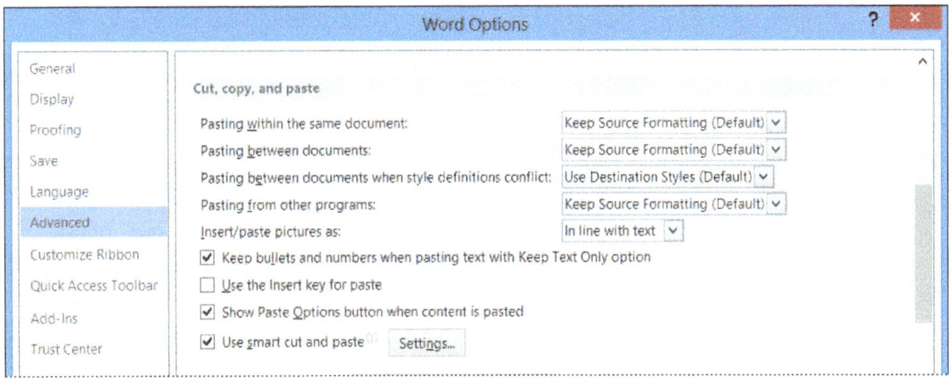


**Figure 3-7**

Word's Paste feature is extremely customizable.

Here you can set the default behavior of Word for a variety of text-handling situations. Note the difference between *Pasting within the same document* and *Pasting between documents* when styles conflict. By default, Word assumes that when moving text around in a single document, you want to preserve its style: you wouldn't want to change the order of two paragraphs and realize you've accidentally turned one into a header. Similarly, when pasting data from another Word document, Word won't interfere with the Style Set you're working with.If the Paste Options toolbar gets in your way, you can turn it off from this same options screen. Finally, if you want to see the technical aspects of the Paste command, which invisibly adjusts word and paragraph spacing every time you move text around, click the *Use smart cut and paste settings* button. These options are meant for advanced users with specific workflow needs; there's no need for you to change these settings now, but it's helpful to know where to find them.

3 Click **OK** to commit changes and **close** the Word Options dialog box.

## Working with columns

**Bottom Line**

In the Page Layout tab, you'll find Word's Columns tool. By default, it provides five modes: one, two, and three-column text, and two asymmetrical two-column layouts. You can use more columns if you need to. Word uses newspaper-style multi-column layouts: text flows from left to right, and lines accumulate top to bottom within a column; the text starts on the next page only when all the columns on the current page are filled.

In other words, Word's text columns do not fill up independently of one another. For example, you wouldn't create a two-column layout with Spanish text on the left and an English translation on the right, and fill them in separately. For layouts built on parallel text streams of that sort, you'd use a specialized layout tool such as Microsoft Publisher or Adobe InDesign.

**Take Note** Strictly speaking, you can make parallel columns from separate text streams in Word. If you have less than a single page of text, for instance, it's no problem: in our translation example, insert a Column Break at the end of one text stream and start the second stream. Alternatively, put each stream in one column of a tall two-column table, or do the same with text boxes, and use the Create Link command to flow text from one to the other. But there's no elegant equivalent to the newspaper-style columns in Word.

Switching to a multi-column layout dramatically changes the feel of the text on-screen and on the page; it will give our info sheet an encyclopedia look.

## STEP BY STEP Working with columns

1. Open **word03a_work.docx** if it is not already open. Press **Ctrl+A** to Select All, including the panda image and caption.
2. Select **Page Layout > Columns > Two**. See Figure 3-8.

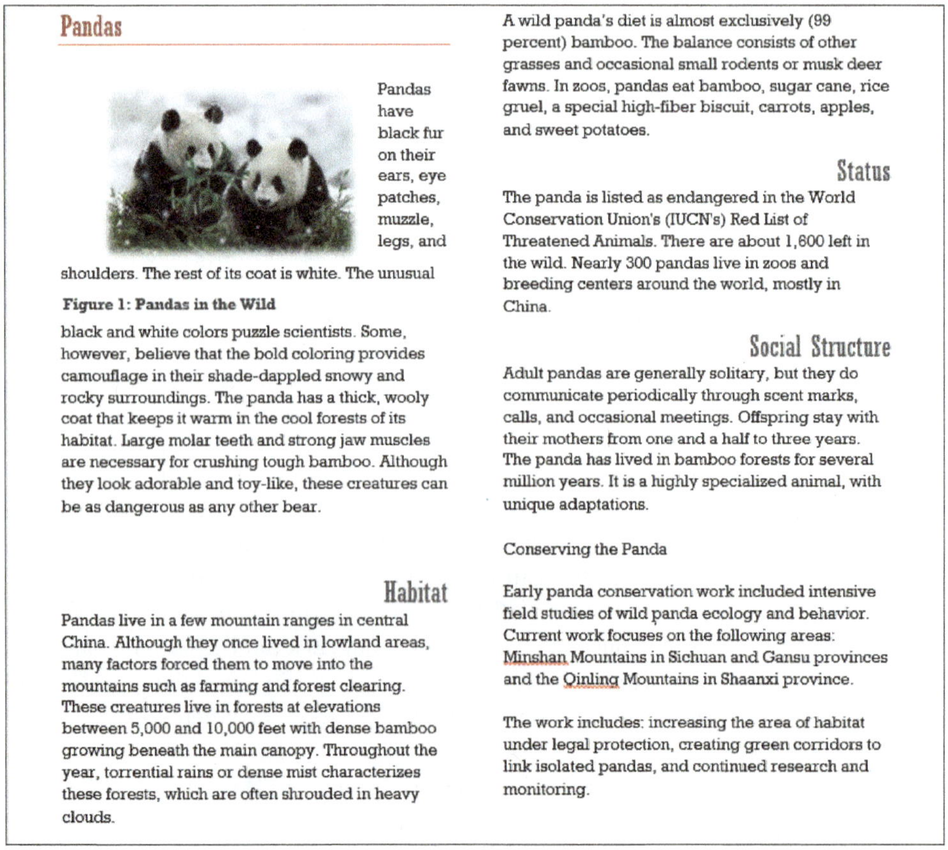
Pandas

Pandas have black fur on their ears, eye patches, muzzle, legs, and shoulders. The rest of its coat is white. The unusual

**Figure 1: Pandas in the Wild**

black and white colors puzzle scientists. Some, however, believe that the bold coloring provides camouflage in their shade-dappled snowy and rocky surroundings. The panda has a thick, wooly coat that keeps it warm in the cool forests of its habitat. Large molar teeth and strong jaw muscles are necessary for crushing tough bamboo. Although they look adorable and toy-like, these creatures can be as dangerous as any other bear.

Habitat

Pandas live in a few mountain ranges in central China. Although they once lived in lowland areas, many factors forced them to move into the mountains such as farming and forest clearing. These creatures live in forests at elevations between 5,000 and 10,000 feet with dense bamboo growing beneath the main canopy. Throughout the year, torrential rains or dense mist characterizes these forests, which are often shrouded in heavy clouds.

A wild panda's diet is almost exclusively (99 percent) bamboo. The balance consists of other grasses and occasional small rodents or musk deer fawns. In zoos, pandas eat bamboo, sugar cane, rice gruel, a special high-fiber biscuit, carrots, apples, and sweet potatoes.

Status

The panda is listed as endangered in the World Conservation Union's (IUCN's) Red List of Threatened Animals. There are about 1,600 left in the wild. Nearly 300 pandas live in zoos and breeding centers around the world, mostly in China.

Social Structure

Adult pandas are generally solitary, but they do communicate periodically through scent marks, calls, and occasional meetings. Offspring stay with their mothers from one and a half to three years. The panda has lived in bamboo forests for several million years. It is a highly specialized animal, with unique adaptations.

Conserving the Panda

Early panda conservation work included intensive field studies of wild panda ecology and behavior. Current work focuses on the following areas: Minshan Mountains in Sichuan and Gansu provinces and the Qinling Mountains in Shaanxi province.

The work includes: increasing the area of habitat under legal protection, creating green corridors to link isolated pandas, and continued research and monitoring.

*© fototravl/iStockphoto*

**Figure 3-8**
Two-column layout radically alters the document's look and feel.

You can now use Undo (Ctrl+Z) and Redo (Ctrl+Y) to toggle back and forth between the one and two-column layouts. The line beneath the top heading stretches across the left-hand column only; there's less whitespace, yielding a denser layout; crucially, the sub-headings stand out much more in a two-column format. However, the image and caption use **absolute placement** on the page, rather than adjusting to the change in text flow, and no longer work in the new layout. Make sure the document is now set to single column.

## TEXT BOXES AND IMAGES

**bottom line**

In previous lessons, we've encountered images, tables, and text boxes: design elements that are separate from the flow of text in a document. When text and other page elements work well together, your documents can be not just functional but beautiful. Here, we'll work with a simple **text box**, the panda caption, and see how it integrates into the flow of our document text.

### Placing text boxes and images

The caption beneath the panda image is formatted as a text box. We'll make several changes to its content and appearance, use the Group tool to link it to the image and streamline our workflow, and then place the photo and caption together.

**STEP BY STEP** **Place text boxes and images**

1. Click the **Figure 1: Pandas in the Wild** text. The outline of the text box appears, along with the Layout Options icon, several handles (small white boxes) to resize the text box, and a handle above to rotate the box.
2. Press **Ctrl+A** (Select All). Change the text to **Wild Pandas**.
3. Click one of the handles on the right-hand side of the box (see Figure 3-9), and then drag it to the left until it's tight with the word *Pandas*, without causing the text to wrap. This resizes the text box, which now takes up only as much space as it needs.

**Figure 3-9**

Resize the text box.

No surprises so far: the text box can be resized like an image, and its content is (initially) an editable text such as any other on the page. Now we'll work on positioning and orientation.

4. With the text box still selected, click **Format > Arrange > Align > Use Alignment Guides** if it is not already checked.

5 Drag the **rotation handle** clockwise until the text runs straight up and down: a 90 degree rotation (See Figure 3-10.) When you're close to 90 degrees, the box will seem to stick a little bit.

**Figure 3-10**

Rotating a text box: Word treats 90° as a likely target amount.

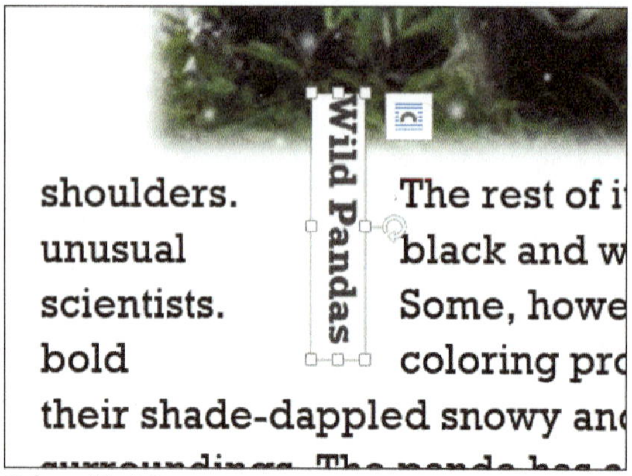


© *fototrav/iStockphoto*

6 Click the **dotted line** around the text box to select the box (rather than the text inside it), and drag it over the pandas, positioning it near the image's rightmost edge.

7 Finally, triple-click once more on the *Wild Pandas* text itself. (The text box will rotate temporarily so the text is readable.) The formatting pop-up menu appears; set the text color to white. Then click **Drawing Tools > Format > Shape Fill > No Fill**.

This series of commands yields a transparent text box with white text running vertically atop the right-hand edge of our panda image. No Fill allows anything that is beneath the text box to show. For more precise control over rotation, we could select the text box and use the Drawing Tools > Arrange > Rotate tool.

8 Without deselecting the text box, Ctrl+click the panda image. Both the panda image and the text box are selected.

9 Click **Drawing Tools > Format > Arrange > Align > Align Middle (not Center)**. The centers of the picture and caption both snap to the same invisible horizontal line, aligning the two objects. Then click **Format > Arrange > Group > Group**. Only a single selection box remains: the one around the image/caption pair. See Figure 3-11 for a comparison of grouped and individual objects.

**Figure 3-11**

Grouped (L) and ungrouped (R) objects in Word.

© *fototrav/iStockphoto*

The caption is nicely placed atop the image, and by **Grouping** them together, we've told Word to move and modify them together, making complex layout tasks somewhat easier. This is just a temporary change; we haven't modified the original image and can use Format > Arrange > Group > Ungroup at a later time if we need to separate image and caption.

**Take Note** In Word, Align Middle refers to vertical alignment; Center refers to horizontal alignment. Everyone's familiar with horizontal alignment, which adjusts the position of an element relative to the margins (of the column, page, table cell, or text box). Vertical alignment works the same way, so when you apply the Align Middle command to an object, note carefully what space's middle you're aligning it to. A variety of weird behaviors can be explained by Word performing an action in a different context from what you expect: centering within a column rather than a line, including trailing spaces in a paragraph-select, and so on.

To close, we'll move the image to the right spot on the page. At this point, the Alignment Guides will come into play.

10. Zoom out to around 70% size using the slider on the bottom-right corner of the window, then drag the image to the top of the Habitat section, along the column's right-hand edge. When the image is in position, green lines will appear along its top and right edges, indicating that it's flush against the margin and aligned with the top of the paragraph. Alignment Guides are shown in Figure 3-12.

**Figure 3-12**

Alignment Guides let you target page and object borders and centers with precision.

© *fototrav/iStockphoto*

The Alignment Guides feature for Word 2013 appear when you line up two objects in some way: their edges or centers at the same horizontal or vertical position.

## Inserting an object directly into a paragraph

**Bottom Line**

In this lesson, we've worked only with absolute positioning: moving the image and caption freely around the page, forcing the text to flow around them. It's a little tricky, but it gives precise control over the layout of a document. Another way to position objects in a Word document is to insert them directly into the text flow. If you've used previous editions of Word, you've probably used this method of placement. Note the difference in presentation:

**STEP BY STEP** **Inserting an object directly into a paragraph**

1. Click the panda image, and then click the **Layout Options** pop-up menu when it appears.
2. Select the **In Line with Text** layout method.
3. Drag the image to a different spot in the document.

In a sense, Word treats your image as an unusually large piece of text, and places it on the text baseline just as any other word. There's no Live Preview either: Word just reflows the paragraph around the image. In this case, the output is terrible: the image is too big to sit comfortably on a line with text. In other circumstances, such as placing a sparkline (a word-sized miniature info-graphic), In Line with Text is the right insertion mode.

4 Choose **File > Save** or press **Ctrl+S** to save your work.

5 Close both documents, but only save the changes to **Word03a_work**.

## What you learned in this lesson:

- Paragraph and Character Formatting
- Line and Paragraph Spacing
- Styles, Themes, and Live Preview
- Cut, Copy, and Paste
- Using the Format Painter
- Formatting Multi-Column Text
- Adding Text Boxes and Images

# Knowledge Assessment

## Fill in the Blanks

**Complete the following sentences by writing the correct word or words in the blanks provided.**

1. A paragraph in Word is a single _____ of text that's wrapped one or more times.
2. To start each paragraph 1" to the right of the left margin, drag the _____ to the appropriate spot on the ruler.
3. To paste text into a document as-is, choose the _____ Paste option.
4. Select a piece of text, then click the _____ command to grab its formatting info for transfer to another text piece.
5. In a multi-column layout, Word won't flow text to the next _____ until it's filled all columns in the current one.
6. Combine several objects to manipulate them all at once for ease of use, using the _____ command.
7. To place an image on/in a grid alongside text characters, rather than freely position it at a specific spot on the "paper," select the _____ layout option.
8. The current Style Set is shown at the _____ side of the _____.
9. The _____ tab of the Paragraph options dialog lets you specify the amount of whitespace before and after each line of text.
10. To remove text from a document and cache it temporarily for insertion later, use the _____ command.

### True/False

**Circle T if the statement is true or F it the statement is false.**

T F 1. Word has built-in support for "parallel" (independent) multi-column layouts.

T F 2. Align Middle refers to horizontal alignment – the middle of a left-right line through the page.

T F 3. Inserting an object In Line with Text can push it off the printable area of a page.

T F 4. In general, sparklines should be inserted In Line with Text.

T F 5. Word gives no visual indication when the current document theme is modified from its original state.

T F 6. Text emphasis refers to formatting like italics, boldface, and underline.

T F 7. The line count in the Status Bar actually counts paragraphs.

T F 8. The leftmost default tab stop is at the far right of the text block.

T F 9. When pasting text into the middle of a paragraph, it makes sense to use the Merge Formatting paste option.

T F 10. By default, when you place a simple text box in a page full of text, Word will wrap the text around the box.

## Competency Assessment

### Project 3-1: Paragraph and Character Formatting

**In this exercise, edit a document at the character and paragraph levels.**

1. Open the project file **glorieta**.
2. Save your document as **project_3-1_formatting**.
3. If you haven't already done so, enable **Show Hidden Characters**.
4. Click somewhere in the first line of the text and select **Bullet** formatting.
5. Do the same for the entire document.
6. Italicize the words **Glorieta, New Mexico**.
7. Add a heading, **Capsule History,** before the first line, with Style Heading 1. Modify the heading to Right Align.
8. Save and close your work.

### Project 3-2: Adding Floats

**Here you'll add floating page elements to a Word file.**

1. Open the project file **3-2-source**. Save your document as **project_3-2_floats**.
2. Insert a Simple Text Box somewhere in the first paragraph. Type **1862** in the box.
3. Open the text box's Layout Options popup and click **See More…**
4. Set the text box's characteristics in the dialog box: Right aligned relative to the Margin, Top aligned relative to the Line, size 1" by 1", Square wrapping, Left wrapping only. Click **OK**. Resize the box vertically so it's just tall enough to fit the text.
5. Select the date in the box and set **Format > Align Text to Middle. Select Home > Align Right**.
6. Finally, select the box, then select **Format > Shape Outline > No Outline**.
7. Save your work.

# Proficiency Assessment

## Project 3-3: More Floats

**This exercise makes further use of floats to lay out content on a page.**

1. Open project file 3-3-source. Save your document as project_3-3_copy_paste. Copy the text box containing 1862 (not the text itself).
2. Paste copies of it next to all the other timeline entries, using the green guideline to align the right edges of each box. Note that Pasting the text boxes doesn't result in perfectly placed, properly aligned copies.
3. Change the text of each float to reflect the date of the paragraph beside it: Autumn instead of "Late 1862," Christmas instead of "Christmas 1862," the same otherwise.
4. Save and close your work.

## Project 3-4: Using Format Painter

**In this exercise you'll duplicate text formatting using the Format Painter.**

1. Open the project file 3-4-source. Save your document as project_3-4_format_painter.
2. Format the first date entry as follows: Bold, Italic, Red, 10pt Calibri Light.
3. Use the Format Painter to apply the same formatting to all the floats.

   Outside of this exercise context, it would make sense to apply this formatting before copying the floats.
4. Change the bullet points from dots to four-part diamonds.
5. Save and close your work.

# Mastery Assessment

## Project 3-5: Indentation

**This exercise has you tweak the presentation of a text block, including text indentation.**

1. Open the project file 3-5-source. Save your document as project_3-5_indentation.
2. Alter the text so it uses a 4" wide text block, with the left margin at the 0.5" mark, fully justified, with no bullets. Delete the boldfaced dates from within the main text block.
3. Insert a rounded rectangle with color Subtle Effect – Green, Accent 6, covering the remaining (red) date entries. Use the Format > Arrange tools to position it behind the dates.
4. Reformat the date floats to have no border and no fill – Shift+clicking will save much time here.
5. Save your work.

## Project 3-6: Creating a Custom Style

**Here you'll create a custom Text Style for your document.**

1. Open the project file 3-6-source. Save your document as project_3-6_custom_style.
2. Create a custom Text Style, Timeline Entry, with the following specs: 11pt Georgia font, left margin 0.75", right margin 5", 12pt spacing before, 8pt after.
3. Apply this custom style to all timeline entries. Save and close your work.

# 4 Structuring Complex Documents

## LESSON SKILL MATRIX

**In this lesson, you will learn the following skills:**

| | |
|---|---|
| Folding Text | Adding a Cover Page |
| Sorting Sections | Viewing Hidden Characters |
| Building an Outline with Headings | Using Page and Section Breaks |
| Managing Master Documents and Subdocuments | Adding Cross-References |
| Adding Captions to Images | Adding and Editing Footnotes and End-notes |
| Using Fields | Building a Table of Contents |
| Hiding and Showing Field Codes | Building a Table of Figures |
| Editing Document Properties | |

## KEY TERMS

- **Subheading**
- **Caption**
- **Table of Figures**
- **Field code**
- **Document Properties**
- **Cover Page**
- **Date/Time Field**
- **Page Break**
- **Section Break**
- **Hidden Characters**
- **Cross-Reference**
- **Footnote**
- **Endnote**
- **invisible Field**

©mbrowe/iStockPhoto

©mbrowe/iStockPhoto

The Contoso School's annual course catalog is a 200-page collection of tabular data, structured text, hundreds of cross-references, thousands of index items, and a 10-page, three-level table of contents, and the same source files generate the Web and print editions. That kind of complexity is only manageable with the tools discussed in this lesson: Word's wide array of features designed for keeping long, densely interlinked documents under control, from planning to printing.

## SOFTWARE ORIENTATION

In this lesson you will discover how to effectively organize table of contents, cross references, fields, captions, and other items to make it easier to work with longer, more complex documents.

**Figure 4-1**

Commands and controls for creating a table of contents

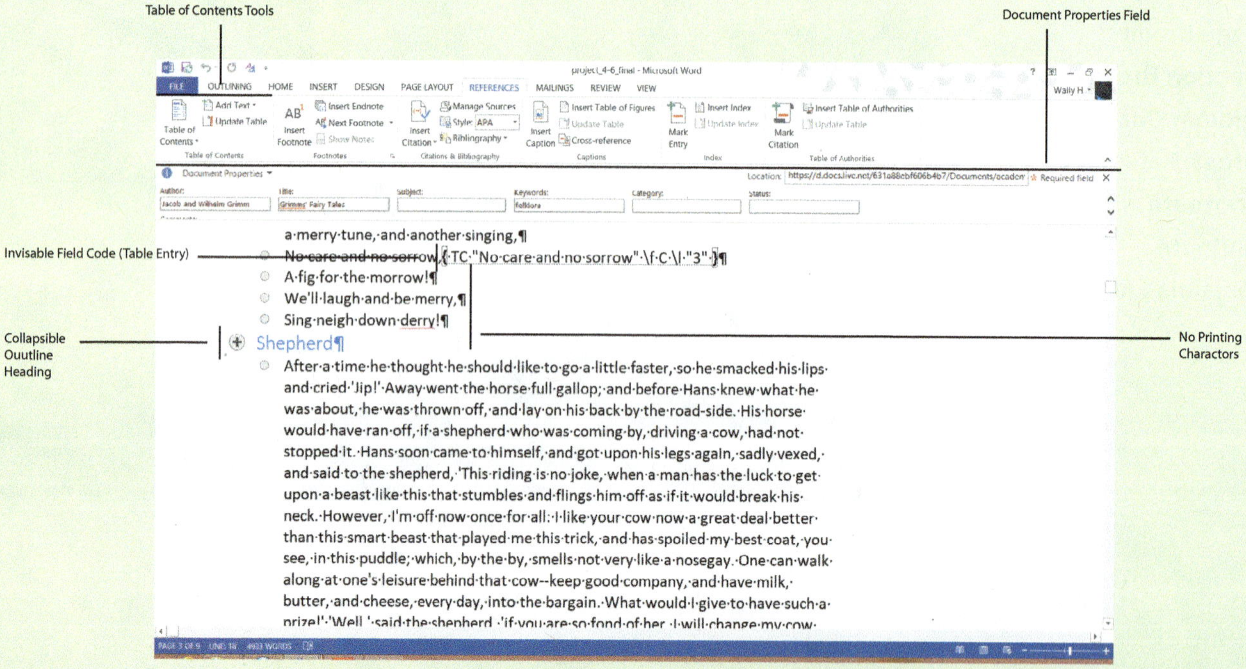

## STARTING UP

In this lesson, you'll work with several files from the Word04lessons folder. Make sure that you have loaded the OfficeLessons folder onto your computer.

## DOCUMENTS ARE DATA

In this lesson, you'll work on a short but complex document with a variety of endnotes, figures, fields, captions, hyperlinks, and cross-references, a cover page, a table of figures, and a table of contents. While each of these document elements is a useful tool in itself, the goal of the lesson isn't to master any one editing technique or feature. Rather, it's to make a transition from thinking about your .docx file as a block of text on a page with stuff stuck to its edges, to thinking of it as a complex program for generating output that looks like a block of text on a page.

The features discussed in this lesson hook into the structure of your Word document; tools such as headings, styles, and fields blur the line between text and data. The advantage of digital publishing tools over pen-and-paper is the ability to manipulate data programmatically; the closer you get to the software itself, the more power you have over your data. In previous lessons, we've mostly worked with abstractions that resemble physical tools: pages, typefaces, pictures, even backstage. The current lesson is the closest we'll get to thinking about your document data the way Word itself does.

Our task for this lesson is to reformat an informal college class handout as a departmental whitepaper. To that end, you'll add a variety of standard document features: tables of contents and figures, cross-references, document metadata, cover page, and more.

Take a little time before proceeding to preview the lesson file for this exercise.

## HEADINGS: LOGICAL DOCUMENT DIVISIONS

As mentioned before, the default behavior in Word 2013 is to treat the built-in Heading styles as special: Word assumes that each heading signifies the beginning of a new section of the document, and uses this assumption to support some best practices for writing and editing. If you use the built-in Heading styles, you can take advantage of a number of tools available in Word to streamline your workflow.

### Text folding

**Bottom Line**

One simple technique for cleanly arranging the content in your workspace is to fold a portion of your document into its heading. In every View mode except Draft, when you mouse over a heading, a triangular handle appears. Clicking the handle temporarily hides all text, images, and other objects between that heading and the next heading of equal level.

**STEP BY STEP** **Text folding**

1 Open **word04a.docx** found in the Word04lessons folder. Choose **File > Save As** and navigate to the Word04lessons folder. Name the file **word04a_work** and click **Save**.

2 Mouse over and click the handle to collapse the first three **subheadings**: **Persuasive Strategies**, **A Note About Cynicism**, and **The Importance of a Good Title**. Figure 4-2 shows the result of this operation.

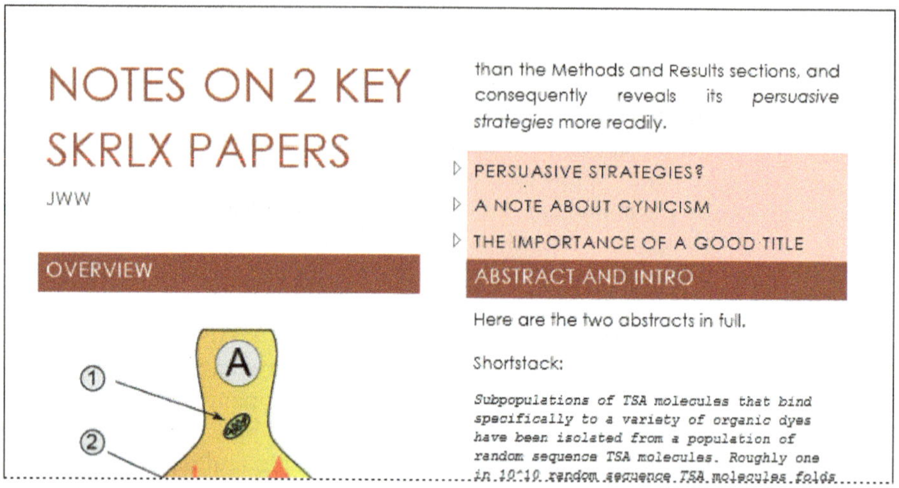


*Image used under Creative Commons license, contributor: Dake*

**Figure 4-2**

Collapse the first three sub-headings.

3 Mouse over and click to collapse the first top-level heading, **Overview**.

As you can see, only the Overview heading remains: Word works forward from the heading and stashes everything it finds until it reaches the next Heading 1 text, Abstract and Intro.

4 Mouse over and click the same triangle on the left of the heading to expand the **Overview** section, and then expand the three collapsed subheadings.

This technique doesn't just clear your workspace: it encourages you to think of your document in terms of high-level organizational units (sections and subsections). In fact, if you triple-click to select a collapsed heading and then Cut it (Ctrl+X), you'll actually cut its entire section, enabling you to move a huge block of laid-out text and images without having to do multiple pages of click-and-drag to select.

Collapsing a section is like grouping multiple objects in a page without changing the data; it just presents it to you in a much more useful way. Because Word is particularly attentive to headings, thinking of a section as a group of objects opens up new possibilities.

**Bottom Line**

## Sorting sections

Here's an example of using the programmatic tools available in Word for manipulating document data: you can alphabetize all the sections of your document. For example, if you were working on an encyclopedia, you could give each entry its own heading, and then use the Sort feature in Word to organize the headings from A to Z.

**STEP BY STEP** **Sorting sections alphabetically**

1 Open **word04a.docx**. Press **Ctrl+A** to select the entire contents of your file.

2 Click **Home > Paragraph > Sort** to bring up a page of options (see Figure 4-3). Select **Sort by > Headings** from the first drop-down menu, and then click **OK**.

**Figure 4-3**

Word's Sort Options screen.

Word automatically rearranges the sections of your document so that it opens with Abstract and Intro instead of Overview. Word won't organize subsections within each section, however; to do so you'll have to switch to Outline View, select the subsections you want to sort, and then click Sort.

3 Press **Ctrl+Z**, or click **Undo** in the Quick Access Toolbar, to return to the original section ordering.

4 Choose **File > Close** to close this document. Do not save your work.

## BUILDING AN OUTLINE WITH HEADINGS

In Lesson 2 you saw how the Navigation pane in Word integrates the built-in heading styles; now we'll look quickly at Outline View. Word doesn't provide a full-featured outliner like OmniOutliner or Microsoft OneNote, but the ability to outline and lay out text in the same application makes for a streamlined writing process.

### Outline view

**Bottom Line**

Outline View is something of a legacy option in Word 2013; for most users, collapsible headings and the mini outline in the Navigation pane will provide all the outline-like functionality they need. That said, it's still quite useful for anyone who wants to rapidly build a document skeleton, and then go straight to drafting in the same app. We'll make a quick change to our SKRLX paper in Outline View to get a feel for its usefulness.

**STEP BY STEP** **Working in outline view**

1 In **word04a_work.docx**, click **View > Views > Outline**.

2 To simplify the view, deselect Show Text Formatting and make sure that **Show First Line Only** is selected , as in Figure 4-4.

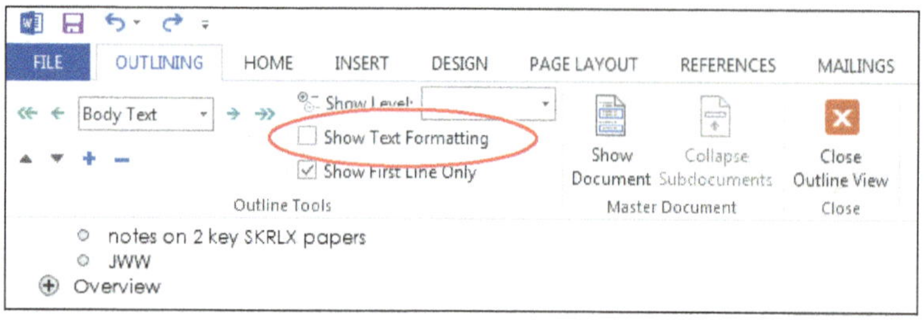


**Figure 4-4**

Make sure Show Text Formatting is deselected and Show First Line Only is selected.

This view is just like any other outline: each level of subheading/subsection is indented slightly from the one above it. For example, and as shown in this exercise file, the Overview section begins with some body text (I'll focus…), which is then followed by three Heading 2 subsections before reaching the next Heading 1 (Abstract and intro). To keep Outline View simple, Word doesn't show our images, but rather a big, potentially confusing bit of whitespace. See Figure 4-5.

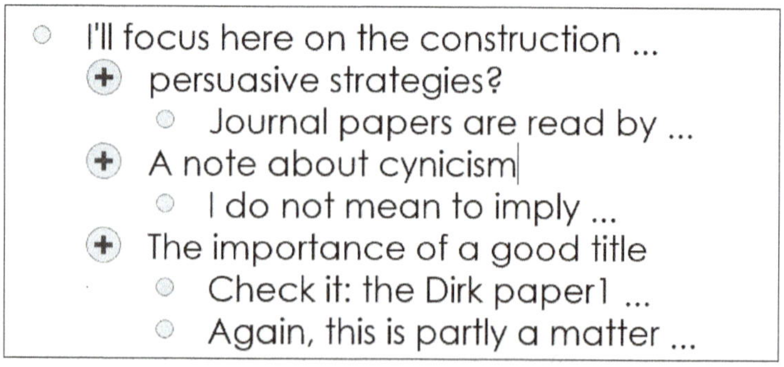


**Figure 4-5**

Outline View is a stripped-down, purely functional angle on your data.

3 Scroll to the top of the document and click the + next to *persuasive strategies?*

Both the subheading and its section text (only a few words of which are visible) are highlighted. The outline is designed to make large-scale changes, like moving this subsection, as easy as possible. Let's switch the order of the selected section and the one following.

4 Drag *persuasive strategies?* to a spot directly above *The importance of a good title*. All three subsections should be vertically aligned as in Figure 4-6, indicating that they have the same heading level.

**Figure 4-6**

These three subsections have the same outline level.

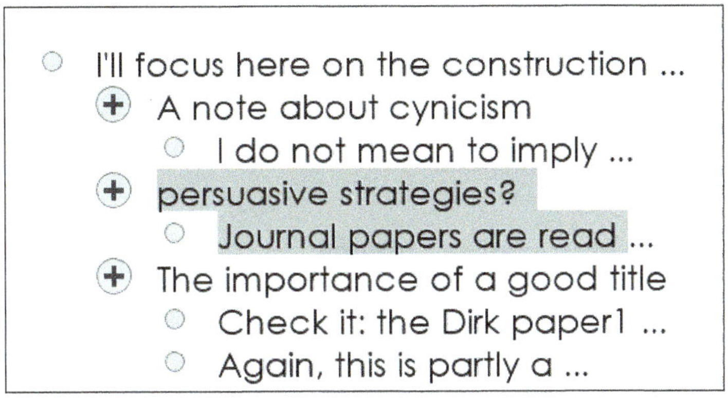


5 Finally, select the **Overview** entry at the top of the document, and then click **Outlining > Outline Tools > Collapse** (or double-click the + next to Overview).

Just as in Print Layout Mode, you can collapse and expand headings to reduce visual clutter. The Outlining > Show Level command takes this minimalism a step further, for example, by letting you work only with specific text levels: Heading 1 only (level 1), Headings 1-3 (level 3), or all heading and body text (All Levels).

At this point, we've got the basic structure we want.

6 Click **Close Outline View** to return to Print Layout Mode and press **Ctrl+S** to save your work.

## CAPTIONS

Word 2013 provides special tools to pair **captions** with images; since a caption will never travel alone, it makes sense to treat it as an extension of the image itself. This approach lets you reposition your images and alter your document layout without needing to manually group image and caption every time.

Because Word knows which text pieces are captions, it always has access to an internal listing of paired images and captions, which makes it easy to generate cross-references or a **Table of Figures** (for example, for a scholarly book or technical paper). We'll add captions to our images now and style them; at the end of this lesson we'll add a new subsection to our document with a Table of Figures

## Tagging images with captions

**Bottom Line**

You can think of captions as tags for objects (such as images and tables). A caption consists of a unique numerical identifier (automatically generated by Word), an optional label (for example, Figure), and an optional title. The caption's number is inserted as a field; in other words, instead of entering the number itself, you insert a placeholder indicating increase the number of captions by one and insert that number here, and Word takes care of the rest.

We'll add captions to all four of our images now:

**STEP BY STEP** **Tagging images with captions**

1. Select the first image in **word04a_work.docx** and click **References > Captions > Insert Caption**, or right-click the image and select **Insert Caption**.
2. Set the caption to **Figure 1: Neurons** and click **OK**.
3. Click the resulting caption and set its paragraph alignment to **Center** (Ctrl+E) , as in Figure 4-7.

**Figure 4-7**

Word formats image captions using the built-in Caption style.

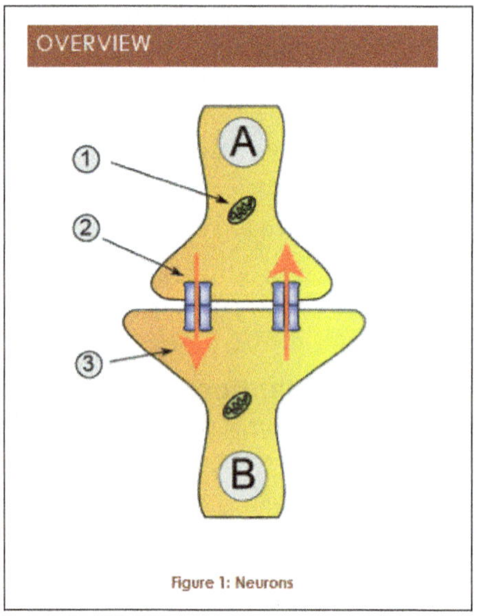


*Image used under Creative Commons license, contributor: Dake*

You can customize Word's handling of captions in the Insert Caption window: the Numbering screen lets you switch from Arabic to Roman numerals, and the Label drop-down menu and New Label button let you switch the word *Field* to another label of your choice. Because there are no other captions in the document, Word assigns this image the number 1.

The Caption style isn't in the Styles gallery by default; it appears when editing a piece of text that uses that style.

**Take Note** Captions without numbers- If you don't want figure numbers in your captions, you can add a caption by inserting a text box below your image and formatting the caption text with the Caption style (or any style you want); there's no built-in command to insert a numberless caption.

Let's add captions to our remaining three images, keeping the default label and centering each caption as we go.

**STEP BY STEP** **Adding captions**

1. Insert the caption **Figure 2: Macromolecule** beneath the second image and center the caption.
2. Insert the caption **Figure 3: Knotty Shape** beneath the third image and center the caption.
3. Insert the caption **Figure 4: No Big Deal** beneath the final image and center the caption.
4. Choose **File > Save** to save your work.

## WORKING WITH FIELDS

**Bottom Line**

Unless you're doing a mail merge (for example, using a database to generate a hundred personalized form letters) you almost certainly won't have to think about how fields (**field codes**) work in Word. But Word uses fields extensively, whether inserting a page number or table of contents, or updating your Document Properties, and the more complex your document, the more useful it is to know what the software is doing behind the scenes.

### Viewing field codes

At this point, you've encountered fields in Word several times. A field is just a placeholder for data that can be altered programmatically. The most oft-used field is the page number: the Insert Page Number command tells Word to calculate which page this field appears on, and insert that number in this spot. Word uses field codes to auto-number captions in the current document.

**STEP BY STEP** **Viewing field codes**

1. Click the **1** in *Figure 1: Neurons*. Instead of placing the cursor as usual, Word selects the figure number, indicating that it's a field rather than a regular character.
2. Right-click the **1**, and select **Toggle Field Codes** from the pop-up menu. Figure 4-8 shows the resulting field code display.

**Figure 4-8**

Field codes are Word's internal representation of your data.

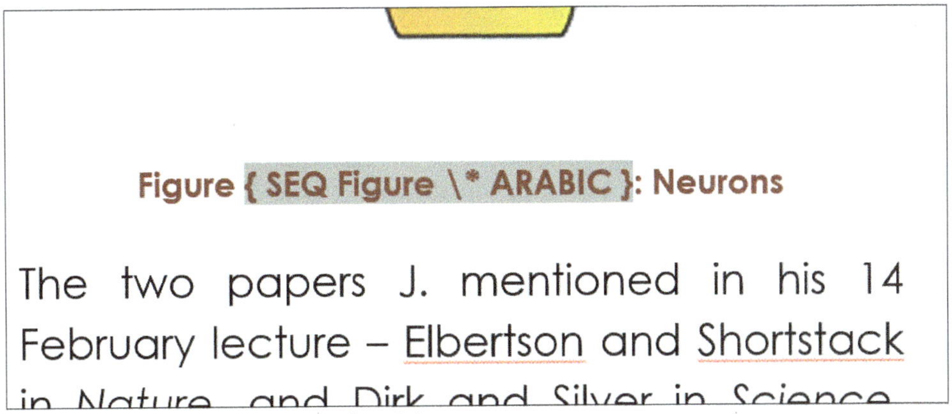


*Image used under Creative Commons license, contributor: Dake*

The SEQ Figure * ARABIC text is Word's internal code to generate the figure number: it adds an entry to a numerical sequence called *Figure*, and renders the entry as an Arabic numeral. Word uses the same kind of internal counter to number footnotes, pages, and bulleted list entries, but masks its computation with user-friendly abstraction: you look at SEQ Figure * ARABIC and see *1*, a number you can actually use.

3 Right-click the field code and toggle it off to reveal Figure 1.

## Setting and accessing document properties

**Bottom Line**

You can also use fields to access your **Document Properties** (or *metadata*), which are viewed through the File > Info command. For instance, if the author's name needs to appear throughout the document, you can insert an Author field anywhere the name should appear; that way the document's writer (or editor) need only type (or change) the document's Author value once, and Word will automatically update every Author field with the corresponding name.

First we'll set the Author and Title properties for the document.

**STEP BY STEP** **Setting and accessing documents properties**

1 With **word04a_work.docx** open, click **File > Info > Properties**, and select **Show Document Panel** from the drop-down menu.

2 In the Author entry field (see Figure 4-9), type your name. In the title entry field, type **SKRLX notes**.

**Figure 4-9**

Editing Properties (metadata) using the Document Panel.

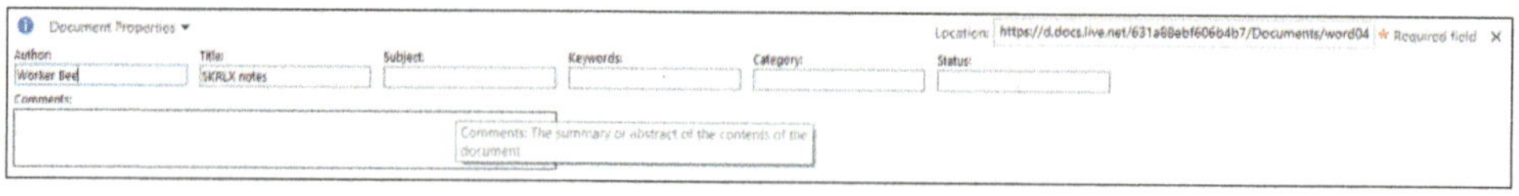


Now scroll to the top of the document. Currently, we have entered the title manually (Notes on 2 Key SKRLX Papers) and author (JWW) listings; we'll update them to use fields instead. This is a common enough task that Word 2013 provides a tool for it in the Insert tab. We'll also insert a subtitle in between.

3 Triple-click the current manually-entered title. Then click **Insert > Text > Quick Parts > Document Property > Title**.

4 Triple-click the second line, **JWW**, and then click **Insert > Text > Explore Quick Parts > Document Property > Subject**. Word inserts a [Subject] field, not yet filled in.

5 In the [Subject] field, type **Spring 2013**. Then press the right arrow key to switch from editing the field contents to working on the page.

6 Press **Enter**, and then Click **Insert > Text > Quick Parts > Document Property > Author**. Apply the Strong style to this line.

Now look at your Document Properties panel still displayed below the Ribbon (see Figure 4-10). The Subject field has been filled in with Spring 2013; you've edited your file's Properties from within the document itself. In general, Word's fields both display data and allow you to edit that data.

**Figure 4-10**

The document's field codes and Document Properties panel are two interfaces to the same metadata.

7 Close your Document Panel and then Save your document.

After setting document properties, we can build a cover page and automatically populate it with data.

## ADDING A COVER PAGE

**Bottom Line**

In Word 2013, a **cover page** is a bundle of especially-formatted text, fields, and images inserted at the front of your document. When you use the Insert > Cover Page command, Word inserts a page full of text/fields/graphics, assigns it page number zero (to keep the first page of the document proper as page 1), inserts a page break to avoid flowing text between the cover and the document itself, and toggles an option to use a separate header and footer for the cover, which you can see by double-clicking your document's header area.

Ideally, you won't notice this background work; you'll just insert the cover page and continue working on your document, with headers and page numbers and pagination intact. But it's good to know exactly what Word is doing, to avoid surprises and troubleshoot if needed.

**STEP BY STEP** **Adding a cover page**

1 With **word04a_work** still open, click **Insert > Pages > Cover Page > Whisp**.

2 Click the [Date] field on the cover, click the arrow to the right of the text field, and in the drop-down menu select **Today**.

**figure 4-11**

When you select a date using the calendar input, it's displayed in the Date field.

*Images and templates used with permission of Microsoft*

Dates are a different type of field: instead of raw text, Word inserts a **Date/Time field** in MM/DD/YYYY format , as in Figure 4-11. If you prefer a different format, you can easily make a change:

3 Click the label above the field to select the placeholder (the field itself) rather than its contents.

4 Click **Insert > Text > Insert Date & Time**. In the options screen, choose the style format **22 January 2013** and click **OK**.

5 At the bottom of the cover page, enter **ABC Company** in the [Company Name] field.

6 Choose **File > Save** or press **Ctrl+S** to save your work.

## PAGE AND SECTION BREAKS

**Bottom Line**

In the previous section, we mentioned that Word inserts a **page break** after the cover page to keep the document text from starting before the second page of the file. Page breaks work much like carriage returns, but instead of moving the cursor to the next line, they move it to the next page of the file. A **section break** is a more complicated play on the same basic idea.

## Seeing breaks and other hidden characters

To see the page break on your cover page, scroll to the top of the handout document and click Home > Paragraph > Show/Hide ¶ (or press Ctrl+*). As in Figure 4-12, you'll see paragraph marks (meaning new line) and a line marked Page Break.

Figure 4-12

*Images and templates used with permission of Microsoft*

Viewing **hidden characters** helps with precise layout tasks.The layout of our cover page is interesting: the title, date, and author/company info are laid out as text boxes, which float above the page, separate from the text. The only actual inline text is the dotted burgundy line at the top of the page. After that is a Page Break, meaning any subsequent text fills in starting on the second page; the floating elements on the cover page are treated more like images than text, and can be placed anywhere on the first page.

## Section breaks

**Bottom Line**

We've been using the word section informally in these lessons, but Word 2013 does have a specific feature called the Section Break, which is worth mentioning, though we don't use Sections in our handout. The purpose of Sections in Word 2013 is to allow you to vary formatting within your document: for instance, you could lay out a scholarly paper with a single-column title and abstract, and then switch to two-column layout for the article text (or do a wide newspaper headline the same way).

Alternatively, you could strip out your document's header just for an 8-page section presenting raw data (by deselecting the Link to Previous option in the Header Design tab); place a decorative border around one section, or switch to a new paper size/orientation; or lay out front matter (Intro, Foreword, Preface, and so on) with Roman page numbers and distinct page dressing. You could even instruct your printer to switch to a different paper source, for example, to insert a sales flyer on purple cardstock into your newsletter. In short, Section Breaks are incredibly powerful tools.

They're also very simple: you insert a Section Break with the Page Layout > Page Setup > Breaks tool; any formatting changes you make will apply only to the current section. Taking out the break is simple: click to show hidden characters, and then delete the break as you would any other character.

**Take Note** When you delete a section break, the two sections are combined into one, and the formatting of the latter section is used; in other words, if Sections 5 and 6 of a document are separated by a break, and you delete the break, the new section that results will absorb the formatting of Section 6 only.

Try experimenting with inserting Section Breaks in your handout to see the flexibility they can provide; just remember to save the document before you add any sections.

## CROSS-REFERENCES

**Bottom Line**

You'll recall that the Insert Caption command is found in the References tab because only specialized documents, such as scholarly papers or technical documentation, tend to make use of image captions. There's a deeper logic at work too: when you add a caption to an image, Word provides hooks to refer to that image or caption using fields; captions are really just labels for referring to images. We'll add a couple of references to see how they work.

**STEP BY STEP** **Inserting a cross-reference**

1 Scroll to page 2, to the section *A note about cynicism*. Place the cursor in the middle of the paragraph between the word ***decisions*** and the comma following it.

2 Insert a space and then the following parenthetical: **(consider the outcome in )**.

3 Now place the cursor before the closing parenthesis, and click **References > Captions > Cross-reference**.

The Cross-reference dialog box pops up; here you can select the target of your reference and customize its appearance. Unlike most pop-up windows, this one stays open until you close it: clicking Insert really does insert the reference, but it doesn't close the window. (The idea is to make it easy to insert multiple references without reopening the dialog box.)

4 In the Cross-reference window (see Figure 4-13), choose Reference type: **Figure**, Insert reference to: **Only label and number**, deselect **Insert as hyperlink**, and select Figure 4: **No Big Deal** from the list below.

**Figure 4-13**

The Cross-reference dialog box.

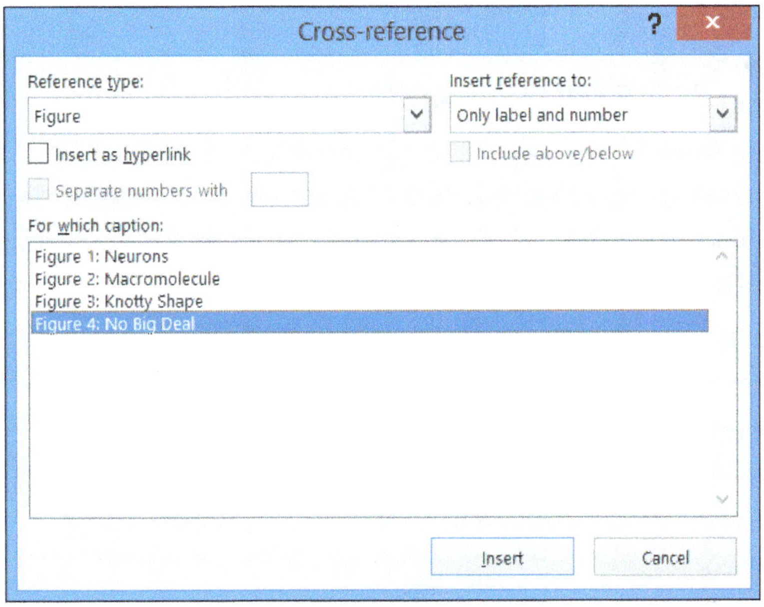


5 Click **Insert**, and then close the box.

You've now played an in-text reference to a figure located elsewhere in the document. It might seem like a lot of work to insert *See Figure 4*, but consider the case of a document with fifty images and a thousand references, each written by hand; now imagine taking one of those images out, renumbering the other 49, and then rewriting a thousand references. This method is a lot less work.

## FOOTNOTES AND ENDNOTES

**Bottom Line**

Many technical or scholarly documents include **footnotes** or **endnotes**. Word generates note numbers using fields, but you can customize the appearance and number scheme of your footnotes and endnotes.

**Take Note**

Sometimes you'll insert a footnote, but it won't appear on the same page; rather, it'll appear several pages later; this tends to happen with very long footnotes, or when a note appears close to the bottom of the text block. Not to worry: you can always travel back and forth between a reference and its associated note by double-clicking their number, and a note will never accidentally appear before its number pops up in the text.

The handout currently contains two footnotes; you should scroll through to see how Word lays them out. Pay special attention to the wrapping and placement: by default, the footnotes are laid out in two-column format, just as the main text, and Word places them beneath the left text column, even if the note number falls in the right-hand column.

In this part of the lesson, we'll make a couple of changes to the notes, but we won't work with Word's bibliography features, which are used by a very small subset of Word users. (If you need a more robust application to manage (shown in Figure 4-14) of scholarly citations, we recommend using an external citations manager such as EndNote; external citations managers are outside the scope of this lesson.)

### Adding and deleting notes

We'll begin by adding and deleting notes, and altering their appearance in the text. Footnotes are simple to use, as long as you don't use special formatting.

**STEP BY STEP** **Adding and deleting nores**

1 In **word04a_work.docx**, insert the cursor at the end of the handout's first sentence (... side-by-side reading.). Click **References > Footnotes > Insert Footnote**.

2 In the notes area, type **This work was funded by the Tortle Foundation**.

3 Click the **arrow** icon in the bottom right corner of the Footnotes group to bring up a window with Footnote and Endnote options.

4 Select **Columns: 1 column**, and the symbols in the Number format drop-down. Press **Enter**.

The footnotes revert to a less awkward one-column format, and Word automatically renumbers when we add a new Note 1; finally, the useful note numbers are replaced by visually appealing, but less practical, asterisks and crosses.

For this exercise, assume that our handout will be distributed along with copies of the Dirk and Shortstack papers, so no citations are needed; let's cut the second footnote. To do so, simply delete the note number from the text block.

5 Click and drag to select the second footnote, marked with a cross located in the The Importance of a Good Title section. Delete the note marking; the note text, at the bottom of the page, disappears along with the mark.

### Endnotes, briefly

Endnotes work much like footnotes, only Word typesets them at the end of the text rather than the bottom of each page. Word can set your endnotes at the end of each section (as in a textbook or anthology) or in one large listing at the end of your entire document. To work with endnotes rather than footnotes, use the Insert Endnote command in the References tab, and set your layout options by clicking the dialog box icon in the lower right corner of the Footnotes group.

## ADDING A TABLE OF CONTENTS

We'll finish this lesson with two consequential mouse clicks: one to generate a Table of Contents (TOC) and one to produce a Table of Figures. The TOC feature in Word makes use of the built-in Heading style hierarchy by default, and mirrors the document structure seen in Outline View, but it offers a high degree of flexibility as well: with a few simple tweaks you could automatically generate a Table of Quotations and Captions, or even a list of First Appearances of Boldfaced Terms.

### From headings to table of contents

**Bottom Line**

The Table of Contents tools are found in the References tab. Each group in the References tab provides tools to generate an analogous table of some resource: the Bibliography, Table of Figures, Index, and Table of Authorities (which lists legal citations): each collect, sort, and nicely lay out every instance of one or more styles in your document. The Table of Figures tool grabs captions; the Index alphabetizes the words you mark as Index Entries, and so on.

By default, the TOC feature in Word builds an outline, with Heading 1 text at the top level, then Heading 2, and so on; just as the Outline View and Navigation pane. Standard-issue TOCs are a single click away.

**STEP BY STEP** **Adding and formatting a table of contents**

1. On page 2 of **word04a_work.docx** place the cursor to the right of your name (the Author field). If the field handle (Author) appears, indicating that you're editing the field, press the **right arrow** to shift focus out of the field.
2. Press **Return** to move to a new line.
3. Click **References > Table of Contents > Table of Contents**. From the drop-down gallery, choose **Automatic Table 1**.

4 Click the new **Contents** heading, and then open **Home > Styles Gallery** (shown in Figure 4-14) to see that a new Style (TOC Heading) has been added.

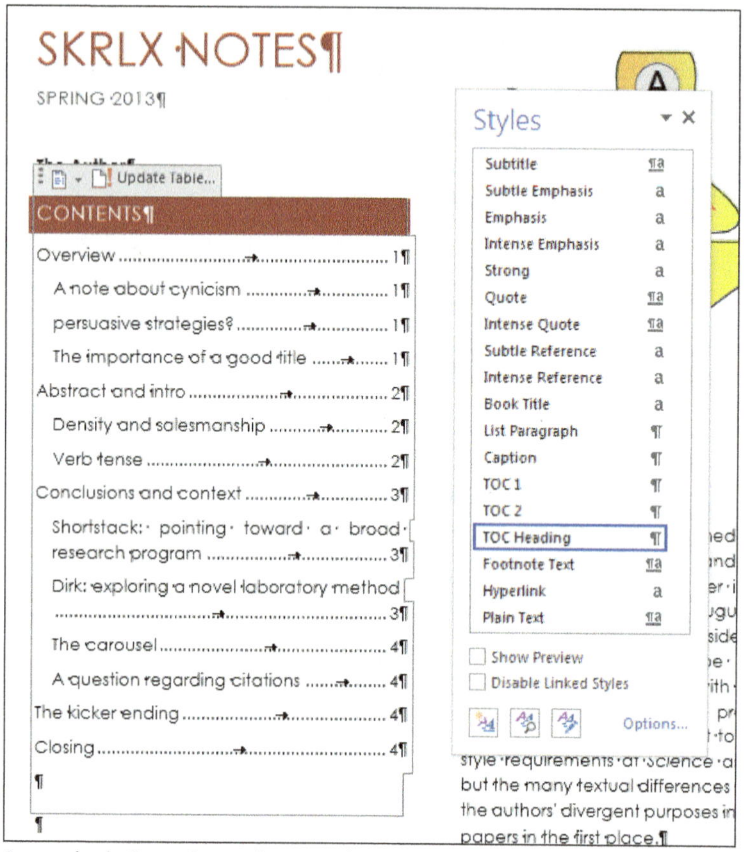


**Figure 4-14**

The TOC uses several special-purpose Styles.

*Image used under Creative Commons license, contributor: Dake*

A grey handle appears around the entire Table of Contents, indicating that it's a large, complex field. This is how Word visually distinguishes between data you've entered manually, such as text, and data that's programmatically generated, such as the Date field on the cover or the content of the TOC.

Word formats the TOC using a variety of TOC-related Styles, which you can see by opening the Styles pane (Alt+Ctrl+Shift+S). You can change the look of the TOC by modifying those Styles, just as with any other aspect of your document. (See below, "Building a Custom TOC.") As you can see, Word uses your current Theme, Style Set, and page formatting to slot the TOC seamlessly into your document.

A couple of things to note about the Table: First of all, because the text isn't styled in all caps (unlike the article's headings), you can see that many section titles use nonstandard capitalization. You can fix it, but it's irrelevant to this lesson. Second, the field handle includes an Update Table... button: if you click it, you'll bring up a dialog box with options to update the entire TOC (if you've added or deleted headings) or just the page numbers (if you've only changed section length). If you want to keep your TOC up to date, you'll need to periodically refresh it using that button.

If you Ctrl+click one of the TOC entries, you'll jump to that spot in the document; the TOC's entries act as hyperlinks, as in a webpage.

Finally, the TOC field has a drop-down menu icon, which lets you choose from a built-in TOC style or create a Manual Table. The latter is just a skeleton for making and maintaining a TOC by hand; unless you have very specific formatting needs, we do not recommend using this feature.

## Building a custom table of contents

**Bottom Line**

Word can restyle an existing TOC, but to set new options, such as how many heading levels to include, you'll need to make a new TOC. We will insert a nonstandard Table of Contents and set its parameters in the Table of Contents dialog.

**STEP BY STEP** **Building a custom table of contents**

1. Remove **Table of Contents** on the TOC field menu, or just select the **TOC** and insert a new one in its place.
2. Click **References > Table of Contents > Custom Table of Contents**. A dialog box appears with custom options as shown in Figure 4-15.

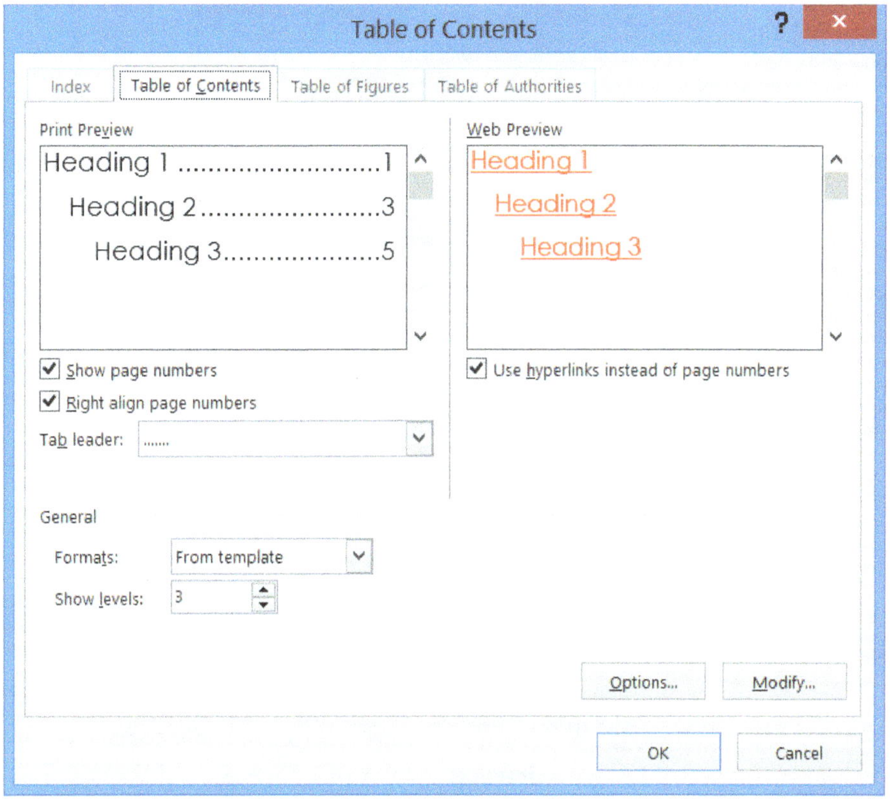


**Figure 4-15**

The Custom Table of Contents dialog box.

3. Try out as many options as you'd like.

The Web Preview shows how the TOC will be styled if you save your .docx file as an HTML webpage; an HTML Table of Contents without hyperlinks isn't much use, so it's wise to leave the *Use hyperlinks* option checked.

The Modify button lets you modify TOC styles just like paragraph styles.

The Options button enables detailed customization: instead of Word's built-in heading hierarchy, you can build your TOC using any other paragraph styles. Only a small fraction of users will ever need to do so; consult the online help at *office.microsoft.com* for instructions.

## Using table fields in your TOC

**Bottom Line**

Finally, the Table Entry fields option lets you add arbitrary text pieces in your TOC by inserting **invisible fields** into your document. We'll add one such field, and then rebuild our TOC.

**STEP BY STEP**

### Marking text for the TOC

1 Scroll to the Density and Salesmanship section of the document, and highlight the words ***culture does matter***.

2 Press **Alt+Shift+O** to mark the selected text as a TOC entry. The resulting dialog box is shown in Figure 4-16.

**Figure 4-16**

Marking text for the TOC with an invisible Table Entry field.

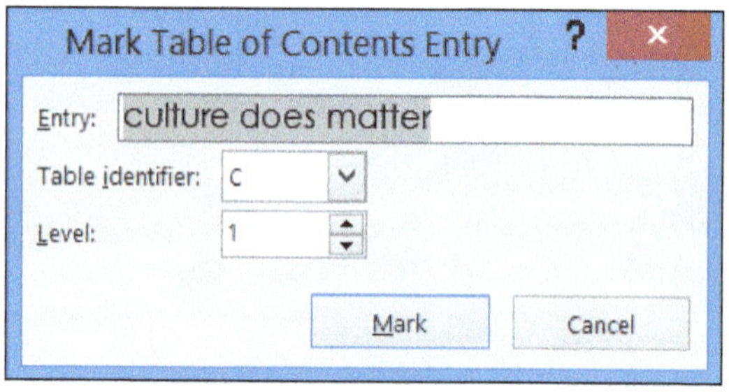


3 In the text field, type **handwaving**, select **3** from the Level drop-down menu, click **Mark**, and then click **Close**.

The Table Identifier option is important only if you use multiple TOCs in a single document, for example, one for chapter headings, another for quotations, a third for dictionary entries, and so on. If so, assign each TOC an identifier and use it to specify which Table your entries will be added to.

Note that Word has turned Show Hidden Characters on; this lets you see the invisible Table Entry code you just entered: {TC "handwaving" \f C \l "3"}. You can edit this text directly, but due to its odd syntax, it's easy to break; to find out what the switches (\f, \l) mean, consult Microsoft's extensive documentation at *office.microsoft.com*.

4 Scroll to the Table of Contents and choose **Remove TOC** from the drop-down menu on the field handle. The cursor will remain in place.

5 Click **References > Table of Contents > Table of Contents > Custom Table of Contents**. Make sure Show levels is set to **3**. Click **Options** and make sure **Table Entry Fields** is selected.

6 Click **OK**, and then click **OK** again.

Your new TOC includes an entry marked *handwaving*; this is the only level 3 entry in the whole Table. You can build an entire TOC out of text pieces marked in this labor-intensive fashion, as long as you spend some time up front deciding on a tagging hierarchy; using the built-in heading/outlining tools will save you a lot of work.

## ADDING A TABLE OF FIGURES

**Bottom Line**

We've already tagged all our images with captions; now we'll finish our lesson by building a Table of Figures, which lists your document's figures with optional numbers. The process is much the same as adding a TOC:

**STEP BY STEP** **Adding a table of figures**

1 Place the cursor on the line below the TOC. Select the **Heading 1** style and type **Table of Figures**.

2 Click **References > Captions > Insert Table of Figures**.

3 Deselect **Include** label and **number**. Click **OK**. The resulting Table of Figures is shown in Figure 4-17.

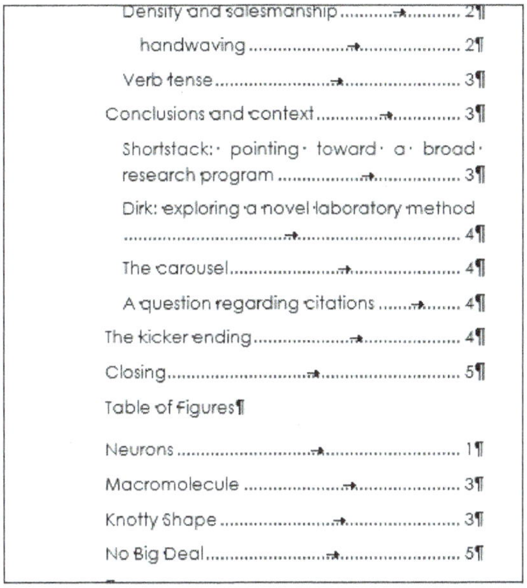


**Figure 4-17**

Table of Contents and Table of Figures with hidden characters displayed.

The options for the Table of Figures are almost the same as for the Table of Contents. You can experiment with the Caption label and Include label and number options to vary the appearance of the Table; for example, cutting out the Figure # prefix is important when space and word count are at a premium.

4 Place the cursor directly below the Table of Figures and click **Page Layout > Page Setup > Breaks > Column** to start the text fresh in the right-hand column.

5 Finally, right-click the **Table of Contents**, choose **Update Field** (F9), select **Update entire table**, and then click **OK**.

That brings our TOC up-to-date with the latest changes (including a new heading), and brings our lesson to a close.

6 Choose **File > Save** or press **Ctrl+S** to save your work. **Close** this document.

## What you learned in this lesson:

- Folding Text
- Sorting Sections
- Building an Outline with Headings
- Managing Master Documents and Subdocuments
- Adding Captions to Images
- Using Fields
- Hiding and Showing Field Codes
- Editing Document Properties
- Adding a Cover Page
- Viewing Hidden Characters
- Using Page and Section Breaks
- Adding Cross-References
- Adding and Editing Footnotes and Endnotes
- Building a Table of Contents
- Building a Table of Figures

# Knowledge Assessment

## Fill in the Blanks

**Complete the following sentences by writing the correct word or words in the blanks provided.**

1. The prefix of a caption, like "Figure" or "Equation," is known as its _____.
2. Section 2, with subsections 2.1 and 2.2, is folded in to save space during editing. The next visible section or subsection is _____.
3. To change the order of multiple subsections of a document, switch to _____ view.
4. To quickly insert the title field of a document (using a field code), use the _____ command.
5. Word provides a collection of pre-formatted cover pages, each tied to a specific document _____.
6. By default, page and section breaks are _____ like carriage returns and tabs.
7. Footnotes have _____ numerals by default, but _____ numerals are available from the Footnote and Endnote options dialog.
8. To insert invisible bookmarks into a document and its TOC, use the _____ field tool.
9. Endnotes are automatically inserted at the end of each _____ by default.
10. Master documents and subdocuments are edited in the _____ view.

## Matching

**Match the document feature to its description.**

1. page break
2. section break
3. hidden character
4. footnote
5. endnote
6. caption
7. label
8. field code
9. Table of Figures
10. subdocumenta. collects image captions/labels for quick reference by reader

a. collects image captions or labels for quick reference by the reader
b. portion of a master document, in a separate file
c. identifying or explanatory text attached to an image
d. typeset at bottom of page on which cite appears
e. typesets subsequent content on next page
f. dynamically inserts content into document, doesn't appear in print itself
g. in-text note or cite typeset at bottom of document or section
h. splits document into independently-formatted subparts
i. for instance, a paragraph break or tab, usually invisible to reader
j. optional category prefix for caption (e.g., Figure or Table)

# Competency Assessment

## Project 4-1: Simple Outlining

1. Open the project file **grimm-source**.
2. Save your document as **project_4-1_outline**.
3. Switch to Outline View. Enable **Outline Tools > Show First Line Only**.
4. Double click the **plus** icon next to each section to collapse it into its heading.
5. Expand "**Hans in Luck**."
6. Before the "After a time he thought" line, insert a new line, Heading 2 (one indent level beyond "Hans in Luck," which has the Heading 1 style), reading **Shepherd**.
7. Similarly, insert Heading 2 **Setting Out** right beneath the title "Hans in Luck," **Goose** before the line "The next man he met was a countryman…," **Grinder** before the line "As he came to the next village," and **Stone** after the line "Then who so blythe."

8. Drag the Stone heading down one line, to just above "Hans took the stone."

   Feel free to experiment with selecting, reordering, and styling the sections in Outline View.
9. Click Close Outline View.
10. Choose File > Save and then File > Close.

## Project 4-2: Document Properties

1. Open the project file 4-2-source. Save your document as project_4-2_document_properties.
2. Open the backstage area and select Info if it's not already selected.
3. In the Properties > Title line, click Add a Title and type Grimms' Fairy Tales.
4. From the Properties dropdown menu, select Show Document Panel.
5. Change the Document Panel's Author: field to Jacob and Wilhelm Grimm.

   If prompted to turn AutoComplete on, dismiss the dialog.
6. Set the Keywords: value to folklore.
7. Close the Document Panel.
8. Add a blank line below the document's title line, and select Insert > Quick Parts > Document Property > Author.
9. Choose File > Save and then File > Close.

# Proficiency Assessment

## Project 4-3: Defining a Custom Field

1. Open the project file 4-3-source. Save your document as project_4-3_custom_field.
2. Click File > Info > Properties > Advanced Properties > Custom tab.
3. In the Name: box, type Edition. In the Value: box, type 1812. Click Add, then OK.
4. Return to the main document editing screen. Add a blank line below the title and place the cursor there.
5. Click Insert > Text > Quick Parts > Field...
6. Select Document Information from the Categories: dropdown, and DocProperty from the Field Names: list.
7. Select the Edition property from the Property: dropdown. Click OK.
8. After the newly-inserted edition date (1812), add a blank space and edition.

   If you wish, alter the "edition" line to have no trailing space (Home > Line and Paragraph Spacing).
9. Choose File > Save and then File > Close.

### Project 4-4: Section Breaks and Headers/Footers

1. Open the project file 4-4-source. Save your document as project_4-4_section_breaks.
2. Insert Odd Page Section Breaks before The Travelling Musicians and Jorinda and Jorindel.
3. Open the document header on the first page and enable both Different First Page and Different Odd & Even Pages in the Header/Footer > Design tab.

   Note that only Section 1's first page will be unique – the other sections of the document will not have unique headers on their first pages.
4. Add the following headers:

   Section 1 Even Page Header: (centered) Hans in Luck

   All Sections, Odd Page Header: (centered) Grimm, {Edition field code} edition

   Section 2 Even Page Header: (centered) Jorinda and Jorindel

   Section 3 Even Page Header: (centered) The Travelling Musicians

   You will have to deselect Header/Footer > Design > Link to Previous for the Section 2 and 3 Even Page headers.
5. Add a centered page number to both the even- and odd-numbered pages (but not page 1), using Insert > Page Number > Bottom of Page > Plain Number 2.
6. Choose File > Save and then File > Close.

## Mastery Assessment

### Project 4-5: Adding a Custom Table of Contents

1. Open the project file 4-5-source. Save your document as project_4-5_toc.
2. Select the first line of each song that appears in the document and tag it as a Table of Contents entry (see the section "Using Table Fields in Your TOC").
3. Below the author line at the top of the document, insert a Custom Table of contents with the Table Entry Fields option selected.
4. Now manually edit the field codes that generate the song entries, to remove the commas from their TOC lines (but not from the printed songs themselves, in the main text), and Update the TOC.
5. Choose File > Save and then File > Close.

### Project 4-6: Bringing It All Together

1. Open the project file 4-6-source. Save your document as project_4-6_final.
2. Add a cover page including Title, Author, and Edition information.
3. Delete and redo the TOC without the song listings.
4. Add a second table at the end of the document, called Songs, which catalogs only the four song lines you tagged.
5. Select an appropriate document theme to go with your cover page.
6. Save your work and close Word.

# 5 Working with Tables

## LESSON SKILL MATRIX

**In this lesson, you will learn the following skills:**

| | |
|---|---|
| Insert and Navigate Tables | Sort Tabular Data |
| Split and Merge Cells | Use Table Styles |
| Integrate Tables into Paragraphs | Customize Cell and Table Borders |
| Position Text Within a Table | Resize Cells and Cell Content |
| Manipulate Columns and Rows | |

## KEY TERMS

- **Row**
- **Column**
- **Heading**
- **Nested Table**
- **Table Style**
- **Select Table Handle**
- **Merge Cells**
- **Eraser tool**
- **Tabular Data**
- **Database**
- **Record**
- **Sort**
- **Table Style Options**
- **Tooltip**
- **Fill**
- **Border Painter**
- **AutoFit**

©Juanmonino/iStockPhoto

Laying out the spring catalog for Northwind Traders's mail-order service means laying out 100 pages full of product descriptions, price lists, images, and other text. To keep this material straight, the designers rely extensively on tables, both for list data and for complex page layout. This lesson covers the somewhat complex behaviors of tables in Word 2013.

## SOFTWARE ORIENTATION

Tables provide an easy way to organize and display groups of data. In this lesson you'll gain an understanding of ways you can use Microsoft Word to present, organize, format and style tables in your Microsoft Word documents.

**Figure 5-1**

Tables and table tools in a Microsoft Word document.

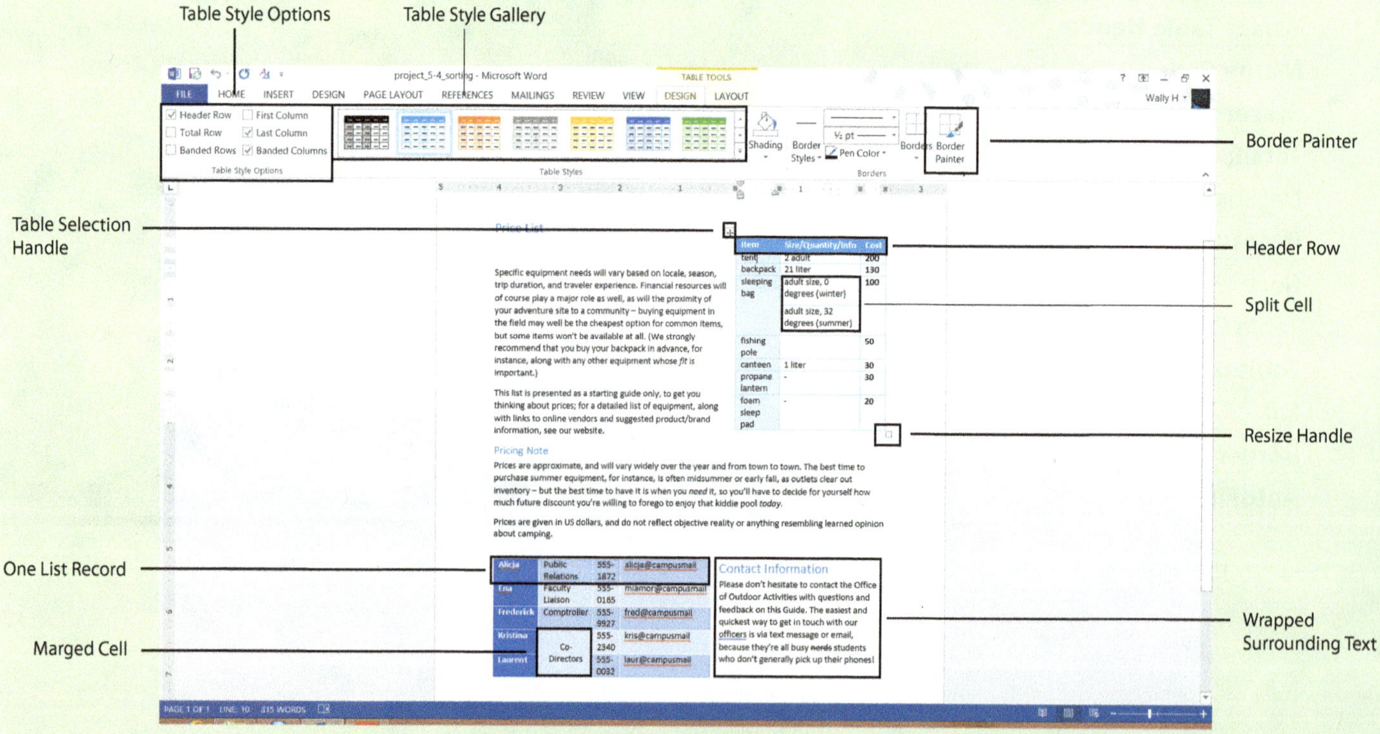

## STARTING UP

You will work with files from the Word05lessons folder. Make sure that you have loaded the OfficeLessons folder onto your computer.

## THE USES OF TABLES

A table in Word is a matrix of **rows** and **columns** with optional column and row **headings**. There are two kinds of tables you might use: invisible grids used to line up elements of a design (such as the implied grid of a newspaper page), and visible grids meant to highlight a collection of structured data, such as a list of phone numbers appearing in a report. Gridded layout is a popular topic in graphic design, particularly web design, where rendering a page in an ever-changing browser window presents a variety of interesting technical and aesthetic problems; but graphic design is beyond the scope of this book. In this lesson, we'll focus solely on tables that are meant to look like tables.

**figure 5-2**

Examples of Word's table formatting.

Table 1: Distances between offices, in miles

| | Doogle | Frapple | TPC | ACME |
|---|---|---|---|---|
| Doogle | - | 5 | 3 | 8 |
| Frapple | 5 | - | 22 | 7 |
| TPIC | 3 | 22 | - | 10 |
| ACME | 8 | 7 | 10 | - |

December

| Sun | Mon | Tue | Wed | Thu | Fri | Sat |
|---|---|---|---|---|---|---|
| | | | | | | 1 |
| 2 | 3 | 4 concert | 5 reception | 6 recover | 7 | 8 |
| 9 | 10 | 11 | 12 | 13 India... | 14 ... | 15 ... |
| 16 ... | 17 ...home | 18 | 19 | 20 | 21 | 22 |
| 23 | 24 | 25 | 26 | 27 | 28 | 29 |
| 30 | 31 | | | | | |

| What? | Where? |
|---|---|
| Art pencil | Pearl |
| Codfish | Star |
| Friendship | Internet |
| Hip hop | Luna |
| Keys | Ace |
| Orangina | Luna |
| Shirt | Coop |
| Textbook | Coop |

## TABLE BASICS

**Bottom Line**

Table are common elements in technical documents Like spreadsheets, tables consist of rectangular regions call cells, organized in rows and columns; indeed, Excel spreadsheets can be inserted into Word documents as tables. We'll create a few tables from scratch to practice maneuvering through them and making basic edits.

## Inserting and navigating tables

A table is an object that can be placed, formatted, and moved just like any other object in Word 2013. But its internal dynamics make it a little more complicated than the average image or text box. We'll start with the commands to insert and navigate tables.

**STEP BY STEP** **Inserting and navigating tables**

1. Open Word 2013 and create a new blank document.
2. Choose **File > Save As** and navigate to the Word05lessons folder. Name the document **word05_work** and click **Save**.
3. Click **Insert > Table**. A drop-down grid appears. Drag your mouse over the grid until a 4 × 4 box is highlighted, and then click.
4. Place the cursor in one of the inner cells of the table and type **This is a test of cell spacing. See how the cell stretches to fit?**
5. Place the cursor in a different cell of the table. Insert a second 4 × 4 table inside the cell, as in Figure 5-3.

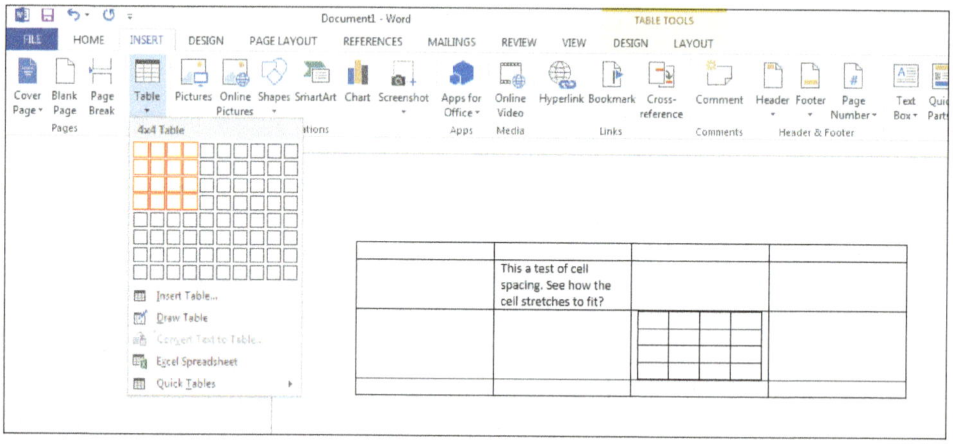


**Figure 5-3**

Live Preview lets you see the result of the Insert > Table command before you commit to adding the table.

6. Use the arrow keys to move right/left and up/down within the tables; then click in the smaller table and use the **Tab** key (and Shift+Tab) to navigate instead. Note that pressing Tab in the bottom-right corner of the table adds another row at the bottom.

**Bottom Line**

This is an important but subtle difference: the arrow keys are for traveling around a table, while Tab is assumed to be used for editing the table.

## Split cells and table styles

Placing one table inside another is called nesting; if you insert a 3 × 3 table into a particular cell of a table, there will still be space within that cell but outside the nested table. You can create a similar structure by splitting one cell, which doesn't create a new table as such, just a more complex region within the outer table.

One key feature of a split cell, as opposed to a nested table, is that the contents of the split cell still inherit the formatting of the surrounding table. A **nested table** is formatted separately from the table where it's embedded, as the following steps will demonstrate.

## STEP BY STEP Splitting cells and changing table styles

1 Click one of the cells of your nested table.

2 Click Table Tools > Layout > Merge > Split Cells. Set both columns and rows to 4, and click OK. The entire split cell, subdivided now into a 4 × 4 matrix, will be selected.

3 Click Table Tools > Design and select Grid Table 5 Dark - Accent 5 from the Table Styles gallery.

As you can see in Figure 5-4, the **Table Style** is applied not just to the selected cells (within the split cell), but to the nested table; yet the outermost table, the one you originally inserted into the blank document, doesn't inherit this formatting.

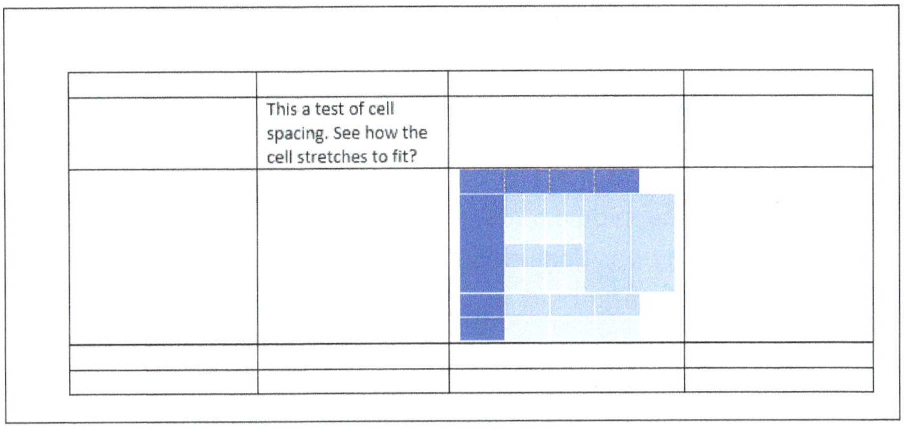


**Figure 5-4**

Applying a Table Style to a nested table doesn't affect the outer table.

4 Finally, select the cell where you inserted text (This is a test…) and split the cell into a 3 × 3 matrix.

The text is pushed into the upper left cell of the 3 × 3 matrix: our first exposure to the interaction of table and text, which we'll explore in the next section.

5 Choose File > Save and then File > Close.

## Working with text in and around tables

**Bottom Line**

You can format text within a table just as you would in the wider space of your document. But the interaction between tables and text can be a little finicky. By default, a table placed with the Insert Table command sits in line with text, but by moving it on the page (or by placing text around it) you turn the table into a floating object, like an absolutely positioned image. The following steps will illustrate this change in behavior.

**STEP BY STEP** **Inserting a table within text**

1. Open **word05a.docx** in your Word05lessons folder.
2. Choose **File > Save As** and navigate to the Word05lessons folder. Name the file **word05a_work** and click **Save**.
3. If you haven't already done so, select **Home > Paragraph > Show Hidden Characters**.
4. Place the cursor after the boldfaced sentence in the first paragraph. Insert a 4 × 4 table at that spot (See Figure 5-5).

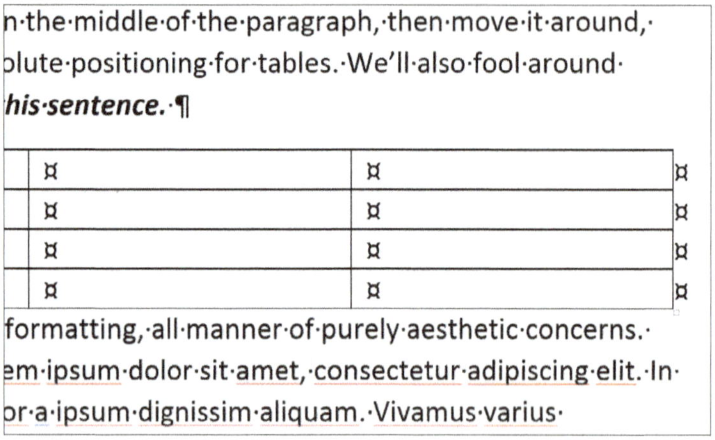


**Figure 5-5**

Inserting a table into a paragraph also adds a line break.

5. Drag the lower-right handle on the table to resize it; make it as small as possible.

Resizing the table has no effect on word wrapping; it's in line with the text, and Word automatically leaves space below the table. But moving the table turns it into a floating object.

6 Select the table, either by mousing over it to reveal the **Select Table** handle in the upper left, or by clicking in one of the cells and then clicking **Table Tools > Layout > Table > Select > Select Table**. Drag it down and to the right, placing it in the center of the page, as in Figure 5-6.

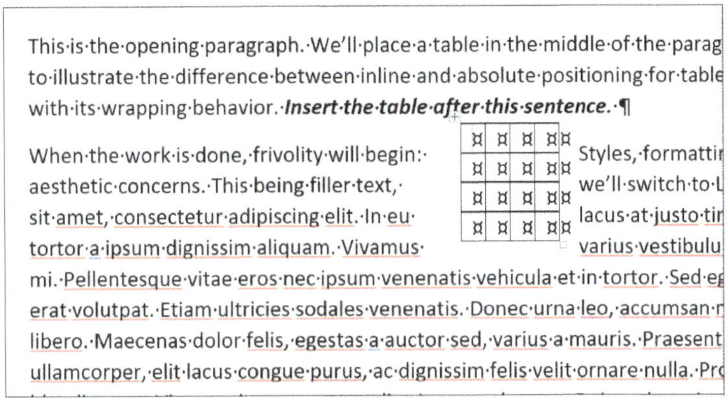

This·is·the·opening·paragraph.·We'll·place·a·table·in·the·middle·of·the·parag
to·illustrate·the·difference·between·inline·and·absolute·positioning·for·table
with·its·wrapping·behavior.·***Insert·the·table·after·this·sentence.***·¶

When·the·work·is·done,·frivolity·will·begin:· Styles,·formatti
aesthetic·concerns.·This·being·filler·text,· we'll·switch·to·L
sit·amet,·consectetur·adipiscing·elit.·In·eu· lacus·at·justo·tir
tortor·a·ipsum·dignissim·aliquam.·Vivamus· varius·vestibulu
mi.·Pellentesque·vitae·eros·nec·ipsum·venenatis·vehicula·et·in·tortor.·Sed·eg
erat·volutpat.·Etiam·ultricies·sodales·venenatis.·Donec·urna·leo,·accumsan·r
libero.·Maecenas·dolor·felis,·egestas·a·auctor·sed,·varius·a·mauris.·Praesent
ullamcorper,·elit·lacus·congue·purus,·ac·dignissim·felis·velit·ornare·nulla.·Pro

**Figure 5-6**

Once a table has been moved, Word applies absolute positioning to it, like a floating text box or image.

Now that the table is a float, you can move it around the page much as you would any image or text box. To return it to inline layout, make a change in the Table Properties dialog:

**STEP BY STEP**

## Using the Table Properties dialog box

1 Select the table, and then click **Table Tools > Layout > Table > Properties**.

2 In the dialog box, set Alignment to Left and Text Wrapping to **None**. Click **OK**.

**Take Note**

Why can't I freely move an in-line table ? Why do tables default to inline positioning and seem to resist absolute positioning? Think of it this way: a table squashes and stretches with its contents; it can be used as a container for other page elements; and it is part of the flow of text in the page in a way images and text boxes aren't. It can also add rows and columns, which would screw up line/paragraph spacing. Think of an inline table as part of the page itself, rather than an object on top of it. To freely position the table, open the Table Properties dialog and uncheck "Move with text" on the Positioning page.

## Text alignment and merged cells

**Bottom Line**

After learning how to move a table in the page and move around inside it, we'll look at the tools Word has for altering a table's internal geography. You've seen how to split cells; it's easy to merge them as well, to create complex cell layouts. Merged cells are simply large cells made by joining smaller ones; they occupy multi-cell regions of tables.

**STEP BY STEP**

## Merging cells and aligning text

1 Open **word05a_work.docx** if it is not already open and resize the table you inserted so that it's about as wide as the text block using the handles that appear in the corner of the table when selected.

2 Click within the upper left cell, and drag to the right to select the first three cells in the top row.

3 Click **Table Tools > Layout > Merge > Merge Cells**.

4 Do the same with the four cells in the bottom right corner of the table: click and drag to select, and then Merge Cells.

5 Place the cursor in the new large cell. Type **Centered Text**. Then open the Table Tools > Layout tab.

In the Alignment group is a 3 × 3 grid of icons, each corresponding to a different text alignment: top center, bottom right, and so on. Remember that text alignment is a paragraph formatting option; you can click inside the cell and set the text alignment without selecting individual characters.

6 Click the center text alignment icon (see Figure 5-7), place the cursor in the first cell in row four, then slowly press **Tab** six times. Carefully observe how the cursor moves.

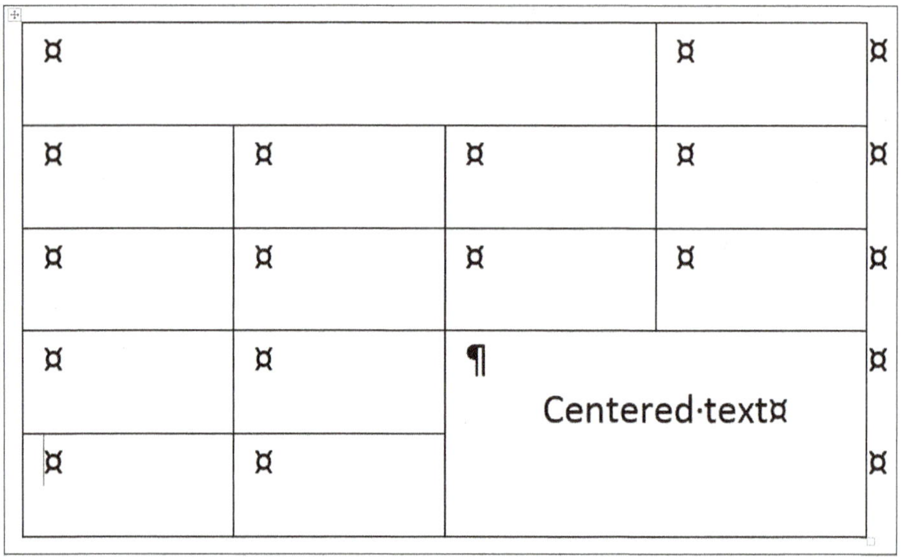


**Figure 5-7**

Merged cells occupy a unique position: you can reach the merged cell by tabbing in from the fourth or fifth row.

Remember that pressing Tab moves the cursor sequentially through the cells, left to right and top to bottom, until the last cell is reached, at which point Tab inserts a new row. (It doesn't insert a Tab character as it would in a normal paragraph.) Word assigns the newly merged cell the position Row 4, Column 3; as you press Tab repeatedly, the cursor moves along the bottom row, *back* through the merged cell, then on to a brand new row. When you turned the 2 × 2 region into one cell, Word created an entity that's a single column wide, but resides in two different rows.

## Merging cells with the Eraser tool

**Bottom Line**

There's another way to merge cells: the **Eraser tool**, which eliminates cell borders unless it can't, in which case it simply renders them invisible.

## STEP BY STEP Merging cells with the eraser tool

1. Select the **Eraser** tool (Table Tools > Layout > Draw > Eraser).
2. Click and drag from the large merged cell upward into the cell directly above it on the left. The top border of the merged cell becomes dotted as in Figure 5-8, meaning it's now a non-printing (invisible) border.

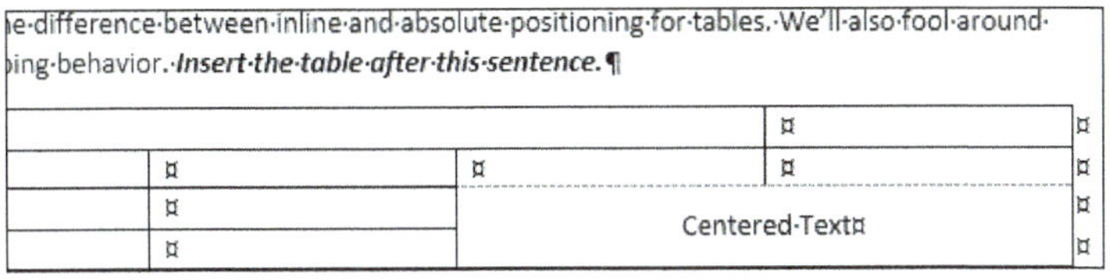


**Figure 5-8**

The Eraser tool merges cells if possible, but it can't merge cells of different sizes, so it hides their shared border instead.

3. Now click and drag the eraser across the vertical line between the two cells above the Centered Text cell. These cells will merge and if they had content, it would be lost.
4. Finally, erase the dotted line between the two merged cells, creating a single empty cell the size of a 3 × 2 region. See Figure 5-9.

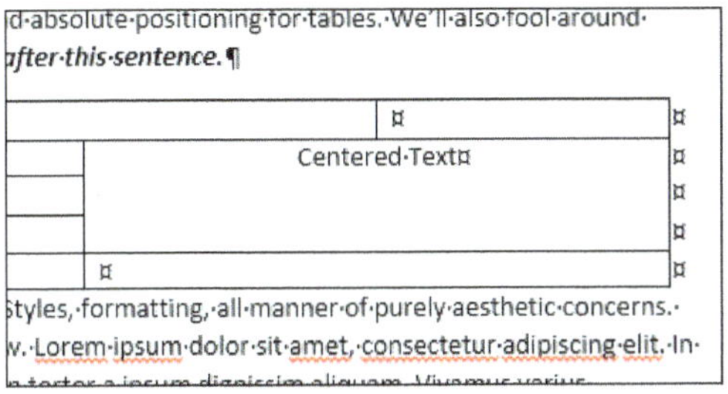


**Figure 5-9**

The Eraser tool knocks down the walls between table cells.

As you can see, you can't merge cells in a table unless their dimensions match; cells must merge horizontally to create a shared two-column southern border before they can merge vertically with the big cell below them.

5. Deselect the **Table Eraser** and choose **File > Save** or press **Ctrl+S** to save your changes.

## PRESENTING AND SORTING TABULAR DATA

**Bottom Line**

The most common use for tables is for presenting **tabular data**. Word treats the contents of a table as a kind of miniature **database**; it will handle each row as a single **record**, for instance with columns corresponding to "fields" (in the database sense, not "field codes"), and can distinguish between records and column/row headings. Our current document contains a small table at the bottom of Page 1 that demonstrates these features: a list of fake chemical elements, along with (fake) Volume/Mass/Energy numbers for each.

The formatting applied to the table is another example of the difference between Word's internal model of an object and its user-friendly visual presentation: this is a 4 × 7 table with a mix of text and numeric data, but because of the formatting, we immediately read it as six records, each of which attaches three data points to a name or label. Word's table formatting tools let you approach a table either way.

### Adding, deleting, and moving columns and rows

**Bottom Line**

Since you can't insert a single cell into the middle of a table without repositioning the columns and rows around it, Word provides hooks to let you manipulate tables by row and by column. We'll alter our chemical data in a handful of ways to see how these tools work: we'll reorder the columns, delete a record, and insert another.

**STEP BY STEP** **Adding, deleting and moving columns and rows**

1. Click the upper border of the **Volume** column; the entire column is selected. (As you mouse over the top border, the pointer should change to a downward-pointing arrow.)
2. Click and drag the column heading to the right and place it in the space between the Mass and Energy columns. The new column order is: Mass, Volume, Energy.
3. Click inside the margin to the left of the Beryllium cell; the entire row is selected. Press **Delete**; the data in the row will vanish, but the empty cells will remain.
4. Press **Ctrl+Z** to Undo, restoring the Beryllium data. Then, with the row still highlighted, press **Backspace**. The row itself will vanish.

Word splits the functions of the Backspace and Delete keys to make a distinction, respectively, between altering the table itself (the size of the database) and altering the contents of a single record. The same behavior occurs when you select a single cell by triple-clicking inside it: you can Delete the data within the cell or Backspace to alter the table grid itself.

Now let's add a replacement record: you can squeeze a record into a table in a couple of ways.

5. Click the word **Paramecium**. Note that the Table Tools > Layout tab offers a number of icons to Insert Rows and Columns next to the selected cell.

6 Instead, mouse over a space just below and to the left of the Paramecium cell. A small icon with a plus sign appears, as in Figure 5-10.

**Figure 5-10**

Inserting a row into a table.

7 Click the **Add Row** icon to add an empty row. The entire row is automatically selected; if you begin typing, Word will insert text into the first cell of the row. Type **Wampum** (press tab), **31** (press tab), **2** (press tab), **9** to populate the row.

## Sorting data in a table

**Bottom Line**

As with a database, you can **sort** the entire contents of a table using one or more columns as keys; for instance, sorting a list of phone numbers by last name, and then first name. We'll sort our table by Energy value (lowest to highest), and then sort Volume from highest to lowest within that ordering.

**STEP BY STEP** **Sorting data in a table**

1 Change the Energy value of the Frustrum record to **88**.

2 Click anywhere in the table, and then click **Table Tools > Layout > Data > Sort**.

3 In the dialog box, Sort By: **Energy (Ascending)**, and **Then By: Volume (Descending)**. Click **OK** The resulting sorted table is shown in 5-11.

**Figure 5-11**

Sorting our chemical info; the sorted data.

| | Mass | Volume | Energy |
|---|---|---|---|
| Wampum | 31 | 2 | 9 |
| Dilithium | 1 | 9 | 12 |
| Tristram | 86 | 123 | 44 |
| Adium | 34 | 23 | 45 |
| Frustrum | 90 | 87 | 88 |
| Paramecium | 66 | 44 | 88 |

If you wanted to sort a single column of data without altering the entire table (in other words, if the table did not contain records as such, just discrete columns) you could do so by selecting the whole column, clicking the Options button in the Sort dialog box, and then selecting the *Sort column only* check box. Note that after doing so, you could treat the resulting table as a database again; be sure to keep track of the changes you've made to your data!

## DESIGNING TABLES

Word 2013 provides a large assortment of Table Styles available from a gallery in the Table Tools > Design tab. Word stocks the gallery with Styles based on the features you select in the Table Style Options group: you decide how your table should be structured, and Word suggests combinations of cell shading, border design, font choices, and so forth. Best of all, once you've chosen a Table Style, Word will modify it if you change the Style Options you want.

### Table style options

**Bottom Line**

The **Table Style Options** group includes six check boxes. You can mouse over each check box to get a **Tooltip** explaining what it does. To see how the various options affect a table's design, start with very basic formatting and iterate through a series of changes.

**STEP BY STEP** **Table style options**

1. Click anywhere in the chemical data table and navigate to the **Table Tools > Design tab**. Open the Table Styles gallery and choose **Clear** (at the bottom of the gallery).
2. Uncheck all six boxes in the Table Styles Options group. Your table appears without any formatting.
3. From the Styles gallery, select **Grid Table 2** (in the Grid Styles section).
4. Click the various Table Styles Options in turn, in various combinations; in particular, try combining Banded Rows and Banded Columns to see how those options conflict.

Our chemical data table suggests a specific set of options: the row and column labels should be set off, and since we're treating the data in terms of records, it makes sense to differentiate table rows rather than columns.

5 Select the **chemical data** table. Check only the **Header Row**, **First Column**, and **Banded Rows** boxes. Open the Table Styles gallery (Figure 5-12) and notice the styles change to reflect the Style options.

**Figure 5-12**

The Table Styles gallery repopulates to reflect our choice of Style Options.

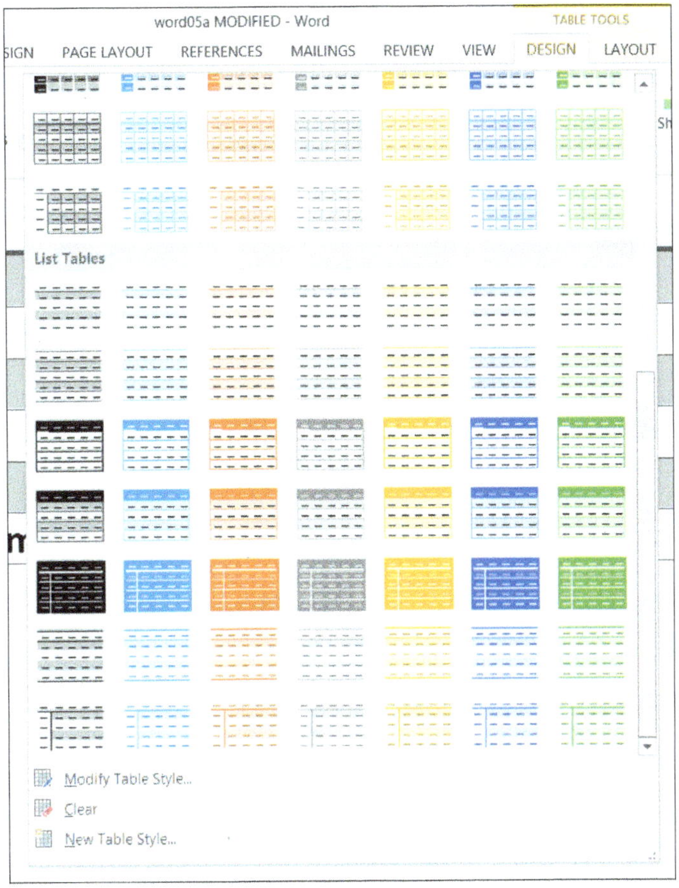


## Applying a table style

**Bottom Line**

After choosing the right Table Styles Options for our data set, we can select a Table Style from the gallery to provide the right visual emphasis. The Grid and List Table Styles vary widely in the intensity of their row/column highlighting and how much emphasis they place on row/column labels. You can experiment with a variety of Table Styles to see how they respond to the constraints you applied in the Table Styles Options group.

## STEP BY STEP Applying a table style

1 Select **Grid Table 3 – Accent 2** from the Table Styles Gallery.

Choosing a Table Style affects the selected table's fonts, colors, shading, and borders. You can change these features individually by right-clicking the Table Style in the gallery and choosing Modify Table Style from the drop-down menu. The options on this screen (see Figure 5-13) should be familiar by now, with the exception of the border design options, which we'll cover in the next section.

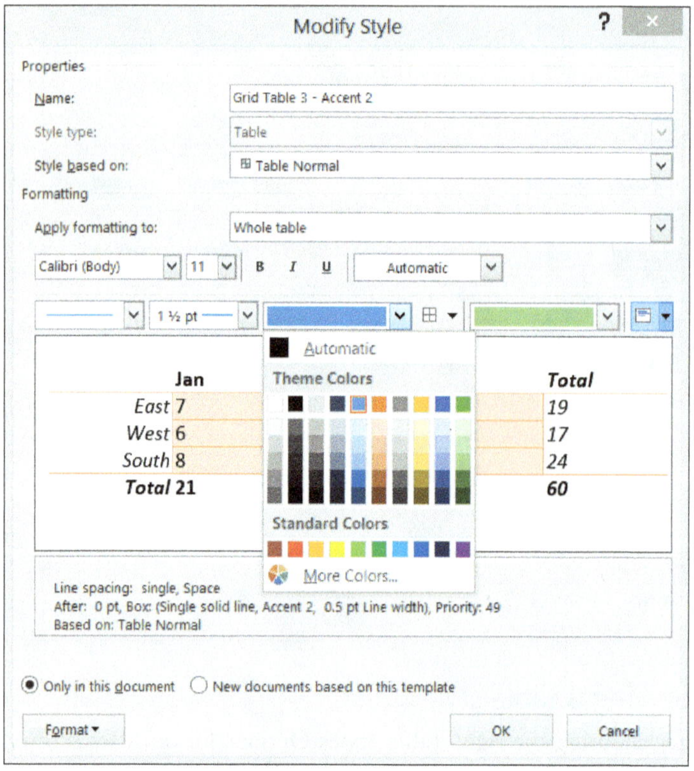


**Figure 5-13**

The Modify Table Style dialog lets you alter the Table Style using your document's Theme Colors.

One thing to note on this screen: the border and cell color options are inherited from the document theme; this is another example of how Office 2013 strives for visual consistency across applications and documents. You can now click Cancel to close this dialog box.

## Setting cell and table borders

**Bottom Line**

A cell has three parts: its **fill** (background color), content (text/images), and border. A cell border is actually four individual segments; you can specify visibility, style, and color for each segment, or handle them all together, cell by cell. Cell borders are set by column/row according to the Table Style, but you can customize them easily.

### STEP BY STEP Setting cell and table borders

1. Place the cursor in the Volume cell of the Dilithium row.
2. Open the **Borders** drop-down menu (Table Tools > Design > Borders > Borders) and select **No Border**.
3. Click and drag to select the Volume cells for Adium and Frustrum; click the Borders icon, which is still set to its last use (No Border).

The borders of the cells you've selected fall away. As you can see in the Borders drop-down menu, you can choose from a variety of border shapes, including diagonal lines.

4. Click and drag to select the data cells (excluding the row/column labels). From the Borders menu, select **No Border**, and then click to enable **Inside Borders**. The outer edges of the table will lose their borders, but inter-cell borders remain.

The terms outside and inside refer to your current selection; if you select multiple contiguous cells, Word can differentiate between the outer border of the shape they make together, and the borders between the region's individual cells. If you click within a single cell, there is no inside to speak of, so for that cell alone, the All Borders and Outside Borders options are equivalent.

Resizing a cell (or rather, its entire row or column) is straightforward: just drag the border in question.

## Using the Border Painter tool

**Bottom Line**

You can also use the **Border Painter** tool (the opposite of the Eraser tool) to draw in individual borders; the Painter takes its color and line information from the options you select in the Borders group.

### STEP BY STEP Using the Border Painter tool

1. Open the Table Tools > Design tab.
2. From the Line Style drop-down menu, select the **double squiggly** line style.
3. Select **Purple** from the Pen Color palette, under Standard Colors.
4. Make sure the **Border Painter** icon is selected, then click and drag various cell and table borders to paint those borders in the selected style, weight, and color.

5 Change the Line Style to a double line style and apply this border style to various cells. See Figure 5-14 for one possible result.

Unlike the Eraser tool, the Border Painter requires precise placement: you drag along a border to paint, rather than across it, so your initial click has to land right on the border to be recognized. For that reason, it's good to use the Zoom slider, on the Status Bar, when painting cell or table borders.

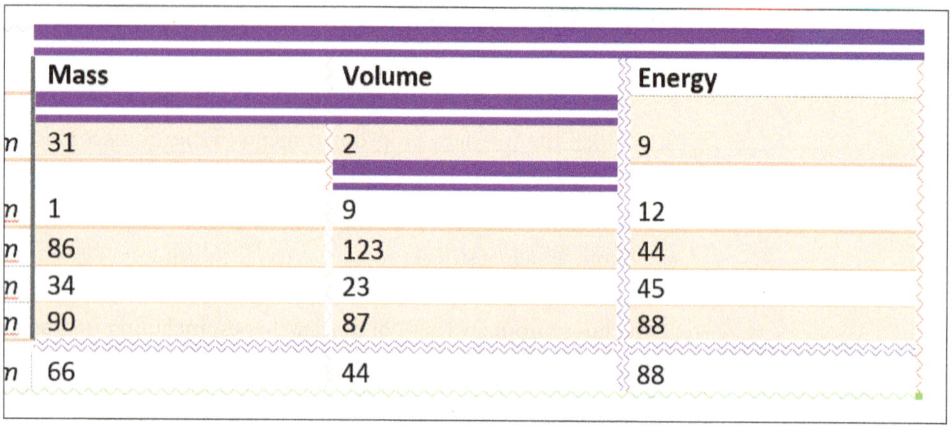

| | Mass | Volume | Energy |
|---|---|---|---|
| n | 31 | 2 | 9 |
| n | 1 | 9 | 12 |
| n | 86 | 123 | 44 |
| n | 34 | 23 | 45 |
| n | 90 | 87 | 88 |
| n | 66 | 44 | 88 |

**Figure 5-14**

The Border Painter lets you add lines in a variety of styles, colors, and weights.

## EDITING CELL CONTENTS

After playing with cell and table borders, we can move on to fills and text. Fills are straightforward: they're just background colors. To change the background color of a cell, select it, and then click Table Tools > Design > Shading. The drop-down palette includes the usual theme colors; clicking the paint icon fills the cell with the selected color.

### Cell text and manual cell sizing

**Bottom Line**

Text formatting within tables is also straightforward; you still use the paragraph/character formatting tools in the Home tab, combined with the cell sizing, alignment, text direction, and margin tools in the Table Tools > Layout tab. We'll add some text to our chemical info table and do some basic formatting.

**STEP BY STEP** **Cell text and manual cell sizing**

1 Continue using **word05a_work.docx** and click to drag the border between the Volume and Energy columns to the left, until the Volume cell is just big enough to contain its heading.

2 In the Dilithium Volume cell, type the words **9 cubic liters, measured by ANS**. The column will stretch horizontally to fit the word measured, and will stretch vertically to include the full entry.

3 Triple-click the new text and chose **Italics** from the formatting popup. Then click **Bullets** in the pop-up menu.

The formatting commands work just as usual, with the added wrinkle of the cell borders shifting slightly around the text. Word started by trying to evenly distribute the four columns, but the column distribution changed when we resized the Volume column.

4 Right-click within the cell you just edited and choose **Table Properties**. Click **Column** (see Figure 5-15) and if not already selected, choose **Percent** in the Measure in drop-down menu. Word is currently trying to apportion 10% of the table's width to Column 3 (Volume). Click **OK**.

**Take Note** If you need a given column or row to have a specific absolute size (for example, 2″ wide), you can set its size in this dialog box.

**Figure 5-15**

Setting absolute and relative column/row sizes in the Table Properties dialog box.

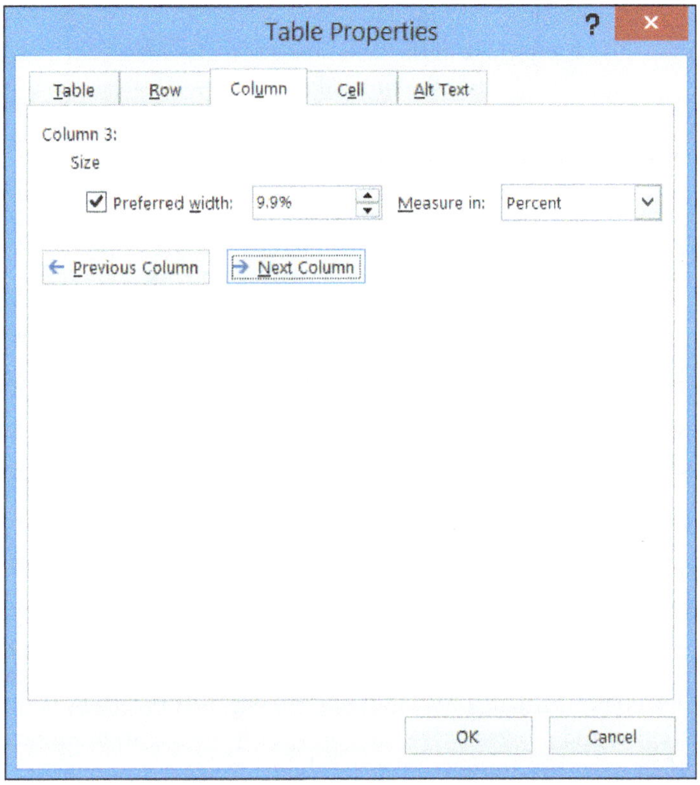


5 With the same cell selected, click **Table Tools > Layout > Alignment > Text Direction** three times to cycle through the possible orientations for table text.

Note that Word doesn't stretch the column to fit the sideways text entirely into the cell.

6 With the Volume Dilithium cell still selected, type **9**. Remove the italics and bullet point.

7 Finally, click **Cell Size > Distribute Rows and Distribute Columns** to even out the cell spacing.

Distribute Rows and Distribute Columns space the table's rows and columns evenly; if you select multiple rows and Distribute Rows, Word will apportion their current vertical space evenly, but won't even out the whole table.

All these commands involve working within a rigid table shape and size. But how do we adjust size and proportions dynamically to the table's contents? By using the AutoFit feature of Word.

8 Choose **File > Save** or press **Ctrl+S** to save your work.

## Using AutoFit and Fit Text

**Bottom Line**

The **AutoFit** tool aims to let you specify general table-sizing behavior without fiddling with absolute sizes or manually tweaking column proportions. By default, a new table will AutoFit Window; it'll stretch between the left and right margins, and stretch and squeeze internally (without changing width) as you change the number of columns. If you manually resize the table, you disable that behavior.

**STEP BY STEP** **Using AutoFit and Fit Text**

1 Click anywhere in the table, and select **Layout > Cell Size > AutoFit > Autofit Window**. The table stretches to full width.

2 Click **Autofit Contents**. The left-hand column will be widest, then Volume. The Mass column, with its short header, will be narrowest.

3 Click **Distribute Columns** found in the same Cell Size section of the Layout tab. The left-hand column becomes a jumble, as the labels no longer fit.

4 Click **Autofit Contents** again to fix the row labels. Select the **Mass**, **Volume**, and **Energy** columns, and click **Distribute Columns**; now the column headings are too big.

5 Finally, click **AutoFit Contents** once more.

AutoFit Contents chooses the same optimally efficient spacing every time; because Distribute Columns applies to a subset of the columns, it can produce variable results.

**Take Note** It's possible to evenly distribute only the data cells in our table—in which case the headings will be out of sync with the data columns. Reverting to AutoFit Contents will fix this error.

6 Choose **File > Save** or press **Ctrl+S** to save your work.

It's worth mentioning one last table text formatting option: Fit Text, which is enabled from the Table Properties dialog box, Cell tab, behind the Options button. Enabling Fit Text will fix the cell's size, and progressively squash or stretch the text to fit inside it. As you can see from Figure 5-16, it tends to adversely affect readability, which is occasionally necessary to fit data to a table's structure.

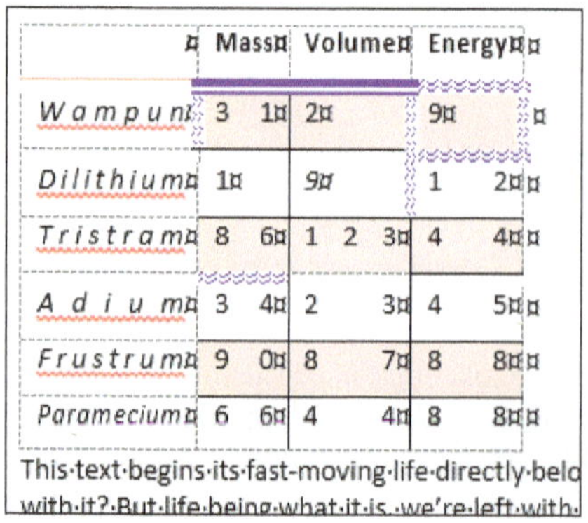


**Figure 5-16**

Using Fit Text forces the contents of a cell to squash and stretch.

## Images in tables

Images in tables behave exactly like images outside of tables. You can even drag an image in and out of a table as if moving it around the page's object layer. To avoid complications, always choose the In Line with Text layout option (enabled by default when you Insert Image).

## What you learned in this lesson:

- Insert and Navigate Tables
- Split and Merge Cells
- Integrate Tables into Paragraphs
- Position Text Within a Table
- Manipulate Columns and Rows
- Sort Tabular Data
- Use Table Styles
- Customize Cell and Table Borders
- Resize Cells and Cell Content

# Knowledge Assessment

### Matching

**Match the function or document element in numbers 1 to 10 to its description in letters a to j.**

1. row
2. Eraser tool
3. AutoFit width
4. Border Painter
5. list
6. column
7. fill
8. Tooltip
9. split cells
10. matrix

a 3x3 specimen would start with nine cells
b. in databases this corresponds to one field in a record
c. pattern, color, or image in a cell's background
d. sortable table of one or more columns
e. in-place help and keyboard shortcut information
f. horizontal cell array
g. adds additional rows/columns within a table region
h. stretches cell border rather than cutting off text
i. drag across inner borders to merge cells
j. subdivides cells as lines are drawn in

### True/False

**Circle T if the statement is true or F is the statement is false.**

T F 1. A 4x4 table with a header row and no split cells will contain 12 data cells.

T F 2. Nested tables automatically share Table Styles.

T F 3. The least visually complex Table Style is a Grid style.

T F 4. A descending alphabetical sort will place periwinkle before quiet.

T F 5. To select an entire column, click the top of the header cell.

T F 6. The Split Cells command creates a new nested table within the original, outer table.

T F 7. The Insert > Table command brings up a dialog box to set the size of the new empty table.

T F 8. "Erasing" the border between two cells creates an invisible border in its place.

T F 9. To position text dead center in a cell, select both Center and Align Middle layout options.

T F 10. Like images, tables are floating objects that can be absolutely positioned on the page.

## Competency Assessment

### Project 5-1: Inserting a Table into a Document

**In this exercise you'll add tables to a Word document and work with the text within and around them.**

1. Open the project files **table-source** and **table-text-source.**
2. Create a new blank document and save it in the working directory as **project_5-1_inserting_table**.
3. Copy the text from **table-text-source** to your project file.
4. Click the selection handle on the first table in **table-source** and copy the entire table, then paste it directly to the right of the words "Price List" in the project file.
5. Right click the handle on the pasted table and select **Table Properties...**
6. Select **Right** alignment and word wrap **Around** the table, and click **OK**.
7. Use the lower right resizing handle on the table and make it as small as you can.
8. Use similar techniques to steps 3-6 and paste the second table from table-text-source next to the "Contact Information" section, with **Left** alignment. You may need to drag the table downward to position it properly.
9. Close the two source files.
10. Save your work and close the file.

### Project 5-2: Merging and Splitting Cells

**This exercise asks you to alter the structure of a table by merging and splitting cells.**

1. Open the project file **5-2-source**. Save your document as **project_5-2_merge_split**.
2. Select the "**adult size, 0 degrees**" cell in the first table and click Table **Tools > Layout > Split Cells**.
3. In the dialog box, select **1** row and **2** columns. Click **OK**.
4. In the newly added cell, type **adult size, 32 degrees (summer).**
5. Add the word **(winter)** to the cell you split in step 2.
6. Click and drag to select the Director and Consiglieri cells in the second table. Merge the two cells.

7. Change the merged cell's text to Co-Directors, then click Table Tools > Layout > Alignment > Center.
8. Save your work and close the file.

# Proficiency Assessment

## Project 5-3: Using Table Styles

**In this exercise, customize the presentation of tabular data with Table Styles and Options.**

1. Open the project file 5-3-source. Save your document as project_5-3_table_styles.
2. Assign the equipment table a Table Style from the fourth row of the Table Styles gallery's Grid Styles section.
3. Select only the following Table Style Options: Header Row, Banded Columns, Last Column.
4. Select an appropriate Table Style and Options for the second table – remember that it has no header row.
5. Save your work and close the file.

## Project 5-4: Sorting List Entries

**In this exercise you'll sort data within a table, and alter a table to make sorting easier.**

1. Open the project file 5-4-source. Save your document as project_5-4_sorting.
2. Sort the two tables on the page by selecting each in turn and using the Table Tools > Layout > Data > Sort command: sort the equipment list in descending order of price, and alphabetize the names on the contact list.
3. If you are prevented from carrying out step 2, make a small change to each table first in order to facilitate sorting – merging or splitting cells in each table – then correct the data after sorting.
4. Save your work and ("CLOSE") the file.

# Mastery Assessment

## Project 5-5: Using Draw Table and the Border Painter

**In this exercise you'll design a variant tic-tac-toe board in which the center cell is claimed by whichever player wins a mini-game of tic-tac-toe within that cell.**

1. Create a new blank document. Save your document as project_5-5_drawing.
2. Draw a tic-tac-toe board using the Draw Table, Border Painter, and Eraser tools.
3. Then embed a copy of the complete tic-tac-toe table into the center cell of the original table.
4. Format the cells for visibility of the Xs and Os.
5. Save your work and close the file.

## Project 5-6: Laying Out Images in a Table

**In this exercise you'll create a "mosaic" using a table to lay out gridded images in a document.**

1. Open the project file **5-4-source** (again). Save your document as **project_5-6_images**.
2. Design a background "mosaic" for the document using a table and fill each cell of the table with a camping-themed image. Use the "Washout" Color effect (**Picture Tools > Format > Color**) to make the different cell images fade into the background as much as possible.
3. Save your work and **close** Word.

# Microsoft Excel 2013

# 1 Getting Started with Excel 2013

## LESSON SKILL MATRIX

**In this lesson, you will learn the following skills:**

| | |
|---|---|
| Getting to Know the Workspace | Using the Quick Access Toolbar |
| Getting to Know the Cell Pointer | Using the Formula Bar |
| Using the Ribbon | Moving Around the Worksheet |
| Exploring the Status Bar | Exploring What's New in Excel 2013 |

## KEY TERMS

- **Workbooks**
- **Worksheet**
- **Columns**
- **Rows**
- **Ribbon**
- **Status bar**
- **Quick access toolbar**
- **Quick analysis**
- **Sparklines**
- **Flash fill**
- **Slicers**

©catenarymedia/iStockPhoto

The accounting department of Fabrikam, Inc. needs to track revenue and expenses for the entire firm and maintain a large volume of employee data. It's also responsible for creating revenue projections and visualizations for the other departments within the firm. Microsoft Excel is an ideal tool for organizing and analyzing such data. In this lesson, you will learn how to enter text and numbers into an Excel worksheet to keep up-to-date employee records.

## SOFTWARE ORIENTATION

This lesson provides you with an introduction to many of the essential tools and capabilities you'll need to use when working in Microsoft Excel.

**Figure 1-1**

The Microsoft Excel interface.

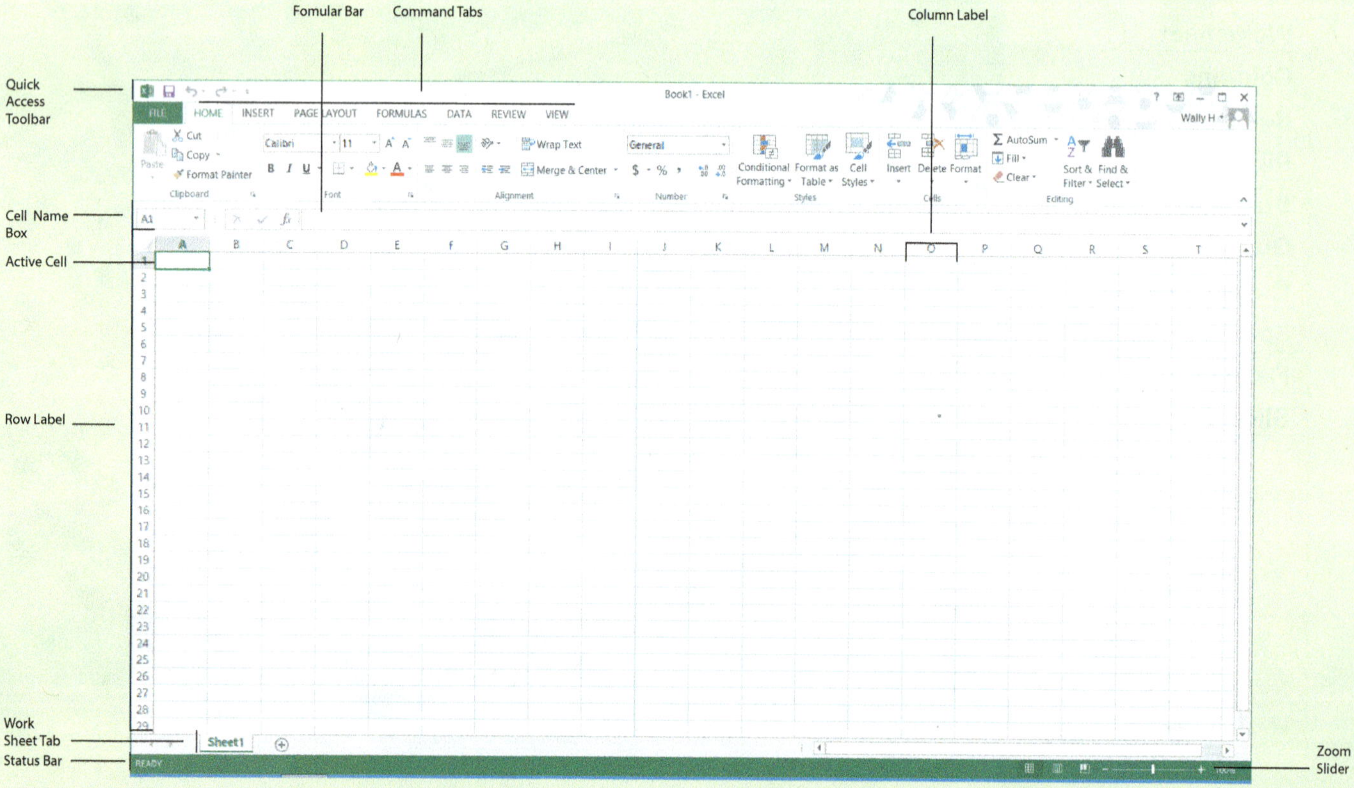

## STARTING UP

In this lesson, you'll work with several files from the Excel01lessons folder. Make sure that you have loaded the OfficeLessons folder onto your computer.

## GETTING TO KNOW THE WORKSPACE

In Microsoft Excel, files are called **workbooks**. In Excel 2013, you can create a new, blank workbook or select from a set of predesigned workbook templates that enable you to quickly get to work. Templates exist for budgets, invoices, lists, reports, and much more. Templates are discussed in greater detail In Lesson 7, "Working with Excel 2013 Templates."

When you create a new file, a blank workbook containing a single **worksheet** is displayed (Figure 1-2). A workbook consists of individual worksheets, each capable of containing its own set of data. By default, each workbook you create contains a single worksheet although a workbook can contain as many as 256 separate worksheets. At the bottom of each worksheet is a tab initially named Sheet1. You can easily rename worksheets by double-clicking the tab and typing the name you wish to use.

**Figure 1-2**

A. Status Bar. B. Row. C. Cell. D. Ribbon Bar. E. Name Box. F. Column. G. Formula Bar.

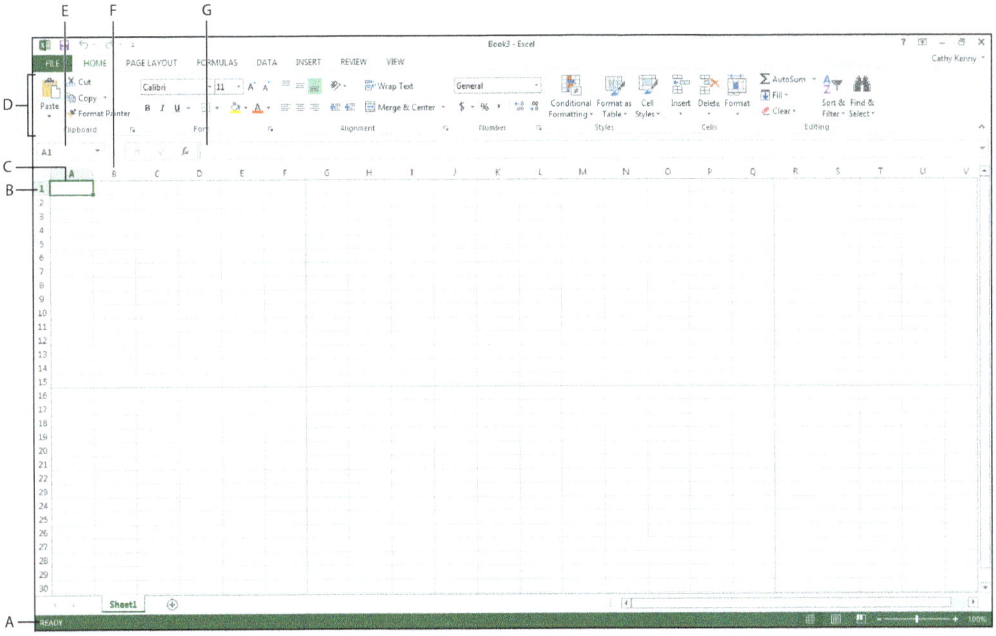


An Excel worksheet is constructed of **columns** and **rows** and is similar in appearance to a grid or bookkeeping ledger. Column headings are arranged along the top of the worksheet window and are labeled alphabetically. Row headings are displayed down the left edge of the worksheet window and are listed numerically.

The basic unit of a worksheet is the **cell**, formed by the intersection of a row and column. Every cell has a cell address named for that intersection, such as A4 or G11. When you click a wcell, the column and row headings appear highlighted, indicating the cell's address. The cell address also appears in the Name box, located just above column A.

**Bottom Line**

To work efficiently in Excel, you need to become familiar with its primary user interface. Knowing your toolkit will let you work more efficiently, and get to work more quickly.

## STEP BY STEP Opening an Excel document

1 Launch Microsoft Excel and see the Backstage view (Figure 1-3).

**Figure 1-3**

The Backstage displays the files you have recently opened.

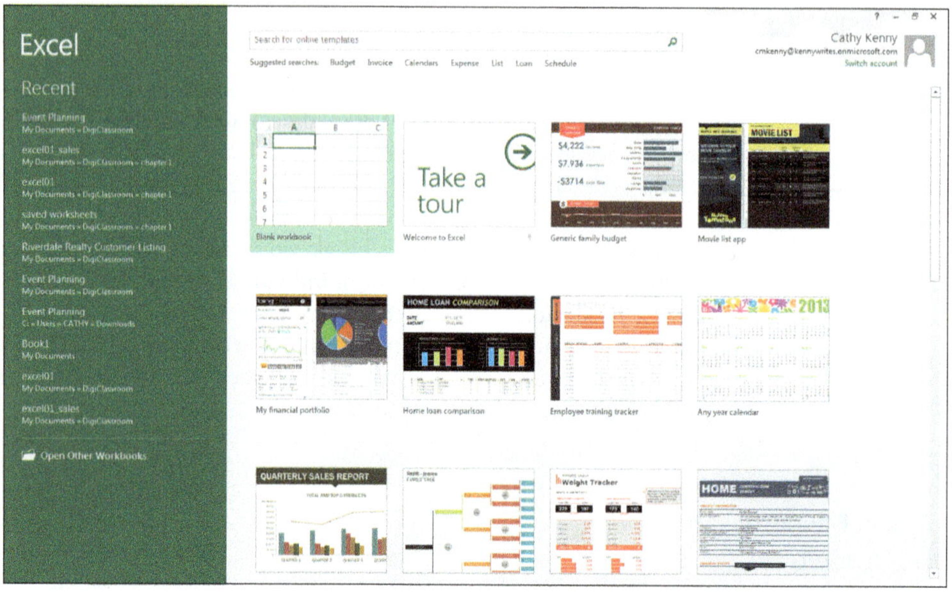


*Templates used with permission of Microsoft*

2 Choose **Open Other Workbooks from the Backstage**.

3 Navigate to the Excel01lessons folder and double-click **excel01**. An Excel document opens to display a worksheet containing three different venue quotes for a fictitious event planning company as shown in Figure 1-4.

**Figure 1-4**

The file named excel01 contains three different pricing quotes for a fictitious events planner.

| | A | B | C | D | E | F | G | H | I | J | K | L | M |
|---|---|---|---|---|---|---|---|---|---|---|---|---|---|
| 1 | Northwind Traders Events | | | | | | | | | | | | |
| 2 | Event | McGrath-Jameson Wedding | | | | | | | | | | | |
| 3 | Date | 6/12/2013 | | | | | | | | | | | |
| 4 | | | | | | | | | | | | | |
| 5 | | | | | | | | | | | | | |
| 6 | | Sapphire Ballroom | | | | Plaza Hotel | | | | Henderson's on the Bay | | | |
| 7 | | Unit Price | Person | Total | | Unit Price | Person | Total | | Unit Price | Person | Total | |
| 8 | Cocktail Hour | | | | | | | | | | | | |
| 9 | Cheese/Crackers | 3.95 | 100 | 395.00 | | 4.50 | 100 | 450.00 | | 4.00 | 100 | 400.00 | |
| 10 | Crudites | 3.95 | 100 | 395.00 | | 4.50 | 100 | 450.00 | | 4.00 | 100 | 400.00 | |
| 11 | Fruit Platter | 2.95 | 100 | 295.00 | | 3.95 | 100 | 395.00 | | 3.25 | 100 | 325.00 | |
| 12 | Dinner | | | | | | | | | | | | |
| 13 | Ceasar Salad | 2.50 | 200 | 500.00 | | 4.00 | 200 | 800.00 | | 3.25 | 200 | 650.00 | |
| 14 | Antipasto | 5.95 | 100 | 595.00 | | 7.95 | 100 | 795.00 | | 6.00 | 100 | 600.00 | |
| 15 | Pasta | 5.75 | 200 | 1150.00 | | 7.25 | 200 | 1450.00 | | 6.50 | 200 | 1300.00 | |
| 16 | Beef | 550 | 2 | 1100.00 | | 750 | 2 | 1500.00 | | 625 | 2 | 1250.00 | |
| 17 | Turkey | 200 | 3 | 600.00 | | 550 | 3 | 1650.00 | | 425 | 3 | 1275.00 | |
| 18 | Ham | 195 | 3 | 585.00 | | 425 | 3 | 1275.00 | | 375 | 3 | 1125.00 | |
| 19 | Potatoes/Veg | 2.00 | 200 | 400.00 | | 4.00 | 200 | 800.00 | | 3.50 | 200 | 700.00 | |
| 20 | Coffee | 32.00 | 6 | 192.00 | | 50.00 | 6 | 300.00 | | 40.00 | 6 | 240.00 | |
| 21 | Subtotal | | | $ 6,207.00 | | | | $ 9,865.00 | | | | $ 8,265.00 | |
| 22 | 18% Admin | | | 1117.26 | | | | 1775.70 | | | | 1487.70 | |
| 23 | Subtotal | | | $ 7,324.26 | | | | $ 11,640.70 | | | | $ 9,752.70 | |
| 24 | 6.25% Meal Tax | | | 457.77 | | | | 727.54 | | | | 609.54 | |
| 25 | Grand Total | | | $ 7,782.03 | | | | $ 12,368.24 | | | | $ 10,362.24 | |
| 26 | | | | | | | | | | | | | |
| 27 | | | | | | | | | | | | | |

4 Choose **File > Save As** and navigate to the Excel01lessons folder. Name the file **excel01_work** and click **Save**.

## GETTING TO KNOW THE CELL POINTER

Before we begin exploring the Excel workspace, it helps to get to know the mouse pointer as it takes many different forms in Excel. The pointer appears as the familiar arrow when you are choosing commands. When you move the mouse pointer within the worksheet area the mouse pointer changes its shape to that of a plus sign. As you enter data in a cell, the mouse pointer takes the shape of a cursor.

Since the mouse pointer takes so many different forms depending on the task you are performing it helps to take a moment to review the most basic shapes. The table below describes the mouse pointer shapes in more detail.

**Mouse pointer shapes**

| SHAPE | ACTION |
|---|---|
|  | Choose a command |
|  | Select a cell |
|  | Enter or edit data in a cell |
|  | Extend a selection with the AutoFill handle |
|  | Resize columns and rows |
|  | Click to select the current row. |
|  | Click to select the current column. |

## USING THE RIBBON

**Bottom Line**

The **Ribbon**, which runs along the top of the worksheet window, contains context-sensitive tools and commands to help you organize, calculate, and format your data. It is made up of a series of named tabs, each of which contains a set of related commands. For instance, the Home tab contains a set of frequently-used commands such as Copy and Paste. The names of the tabs are Home, Insert, Page Layout, Formulas, Data, Review, and View. Additional tabs are also displayed when working Charts, Images, and PivotTables.

**Figure 1-5**

Use the Ribbon to choose commands.

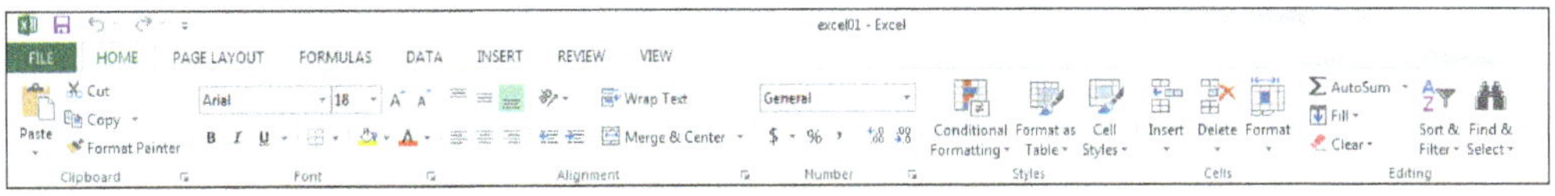

The table below describes the options on the Ribbon in more detail.

| TAB | DESCRIPTION |
|---|---|
| Home | Contains commonly used commands such as format cells, copy and paste, text alignment, and number formats. |
| Insert | Commands that enable you to insert items into your worksheet including charts, images, text boxes, and SmartArt. |
| Page Layout | Contains commands that enable you to change the appearance of your printed page. You can set margins, apply themes, change the page orientation, and insert page breaks |
| Formulas | Contains function library and other commands related to performing calculations. |
| Data | Contains commands for managing lists of data. |
| Review | Contains commands such as Spell Checker, Grammar Checker, etc. |
| View | Commands that enable you to change the display of the worksheet window. |

## Customizing the Ribbon display

You can collapse the Ribbon, by clicking the Ribbon Display Options button located in the far right corner of the title bar, so that only the named tabs appear across the top of the worksheet window. When you need to choose a command, just click the tab to redisplay the Ribbon and its options. You can also choose to Auto-Hide the Ribbon when you need additional viewing space. When you click the top of the worksheet window the Ribbon is redisplayed.

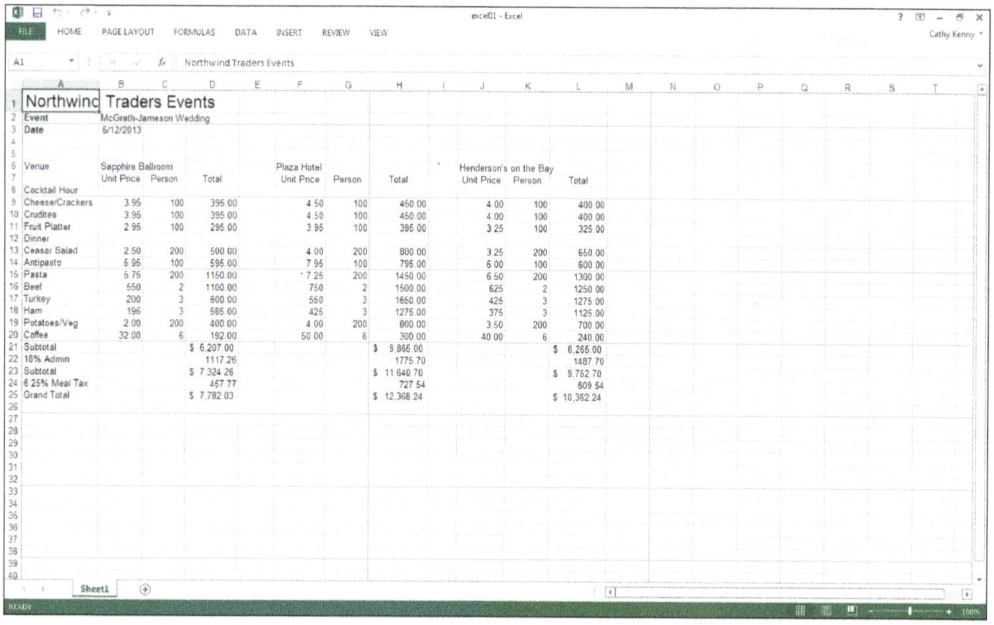

**Figure 1-6**

Collapse the Ribbon to display the named tabs only.

The table below describes the Ribbon Display Options found in the top-right corner of Excel.

| OPTION | ICON | WHAT IT DOES |
|---|---|---|
| **Auto-Hide Ribbon** |  | Hides the Ribbon. Click at the top of the Excel window to redisplay it. |
| **Show Tabs** |  | Display tabs only. Click a tab to redisplay the Ribbon. |
| **Show Tabs and Commands** |  | Displays both the Tabs and Commands at all times. |

## STEP BY STEP Collapsing the Ribbon

1 Click the **Ribbon Display Options** button.

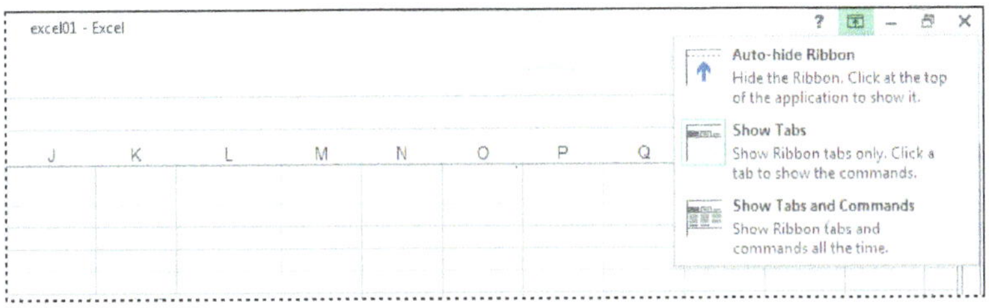


**Figure 1-7**

The Ribbon Display Options button allows you to alter the Ribbon's appearance.

2 Choose **Show Tabs** and then select cell **A1**.

3 Click the **Home** tab to redisplay the Ribbon and choose **Bold** in the Font group.

The Show Tabs command shows the tabs but doesn't display the Ribbon unless a specific tab is selected. Once a command is selected on the Ribbon or you click elsewhere on the worksheet, the Ribbon disappears.

## STEP BY STEP Hiding the Ribbon

1 Click the **Ribbon Display Options** button.

2 Choose **Auto-Hide Ribbon**.

3 Click the top of the Excel window to redisplay the Ribbon.

The Auto-Hide Ribbon command hides the Ribbon from view. When you click the top of the worksheet window, the Ribbon is redisplayed.

Once you choose a command or click elsewhere on the worksheet, the Ribbon disappears.

**Take Note** To quickly collapse the Ribbon, right-click anywhere within the Ribbon and choose Collapse the Ribbon.

## EXPLORING THE STATUS BAR

**Bottom Line**

The **Status bar** appears at the bottom of the worksheet window and provides updates on the current worksheet. Messages appear in the lower left corner to tell you what a command does, or what you should do next, to execute a command. For instance, when entering data in a cell the

Status bar displays ENTER in the lower left corner.

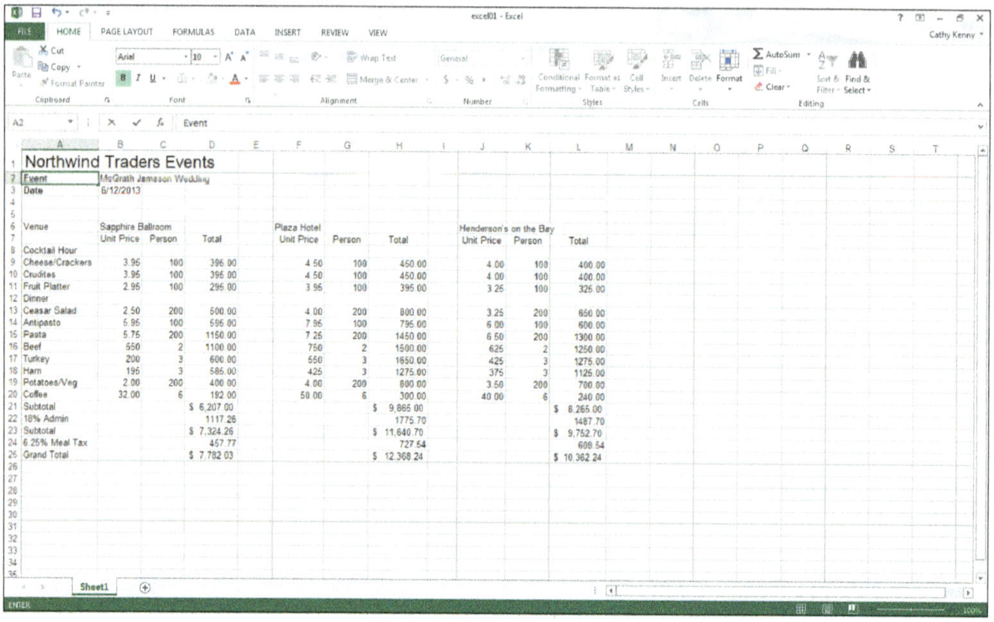


**Figure 1-8**

The Status bar displays the word ENTER when entering data in a cell.

The Status bar also contains a set of buttons that enable you to change the view of your worksheet. You can switch between Normal, Page Layout, and Page Break Preview modes. Using the Zoom slider, you can enlarge or reduce the size of the worksheet display.

## Switching display modes

The default viewing mode in Excel is the Normal mode, and it is primarily used when you are working with your data. There are times when you want to switch the display to see what your worksheet will look like when printed, or you may just want to view where the page breaks will occur, and you can use various display modes to see these things. You can quickly change the viewing mode of your worksheet by using the buttons in the Status bar. You'll learn more about printing in Lesson 2, "Creating a Worksheet in Excel 2013."

### STEP BY STEP Switching display modes

1 Switch to Page Layout mode by clicking the **Page Layout** button.

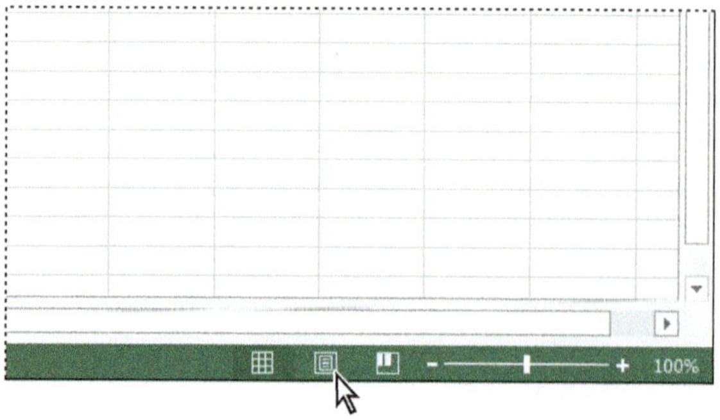


**Figure 1-9**

Choose the Page Layout mode.

2 Switch to Page Break Preview mode by clicking the **Page Break Preview** button.

3 Click **Normal** to return the regular viewing mode.

### Change the size of the worksheet display

You may need to change the size of your worksheet display, especially if you are working with data that extends beyond the visible area. Using the Zoom tool in the Status bar, you can quickly reduce or enlarge the worksheet display.

**Figure 1-10**

Change the size of your worksheet display by dragging the Zoom slider.

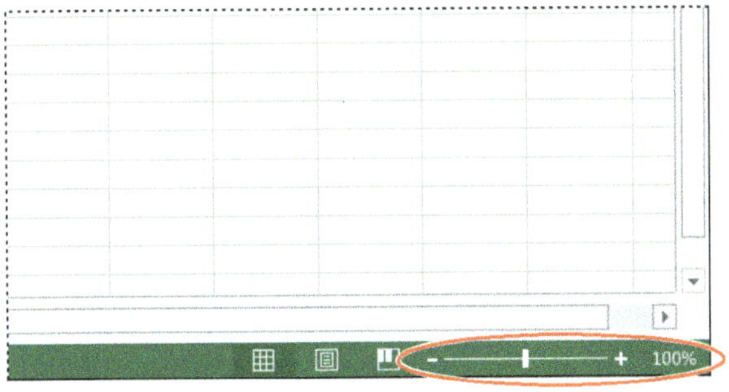


**STEP BY STEP** **Changing the size of the worksheet display**

1 Click and drag the **Zoom** slider to enlarge the display area to **125%**.

2 Drag the slider to **100%** to return the view to its original size.

## USING THE QUICK ACCESS TOOLBAR

**Bottom Line**

The **Quick Access Toolbar** is displayed at the top left of the Excel window and provides single-click access to frequently-used commands such as Save and Undo. You can customize the toolbar to add additional commands that you use frequently.

**STEP BY STEP** **Customizing the Quick Access Toolbar**

1 Click the **Customize Quick Access Toolbar** button.

**Figure 1-11**

Add your favorite commands to the Quick Access Toolbar to gain single-click access.

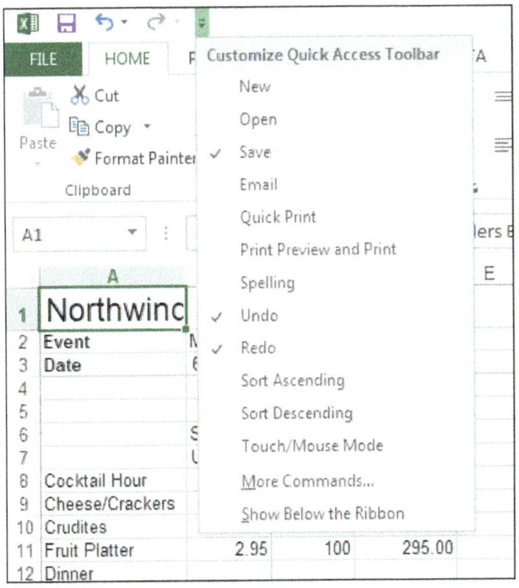

2 Click **New** to add the New command to the toolbar.

3 Click the **Customize Quick Access Toolbar** again and click **Open** to add the Open command to the toolbar.

## USING THE FORMULA BAR

**Bottom Line**

The Formula bar appears just below the Ribbon and displays the contents of the active cell. When you type data in a cell, the Formula bar activates and displays the data as you type.

### STEP BY STEP Using the Formula bar

1 Click in cell A6 and type **Venue**.

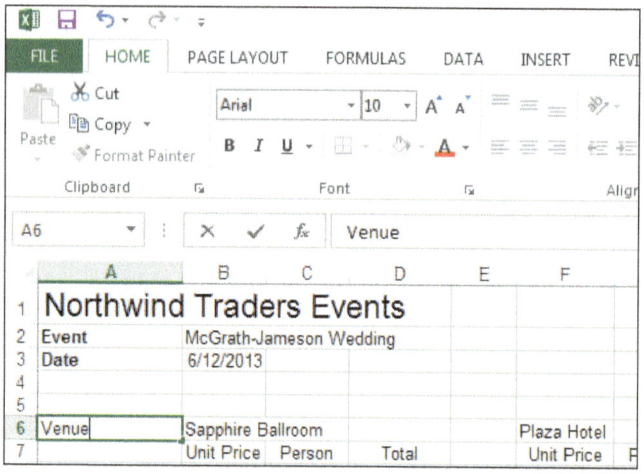


**Figure 1-12**
As you type, the data appears in the Formula bar.

Notice also the appearance of three buttons to the left of the Formula bar. These buttons enable you to confirm or cancel what you are entering or a Function within the cell. Formulas will be discussed in greater detail In Lesson 4, "Using Formulas in Excel 2013."

**The buttons in the Formula bar**

| BUTTON | ACTION |
|---|---|
| ✓ | Confirms the current entry. Equivalent to pressing Enter. |
| × | Cancels the current entry. Equivalent to pressing Esc. |
| fx | Opens the Insert Function dialog box. |

### STEP BY STEP Activating the Formula bar

1 Activate the cell by clicking it.

2 Move the mouse pointer to the Formula bar area.

3 When the cursor appears, click within the Formula bar to set the insertion point.

## MOVING AROUND THE WORKSHEET

The active cell in a worksheet always appears with a dark outlined border. To activate another cell using the mouse, move the mouse pointer to the cell you wish to use and click it. For example, you can click cell F13 to make it active.

**Bottom Line**

If you wish, you can navigate through an Excel worksheet using only its wide variety of keyboard commands, but the mouse remains an option for selecting cells and regions.

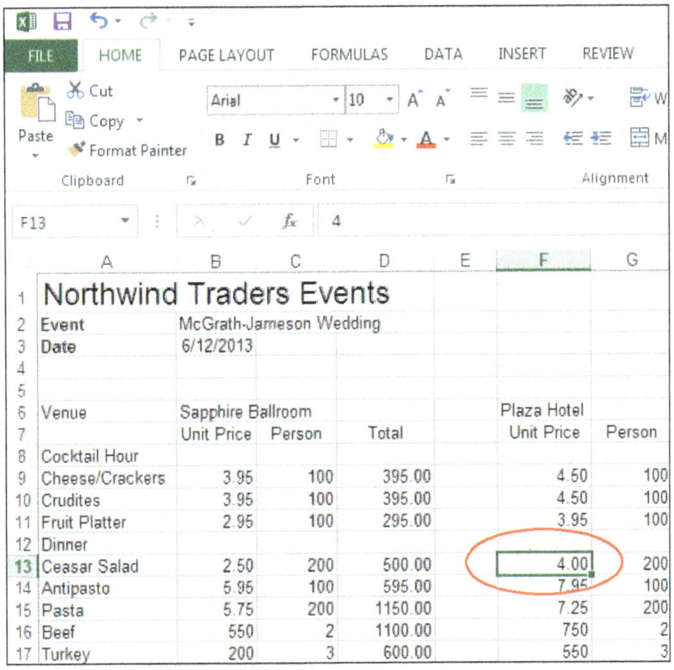


**Figure 1-13**

The active cell in a worksheet appears with an outlined border.

You can also move the cell pointer around the worksheet by using the keyboard. The table below discusses the keys for navigating the worksheet with the keyboard.

## Navigating the worksheet with the keyboard

| KEY | MOVEMENT |
|---|---|
| Up, Down, Left, Right | Moves one cell to the left, right, up or down |
| Ctrl Up, Down, Left, Right | Moves to the next cell of data separated by a blank cell |
| Tab | Moves one cell to the right |
| Shift Tab | Moves one cell to the left |
| Home | Moves to the first cell in the row |
| Ctrl + Home | Moves to cell A1 |
| End + Left | Moves to the next non-blank cell to the left |
| End + Right | Moves to the next non-blank cell to the right |
| End + Up | Moves to the next non-blank cell above. |
| End + Down | Moves to the next non-blank cell below. |
| Ctrl + End | Moves to the last cell containing data |
| PgUp | Moves up one screen |
| PgDn | Moves down one screen |
| Ctrl + PgUp | Moves to the next worksheet |
| Ctrl + PgDn | Moves to the previous worksheet |

## Moving to a specific cell

You can quickly move to a specific cell within a worksheet by typing the cell address in the Name box that appears to the left of the Formula bar.

**STEP BY STEP** **Moving to a specific cell**

1 Click the **Name** box.

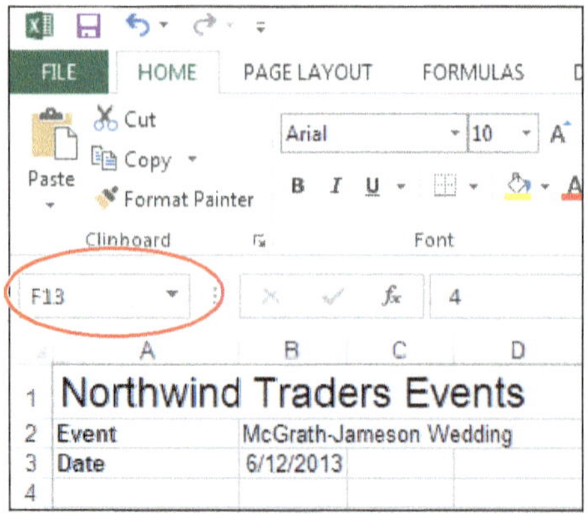


**Figure 1-14**
To quickly move to a specific cell, type the cell address in the Name box.

2 Type **D11** and press **Enter** or **Return** on your keyboard to move to cell D11.

## Using the scroll bars

The scroll bars, located along the right edge and bottom of your worksheet window, offer the quickest way to navigate a worksheet with the mouse or touch screen. Each scroll bar consists of a scroll box, scroll arrows, and the scroll bar. The scroll box, located within the scroll bar, changes size depending on where you are in the worksheet. When you are at cell A1, the scroll box fills the entire scroll bar. As you drag the bar further away from A1, the scroll box decreases in size.

**Figure 1-15**

A. Scroll Arrow. B. Scroll Box. C. Scroll Bar.

## EXPLORING WHAT'S NEW IN EXCEL 2013

Microsoft has been busy adding new features designed to help you display your data visually, and has provided you with a new streamlined interface. Let's take a quick look at some of the new features Excel 2013 has to offer.

## Templates help you get started right away

Excel's Backstage view, which appears whenever you launch Excel or choose File > New, displays a set of professionally designed worksheet templates. When you create a worksheet from a template, you need only plug in your data and the worksheet will update automatically.

**Figure 1-16**

Excel's Templates take the design-work out of your hands and let you get started immediately.

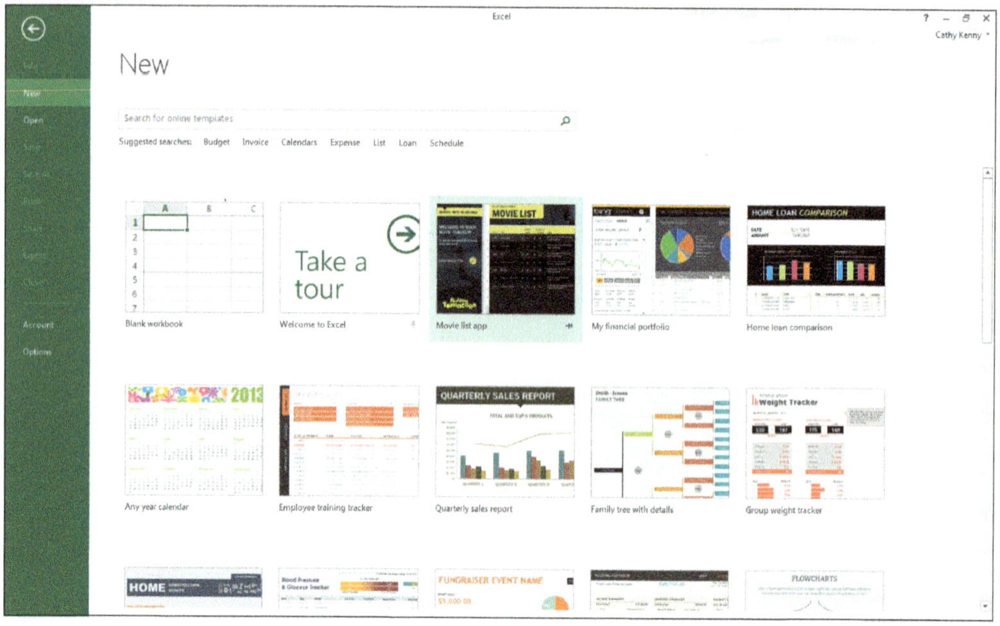


*Templates used with permission of Microsoft*

Excel offers thousands of template choices to help you get up and running. From Invoices and Budgets, to Sales Reports and Cash Flow Statements, Excel has templates for virtually every type of business or organizational need. There are also a wide assortment of personal templates, such as a Home Construction Budget, a Group Weight Loss Tracker, and the ability to keep track of your movie collection with the Movies List. Excel also makes it easy to search through thousands of online templates with its built in Search box. For more information on using Excel's templates, see Lesson 7, "Working with Excel 2013 Templates."

## Quick analysis gets down to business

With the new **Quick Analysis** button, you can instantly produce visual snapshots of your data. After selecting a range of data, click the Quick Analysis Button and choose from the selected options. Add special Formatting, create a quick Chart, add a line of Totals, produce a PivotTable, or add **Sparklines**. For more information on the Quick Analysis Tools, see Lesson 8, "Advanced Data Analysis in Excel 2013."

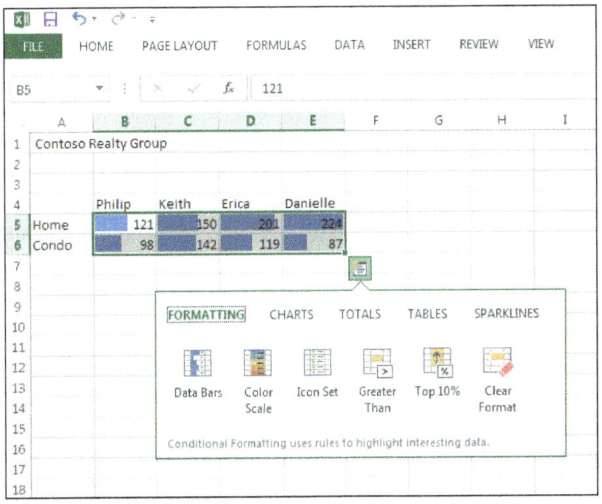


**Figure 1-17**

Get a quick visual of your data with the new Quick Analysis tools.

## Flash Fill reduces data entry drudgery

One of the more tedious aspects of working with a program like Excel is that before you can analyze your data, you first have to enter it into your worksheet. Excel 2013 introduces **Flash Fill**, which aims to reduce the drudgery that is data entry. As you enter data, Excel analyzes the data for any patterns that may exist and if it detects any, fills the rest of the Information for you. For more information on using Flash Fill, see Lesson 6, "Working with Data."

**Figure 1-18**

Excel aims to reduce data entry time by anticipating patterns and filling the remainder in for you.

## Chart recommendations remove the guesswork

Not sure which chart type is the best fit for your data and the message you want to convey? With Excel's new Chart recommendations, you needn't ever second guess yourself again. Just select the data you want to chart and choose Recommended Chart's, from the Insert tab. Excel will recommend a set of charts based on your data. For more Information on charts, see Lesson 5, "Working with Charts."

**Figure 1-19**

Use Chart Recommendations when you are not sure which chart type best suits your data.

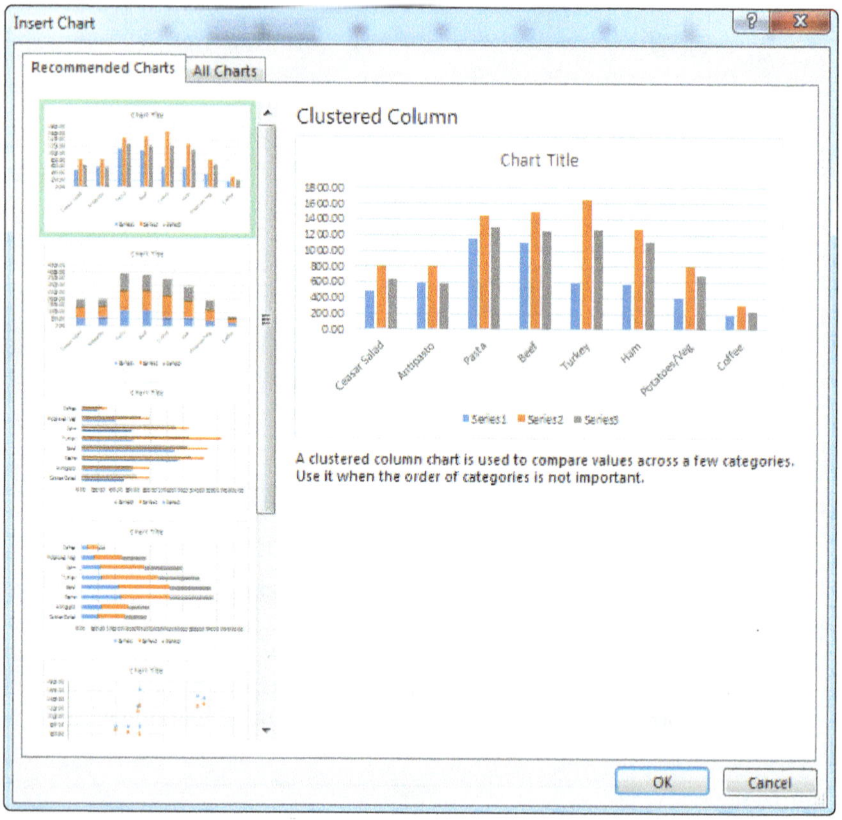

## Filter your data with slicers

You can use **slicers** to filter your data using more than one value. The slicer is built-in to the Table feature and an icon is displayed to let you know when your data has been filtered. To learn more about Data Slicers, see Lesson 8, "Advanced Data Analysis in Excel 2013." While the slicer functionality first appeared in Office 2010, it has been streamlined significantly for Office 2013.

**Figure 1-20**

Filter your data on multiple values using the new Data Slicers.

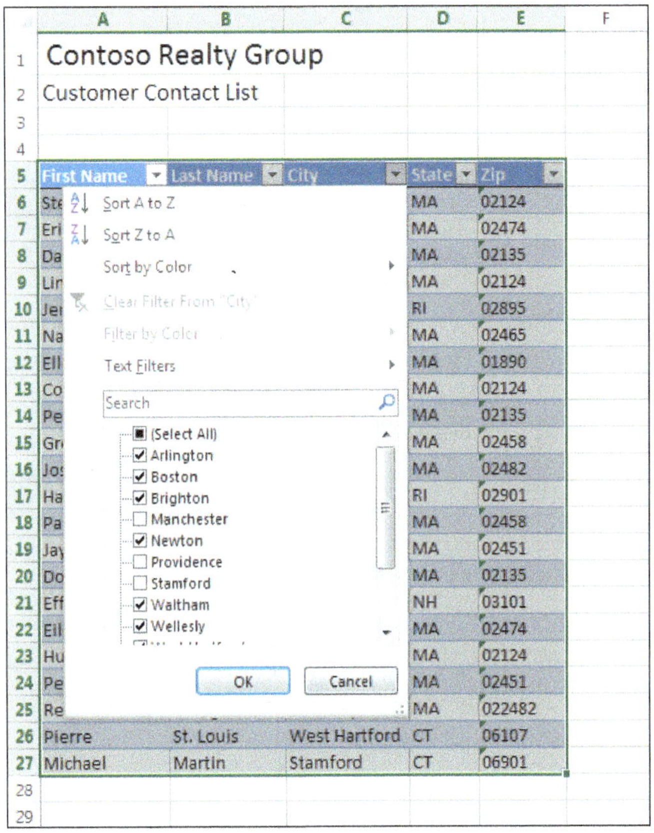


You've now completed this lesson. Now that you are familiar with the workspace in Excel, you are ready to begin creating new worksheets and working with your data.

## What you learned in this lesson:

- Getting to Know the Workspace
- Getting to Know the Cell Pointer
- Using the Ribbon
- Exploring the Status Bar
- Using the Quick Access Toolbar
- Using the Formula Bar
- Moving Around the Worksheet
- Exploring What's New in Excel 2013

# Lesson 1 Knowledge Assessment

## Fill in the Blank

**Complete the following sentences by writing the correct word or words in the blanks provided.**

1. Excel files are also known as ________.
2. Excel's commands are organized by topic in the ________.
3. The ________ can be customized with often-used commands like Quick Print.
4. Data can be entered directly into a cell, or into the ________.
5. The ________ view appears whenever you launch Excel.
6. Excel's new ________ tool will analyze your data for patterns and attempt to fill in the rest of your information.
7. To jump to a specific cell in the worksheet, enter its address in the ________.
8. When you mouse over the row number at the left of the screen, the pointer changes to a ________.
9. Rows are labeled numerically; columns are labeled ________.
10. Pre-formatted Excel documents can be downloaded through the ________ Gallery.

## True/False

**Circle T if the statement is true or F it the statement is false.**

T F 1. Every Excel command can be accessed from the Home tab.
T F 2. Workbooks can contain multiple worksheets.
T F 3. To add charts and images to a worksheet, use the View tab.
T F 4. The zoom slider is located within the Status Bar.
T F 5. Cell M4 is located directly below cell L4.
T F 6. A new, blank Excel file contains two workbooks holding two worksheets each.
T F 7. When you input data in a cell, the Status Bar displays the word ENTER.
T F 8. A command like "add cells F5 and F6 and display the result here" is called a function.
T F 9. Pressing the Home button moves the cursor to the top left cell.
T F 10. As you type data into a cell, it also appears in the Address bar.

# Competency Assessment

## Project 1-1: Creating and Saving a Workbook

**Use this exercise to familiarize yourself with the Save function and Backstage view.**

1. Launch Excel if it is not already open and create a new document by selecting **Blank workbook** from the launch screen, or pressing **Ctrl+N**.
2. Add two worksheets (Sheets 2 and 3) by clicking the ⊕ symbol at the bottom of the Excel window.
3. Click in cell A1 and drag to C3 to select nine cells.
4. In the Font group of the Home tab, click the **paint bucket** icon to change the color of the selected cells.

5. Click the **File** tab to open the Backstage view, then select **Save**. Note that "Save As" remains highlighted.
6. In the left column, select **Computer**. Then click **Browse**.
7. Browse to the Excel01lessons folder on your computer.
8. In the File name: text area, type **1_1**. Click the **Save as type**: drop-down to view the many save formats available in Excel 2013.
9. Select **Excel Workbook** from the Save as type: drop-down and click **Save**.
10. Close the workbook.

## Project 1-2: Utilizing the Ribbon

**In this exercise you'll work with the Ribbon tabs.**

1. Open Excel and create a new blank document. (No need to save.)
2. Click the File tab (Backstage) and survey the file-management options available.
3. Press **Escape** to return to the main editing screen. Add a title to Slide 1, then select the new title text.
4. In the Home tab, expand the font gallery. Press **T** to jump down the font list. Choose **Times New Roman** and note the font change in the title box.
5. Select **Undo** from the Quick Access Toolbar (or press **Ctrl+Z**).
6. Experiment with commands in the Insert, Design, and other tabs.
7. Click **File > Exit**. When prompted, elect not to save the document.

# Proficiency Assessment

## Project 1-3: Entering Data

**You will create an Excel worksheet containing a list of items sold at a recent garage sale. Excel's tools for quick data entry speed up the process.**

1. Create a new workbook. Click the **File** tab, choose **Save**, navigate to Excel01lessons folder, and name the workbook **Sale_Items_1**.
2. In cell A1, type **Item**. Press **Tab**.
3. In cell B1, type **Cost**. Press **Tab**.
4. In cell C1, type **Quantity**. Press **Tab**.
5. In cell D1, type **Total Cost**. Press **Return** to move the cursor to A2.
6. Type each of the following item names and press **Return** after each: **sneakers**, **shirt (L)**, **shirt (S)**, **books**. The last entry will appear in A5.
7. Click in B2, type **$5**, and press **Return**.
8. Type **$2**, then click on the small handle at the lower right of the selected cell, called the AutoFill handle, and drag it down to B5. All three cells will display $2.
9. Click in cell C2, then click in the Formula bar and type **2**.
10. Hit **Return**. Type the following values, hitting **Return** after each one: **1**, **3**, **10**.
11. Save the file and close the workbook.

### Project 1-4: Editing and Extending a Workbook

**In this exercise, you will add formulas to the previously created workbook.**

1. Click the **File** tab. A list of recent locations and documents will appear. Under Recent Workbooks, select **Sale_Items_1**.
2. Select cell **D2**. In the Formula bar, type **=product(** but do not press Return.
3. Click and drag from B2 to C2 to select those cells. The Formula bar now reads =product(B2:C2.
4. Press **Return**. Cell D3 is selected, and D2 displays the number 10.
5. Click cell D2 and drag its AutoFill handle down to D5. The column fills with numbers representing total sales cost: 2, 6, and 20.
6. Click cell **B4** and type **5**, then press **Return**. The values in B4 and D4 will update.
7. Choose **Save As** and name the file **Sales_Items_2**. Close the file.
8. Leave Excel open for the next exercise.

## Mastery Assessment

### Project 1-5: Using Display Modes

1. Hit **Ctrl+N** to create a new file.
2. In cell A1, type **Sample entry 1**.
3. Drag its AutoFill handle down to populate the first 60 cells of column A.
4. Open the View tab and click **Page Layout**. Note that Excel fills up the entire first page with dozens of rows before breaking for page 2.
5. Select **Page Break Preview**. Drag the blue dotted line, which indicates a page break, up to roughly row 10.
6. Reselect **Page Layout**. Excel has moved the page break to its new location.
7. Press **Ctrl+W** to close the document. When prompted to save, select **Don't Save**. Leave Excel open for the next exercise.

### Project 1-6: Customizing the Quick Access Toolbar

1. Click the arrow on the Quick Access Toolbar to open the Customize Quick Access Toolbar drop-down menu.
2. Select **Sort Ascending** from the menu.
3. Reopen the dropdown menu and select **More Commands...**
4. From the left-hand list, select **Create Chart** and click **Add>>**.
5. Click **Customizations: Reset** and select **Reset only Quick Access Toolbar**. Click **Yes** at the prompt, then click **OK**.
6. Close Excel.

# 2 Creating a Worksheet in Excel 2013

## LESSON SKILL MATRIX

**In this lesson, you will learn the following skills:**

- Creating a Worksheet
- Entering Data in a Cell
- Working with Cell Ranges
- Saving Workbooks
- Opening Workbooks
- Editing Data
- Using Undo/Redo
- Working with Rows and Columns
- Creating Additional Worksheets
- Printing Worksheets and Workbooks

## KEY TERMS

- **AutoFill**
- **AutoSum**
- **Cell Address**
- **Copy**
- **Cut**
- **Footer**
- **Formula**
- **Freeze (row or column)**
- **Handle**
- **Header**
- **Operator**
- **Page Layout Mode**
- **Page Orientation (portrait, landscape)**
- **Paste**
- **Print Area**
- **Range**

©LawrenceSawyer/ iStockPhoto

The staff at Contoso Partners are preparing a report on campaign contributions, broken down geographically and by age group. They lay out Excel documents that combine scratch data-entry spaces, complex calculations, and carefully sorted final numbers. Excel's data-entry and analysis tools, screen/print layout tools, and features like AutoSum and AutoFill let the staff build these complex documents quickly and efficiently.

## SOFTWARE ORIENTATION

Understanding how Microsoft Excel helps you organize and compute data saves you time while helping you to be more accurate in the work you perform.

**Figure 2-1**

New document workspace.

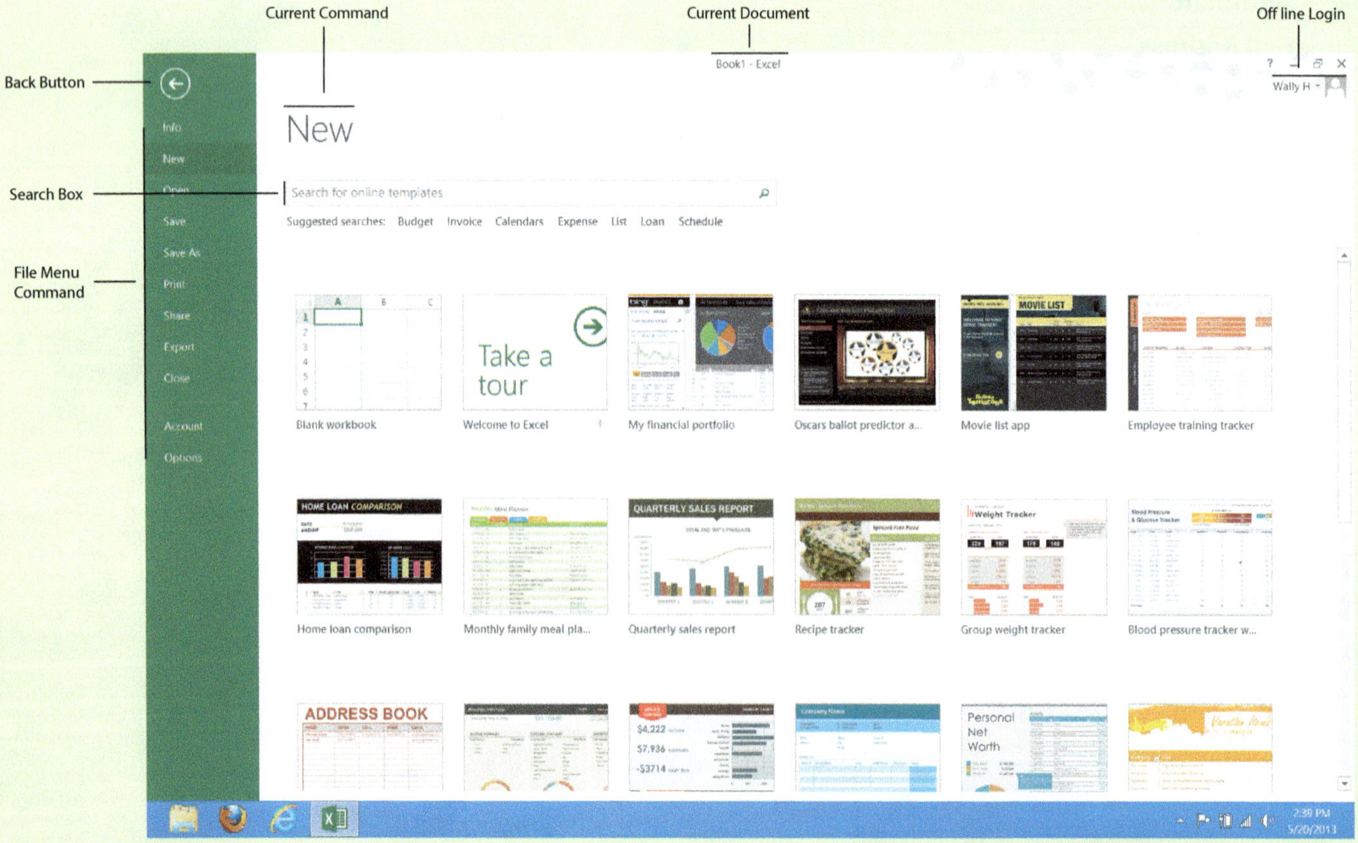


*Templates used with permission of Microsoft*

## STARTING UP

In this lesson, you'll work with several files from the Excel02lessons folder. Make sure that you have loaded the OfficeLessons folder onto your computer.

**Bottom Line**

## CREATING A WORKSHEET

In this first lesson, we will create a new blank workbook to practice some basic data entry skills.

**STEP BY STEP** **Creating a new workbook**

1 Launch Microsoft Excel.

2 Choose **Blank workbook** from the New Backstage (See Figure 2-2.).

**Figure 2-2**

Excel 2013 offers thousands of predesigned templates to choose from. Choose Blank Workbook to start from scratch.

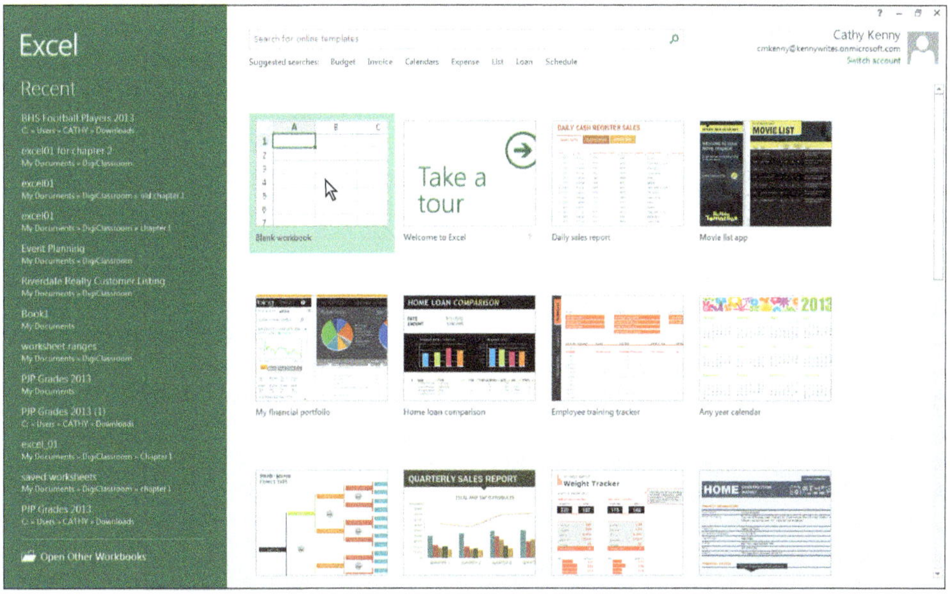


*Templates used with permission of Microsoft*

3 Excel opens a new window and displays a blank workbook containing a single worksheet.

**Bottom Line**

## ENTERING DATA IN A CELL

Entering data in Excel is fairly straightforward, once you understand a few simple concepts. Before you can enter data, you must first select the cell in which you want the data to appear. As discussed in Lesson 1, "Getting Started with Excel 2013," the active cell appears outlined and the cell pointer changes its shape to that of a plus sign when it is within the worksheet window. To select a cell, click it or use the arrow keys on your keyboard to move the cell pointer to that cell.

When you start typing, the data appears in both the active cell and in the Formula bar. You can enter text, numbers, dates, times, or formulas in a cell.

### Entering text

As you enter text within a cell, the text continues to be displayed in adjacent columns until it meets a non-blank cell. Although the text appears to be in more than one cell, it is contained within the active cell only. Note also that Excel aligns the text to the left edge of the cell border.

## STEP BY STEP Entering text in cells

1. Click cell **A1**.
2. Type **Contoso Realty Group** and press **Enter**.
3. In your Excel spreadsheet, enter the words shown in the right column (Type) into the cells indicated by the left column (Cell), as in Figure 2-3.

| Cell | Type |
|---|---|
| B4 | Philip |
| C4 | Keith |
| D4 | Erica |
| E4 | Danielle |
| A5 | House |
| A6 | Condo |
| A7 | Total |
| F4 | Total |

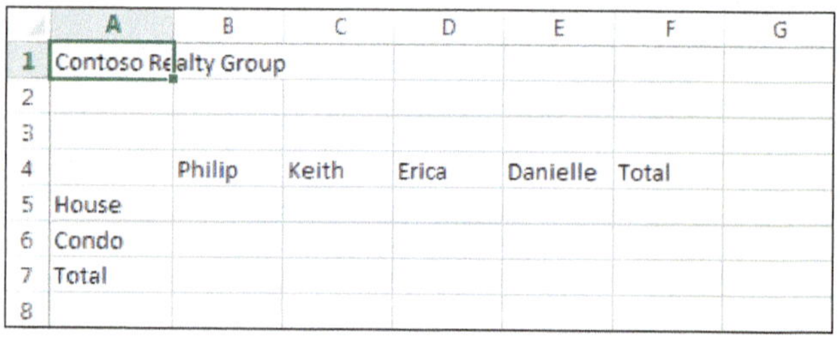


**Figure 2-3**
Use text to label the data in your worksheets.

### Entering numbers

When you type numbers or values in a cell, you can type them with or without accompanying symbols, such as commas, decimals, or dollar signs. You can format the cell after the fact to display the symbols that we discuss in Lesson 3, "Formatting Excel Worksheets." If you do enter the value with accompanying symbols, Excel automatically assigns the appropriate numeric format. In addition, Excel automatically aligns the values to the right side of the cell.

## STEP BY STEP Entering numbers in cells

1. Click cell **B5**.
2. Type **121** and press **Enter**.

3 In your Excel spreadsheet, enter the values shown in the right column (Type) into the cells indicated by the left column (Cell). The resulting table is shown in Figure 2-4.

| Cell | Type |
|---|---|
| B6 | 98 |
| C5 | 150 |
| C6 | 142 |
| D5 | 201 |
| D6 | 119 |
| E5 | 224 |
| E6 | 87 |

**Take Note** If you enter a large value, Excel displays the symbols ##### in the cell, indicating that the value is wider than the current column width

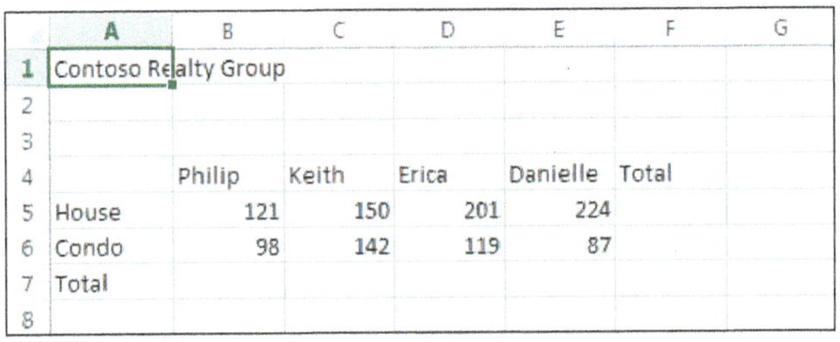

| | A | B | C | D | E | F | G |
|---|---|---|---|---|---|---|---|
| 1 | Contoso Realty Group | | | | | | |
| 2 | | | | | | | |
| 3 | | | | | | | |
| 4 | | Philip | Keith | Erica | Danielle | Total | |
| 5 | House | 121 | 150 | 201 | 224 | | |
| 6 | Condo | 98 | 142 | 119 | 87 | | |
| 7 | Total | | | | | | |
| 8 | | | | | | | |

**Figure 2-4**

Values appear right-aligned within a cell.

## Entering dates and times

Excel accepts a number of different formats for entering date and time values. You can enter dates and times with accompanying symbols, such as dashes (-), slashes (/), or colons (:) or type the entry as text, for example, March 30, 2013 or 12:15 PM. Excel recognizes any of these entries as a date or time and applies the appropriate date format.

**STEP BY STEP** **Entering numbers in cells**

1 Type 3/20/13 in cell A2.

2 Press Enter to enter the date.

**Take Note** To quickly enter Today's date, select a cell and press Ctrl+;.

## Entering formulas

The final type of data you can enter into Excel is a **formula**, which is a calculation using a combination of values and mathematical **operators**. Formulas must follow a particular syntax to be recognized by Excel, and they begin with the equal sign (=) followed by the values and operators. For example, the formula =750*34 multiplies the value 750 by 34. When you press Enter, Excel displays the result, or in this case, the product of the two values. Formulas will be discussed in greater detail in Lesson 4, "Using Formulas in Excel 2013."

If you don't want to enter fixed, specific values into your formula, you can enter the cell address of applicable values. When you use **cell addresses** in a formula, Excel refers to them as cell references, and uses whatever value is in the cell. If the value contained in the cell changes, Excel automatically updates the formula.

To perform quick calculations in Excel, you can use the **AutoSum** command. To use it, click in a cell directly adjacent to the values you want to summarize. Choose AutoSum from the Home tab and click the appropriate summarizing function. Excel automatically includes the range of cells above or to the left of the current cell in the calculation. Press Enter to complete the formula.

**STEP BY STEP**

### Using formulas

1 Click in cell B7.

2 Choose **AutoSum** from the Editing group in the Home tab, and click **Sum** from the resulting menu.

**AutoSum options**

| BUTTON | WHAT IT DOES |
|---|---|
| **Sum** | Sums the value of a range. |
| **Average** | Finds the average value in a range. |
| **Count Numbers** | Counts up the numbers in a range. |
| **Max** | Finds the maximum value. |
| **Min** | Finds the minimum value. |

Excel automatically selects cells B5 and B6, the values directly above the current cell.

3 Press **Enter** to calculate the sum.

4 Click in **F5**, choose **AutoSum** again, and click **Sum** from the resulting menu.

5 Excel automatically selects cells B5 through E5, the cells directly to the left of the current cell (see Figure 2-5).

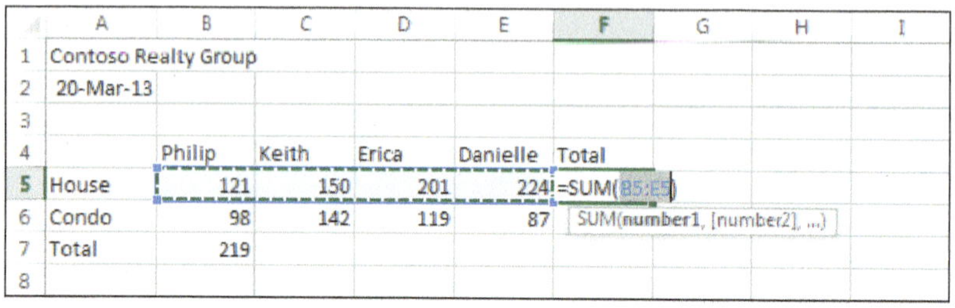


**Figure 2-5**

The AutoSum command selects the values in adjacent cells.

6 Press **Enter** to calculate the Total amount.

Rather than enter the same formula for columns C, D, and E, you can copy the formula instead.

When you do, Excel automatically updates the cell addresses in the formula to refer to the proper range of cells.

7. Click cell **B7** and choose **Copy** from the Home tab.
8. Click and drag from cell C7 to cell E7 and choose **Paste**. Excel calculates the total amounts for columns C, D, and E.
9. Click in cell F5, choose **Copy** from the Home tab, click and drag from cell F6 to F7 and choose **Paste**.

## WORKING WITH CELL RANGES

**Bottom Line**

Before you can use many of the features in Excel, you must first select the cells with which you want to work. Excel refers to a collection of selected cells as a range. Cell **ranges** are designated by first and last cell in the range, separated by a colon. For instance, a selection of cells spanning from A1 through cell G8 would be referred to as A1:G8.

When you select a range of cells, the selection appears highlighted and a dark border surrounds the entire range. Once you select a cell or range of cells, any command or action you perform affects the entire selection.

### Selecting a range of cells

The easiest way to select a range of cells is to click the first cell in the range and drag to the last cell in the range. You can also use the keyboard to select a range of cells. To do so, move to the first cell in the range, press and hold the Shift key, and move to the last cell in the range.

**STEP BY STEP** **Selecting a range of cells**

1. Click in cell A4, drag to cell F7 and release. The range is now selected.
2. Select cell **B5**, press and hold the **Shift** key, use the right arrow key to extend the selection to cell F5, and release the Shift key. This is another method of selecting a range of cells.

When you need to select more than one range of cells at a time that are not contiguous, you can use the Ctrl key.

## STEP BY STEP Selecting multiple ranges

1 Click in cell B4 and drag to cell F4 to select the first range of data.

2 Press and hold the **Ctrl** key, click in cell B7 and drag to cell F7. Both ranges appear selected, as in Figure 2-6.

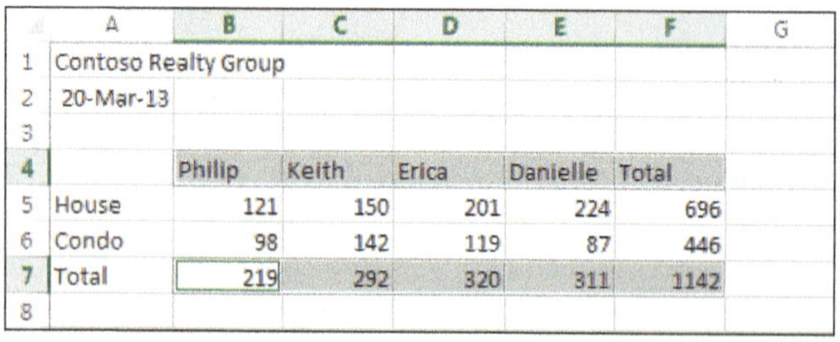

| | A | B | C | D | E | F | G |
|---|---|---|---|---|---|---|---|
| 1 | Contoso Realty Group | | | | | | |
| 2 | 20-Mar-13 | | | | | | |
| 3 | | | | | | | |
| 4 | | Philip | Keith | Erica | Danielle | Total | |
| 5 | House | 121 | 150 | 201 | 224 | 696 | |
| 6 | Condo | 98 | 142 | 119 | 87 | 446 | |
| 7 | Total | 219 | 292 | 320 | 311 | 1142 | |
| 8 | | | | | | | |

**Figure 2-6**

Press and hold the Ctrl key to select multiple ranges of cells that are not contiguous

## STEP BY STEP Select an entire row

1 Point at the row heading such as row 4.

2 Click to select the row when the pointer turns into a forward-facing arrow ( ).

Excels selects the entire row.

## STEP BY STEP Select a column

1 Point at the column heading such as column E.

2 Click to select the column when the pointer turns into a downward-facing arrow ( ).

Excel selects the entire column.

**STEP BY STEP** **Select the entire worksheet**

1 Click the area just below the Name box (see Figure 2-7) to select the entire worksheet.

**Figure 2-7**

Select the entire worksheet with one click

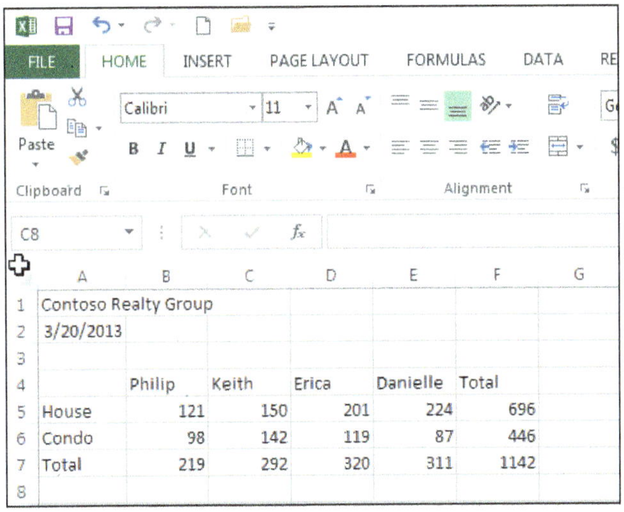


**Take Note** Use caution after selecting the entire worksheet, since any action you perform affects the entire selection.

### Selecting Cells using the Keyboard

| KEY | ACTION |
|---|---|
| **Shift+left arrow** | Selects the cell to the left |
| **Shift+right arrow** | Selects the cell to the right |
| **Shift+up arrow** | Selects the cell above |
| **Shift+down arrow** | Selects the cell below |
| **Shift+Spacebar** | Selects the current row |
| **Ctrl+Spacebar** | Selects the current column |
| **Ctrl+Shift+Spacebar** | Selects the entire sheet |

## Using AutoFill to fill a range with data

One of the quicker ways to enter data in a worksheet is to use the **AutoFill** feature. With AutoFill, Excel looks for patterns in your data and quickly fills in the remainder of the data based on that pattern. For instance, to enter a series of dates each a week apart, enter the first date followed by the next date 7 days later. Select both cells and click and drag the AutoFill handle to fill in the remaining dates.

**STEP BY STEP** **Using AutoFill**

1. Enter the value 1 in cell J1.
2. Enter the value 2 in cell J2.
3. Select cells J1 and J2.
4. Click the AutoFill **handle**, located at the lower-right corner of the selected range, and drag down to cell A20 as in Figure 2-8. Excel fills in the values 1 through 20 in the range of cells.

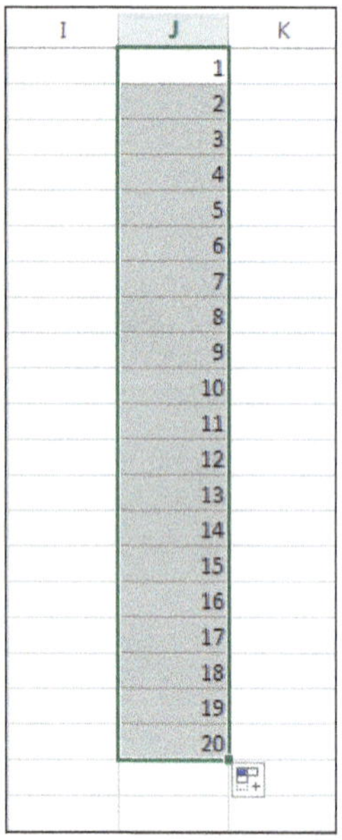


**Figure 2-8**

AutoFill quickly fills in a range of data when it senses a pattern.

## SAVING WORKBOOKS

**Bottom Line**

When you save a workbook for the first time, Excels prompts you to assign a name to the file and indicate where you want the file stored. Once you assign a name to the file, it appears in the title bar of your workbook. You don't need to assign a name each time you save a file. After a file has been named, the next time you save the file Excel will not prompt you for a name and will simply save it using the assigned name.

## STEP BY STEP Saving Workbooks

1 Choose **Save** from the File tab.

2 Click **Computer** in the Office Backstage, and then click the **Browse** button.

3 In the Save As dialog box, navigate to the Excel02lessons folder.

4 Type **excel_practice** in the File name text box (See Figure 2-9.).

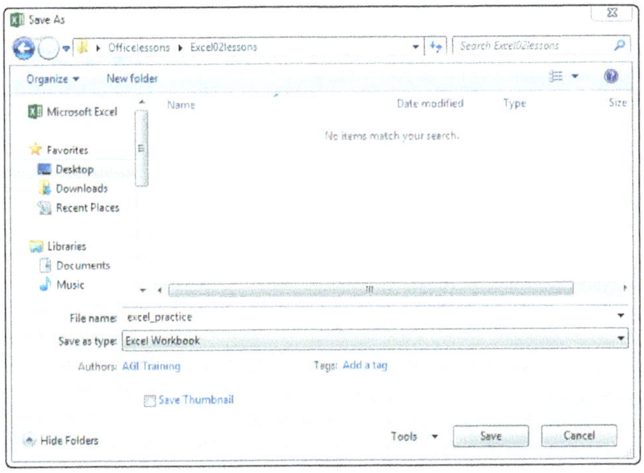


**Figure 2-9**

In the Save As dialog box, enter a name for the file and indicate where it should be saved.

5 Click **Save** to save the file and choose **File > Close** to close this file.

### A word about Save vs. Save As

The Save As command and the Save command can be confusing because the first time you use the Save command to save your file, Excel displays the Save As dialog box instead of a Save dialog box. Excel doesn't really have a Save dialog box; when you choose the Save command for the first time, Excel displays the Save As dialog box because you have not yet specified a name or location.

If you use the Save As command when you want to save a file, Excel will again ask you to supply the name and location and this is where you may run into some trouble. The Save As command should really only be used if you want to make a copy of the file with a new name, leaving the original file intact.

## OPENING WORKBOOKS

There are two ways to open an Excel workbook. You can navigate to the file in your Documents folder and double-click the icon to both launch Excel and open the file. Alternatively, you could launch Excel and then use the Open command to open a file within the Excel window.

## STEP BY STEP Opening an existing worksheet

1 Launch Microsoft Excel if it is not already opened.

2 From the Backstage, choose **Open** (see Figure 2-10) and navigate to the Excel02lessons folder on the desktop.

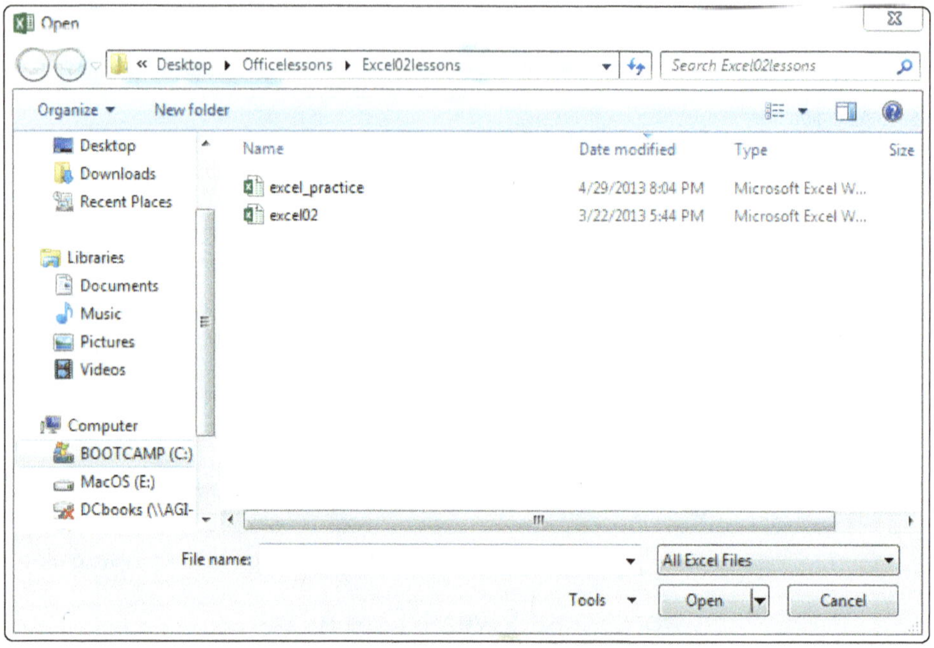


**Figure 2-10**

The Open dialog box appears to allow you to find an Excel file.

3 Double-click the file named **excel02**, shown in Figure 2-11. An Excel document opens to display a worksheet containing the customer list for a fictitious real estate company.

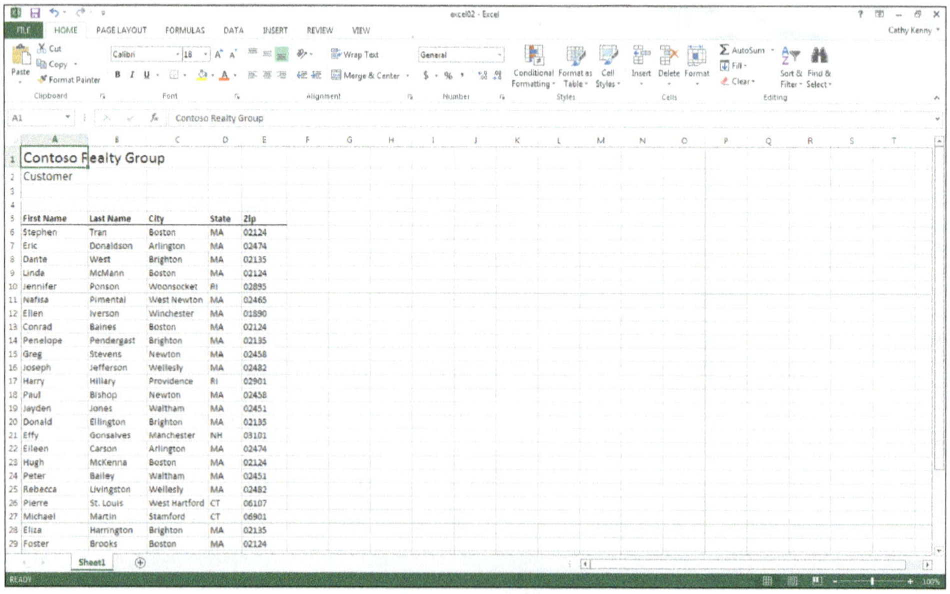


**Figure 2-11**

Open an existing file in Excel using the Open command in the File tab.

Since we will be altering the file in this lesson, we will use the Save As command to save the file with a new name. By doing so, the original file will remain intact and the changes that we will make throughout the course of the lesson will only be saved in the new version.

**STEP BY STEP** **Using Save As**

1. Choose **Save As** from the File tab.
2. From the Office Backstage, choose **Computer** and then click **Browse** and locate the Excel02lessons folder.
3. In the File Name text box, add **_customers** to the end of the file name.
4. Click the **Save** button.

## EDITING DATA

**Bottom Line**

A common occurrence when constructing worksheets is the need to edit, rearrange, or work with data that has already been entered. For instance, you might need to move a range of cells from one location to another, copy a collection of cells so they can be reused in another section, or even clear a selection of cells altogether.

### Editing data in a cell

To edit existing data in a cell, you have two options. You can edit the data directly in the cell, or you can use the Formula bar. Before you can edit data, though, you must first select the cell containing the data.

To edit data directly in the cell, double-click the cell you want to edit. When the cursor appears in the cell, make your changes.

**STEP BY STEP** **Editing data in a cell**

1. In the file **excel02_customers**, double-click cell **A2**.
2. Type **List** after Customer and press **Enter**.

To edit data in the Formula bar, click the cell you want to edit and move the pointer up to the Formula bar. When it changes into the cursor shape, click to set the insertion point and make your changes.

**STEP BY STEP** **Editing data in the Formula bar**

1. Click cell **A2**.
2. Click in the Formula bar to set the insertion point between Customer and List.
3. Type **Contact**, add a space and press **Enter**.

### Using cut, copy, and paste

The Cut, Copy, and Paste commands allow you to rearrange existing worksheet data. With **Cut**, you can move data from one location to another; **Copy** allows you to make multiple copies of a range of data. When you use Cut and Copy, Excel uses the Clipboard to temporarily store the data until the next time you use the Cut or Copy command. Data you have selected to be cut or copied appears highlighted by a dashed line border instead of the usual solid border.

To move a range of data from one location to another, use the Cut and **Paste** commands. Excel removes the selected data from its original location and inserts it into the new one. Note that you can only paste a range of data that has been cut once.

## STEP BY STEP Using Cut

1 Select range A5:E37 (see Figure 2-12).

2 Choose Cut from the Clipboard group on the Home tab.

**Figure 2-12**

When you select a range of cells to Cut or Copy, Excel uses a dashed border to indicate the selected range.

| | A | B | C | D | E | F |
|---|---|---|---|---|---|---|
| 1 | Contoso Realty Group | | | | | |
| 2 | Customer Contact List | | | | | |
| 3 | | | | | | |
| 4 | | | | | | |
| 5 | First Name | Last Name | City | State | Zip | |
| 6 | Stephen | Tran | Boston | MA | 02124 | |
| 7 | Eric | Donaldson | Arlington | MA | 02474 | |
| 8 | Dante | West | Brighton | MA | 02135 | |
| 9 | Linda | McMann | Boston | MA | 02124 | |
| 10 | Jennifer | Ponson | Woonsocket | RI | 02895 | |
| 11 | Nafisa | Pimental | West Newton | MA | 02465 | |
| 12 | Ellen | Iverson | Winchester | MA | 01890 | |
| 13 | Conrad | Baines | Boston | MA | 02124 | |
| 14 | Penelope | Pendergast | Brighton | MA | 02135 | |
| 15 | Greg | Stevens | Newton | MA | 02458 | |
| 16 | Joseph | Jefferson | Wellesly | MA | 02482 | |
| 17 | Harry | Hillary | Providence | RI | 02901 | |
| 18 | Paul | Bishop | Newton | MA | 02458 | |
| 19 | Jayden | Jones | Waltham | MA | 02451 | |
| 20 | Donald | Ellington | Brighton | MA | 02135 | |
| 21 | Effy | Gonsalves | Manchester | NH | 03101 | |
| 22 | Eileen | Carson | Arlington | MA | 02474 | |
| 23 | Hugh | McKenna | Boston | MA | 02124 | |
| 24 | Peter | Bailey | Waltham | MA | 02451 | |
| 25 | Rebecca | Livingston | Wellesly | MA | 02482 | |
| 26 | Pierre | St. Louis | West Hartford | CT | 06107 | |
| 27 | Michael | Martin | Stamford | CT | 06901 | |
| 28 | Eliza | Harrington | Brighton | MA | 02135 | |
| 29 | Foster | Brooks | Boston | MA | 02124 | |

3 Click in cell B5 and choose Paste.

To reuse a range of cells in another area of your worksheet, use Copy and Paste. Excel keeps the original selection intact and inserts a copy in the new location. You can paste as many copies of the selected data as you need.

## STEP BY STEP Using Copy and Paste

1 Select range B37:F37.

2 Choose Copy from the Home tab.

3 Click in cell B38 and choose Paste.

4 Enter Kelvin in cell B38 and Davis in cell C38.

**Take Note** Notice that the contents of column D have been truncated. This occurs because the contents are longer than the current column width can accommodate. To resize the column width, double-click the border separating column D and E. Excel automatically adjusts the width to the widest entry. (For more information on changing column widths, see Lesson 3, "Formatting Excel Worksheets.")

## Inserting cells

Another way to reorganize a worksheet is to insert cells within an existing range of data when you need to add new information. You can insert a new cell one at a time or insert a range of cells all at once. When you do, you can shift existing cells to the right or down to accommodate the new cells.

**STEP BY STEP** **inserting cells**

1. Select range **B8:F8**.
2. Click the arrow just below the Insert command in the Cells group on the Home tab.
3. Choose **Insert Cells** from the resulting menu.
4. From the Insert dialog box (see Figure 2-13), click **Shift cells down**.

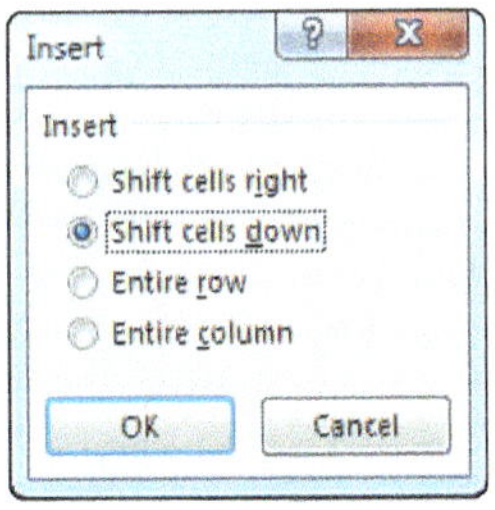


**Figure 2-13**

Insert a range of cells to add data to an existing worksheet.

5. Click **OK** and then choose **File > Save** to save your work.

## Deleting cells

When you need to remove a range of cells from a worksheet altogether, you can delete them. Excel then automatically adjusts the existing data.

**STEP BY STEP** **Deleting cells**

1. Select range **B8:F8**.
2. Click the arrow just below the Delete command in the Cells group of the Home tab.
3. Choose **Delete Cells** from the resulting menu.
4. From the Delete dialog box, click **Shift cells up** and then click **OK**. Excel shifts the existing cells automatically.

## Clearing cells

If you need to remove data from a range of cells without deleting them from the worksheet range, you can choose to clear them.

**STEP BY STEP** **Clearing cells**

1. Select range **B8:F8**.
2. Click the arrow just below the Clear command in the Editing group on the Home tab.
3. Select **Clear Contents** from the resulting menu.

## USING UNDO AND REDO

**Bottom Line**

The Undo command is an extremely important tool when working in Excel. As its name implies, Undo allows you to reverse the last action you have performed. For example, if you mistakenly delete a range of cells, you can immediately click Undo to have them reinserted.

Excel records the last 100 actions performed, allowing you to cycle through the commands until you restore the worksheet to its intended order. You can click the arrow to the right of the Undo button to see the list of actions performed. Click the action you want to Undo; Excel reverses all actions up to that point. If you realize that you really did mean to do what you did, Redo will redo the action that you undid.

Perform the following set of steps to see how the Undo and Redo commands work.

**STEP BY STEP** **Using undo and redo**

1. Select range **B8:F8**.
2. Choose **Insert** from the Cells group on the Home tab and select **Insert Sheet Rows**.
3. Click the **Undo** button () found on the Quick Access Toolbar to reverse the action.
4. Click the **Redo** button () to re-insert the range of cells.
5. Click **OK** and then choose **File > Save** to save your work.

## WORKING WITH ROWS AND COLUMNS

**Bottom Line**

As discussed in Lesson 1, a worksheet is constructed of a series of rows and columns, the intersection of which forms a cell. When constructing worksheets, you might need to rearrange your existing data to accommodate new information.

While you could use the Cut and Paste commands to move your data, many times the simplest way to add new information is to insert a new row or column into the existing data structure. When you do, Excel automatically moves existing data and updates formulas as necessary. (For more details on formulas, see Lesson 4, "Using Formulas in Excel 2013.")

## Inserting rows and columns

Before inserting a new row or column, you must first indicate where you want the new row or column to appear. To do so, select a cell in the row *below* where you want the new row to appear. For example, to insert a new row between rows 1 and 2, click any cell in row 2. Prior to inserting a new column, select a cell in the column *to the right* of where you want the new column to appear. For example, if you want to insert a column between columns B and C, click any cell in column C to select it.

**STEP BY STEP** **Inserting rows and columns**

1. Click in cell B8.
2. On the Home tab, in the Cells group, choose **Insert** and select **Insert Sheet Rows** from the resulting menu.
3. In cell B8, type **Stephanie**; in cell C8 type **Walker**; in cell D8 type **Boston**; in cell E8 type **MA**; and in cell F8 type **02124**.
4. Move the cell pointer to cell D6, choose **Insert** from the Home tab, and select **Insert Sheet Columns** from the resulting menu. Excel inserts a column between columns C and E.

**Take Note** To quickly insert a row or column, right-click the row or column heading and choose Insert from the resulting menu. To insert more than one row or column at a time, select the number of rows or columns you want to insert before you choose the Insert command. For example, if you want to insert two rows, select two existing rows, and then choose Insert.

## Deleting rows and columns

Before you can delete a row or column, you must select a cell within the row or column to be deleted.

**STEP BY STEP** **Deleting rows and columns**

1. Click cell **B3**.
2. From the Home tab, choose **Delete**, and then select **Delete Sheet Rows** from the resulting menu.

Excel removes the row and shifts existing data up one row.

3. Click cell **D2**.
4. From the Home tab, choose **Delete**, and select **Delete Sheet Columns** from the resulting menu.

Excel removes the column and shifts existing data one column to the left.

5. Delete any blank rows that may appear in the middle of your chart.

## Hiding and unhiding rows and columns

Another option available when constructing worksheets is to hide certain rows or columns from view. By hiding rows and columns rather than deleting them, the data remains within the worksheet, but no one will see it.

The following set of steps illustrate how hiding a row or column works.

## STEP BY STEP Hiding rows and columns

1. Select column **D**.
2. Choose **Format** from the Home tab, choose **Hide & Unhide** from the resulting menu as in Figure 2-14, and click **Hide Columns**.

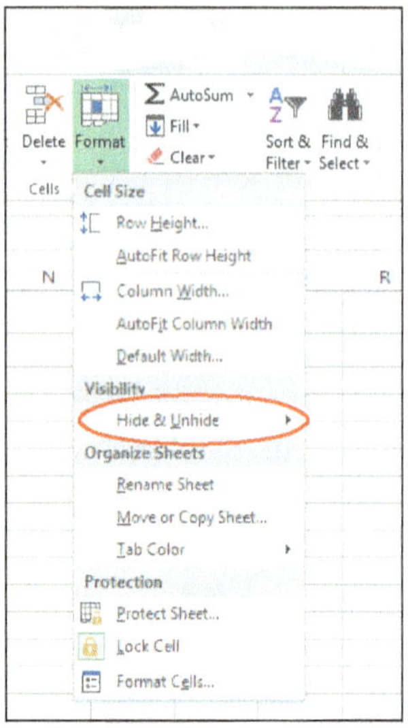


**Figure 2-14**

Hide a column or row when you want to prevent the data from being displayed.

3. Select row **6**, choose **Format** from the Home tab, choose **Hide & Unhide**, and click **Hide Rows**.

Redisplaying columns is a little trickier. You must first select cells on either side of the hidden row or column before you can unhide them.

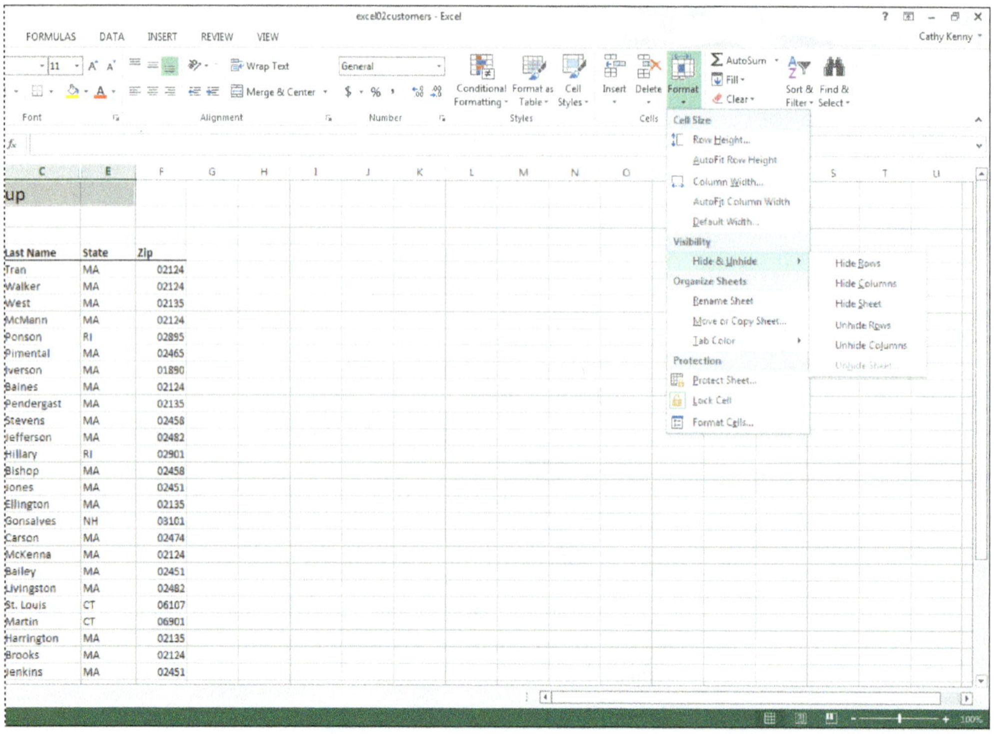


**Figure 2-15**

When columns and rows are hidden in the worksheet, you must select a range of cells on either side before you can redisplay them.

**STEP BY STEP** **Redisplaying rows or columns**

1 Select range **C1:E1** as shown in Figure 2-15.

2 From the Home tab, choose **Format**, choose **Hide & Unhide**, and click **Unhide Columns**.

3 Select range **A5:A7**.

4 Again from the Home tab, choose **Format**, choose **Hide & Unhide**, and click **Unhide rows**.

## Freezing and unfreezing rows and columns

If your worksheet data spans beyond a single screen display, you can **freeze** the column and row headings so they continue to be displayed when you scroll to other areas of the worksheet. You can specify that the top row or first column of the worksheet be frozen or select a specific range of cells to remain displayed.

**STEP BY STEP** **Freezing and unfreezing rows and columns**

1 Select range **B5:F5**.

2 Choose **Freeze Panes** from the View tab.

3 From the resulting menu choose **Freeze Panes**.

4 Excel freezes everything above row 5.

5 Scroll down to row 25 and notice that the titles at the top of the worksheet remain displayed.

6 Choose **Freeze Panes** from the View tab and choose **Unfreeze Panes**.

**Freeze options**

| OPTION | ACTION |
|---|---|
| Freeze Panes | Keeps rows and columns visible above the current selection |
| Freeze Top Row | Keeps the first row in the worksheet visible. |
| Freeze First Column | Keeps the first column in the worksheet visible. |

# CREATING ADDITIONAL WORKSHEETS

**Bottom Line**

Each new workbook file you create consists of a single worksheet. You can insert additional worksheets into a workbook file when you need to manage a new set of related data.

## Inserting worksheets

**STEP BY STEP** **Inserting worksheets**

1 Choose **Insert** from the Home tab and select **Insert Sheet**.

2 A new blank worksheet is displayed to the left of the current worksheet named Sheet2.

You can also click the plus sign located at the bottom of the worksheet window, adjacent to the worksheet tab. Excel inserts a new worksheet to the right of the current worksheet tab (see Figure 2-16).

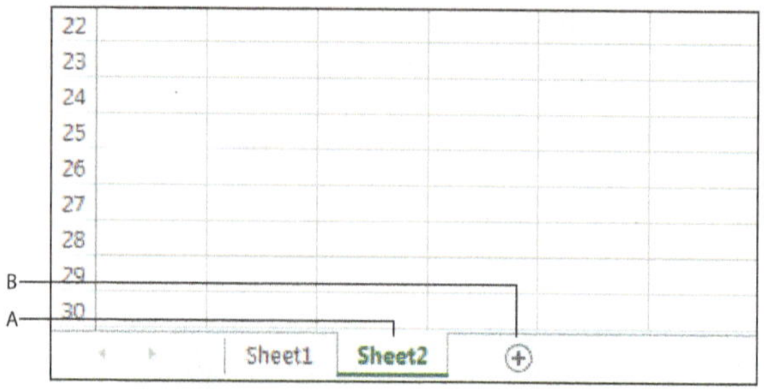


**Figure 2-16**

A. Worksheet tab.

B. New Sheet button.

## Renaming worksheets

Each worksheet you create is assigned a consecutively numbered name, such as Sheet1, Sheet2, and Sheet3. You can assign more meaningful names to your worksheets.

**STEP BY STEP** **Renaming worksheets**

1. Click the tab labeled **Sheet1**.
2. Choose **Format** from the Home tab and select **Rename Sheet**.
3. Excel highlights the current worksheet tab. Type **Customers** and press **Enter**.
4. Double-click the tab labeled **Sheet2**.
5. Type **Listings** and press **Enter**.

## Moving and copying worksheets

When you are working with multiple worksheets in a workbook, you might need to rearrange the order of their appearance. Moving a worksheet requires you to click and drag the tab to the new location in the workbook. You can also make a copy of a worksheet in your workbook.

**STEP BY STEP** **Moving and copying worksheets**

1. Click and drag worksheet **Customers** and drop it right before tab Listings. Notice that as you drag the tab, a small black triangle appears as a guide. When the triangle is at the point where you want it, let go of the tab to drop the worksheet into place. The result is shown in Figure 2-17.

| | | | | | |
|---|---|---|---|---|---|
| 21 | Effy | Gonsalves | Manchester | NH | 03101 |
| 22 | Eileen | Carson | Arlington | MA | 02474 |
| 23 | Hugh | McKenna | Boston | MA | 02124 |
| 24 | Peter | Bailey | Waltham | MA | 02451 |
| 25 | Rebecca | Livingston | Wellesly | MA | 02482 |
| 26 | Pierre | St. Louis | West Hartford | CT | 06107 |
| 27 | Michael | Martin | Stamford | CT | 06901 |
| 28 | Eliza | Harrington | Brighton | MA | 02135 |
| 29 | Foster | Brooks | Boston | MA | 02124 |

Customers Listings

READY

**Figure 2-17**

Move the Customers tab in front of the Listings tab.

2. Choose **File > Save** to save your work.

## Changing the color of worksheet tabs

You can color code your Excel worksheet tabs for organization purposes just as you would paper-based filing systems. When managing data in a workbook containing multiple tabs, you can rely on color coding to help you find your information quickly and easily. For instance, in a Budget worksheet, you could change the color of a tab containing Income to Blue and the tab containing expenses to Red.

**STEP BY STEP** **Changing the color of worksheets tabs**

1 Click the **Customers** worksheet.

2 From the Home tab, choose **Format**.

3 Choose **Tab Color** and select **Blue** from the resulting color menu, as in Figure 2-18.

4 Change the color of the Listings worksheet to **Orange**.

**Figure 2-18**

Assign color-coding to worksheet tabs to help keep data organized.

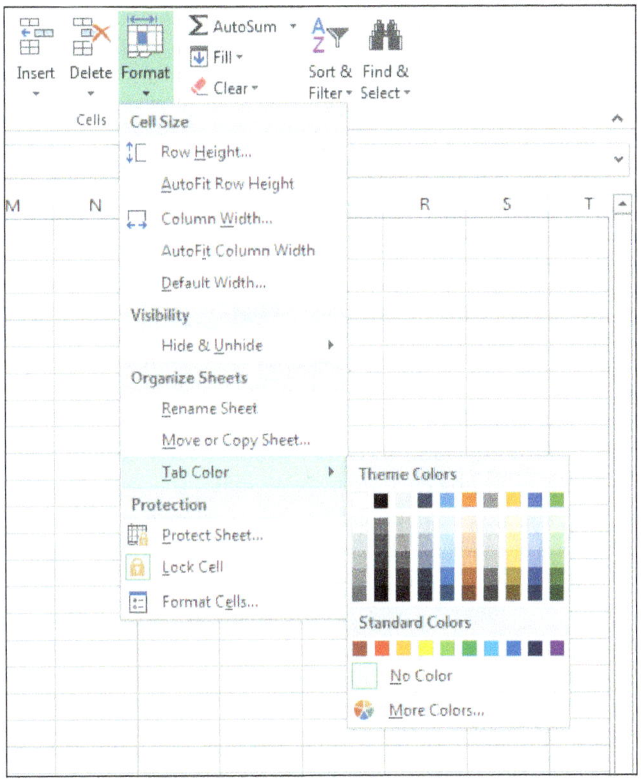

### Hiding sheets

You can hide worksheets from view just as you do with rows and columns.

**STEP BY STEP** **Hiding sheets**

1. Click the **Listings** tab.
2. From the Home tab, choose **Format**.
3. From the Visibility section of the Format menu, choose **Hide & Unhide**.
4. Select **Hide Sheet** from the resulting menu. Excel removes the worksheet and its tab from view.

### Unhiding sheets

Unhiding sheets is just as simple as hiding them.

**STEP BY STEP** **Unhiding sheets**

1. From the Home tab, choose **Format**.
2. From the Visibility section of the Format menu, choose **Hide & Unhide**.
3. Select **Unhide Sheet** from the resulting menu.
4. In the Unhide dialog box, select **Listings**, and then click **OK**. Excel redisplays the hidden worksheet.

### Deleting worksheets

You can delete existing worksheets that you no longer need. To delete a worksheet, you must first make it the active sheet by clicking it. Note that if the worksheet you want to delete contains data, Excel displays a dialog box reminding you that once you delete a worksheet, you cannot get it back. Click Cancel to keep the worksheet and Delete to continue deleting the worksheet.

**STEP BY STEP** **Deleting worksheets**

1. Click the worksheet tab named **Listings** and choose **Delete** from the Home tab. You can also right-click Listings to display a context-sensitive menu. Select **Delete**.
2. Choose **Delete Sheet** from the resulting menu.

## PRINTING WORKSHEETS AND WORKBOOKS

If you want to print your worksheet, you might find that you have more data than easily fits onto a standard piece of paper. When your worksheets contain a great deal of information, you'll need to specify details about the data you want to print and how you want it to fit on the page. This makes the printing process a bit more detailed than many other applications.

### Printing a range of data

By default, Excel prints the entire worksheet. If you want to print a specific range of data, you need to select it.

## STEP BY STEP Printing a range of data

1 Select range **A1:F38**.

2 Click the **File** tab and choose **Print**.

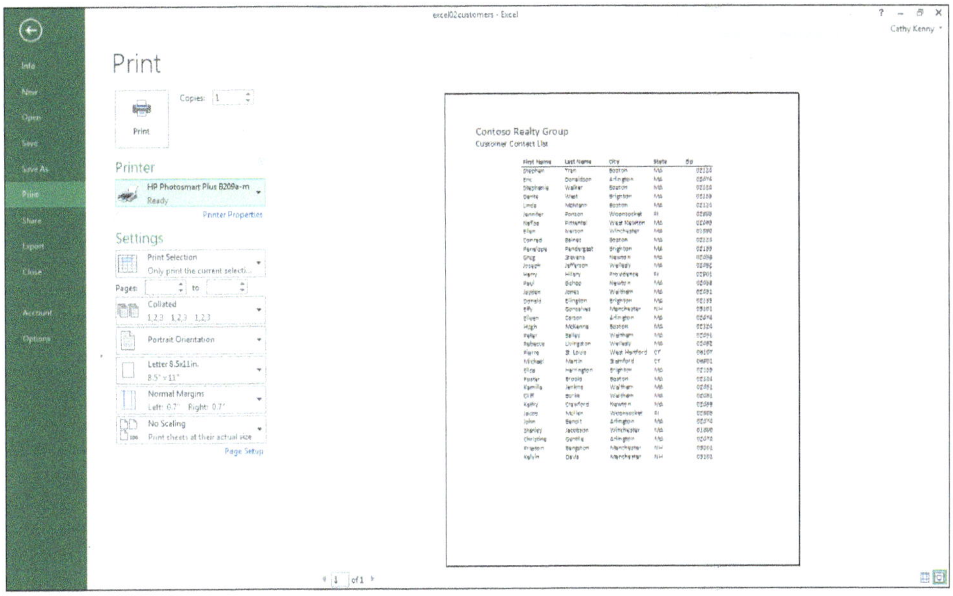


**Figure 2-19**

Excel shows you a static preview of what your worksheet will look like when printed.

3 In the Settings section of the Print Backstage view (see Figure 2-19), click the drop-down arrow and choose **Print Selection**.

4 In the Printer section, specify your printer.

5 Click **Print** to print your worksheet.

### Defining the print area

If you frequently need to print the same range of data, define it as the **Print Area** so you don't have to select the same range every time you're ready to print.

## STEP BY STEP Defining the print area

1 Select range **A1:F38**.

2 From the Page Layout tab, choose **Print Area**.

3 Select **Set Print Area** from the resulting menu. Each time you elect to print, Excel automatically selects the range you defined as the Print Area.

4 To clear the print area, choose **Print Area** from the Page Layout tab and select **Clear Print Area** from the resulting menu.

### Viewing the page layout

As stated above, the Print menu option now incorporates a preview of the worksheet as it will appear when printed. If you need to make changes to the worksheet based on your preview, you'll need to exit Preview mode.

The **Page Layout** mode in Excel displays a fully-editable preview of your printed page. When you switch to Page Layout, guides indicate the current margins and page breaks, and you can continue working on your worksheet as well.

## STEP BY STEP Viewing the page layout

1 Select range **A1:F38**.

2 In the Status bar, click the **Page Layout** button. Excel switches to Page Layout mode (shown in Figure 2-20), displaying the worksheet as it will appear when printed.

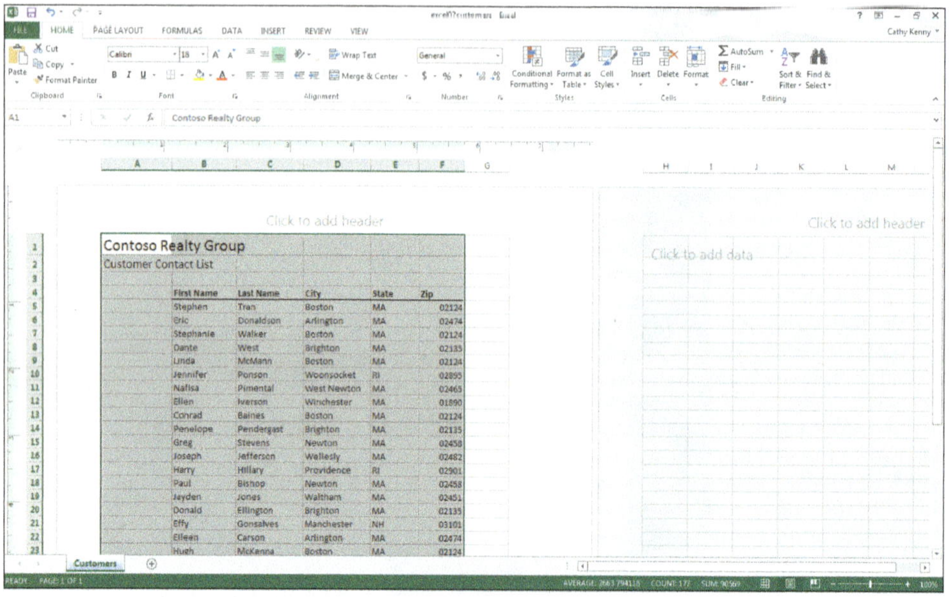


**Figure 2-20**
The dynamic Page Layout Mode allows you to preview and work on your data.

3 Click **Normal** on the Status bar to return to the default worksheet display mode.

### Adding headers and footers

**Headers** and **footers** are text that appear in the top and bottom margins of your worksheets. You can add the current date and time, page numbers, and other specific text to this area. The easiest way to add headers and footers to your worksheet is to switch to Page Layout mode.

## STEP BY STEP Adding headers and footers

1 In the Status Bar, click the **Page Layout** button.

2 On your preview page, click the area labeled **Click** to add header to display the Header & Footer Tools tab.

3 From the Design tab, choose **Header** to display a list of sample headers (See Figure 2-21.).

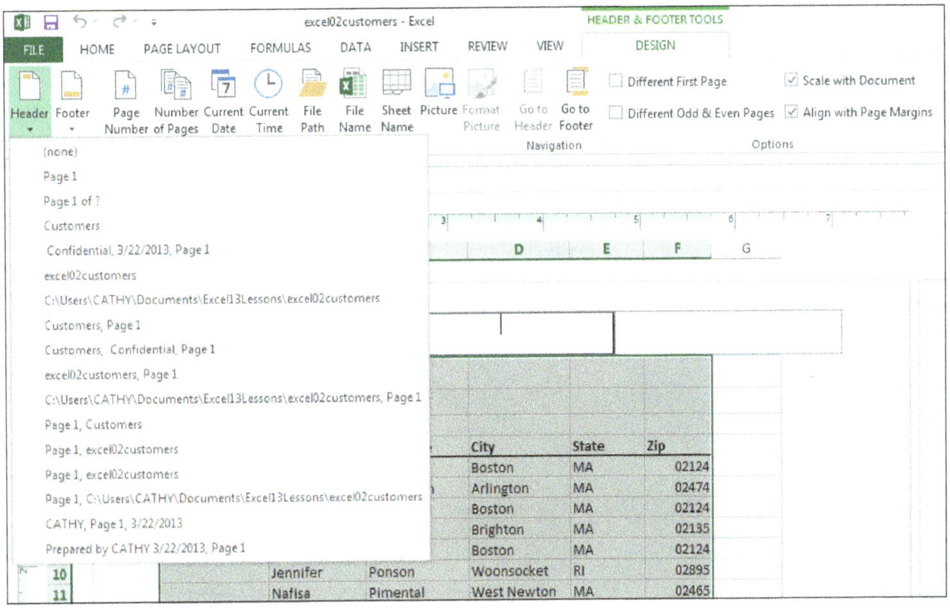


**Figure 2-21**

Add headers and footers directly to your worksheet in Page Layout mode.

4 Choose **excel02_customers** from the displayed list to add the file name to the header.

### Header and footer tools

| TOOL | ACTION | EXAMPLE |
|---|---|---|
| **Page Number** | Inserts the current page number | Page 1 |
| **Number of Pages** | Inserts the current page out of the total number of pages | Page 1 of 3 |
| **Current Date** | Inserts the current date | 3/20/2013 |
| **Current Time** | Inserts the current time | 2:30 pm |
| **File Path** | Inserts the file name, including the entire path | C:\users\username\document\budget2013 |
| **File Name** | Inserts the file name only | Budget2013 |
| **Sheet Name** | Inserts the name of the current sheet | Expenses |
| **Picture** | Inserts an image | |

5 Scroll to the bottom of the Page Layout view and click the area labeled **Click** to add footer to display the Header & Footer Tools tab.

6 From the Design tab, choose **Footer** to display a list of sample footers.

7 Choose **Page 1** from the displayed list.

8 Click the **Normal** view button from the Status bar.

## Changing margins

Depending on the amount of data you have or the manner in which you want your worksheet printed, you can change the margin settings.

**STEP BY STEP** **Changing margins**

1. Choose **Margins** from the Page Layout tab.
2. Choose **Narrow** from the resulting menu.

## Changing the orientation

Many times, you can fit more data on the printed page by switching the **Page Orientation** from Portrait to Landscape.

**STEP BY STEP** **Changing the page orientation**

1. From the Page Layout tab, choose **Orientation**.
2. Choose **Landscape**.

## Printing titles

If the data in your worksheet spans multiple pages, you can add print titles to your print job so the column or row headings appear on each page of the printout. To indicate Print Titles, select the row or column that contains the headings.

**STEP BY STEP** **Printing titles**

1. From the Page Layout tab, choose **Print Titles**.
2. Click **Rows** to repeat at top to set the insertion point inside the text box.

3 Click the row heading for row 4. You will see the range $4:$4 indicated, as in Figure 2-22.

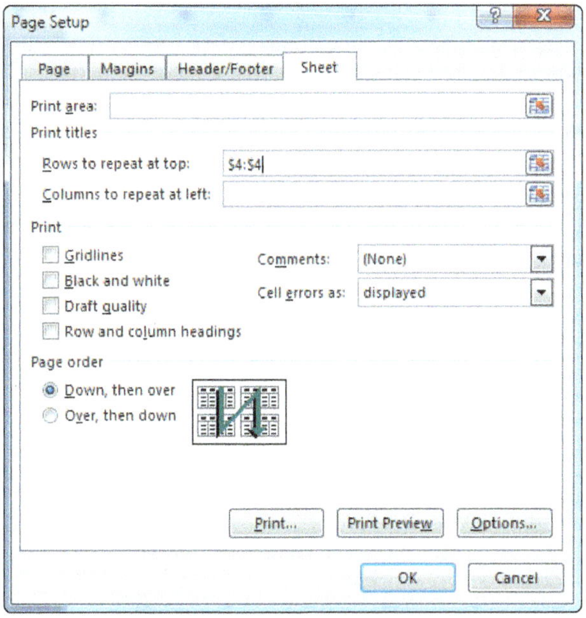


**Figure 2-22**

Designate Print Titles in your worksheet so that column headings appear on every page of the printout.

4 Click **OK**.

5 From the File tab, choose **Print** and then click the **Print** button to print the worksheet.

6 To turn off Print Titles, choose **Print Titles** again and remove the row reference from the Rows to repeat at top box.

## Turning gridlines off and on

Excel automatically turns off the worksheet gridlines when you print. You can, however, elect to include the gridlines in your printout.

**STEP BY STEP** **Turning gridlines off and on**

1 Click the Page Layout tab.

2 Select **Print** in the Gridlines section to have Excel print the gridlines on your paper.

3 Select **Print** again to turn them off in the printouts.

4 Choose **File > Save** to save your work.

You've now completed this lesson. Now that you are familiar with entering and editing data and selecting worksheet ranges, you are ready to begin learning how to format your worksheets to give them a professional appearance.

## What you learned in this lesson:

- Creating a Worksheet
- Entering Data in a Cell
- Working with Cell Ranges
- Saving Workbooks
- Opening Workbooks
- Editing Data
- Using Undo/Redo
- Working with Rows and Columns
- Creating Additional Worksheets
- Printing Worksheets and Workbooks

# Knowledge Assessment

### Matching

**Match the Excel function in numbers 1 to 10 to its keyboard or mouse command in letters a to j.**

1. Turn gridlines on/off in printed output
2. Unhide a worksheet
3. Print only specific cell range
4. Insert a worksheet into a workbook
5. Print short, wide pages
6. Select a range of cells
7. Reduce printed whitespace
8. Enter formula into a cell
9. Delete a row
10. Freeze a range of cells

a. Print > Settings > Print Selection
b. Page Layout > Margins > Narrow
c. Home > Delete > Delete Sheet Rows
d. Type =, function name, then parameters
e. Page Layout > Orientation > Landscape
f. Page Layout > Gridlines > Print
g. Shift+click opposite corners
h. Home > Insert > Insert Sheet
i. Select cells, then View > Freeze Panes
j. Home > Cells > Format > Visibility > Unhide Sheet...

### Fill in the Blanks

**Complete the following sentences by writing the correct word or words in the blanks provided.**

1. To create a new workbook at any time, press _____.
2. When you type $15 into a cell, Excel automatically applies the _____ data format.
3. The range A6:D6 includes _____ cells.
4. Hold the _____ key while click/dragging to select multiple cell ranges.
5. The _____ command adds data to the clipboard while removing the original content.
6. To add a row or column to a worksheet, use the _____ command.
7. The _____ command, found in the Quick Access Toolbar, returns the document to a previous state.
8. A _____ column heading stays visible even when you scroll several pages down the worksheet.
9. When you create a workbook and add two additional worksheets, the worksheets' default names are _____ and _____.
10. The _____ command to recolor worksheet tabs is found in the _____ group of the _____ tab.

## Competency Assessment

### Project 2-1: Rapidly Populating a Worksheet

**In this exercise you will use AutoFill to fill two columns of a worksheet.**

1. Create a new document by selecting **Blank workbook** from the launch screen, or pressing **Ctrl+N** if Excel is running.
2. Select cell **A1**. Type **Date** and press **Tab**.
3. Type **Amount** and press **Return** or **Enter**.
4. Type **mar 11 <Tab> 3 <Enter>**.
5. Type **mar 12 <Tab> 6 <Enter>**.
6. Select cell **A3** and drag the AutoFill handle straight down until the date 4-Apr appears.
7. Click and drag to select both **B2** and **B3**.
8. Drag the AutoFill handle straight down until the number 75 appears next to the date 4-Apr.
9. Save your file as **project_2-1_autofill** and close it.

### Project 2-2: Using Undo and Redo

**In this exercise you will modify a document and experiment with the Undo/Redo tools.**

1. Open the project file **2-2-source** and save it as **project_2-2_undo**.
2. Select cell **C27** and type **April total**. Press **Tab**.
3. Click **Formulas > AutoSum > Sum**.
4. Click and drag to select the range **B2:B26**. Press **Enter** or **Return**.
5. Click on the row number **27** to select the entire row, and press **Ctrl+B**. Now we will use the **Undo** function to "take back" steps 4-5.
6. Click the drop-down arrow beside the Undo command in the Quick Access Toolbar.
7. Select Typing **'=SUM(B2:B26)'** in D27 from the Undo dropdown menu.
8. Select cell **D27**.

9. Click Formulas > AutoSum > Sum, then select the range B23:B26. Press Return.
10. Save and close your document.

## Proficiency Assessment

### Project 2-3: Working with Rows

**In this exercise you will work with several rows of data at once.**

1. Open the project file 2-3-source and save it as project_2-3_rows.
2. Select row 1 by clicking on the row label "1." Apply boldface formatting to the row (Ctrl+B).
3. Freeze row 1 (View > Freeze Panes > Freeze Top Row).
4. Select row 23. Right click the label and select Insert Row.
5. Insert three more empty rows in the same spot.
6. Select row 31 and Copy its contents.
7. Select row 23 and Paste the clipboard contents.
8. Change the contents of cell C23 to March total.
9. Select cell D23. Click in the Formula bar. Drag the handles of the blue bounding box to change the selected cell range to B2:B22. Press Return.
10. Select the column C heading and click Home > Cells > Format > AutoFit Column Width to resize the column.
11. Select rows 2 through 22. Right click in the selected range and choose Hide.
12. Repeat step 11 for rows 27 through 30 (the April data).
13. Save and close your document.

### Project 2-4: Rows and Columns

**In this exercise you will reformat rows and columns in a worksheet.**

1. Open the project file 2-4-source and save it as project_2-4_columns.
2. Click and drag to select the labels for rows 26 and 31 (and the hidden rows between). Right click one of the labels and select Unhide.
3. Click and drag to select the headings for columns C and D.
4. Press Ctrl+X to cut.
5. Click the heading for column E and press Ctrl+V to paste.
6. Select cells A27:A30. From the Home > Number group, select Short Date from the drop-down menu. Note that applying the Date data format to the whole column would mislabel the header cell as a Date.
7. Save and close your document.

# Mastery Assessment

## Project 2-5: Worksheet Layout

**In this exercise you will experiment with Excel's formatting tools: AutoFit, page breaks, gridlines, and so forth.**

1. Open the project file 2-5-source and save it as project_2-5_layout.
2. Copy all the data from Sheet1 to a new sheet in the same workbook, Sheet2. You will work with Sheet2 for the rest of this exercise.
3. Rename Sheet2 **Printable**.
4. Change the fill color of row 1 to **Grey 25% - Background 2**.
5. Fix column E's width with AutoFit.
6. Insert a page break between rows 26 and 27 (above the April monthly data).
7. Turn off gridlines.
8. Save and close your document.

## Project 2-6: Print Layout

**In this exercise you'll prep a document for print.**

1. Open the project file 2-6-source and save it as project_2-6_layout2.
2. Hide Sheet1.
3. Add a centered Header: **Daily Totals**.
4. Add a footer to the lower right of every page: **<page number> of <total pages>**.
5. Resize column A so all its data appears in Page Layout view (rather than ####).
6. Select **Narrow margins** and **Landscape orientation**.
7. Use the Print Titles tool to repeat row 1 at the top of every page.
8. AutoFit column E's width.
9. Click **File > Export** and create a PDF, using all default options, also entitled project_2-6_layout2.
10. Save and close your Excel document.

# 3 Formatting a Worksheet

## LESSON SKILL MATRIX

**In this lesson, you will learn the following skills:**

- Understanding Cell Formats
- Changing Number Formats
- Changing the Font and Font Size
- Modifying Row Heights and Column Widths
- Cell Alignment
- Borders & Shading
- Copying Cell Formats
- Working with Cell Styles
- Using Conditional Formatting
- Using Page Themes

## KEY TERMS

- Accounting Format
- Alignment
- AutoFit
- Color Scheme
- Conditional Formatting
- Effects
- Fill Color
- Font Set
- Format
- Format Painter
- Merge (cells)
- Separator
- Cell Style
- Text Attributes
- Theme
- Values
- Wrap

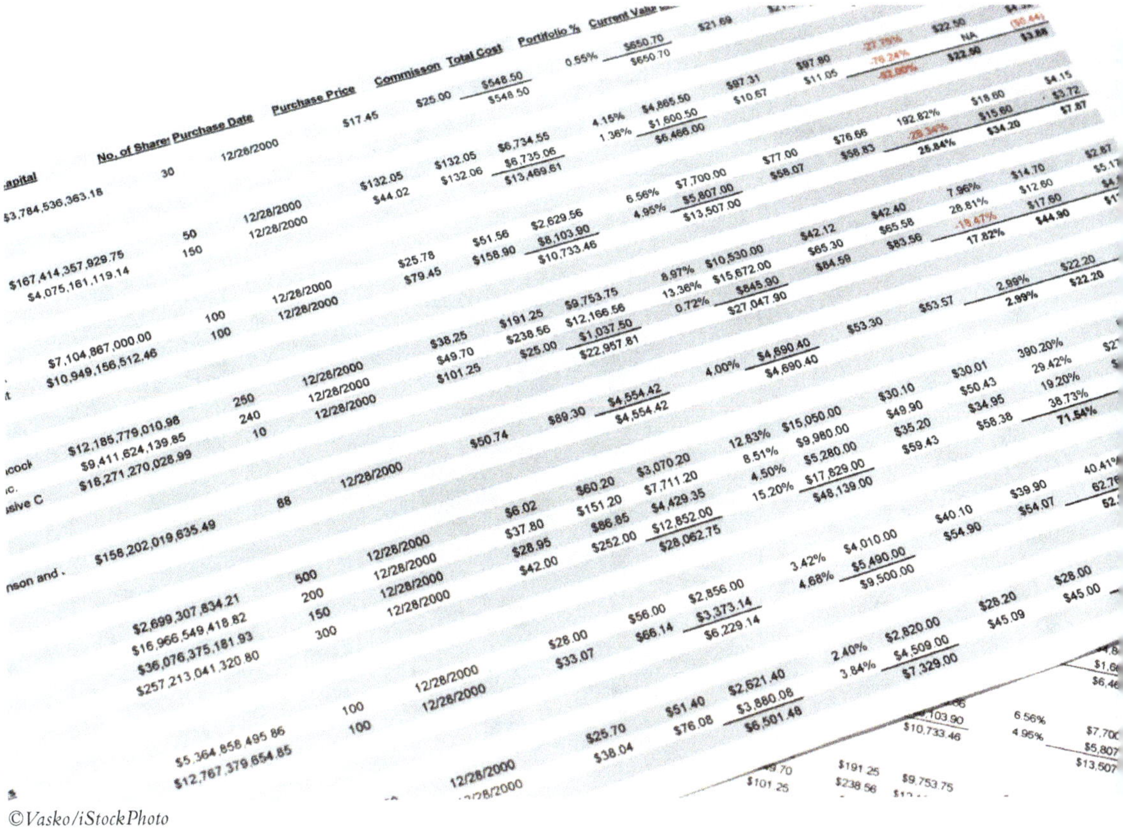


©Vasko/iStockPhoto

©Vasko/iStockPhoto

A large crew of contractors submit complex data sheets several times a day to the central desk at Northwind Traders, which a small team then cleans up and consolidates into a daily master spreadsheet for the analysts downstairs. Smart, robust, consistent data formatting is essential to this process. Excel 2013's cell and document formatting tools help the Northwind team produce readable, flexible documents as quickly as possible.

## SOFTWARE ORIENTATION

Data needs to be clear and easily understood. Formatting your spreadsheets helps readers understand and work with the data you organize in Microsoft Excel.

**Figure 3-1**

Formatting controls

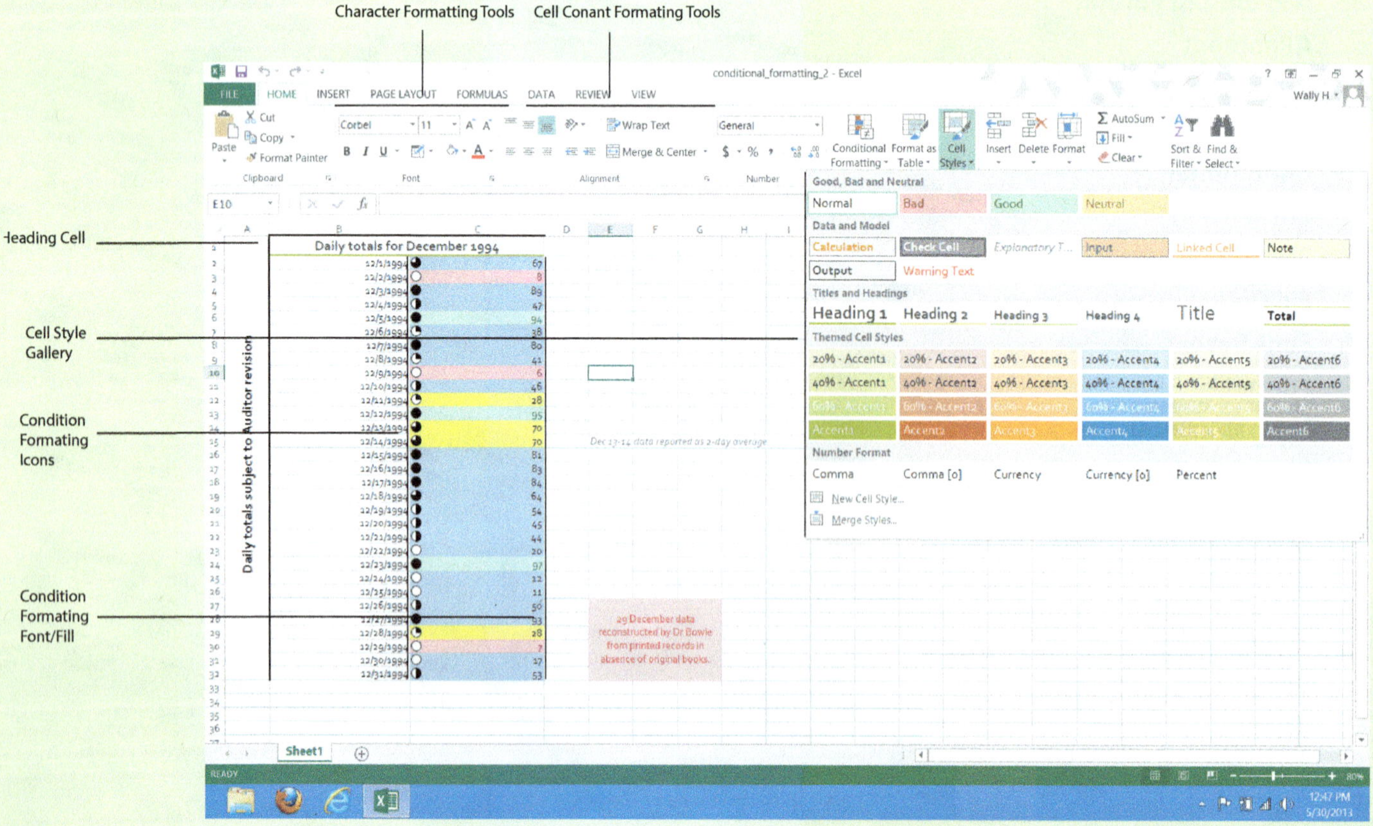

## STARTING UP

In this lesson, you'll work with several files from the Excel03lessons folder. Make sure that you have loaded the OfficeLessons folder onto your computer.

## UNDERSTANDING CELL FORMATS

**Bottom Line**

Before we talk about cell formatting, you must understand how Excel treats data. Excel categorizes data into three different types: numbers, text, and dates or times. Numbers, or **values**, consist of numeric data that will be used in calculations or formulas. There are also numbers on which you would never perform calculations, such as zip codes, social security numbers, product codes, or phone numbers.

Text also appears to be a straightforward concept. Text includes alphanumeric data that can be used in headings and other descriptive labels, for example, Sales 2001 or Northwest Region. When you enter a date, you might also think of it as a text-based entry, for example, March 27, 2013 or even 3/27/2013. Dates, in all actuality, are converted to a date value when entered, since you can perform calculations with dates.

When numbers are entered in a worksheet cell, Excel automatically applies a General format, unless it recognizes the value in some other way. For instance, if you enter a dollar ($) sign with the value, Excel assigns the Currency format. If you enter a percent (%) sign, it applies a percentage format. If you enter a value with a decimal point, Excel assigns the Number format.

When you enter numbers such as zip codes and social security numbers in a cell, Excel thinks they are values and treats them as such. In the case of zip codes, Excel automatically removes any leading zeroes from the number, (for example, 02124 becomes 2124), and converts it to a number. In these cases, you must intervene and let Excel know that the data you are entering is actually a text entry.

The following table explains the different types of cell formats that Excel uses.

**Cell formats**

| FORMAT | DESCRIPTION |
|---|---|
| **General** | Applies no specific format. Will display decimal point if initially entered. |
| **Number** | Displays decimal point and two decimal places. |
| **Currency** | Displays the currency symbol to the immediate left of the value and a minus sign in front of negative numbers. |
| **Accounting** | Displays the currency symbol to the left edge of the cell, lines up decimal points, and encloses negative values in parentheses. |
| **Short Date** | Displays the date in mm/dd/yyyy format: 3/24/2013 |
| **Long Date** | Displays date in expanded format: Monday, March 25, 2013 |
| **Time** | Displays time in hh:mm:ss format: 12:19:20 PM |
| **Percentage** | Displays the percent symbol and rounds up |
| **Fraction** | Displays the value as a fraction |
| **Scientific** | Displays the value using scientific notation |
| **Text** | Data entered will be treated as text and will not be used in calculations. |

## CHANGING NUMBER FORMATS

**Bottom Line**

You can format your numeric entries using a variety of predefined formats. You can also create and apply custom numeric formats for values such as phone numbers and zip codes.

In this first lesson, we will format a range of values using a variety of number formats.

### Applying a numeric format

The next steps show an example of how to use this feature.

**STEP BY STEP** **Applying a numeric format**

1 Launch Excel and open the file named **excel03** from the Excel03lessons folder.

2 Select range **B9:B20**.

3 In the Number section of the Home tab, click the arrow to display the Format drop-down menu (See Figure 3-2.).

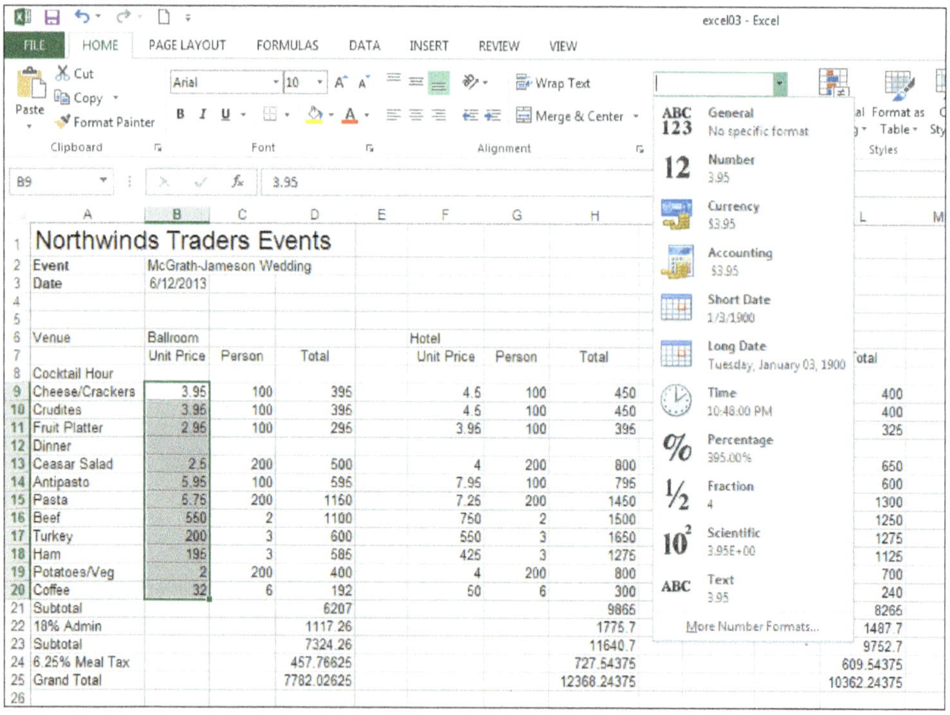


**Figure 3-2**

First select the range of cells and then assign a format to your values.

4 Choose **Number**.

Excel adds a decimal point and two digits (two decimal places) after each value in the range.

**Commonly-used numeric formats**

| ICON | NAME | ACTION |
|---|---|---|
| $ | Accounting (Currency) | Adds the currency symbol and two decimal places |
| % | Percent | Adds the percent sign and zero decimal places |
| , | Comma | Adds the thousands separator and two decimal places |
| ←.0 .00 | Increase Decimal | Increases the decimal place setting by 1 |
| .00 →.0 | Decrease Decimal | Decreases the decimal place setting by 1 |

## Changing the number of decimal places

By default, Excel rounds values with the Number format to two decimal places. You can increase or decrease the decimal place value accordingly. The following steps show an example of how to use this feature.

**STEP BY STEP** **Changing the number of decimal places**

1. Select range **D24:D25**. Notice that all numbers in this range have four decimal places.
2. In the Number section of the Home tab, click the **Decrease Decimal** button (.00→.0) three times.
3. Excel rounds down the value and displays the result with two decimal places instead of the original four. The value in cell D25 now reads 7782.03.
4. Perform steps 1–3 for ranges H24:H25 and range L24:L25.

## Adding the thousands separator

Excel automatically adds the thousands **separator** when the Currency or Accounting format is applied. The Comma Style format can be used when you want the thousands separator but not a currency symbol. Follow the next steps for an example of how to use this feature.

**STEP BY STEP** **Adding the thousands separator**

1. Select range **D9:D20**.
2. Press and hold the **Ctrl** key and select ranges **H9:H20** and **L9:L20**.
3. In the Number section of the Home tab, click the **Comma Style** button. Excel adds the thousands separator to the values and adds two decimal places.

4 Click the **Decrease Decimal** button on the Home tab twice to remove the decimal place setting. The result is shown in Figure 3-3.

**Figure 3-3**

Click the Decrease Decimal button to remove the two decimal spaces.

| Ballroom Unit Price | Person | Total |
|---|---|---|
| 3.95 | 100 | 395 |
| 3.95 | 100 | 395 |
| 2.95 | 100 | 295 |
| | | |
| 2.50 | 200 | 500 |
| 5.95 | 100 | 595 |
| 5.75 | 200 | 1,150 |
| 550.00 | 2 | 1,100 |
| 200.00 | 3 | 600 |
| 195.00 | 3 | 585 |
| 2.00 | 200 | 400 |
| 32.00 | 6 | 192 |
| | | 6207 |
| | | 1117.26 |
| | | 7324.26 |
| | | 457.77 |
| | | 7782.03 |

## Assigning the currency format

The next steps show an example of how to assign the currency format.

**STEP BY STEP** **Assigning the currency format**

1 Select range **D21:D25**.

2 Press and hold the **Ctrl** key and select ranges **H21:H25** and **L21:L25**.

3 From the Home tab, choose **Number Format**.

4 From the Number Format list, choose **Currency** to apply this style to the selected cells, as in Figure 3-4.

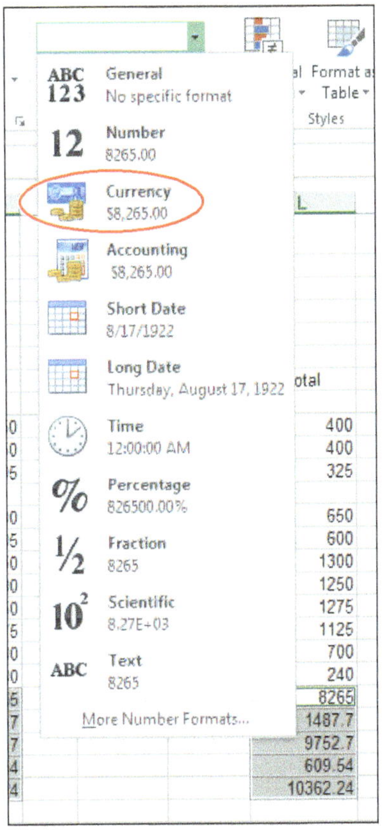


**Figure 3-4**

Assign the Currency format to a range of cells.

## Assigning the accounting format

The next steps show an example of how to assign the **accounting format**.

## STEP BY STEP Assigning the accounting format

1 Select range **D21:D25**.

2 Press and hold the **Ctrl** key and select ranges **H21:H25** and **L21:L25**.

3 From the Home tab, choose **Number Format**.

4 From the Number Format list, choose **Accounting**. See Figure 3-5. Notice how the Accounting format looks slightly different than the Currency format but the dollar signs, commas and decimals remain.

**Figure 3-5**

Values assigned the Accounting format look slightly different than the Currency format.

| | A | B | C | D | E | F | G | H | I | J | K | L | M |
|---|---|---|---|---|---|---|---|---|---|---|---|---|---|
| 1 | Northwinds Traders Events | | | | | | | | | | | | |
| 2 | Event | McGrath-Jameson Wedding | | | | | | | | | | | |
| 3 | Date | 6/12/2013 | | | | | | | | | | | |
| 4 | | | | | | | | | | | | | |
| 5 | | | | | | | | | | | | | |
| 6 | Venue | Ballroom | | | | Hotel | | | | Restaurant | | | |
| 7 | | Unit Price | Person | Total | | Unit Price | Person | Total | | Unit Price | Person | Total | |
| 8 | Cocktail Hour | | | | | | | | | | | | |
| 9 | Cheese/Crackers | 3.95 | 100 | 395 | | 4.5 | 100 | 450 | | 4 | 100 | 400 | |
| 10 | Crudites | 3.95 | 100 | 395 | | 4.5 | 100 | 450 | | 4 | 100 | 400 | |
| 11 | Fruit Platter | 2.95 | 100 | 295 | | 3.95 | 100 | 395 | | 3.25 | 100 | 325 | |
| 12 | Dinner | | | | | | | | | | | | |
| 13 | Ceasar Salad | 2.50 | 200 | 500 | | 4 | 200 | 800 | | 3.25 | 200 | 650 | |
| 14 | Antipasto | 5.95 | 100 | 595 | | 7.95 | 100 | 795 | | 6 | 100 | 600 | |
| 15 | Pasta | 5.75 | 200 | 1,150 | | 7.25 | 200 | 1450 | | 6.5 | 200 | 1300 | |
| 16 | Beef | 550.00 | 2 | 1,100 | | 750 | 2 | 1500 | | 625 | 2 | 1250 | |
| 17 | Turkey | 200.00 | 3 | 600 | | 550 | 3 | 1650 | | 425 | 3 | 1275 | |
| 18 | Ham | 195.00 | 3 | 585 | | 425 | 3 | 1275 | | 375 | 3 | 1125 | |
| 19 | Potatoes/Veg | 2.00 | 200 | 400 | | 4 | 200 | 800 | | 3.5 | 200 | 700 | |
| 20 | Coffee | 32.00 | 6 | 192 | | 50 | 6 | 300 | | 40 | 6 | 240 | |
| 21 | Subtotal | | | $ 6,207.00 | | | | $ 9,865.00 | | | | $ 8,265.00 | |
| 22 | 18% Admin | | | $ 1,117.26 | | | | $ 1,775.70 | | | | $ 1,487.70 | |
| 23 | Subtotal | | | $ 7,324.26 | | | | $ 11,640.70 | | | | $ 9,752.70 | |
| 24 | 6.25% Meal Tax | | | $ 457.77 | | | | $ 727.54 | | | | $ 609.54 | |
| 25 | Grand Total | | | $ 7,782.03 | | | | $ 12,368.24 | | | | $ 10,362.24 | |
| 26 | | | | | | | | | | | | | |
| 27 | The above bids are based on a head count of 200 guests. Should the guest list head count change the administration fee will also change based on the new nu | | | | | | | | | | | | |
| 28 | | | | | | | | | | | | | |

## Assigning the text format

The next steps show an example of how to format the text.

**STEP BY STEP** **Assigning the text format**

1 Type the label **Contact Number** in cell A4.

2 Click in cell **B4**.

3 From the Home tab, choose **Number Format**.

4 From the Number Format list, choose **Text**.

5 Type **(800) 555-1212** in cell B4 and press **Enter**.

## Creating custom formats

When formatting data, you can choose from among the built-in formats or you can assign a custom format for specialized data. Follow the next set of steps for an example of how to create custom formats.

**STEP BY STEP** **Creating custom formats**

1 Click in cell B4.

2 From the Editing group on the Home tab, choose **Clear**.

3 From the Clear list, choose **Clear All**.

4 Type **8005551212** in cell B4 and press the **Enter** key.

5 Click back on cell B4 and from the Home tab, choose **Number Format**.

6 In the drop-down menu choose **More Number Formats**.

**Figure 3-6**

Use Special Formats for items such as zip codes and phone numbers.

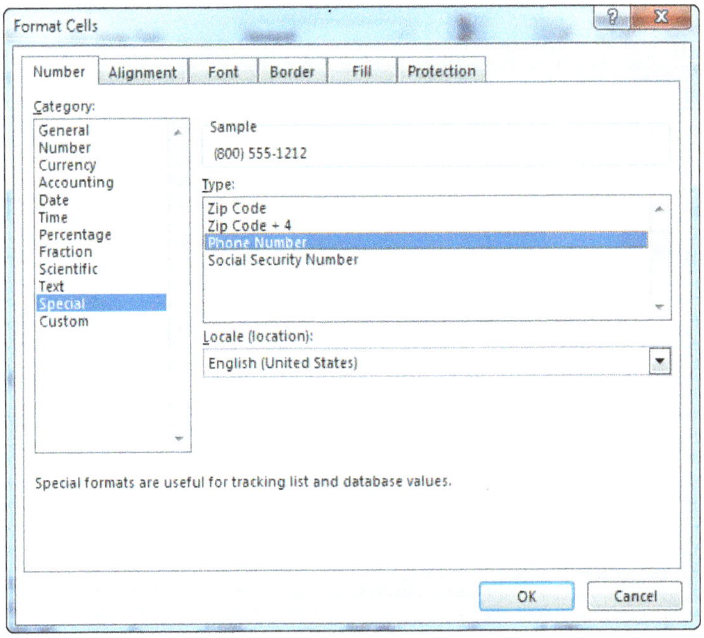


7 In the Format Cells dialog box (shown in Figure 3-6), select **Special as the Category**.

8 From the Type section, select **Phone Number**.

9 Click **OK** to apply the format.

## CHANGING THE FONT AND FONT SIZE

**Bottom Line**

In addition to changing the display of numeric data, you can add visual interest to your worksheets. Some of the changes you can make include font and font size, the color of the text, the background color of the cell, and text attributes such as bold, italic, and underline.

### Changing the font

The following set of steps show an example of how to change the font.

**STEP BY STEP** **Changing the font**

1 Select range **A1:L27**.

2 From the Home tab, choose **Font** from the Font group.

3 Select **Calibri** from the list (shown in Figure 3-7). Notice that your selected worksheet cells display a preview of the font as you move over a font name in the list.

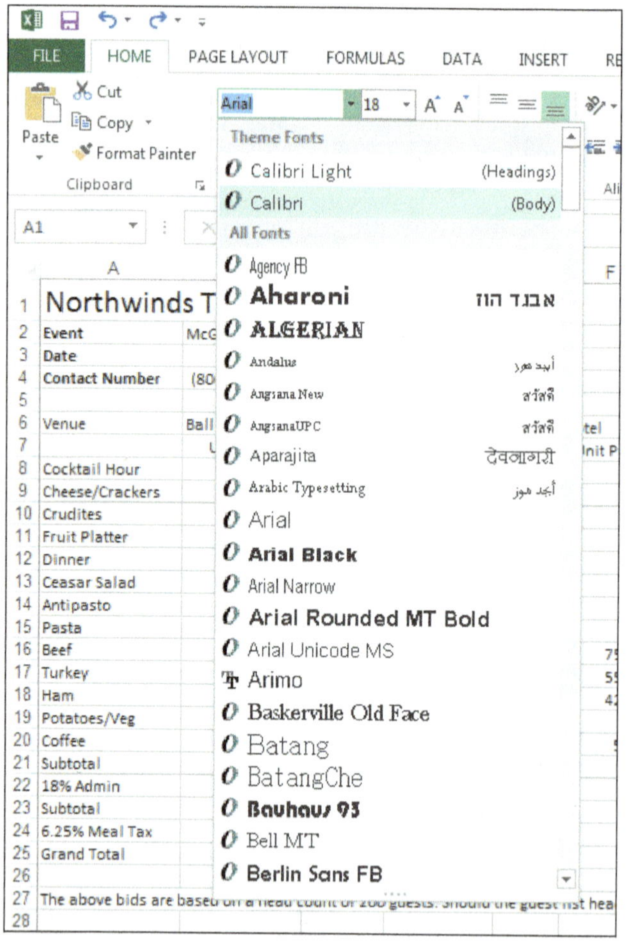

**Figure 3-7**

Change the manner in which your data is displayed with the Font option.

## Changing the font size

The following set of steps show an example of how to change the size of the font.

**STEP BY STEP** **Changing the font size**

1 Select range **A2:L27**.

2 From the Home tab, choose **Font Size** to display the drop-down list of font sizes.

3 Select **12**.

**Take Note** Click the **Increase Font Size** or **Decrease Font Size** buttons to quickly adjust the size accordingly.

## Changing the color of your text

The following set of steps show an example of how to change the color of text.

**STEP BY STEP** **Changing the color of your text**

1. Select range **A1:B4**.
2. From the Home tab, click the arrow to the right of the Font Color button to display the color palette, as in Figure 3-8.
3. Select **Blue**. Notice that the Font Color icon now reflects the change in color. You can apply the same color to another range of cells by clicking the icon because Excel saves the color that was last used.

**Figure 3-8**

For on-screen displays, make use of color.

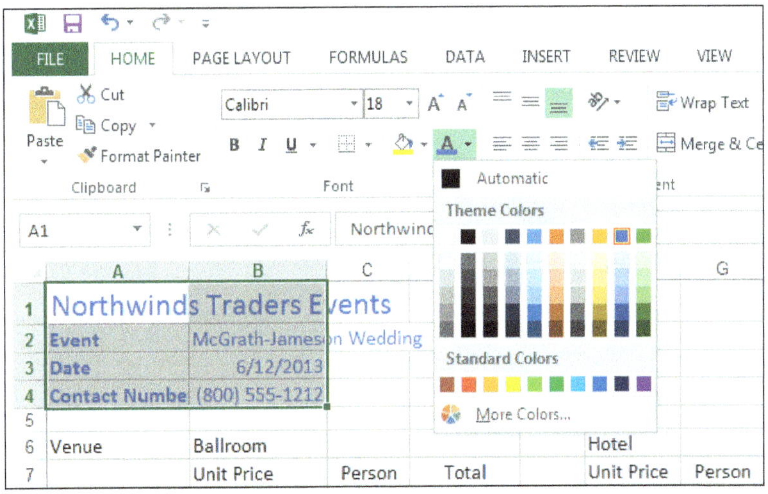


## Changing the background color of cells

The following set of steps show an example of how to change the background color of cells.

**STEP BY STEP** **Changing the background color of cells**

1. Click cell **D25**.
2. From the Home tab, click the arrow to the right of the Fill Color button to display the color palette See Figure 3-9.

3 From Standard Colors, select **Orange**. Notice that the Fill Color icon now displays the paint color you selected.

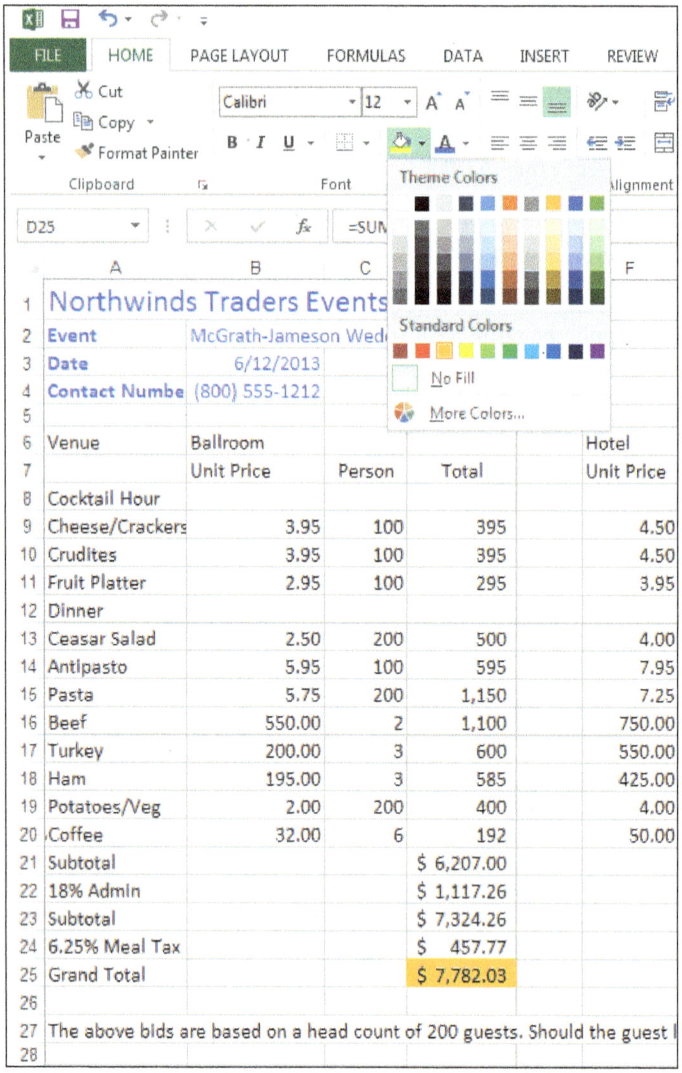

**Figure 3-9**

Change the background color of cells to draw attention to important data.

## Changing text attributes

Another way to add visual interest to your worksheets is to use **text attributes**, which works regardless of the font you have chosen. Your choices are bold, italics, underline, and double-underline (See Figure 3-10 for an example of formatting a heading.). The next set of steps show an example of how this feature works.

**STEP BY STEP** **Changing text attributes**

1 Select range **B7:D7**.

2 Press and hold the **Ctrl** key and select ranges **F7:H7** and **J7:L7**.

3 From the Home tab, choose **Bold**.

4 Select ranges **A9:A11** and **A13:A20**.

5 From the Home tab, choose **Italic**.

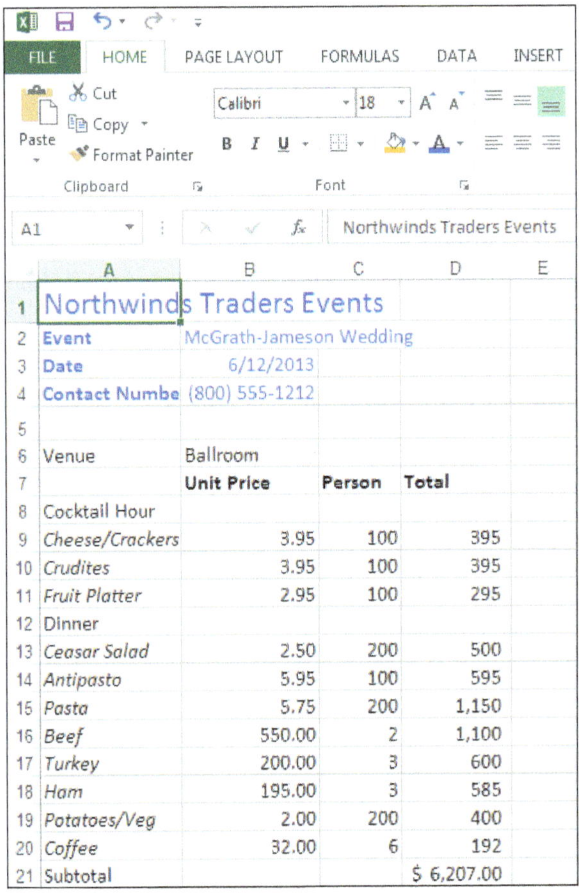


**Figure 3-10**

Text attributes can help set headings apart from the rest of the worksheet data.

**Bottom Line**

## MODIFYING ROW HEIGHTS AND COLUMN WIDTHS

By default, column widths and row heights are set to predefined measurements. If the data in a worksheet is larger than the column width or row height allows, Excel will alert you depending on the data type. If text is longer than the column width, Excel truncates the text if the cell to the immediate right contains data. Otherwise, the text continues to be displayed. If a numeric entry is longer than the current column width, Excel displays a series of number signs (########) in the cell. Row heights are set to adjust automatically when you change the size of your data.

### Change the column width

The next set of steps show an example of how to change the width of columns.

**STEP BY STEP** **Change the column width**

1 Click in cell L25.

2 From the Cells group on the Home tab, choose **Format**.

3 Select **Column Width** from the resulting menu to display the Column Width dialog box, shown in Figure 3-11.

Figure 3-11

Change the width of a column by typing an amount in the Column Width dialog box.

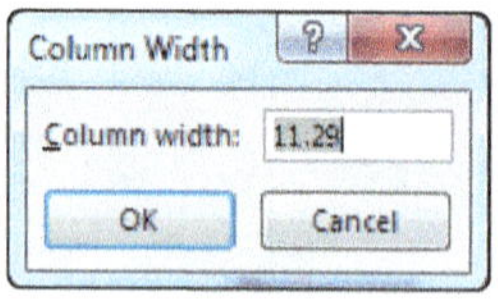


4 Type **12** In the Column Width text box, and then click **OK**.

## Changing the column width with the mouse

The next set of steps show an example of how to change the width of columns with the mouse.

**STEP BY STEP** **Changing the column width with a mouse**

1 Click the border separating columns A and B.

2 Click and drag the mouse to the right as in Figure 3-12.

3 Release when column A displays the label Contact Number in its entirety.

Figure 3-12

Change the width of a column by clicking and dragging the column border.

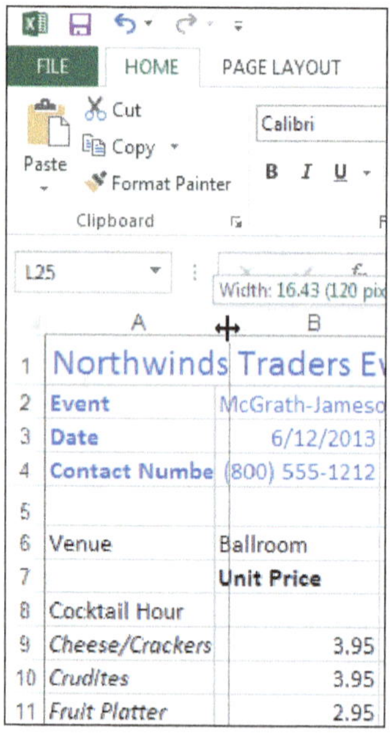


## Changing the column width automatically

You can quickly adjust the column width to accommodate the longest entry.

**STEP BY STEP** **Changing the column width automatically**

1 Select any column from the worksheet.

2 From the Cells group on the Home tab, choose **Format**.

3 Select **AutoFit Column Width** to set that column to auto-fit the width depending on the contents.

**Take Note** You can also double-click the border between the column headings to adjust the column width to the widest entry

### Changing the row height

The next set of steps show an example of how to adjust the height of a row.

**STEP BY STEP** **Changing the row height**

1. Click the border separating rows 5 and 6.
2. Click and drag the mouse down.
3. Release when the row is the height you desire.

**Take Note** Excel automatically adjusts the height of a row when you change the size of the data within the row.

### Changing the row height automatically

You can quickly adjust the row height to accommodate the tallest entry.

**STEP BY STEP** **Changing the row height automatically**

1. Select row **5** from the worksheet.
2. Choose **Format** from the Cells group of the Home tab.
3. Select **AutoFit Row Height**.

**Take Note** Double-click the border between the row headings to automatically adjust the height of a row.

## CELL ALIGNMENT

**Bottom Line**

By default, Excel automatically **aligns** numeric data to the right edge of a cell and text entries to the left. For the most part, numeric entries generally stay aligned to the right for consistency's sake (See Figure 3-13.). There are many different options for aligning text within a worksheet. Text can be aligned within a cell or across a range of cells. You can change the horizontal and vertical placement of text within a cell and you can also wrap extra-long text entries within a single cell.

**Figure 3-13**

Excel automatically aligns text to the left edge of the cell and numbers to the right.

## Aligning text within cells

You can change the alignment of text both within the columns and rows. That is, between the column widths and the row heights. When you increase the **width** of a row, data can be aligned between the top and bottom edges of the cell.

**STEP BY STEP** **Aligning text within cells**

1. Select range B7:D7.
2. Press and hold the Ctrl key and select ranges F7:H7 and J7:L7.
3. On the Home tab in the Alignment group, click the Center button. Excel centers the headings within the selected cells.

## Merging and centering columns

You can center a heading over multiple columns with the Merge and Center command. When you **merge** a range of cells, all the cells are converted to a larger single cell. For instance, in our example we want the heading for the venue type to be centered over the column headings Unit Price, Person, and Total.

**STEP BY STEP** **Merging and centering columns**

1. Select range B6:D6, which contains both the heading we want to center and the columns to center it over.
2. From the Home tab, choose the Merge & Center command from the Alignment group.
3. Excel merges cells B6, C6, and D6 and centers the heading Ballroom over all three columns.
4. Merge and Center range F6:H6 and J6:L6. The result is shown in Figure 3-14.

**Figure 3-14**

When a heading spans multiple columns, use the Merge & Center command to center the heading over all the columns.

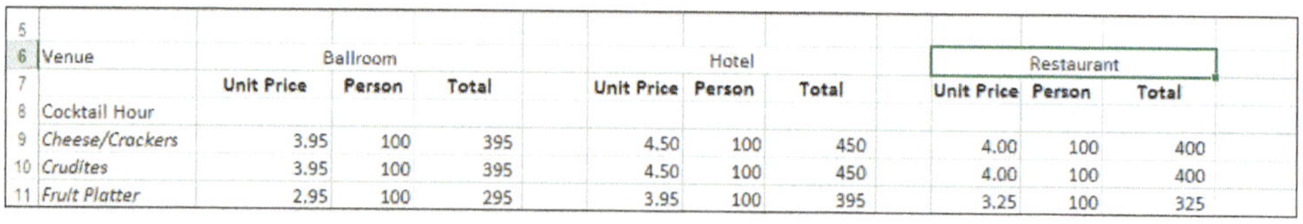

| | | | | | | | | | | | | |
|---|---|---|---|---|---|---|---|---|---|---|---|---|
| 5 | | | | | | | | | | | | |
| 6 | Venue | Ballroom | | | | Hotel | | | | Restaurant | | |
| 7 | | Unit Price | Person | Total | | Unit Price | Person | Total | | Unit Price | Person | Total |
| 8 | Cocktail Hour | | | | | | | | | | | |
| 9 | *Cheese/Crackers* | 3.95 | 100 | 395 | | 4.50 | 100 | 450 | | 4.00 | 100 | 400 |
| 10 | *Crudites* | 3.95 | 100 | 395 | | 4.50 | 100 | 450 | | 4.00 | 100 | 400 |
| 11 | *Fruit Platter* | 2.95 | 100 | 295 | | 3.95 | 100 | 395 | | 3.25 | 100 | 325 |

## Wrapping text

Excel has a number of sophisticated text handling tools that you would normally only find in a word processing program such as Microsoft Word. As Excel has grown more powerful and easier to use, it has added the ability to manipulate text within worksheet cells. For example, the Wrap Text command allows you to wrap extra-long text within a single cell.

The following set of steps shows an example of how to wrap text.

**STEP BY STEP** **Wrapping text**

1. Click cell A27.
2. Choose Wrap Text from the Alignment group on the Home tab.

Excel enlarges the height of row 27 and wraps the extra-long notation within cell A27.

### Rotating text

Another advanced text editing tool is the ability to rotate text within a cell. This can be useful when a heading is much longer than the data it is describing, or when you'd like to fit more data on a single page.

Follow the next set of steps for an example of how to rotate text.

**STEP BY STEP** **Rotating text**

1 Select range **B7:D7**.

2 Choose **Orientation** from the Alignment group on the Home tab.

3 Select **Angle Counterclockwise**. The result is shown in Figure 3-15.

**Figure 3-15**

Text alignment helps when you need to make more room on a page.

**Take Note** When you apply formatting to a cell, the format is either On or Off. A format that is applied to the current cell will appear highlighted to indicate that it is on.

4 Click the **Orientation** button again and choose **Angle Counterclockwise** again to turn off the format from range B7:D7.

## BORDERS AND SHADING

**Bottom Line**

Just as text and number formats can help guide the eye in a worksheet, so too can the use of borders. A border can be applied to all four sides of a cell in a variety of line styles.

There are two ways to add a Border: you can add a predesigned border to a selected range of cells or you can draw your own, changing the line style and color yourself.

### Applying a border

The following steps show an example of how to add a border.

**STEP BY STEP** **Applying a border**

1 Select range **B6:D7**.

2 Choose **Borders** from the Font group on the Home tab.

3 Select **Outside Borders**, as in Figure 3-16.

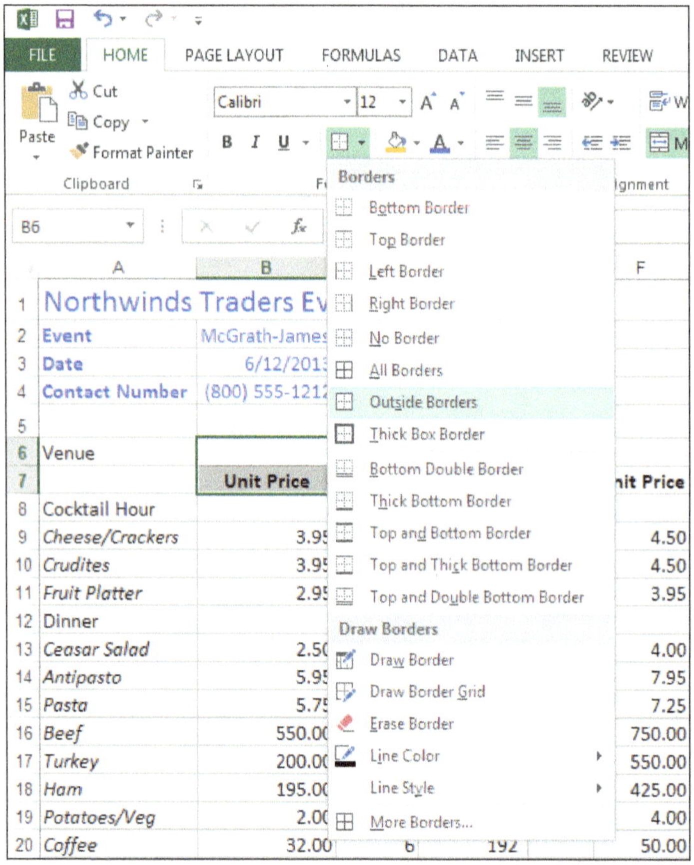

**Figure 3-16**

Add borders to your worksheet to help draw the eye.

4 Click another cell so you can view the thin border.

**Take Note** Once you select a Border style, the Border icon maintains that style until you pick a new one. Select each range of cells and click the Border icon to apply the style.

## Drawing a border

Excel automatically uses a single black line style when you draw a border. You can change both the line style and color of a border you drawn, as illustrated by the next set of steps.

**STEP BY STEP** **Drawing a border**

1 From the Font group choose **Borders**.

2 Choose Line Style and select the **Thick-Dashed** line style. The cell pointer changes its shape into that of a pencil.

3 Choose **Borders** again, click **Line Color** and select **Green**.

4 Click and drag the pencil around range F6:H7 to add the border See Figure 3-17.

5 Press the **Esc** key on the keyboard when you have finished to remove the pencil cell pointer.

**Figure 3-17**

Draw a custom border around a range of cells.

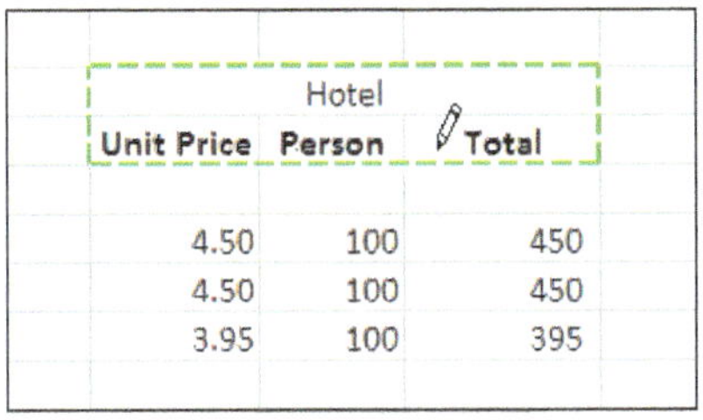


## Erasing a border

Just as there are two ways to add a border, there are two ways to remove a border. When you apply a border, you select the range of cells and then pick the border you want to use. To remove a border, select the range of cells and choose No Border from the Border command. You can also use the Erase Border command to erase the border by clicking each cell that has a border.

Here is an example of erasing a border using the No Border option:

### STEP BY STEP Removing a border

1 Select range **B6:D7**.

2 From the Home tab, choose **Border**.

3 Choose **No Border** from the displayed list.

### STEP BY STEP Erasing a border

1 From the Home tab, choose **Border**.

2 Choose **Erase Border**. The mouse pointer is displayed as an eraser , as in Figure 3-18.

3 Click the eraser on the edge of each cell in range F6:H7 to remove the border.

**Figure 3-18**

Remove a border from a range of cells with the Eraser.

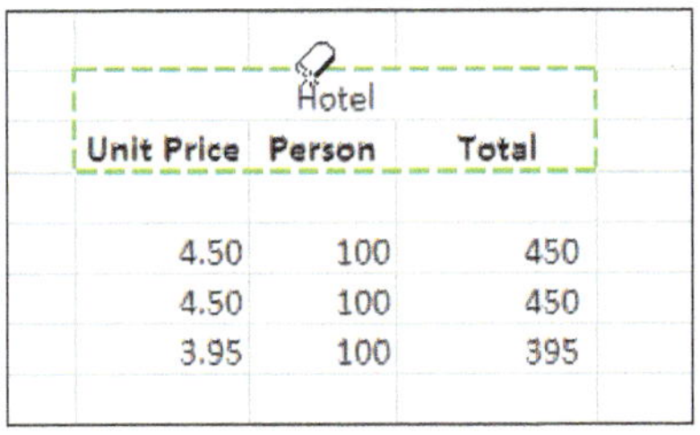


4 Press the **Esc** key when finished to return the pointer back to normal.

## COPYING CELL FORMATS

**Bottom Line**

Excel's **Format Painter** tool is essential when formatting a worksheet. With this tool, you can quickly and easily copy a format from one cell to another with a single click. Follow the next set of steps for an example.

**STEP BY STEP** **Copying cell formats**

1. Select cell D25.
2. In the Clipboard group, choose the Format Painter. The mouse pointer now includes a paint brush, shown in Figure 3-19.

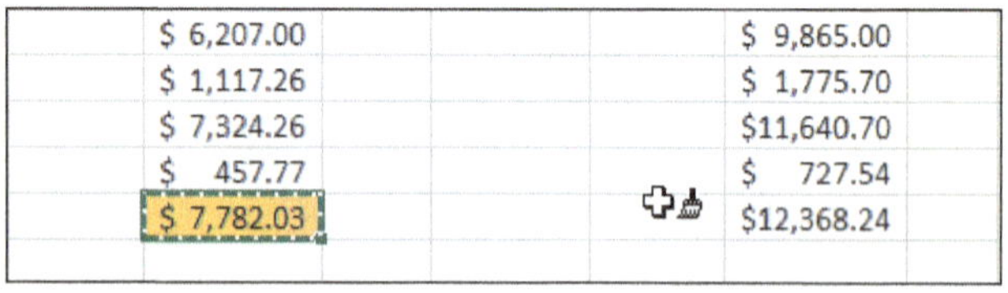


**Figure 3-19**

Copy formats from one cell to another with the Format Painter command.

3. Click cell H25 to apply the formatting.
4. Repeat step 2 and 3 to copy the format to cell L25.

**Take Note** To apply formatting to multiple cells, double-click the Format Painter and click each cell to apply. Press Esc when you are done.

## WORKING WITH CELL STYLES

**Bottom Line**

A **style** is a collection of formatting stored under a single name. A style can consist of alignment, numeric formats, borders, fonts, shading, and a host of other attributes. To apply that collection of attributes, you need to assign the style rather than each attribute individually.

Excel comes with a number of predefined styles from which to choose; you can also create your own.

## Applying cell styles

Follow the next set of steps for an example of how to apply styles to cells.

### STEP BY STEP Applying a style to a range of cells

1 Select range **A8:A11**.

2 From the Styles group choose **Cell Styles**. The drop-down gallery is shown in Figure 3-20.

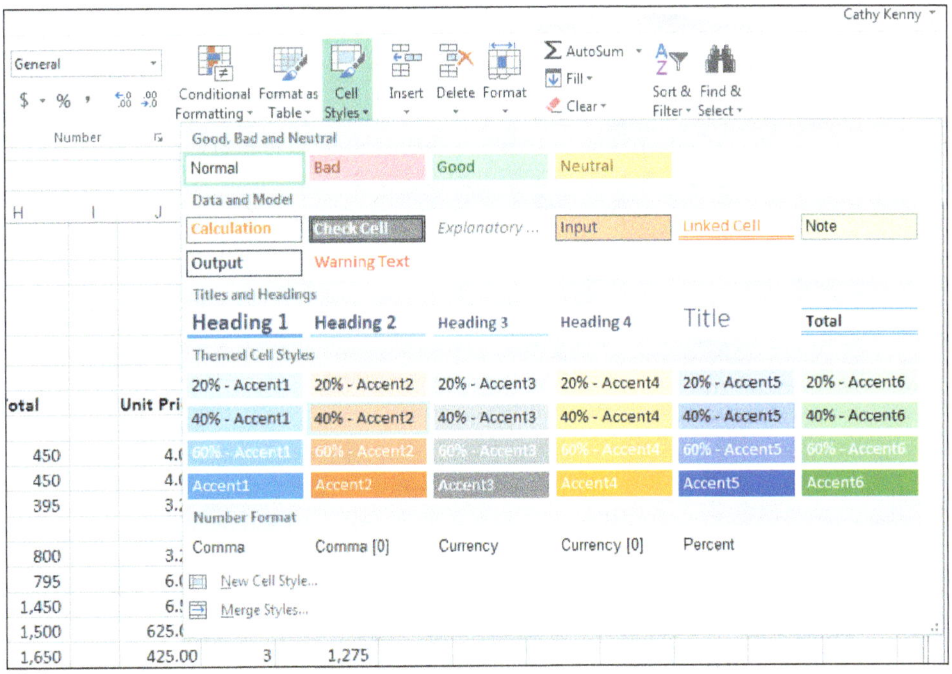


**Figure 3-20**
Assign cell styles to maximize visibility.

3 Select **40% - Accent 2**.

4 Select range **A12:A20**.

5 From the Home tab, choose **Cell Styles**.

6 Select **40% - Accent 1**.

7 Click cell **A8**, press and hold the **Ctrl** key, and click cell **A12**.

8 From the Home tab, choose **Cell Styles**.

9 Select **Heading 3**.

10 Click on cell **A21**. Hold the **Ctrl** key and click cells **A21** and **A25**.

11 From the Home tab, choose **Cell Styles**.

12 Select **Total**.

## Clearing a style

You can easily remove the formatting from a cell without removing its contents with the Clear command, as the following set of steps illustrates.

**STEP BY STEP** **Clearing a style**

1. Select range **A9:A11**.
2. From the Editing group, choose **Clear**.
3. Select **Clear Formats** from the resulting menu to remove the themed cell style.

## Creating a style

If you don't want to use any of Excel's built-in styles, you can create your own styles and save them for future use. Once you create a style, it appears at the top of the Styles menu under the Custom category. The easiest way to create a style is to assign the appropriate formats to the cell first, as demonstrated by the following steps.

**STEP BY STEP** **Creating a style**

1. Click cell **B6**.
2. Change the Font to **Bauhaus 93**, the size to **14**, the color to **Blue**, and add a Border to the Bottom of the cell.
3. From the Styles group, choose **Cell Styles**, and then click **New Cell Style**.
4. Type **Heading Column** in the Style name text box (see Figure 3-21) and click **OK**.

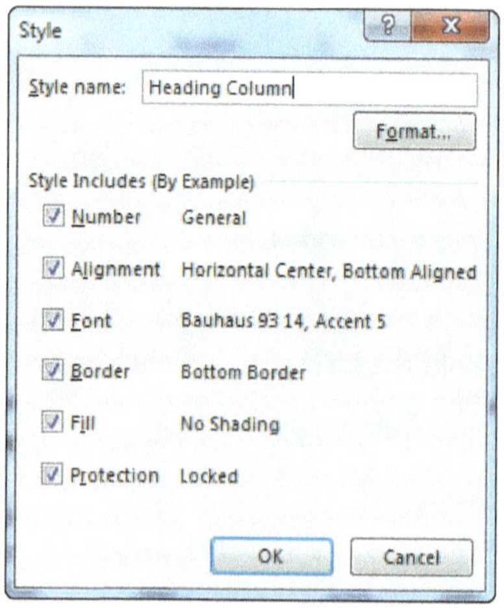


**Figure 3-21**

You can create your own custom styles and save them for future use.

## Modifying a style

Another way to create a custom style is to take an existing style, change an attribute or two, and save it as a new style.

**STEP BY STEP** **Modifying a style**

1 From the Styles group, choose **Cell Styles** to display the Style Gallery.

2 Right-click the new **Heading Column** style at the top of the Style Gallery and choose **Modify** (See Figure 3-22.).

**Figure 3-22**

Rather than start from scratch, modify an existing style to suit your needs.

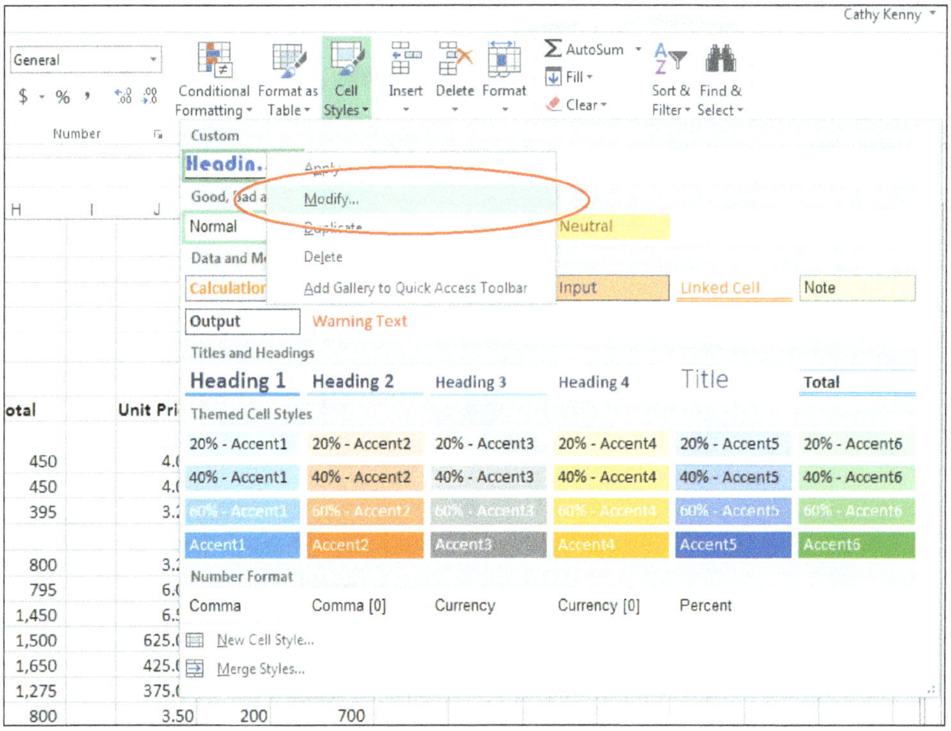


3 Click **Format** in the resulting dialog box, and then click the **Font** tab.

4 Change the size to **12**.

5 Click **OK** twice to save the modifications.

## Merging styles from other worksheets

When you create a style, Excel stores the style in the worksheet in which it was created. You can use custom styles with other worksheets, but you must first merge them in to the current worksheet.

**STEP BY STEP** **Merging styles from other worksheets**

1 Open a new worksheet using the **File > New** command. Choose **Blank workbook**.

2 Choose **Cell Styles** from the Styles group.

3 Select **Merge Styles**. The Merge Styles dialog box is shown in figure 3-23.

4 Select **excel03** to copy the styles into the new, blank workbook.

**Figure 3-23**

You can merge cell styles from other workbooks into the current file.

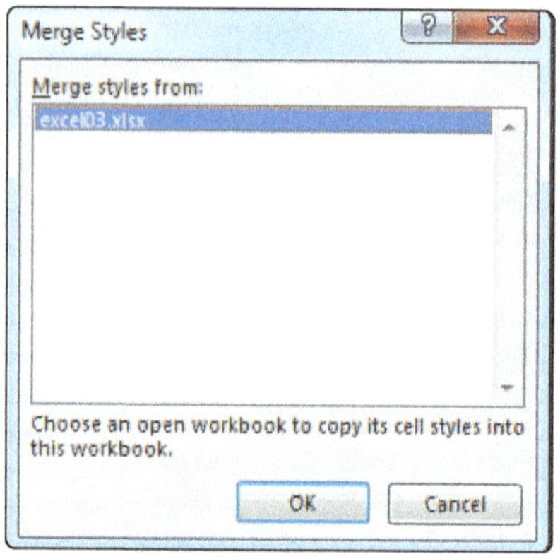


5 Click **OK**.

6 In the resulting dialog box, click **No** to keep the styles in the current workbook intact and merge the custom styles only.

7 Choose **File > Close**. We won't be working with this file so you don't need to save it.

## USING CONDITIONAL FORMATTING

**Bottom Line**

Excel's **conditional formatting** options let you draw attention to important points in your data set based on a certain set of criteria. You could, for instance, highlight values that are greater than a certain value; highlight sales data that falls within the top 10%; or highlight testing values that are above average. By using color, symbols, and other special attributes, you can show data at a glance that might be on the rise or falling below expectations.

Conditional formatting is based on a set of predefined rules. For instance, the rule that states Format All Cells Based on Their Values formats cells using a graduated color scale based on a set of defined values. There are five different categories of rules and a number of options within each category that you can use.

**Conditional formatting rules**

| ICON | HIGHLIGHT CELL RULES | DESCRIPTION |
|---|---|---|
| | Highlight Cells Rules | Highlights cells based on a defined value. |
| | Top/Bottom Rules | Highlights values based on a defined ranking. |
| | Data Bars | Adds a data bar to the cell to represent the value; the longer the bar, the larger the value. |
| | Color Scales | Applies a gradient color scale to a value and the color indicates where the value falls within a range. |
| | Icon Sets | Adds a set of icons to represent the values in a range of cells. |

To demonstrate conditional formatting, we will open a new worksheet from the Excel03lessons folder. But first, save and close the current event planning worksheet we have been using.

**STEP BY STEP** **Saving a worksheet**

1 Go back to the **excel03** worksheet and choose **File > Save As**.

2 In the Office Background, click **Computer** and navigate to the Excel03lessons folder.

3 In the file name text box, type **_formats** at the end of the current file name.

4 Click **Save**, and then choose **File > Close**.

## Using conditional formatting

Follow the next set of steps for an example of how to use this feature.

**STEP BY STEP** **Using conditional formatting**

1 Choose **File > Open**.

2 Navigate to the Excel03lessons folder and double-click the file named **excel03_grades**.

3 Select range **A4:E37**.

4 From the Style group, choose **Conditional Formatting**.

5 Select **Top/Bottom Rules** (see Figure 3-24) and select **Top 10%**.

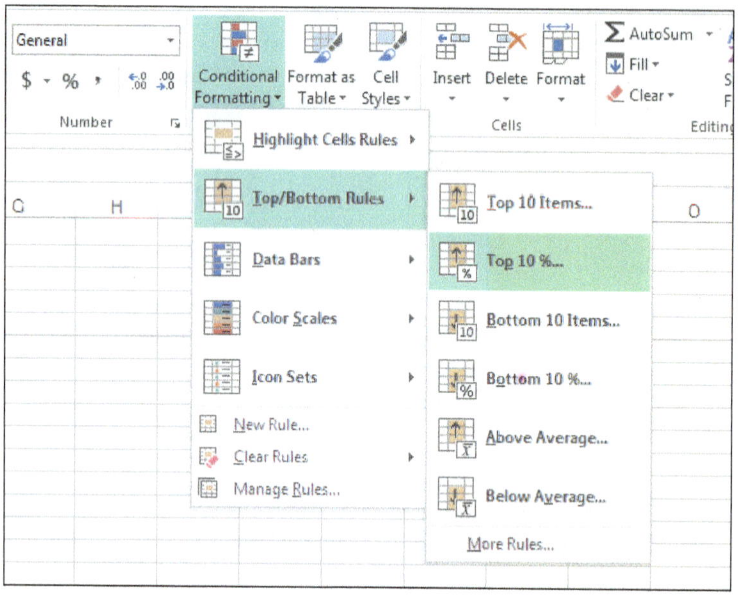


**Figure 3-24**

Instantly highlight important data with Conditional Formatting.

6 Click **OK**. Excel highlights the grades that fall within the Top 10%.

## Removing conditional formatting

You can remove conditional formatting from an entire worksheet or a specified range, as the follow example indicates.

**STEP BY STEP** **Removing conditional formatting**

1 Select range **A4:E37**.

2 Choose **Conditional Formatting** again.

3 Choose **Clear Rules**.

4 Select **Clear Rules** from Selected Cells.

## Creating a new rule

If the predefined rules are not what you are looking for, you can create your own, including specifying the formatting you want to apply should the conditions be met. The next set of step shows you an example of how to use this feature.

**STEP BY STEP** **Creating a new rule**

1. Select range **E4:E37**.
2. From the Style group choose **Conditional Formatting** again.
3. Choose **New Rule**.
4. From the Rule list, select **Format only cells that contain**.
5. In the **Format only cells with:** section, select **Greater Than** from the drop-down menu adjacent to the Cell Value field (See Figure 3-25.).

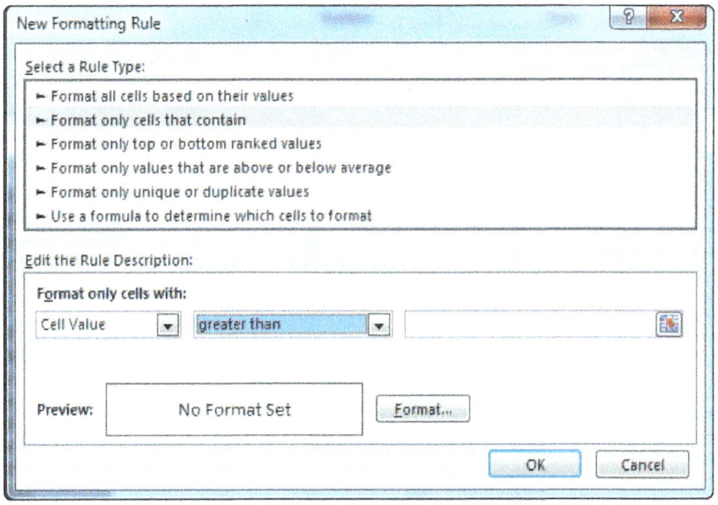


**Figure 3-25**

Create a New Rule to make your data standout when it meets specific criteria.

6. Type **2000** in the box adjacent to Greater Than.
7. Click **Format** and choose the **Fill** tab.
8. Select the color **Blue**.
9. Click **OK** twice. Excel highlights all scores that are higher than 2000.

## USING PAGE THEMES

Page **themes** are a collection of color-coordinated color schemes and font families for use in a single worksheet. Each theme contains a set of predefined colors, fonts, and attributes that have been professionally designed and coordinated. You can also swap out different parts of each theme to suit your individual needs. You can, for instance, pick a new font set to use or select a different color scheme. You can also adjust the settings for objects added to your worksheets with the Drawing tools.

### Applying a theme

Follow the next set of steps for an example of how to apply a theme.

**STEP BY STEP** **Applying a theme**

1 From the Page Layout tab, choose **Themes** from the Themes group.

**Figure 3-26**

Use Page Themes to design color-coordinated worksheets.

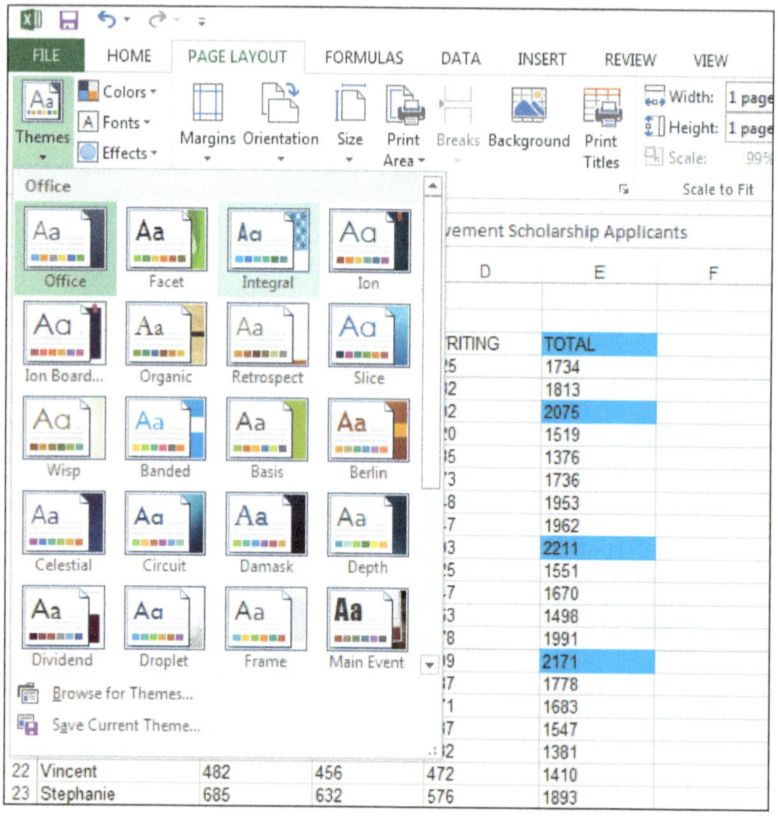


2 Select **Integral** from the gallery, shown in Figure 3-26

Excel changes the appearance of your worksheet, including any cells that make existing use of Cell Styles or colors.

## Changing the color scheme

Follow the next set of steps for an example of how to change the **color scheme** of your worksheet.

**STEP BY STEP** **Changing the color scheme**

1. From the Page Layout tab in the Themes group, choose **Colors**.
2. Select **Blue Green** (See Figure 3-27.).

**Figure 3-27**

Swap out one color set for another in the Page Theme.

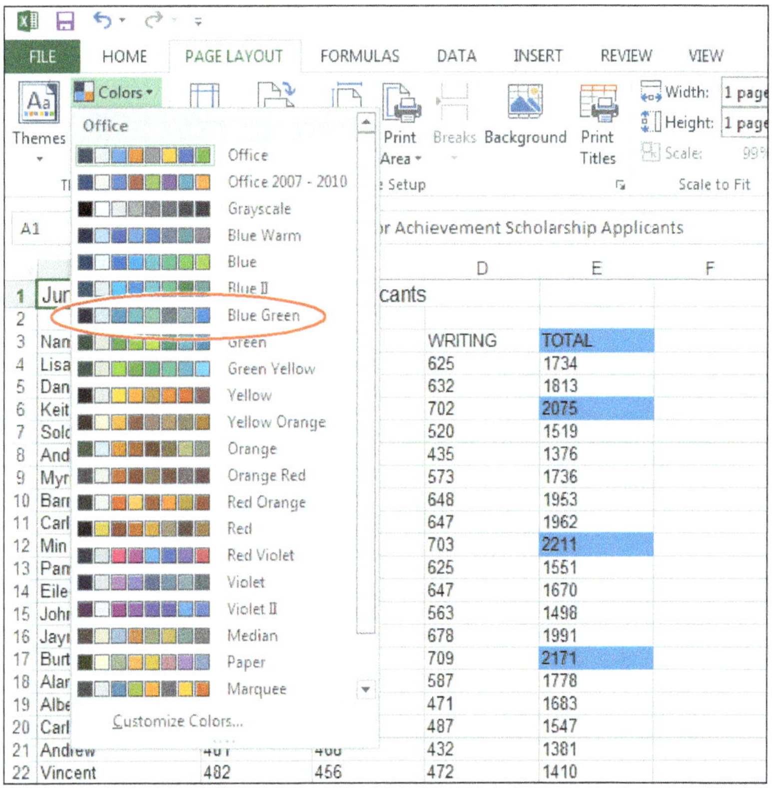

## Changing the font set

Follow the next set of steps for an example of how to change the **font set** used by your worksheet.

### STEP BY STEP Changing the font set

1. From the Page Layout tab, choose Fonts.
2. Select Corbel from the Fonts gallery, shown in Figure 3-28.

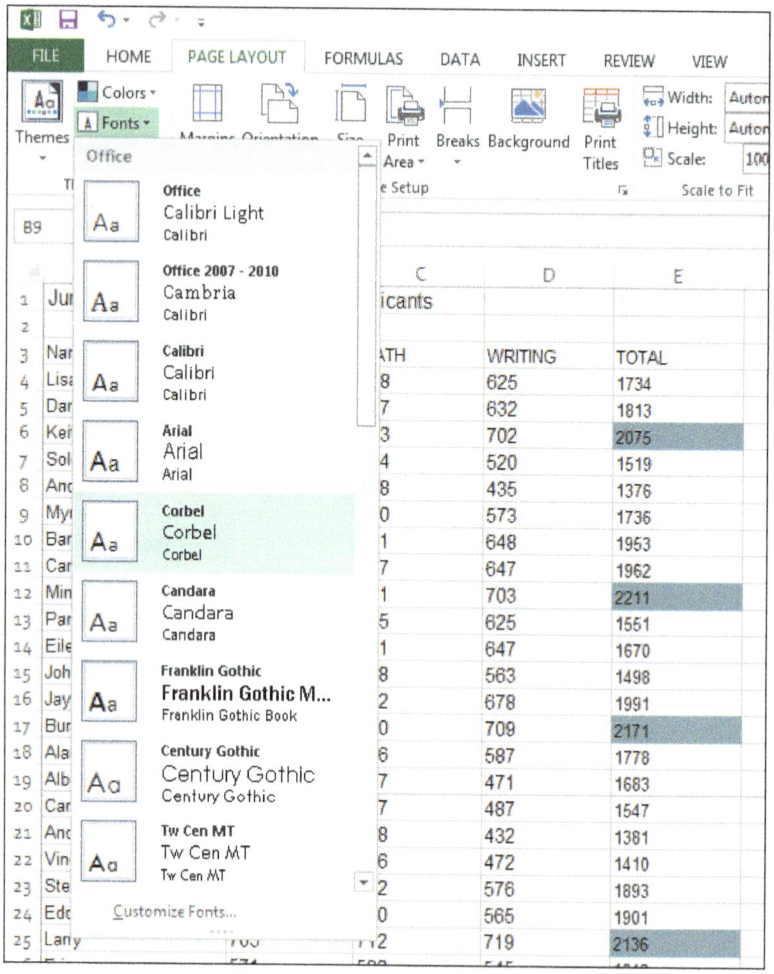


Figure 2-28

Pick a new Font family to use in the Page Theme.

## Changing the effects

Follow the next set of steps for an example of how to change the **effects** used in your worksheet.

**STEP BY STEP** **Changing the effects**

1 From the Page Layout tab in the Themes group, choose Effects.

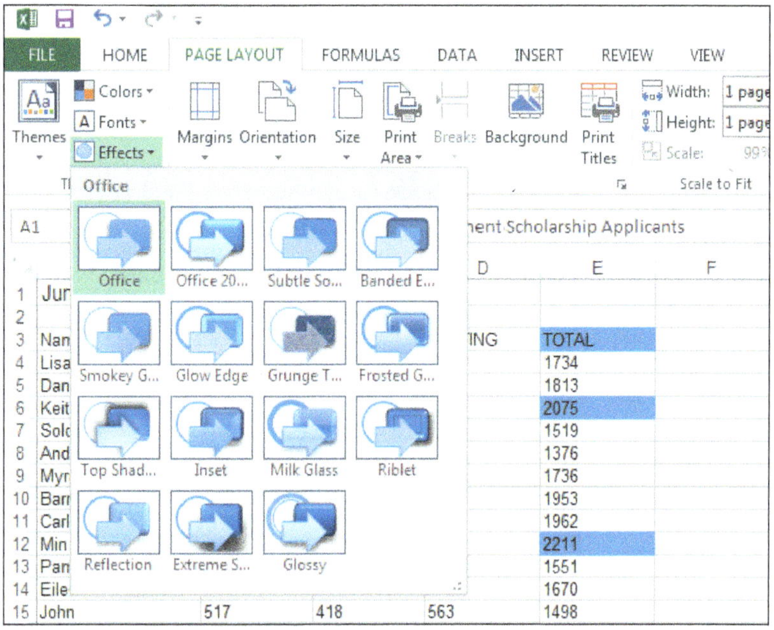


Figure 3-29

Select the effects to add to drawn objects in a worksheet.

2 Select **Glow Edge** from the gallery. See Figure 3-29.

3 Choose **File > Save As**, and navigate to the Excel03lessons folder. Type **excel03_grades_format** as the file name, and click **Save**.

## What you learned in this lesson:

- Understanding Cell Formats
- Changing Number Formats
- Changing the Font and Font Size
- Modifying Row Heights and Column Widths
- Cell Alignment
- Borders & Shading
- Copying Cell Formats
- Working with Cell Styles
- Using Conditional Formatting
- Using Page Themes

# Knowledge Assessment

## True/False

**Circle T if the statement is true or F it the statement is false**

T F 1. A number with a thousands separator but no currency symbol has the Comma Style.

T F 2. Accounting Format aligns both currency symbols and decimal points.

T F 3. Excel offers Social Security and Phone Number format support.

T F 4. The background color of a cell is called the Cell Shade.

T F 5. Merge & Center adds up the contents of several cells and displays the sum in a single large cell.

T F 6. To add a thick borderline around the edges of a multi-cell selection, use the All Borders option.

T F 7. You can modify the borders of a cell range using the Border Eraser tool.

T F 8. To copy the fill color and data format between cells, use the Format Painter.

T F 9. Selecting a new Page Theme will clear the data formatting in a document.

T F 10. Conditional Formatting uses rules to determine the content or style of a cell.

## Fill in the Blanks

**Complete the following sentences by writing the correct word or words in the blanks provided.**

1. Themes and Color Schemes can be selected from galleries in the _____ tab.
2. A Font Set consists of default fonts for _____ and _____ cells.
3. The command for adjusting text wrapping is found in the _____ group of the _____ tab.
4. To automatically expand a column to display its entire contents, use the _____ tool.
5. In addition to changing font, size, and color, you can alter your data's text attributes. Options include _____, _____, _____, and _____.
6. Data formatted with the Text format will not be used in _____.
7. To display $5 as $5.00, apply the _____ command twice.
8. Calendar entries can be formatted as _____ (e.g., 2/13/1979) or _____ (e.g., Tuesday, February 13, 1979).
9. In Excel, numbers are also known as _____.
10. To format a calendar date like 21 /:/ December /:/ 2005, use a _____ number format.

# Competency Assessment

## Project 3-1: Formatting Numeric Data

**In this exercise you will apply a variety of number formats to the same data.**

1. Create a new blank workbook.
2. Fill the range A1:A7 with the following text labels, one per cell: **General**, **Date**, **Currency**, **Percentage**, **Scientific**, **Accounting**, **Time**.
3. Type the number **4509.334** in cell B1.
4. Drag the AutoFill handle down to fill cells B2:B7 with the same number.
5. Select cell **B2**.
6. From the drop-down menu in the Home > Number group, select **Short Date**.

7. Repeat steps 6-7 to format cell B3 with the **Currency** format, B4 as a **Percentage**, B5 with **Scientific notation**, B6 with **Accounting**, and B7 with the **Time format**.
8. AutoFit column A's width to its contents.
9. Press **Ctrl+W**. Save your file as **project_3-1_numberformats**.

### Project 3-2: Simple Conditional Formatting

**In this project you'll use conditional formatting to highlight top and bottom 10% values.**

1. Open the exercise file **cond_formatting_1** and save it as **project_3-2_conditional**.
2. Select cells **B2:B32**.
3. Click **Home > Styles > Conditional Formatting**. From the Top/Bottom Rules list, select **Top 10%**.
4. Format the top 10% of cells with **Green Fill with Dark Green Text**. Click **OK**.
5. Repeat steps 3-4 to format the bottom 10% of cells with **Light Red Fill with Dark Red Text**.
6. Finally, from the Conditional Formatting dropdown, select the **5 Quarters** icon set.
7. Save and close your document.

## Proficiency Assessment

### Project 3-3: Applying Themes and Styles

**In this exercise you'll apply themes and styles to your worksheet data.**

1. Open the project file **3-3-source** and save it as **project_3-3_themes**.
2. Apply the **Heading 1** style to cell A1.
3. Select cells **B2:B32**.
4. Apply the "**40% - Accent 4**" themed cell style.
5. In cell D15, type **Dec 13-14 data reported as 2-day average**.
6. Apply the **Explanatory Text** style to cell D15.
7. Select the **Basis** theme from the Page Layout tab.
8. Save and close your document.

### Project 3-4: More Cell Formatting

**In this exercise you'll format cell contents.**

1. Open the project file **3-4-source** and save it as **project_3-4_cellformatting**.
2. Insert a column to the left of column A.
3. In any cell in the range A1:A32, type the text **Daily totals subject to Auditor revision**.
4. Select the cell you edited in step 3 and rotate the text 90 degrees counterclockwise, so it reads bottom to top.
5. Apply the **Merge and Center** tool to A1:A32.
6. Middle Align the newly merged cell.
7. Select the thickest Line Style from the Cell Borders tool, then draw a border along the right hand edge of the merged cell.
8. Click on the merged cell **B1** and determine its font size and text characteristics from the Home > Font group.
9. Format merged cell A1 with the same font size and boldface type.
10. Save and close your document.

# Mastery Assessment

## Project 3-5: Custom Cell Styles

**In this exercise you will create custom cell styles.**

1. Open the project file **3-5-source** and save it as **project_3-5_customcellstyles.**
2. Merge cells **E27:G32**.
3. Open the exercise file **bowie_data.**
4. Copy the cell text ("29 December data…") from bowie_data into the newly merged cell in themes_styles_3.
5. Format the new merged cell as follows: **Text data format**; **Word Wrap on**; **9pt Corbel**; "**Red**, **Accent 2**, **Lighter 80%**" **fill**; **red text**; **Center text**; **Middle Align text**.
6. Select the new merged cell and save its formatting as a custom Cell Style called **data_notice.**
7. Save and close your document.

## Project 3-6: Advanced Conditional Formatting

**In this exercise, create more complex conditional formatting rules.**

1. Open the project file **3-6-source** and save it as **project_3-6_conditional2**.
2. Select the data in column C.
3. Create a new Conditional Formatting rule to add a bright yellow fill to any cells with duplicate daily values.

   (Four cells should be emphasized with this rule, in rows 12, 14, 15, and 29.)
4. Open the Manage Cells… dialog and change the order in which conditional formatting rules are applied, so the duplicate cells rule is applied last. (This will not affect the spreadsheet's formatting.)
5. Save and close your document.

# 4 Using Formulas in Excel 2013

## LESSON SKILL MATRIX

In this lesson, you will learn the following skills:

| | |
|---|---|
| Understanding Formulas | Using Common Functions |
| Entering Simple Formulas | Working with Ranges |
| Referencing Cells from Other Worksheets/Workbooks | Copying Formulas |
| Using Functions | Formula Auditing |
| Using the Function library | Using the AutoSum Tool |

## KEY TERMS

- Absolute Cell Reference
- Arguments
- Auditing (tools)
- Average
- Cell Reference
- Comparison Formula
- COUNTIF
- Formula
- Function Library
- If
- Max
- Median
- Min
- Name Manager
- NOW
- PMT
- Range Name
- Relative Cell Reference
- Sum

ResearchersField researchers at Fabrikam receive enormous amounts of raw sensor data each day. To turn it into something meaningful for humans, they must transform the data in a variety of ways, ranging from simple sums and averages to advanced statistical analysis. Excel's Function Library offers the combination of Excel's robust Function Library contains the tools they need for their mathematical work – and back at HQ, the financial and HR teams will use the same Library for their own ends.

## SOFTWARE ORIENTATION

You can use formulas to perform basic or complex calculations within Microsoft Excel.

**Figure 4-1**

Formula controls in Microsoft Excel 2013.

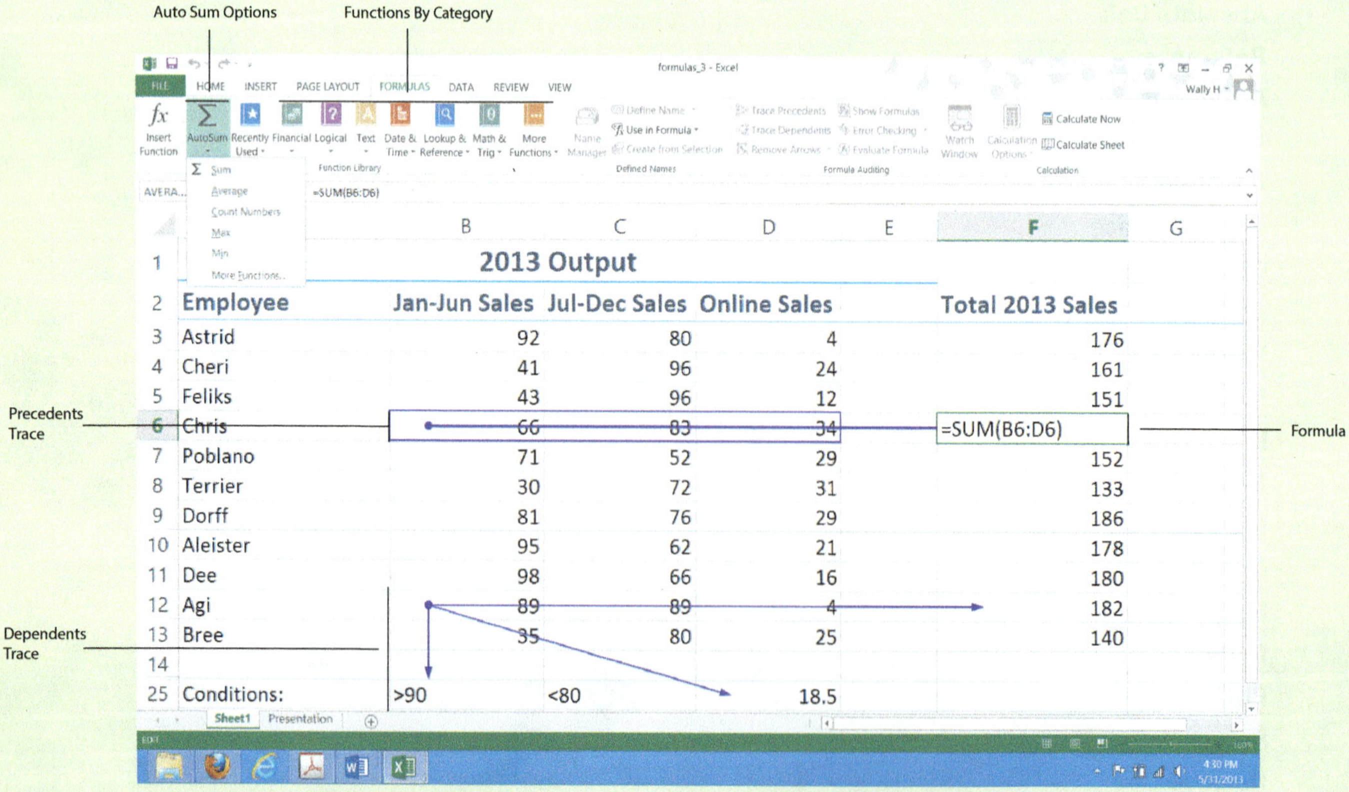

## STARTING UP

In this lesson, you'll work with several files from the Excel04lessons folder. Make sure that you have loaded the OfficeLessons folder onto your computer.

The most useful feature of Excel is its ability to perform calculations. Through formulas, you can use Excel to calculate any range of values. Excel's extensive Function library, which is a set of predefined formulas, enables you to perform sophisticated data analysis with little or no experience.

## FORMULAS

**Bottom Line**

A **formula** is a mathematical equation used to calculate a value. In Excel, a formula must always begin with the equal sign (=), which indicates to Excel that it must interpret the data in the cell as a formula.

When you enter a formula, Excel displays the result of the formula in the cell rather than the formula itself. For example, if you type =2+6 in a cell, Excel displays the result of that calculation (8). The Formula bar, located at the top of the worksheet window, is the area in which you can view, enter, and edit formulas.

Excel also provides hundreds of predefined functions that allow you to perform calculations, from easy to complex, without having to build the formulas from scratch. For instance, the SUM function quickly adds together a range of cells, so you don't have to add each cell individually.

Before we begin creating formulas, you should become familiar with some key terms.

### Operator

An operator is a sign or symbol that specifies the type of calculation that should be performed, such as an addition (a plus sign +) or a multiplication (*). For example, in the formula =150+25, the operator is the plus sign, and it adds together the values 150 and 25.

### Operand

Every Excel formula includes at least one operand, which is the data that Excel uses in the calculation. The simplest type of operand is a number; however, you can also include a reference to worksheet data, such as a cell address (B1), as an operand.

### Arithmetic formula

An arithmetic formula combines a numeric operand (a number or a function that returns a numerical value as a result) with an operator to perform a calculation. As you can see in the following table, there are six arithmetic operators you can use to construct arithmetic formulas.

**Mathematical operators in formulas**

| OPERATOR | PURPOSE |
|---|---|
| + | Addition |
| - | Subtraction |
| * | Multiplication |
| / | Division |
| % | Percentage |
| ^ | Exponentiation |

### Order of operations

Many errors occur in formulas when mathematical operators are not entered in the proper order. When creating formulas, you must keep in mind the *order of operations*: exponentiation occurs before multiplication or division, and multiplication occurs before addition and subtraction. You can alter the order of operations by enclosing segments of the formula in parentheses. For example, the formula =(4+10)*2 forces Excel to first add 4 and 10 and then multiply the result by 2.

### Comparison formula

A **comparison formula** combines a numeric operand, such as a number, with special operators to compare one operand to another. The most common comparison operators are greater than (>), less than (<), and equal to (=) or some combination thereof. A comparison formula returns a logical result of 1 or 0. If the comparison is true, the formula returns a value of 1. If the comparison is false, the formula returns a value of 0.

Comparison formulas often consist of *If...Then* statements. For example, the formula =IF(C2>D2,"Yes","No") returns the label Yes if the value in cell C2 is greater than the value in cell D2; otherwise, it returns the label "No."

## ENTERING SIMPLE FORMULAS

You can create formulas by using the mouse or the keyboard.

### Building a formula by typing

The following example shows how to build a formula by typing.

**STEP BY STEP** **Entering a formula**

1 Launch Microsoft Excel and open a Blank workbook.

2 Type **24** in cell A2 and **12** in cell A3.

3 Type =24*12 in cell A4, as in Figure 4-2.

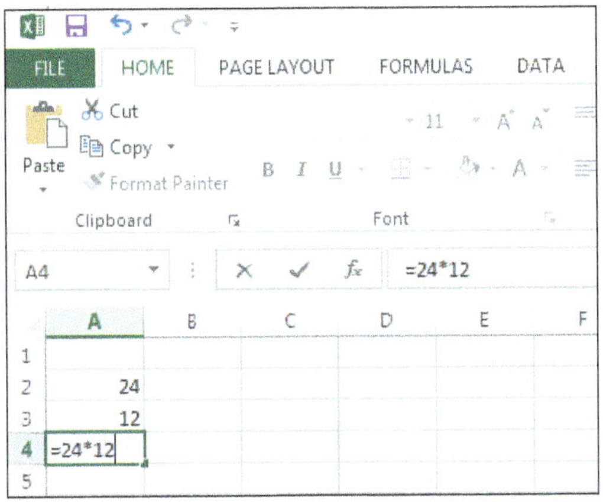


**Figure 4-2**

When you enter a formula, Excel displays the result of the formula in the cell and the formula in the Formula bar.

4 Press Enter. Excel displays the result of the formula, 288, in cell A4.

Another way to create a formula is to refer to the cell that contains the value, rather than enter the value itself. When you do, Excel updates the formula automatically when the original value changes. For instance, the values used for the formula in cell A4 actually reside in cells A2 and A3. Note that Excel also color-codes each cell reference in the formula to help you keep track of the data in your worksheet.

Follow the next set of steps to see how this feature works.

**STEP BY STEP** **Using a formula**

1 Type = in cell A5.

2 Continue typing A2*A3 in cell A5 and press Enter. Excel displays the result of 288.

3 Type 57 in cell A2 and press Enter. Excel updates the result in cell A5 to 684.

## Building a formula by pointing

In addition to typing the **cell reference**, you can also build a formula by pointing to the cell that contains the data you want to use, as shown by the following set of steps.

**STEP BY STEP** **Building a formula by pointing**

1 Type = in cell A6.

2 Using the arrow keys or the mouse, move the cell pointer to cell A2.

3 Type the multiplication operator, (*) and move the cell pointer to cell A3.

4 Press Enter on your keyboard. Excel displays the result 684.

## REFERENCING CELLS FROM OTHER WORKSHEETS OR WORKBOOKS

**Bottom Line**

When building formulas, you can also reference data from other worksheets or workbooks.

### Referencing a cell in another worksheet

Perform the following set of steps to practice referencing a cell in another worksheet.

**STEP BY STEP** **Referencing a cell in another worksheet**

1. Click the **New Sheet** button at the bottom of the worksheet window.
2. Type **823** in cell A2.
3. Type = in cell B2.
4. Click cell **A2** and type *.
5. Click the tab labeled **Sheet1**.
6. Click cell **A2**. Excel appends the sheet name to the cell address in the formula bar. Your formula should now read: =A2*Sheet1!A2.
7. Press **Enter** on your keyboard. Excel switches back to Sheet2 and multiplies the value in cell A2 of Sheet1 by the value in cell A2 of Sheet2.

### Referencing a cell in another workbook

Perform the following set of steps to practice referencing a cell in another workbook.

**STEP BY STEP** **Referencing a cell in another workbook**

1. Choose **File > Open**, click **Computer** in the Backstage view, and click **Browse**.
2. Navigate to the Excel04lessons folder and open the file named **excel04_formulas**.
3. Point to the Excel icon in the Windows Taskbar at the bottom of your screen (see Figure 4-3) and click the file named **Book1** to maximize the workbook.

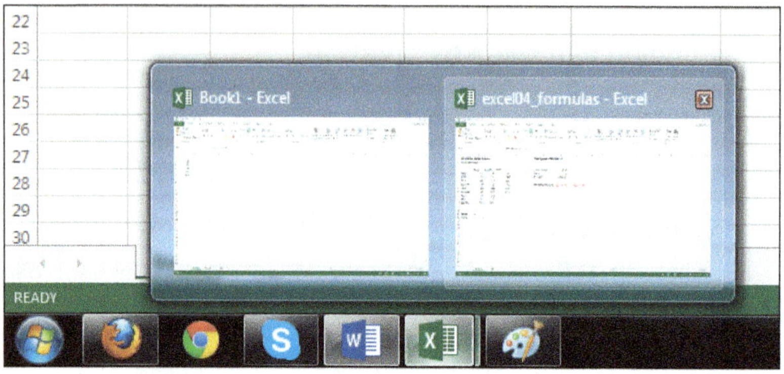


**Figure 4-3**

Switch between open workbooks in the Windows Taskbar.

4. On Sheet1 of **Book1**, click in cell A7 and type **=**.
5. Point to the Excel icon in the Windows Taskbar, and click the file named **excel04_formulas** to maximize the workbook.
6. Click in cell B5. Excel appends the file name, sheet name, and cell address to the formula. Your formula should now read: =[Excel04_formulas.xlsx]Sheet1!$B$5.
7. Type *.
8. Switch back to Sheet1 in the workbook named **Book1** and click in cell A6.
9. Press **Enter** on your keyboard. Excel multiplies the value in cell B5 of the workbook named **excel04_formulas** by the amount in cell A6.

## USING FUNCTIONS

**Bottom Line**

Functions are predefined formulas that perform a specific calculation, such as determining the average value in a range or calculating a mortgage payment. Excel includes over 200 functions in categories such as financial, statistical, scientific, and engineering. The table below details some of the most commonly-used functions.

**Common Excel functions**

| FUNCTION | DESCRIPTION | SYNTAX AND EXAMPLE OF SYNTAX |
|---|---|---|
| SUM | Adds together values within a range | =SUM(*range*)<br>=SUM(A1:A50) |
| IF | Tests whether a condition is met and returns the first result if the value is true and the second result if the value is false | =IF(*test,true,false*)<br>=IF(A1>B1,500,5000) |
| AVERAGE | Returns the average of a range | =AVERAGE(*range*)<br>=AVERAGE(A1:A10) |
| MAX | Returns the largest value in a range | =MAX(*range*)<br>=MAX(A1:A30) |
| MIN | Returns the smallest value in a range | =MIN(*range*)<br>=MIN(A1:A10) |
| MEDIAN | Returns the median value in a range | =MEDIAN(*range*)<br>=MEDIAN(A1:A10) |
| DATE | Returns the value that represents the date | =DATE(*year,month,day*)<br>=DATE(2013,4,23) |
| NOW | Returns the current date and time | =NOW() |
| COUNTIF | Counts the number of cells within a range that meet a given condition | =COUNTIF(*range,criteria*)<br>=COUNTIF(A1:A45,">20") |
| PMT | Calculates the payment for a loan | =PMT(*rate,nper,fv*)<br>=PMT(.08/12,12,100000) |

## USING THE FUNCTION LIBRARY

**Bottom Line**

The **Function Library** in the Formulas tab, shown in Figure 4-4, organizes functions by type. To use the Function Library, select the category containing the function you want to use, and click it. When you do, Excel displays the list of functions assigned to that category. Select the function you want to use by clicking it. Excel displays a Function Arguments dialog box, where you can indicate the ranges containing the arguments.

**Figure 4-4**

The Function Library group on the Formulas tab.

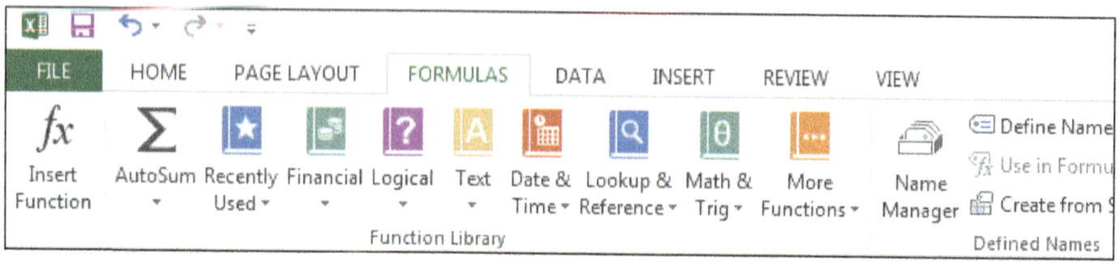


**Take Note** If you know the Function you want to use and its syntax, you can type the function and its required arguments directly in the cell, without using the Function Library at all.

**The Function Library**

| TYPE | DESCRIPTION |
|---|---|
| AutoSum | Commonly-used functions such as SUM, AVERAGE, COUNT, MAX, and MIN. |
| Recently-Used | The most recently-used functions. |
| Financial | Financial calculations such as loan payments (PMT) and net present value (NPV). |
| Logical | Formulas that perform logical tests including IF, TRUE, and NOT. |
| Text | Formulas that manipulate text strings including FIND, EXACT, and SEARCH. |
| Date & Time | Date and time calculations including NOW, MONTH, and DAYS. |
| Lookup & Reference | Formulas that help find matching values, including VLOOKUP, MATCH, and CHOOSE. |
| Math & Trig | Mathematical calculations, including SUM, PRODUCT, and COS. |

## Creating a formula with a function

Creating formulas with functions is very similar to creating regular formulas, with the exception that each function follows a specific syntax. All functions consist of the equal sign followed by the function name and the **arguments** within a set of parentheses. For instance, the formula to calculate the average in a range of data would be similar to: =AVERAGE(A1:A50).

You can create a formula using a function by typing the function name and arguments yourself, or you can use the Function Library to build the function step by step. In the following example, we will use the NPER function to determine how long it will take to pay back a loan of $15,000 if monthly payments of $100 are made and the interest rate is 2.5% per year.

**STEP BY STEP** **Creating a formula with function**

1 In **Book1**, click in cell A8.

2 Choose **Financial** from the Formulas tab.

3 Select **NPER** from the Function list. In the formula bar Excel displays a description and the syntax for the NPER function, which calculates the number of payment periods to pay off a loan.

The Function Arguments dialog box for the selected function NPER is displayed. See Figure 4-5.

4 Enter **.025/12** in the Rate box; enter **100** in the Pmt box; and **15000** in the Pv box.

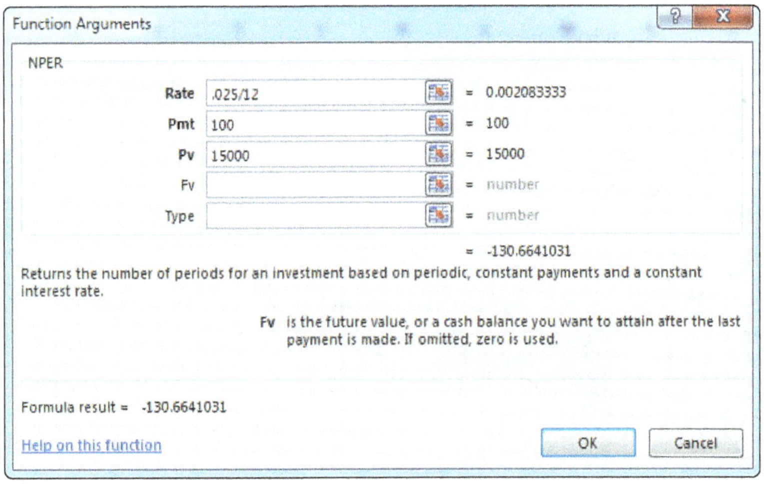


**Figure 4-5**

The Function Arguments dialog box helps you build a formula step by step.

5 Click **OK**. Excel enters the formula in cell A8 and calculates the result of 130 pay periods.

## USING THE AUTOSUM TOOL

**Bottom Line**

The AutoSum tool, which you'll find on both the Home tab and Formulas tab of the Ribbon, contains a set of quick single-click functions. To use these commands, select the range of data and then choose the appropriate function. The following table describes what each function does.

**The AutoSum functions**

| COMMAND | DESCRIPTION |
|---|---|
| AutoSum | Adds up the values in a range. |
| Average | Finds the average value in a range. |
| Count Numbers | Counts the number of values in a range. |
| Max | Returns the maximum value in a range. |
| Min | Returns the minimum value in a range. |

### Quickly adding up a range of values

Perform the next set of steps to understand how you can quickly add up a range of values in Excel using the AutoSum function.

**STEP BY STEP** **Using the AutoSum Tool**

1 Select range **A2:A8**.

2 Choose **AutoSum** from the Formulas tab. From the drop-down menu shown in Figure 4-6, choose **Sum**.

Excel adds up the values in range A2:A8 and enters the result in cell A9, which is the cell immediately below the selected range.

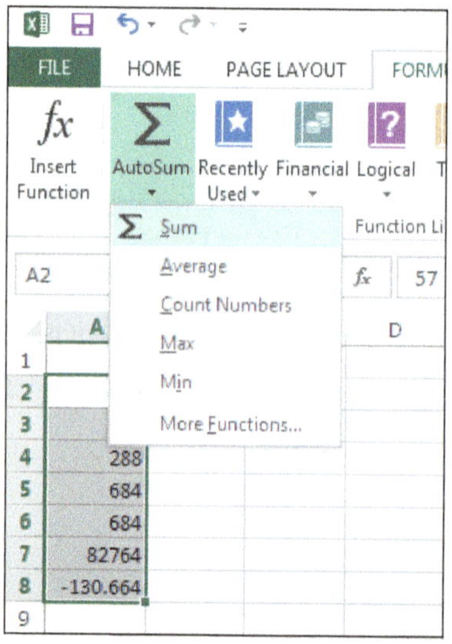


**Figure 4-6**

Quickly calculate a range of values with the AutoSum command.

## USING COMMON FUNCTIONS

Before we review some of the more commonly-used functions and how to use them, we need to save the worksheet we have been using to experiment with creating formulas.

## STEP BY STEP Saving your work

1. Choose **File > Save**, and choose **Computer**.
2. Click the **Browse** button, navigate to the Excel04lessons folder, name the file **excel04_sample**, and click **Save**.
3. Choose **File > Close** to close the worksheet. We will continue working with the file named **excel04_formulas**.

### SUM

The **Sum** function adds together the values in a range of cells, as the following steps show.

## STEP BY STEP Using the SUM function

1. Click in cell B9.
2. Click the arrow next to the AutoSum button in the Editing group of the Home tab, and select **Sum** from the drop-down menu, shown in Figure 4-7.

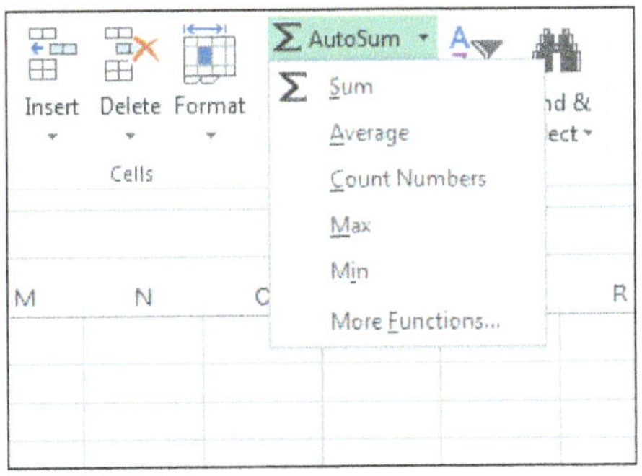


**Figure 4-7**
AutoSum button found in the Editing group of the Home tab.

3. Excel automatically selects the range of cells immediately adjacent to the current cell, in this case the values directly above cell B9, or range B5:B8 (See Figure 4-8.).

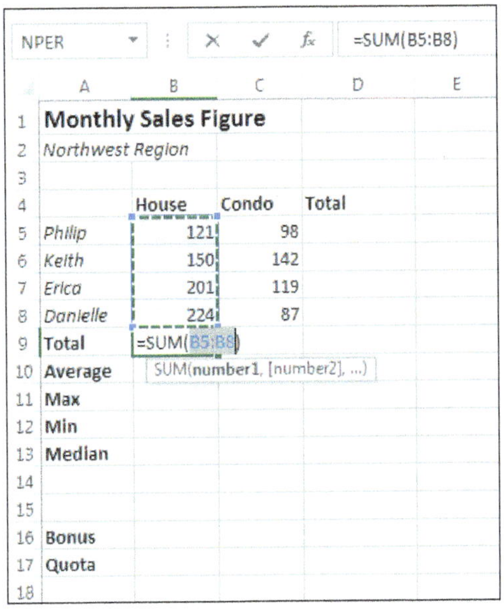


**Figure 4-8**
Excel automatically selects the range of cells adjacent to the current cell.

4. Press **Enter** on your keyboard to sum the range.

## AVERAGE

The **Average** function finds the average value in a range of cells, as the following example shows.

**STEP BY STEP** **Using the AVERAGE function**

1. Click in cell B10.
2. Click the arrow next to the AutoSum button in the Editing group, and select **Average** from the drop-down menu.

Excel automatically selects the range of cells immediately adjacent to the current cell, in this case the values directly above cell B10, or range B5:B9.

3. Change the range to B5:B8.
4. Press **Enter** on your keyboard. Excel displays the average amount in cell B10.

## MAX

The **Max** function finds the maximum value in a range of cells, as the following example shows.

**STEP BY STEP** **Using the MAX function**

1. Click in cell B11.
2. Click the arrow next to the AutoSum button, and select **Max** from the drop-down menu.

Excel automatically selects the range of cells immediately adjacent to the current cell, in this case the values directly above cell B11, or range B5:B10.

3. Change the range to B5:B8.
4. Press **Enter** on your keyboard. Excel displays the Maximum value in cell B11.

## MIN

The **Min** function finds the minimum value in a range of cells, as the following example shows.

**STEP BY STEP** **Using the MIN function**

1. Click in cell B12.
2. Click the arrow next to the AutoSum button and select **Min** from the drop-down menu.

Excel automatically selects the range of cells immediately adjacent to the current cell, in this case the values directly above cell B12, or range B5:B11.

3. Change the range to B5:B8.
4. Press **Enter** on your keyboard. Excel displays the minimum value in cell B12.

## MEDIAN

The **Median** function finds the middle value in a range of cells, as shown by the next set of steps.

## STEP BY STEP Using the MEDIAN function

1. Click in cell B13.
2. Type =MEDIAN(.
3. Select range B5:B8.
4. Type ) and press Enter on your keyboard.
5. Excel displays the median value in cell B13.

### IF

The **If** function performs a logical test on a cell or range of cells to determine whether a specified condition has been met. For example, suppose you have decided that a Bonus will be granted to the individual who sells more than 700 units of certain product. The example below shows how you can use the If function to calculate whether the value in cell B9 meets this criteria.

## STEP BY STEP Using the IF function

1. Click in cell B16.
2. Type =IF(B9>700,"Yes","No") and press Enter on the keyboard.

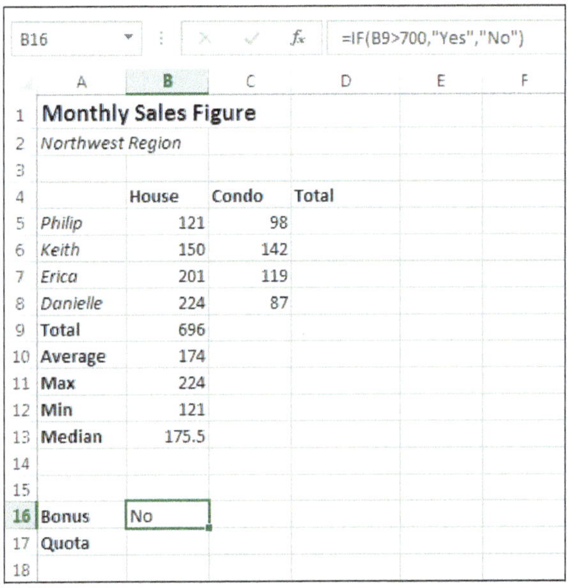

B16 =IF(B9>700,"Yes","No")

| | A | B | C | D | E | F |
|---|---|---|---|---|---|---|
| 1 | Monthly Sales Figure | | | | | |
| 2 | Northwest Region | | | | | |
| 3 | | | | | | |
| 4 | | House | Condo | Total | | |
| 5 | Philip | 121 | 98 | | | |
| 6 | Keith | 150 | 142 | | | |
| 7 | Erica | 201 | 119 | | | |
| 8 | Danielle | 224 | 87 | | | |
| 9 | Total | 696 | | | | |
| 10 | Average | 174 | | | | |
| 11 | Max | 224 | | | | |
| 12 | Min | 121 | | | | |
| 13 | Median | 175.5 | | | | |
| 14 | | | | | | |
| 15 | | | | | | |
| 16 | Bonus | No | | | | |
| 17 | Quota | | | | | |
| 18 | | | | | | |

**Figure 4-9**

Perform logical tests on data using IF and COUNTIF functions. Here, data is analyzed to see if sales quotas have been met.

Excel evaluates the Total amount in cell B9 to determine whether more than 700 units have been sold (in other words, whether the value in B9 is greater than 700). If the value in B9 is greater than 700, (meaning that more than 700 units have been sold), the formula returns the label Yes, and you can give the individual his or her bonus. However, if the value in B9 is 700 or less as in Figure 4-9,, the function returns the label No, and you can decide not to grant the individual his or her bonus.

## COUNTIF

**COUNTIF** is similar to IF in that the function evaluates a cell or range of cells to test for a specific condition. However, the COUNTIF function returns the number of times the condition has been meet in the range, not whether the condition has been met at all. For example, suppose you want to figure out how many brokers have met a sales quota of 200 units. The following set of steps illustrates how to apply the COUNTIF formula to make this determination.

**STEP BY STEP** **Using the COUNTIF function**

1 Click in cell B17.

2 Type **=COUNTIF(B5:B8,">200")** and press **Enter** on the keyboard.

Excel evaluates the values in range B5:B8 to determine how many of the cells within this range have values that are greater than 200 (in other words, how many brokers met the sales quota of 200 units.)

## NOW

The **NOW** function enters the current date and time in a worksheet cell and it's updated whenever the workbook is opened. An example is shown below.

**STEP BY STEP** **Using the NOW function**

1 Click in cell G2.

2 From the Formulas tab, choose **Date & Time**.

3 From the drop-down list that appears, select **NOW**. Note that the function does not take any arguments.

4 Click **OK** in the resulting dialog box.

Excel enters the current date and time in cell G2.

## PMT

The **PMT** function calculates the monthly payment amount on a loan. The arguments it uses are the Interest Rate (*rate*), Term (*nper*), and Principal (*pv*) amount. You must adjust the interest rate period and payments to use the same number units. For example, if you make monthly payments on the loan, the interest rate needs to be adjusted to *rate*/12 and the term or Nper adjusted to *nper**12. In the following example, you will calculate the monthly payment for a 30-year loan of $425,000 at a 4.25% interest rate.

**STEP BY STEP** **Using the PMT function**

1 Click in cell H8.

2 From the Formulas tab, choose **Financial**.

3 From the list of functions that appears, select **PMT**.

4 In the Functions Argument dialog box (see Figure 4-10), enter the following: **H4/12** in Rate; **H5*12** in Nper; and **H6** in Pv.

5 Click **OK**. Excel calculates the monthly payment of -$2,090.74. (The amount is displayed as a negative number to indicate that it is a payment.)

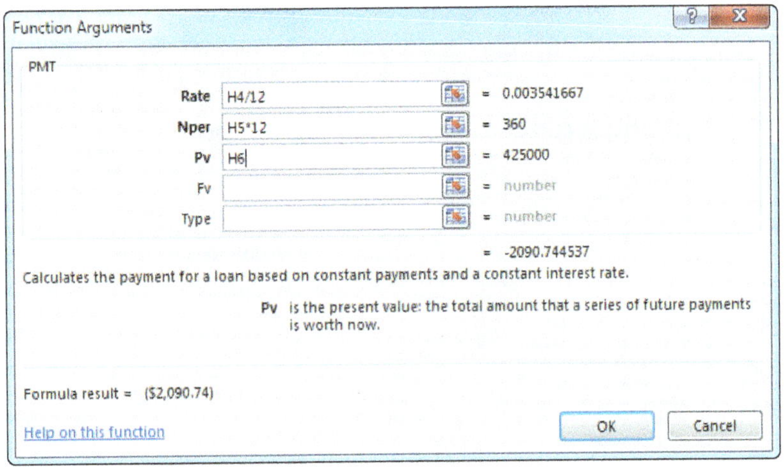


**Figure 4-10**

Calculate the monthly payment on a loan using the PMT function.

## WORKING WITH RANGES

**Bottom Line**

You can assign names to particular ranges within a worksheet. By assigning a name to a range, you can more easily describe data. In particular, you can use **range names** in formulas rather than cell references to describe the data being used in the formula.

For instance, in the worksheet shown in the figure below, range B5:B8 contains data for the number of individual houses sold. If you assign the name House to that range, we can easily construct the formula =SUM(House) to calculates the total number of houses sold.

### Naming a range of cells

The following set of steps shows an example of how to name a range of cells.

**STEP BY STEP** **Naming a range of cells**

1 Select range **B5:B8**.

2 From the Formulas tab, choose **Define Name**.

3 In the Name box (see Figure 4-11), type **House**.

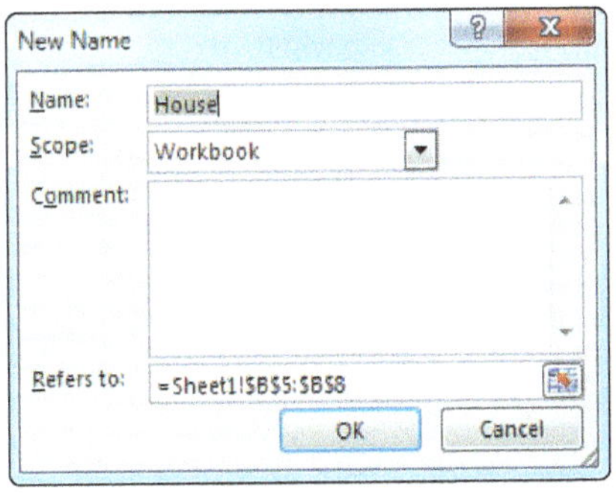


**Figure 4-11**

Name a range of cells to describe the data in your worksheet.

4 Click **OK**.

## Naming a range of cells from a selection

You can quickly convert row or column headings to range names. To do so, first select the range of cells to name, including the heading you want to use as the name. Here's an example.

**STEP BY STEP** **Naming a range of cells for a selection**

1. Select range **C4:C8**.
2. In the Formulas tab, choose **Create from Selection**. If Excel doesn't automatically select Top Row, select **Top Row now** (See Figure 4-12.).

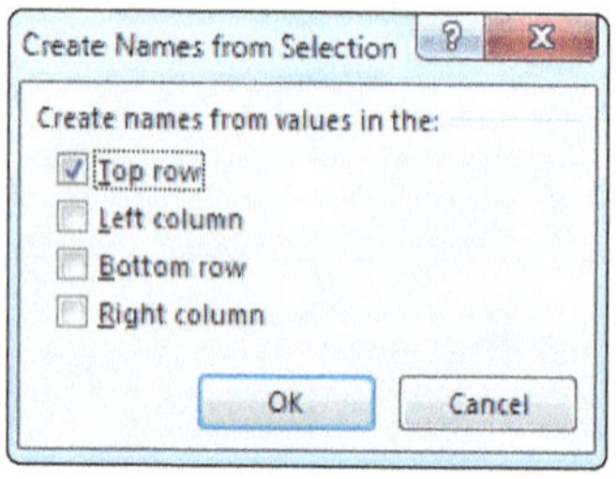


**Figure 4-12**
Quickly name a range of cells using existing headings.

3. Click **OK**. Excel creates the range name *Condo* for range C5:C8.
4. Select range **A5:C8**.
5. In the Formulas tab, choose **Create from Selection**. Excel automatically selects Left column.
6. Click **OK**. Excel creates range names for each row of broker's sales.

## Using a range name in a formula

When using a name in a formula, you can type the range name or select the name from a list, as the next set of steps illustrates.

**STEP BY STEP** **Using a range name in a formula**

1. Click in cell C9.
2. Type **=SUM(** to begin the formula.
3. From the Formulas tab, choose **Use in Formula**.

4 From the list that appears (see Figure 4-13), select **Condo**, and then type **)**.

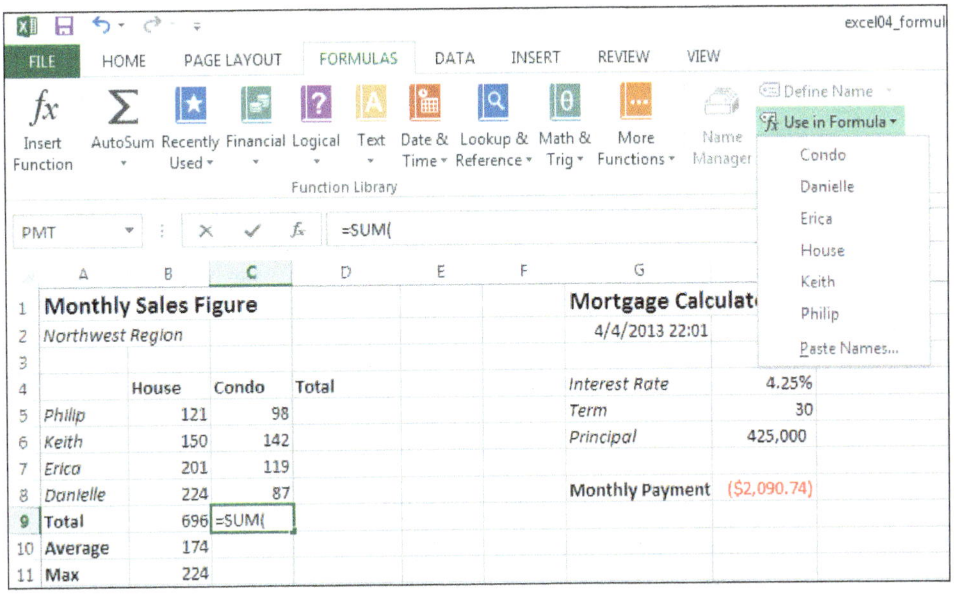


**Figure 4-13**

Select the Range Name to use in the formula instead of typing the cell addresses.

5 Press **Enter**. Excel calculates the Total number of Condo units sold.

## Editing a range name

You can use the **Name Manager** in the Formulas tab to adjust the range addresses or to rename your range names. Note that when you rename a range, you must update any formulas that use the range names.

**STEP BY STEP** **Editing a range name**

1 From the Formulas tab, choose **Name Manager**. The resulting dialog box is shown in Figure 4-14.

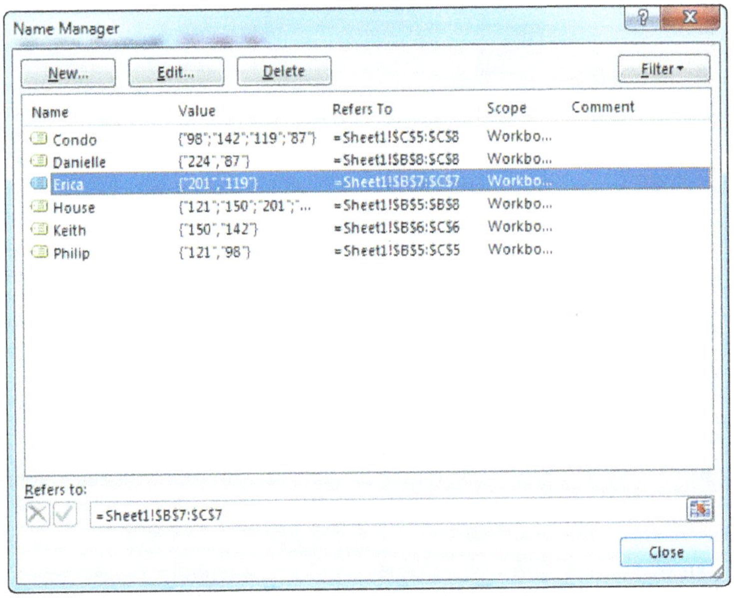


**Figure 4-14**

The Name Manager is used to modify existing range names.

2 Select the range name **Erica** and click **Edit**.

3 Type **EricaM** in the Name box and click **OK**.

4 Click **Close** to close the Name Manager.

### Extending a range

Range names automatically adjust to accommodate new cells when you add a cell to an existing range of cells. You will need to extend a range name to include new data if you add that data to the bottom of an existing range.

**STEP BY STEP** **Extending a range**

1. From the Formulas tab, choose **Name Manager**.
2. Select the range name **Danielle**.
3. In the Refers to box, edit the range to include column D. (Change the C in the range to a **D**.)
4. Click the **Accept** button which looks like a checkmark to the left of the Refers to text box.
5. Click **Close** to close the Name Manager.

### Deleting a range name

The next set of steps shows an example of how to delete range names.

**STEP BY STEP** **Deleting a range name**

1. From the Formulas tab, choose Name Manager.
2. Select **Philip** and click **Delete**.
3. Click **OK** in the resulting dialog box to confirm the deletion.
4. Click **Close** to close the Name Manager.

**Take Note** When you delete a range name, any formula that refers to that range name will result in an Error. (The error message #NAME? is returned in the cell.) To correct the error, you must redefine the name or replace the range name in the formula with the appropriate range address.

## COPYING FORMULAS

**Bottom Line** After creating a formula in Excel, you can use the Copy and Paste commands to duplicate or transfer the formula in/to other areas of your worksheet. When you copy formulas that contain cell references, the references adjust to their new location, unless you specify otherwise.

### Using absolute and relative cell references

When you use cell references in your formulas, Excel uses the data stored in that location in its calculations. The benefit is that when you change the original data, the formula is updated as well.

If you copy a formula from one location to another, Excel adjusts the cell reference based on its new location. For instance, the formula =B2*B3 entered in cell B5 would be adjusted to =C2*C3 when copied to cell C5. However, you can modify the cell reference so it remains fixed to its original location.

An **absolute cell reference** in a formula remains fixed even when the formulas are copied or moved. A **relative cell reference adjusts to its new location.**

The dollar sign ($) is used to indicate that the cell reference should remain absolute. Use the dollar sign to indicate the portion of the address (the row reference, the column reference, or both) that should remain fixed. The following table shows some examples.

**Absolute and relative cell references**

| REFERENCE | WHAT IT MEANS |
|---|---|
| $A6 | Column A remains fixed, row 6 adjusts |
| A$6 | Row 6 remains fixed, column A adjusts |
| $A$6 | Cell A6 remains fixed |
| A6 | The reference to column A and row 6 adjusts to its new location |

## Making a cell reference absolute

The following example shows how to make a cell reference absolute.

**STEP BY STEP** **Making a cell reference absolute**

1 Type = in cell D5.

2 Point to cell B5 and then press the **F4** function key on your keyboard. Excel inserts a dollar sign ($) between the row and column reference.

3 Type + and point to cell C5.

4 Press **Enter** on the keyboard. The formula in cell D5 now reads =$B$5+C5.

**Take Note** When you use a range name in a formula, Excel automatically makes the range absolute. In other words, when you copy a formula that makes use of a range name, the range reference will not adjust to its new location

## Copying formulas with AutoFill

The AutoFill command lets you quickly copy a formula to a range of adjacent cells. Perform the following set of steps to practice using the AutoFill command.

**STEP BY STEP** **Copying formulas with AutoFill**

1 Click in cell D5.

2 From the Formulas tab, choose **AutoSum**. Excel adds up the cells immediately adjacent to the current cell, which in this case is range B5:C5. Press **Enter**.

3 Click in cell D5 and drag the AutoFill handle (see Figure 4-15) down to cell D9 and release. Excel copies the formula from cell D5 and adjusts the cell references accordingly.

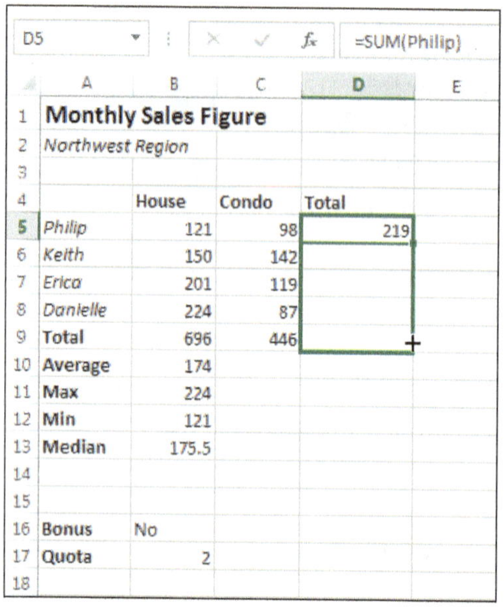


| | A | B | C | D | E |
|---|---|---|---|---|---|
| 1 | Monthly Sales Figure | | | | |
| 2 | Northwest Region | | | | |
| 3 | | | | | |
| 4 | | House | Condo | Total | |
| 5 | Philip | 121 | 98 | 219 | |
| 6 | Keith | 150 | 142 | | |
| 7 | Erica | 201 | 119 | | |
| 8 | Danielle | 224 | 87 | | |
| 9 | Total | 696 | 446 | | |
| 10 | Average | 174 | | | |
| 11 | Max | 224 | | | |
| 12 | Min | 121 | | | |
| 13 | Median | 175.5 | | | |
| 14 | | | | | |
| 15 | | | | | |
| 16 | Bonus | No | | | |
| 17 | Quota | 2 | | | |
| 18 | | | | | |

**Figure 4-15**

The AutoFill feature lets you quickly copy a formula to adjacent cells.

## Copying formulas with Copy and Paste

When you use the Copy command, Excel stores a copy of the selection on the clipboard, allowing you to paste the data multiple times. Perform the following set of steps to practice copying and pasting data.

**STEP BY STEP** **Duplicating data with Copy and Paste**

1 Click in cell B10.

2 From the Home tab, choose **Copy** from the Clipboard group.

3 Select range **C10:D10**.

4 Choose **Paste** from the Clipboard group. Excel pastes the formula from cell B10 and adjusts the cell references accordingly.

**Take Note** You can also press the Enter key on your keyboard to paste the data in a worksheet cell. However, Excel will remove the stored item from the clipboard.

## Pasting formula results

With the Paste Values command, you can copy a formula and then paste the results of the formula in another cell. Perform the following set of steps to practice copying and pasting formula results.

**STEP BY STEP** **Pasting formula results**

1 Select cell **H8** and choose **Copy** from the Home tab.

2 Click in cell I8, choose **Paste** from the Clipboard group, and then select **Paste Special**. The Paste Special dialog box appears. See Figure 4-16.

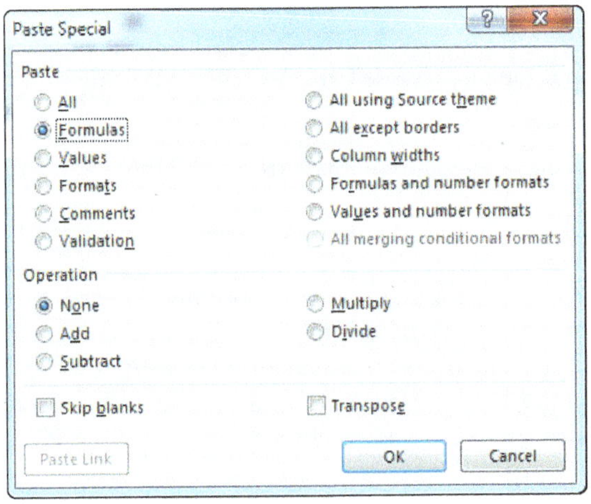


**Figure 4-16**

Paste the results of formulas in a separate cell.

3 Select **Values** from the Paste Special dialog box and click **OK**. Excel pastes the result of the PMT formula, (2,090.74) in cell I8.

## Moving worksheet formulas

Unlike copying a formula, Excel does not adjust cell references when a formula is moved. There are two ways to move a formula in Excel: with the Cut and Paste command, or by dragging and dropping the formula to its new location.

To drag and drop a formula:

### STEP BY STEP Moving worksheet formulas

1 Select range **D4:D10**.

2 Position the mouse pointer on the edge of the selected range; when the mouse pointer changes to a four-headed arrow, click and drag the selection to cell E4, as in Figure 4-17.

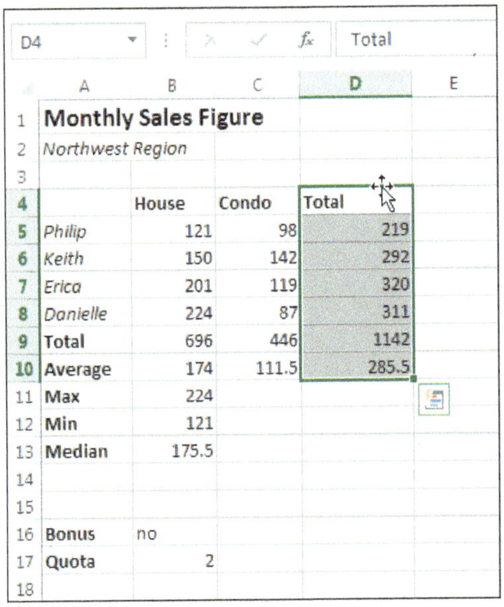


**Figure 4-17**

Quickly move a range of cells to a new location with click, drag and drop.

3 Release to drop the range in its new location.

To move a formula with Cut and Paste:

**STEP BY STEP** **Moving a formula with Cut and Paste**

1 Select range **E4:E10**.

2 From the Home tab, choose **Cut**. A flashing dashed border appears around the selected range.

3 Click in cell D4 and choose **Paste** from the Home tab. Excel pastes the selected range.

## FORMULA AUDITING

**Bottom Line**

When you begin to work with more complex formulas in your worksheets, Excel provides a set of **Auditing** tools to help you verify cell formulas and to track down errors in syntax or use. When you use the Auditing tools, Excel makes use of Tracer Arrows to show the relationship between cells and the formulas that reference them. The table below details the Auditing tools and the actions they perform.

**Excel formula auditing tools**

| COMMAND | TOOL | ACTION |
|---|---|---|
| Trace Precedents | | Indicates cells that are referred to in the formula. |
| Trace Dependents | | Indicates cells that are dependent on the formula. |
| Remove Arrows | | Removes the auditing arrows from the worksheet. |
| Show Formulas | | Displays the formulas in the worksheet instead of the results. |
| Error Checking | | Runs through the worksheets looking for errors. |
| Evaluate Formula | | Runs through a formula argument by argument to ensure its accuracy. |

### Tracing formula precedents

The following is an example of how to trace formula precedents.

**STEP BY STEP** **Tracing formula precedents**

1 Click in cell B9 and choose **Trace Precedents** from the Formula Audition group on the Formulas tab See Figure 4-18.

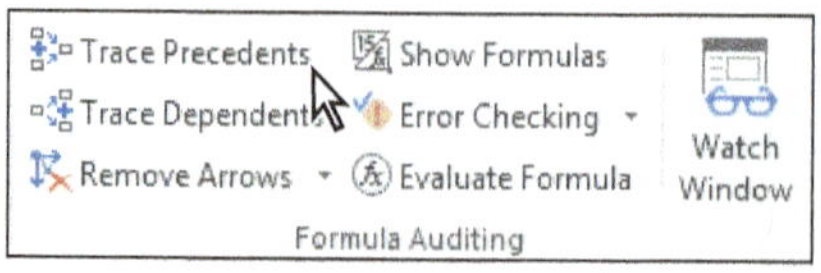


**Figure 4-18**

Choose Trace Precedents.

Excel overlays a tracer arrow on range B5:B8, showing the cells that are used in the SUM function in cell B9.

## Tracing formula dependents

The following is an example of how to trace formula dependents.

**STEP BY STEP** **Tracing formula dependents**

1 Click in cell B9 and choose **Trace Dependents** from the Formulas tab.

Excel overlays a tracer arrow from cell B9 pointing to cell B16; the IF function that relies on data in cell B9 for its conditional formula; and cell D9, which calculates the total amount. See Figure 4-19.

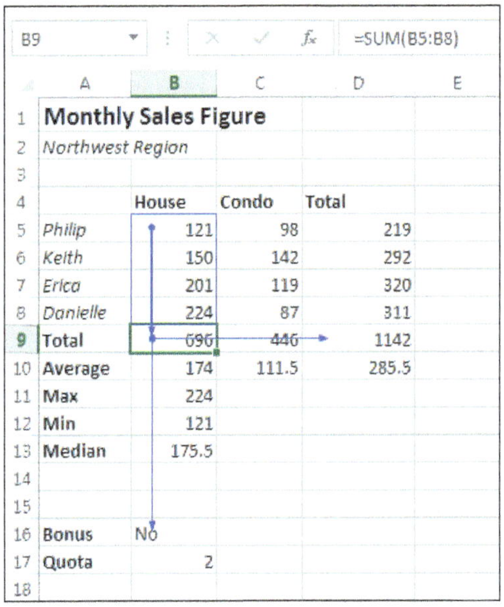


**Figure 4-19**

The Trace Precedents and Trace Dependents tools display the relationships between formulas and the cells that the formulas reference.

## Removing tracer arrows

Tracer arrows can be removed from the entire worksheet or one at a time from specific cells.

**STEP BY STEP** **Removing tracer arrows**

1 Click in cell B9 and then click the arrow to the right of the Remove Arrows command on the Formulas tab.

2 Choose **Remove Precedent Arrows**.

## STEP BY STEP Removing dependent arrows

1 Click in cell B9 and then click the arrow to the right of the Remove Arrows command on the Formulas tab.

2 Choose **Remove Dependent Arrows**.

## STEP BY STEP Removing all tracer arrows

1 From the Formulas tab, choose **Remove Arrows**.

### Viewing formula references

The Tracer Arrows offer a visual display of the relationships between formulas and the cells that reference them, but sometimes the easiest way to view these relationships is to switch to Edit mode. To do so, double-click the cell you want, press the F2 key on your keyboard, or click in the formula bar. When you do, each cell referenced by the formula is displayed.

## STEP BY STEP Viewing formula references

1 Click in cell H8.

2 Press the **F2** key on your keyboard. Alternatively, double-click in the Formula bar or on the cell itself. Excel color-codes each cell referenced by the formula, as in Figure 4-20.

**Figure 4-20**

When you enter Edit mode, Excel color-codes each cell referenced by the formula.

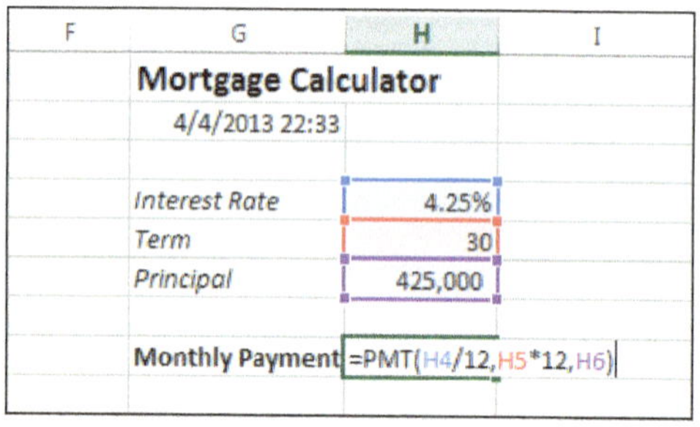


3 Press **Esc** on your keyboard to exit Edit mode.

### Displaying worksheet formulas

As mentioned previously, Excel displays the result of the formula in a cell rather than the formula itself. With the Show Formulas auditing tool, you can switch the worksheet display so that it displays the formulas as entered.

## STEP BY STEP Displaying worksheet formulas

1 From the Formulas tab, choose **Show Formulas**. Excel displays all formulas in the cells as entered. See Figure 4-21.

**Figure 4-21**

Switch the worksheet view to Show Formulas when you want to view the formulas and not the results.

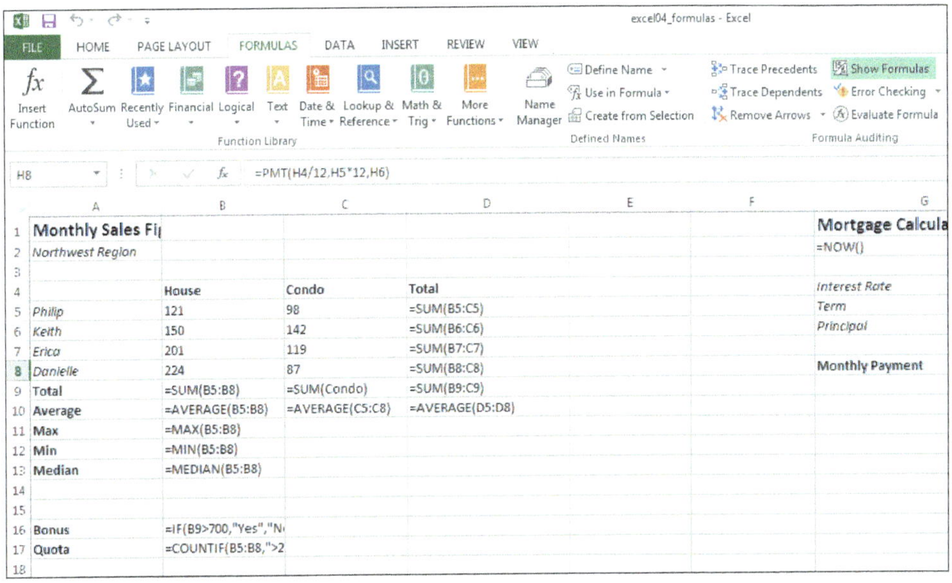


2 Choose **Show Formulas** again display the formula results.

3 Choose **File > Save As**, navigate to the Excel04lessons folder.

4 Type **excel04_formulas_final** as the file name, and click **Save**.

You've now completed this lesson. Now that you have learned how to work with formulas to perform calculations, you are ready to learn how to produce charts and graphs with your worksheet data, which you will learn in Lesson 5, "Working with Charts."

## What you learned in this lesson:

- Understanding Formulas
- Entering Simple Formulas
- Referencing Cells from Other Worksheets/Workbooks
- Using Functions
- Using the Function library
- Using the AutoSum Tool
- Using Common Functions
- Working with Ranges
- Copying Formulas
- Formula Auditing

# Knowledge Assessment

## Matching

**Match the function in numbers 1 to 10 to its output in letters a to j.**

1. =AVERAGE(5,6,7)
2. =SUM(2,4,9)
3. =MIN(4,2,8,3,0)
4. =MAX(5,5,5,3,4,9,6)
5. =MIN(B4:B9)
6. =MEDIAN(A1:A10)
7. =IF(B1=5, "yes", "no") ; B1=7
8. =COUNTIF(A5,">10"); A5=12
9. =NOW()
10. =NOW

a. no
b. 15
c. 6
d. returns an error
e. shows current date/time
f. 0
g. displays lowest value in range
h. 1
i. displays middle value in range
j. 9

## Fill in the Blanks

1. The AutoSum tool offers quick access to sum, count, ______, ______, and ______ functions.
2. Indicate a range of cells by listing the first and last cells separated by a ______.
3. Cell A4 of Sheet3 in the file data.xlsx is indicated by the cell reference ______.
4. Calculations like loan payments, interest rates, and security yields are performed using functions from the ______ category of the Function Library.
5. Excel recognizes the contents of a cell as a formula if it begins with the ______ character.
6. The RAND() function generates a random number. To paste the number's value rather than the formula, use the ______ command.
7. To see the cells that a formula refers to, use Excel's Auditing command to trace its ______.
8. Cell C3 contains a formula, but displays its output value. To edit the formula itself, highlight cell C3 and press ______.
9. The ______ function traverses a cell range and returns a count of how many values in that range meet an IF/THEN condition.
10. A formula's ______ is the symbol of the operation it performs (e.g., multiplication); its ______ are the numbers, cells, or ranges it acts upon.

# Competency Assessment

## Project 4-1: Basic Formulas

**In this exercise you will build formulas using text, numeric data, and cell references.**

1. Open the practice file **2013_output** and save your document as **project_4-1_formulas.**
2. In cell F3, type =SUM(.
3. Select cells B3:D3 and type ).
4. Drag F3's AutoFill handle down to reuse its formula in F4:F13.
5. Select B15 and use the AutoSum > Sum command over the range B3:B13.
6. Drag B15's AutoFill handle to C15.
7. Select cell C15 and press Ctrl+C to copy.
8. Select D17 and press Ctrl+V, then edit D17's formula to =SUM(D3:D13).
9. Select F19 and click **AutoSum**.
10. Select B23 and add the formula =COUNTA(A3:A13).
11. Click B24.
12. Type =. Click cell F19. Type /. Click cell B23. Press **Return**.
13. Save and close your document.

## Project 4-2: Range Names

**In this exercise you'll create named ranges for ease of use.**

1. Open the project file **4-2-source** and save it as **project_4-2_range_names.**
2. Press Ctrl+A and change the fill color to **No Fill**.
3. Select B3:D3.
4. Click **Formulas > Define Name** and name the range **AstridSales**. Note that Astrid-Sales appears in the Name Box.
5. Select B3:B13 and name the range **JanJunSales**.
6. Do the same for C3:C13 (**JulDecSales**) and D3:D13 (**OnlineSales**).
7. Open the Name Manager. Double click the Astrid entry and add a comment ("**label not included**").
8. Close the Name Manager.
9. Save and close your document.

## Proficiency Assessment

### Project 4-3: Cell References

**In this exercise you'll use cell references to simplify formula building.**

1. Open the project file **4-3-source** and save it as **project_4-3_references**.
2. Create a new worksheet within the file and name it **Presentation**.
3. Select the **Presentation** worksheet. In cell A1, type **Astrid total sales:**.
4. In cell C1, type **=AstridSales**. The error message indicates that Excel expects a single value; you've inserted a reference to a range of cells.
5. Change C1's content to **=SUM(AstridSales)**. You can insert the range name with the Formulas > Use in Formula command.
6. Type **Bree total sales:** in A2.
7. In C2, add a Sum formula, and select **Sheet1!B13:D13** as the range.
8. Save and close your document.

### Project 4-4: Formula Auditing

**In this exercise you'll perform Formula Audits on a worksheet.**

1. Open the project file **4-4-source** and save it as **project_4-4_trace**.
2. Switch to Sheet1. Select **Formulas > Formula Auditing > Show Formulas**.
3. Select cell **F19**, then select **Trace Precedents**.
4. Do the same for F3:F13 to generate a complete map of the 2013 Sales Total's formula precedents.
5. Run Trace Precedents for Presentation!C1 and Presentation!C2.
6. Clear **Arrows**, deselect **Formulas**, then Trace Precedents for Sheet1!B24.
7. Save and close your document.

## Mastery Assessment

### Project 4-5: Advanced Formulas

**In this exercise you'll construct a complex formula using the Function Library.**

1. Open the project file **4-5-source** and save it as **project_4-5_formulas2**.
2. Hide rows 15-24 in Sheet1.
3. Type **Conditions:** in A25.
4. Type **>90** in B25 and **<80** in C25.
5. Click **D25** and use Insert Function to call the AVERAGEIFS function.
6. Build the function using the Online Sales data (**OnlineSales**) as the Average_range, **JanJunSales** as Criteria_range1, **B25** as Criteria1, **JulDecSales** as Criteria_range2, and **C25** as Criteria2.

   The output of this function is the average online sales of those employees who sold >90 units Jan-Jun but <80 units Jul-Dec – the average of D10 and D11.
7. Save and close your document.

## Project 4-6: Operations with Text

**In this exercise you'll perform some complex operations on text data.**

1. Open the project file **4-6-source** and save it as **project_4-6_text**.
2. In I3, use the REPLACE(...) function to replace the first letter in Astrid's name with X, then use AutoFill to extend that operation down column I to all 12 employee names.

   Hint: the first letter in Astrid is character 1, and the replacement string must be in quotes: "X."
3. Add a single cell that displays the average length of the employee names.

   Hint: the LEN() command will prove useful here, as will the "Search for a function" feature of the Insert Function command.
4. Choose **File > Save** and then **File > Close**.

# 5 Working with Charts

## LESSON SKILL MATRIX

**In this lesson, you will learn the following skills:**

| | |
|---|---|
| Understanding Chart Types | Editing a Chart |
| Creating a Chart | Customizing the Chart |
| Understanding Chart Elements | Printing a Chart |
| Using Chart Recommendations | Enhancing a Chart |
| Moving and Resizing Charts | |

## KEY TERMS

- **Linked data**
- **Chart area**
- **Chart title**
- **Data series**
- **Vertical axis**
- **Gridlines**
- **Horizontal axis**
- **Legend**
- **Plot area**
- **Data marker**
- **Plot**
- **Data source**
- **Scale (i.e. chart scale – along axis)**
- **Sparkline**

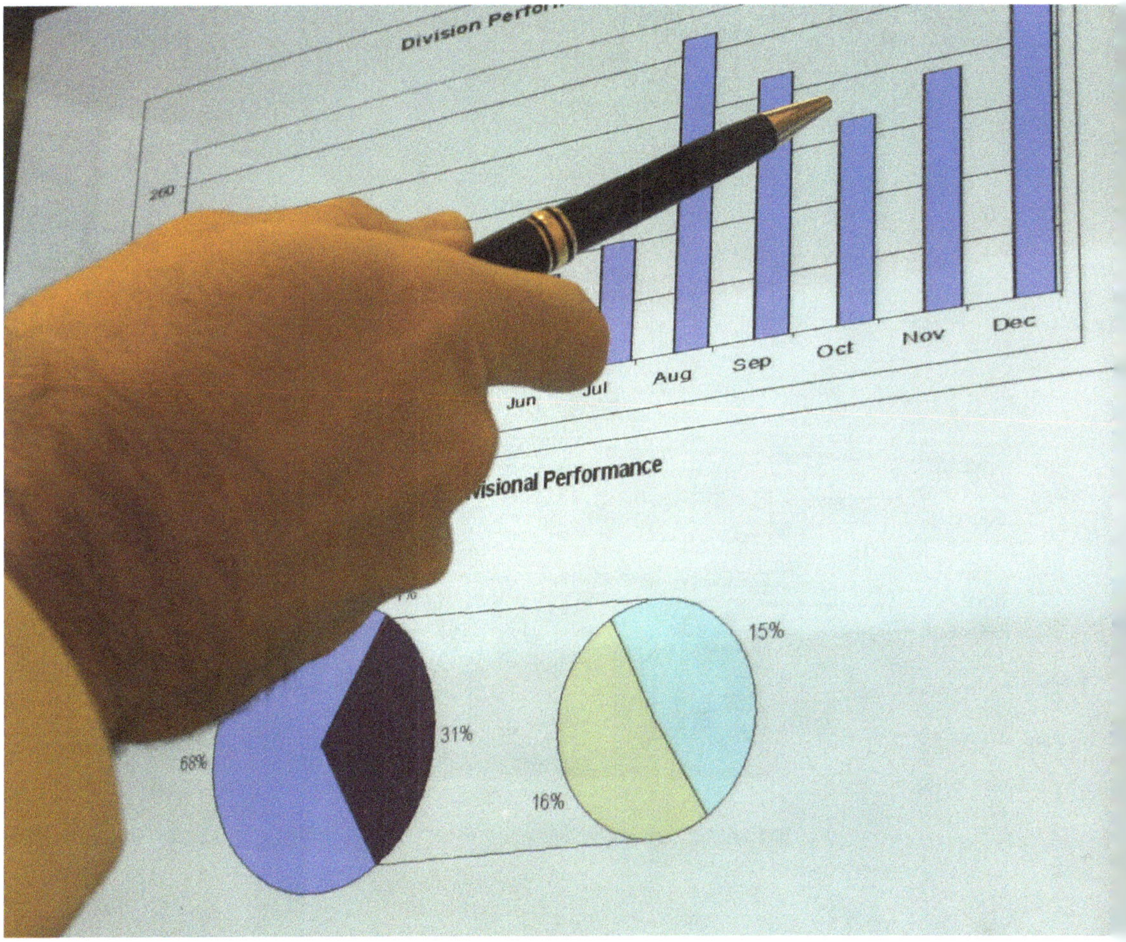


©RBFried/iStockPhoto

©RBFried/iStockPhoto

The new management team at Northwind Traders needs to quickly get a handle on the yearly financial data – but they're in Springville and Northwind's accountants are in Ellicottville, so meeting time is in short supply. Turning the raw data into memorable visuals is the solution. Luckily, Excel has an extensive suite of tools to do just that – and an even wider variety of tools to nudge, tweak, style, and emphasize infographic elements in order to make sure the managers know exactly what the data means, and why it matters.

## SOFTWARE ORIENTATION

Charts and graphs help you to express numbers and data visually.

**Figure 5-1**

Working with charts in Excel.

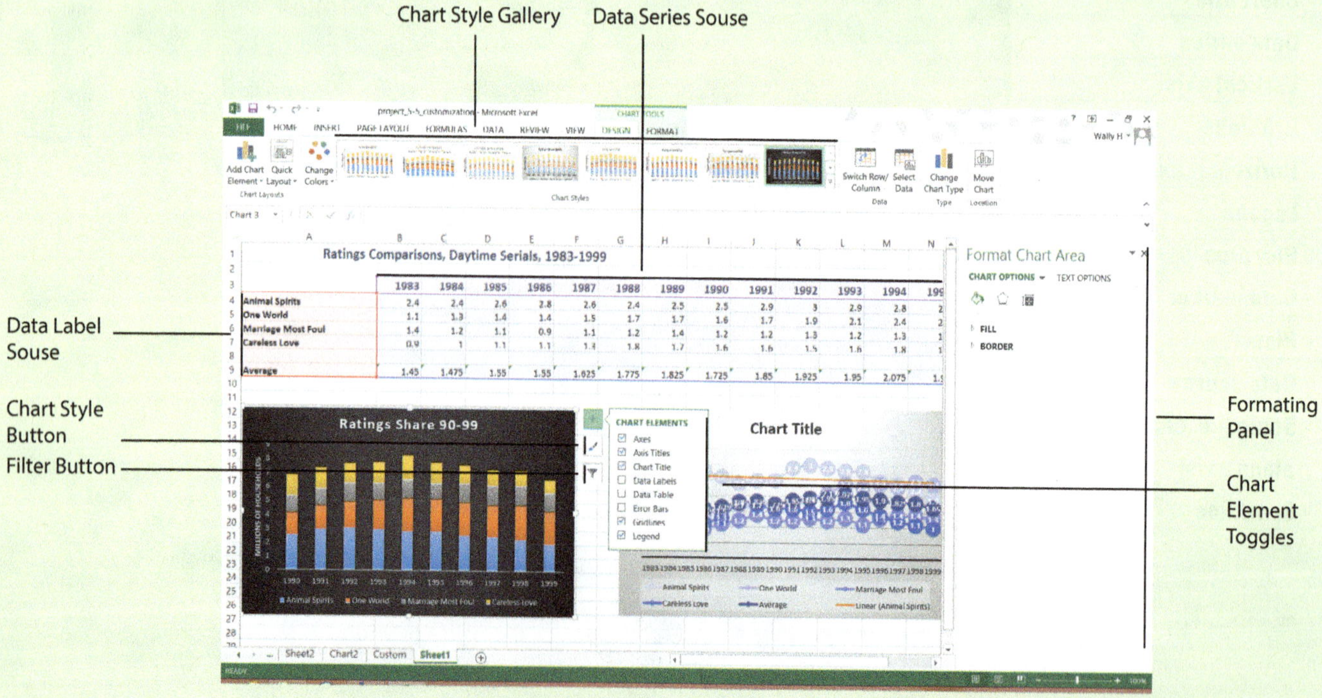

## STARTING UP

In this lesson, you'll work with several files from the Excel05lessons folder. Make sure that you have loaded the OfficeLessons folder onto your computer.

## UNDERSTANDING CHART TYPES

**Bottom Line**

Excel offers a number of different chart types. From bar graphs and pie charts to scatter plots and area charts, Excel provides a chart type for the data you want to present. The new Recommended Charts feature helps to remove some of the guesswork by offering a number of chart types based on your selected data. You can also change the chart from one type to another once it is complete. The following table lists the 12 chart types that Excel offers.

**Chart types**

| TYPE | ICON | DESCRIPTION |
|---|---|---|
| **Area** | | Shows the relative importance of values over time. An area chart emphasizes the magnitude of change over time more than a line chart does. |
| **Bar** | | Illustrates individual values at a specific point in time. |
| **Bubble** | | A type of XY chart that uses three values instead of two. In the third data series, Excel displays the plot points as bubbles; the larger the bubble, the larger the value. |
| **Column** | | Shows variations in data over time or compares individual items. |
| **Combo** | | Highlights different types of information in a single chart. |
| **Doughnut** | | Shows how individual parts relate to a whole. A doughnut chart can display multiple data series, with each ring representing a different series. |
| **Line** | | Illustrates changes in a large number of values over time. |
| **Pie** | | Shows the relationship of each part to the whole. |
| **Radar** | | Shows changes in multiple data series relative to a center point as well as to each other. |
| **Stock** | | Shows the fluctuation of values over a certain time period, such as stock prices or temperature fluctuations. |
| **Surface** | | Plots trends in values across two dimensions in a continuous curve, and applies color to indicate where data series are in the same range. This is useful for comparing two data series to find the best combinations between them. |
| **XY Scatter** | | Shows the relationship between numeric values in multiple data series that may not be apparent from looking at the data. |

## CREATING A CHART

**Bottom Line**

Charts enable you to present worksheet data in graphical form. They also allow you to highlight trends, see the parts that make up a whole, or show comparisons. When you create a chart, the source worksheet data is **linked** to the chart. So when you update the data in your worksheet, the chart gets updated, too. In Excel, you can add a chart directly to the worksheet as an object or you can create a separate chart worksheet.

## STEP BY STEP Creating a chart

You will now create a Clustered Column type of chart from a range of data contained within the exercise file.

1. Choose **File > Open**, click **Computer** in the Backstage view, and click **Browse**.
2. Navigate to the Excel05lessons folder and open the file named **excel05_charts**.
3. Choose **File > Save As**, and choose **Computer**.
4. Click the **Browse** button, navigate to the Excel05lessons folder, name the file **excel05_charts_final**, and click **Save**.
5. Select range **A4:C8**.
6. From the Insert tab, choose **Insert Column Chart** as shown in Figure 5-2

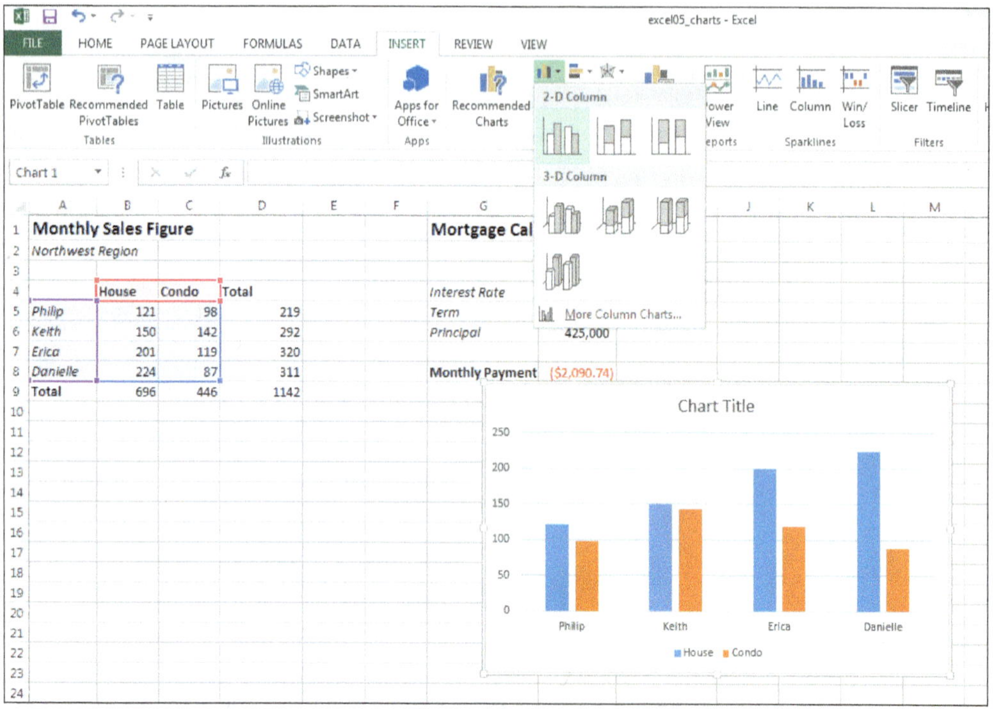


**Figure 5-2**

Convert your worksheet data into easy-to-read charts.

7. From the 2-D Column section of the drop-down menu, select **Clustered Column**.

Excel adds the chart to the worksheet and highlights the source data used by the chart.

**Take Note** When you select the data for a chart, include headings and labels but do not include totals and subtotals.

## UNDERSTANDING CHART ELEMENTS

**Bottom Line**

When you create a chart, Excel adds it to the worksheet as an object, which then sits on top of the worksheet and can be manipulated separately from the worksheet data. The Key Charting Terms table details key terms related to working with charts and are also displayed in Figure 5-3.

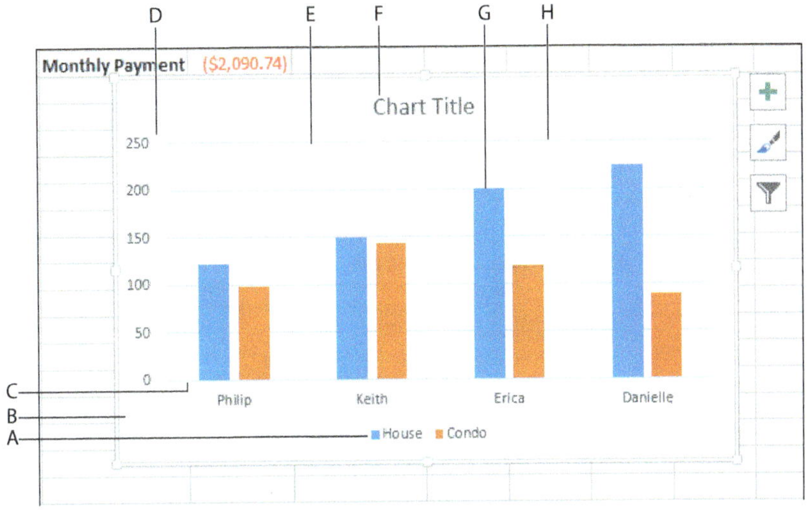


**Figure 5-3**

A. Legend. B. Chart Area. C. Horizontal Axis. D. Vertical Axis. E. Gridline. F. Chart Title. G. Data Marker. H. Plot Area.

| TERM | DEFINITION |
|---|---|
| **Chart area** | Everything inside the chart window. |
| **Chart title** | Identifies the subject of the chart. |
| **Data Series** | A set of values used to plot the chart. |
| **Vertical (value) axis** | Also known as the value or y-axis, shows the data values in the chart, such as hours worked or units sold. |
| **Gridlines** | Horizontal and vertical extensions of the tick marks on each axis; they make the chart easier to read. |
| **Horizontal (category) axis** | Also known as the category or x-axis, shows the categories in the chart, such as months of the year or branch offices. |
| **Legend** | A key that identifies patterns, colors, or symbols associated with a data series. |
| **Plot area** | The area in the chart where the data is plotted; includes the axes and data markers. |
| **Data marker** | A symbol on the chart that represents a single value in the worksheet, such as a bar in a bar chart or a wedge in a pie chart. A group of related data markers (such as all the green columns in the example on the previous page) constitute a single data series. |

## USING CHART RECOMMENDATIONS

**Bottom Line**

The most difficult part in creating charts is deciding the type that best suits your data and the message you want to convey. When you use Recommended Charts, Excel suggests a set of chart types based on your selected data. Follow the steps below for an example of how this works.

**STEP BY STEP** **Using chart recommendations**

1 Using **excel05_charts_final**, select range **A4:C8**.

2 From the Insert tab, choose **Recommend Charts**.

3 In the resulting Change Chart Type dialog box, select **Clustered Bar** from the Recommended Charts tab (Figure 5-4) and click **OK**.

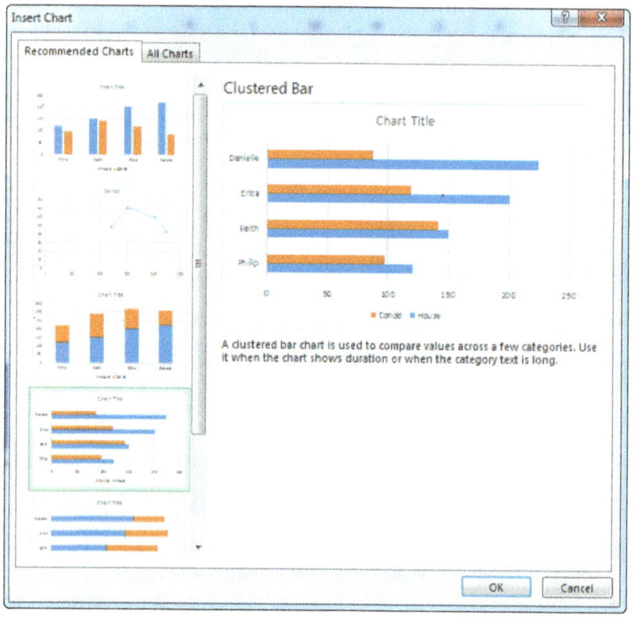


**Figure 5-4**

Chart recommendations suggest chart types based on your data.

Excel inserts a clustered bar graph in your worksheet. Note that the bar graph is now sitting directly on top of the column chart you created in the previous exercise.

## MOVING AND RESIZING CHARTS

**Bottom Line**

When you add a chart to a worksheet, Excel adds it to the middle of the workspace area. To move the chart to another location, click and drag the chart object. Alternatively, you can manually move the chart to a new worksheet.

When you click a chart, Excel displays a set of selection handles around the chart area and a set of Chart Tools appear in the Ribbon bar (Figure 5-5). The Design and Format tabs contain context-sensitive tools for editing and formatting charts.

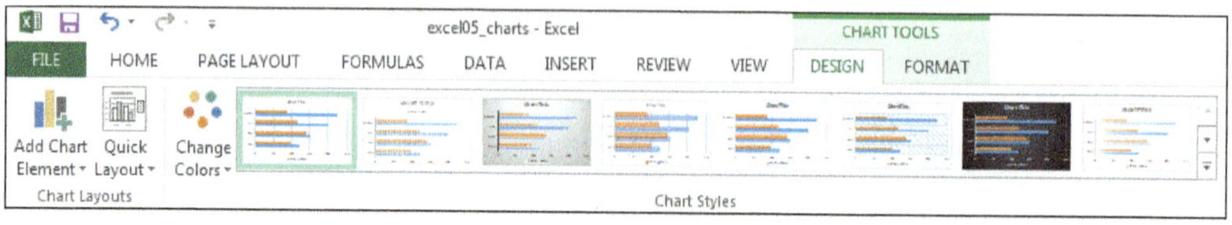


**Figure 5-5**

When you click a chart to select it, two new tabs appear in the Ribbon bar.

For the next four exercises (Moving a Chart, Resizing a Chart, Creating a Chart Sheet, and Deleting a Chart), use the same Excel exercise file that you used for the previous exercises, so don't close the file at the end of each set of steps.

## Moving a chart

**STEP BY STEP** **Moving a chart**

1 Click near the outside edge of the Clustered Bar chart to select it.

2 Position the pointer within the chart area. When the pointer changes into a four-headed arrow, click and drag the chart to the vicinity of B13.

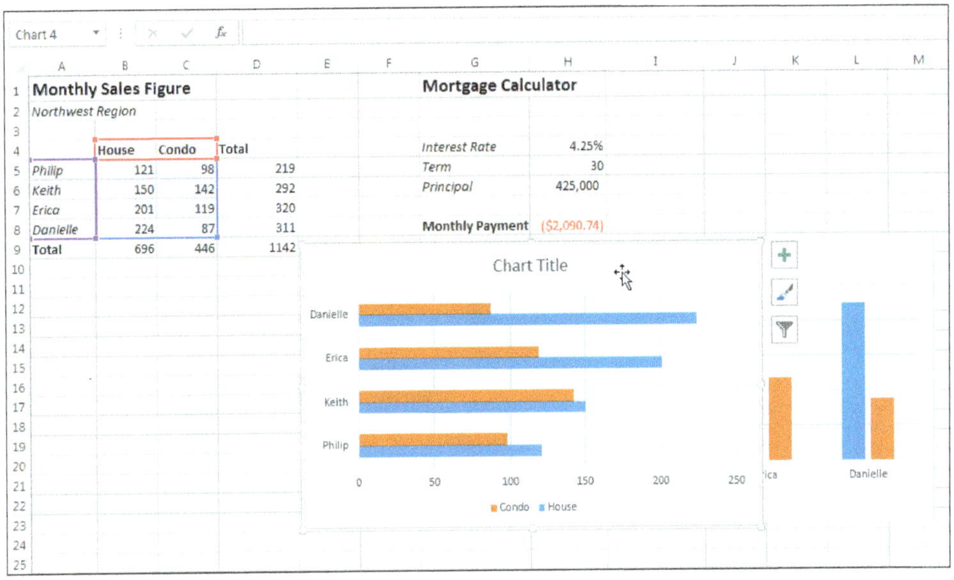


**Figure 5-6**

Click and drag the chart object to move it to a new position.

3 Click and drag the Clustered Column graph to the vicinity of I13.

## Resizing a chart

**STEP BY STEP** **Resizing a chart**

1 Click the **Clustered Bar** chart to select it.

2 Point at the corner of the chart area. When the pointer changes into a double-headed arrow, click and drag to resize the chart. Release when the chart is the desired size.

## Creating a chart sheet

**STEP BY STEP** **Creating a chart sheet**

1 Make sure the Clustered Bar chart is still selected.

2 From the Design tab, choose **Move Chart** in the Location group.

3 In the Move Chart dialog box, select **New Sheet** and type **Total Sales** in the name box as shown in Figure 5-7.

**Figure 5-7**

Enter a name for the chart sheet.

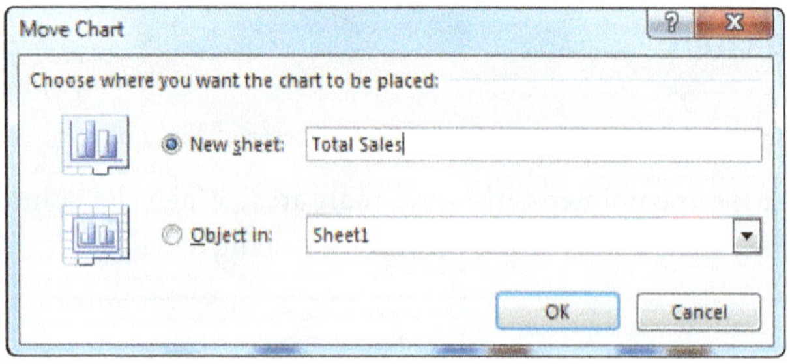


4 Click **OK**. The Clustered Bar chart appears on a Chart Sheet (Figure 5-8).

**Figure 5-8**

When you create a Chart sheet, the chart is displayed on its own sheet.

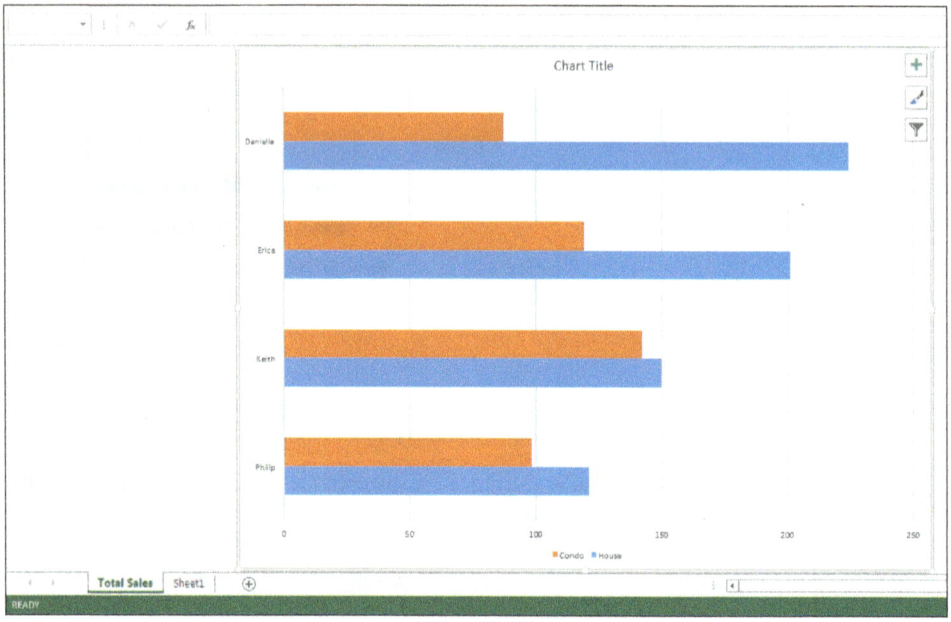


5 From the Design tab, choose **Move Chart**.

6 From the Move Chart dialog box, select **Object** in and click **OK**. The Clustered Bar is moved back to the worksheet.

**Take Note** When you move a chart from a chart sheet to a worksheet, Excel deletes the chart sheet from the workbook.

## Deleting a chart

**STEP BY STEP** **Deleting a chart**

1 Click the **Clustered Bar** chart to select it.

2 Press the **Delete** key. Excel removes the chart object from the worksheet.

3 Save your exercise file, but don't close it. You will continue using it in the next section.

## ENHANCING A CHART

**Bottom Line**

An important step when creating charts is to provide adequate explanations of the data represented in the chart. Excel enables you to add descriptive titles and legends, adjust the scale and orientation, and add data labels and gridlines. These chart elements are in either an on or off state. That is, to add an element, click the check box to mark it; to remove an element, click the check box to clear it.

For all seven exercises in this section, use the same exercise file you have been using till now. Don't close the file at the end of each exercise.

### Using Quick Layouts

The Quick Layouts feature contains a set of predefined layout options that you can assign to a chart with a single click.

**STEP BY STEP** **Using Quick Layouts**

1. Click the **Clustered Column** chart to select it.
2. From the Chart Layouts group on the Design tab, choose **Quick Layout**.
3. As you hover over each option, your chart is updated to reflect the layout as displayed in Figure 5-9.

**Figure 5-9**

Quick Layouts allow you to quickly change the layout of the chart.

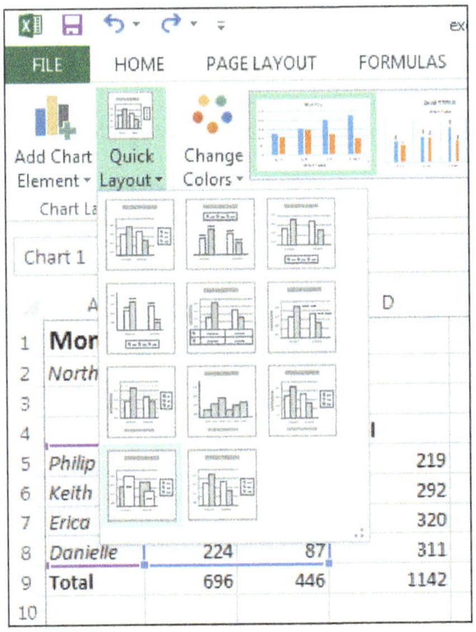


4. Click **Layout 10** to select it.

### Adding a chart title

**STEP BY STEP** **Adding a chart title**

1. In the **Clustered Column** chart, click the text box labeled **Chart Title**.
2. Click inside the box to set the insertion point.

3 Type **Monthly Sales** (Figure 5-10).

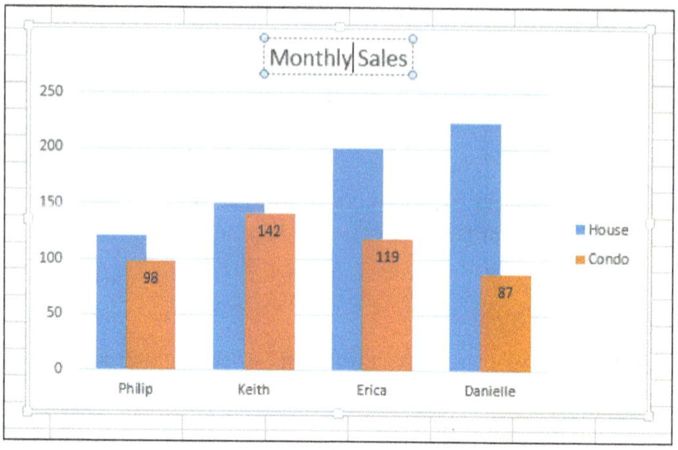


**Figure 5-10**
Click to set the Chart Title.

## Displaying a data table

When you add a data table to your chart, Excel adds the source data to the chart area in table form.

**STEP BY STEP** **Displaying a data table**

1 Click the **Monthly Sales** chart to select it.

2 From the Design tab, choose **Add Chart Element**; or click the **Chart Elements** button that appears to the right of the chart.

3 Select **Data Table** and and in the Data Table drop-down menu, choose **No Legend Keys** (Figure 5-11).

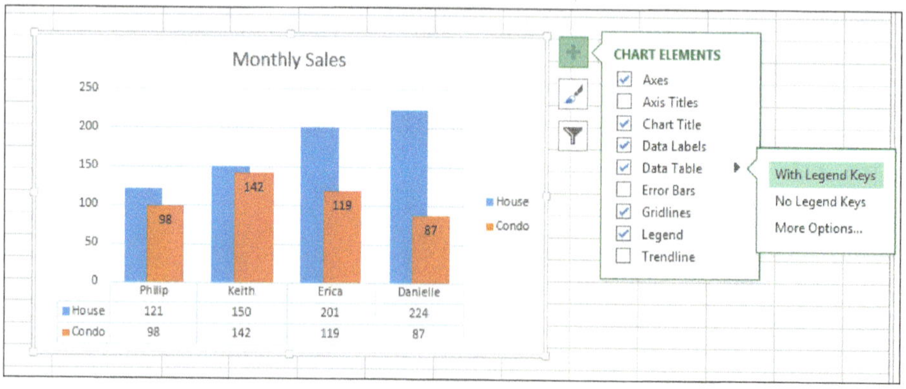


**Figure 5-11**
Data tables display the source data used to generate the chart.

## Adding data labels

With Data Labels, Excel labels each data marker in the chart with the source value. The Quick Layout we selected before added Data Labels to the Condo Data Series. Here, we will add Data Labels to the House Data Series.

**STEP BY STEP** **Adding data labels**

1 Click the **Monthly Sales** chart to select it.

2 From the Design tab, choose **Add Chart Element**; or click the **Chart Elements** button.

3 Click the drop-down arrow next to Data Labels and choose **Inside End** as shown in Figure 5-12.

**Figure 5-12**

Data Labels include the data values behind the chart.

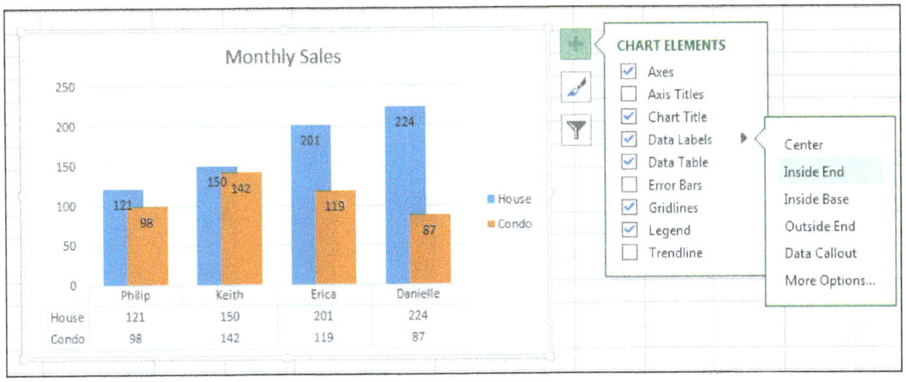


## STEP BY STEP Adding gridlines

1 Click the **Monthly Sales** chart to select it.

2 From the Design tab, choose **Add Chart Element**; or click the **Chart Elements** button.

3 Click the drop-down arrow next to Gridlines and choose **Primary Minor Horizontal** as shown in Figure 5-13.

**Figure 5-13**

Gridlines help to guide the eye along the data points.

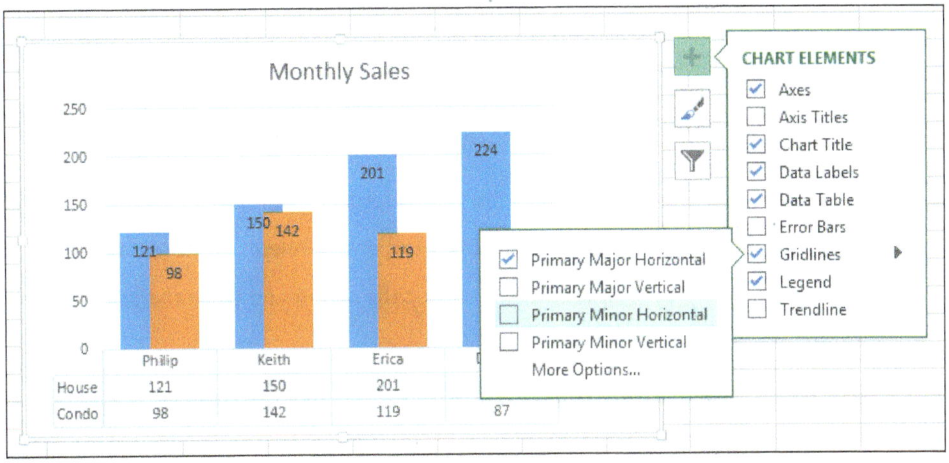


## Adding or moving legends

Legends describe the color-coded data series in each chart.

## STEP BY STEP Adding and moving legends

1 Click the **Monthly Sales** chart to select it.

2 From the Design tab, choose **Add Chart Element**; or click the **Chart Elements** button.

3 Click the drop-down arrow next to Legend and choose **Left** to place the Legend box to the left of the chart area (Figure 5-14).

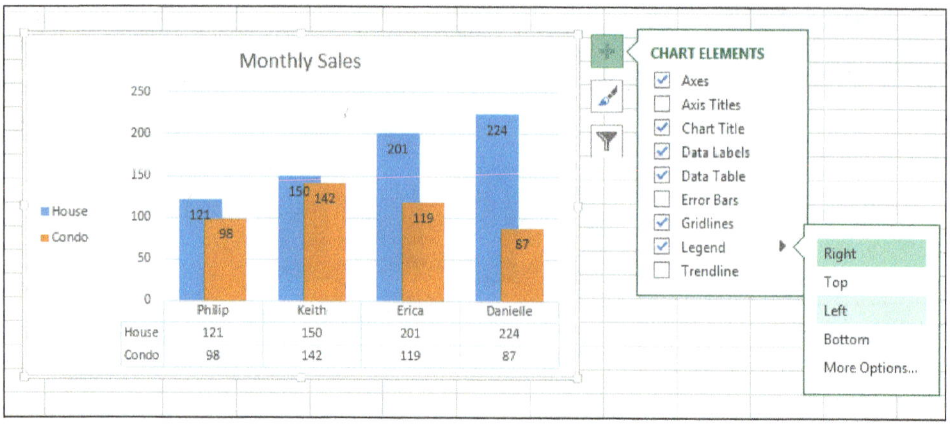


**Figure 5-14**

Legends contain descriptive data that explains the data series.

## Removing chart elements

You can remove chart elements from the chart display by deselecting the item. For instance, when you click the Chart Elements button, any element that is currently employed has a check mark indicating it is selected. To remove the element, deselect it.

You can also remove a chart element by selecting the element you want to remove and pressing the Delete key. When you select an element, selection handles are displayed around the selected object.

**STEP BY STEP** **Removing an element with the Delete key**

1 Click the **Monthly Sales** chart to select it.

2 Click the gridlines and press **Delete**. Excel removes the gridlines from the chart object.

3 Click **Undo** to revert the action and place the gridelines back into the chart.

**STEP BY STEP** **Removing an element via Chart Elements**

1 Click the **Monthly Sales** chart to select it.

2 Click the **Chart Elements** button.

3 Deselect **Data Labels** and **Data Table** as shown in Figure 5-15.

**Figure 5-15**

To remove an element from the chart, deselect the option.

4 Save the exercise file, but don't close it.

## FORMATTING A CHART

**Bottom Line**

Excel provides many formatting options and commands that allow you to make charts visually appealing. You can change the colors used by the data series, change text attributes, and adjust alignment, among other options. You can also apply a chart style, which is a set of predefined formatting options that help to maintain uniformity of design.

**Take Note** For all four exercises in this section, use the same exercise file you have been using till now. Don't close the file at the end of each exercise.

### Applying chart styles

**STEP BY STEP** **Applying chart styles**

1 Click the **Monthly Sales** chart to select it.

2 Click the **Chart Styles** button (Figure 5-16) and select the second style option displayed.

**Figure 5-16**

Chart styles consist of a collection of related formatting options.

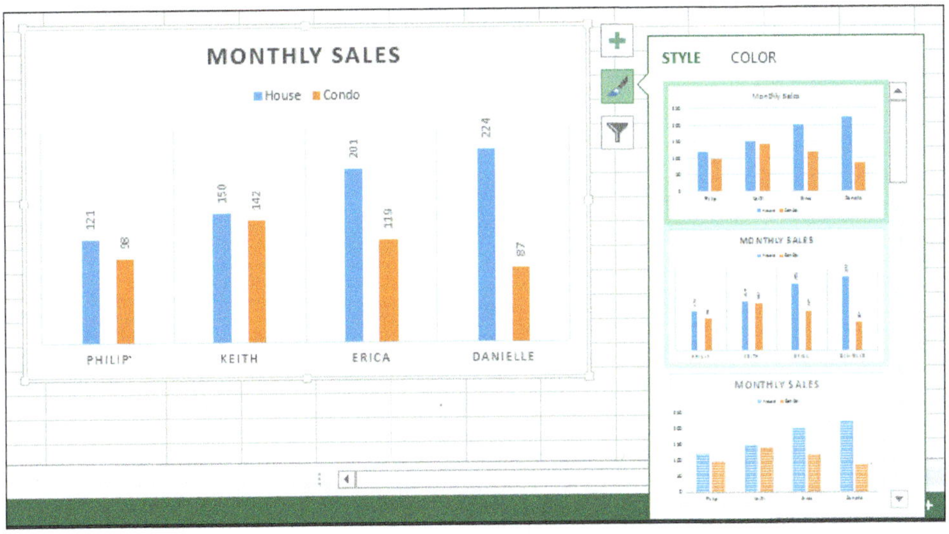


3 Click the **Chart Styles** button again to close the menu.

## Changing the color scheme

**STEP BY STEP** **Changing the color scheme**

1 Click the **Monthly Sales** chart to select it.

2 Click the **Chart Styles** button.

3 From the Chart Styles menu, select **Color**; from the Colorful section, choose **Color 4** (Figure 5-17).

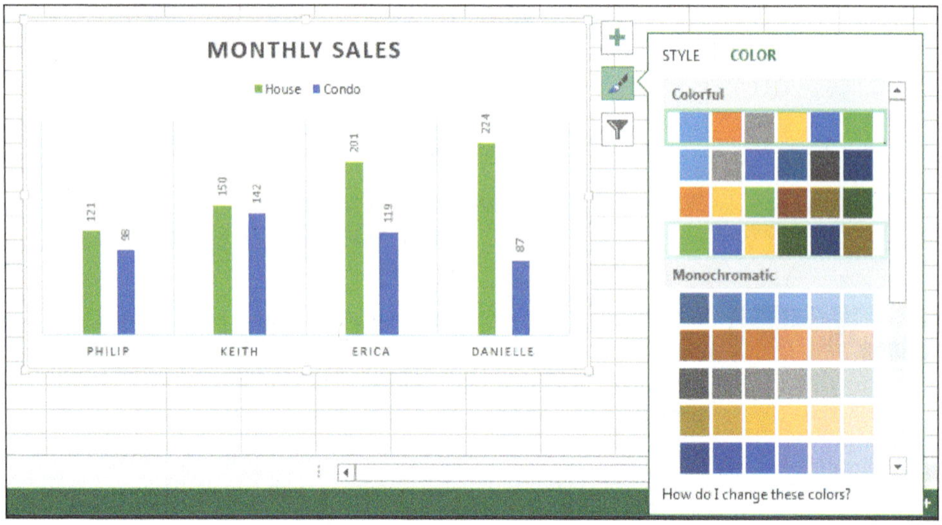


**Figure 5-17**

Change the color scheme used by your chart style.

4 Click the **Chart Styles** button again to close the menu.

## Adding borders

**STEP BY STEP** **Adding borders**

1 Click the **Monthly Sales** chart to select it.

2 From the Format tab, choose **Format Selection** in the Current Selection group.

3 In the **Format Chart Area** window, select **Chart Options**.

4 Click **Border**, select **Solid Line**, and change the width to **4 pt**.

5 Click the **Outline Color** button and select **Black** as shown in Figure 5-18.

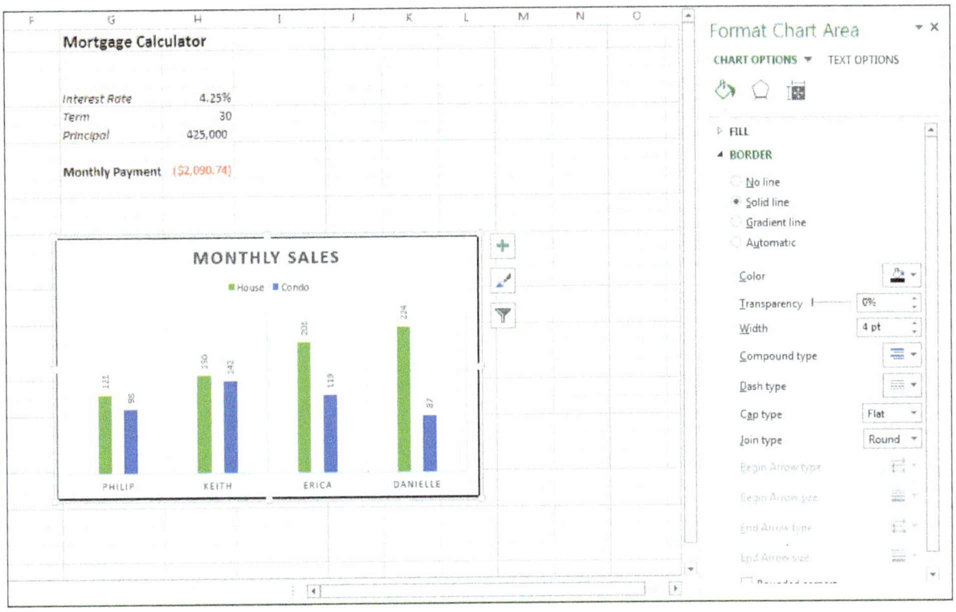


**Figure 5-18**

Add borders to the chart area to set it apart from the rest of the worksheet.

6 Close the Format Chart Area window by clicking the **X** in the upper-right corner.

## Formatting text

**STEP BY STEP** **Formatting text**

1 Click the **Monthly Sales** title box.

2 On the Home tab, click the **Font** button.

3 Select the **Candara** font and **Blue** for the text color as displayed in Figure 5-19.

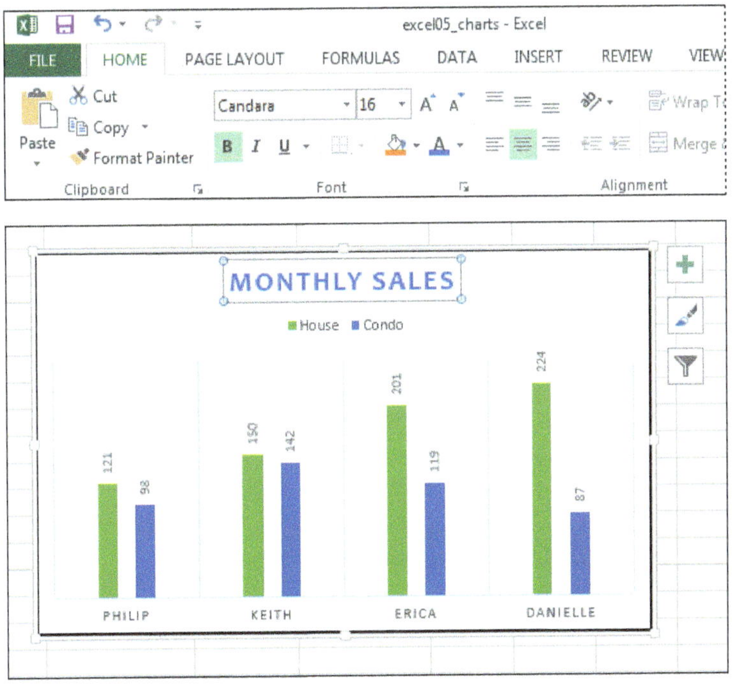


**Figure 5-19**

Change the text in your chart using the Font menu.

## EDITING A CHART

**Bottom Line**

When you create a chart, Excel **plots** the data according to the selected data range. When you edit the source data in the worksheet, the chart is updated to reflect those changes.

You can also add a new data set to an existing chart. If the range of data you want to add is adjacent to the source data, you can click and drag to extend the selection so it includes the additional data. If the new data set is not adjacent, you can add the data via the Data Source dialog box.

First, let's add an additional data series to the worksheet you have been using for all the previous exercises.

### STEP BY STEP Editing a chart

1. Click to select **Column D**, and in the Cells group of the Home tab, choose **Insert**.
2. Enter the following: **Apt** in cell D4, **75** in cell D5, **112** in cell D6, **98** in cell D7, and **42** in cell D8. As you can see, Excel's automatic error checker detects problems with the Total values we moved from column D to E.
3. Click in cell E5 and choose **Update Formulas** to Include Cells from the Error Check menu.
4. Do the same for cells E6:E8.
5. Finally, copy the formula in cell C9 to range D9:E9.

### STEP BY STEP Adding a data series by selecting the adjacent data

1. Click the **Monthly Sales** chart to select it. Excel highlights the source data, range A4:C8, in the worksheet.
2. Click and drag the sizing handle to include the new data in range D4:D8 as displayed in Figure 5-20. The chart is automatically updated.

**Figure 5-20**

Click and drag to extend the data range to add a new data series to the chart.

| | A | B | C | D | E | F |
|---|---|---|---|---|---|---|
| 1 | Monthly Sales Figure | | | | | |
| 2 | *Northwest Region* | | | | | |
| 3 | | | | | | |
| 4 | | House | Condo | Apt | Total | |
| 5 | *Philip* | 121 | 98 | 75 | 294 | |
| 6 | *Keith* | 150 | 142 | 112 | 404 | |
| 7 | *Erica* | 201 | 119 | 98 | 418 | |
| 8 | *Danielle* | 224 | 87 | 42 | 353 | |
| 9 | Total | 696 | 446 | 327 | 1469 | |
| 10 | | | | | | |

3. Click **Undo** to revert the action so the Monthly Sales chart only shows the data in range A4:C8. (You need the Monthly Sales chart to only show this data for the next exercise.)

### STEP BY STEP Adding a data series manually

1 Click the **Monthly Sales** chart to select it. Excel highlights the source data, range A4:C8, in the worksheet.

2 From the Design tab, choose **Select Data** in the Data group.

3 In the Select Data dialog box that appears (Figure 5-21), choose **Add**.

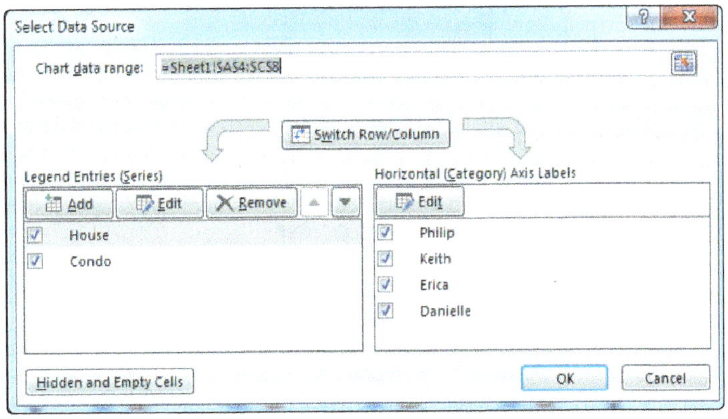


**Figure 5-21**

Use the Data Source dialog box when the data you want to add to the chart is not nearby.

4 Click in the **Series Name** box and select cell D4.

5 Click in the Series Values box removing any text that was prepopulated and select range D5:D8. Then click **OK**.

6 Click **OK** to close the dialog box. The Monthly Sales chart now includes the new data series.

**STEP BY STEP** **Changing the order of a data series**

You can rearrange the order of the data series in your chart.

1 Click the **Monthly Sales** chart to select it.

2 From the Design tab, choose **Select Data**.

3 From the Legend Entries box, select **Condo** as done in Figure 5-22.

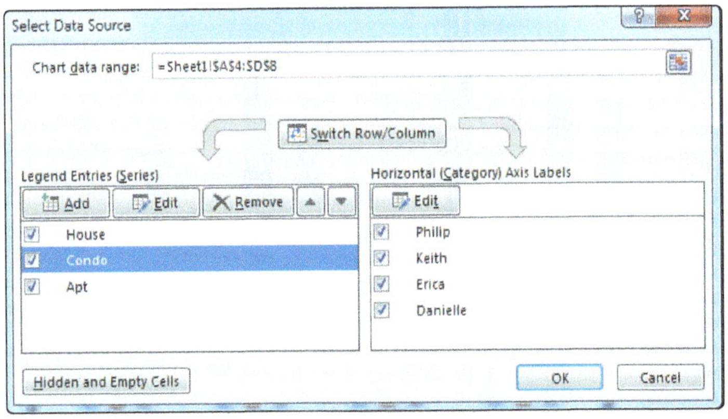


**Figure 5-22**

Rearrange the order of the series by clicking the Move Up and Move Down buttons.

4 Click the **Move Up** button to move the Condo series to the first position, and then click **OK**.

## Removing a data series

The easiest way to remove a data series from a chart is to click the data series in the chart window and then press Delete; Excel adjusts the chart accordingly. You can also remove a data series via the Data Source dialog box.

**STEP BY STEP** **Removing a data series**

1 Click the **Monthly Sales** chart to select it.

2 From the Design tab, choose **Select Data**, click in the Chart data range text box and select range **A4:D8**. Then click **Apt** series.

3 Click **Remove**, and then click **OK** to update the chart.

## Rearranging the data series order

**STEP BY STEP** **Rearranging the data series order**

You can switch the order of the data as it appears on the x and y axes.

1 Click the **Monthly Sales** chart to select it.

2 From the Design tab, choose **Switch Row/Column**. As displayed in Figure 5-23, Excel swaps the order of the data.

**Figure 5-23**

Swap out the series on the axis to get another look at your data.

| | A | B | C | D | E |
|---|---|---|---|---|---|
| 1 | **Monthly Sales Figure** | | | | |
| 2 | *Northwest Region* | | | | |
| 3 | | | | | |
| 4 | | House | Condo | Apt | Total |
| 5 | *Philip* | 121 | 98 | 75 | 294 |
| 6 | *Keith* | 150 | 142 | 112 | 404 |
| 7 | *Erica* | 201 | 119 | 98 | 418 |
| 8 | *Danielle* | 224 | 87 | 42 | 353 |
| 9 | **Total** | 696 | 446 | 327 | 1469 |
| 10 | | | | | |

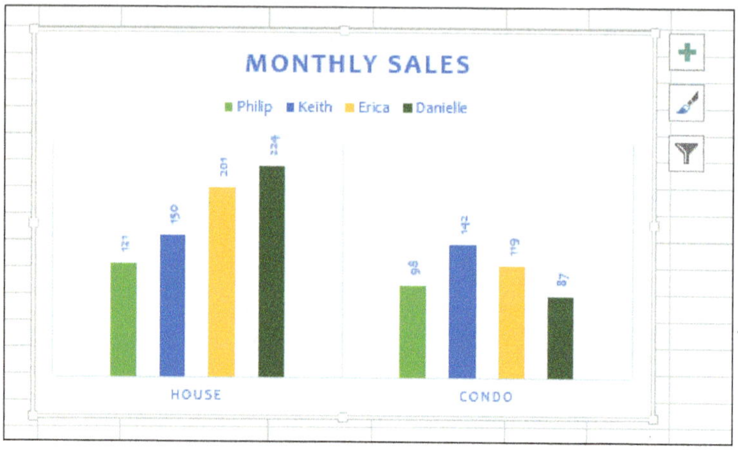

## Filtering data in a chart

When you filter data in a chart, you can hide the display of the data series rather than remove it outright.

**STEP BY STEP** **Filtering data in a chart**

1. Click the **Monthly Sales** chart to select it.
2. Click the **Chart Filters** button as shown in Figure 5-24.

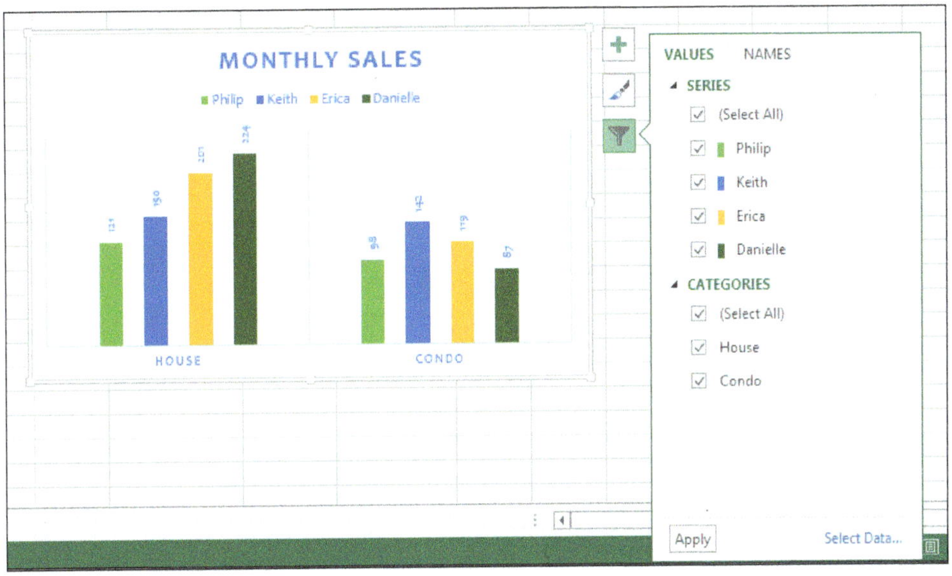


**Figure 5-24**

Filter your charts to only display the series or categories you want.

3. Click the check box adjacent to Erica to remove her data from the chart, and then click **Apply**. Erica's data no longer appears in the chart.
4. Click the **Chart Filters** button again to close the tab.

## Changing the chart type

**STEP BY STEP** **Changing the chart type**

1. Click the **Monthly Sales** chart to select it.
2. From the Design tab, choose **Change Chart Type**.

3 Select **Bar**, choose **Clustered Bar** (Figure 5-25), and then click **OK**.

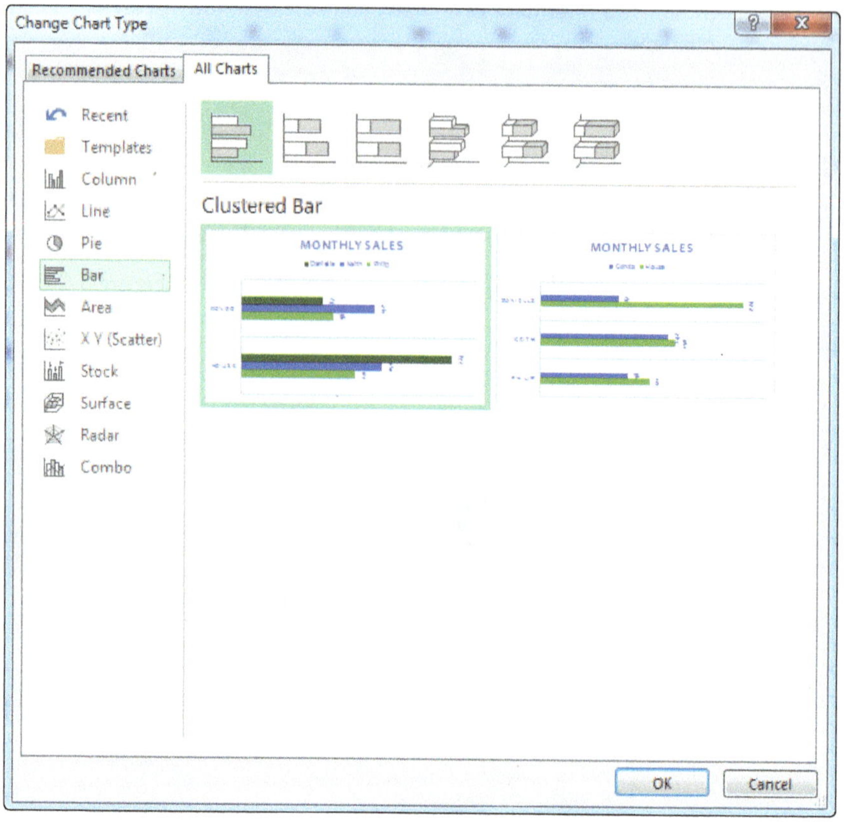


**Figure 5-25**

Switch the Chart Type via the Change Chart dialog box.

4 You can choose to save the exercise file, but don't close it, since you will need it for the next section.

## CUSTOMIZING THE CHART

**Bottom Line**

Excel automatically plots the data along the axes according to the data used to create the chart. You can adjust the values used in the chart **scale** and change the numeric format of those values. Before we customize the chart, we will revert some earlier changes.

**Take Note** For this section, use the same exercise file you have been using till now. Don't close the file at the end of each exercise.

**STEP BY STEP** **Reverting earlier changes**

1 Click the **Monthly Sales** chart to select it and choose **Switch/Row Column** from the Design tab.

2 Choose **Change Chart Type** and select **Column > Clustered Column** and click **OK**.

3 Click the **Chart Elements** button and deselect the **Data Labels** option.

4 Click the **Chart Filters** button, select **Erica** and click **Apply** to add her data back to the chart.

## STEP BY STEP Changing the chart scale

1. Click the **Monthly Sales** chart to select it.
2. Click the **Chart Elements** button, select **Axes**, and choose **Primary Vertical**.
3. Choose **Gridlines**, select **Primary Major Horizontal**, and deselect **Primary Major Vertical**. Click the **Chart Elements** button again to close the menu.
4. Double-click the vertical axis scale.
5. Select the **Axis Options** tab and under Bounds enter **300** as the Maximum value.
6. Change the Major value to **25** in the Units section as shown in Figure 5-26.

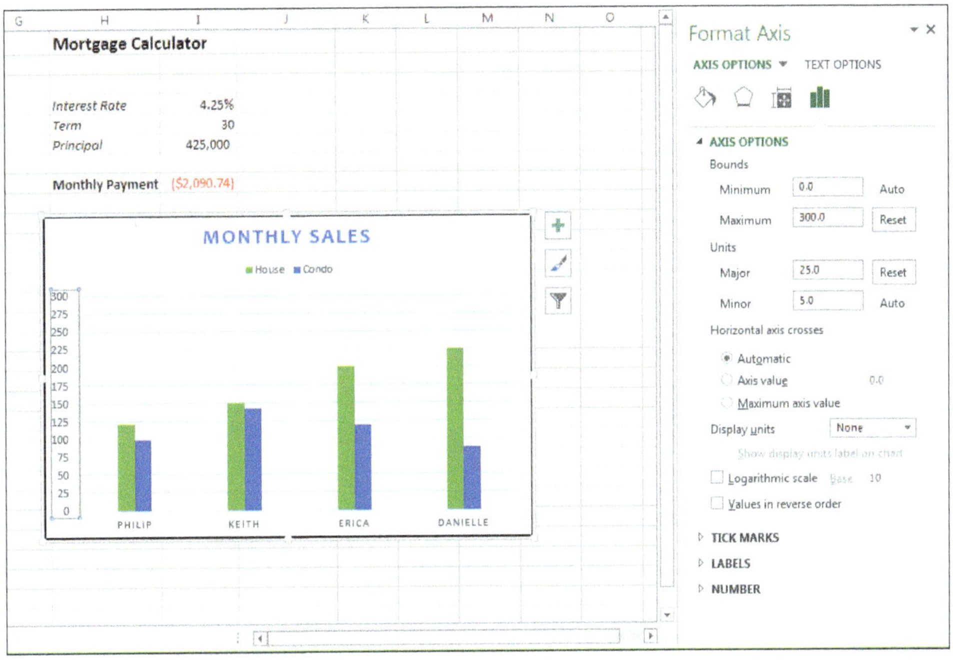


**Figure 5-26**

Adjust the values in the chart scale to highlight your data.

7. Click the **X** to close the Format Axis pane.

**STEP BY STEP** **Formatting the scale**

1. Click the **Monthly Sales** chart to select it.
2. Double-click the **Vertical Axis** scale.
3. From the Axis Options tab and at the very bottom of the tab, select **Number**.
4. From the Category box, choose **Number** and change the number of decimal places to **0** as displayed in Figure 5-27.

**Figure 5-27**

Change the numeric format of your axis scales.

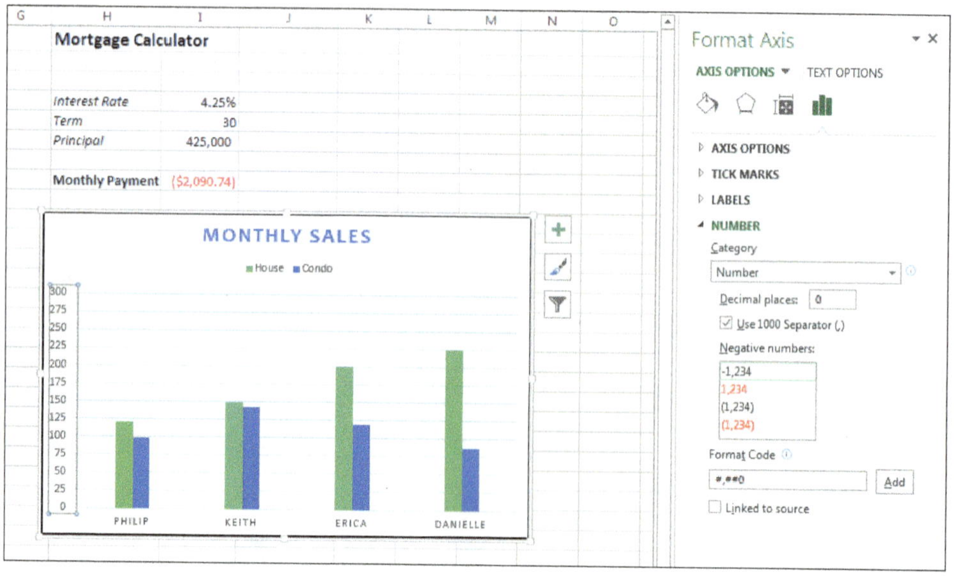


5. Click the **X** to close the Format Axis pane.
6. You can choose to save the exercise file, but don't close it, since you will need it for the next section.

**Bottom Line**

## PRINTING A CHART

You have two options for printing charts. You can print the chart alongside the worksheet data, or you can print the chart itself. When you choose the latter, the chart is printed in full page version.

**STEP BY STEP** **Printing with worksheet data**

1. Select range **A1:M29**.
2. Choose **File > Print**.
3. From the Printer Properties menu, select the printer you want to use.
4. In the Scaling box, choose **Fit Sheet On One Page**; then click **Print**.

**STEP BY STEP** Printing the chart

1 Click the **Monthly Sales** chart to select it.

2 Choose **File > Print**.

3 From the Printer Properties menu, select the printer you want to use, and then click **Print**.

4 Choose **File > Save** to save your work.

5 Choose **File > Close** to **close** the worksheet.

## USING SPARKLINES

**Bottom Line**

Sparklines are mini charts placed in a single cell, each representing a row of data in your worksheet. They are useful when you want to show trends in your data without having to create a full-blown chart. You can add markers, such as high points and low points, and adjust the color to draw attention to important details.

**Sparkline chart types**

| TYPE | ICON | DESCRIPTION |
|---|---|---|
| **Line** | 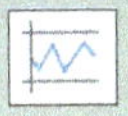 | Illustrates change. |
| **Column** | 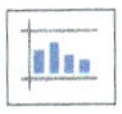 | Compares items. |
| **Win/Loss** |  | Compares items, with all of the positive values displayed above the line and negative values below. |

**STEP BY STEP** Creating a Sparkline

In this exercise, you will create a Sparkline.

1 Choose **File > Open**, click **Computer**, and click **Browse**.

2 Navigate to the Excel05lessons folder and open the file named **excel05_MonthlySalesCharts**.

3 Choose **File > Save As**, and choose **Computer**.

4 Click the **Browse** button, navigate to the Excel05lessons folder, name the file **excel05_MonthlySalesCharts_final**, and click **Save**.

5 Select range **B6:M9**.

6 Click the **Quick Analysis** button that appears in the bottom right corner of the chart.

7 Choose **Sparklines** and select **Line** as shown in Figure 5-28.

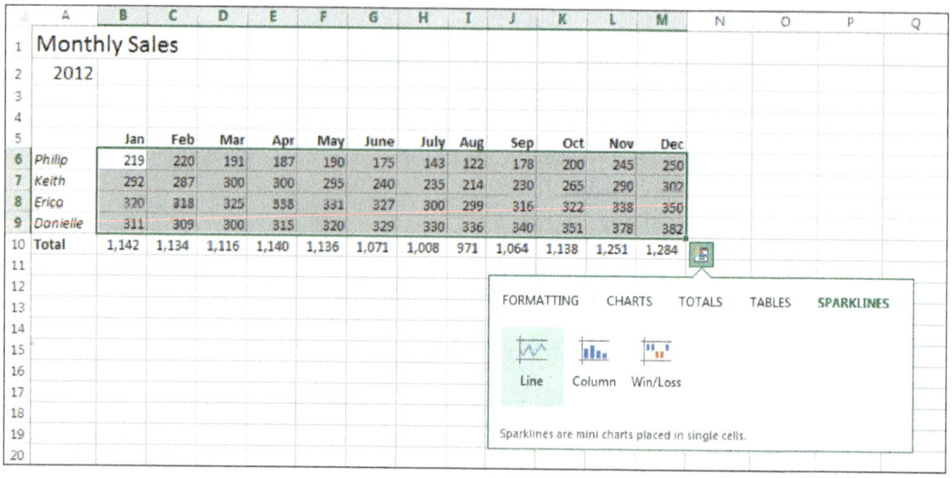


**Figure 5-28**

Choose Sparkline from the Quick Analysis button to add a Sparkline to the worksheet.

As shown in Figure 5-29, Excel adds the Sparkline to the cells immediately adjacent to the selected range, beginning in cell N6 and a Sparkline Tools tab is added to the Ribbon.

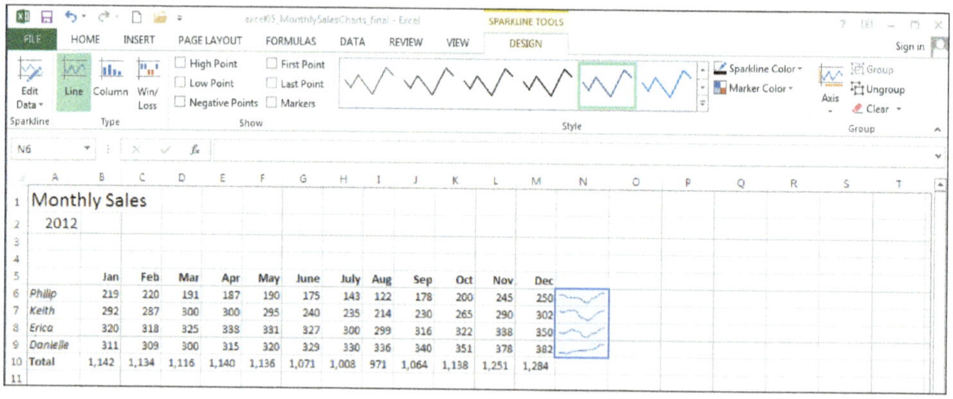


**Figure 5-29**

The Sparkline Tools tab is added to the Ribbon bar when you add a Sparkline to the worksheet.

**Take Note** Excel treats Sparklines applied to a multi-row range as a single group, so any changes you make affects the entire group. To treat the charts individually, you must first ungroup them by choosing Ungroup from the Sparkline Tools tab.

## STEP BY STEP Adding data markers

1 Using **excel05_MonthlySalesCharts_final**, select cell **N6**. Notice that N6 through N9 are selected.

2 From the Show group of the Sparkline Tools tab, select **High Point**, **Low Point**, and **First Point**. As displayed in Figure 5-30, Excel adds these details to your Sparkline.

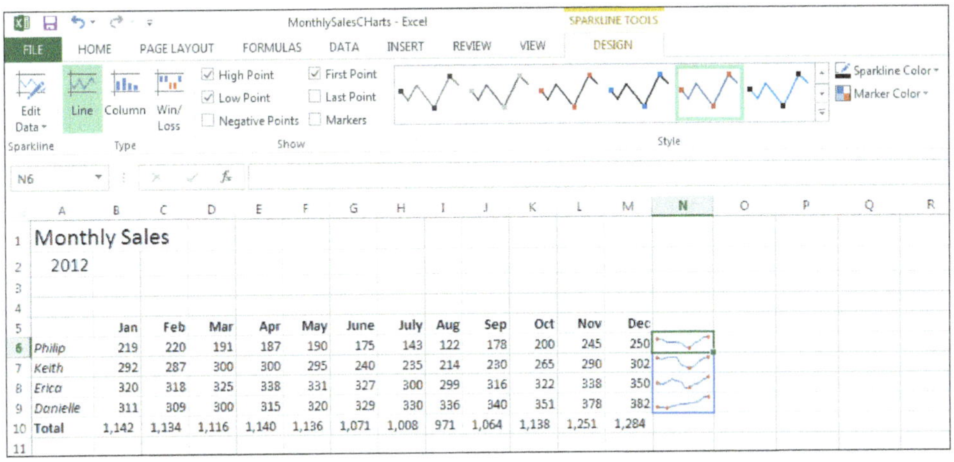


**Figure 5-30**

Add details such as High Point and Low Point values to make your Sparkline pop.

## STEP BY STEP Changing the Sparkline type

1 Make sure N6:N9 is still selected.

2 From the Sparkline Tools tab, choose **Column** from the Type group. As shown in Figure 5-31, Excel switches to a columnar display and retains the Marker options.

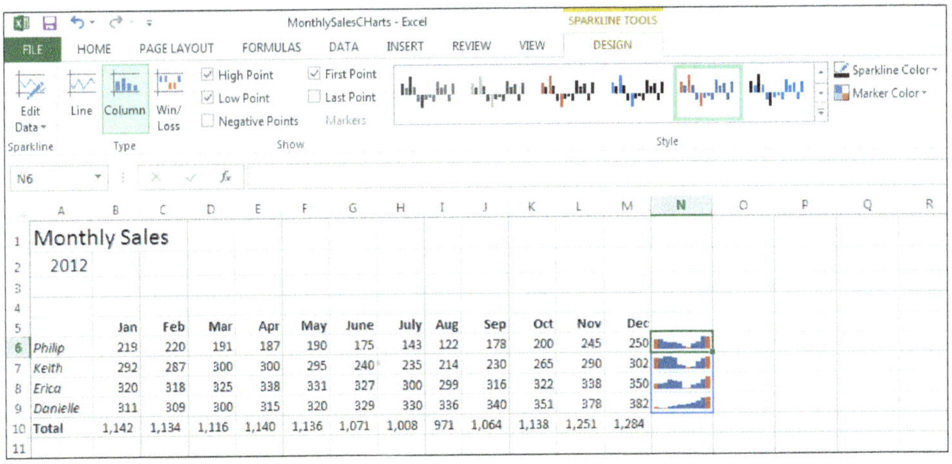


**Figure 5-31**

When you switch the Sparkline type, Excel retains the Marker settings.

## STEP BY STEP Removing the Sparklines

1 Make sure N6:N9 is selected.

2 Choose **Clear** from the Sparkline Tools tab and choose **Clear All** from the drop-down menu. Excel removes the Sparklines from the worksheet.

3 Choose **Undo** to place the Sparklines back into the spreadsheet.

4 Choose **File > Save** to save the current worksheet.

## What you learned in this lesson:

- Understanding Chart Types
- Creating a Chart
- Understanding Chart Elements
- Using Chart Recommendations
- Moving and Resizing Charts
- Enhancing a Chart
- Formatting a Chart
- Editing a Chart
- Customizing the Chart
- Printing a Chart

# Knowledge Assessment

### True/False

**Circle T if the statement is true or F it the statement is false.**

T F 1. The collection of values used to plot a chart is called the data series.
T F 2. A chart must remain on the worksheet that contains its source data.
T F 3. Quick Layouts for charts are found in the Page Layout tab.
T F 4. Chart Style and Chart Color can be selected independently.
T F 5. A chart's vertical axis is marked in increments called Labels.
T F 6. You can customize a sparkline with titles and labels.
T F 7. Bar graphs are also known as area charts.
T F 8. The vertical axis of a graph generally tracks magnitudes or values.
T F 9. By default, Excel creates a new workbook for each new chart.
T F 10. You can enhance a chart with a display of its numeric source data, called a Chart Sheet.

### Fill in the Blanks

**Complete the following sentences by writing the correct word or words in the blanks provided.**

1. A _____ chart plots points with three values, using X and Y coordinates and points of different sizes.
2. The _____ includes the entire contents of the chart window.
3. Select a chart, then click on its _____ button to toggle the title, gridlines, and data labels.
4. Text formatting commands for charts are found in the _____ tab.
5. Commands for styling an entire chart are found in the _____ contextual tab; commands to style individual chart elements reside in the _____ contextual tab.

6. Temporarily remove individual elements from a chart's data series with the _____ tool.
7. The command to switch a chart from Bubble Chart to Clustered Bar is _____.
8. A _____ sparkline displays positive values above a dividing line and negative values below it.
9. Create a sparkline without opening the Ribbon by selecting a data range and clicking the _____ button.
10. A single graph with both line and column plots is called a _____ Chart.

## Competency Assessment

### Project 5-1: Creating a Simple Chart

**In this exercise you will create a simple chart in a new worksheet.**

1. Open Excel and create a new blank worksheet.
2. Save your document as **project_5-1_simple_chart.**
3. In A1, type **Date**. In B1, type **Calls**.
4. Populate A2:A9 with the dates **December 1-8**.
5. Populate B2:B9 with the data series **6, 4, 4, 9, 6, 2, 6, 9**.
6. Apply the Heading 2 cell style to A1:B1.
7. Select **A1:B9**. Click the **Quick Analysis** button, then select **Charts > Line**.
8. Save and close your document.

### Project 5-2: Chart Elements

**In this exercise you'll begin to customize the content and presentation of your chart.**

1. Open the document **5-2-source** and save it as **project_5-2_elements.**
2. Click on the chart's **Chart Elements** button.
3. Deselect **Gridlines**. Select **Axis Titles > Primary Vertical** (not Horizontal).
4. Select the chart's title (Calls), the double click it to edit the text. Type **Daily Sales Calls**.
5. Similarly edit the vertical axis title to **Only completed calls are counted**.
6. Click the **Chart Styles** button and select **Style 2**.
7. Under **Chart Styles > Color**, select **Color 3 (orange)**.
8. Press **Ctrl+W** to close the document. When prompted, save your work.

## Proficiency Assessment

### Project 5-3: Recommended Charts

**In this exercise you'll take advantage of Excel's ability to recommend chart types.**

1. Open the practice file **ratings_comparison**.
2. Save the file as **project_5-3_recommended_charts**.
3. Use AutoFill to extend the =AVERAGE() function to the other cells in row 9.
4. Select **A3:R7** and preview Recommended Charts. Add a **Line Chart** to the worksheet.
5. Select **A3:R9** and preview Recommended Charts. Add a **Clustered Column Chart** for the new range.

   Note the difference in Excel's handling of the raw yearly data and the AVERAGE() output.
6. Experiment with selecting different ranges (e.g., R4:R7, P3:R7) to see which chart styles Excel recommends.
7. Save and close your document.

### Project 5-4: Altering Meaning with Chart Elements

**This exercise will demonstrate how the meaning of a chart can be altered by a subtle change to its construction.**

1. Open the project file **5-4-source** and save it as **project_5-4_chart_elements_2.**
2. Move the chart with no AVERAGE() data to worksheet Chart1, and the other chart to Chart2.
3. Change Chart1's Chart Type to **100% Stacked Area**.
4. Hide the data series for Animal Spirits with the **Select Data** command.

   The graph now depicts the other three shows' share of the "leftover" viewers not watching the top-rated series.
5. Copy Chart1 to a new worksheet (Sheet2). In the new version of the graph, restore the fourth data series and switch rows/columns. What kind of relationships does the new chart in Sheet2 depict?
6. Save and close your document.

## Mastery Assessment

### Project 5-5: Further Chart Customization

**In this exercise you'll carefully tailor a pair of charts to project specifications.**

1. Open the project file **5-5-source** and save it as **project_5-5_customization**.
2. Add a sheet to your document and name it **Custom**.
3. Create two new charts in the Custom sheet, each from the full data set, according to the following specifications:
   * Stacked Column, Layout 10, Style 8, Title **Ratings Share 90-99,** Vertical axis **Millions of households**, exclude Average data series and dates 1983-1989
   * Line, Layout 1, Style 2, Color 16, no gridlines, no title, add bright orange trend-line for Animal Spirits
4. Save and close your document.

## Project 5-6: Choosing the Right Chart

**This exercise challenges you to build a chart to achieve a specific informational effect.**

1. Open the project file **5-6-source** and save it as **project_5-6_design**.
2. Experiment with different types of charts available and use different chart and text options to creatively style your charts.
3. Save and close your document.

# 6 Working with Data

## LESSON SKILL MATRIX

| In this lesson, you will learn the following skills: | |
|---|---|
| Working with Lists | Sorting Records |
| Filtering Records | Searching Records |
| Deleting Records | Removing Duplicates |
| Extracting Records | Subtotaling Data |
| Grouping Records | Using Data Validation |
| Converting Text to Columns | Using Flash Fill |

## KEY TERMS

- List
- Database
- Field
- Record
- Custom sort
- Filter
- Criteria range
- Subtotal
- Grand total
- Data validation
- Input message
- Error alert
- Columnar form
- Delimiter
- Flash fill

©cmcderm1/iStockPhoto

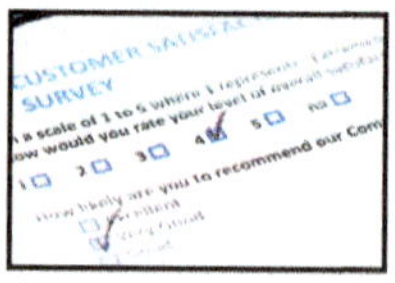

©cmcderm1/iStockPhoto

Contoso's customer database has grown unwieldy – ten thousand records, each with thirty fields, some updated weekly. Their data handlers can only work with a subset of the data at once, and need to reorder and cut down the data for quick reading. Excel's sorting, filtering, and data validation tools keep the database under control, and prevent errors from sneaking in where they'll be impossible to fix.

## SOFTWARE ORIENTATION

You can use powerful tools to sort, organize, and manage data within Microsoft Excel.

**Figure 6-1**

Filtered data

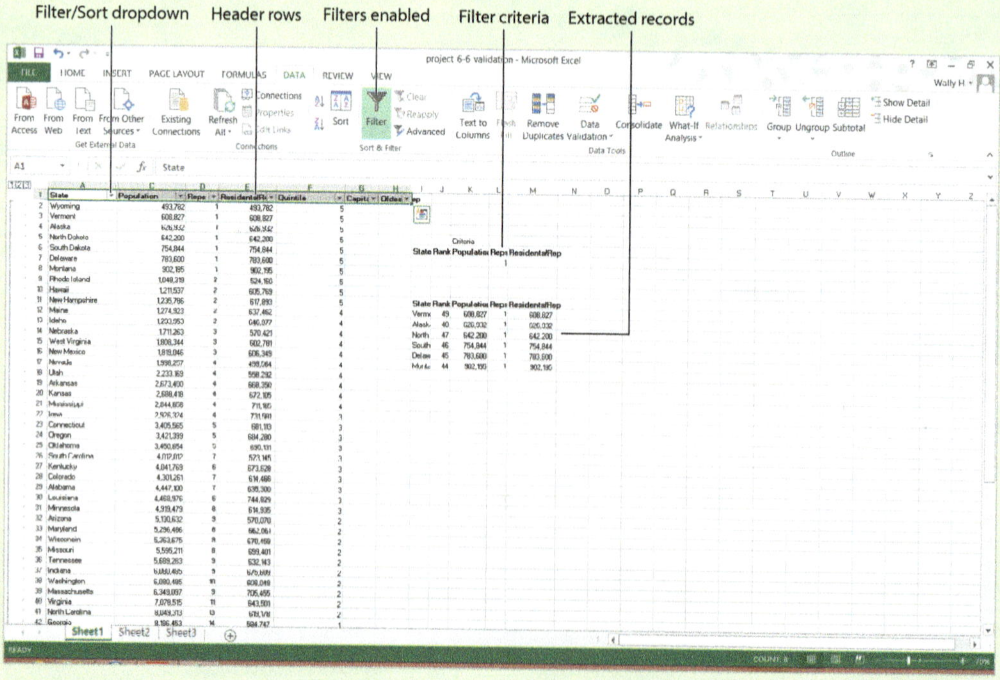

## STARTING UP

In this lesson, you'll work with several files from the Excel06lessons folder. Make sure that you have loaded the OfficeLessons folder onto your computer.

## WORKING WITH LISTS

**Bottom Line**

With Excel, you can easily manage data in a **list**. After information is organized into a list format, you can find and extract data that meets certain criteria. You can also sort information in a list to put into a specific order, and you can extract, summarize, and compare data.

### Database terms

A list, also known as a **database**, is information that contains similar sets of data, such as a phone directory. Information in a list is organized by categories or **fields**. Each column in a list contains a heading or field name that determines the type of information entered in that column. You enter data in a row to form a record. Once information is organized in a list, you can filter, sort, extract, and summarize the data. Figure 6-2 shows 24 records of a database containing four fields.

| | A | B | C | D | E |
|---|---|---|---|---|---|
| 1 | Northwind Traders | | | | |
| 2 | *Employee Expense Reports* | | | | |
| 3 | | | | | |
| 4 | | | | | |
| 5 | First Name | Last Name | Department | Amount | |
| 6 | Stephen | Tran | Sales | $245 | |
| 7 | Eric | Donaldson | Accounting | $300 | |
| 8 | Dante | West | Marketing | $260 | |
| 9 | Linda | McMann | Editorial | $320 | |
| 10 | Jennifer | Ponson | Marketing | $140 | |
| 11 | Nafisa | Pimental | Marketing | $340 | |
| 12 | Ellen | Iverson | Sales | $180 | |
| 13 | Conrad | Baines | Editorial | $280 | |
| 14 | Penelope | Pendergast | Editorial | $254 | |
| 15 | Greg | Stevens | Sales | $167 | |
| 16 | Joseph | Jefferson | Accounting | $100 | |
| 17 | Harry | Hillary | Sales | $189 | |
| 18 | Paul | Bishop | Marketing | $349 | |
| 19 | Jayden | Jones | Marketing | $415 | |
| 20 | Donald | Ellington | Editorial | $620 | |
| 21 | Effy | Gonsalves | Editorial | $430 | |
| 22 | Eileen | Carson | Editorial | $300 | |
| 23 | Hugh | McKenna | Sales | $150 | |
| 24 | Peter | Bailey | Accounting | $780 | |
| 25 | Rebecca | Livingston | Marketing | $450 | |
| 26 | Pierre | Louis | Sales | $309 | |
| 27 | Michael | Martin | Accounting | $500 | |
| 28 | Eliza | Harrington | Editorial | $550 | |
| 29 | Foster | Brooks | Sales | $425 | |

**Figure 6-2**
A list contains similar sets of data.

## CREATING A LIST

**Bottom Line**

Creating a list is very simple. The first step is to determine the categories of information that you want to capture, and then enter a label in each column of the list. For instance, you could have a file with information about your sales force, where the columns are labeled First Name, Last Name, Department, and Amount.

The row that contains the column headings or field names is referred to as the Header Row. The header row is important when you begin to work with your data, since it is used to specify fields to sort by or records to filter.

## STEP BY STEP Adding records to a list

When creating a list, the first step is to create the header row; you can then enter **records** in the rows directly beneath.

To move to the next field in the list, press the Tab key on your keyboard. To move down the list, you can press the Enter key: Excel recognizes the data entry pattern as a list and automatically moves the cell pointer to the first field in the next row.

Here's an exercise for you to practice creating lists in Excel.

1. Open Excel, choose **File > Open** and navigate to the Excel06lessons folder. Open the file named **excel06_list.**
2. Choose **File > Save As** and navigate to the Excel06lessons folder again. Name the file **excel06_list_work**.
3. Click in cell A38 and type **James**.
4. Press **Tab** and type **Gilford** in cell B38.
5. Press **Tab** and type **Sales** in cell C38. Notice that when you begin typing **Sales**, Excel automatically fills in the remainder for you with its AutoComplete feature.
6. Press **Tab** and type **345** in cell D38.
7. Press **Enter** to move to cell A39. See Figure 6-3.
8. Save the file, but don't close it; you'll use it in the next section.

| | A | B | C | D | E |
|---|---|---|---|---|---|
| 1 | Northwinds Traders | | | | |
| 2 | Employee Expense Reports | | | | |
| 3 | | | | | |
| 4 | | | | | |
| 5 | First Name | Last Name | Department | Amount | |
| 30 | Kamilla | Jenkins | Accounting | $375 | |
| 31 | Cliff | Burke | Accounting | $345 | |
| 32 | Kathy | Crawford | Sales | $125 | |
| 33 | Jacob | Mullen | Marketing | $600 | |
| 34 | John | Benoit | Marketing | $450 | |
| 35 | Stanley | Jacobson | Marketing | $235 | |
| 36 | Christine | Gentile | Marketing | $350 | |
| 37 | Preston | Bangston | Editorial | $230 | |
| 38 | James | Gilford | Sales | $345 | |
| 39 | | | | | |
| 40 | | | | | |

**Figure 6-3**
When you press the Enter key, Excel moves the cell pointer to the next record.

## SORTING RECORDS

**Bottom Line**

Excel enables you to organize the data in a list to suit your needs. You can sort the data so it appears in a certain order, either alphabetically or numerically, and in ascending or descending order. You can also create a custom sort to arrange records on multiple fields.

**Take Note** For all four exercises in this section, use the same exercise file you used in the previous section. Don't close the file at the end of each exercise.

## STEP BY STEP Sorting records in ascending order

1. Position the cell pointer in cell B6 to sort the records by Last Name.
2. From the Data tab, choose **Sort A to Z**. Excel sorts the list alphabetically by last name, as in Figure 6-4.

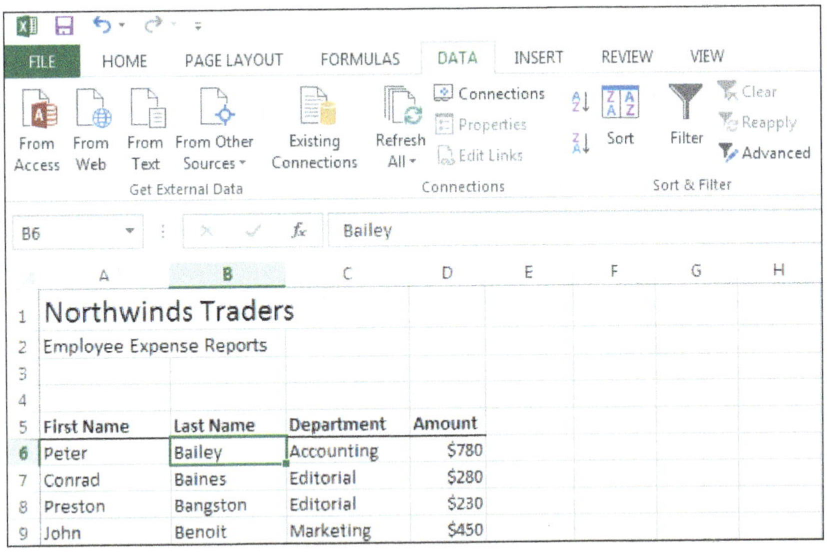


**Figure 6-4** Sort records in a list to rearrange the order alphabetically.

## STEP BY STEP Sorting records in descending order

1. Position the cell pointer in cell D6 to sort by the Amount field.
2. From the Data tab, choose **Sort Z to A**. Excel sorts the list from highest to lowest by the Amount field. (See Figure 6-5.)

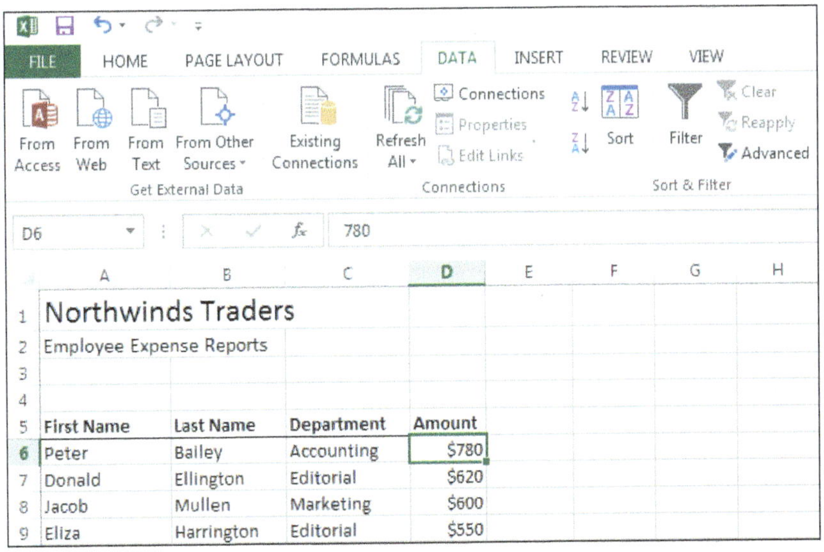


**Figure 6-5** Sort numeric values in a list in descending order to rearrange the order from highest to lowest.

## STEP BY STEP Sorting selected records

You can also sort a subset of records rather than the entire list. When you sort a select group and choose the Sort A to Z or Sort Z to A commands, Excel automatically sorts by the first field in the list. To sort by a different field you must use the Sort command.

1. Select range **A6:E16**.
2. From the Data tab, choose **Sort**. (See Figure 6-6.)
3. In the Sort By field, select **Last Name**.
4. Change the Order to **A to Z** and click **OK**.

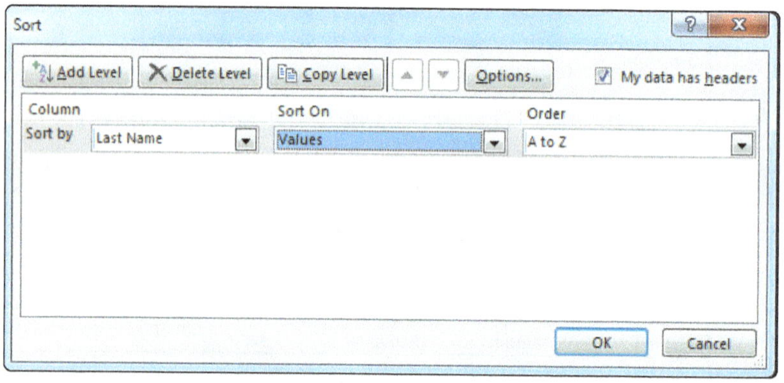


**Figure 6-6**
Sort a subset of records with the Sort command.

## STEP BY STEP Creating a custom sort

When you want to sort records by more than one field, (for instance, by Department and then Last Name), you can create a **custom sort**.

1. Position the cell pointer in cell A6.
2. From the Data tab, choose **Sort**; then, select **Department** in the Sort by field.
3. Click the **Add Level** button.

4 In the **Then By** field, select **Last Name**, and then click **OK**. The data is now sorted alphabetically by the department and then alphabetically by the last name.

**Figure 6-7**

With the Sort command, you can sort records by more than one field.

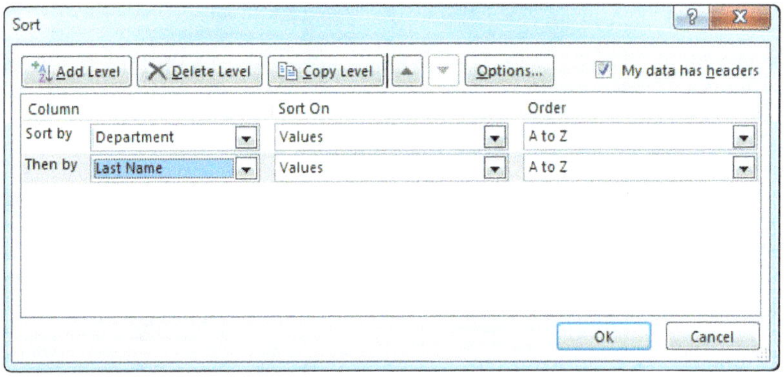


**Figure 6-8**

Sort records by more than one field when you want view records by multiple order.

| | A | B | C | D | E |
|---|---|---|---|---|---|
| 1 | Northwinds Traders | | | | |
| 2 | Employee Expense Reports | | | | |
| 3 | | | | | |
| 4 | | | | | |
| 5 | First Name | Last Name | Department | Amount | |
| 6 | Peter | Bailey | Accounting | $780 | |
| 7 | Cliff | Burke | Accounting | $345 | |
| 8 | Eric | Donaldson | Accounting | $300 | |
| 9 | Joseph | Jefferson | Accounting | $100 | |
| 10 | Kamilla | Jenkins | Accounting | $375 | |
| 11 | Michael | Martin | Accounting | $500 | |
| 12 | Conrad | Baines | Editorial | $280 | |
| 13 | Preston | Bangston | Editorial | $230 | |
| 14 | Eileen | Carson | Editorial | $300 | |
| 15 | Donald | Ellington | Editorial | $620 | |
| 16 | Effy | Gonsalves | Editorial | $430 | |
| 17 | Eliza | Harrington | Editorial | $550 | |
| 18 | Linda | McMann | Editorial | $320 | |
| 19 | Penelope | Pendergast | Editorial | $254 | |
| 20 | John | Benoit | Marketing | $450 | |
| 21 | Paul | Bishop | Marketing | $349 | |
| 22 | Christine | Gentile | Marketing | $350 | |
| 23 | Stanley | Jacobson | Marketing | $235 | |
| 24 | Jayden | Jones | Marketing | $415 | |
| 25 | Rebecca | Livingston | Marketing | $450 | |
| 26 | Jacob | Mullen | Marketing | $600 | |
| 27 | Nafisa | Pimental | Marketing | $340 | |
| 28 | Jennifer | Ponson | Marketing | $140 | |
| 29 | Dante | West | Marketing | $260 | |

5 Save the file, but don't close it; you'll use it in the next section.

**Bottom Line**

## FILTERING RECORDS

By **filtering** records, you can select the records to view in your list. Filtering records is similar to sorting in that you indicate the field by which you want to filter. You can also create multiple levels of filtering so you can view records by more than one criterion. For example, you can view records by specific departments or by a certain amount. When you apply a filter, Excel hides the records that do not meet the filter.

**Take Note** For all exercises in this section, use the same exercise file you have been using till now. Don't close the file at the end of each exercise.

**STEP BY STEP** **Creating a filter**

1 Position the cell pointer in cell A6.

2 From the Data tab, choose **Filter**. Excel adds filter buttons to the field names in row 5 in your list.

3 Click the **Department** filter button.

4 Click **Select All** to deselect it; select **Marketing**, as in Figure 6-9.

**Figure 6-9**

Filtering allows you to designate the records you want to view.

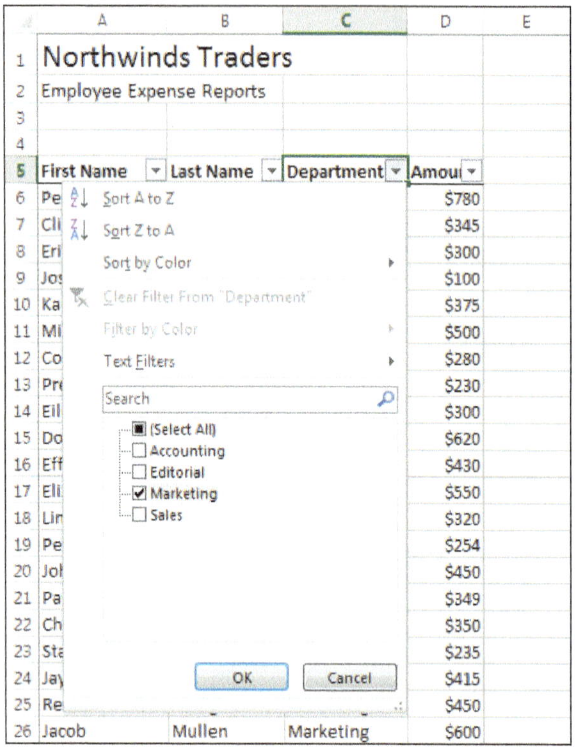

5 Click **OK**. As in Figure 6-10, Excel displays only the records from the Marketing department.

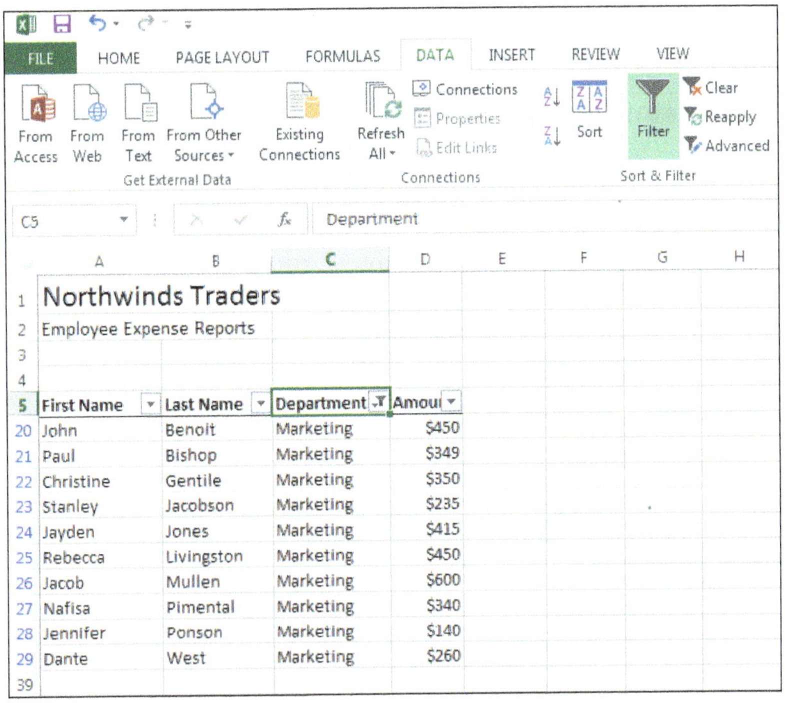


**Figure 6-10**

Filtered records only display the records containing the filter you specified.

**STEP BY STEP**

## Clearing a filter

Excel indicates when a filter is in place by adding the filter symbol to the field heading you are filtering by. When you hover the pointer over the field heading, a box pops up telling you the current filter that is in place.

1 Click in cell A20.

2 From the Sort & Filter group in the Data tab, choose **Clear**. Excel redisplays all the records in the list.

**STEP BY STEP**

## Custom filtering

You can define a custom filter when the data must meet specific criteria. For instance, you can locate records that fall within a certain range of values or contain a certain string of text.

1 Position the cell pointer in cell A6.

2 From the Data tab, make sure Filter is selected.

3 Click the **Amount** filter, select **Number Filters**, and then choose **Greater Than**.

4 In the Custom AutoFilter dialog box, type **400** in the box adjacent to is greater than. See Figure 6-11.

**Figure 6-11**

AutoFilters let you search for specific records.

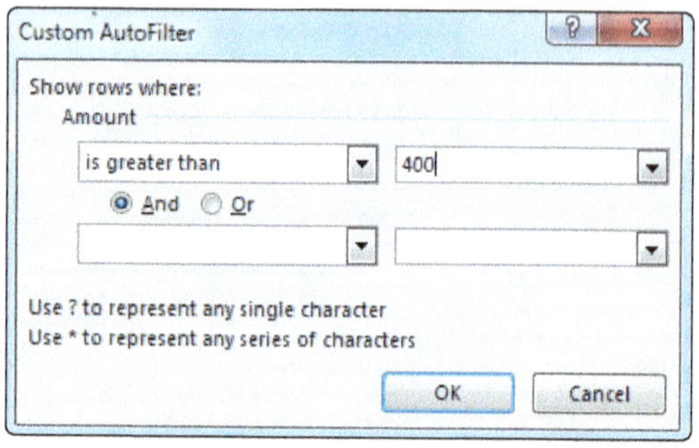


5 Click **OK** to only show records that have amounts over $400, as in Figure 6-12.

**Figure 6-12**

Filtered records display only those where the amount is greater than $400.

| | A | B | C | D | E |
|---|---|---|---|---|---|
| 1 | Northwinds Traders | | | | |
| 2 | Employee Expense Reports | | | | |
| 3 | | | | | |
| 4 | | | | | |
| 5 | First Name | Last Name | Department | Amou | |
| 6 | Peter | Bailey | Accounting | $780 | |
| 11 | Michael | Martin | Accounting | $500 | |
| 15 | Donald | Ellington | Editorial | $620 | |
| 16 | Effy | Gonsalves | Editorial | $430 | |
| 17 | Eliza | Harrington | Editorial | $550 | |
| 20 | John | Benoit | Marketing | $450 | |
| 24 | Jayden | Jones | Marketing | $415 | |
| 25 | Rebecca | Livingston | Marketing | $450 | |
| 26 | Jacob | Mullen | Marketing | $600 | |
| 30 | Foster | Brooks | Sales | $425 | |
| 39 | | | | | |

6 Save the file, but don't close it; you'll use it in the next section.

## SEARCHING RECORDS

**Bottom Line**

To quickly find records in your list, use the Search feature.

## STEP BY STEP Using the Search filter

1. Click in cell A6.
2. From the Data tab, click **Filter** twice. Excel removes the last filter setting and then adds filter buttons to the field names in your list again and removes the current filter.
3. Click the **Last Name** filter.
4. In the Search box, type **Gonsalves** and click **OK**. (See Figure 6-13.) Excel displays only those records that meet the specified search criteria.

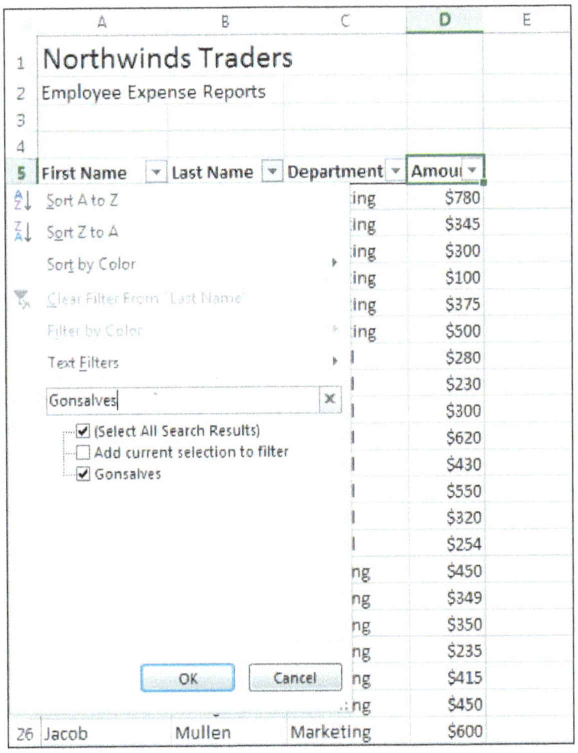


**Figure 6-13**

Find specific records with the Search filter.

5. Save the file, but don't close it; you'll use it in the next section.

## DELETING RECORDS

**Bottom Line**

When you need to delete records from a list, you can delete them directly from the worksheet, just as you would any data you no longer need. If you're working with a large list, you should first filter the list to display only those records you want to delete. Use the Delete command to remove the filtered records from the list.

## STEP BY STEP Deleting Records

1. Click in cell A16.
2. From the Data tab, click **Filter** twice to clear the previous filter settings and begin a new filter.
3. Click the **Department** filter.
4. Click **Select All** to deselect it and choose **Accounting**.
5. Click **OK**. Excel filters the list to display only those records from the Accounting department.
6. Highlight range **A6:E11** and in the Cells group on the Home tab, choose **Delete**.
7. Click **OK** when prompted to delete the rows (see Figure 6-14). Excel removes the records from the Accounting department. Click the **Undo** button to restore the deleted records.

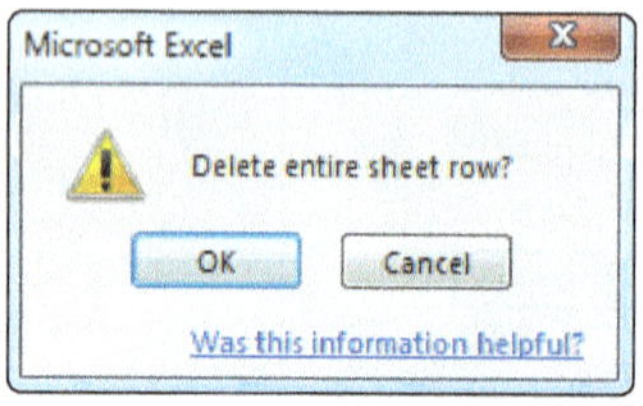


**Figure 6-14**
Delete filtered records from a list with the Delete command.

8. Click the **Filter** button on the Data tab to clear the current filter.
9. Save the file, but don't close it; you'll use it in the next section.

## REMOVING DUPLICATES

**Bottom Line**

Excel can scan a list and search for duplicate entries. If it finds any, you can instruct Excel to remove them from the list.

## STEP BY STEP Removing records that contain duplicate values

1. Click in cell A6.
2. From the Data tab, choose **Remove Duplicates**.
3. Click the **Unselect All** button.
4. From the Columns section of Remove Duplicates dialog box, shown in Figure 6-15, select **First Name** and **Last Name**.

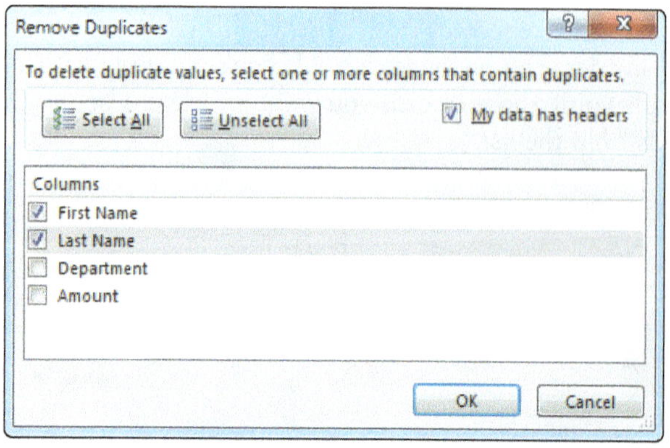


**Figure 6-15**
Remove records that contain duplicate values.

5 Click **OK**. If there were records with duplicate first name and last name entries, they would be removed.

6 In the resulting dialog box, click **OK** to acknowledge that no duplicate values were found.

## EXTRACTING RECORDS

**Bottom Line**

Organizing data in a list is very important, and so is pulling data out when needed. With Advanced sort, you can pull data from a list and store it in another area of the worksheet. By extracting specific records, we can analyze a subset of the data.

Before you can use the Advanced Sort feature, you must define a **criteria range** in the worksheet. The criteria range is identical to the header row in the list in that it contains a copy of the field names used in the list. To define the criteria, enter the data or criteria you want to find immediately below each column heading. You can indicate that the records be copied to another location for further analysis.

### STEP BY STEP Defining the criteria range

1 Select range A5:D5 and choose **Copy** from the Home tab.

2 Click in cell G5 and press **Enter** to paste the copied headings.

3 In cell J6, enter **>400**.

### STEP BY STEP Extracting records defined in the criteria range

1 Click in cell L5.

2 From the Sort & Filter group of the Data tab, choose **Advanced**. Excel automatically selects range A5:D38 as the List range.

3 Change Excel's automatic selection to indicate range G5:J6 as the Criteria range.

4 Select **Copy to Another Location**.

5 Indicate cell L5 as the Copy to range. (See Figure 6-16.)

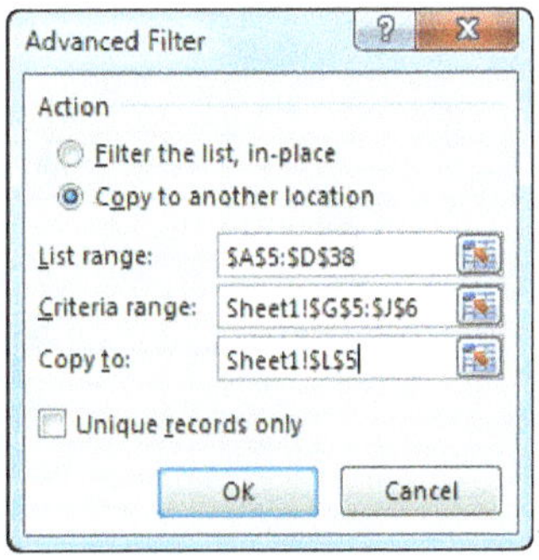


**Figure 6-16**

Use Advanced Filter to extract a range of records from a list.

6 Click **OK**. Excel pulls the records that match the criteria and copies them over under cell L5, as in Figure 6-17.

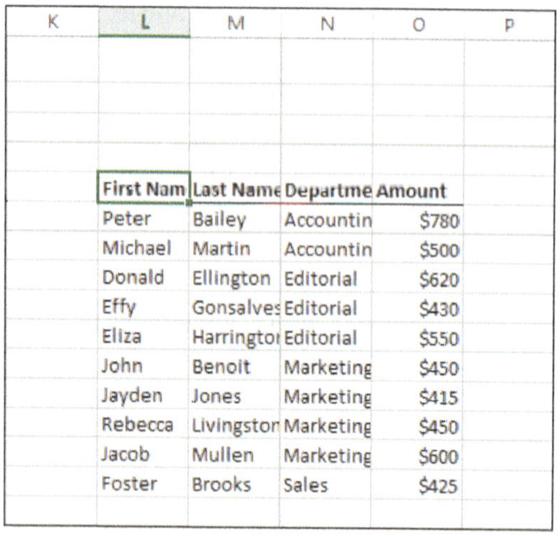

| First Nam | Last Name | Departme | Amount |
|---|---|---|---|
| Peter | Bailey | Accountin | $780 |
| Michael | Martin | Accountin | $500 |
| Donald | Ellington | Editorial | $620 |
| Effy | Gonsalves | Editorial | $430 |
| Eliza | Harringtoı | Editorial | $550 |
| John | Benoit | Marketing | $450 |
| Jayden | Jones | Marketing | $415 |
| Rebecca | Livingstor | Marketing | $450 |
| Jacob | Mullen | Marketing | $600 |
| Foster | Brooks | Sales | $425 |

**Figure 6-17**

Extract a range of records for further analysis.

7 Save the file, but don't close it; you'll use it in the next section.

## SUBTOTALING DATA

**Bottom Line**

Excel's Subtotal command allows you to summarize data in your lists by calculating **subtotal** and **grand total** amounts for numeric fields. When you summarize a list in such a manner, Excel calculates subtotals on subsets of data. For example, you can quickly determine sales revenue by department or determine the average number of units sold by branch.

**STEP BY STEP**

### Alphabetically sort the list

Prior to adding subtotals, you must sort the list by the appropriate field.

1 Click in cell C6.

2 From the Home tab, choose **Sort A to Z**. Excel sorts the list by department if this was not already done.

**STEP BY STEP**

### Adding subtotals

1 Click in cell A6.

2 From the Outline group on the Data tab, choose **Subtotal**.

3 From the "At each change in" drop-down menu, select **Department**.

4 In the Add subtotal to box, select **Amount**. See Figure 6-18.

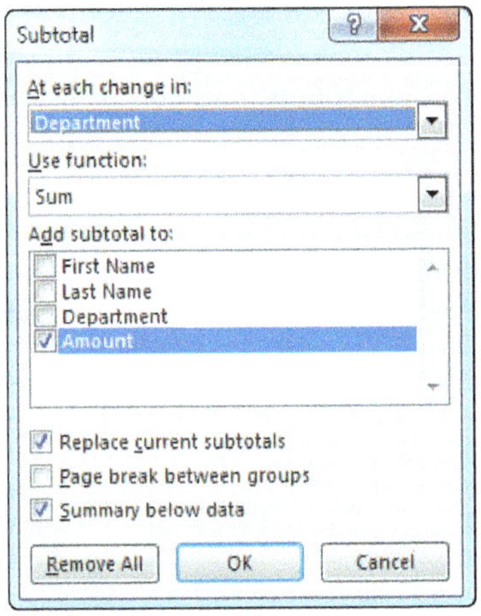


**Figure 6-18**

You can add subtotal amounts at each change in Department.

5 Click **OK**. As Figure 6-19 shows, subtotals are now added to the list below each department.

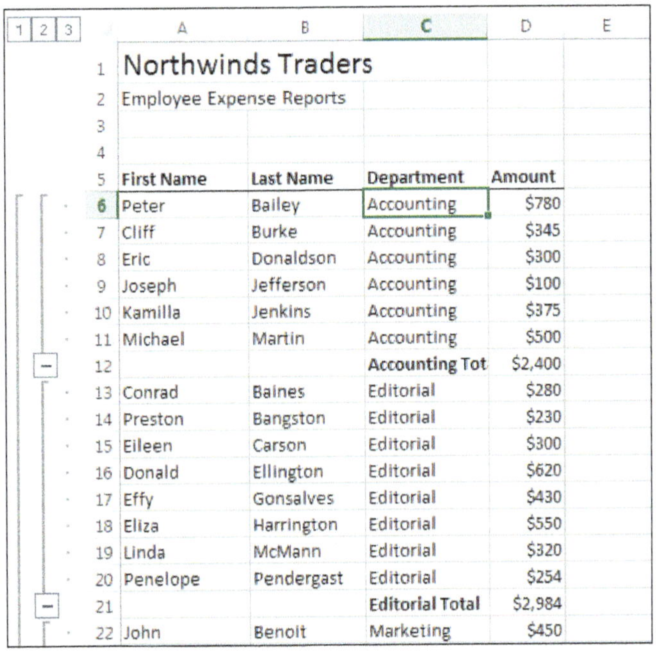

| | A | B | C | D | E |
|---|---|---|---|---|---|
| 1 | Northwinds Traders | | | | |
| 2 | Employee Expense Reports | | | | |
| 3 | | | | | |
| 4 | | | | | |
| 5 | First Name | Last Name | Department | Amount | |
| 6 | Peter | Bailey | Accounting | $780 | |
| 7 | Cliff | Burke | Accounting | $345 | |
| 8 | Eric | Donaldson | Accounting | $300 | |
| 9 | Joseph | Jefferson | Accounting | $100 | |
| 10 | Kamilla | Jenkins | Accounting | $375 | |
| 11 | Michael | Martin | Accounting | $500 | |
| 12 | | | Accounting Tot | $2,400 | |
| 13 | Conrad | Baines | Editorial | $280 | |
| 14 | Preston | Bangston | Editorial | $230 | |
| 15 | Eileen | Carson | Editorial | $300 | |
| 16 | Donald | Ellington | Editorial | $620 | |
| 17 | Effy | Gonsalves | Editorial | $430 | |
| 18 | Eliza | Harrington | Editorial | $550 | |
| 19 | Linda | McMann | Editorial | $320 | |
| 20 | Penelope | Pendergast | Editorial | $254 | |
| 21 | | | Editorial Total | $2,984 | |
| 22 | John | Benoit | Marketing | $450 | |

**Figure 6-19**

Subtotal amounts are added to the list.

## GROUPING RECORDS

**Bottom Line**

When Subtotals are added to an Excel list, each set of records is automatically grouped on the field by which they are subtotaled. When records are grouped in such a way, you can collapse the details of the group to display the subtotals only, and you can expand each group to display the detailed data.

Excel automatically applies an outline view to the worksheet list after subtotals are added. This view offers you single-click access to hiding and expanding details. You can collapse and expand outline levels with the Outline symbols or with the Show Detail and Hide Detail commands from the Data tab.

### STEP BY STEP Hiding and showing details

1 Click in cell C7 and choose **Hide Detail** ( ) from the Data tab. Excels hides rows 6 through 11 and displays the Subtotal amount for the Accounting department in row 12. (See Figure 6-20.)

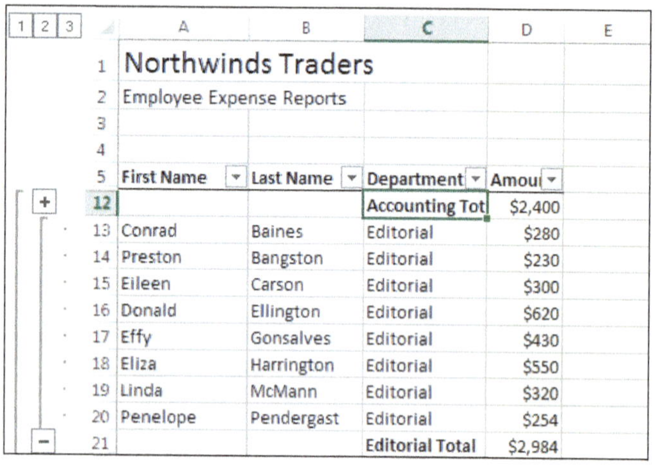

| | A | B | C | D | E |
|---|---|---|---|---|---|
| 1 | Northwinds Traders | | | | |
| 2 | Employee Expense Reports | | | | |
| 3 | | | | | |
| 4 | | | | | |
| 5 | First Name | Last Name | Department | Amou | |
| 12 | | | Accounting Tot | $2,400 | |
| 13 | Conrad | Baines | Editorial | $280 | |
| 14 | Preston | Bangston | Editorial | $230 | |
| 15 | Eileen | Carson | Editorial | $300 | |
| 16 | Donald | Ellington | Editorial | $620 | |
| 17 | Effy | Gonsalves | Editorial | $430 | |
| 18 | Eliza | Harrington | Editorial | $550 | |
| 19 | Linda | McMann | Editorial | $320 | |
| 20 | Penelope | Pendergast | Editorial | $254 | |
| 21 | | | Editorial Total | $2,984 | |

**Figure 6-20**
Hiding the rows will adjust the total of your spreadsheet.

2 Choose **Show Detail** ( ) to expand the detail items for the Accounting group; in this case, rows 6 through 11.

**Take Note** Click the Level 1 symbol to hide all details and display the Grand Total amount only. Click the Level 2 symbol to show subtotal amounts for each group. Click the Level 3 symbol to display all detail data.

### STEP BY STEP Removing an outline

You can remove the outline from your worksheet list without removing the subtotal and grand total calculations. However, prior to removing the outline, make sure you expand the outline to include all your worksheet data. The quickest way to do this is to click the lowest level number displayed in your outline. For the exercise file you've been using throughout this lesson, this would be Level 3.

1 Click the drop-down arrow under the Ungroup button from the Data tab.

2 Select **Clear Outline**. Excel clears the outline from the display and retains the subtotal rows and data.

3 Choose **Subtotal** from the Data tab and click **OK** to add the Outline back to the list. Choose **Subtotal** and click **Remove All** from the resulting Subtotal dialog box. Excel removes both the outline and subtotals from the list.

4 Save the file, but don't close it; you'll use it in the next section.

## USING DATA VALIDATION

**Bottom Line**

Excel's **Data Validation** tools enable you to restrict the type of data that users enter into the field of a list. By doing so, you can streamline data entry and ensure that the data meets a certain level of authentication. Data Validation can also help cut down on data entry errors. For instance, you can create a list of choices from which users can make a selection for a field such as Department. Or impose a restriction on the highest amount that can be entered into a field that captures expense-related items.

### STEP BY STEP Creating data validation rules

1 In cell E5, type **Date Submitted** and press **Enter**.

2 Select range **E6:E38** and click **Data Validation** in the Data tab.

3 Select **Date** in the Allow field; select **between** in the Data field.

4 Type **1/1/13** in the Start Date field; type **1/31/13** in the End Date field. Click **OK**. (See Figure 6-21.)

**Figure 6-21**

Restrict data entry to specific dates with Data Validation.

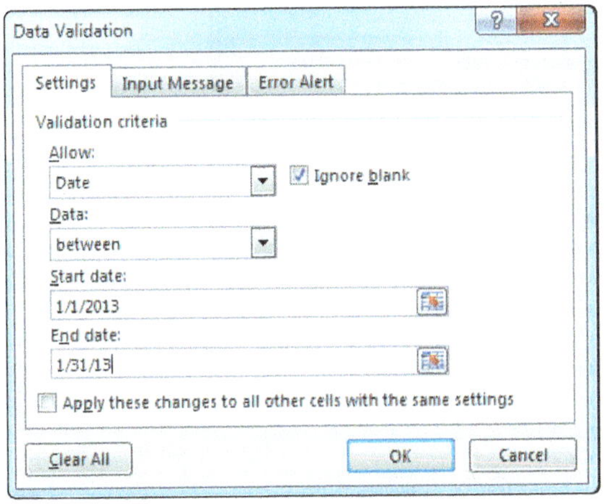


### STEP BY STEP Entering data using data validation

1 Click in cell E6.

2 Type **1/2/13** and press **Enter**.

3 Type **1/4/13** in cell E7 and press **Enter**.

4 Type **2/2/13** in cell E8 and press **Enter**. Excel displays an error message (Figure 6-22) alerting you that the value you entered is not valid.

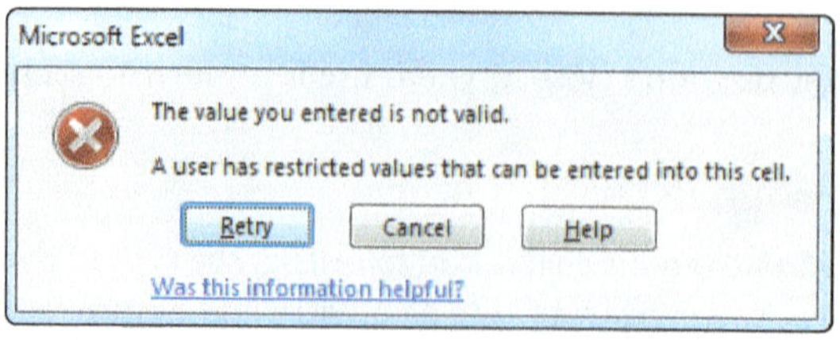


**Figure 6-22**

Error messages are displayed when a user breaks a Data Validation rule.

5 Click **Cancel** and enter **1/2/13** in cell E8 and press **Enter**.

## STEP BY STEP Creating an input message

You can define the message that a user sees when the cell pointer moves to a range that has data validation enabled.

1 Select range **E6:E38**.

2 In the Data tab, choose **Data Validation**, and then click the **Input Message** tab.

3 Type **Date Submitted** in the Title field; type **Enter dates for the current month only.** in the Input message field, as in Figure 6-23.

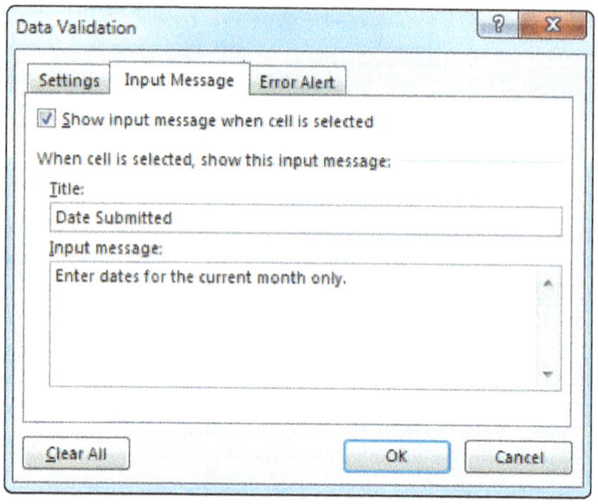


**Figure 6-23**

Define the message that users will see when they point to a cell with data validation rules.

4 Click **OK**. The custom message you created is displayed explaining the data validation rules as in Figure 6-24.

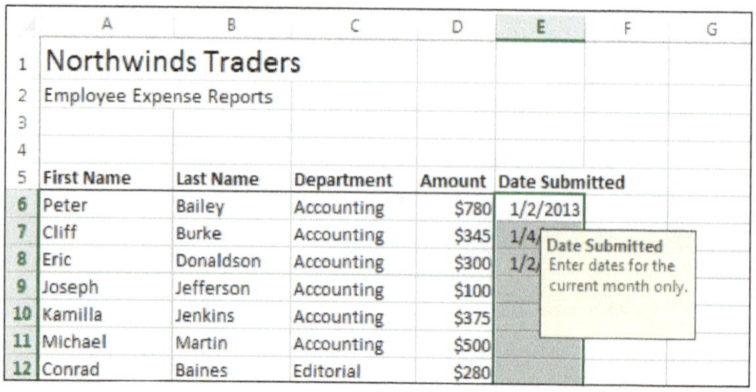


**Figure 6-24**

Define the message that users will see when they point to a cell with data validation rules.

STEP BY STEP

## Creating the error alert

In addition to creating a specialized message when users enter a cell using Data Validation, you can create a custom error message when users break the data entry rule.

1 Make sure range **E6:E38** is selected.

2 In the Data tab, choose **Data Validation**.

3 Click the **Error Alert** tab and select **Stop** from the Style drop-down menu.

4 Type **Invalid Date** in the Title field; type **Enter a date from the current month only.** in the Error Message field. See Figure 6-25.

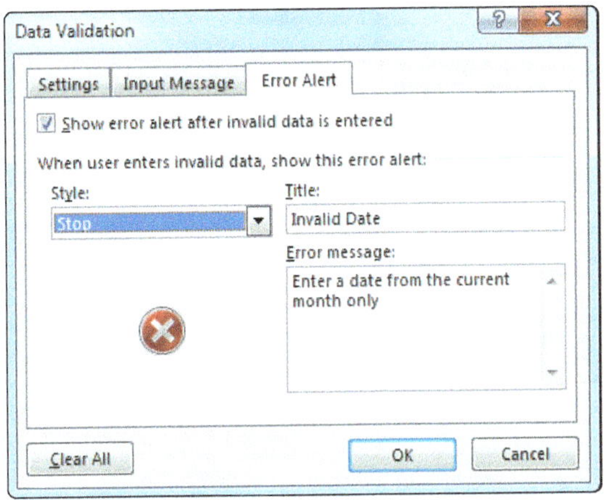


**Figure 6-25**

Create a custom error message for when users type the incorrect data.

5 Click **OK**. Test by typing **2/5/13** in cell E9 and press **Enter**. The resulting dialog box is shown in Figure 6-26.

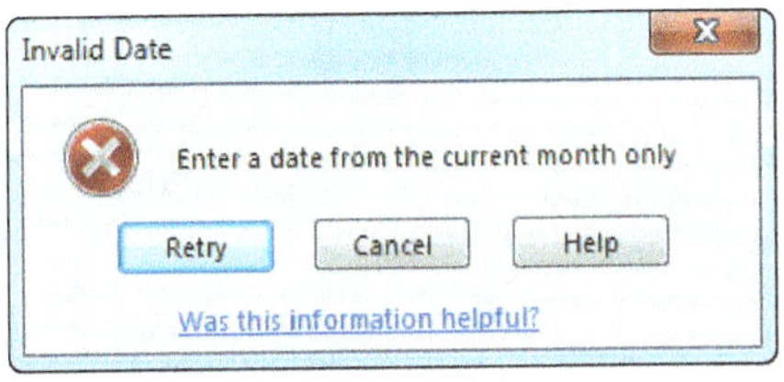


**Figure 6-26**

A custom error message alerts the user to invalid entries.

6 Click **Retry** and type **1/5/13** and press **Enter**.

7 Choose **File > Save** and then **File > Close**.

## CONVERTING TEXT TO COLUMNS

**Bottom Line**

Many times, the data we want to work with in an Excel list comes from other sources. To manipulate the information in the column and row worksheet structure of Excel, we need to clean up the data and convert it so that it can be more readily used.

For example, suppose that you import a mailing list that contains both the first and last name of the customer in the same field. In a list such as this, you can't sort the records by last name. The best option is to split the complete name into two separate fields: First Name and Last Name.

## STEP BY STEP To convert text into columnar form

Before you convert text into multiple columns, you must make sure that there are enough blank columns to hold the split data; otherwise, existing information will be overwritten.

In this exercise, you will begin by opening the practice file, save it, and rename it so you have your own working copy. Then you will add a blank column to your working copy so you have enough columns to hold the split data; and finally, you will split the data.

1. Choose **File > Open** and navigate to the Excel06lessons folder on your Computer. Open the file named **excel06_customers**.
2. Choose **File > Save As** and navigate back to the Excel06lessons folder. Name the file **excel06_customers_work**.
3. Click in column B and click the down arrow below Insert from the Home tab. Select **Insert Sheet Columns**.
4. Select range **A4:A32** and choose **Text to Columns** from the Data tab.
5. In the Covert Text to Columns wizard, choose **Delimited**. (See Figure 6-27.) Then, click **Next**.

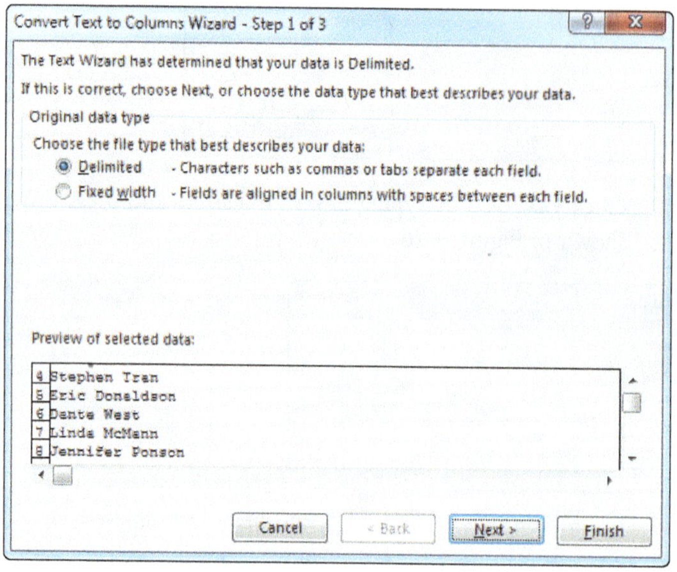


**Figure 6-27**
Convert text entries into multiple columns.

6 Select **Space** as the only **Delimiter** and click **Next**. Click **Finish**. As in Figure 6-28, Excel splits the names from column A into first and last name entries in columns A and B.

**Figure 6-28**

Convert multi-word text entries into separate columns for easy manipulation.

| | A | B | C | D | E | F |
|---|---|---|---|---|---|---|
| 1 | Contoso Realty Group | | | | | |
| 2 | Customer Contact List | | | | | |
| 3 | | | | | | |
| 4 | Stephen | Tran | Boston | MA | 02124 | |
| 5 | Eric | Donaldson | Arlington | MA | 02474 | |
| 6 | Dante | West | Brighton | MA | 02135 | |
| 7 | Linda | McMann | Boston | MA | 02124 | |
| 8 | Jennifer | Ponson | Woonsocket | RI | 02895 | |
| 9 | Nafisa | Pimental | West Newton | MA | 02465 | |
| 10 | Ellen | Iverson | Winchester | MA | 01890 | |
| 11 | Conrad | Baines | Boston | MA | 02124 | |
| 12 | Penelope | Pendergast | Brighton | MA | 02135 | |
| 13 | Greg | Stevens | Newton | MA | 02458 | |
| 14 | Joseph | Jefferson | Wellesly | MA | 02482 | |
| 15 | Harry | Hillary | Providence | RI | 02901 | |
| 16 | Paul | Bishop | Newton | MA | 02458 | |
| 17 | Jayden | Jones | Waltham | MA | 02451 | |
| 18 | Donald | Ellington | Brighton | MA | 02135 | |
| 19 | Effy | Gonsalves | Manchester | NH | 03101 | |
| 20 | Elleen | Carson | Arlington | MA | 02474 | |

7 Save the file, but don't close it; you'll use it in the next section.

## USING FLASH FILL

**Bottom Line**

The **Flash Fill** command is another time-saving technique for working with data imported from other programs. Flash Fill evaluates a range of cells for any patterns or consistencies that it might find. When it senses a pattern, it automatically fills in the remainder of the data for you.

For example, in the following exercise, column A will contain the first and last name in the same field. We will use Flash Fill to fill column B with the first name and column C with the last name.

1 Click the **Undo** button two times to revert the worksheet you used in the previous exercise back to its original state.

2 Click in cell B4 and choose **Insert > Insert Sheet Columns** twice from the Home tab.

3 Click in cell B4 and type **Stephen**.

4 Click in cell B5 and type **Eri**. Excel senses the pattern and fills in the remainder of first names in column B, as in Figure 6-29. To accept the fill, press **Enter**.

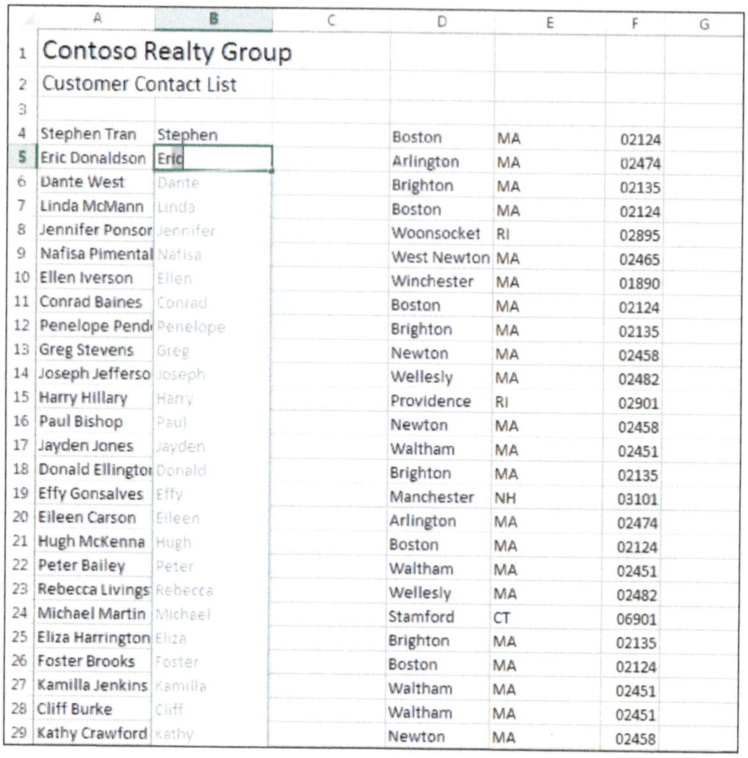

| | A | B | C | D | E | F | G |
|---|---|---|---|---|---|---|---|
| 1 | Contoso Realty Group | | | | | | |
| 2 | Customer Contact List | | | | | | |
| 3 | | | | | | | |
| 4 | Stephen Tran | Stephen | | Boston | MA | 02124 | |
| 5 | Eric Donaldson | Eric | | Arlington | MA | 02474 | |
| 6 | Dante West | Dante | | Brighton | MA | 02135 | |
| 7 | Linda McMann | Linda | | Boston | MA | 02124 | |
| 8 | Jennifer Ponsor | Jennifer | | Woonsocket | RI | 02895 | |
| 9 | Nafisa Pimental | Nafisa | | West Newton | MA | 02465 | |
| 10 | Ellen Iverson | Ellen | | Winchester | MA | 01890 | |
| 11 | Conrad Baines | Conrad | | Boston | MA | 02124 | |
| 12 | Penelope Pendl | Penelope | | Brighton | MA | 02135 | |
| 13 | Greg Stevens | Greg | | Newton | MA | 02458 | |
| 14 | Joseph Jefferso | Joseph | | Wellesly | MA | 02482 | |
| 15 | Harry Hillary | Harry | | Providence | RI | 02901 | |
| 16 | Paul Bishop | Paul | | Newton | MA | 02458 | |
| 17 | Jayden Jones | Jayden | | Waltham | MA | 02451 | |
| 18 | Donald Ellingtoi | Donald | | Brighton | MA | 02135 | |
| 19 | Effy Gonsalves | Effy | | Manchester | NH | 03101 | |
| 20 | Eileen Carson | Eileen | | Arlington | MA | 02474 | |
| 21 | Hugh McKenna | Hugh | | Boston | MA | 02124 | |
| 22 | Peter Bailey | Peter | | Waltham | MA | 02451 | |
| 23 | Rebecca Livings | Rebecca | | Wellesly | MA | 02482 | |
| 24 | Michael Martin | Michael | | Stamford | CT | 06901 | |
| 25 | Eliza Harrington | Eliza | | Brighton | MA | 02135 | |
| 26 | Foster Brooks | Foster | | Boston | MA | 02124 | |
| 27 | Kamilla Jenkins | Kamilla | | Waltham | MA | 02451 | |
| 28 | Cliff Burke | Cliff | | Waltham | MA | 02451 | |
| 29 | Kathy Crawford | Kathy | | Newton | MA | 02458 | |

**Figure 6-29**

Flash Fill cuts down on data entry by sensing patterns in your data.

5 Click in cell C4 and type **Tran**.

6 Click in cell C5 and type **Dona**. Again, Excel senses the pattern and fills in the remainder of last names in column C. Press **Enter** to accept the pattern.

7 Select range **A4:A32** and choose **Delete > Delete Cells** from the Home tab.

8 Select **Shift cells left** and click **OK**. This removes the data in column A, which had become obsolete.

You've now completed Lesson 6. In our next lesson, "Using Templates," you will learn how to use and customize the templates included in Excel 2013.

## What you learned in this lesson:

- Working with Lists
- Sorting Records
- Filtering Records
- Searching Records
- Deleting Records
- Removing Duplicates
- Extracting Records
- Subtotaling Data

- Grouping Records
- Using Data Validation
- Converting Text to Columns
- Using Flash Fill

## Knowledge Assessment

### Matching

**Match the function in numbers 1 to 10 to its output in letters a to j.**

1. database
2. input message
3. delimiter
4. record
5. filter
6. field
7. columnar form
8. custom sort
9. descending order
10. subtotal

a. single line in a database
b. character that separates entries in a series
c. orders data based on multiple criteria
d. list of entries, each w/several fields
e. splitting data into multiple fields per line
f. sorting from Z to A, or greater to lesser numbers
g. prompt for data entry
h. one column/category in a database
i. criteria for viewing records
j. summary of part of a dataset

### Fill in the Blanks

**Complete the following sentences by writing the correct word or words in the blanks provided.**

1. An Ascending Sort of the series (3, 5, 1, 8, 2, 2, 0, 4) produces the series ______.
2. To enable the Hide/Show Detail commands, you must ______ data in your spreadsheet, or calculate ______ for some subset of the data.
3. The ______ tool can, for instance, force the user to enter dates in a certain range into a cell.
4. The most flexible way to include mailing addresses in an Excel list is to first break them into ______ form.
5. Using the / (forward slash) character as a delimiter when breaking up the string "3:00pm on 5/30/99" yields the following entry: ______.
6. The Data Validation will throw up an ______ when data outside its acceptable range is entered.
7. After subtotals are applied to a list, Excel converts it automatically to ______ view.
8. To create an Advanced sort, first preselect or ______ part of the data.
9. The ______ command lets you clear redundant/repeated data within a column.
10. Clicking the dropdown arrow in a column's header cell displays a set of commands to ______ the entries in the column.

## Competency Assessment

### Project 6-1: Filtering Lists

**In this exercise you'll filter and sort data in a list.**

1. Open the practice file **state_rankings** and save a copy called **project_6-1_filters**.
2. Select cell **A1** and click **Data > Filter**.
3. Hide column B.
4. Select the **filter** dropdown arrow for column C, and choose **Number Filters > Top 10**. In the Top 10 Autofilter dialog box, click **OK**.
5. Click the column **A** filter dropdown and select **Sort Z to A**.
6. Save and close your document.

### Project 6-2: More Sorts

**In this exercise you'll create a custom sort for your database.**

1. Open the exercise file **6-2-source** and save your document as **project_6-2_sorting**.
2. Click **Data > Sort & Filter > Clear**, then Unhide column B.
3. Open the project file **state_reps** and copy column A.
4. Paste the copied column into your working document.
5. Select cell **D1**, select **Data > Filter**, then reselect it.
6. Click **Data > Sort**.
7. On the first sort line, sort by Reps, from largest to smallest.

8. Add a Level. Sort by **Population, smallest to largest**. Click **OK**.

   This sort uses state population as a "tiebreaker" when two states have the same number of representatives.

9. Save your work and close all open files.

# Proficiency Assessment

## Project 6-3: Extracting Records

**In this exercise you'll extract a handful of records meeting specific numeric criteria.**

1. Open the exercise file **6-3-source** and save your document as **project_6-3_extracting**.
2. Clear the filter/sort settings for the worksheet.
3. Add the heading **Residents/Rep** to column E and AutoFit the column's width.
4. In E2, add a formula that divides the state's population by its representative count.
5. Format E2 as a Number, comma style, with no decimal spaces. Use AutoFill to apply the E2 formula/formatting to the whole column.

   Note that District of Columbia shows a "divide by zero" error in this field.
6. Copy A5:D5 to I7:M7.
7. Type **>5000000** in K8 and **<600000** in M8.
8. Click anywhere in the main dataset and select **Data > Sort & Filter > Advanced**.
9. Select **Copy to Another Location**, use **I7:N8** for the Criteria range, and Copy to: **I12**. Click **OK**.

   Excel automatically uses the main dataset, A1:E52, as the List Range.
10. Save and close your document.

## Project 6-4: Subtotals and Groups

**In this exercise you will sort, filter, and add subtotals to a database.**

1. Open the exercise file **6-4-source** and save your document as **project_6-4_subtotals**.
2. Sort the dataset by **Population, smallest to largest**.
3. Click the **State** dropdown, and filter the list so only District of Columbia is displayed. Delete its row.
4. Clear the filter/sort info, then sort the dataset by **Rank**.
5. Add column F, heading **Quintile**.

   "Quintile" simply means "fifth": the bottom or 5th quintile is the 1/5 of the dataset with the lowest population.
6. Fill F2:F11 with the number **5**, F12:F21 with **4**, F22:F31 with **3**, and so forth.
7. Click in the main dataset, and select **Data > Subtotal**.
8. At each change in **Quintile**, use function **Average**, add subtotal to **Residents/Rep**.
9. AutoFit column F's width.
10. Save and close your document.

# Mastery Assessment

## Project 6-5: Advanced Filtering

**In this exercise you'll extract records from a list according to a complex set of criteria.**

1. Open the exercise file **6-5-source** and save your document as **project_6-5_filters_2**.
2. Delete the subtotal and grand average rows and hide the Rank column.
3. Use a combination of filter dropdowns and new filter criteria to extract all records of states with a single representative and an above average residents/reps ratio. Copy the results to I11.
4. Save and close your document.

## Project 6-6: Data Validation

**This exercise challenges you to add data validation to a column in a database.**

1. Open the exercise file **6-6-source** and save your document as **project_6-6_validation**.
2. Add two new columns to your worksheet, header cells **Capital** and **Oldest Rep**.
3. Set up Data Validation for the Oldest Rep column, allowing only Date entries in the 20th century, with Input title **oldest rep's birthdate**, message **Please enter a valid 20th century date**, and Stop-style error alert (title **invalid date**, message **Please try again!**).
4. Save and close your document.

# Microsoft PowerPoint 2013

# 1 Microsoft PowerPoint 2013 Jumpstart

## LESSON SKILL MATRIX

| In this lesson, you will learn the following skills: | |
|---|---|
| Selecting and Opening a Template | Adding Animations and Transitions |
| Adding Slides | Switching presentation Themes |
| Editing Slide Text | Presenting a Slide Show |
| Placing Images into Slides | Adding Speaker Notes |

## KEY TERMS

- Variant
- Widescreen
- Change Case
- WYSIWYG
- Speaker Notes
- Exit Animation
- Transition
- Slide Sorter

©kzenon/iStockPhoto

Contoso's one thousand employees are spread over four buildings and a dozen departments. Staying on top of other groups' progress, even within a single project, can be daunting, especially when two groups have wildly different areas of expertise. Workplace presentations – from slide shows online to point-by-point in-person talks – are vital to Contoso's operations. PowerPoint helps engineers, marketers, researchers, admins, accountants, and managers make their ideas "stick." It's a tool for that most memorable workplace activity: show-and-tell.

## SOFTWARE ORIENTATION

You'll quickly create your first presentation using PowerPoint in this lesson where you'll discover the process for adding slides, editing text, importing images, and using presentation themes.

**Figure 1-1**

Microsoft PowerPoint 2013 Workspace.

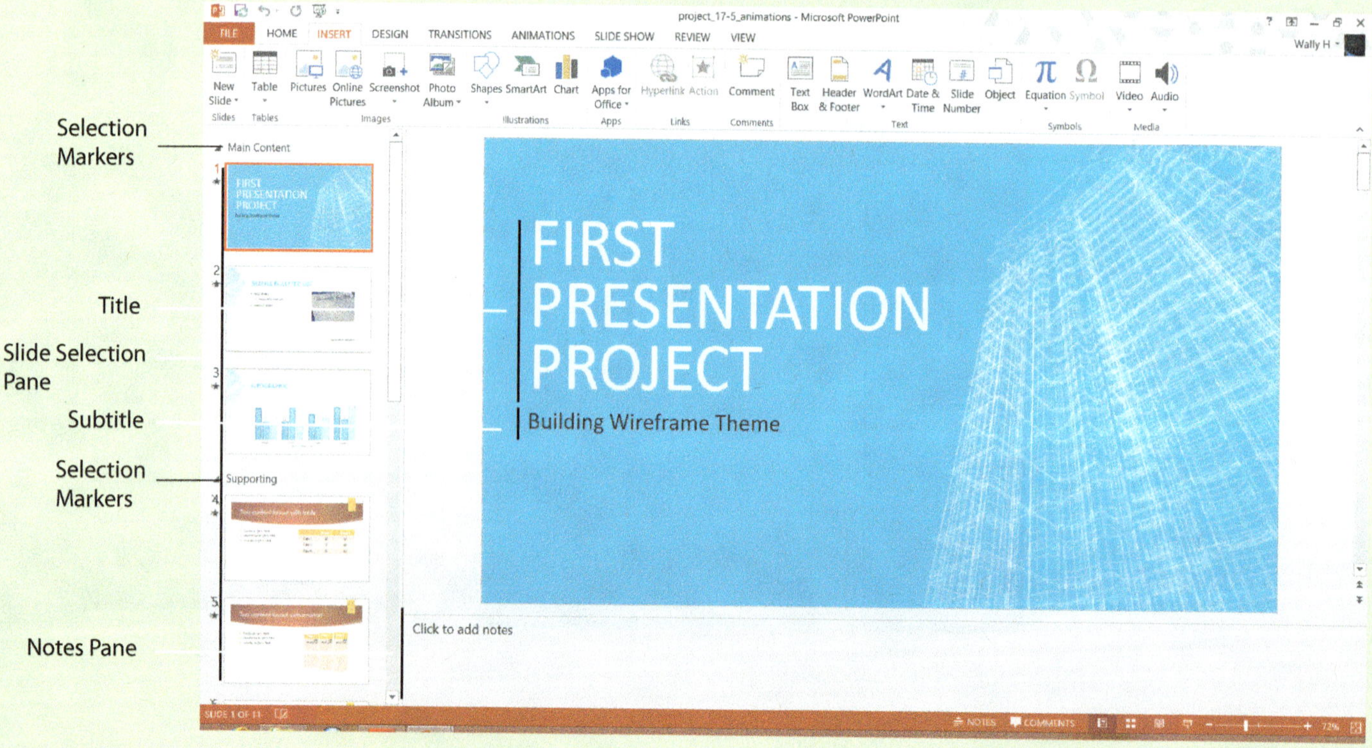

## STARTING UP

In this lesson, you'll work with several files from the PPT01lessons folder. Make sure that you have loaded the lessson files onto your computer.

This Jumpstart lesson contains minimal explanation of the basic functions you'll use in every PowerPoint 2013 presentation: selecting a theme, adding slides, editing text, inserting images, applying basic animations, and starting a slide show. Most PowerPoint presentations are no more complicated than the sample file in this lesson. The remaining lessons explore these functions in greater detail, introduce some of PowerPoint's more advanced features, and introduce you to topics such as presentation style and visual design.

After completing the work in this lesson, you'll have a file that looks like **pp01c-finished.pptx**; feel free to consult that file at any point. Now launch PowerPoint 2013. The launch screen is shown in Figure 1-2.

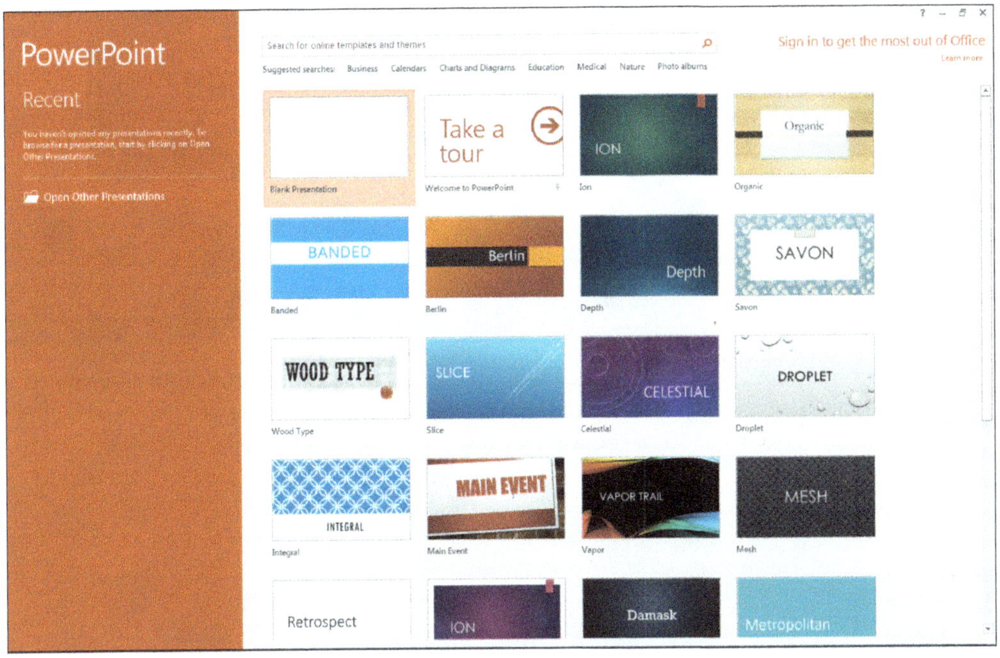


**Figure 1-2**

Rather than a blank document, PPT 2013's launch screen offers templates and recent files.

### Choosing a template

**Bottom Line**

We'll use one of PowerPoint's ready-made templates to structure and style our slides. Templates are premade documents, ready to be filled in with your content. Office 2013 offers templates with multiple color schemes (**Variants**), providing some flexibility within each design.

## STEP BY STEP Choosing a template

1 From the Template Gallery, select the **Ion** template.

2 A window pops up with four color choices. Select the purple variant (see Figure 1-3) and click **Create**.

**Figure 1-3**

Select the purple variant of the Ion template.

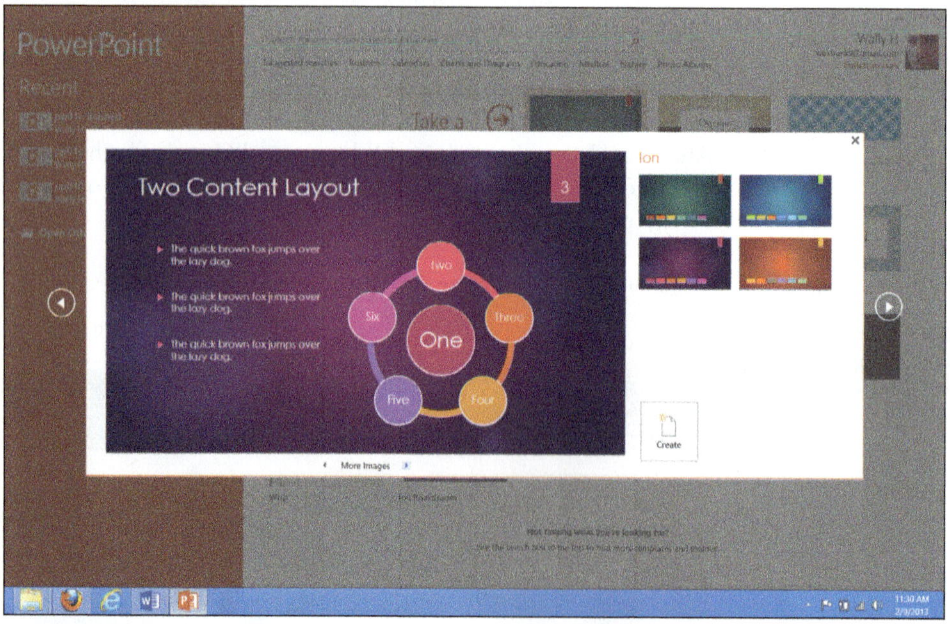


The main document screen appears, initially split into three parts: Ribbon and toolbar at the top, a pane containing all the presentation's slides at left, and the document editing area taking up most of the screen.

**Take Note** Previous editions of PowerPoint supported **widescreen** presentations as a supplementary option: you had to tweak aspect ratios manually to get to a widescreen format. As you can see, we're starting the lesson with a widescreen template, and you can move fluidly between widescreen (16:9) and old-fashioned TV (4:3) formats with the Design > Slide Size button.

### Editing the title slide

By default, templates open with a Title Slide. The title slide skeleton contains two text boxes (title and subtitle) with minimal empty space for visual decoration. The Slides pane displays a preview of the slide with all elements in place: the placeholder text (Click to add title) appears only in the editing area.

## STEP BY STEP Editing the title slide

1 Click in the Title text box and type **Digital Publishing**.

2 Click in the Subtitle text box and type **From raw text to printed output**.

Note that the subtitle is formatted in all caps. You can change the look of the subtitle with the Home > Font > Change Case command.

3 Choose File > Save As and navigate to the PPT01lesson folder. Name the document **Publishing-Markup** and press Enter.

## Adding slides

**Bottom Line**

To add a slide, you can select a slide type from the New Slide drop-down menu or press Ctrl+M to insert a new slide with the current slide's layout, then change its layout afterward.

**STEP BY STEP** **Adding slides**

1 Press **Ctrl+M** three times to insert three slides after the current slide. Leave slide 2 as is.

Pressing Ctrl+M with the title slide selected inserts a blank heading/content block slide. PowerPoint is smart enough to know you don't want two title slides.

2 Select slide **3** in the Slides pane and change its layout by clicking **Home > Slides > Layout > Comparison**. (You can also right-click the **slide preview** and choose **Layout** from the context menu.)

3 Use the same command to change slide 4 to the Panoramic Picture with Caption layout.

## Adding text to your presentation

**Bottom Line**

Now we can add content to our slides. As you've already seen from adding slides after the title slide, PowerPoint makes some simplifying assumptions about your document; these will streamline the process of building your presentation.

**STEP BY STEP** **Adding text to your presentation**

1 Select slide **2**. Click in the slide title box and type **why work with plain text?**

2 Select the text you just entered and select **Home > Font > Change Case > Capitalize Each Word**, and then correct the resulting capitalization by changing With to **with**.

PowerPoint can also automatically capitalize certain paragraph styles (for instance, the title slide's subtitle) but the **Change Case** command is for quick changes.

3 Click in the main text area of slide 2, which is formatted to produce bulleted text by default. Enter the following text (remember that Tab increases indent level, Shift+Tab decreases it):

- **Portable**
- **Easy to Edit**
- **Modern markup**
  - **Single source**
  - **Human readable**

**Take Note** Picking a font size for a PowerPoint presentation is slightly more complex than sizing for the printed page; 12 point text should be the same size on notebook paper and in a 6×9 trade paperback, but the readability (indeed, the size) of slide text is highly dependent on the size and quality of the projection screen. We strongly suggest following this general principle: go big for those in the back row of the auditorium.

4 Select all the text in the bulleted list and click **Home > Font > Increase Font Size** (**Ctrl+Shift+>**) five times; the list should nearly fill the text area, as in Figure 1-4.

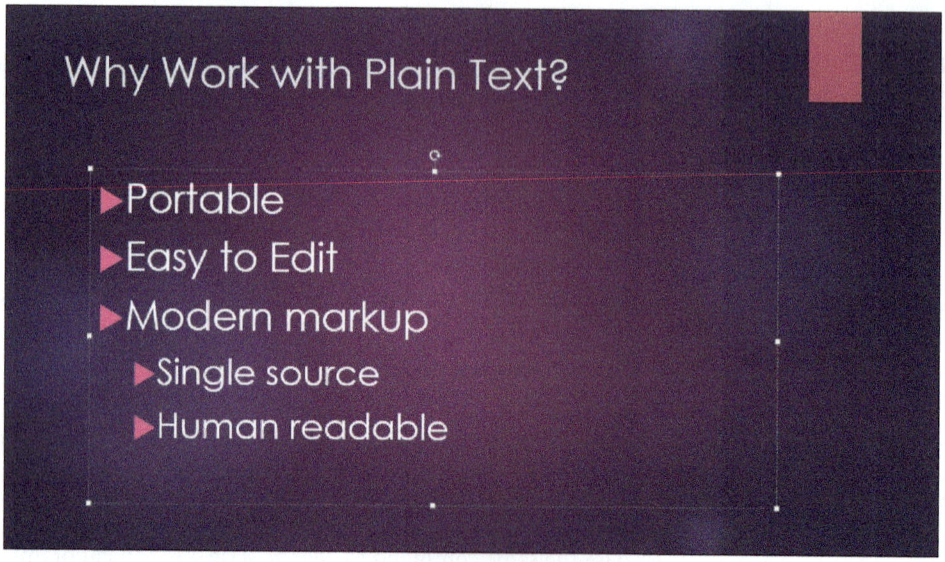


**Figure 1-4**

Increase the font size five times.

Now we'll add the slide number to all but the first slide; since we're using a built-in template, there's already a spot set aside for it on every slide.

5 Click **Insert > Text > Header & Footer**. Make sure the Slide number and Don't show on title slide check boxes are marked as in Figure 1-5. Click **Apply to All**.

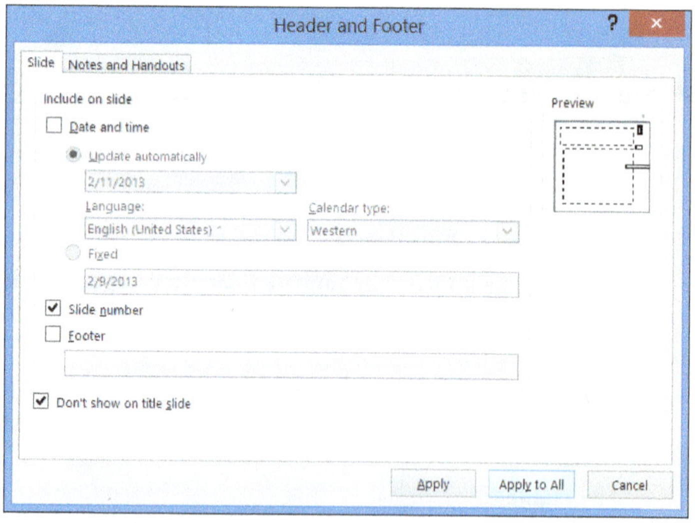


**Figure 1-5**

Adding slide numbers to our presentation.

6 Choose **File > Save** or press **Ctrl+S** to save your work.

## Adding visuals to a slide

Most built-in PowerPoint 2013 slide layouts include content areas with buttons to add standard visual elements: images, video, Excel data, charts, etc. (Title slides, on the other hand, are laid out with the assumption that they'll include only text.) Just as in the other Office 2013 applications, you can use the Insert tools to add objects to a slide, but if you don't want to bother with formatting, the content area controls (shown in Figure 1-6) will let you add visuals easily.

**Figure 1-6**

Use the content controls to insert charts, graphs, images, spreadsheets, and video in a slide content area.

**STEP BY STEP** **Adding visuals to a slide**

1. Switch to slide **3**. In the title box, type **Visual Editing vs Markup**.
2. Type **WYSIWYG** (short for What You See Is What You Get) in the heading area to the left, and **Markup** in the right.
3. In the content area to the left, click the **Pictures** control. Navigate to your PPT01lessons folder and select **pp01a.png**. Click **Insert**.
4. Do the same in the box to the right, but insert the image **pp01b.png**.

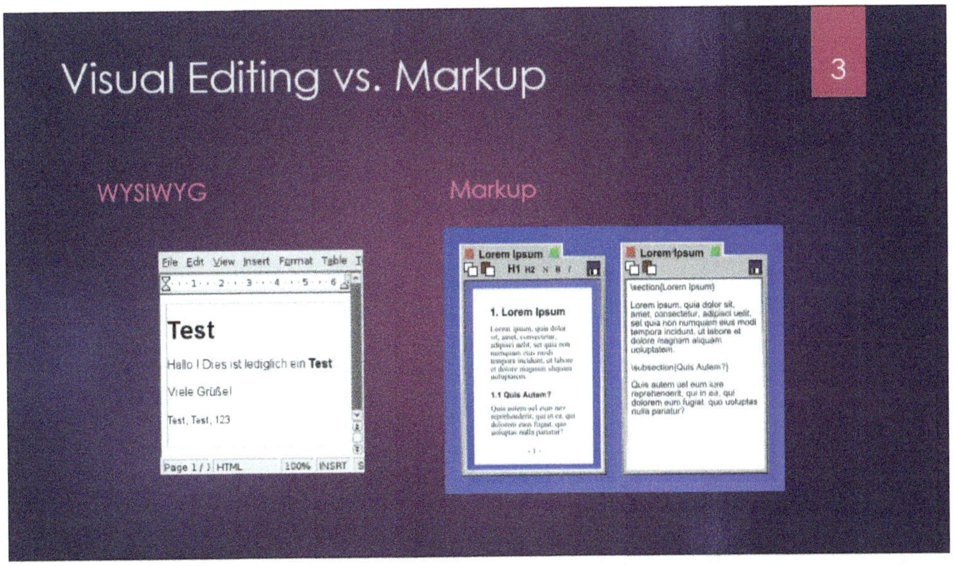


**Figure 1-7**

Add Pictures to your slides using the Pictures control.

The two images aren't the same size or proportion (see Figure 1-7), so the slide is currently unsightly. With help from PowerPoint's layout guides and basic image editing tools, you can quickly and easily make rudimentary layout corrections.

5. Click **View > Show > Guides** to turn on responsive guidelines. Drag the left hand image up and to the left until its top edge is flush with the other image's and its left edge is flush with the word **WYSIWYG**. Orange dotted guidelines will appear when you get close. (You can Use the zoom slider on the Status Bar to zoom in on the slide for fine control over positioning.)

6 Use the image handles to make the right image (Markup) the same height as the WYSIWYG image; again, an orange guideline will appear along the bottom edge of the two images to indicate when you've matched the size.

7 Choose **File > Save** to save your work.

The Show Guides feature works the same in PowerPoint and Word; it's most obviously useful when laying out complex pages, but PowerPoint slides are rarely as complex as, say, a newsletter. We'll see its full usefulness in later lessons.

## FROM SLIDE DECK TO PRESENTATION

As you build your slide deck, we recommend stopping periodically and clicking through the presentation as if you were presenting to an audience; even without your commentary, this practice will give you a sense for the flow of the slides. Viewing the presentation without busy user interface elements like the Ribbon and Status Bar will also let you see and think about the look and feel of the slides themselves.

### Including speaker notes

**Bottom Line**

**Speaker notes** are additional text pieces attached to your slides. You can use them as prompts or scripts while you give your talk. They're for your eyes only; the audience won't see them. We'll add an image and caption to slide 4, and then start to annotate our presentation with speaker notes. When we've finished designing the slides and making notes, we'll run through the rough draft of the presentation.

**STEP BY STEP** **Adding speaker notes**

1 Turn off guidelines by deselecting **View > Show > Guides**. Click to select slide **4**. In the large content area, click the icon to add a picture. Navigate to the PPT01lessons folder and select **pp01d.png**. Click **Insert** or press **Enter** to add the image.

2 In the title box, type **Live Preview: best of both worlds**. In the bottom content area, type **Modern apps let you see multiple (beautiful) outputs from a single readable text source**.

As you can see from Figure 1-8, this is a fairly lengthy piece of text, and probably too small for easy reading onscreen; we'll see when we test out the presentation. Next we'll add notes to each slide.

3 Click **View > Show > Notes** to display a pane with speaker notes. Add the following note to slide 4: **Stress cross-platform for corporate audience**.

**Figure 1-8**

Add speaker notes to each slide.

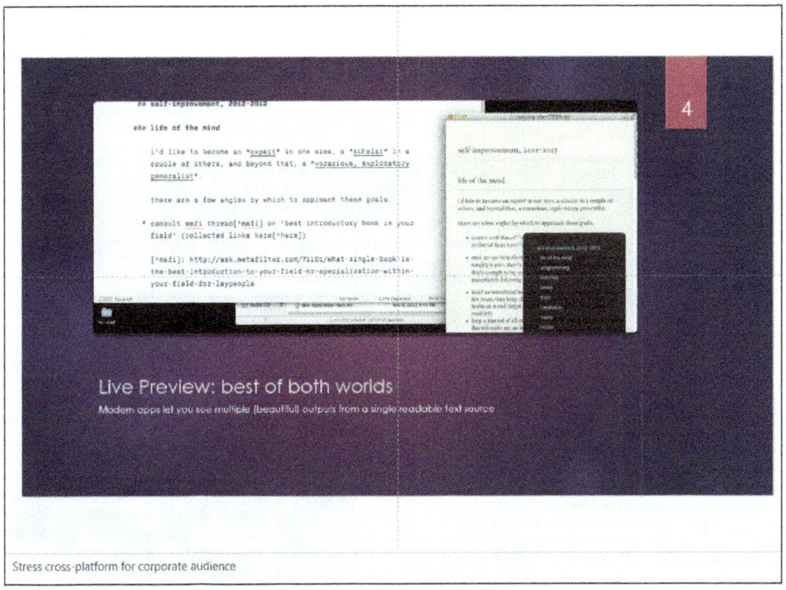


4 Add the note **Final bullet: analogy to HTML** to slide 2, and **Dynamic numbering makes outlining less stressful** to slide 3.

5 Finally, add the following note to the title slide: **MAKE SURE TO THANK THE MONEY GUYS** (don't forget all caps). Save your work.

## Practicing the slide show

**Bottom Line**

The Slide Show tab is full of tools to configure and run the presentation (Slide Show) itself. The Set Up Slide Show command lets you configure the presentation for different viewing modes: projecting onscreen at a talk, running repeatedly at a kiosk, or simply viewed on a single user's screen. We'll use the default options for now, and view the slide show in Presenter Mode to see what the tool offers.

**STEP BY STEP**

## Playing the slide show

1 Using the **Publishing-Markup** file, open the Slide Show tab and select **Start Slide Show > From Beginning** to start the presentation. The slide show runs in full screen mode; to return to the editing screen, press **Escape**.

What you see in the basic Slide Show view is essentially the same as what an audience would see on a mirrored display device; but when you mouse over the lower-left part of the screen, a set of presenter tool icons appear on the presenter screen only. Click the mouse or press space/return/right arrow to advance; press the left arrow to go back. Because your presentation doesn't yet contain animations or transitions, each time you press the spacebar or right arrow you'll advance one slide.

**Figure 1-9**
Presenter tools in the basic Slide Show view.

When you move the mouse in the Slide Show, a set of controls is revealed in the lower left of your (presenter) screen, but hidden from the audience. These controls, shown in Figure 1-9, provide access to the Pen Tools (laser pointer, highlighter, pen), zoom mode (zoom in on part of the screen), slide selector, and an options screen that includes Presenter View, shown in Figure 1-10.

## STEP BY STEP Using the Presenter View

1 Click the (...) button and select **Show Presenter View**.

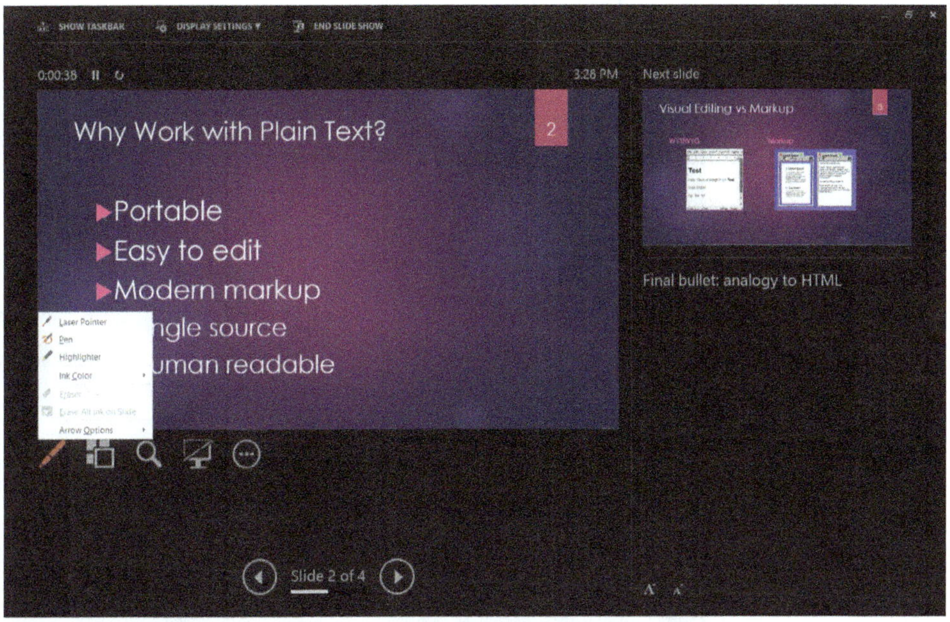


**Figure 1-10**

The revamped Presenter View emphasizes presentation flow along with the current slide content.

Presenter View is a private view of your presentation: a control center for the presenter. It provides ready access to speaker notes, a view of the next slide, a timer and clock, an overall status bar, and access to pen tools, zoom, and slide sorter. It's meant to keep you abreast of your presentation as an audience (theatrical) event rather than a series of static images.

Take special note of the timer; it can be paused and reset, letting you time individual slides while you practice your talk, or pause while you clean up some infelicity of text or speech.

**Take Note** Of all the Office 2013 applications, PowerPoint is the obvious candidate for deep touchscreen integration: slides can naturally be manipulated directly by fingertips or pen. If you're working on a Surface or other Windows tablet, Presenter View provides a nice showcase for Office 2013's new touch-based UI.

2 Advance to slide 2. From the Pen Tool menu, select the **Highlighter** and highlight a couple of bulleted lines. Then select the pen tool and circle the words *Modern markup*. This is the point where, according to your speaker notes, you'd emphasize the ease of translating between markup languages for humans and those for machines (like HTML). The slide with handwritten annotations is shown in Figure 1-11.

**Figure 1-11**

Pen Tools let you emphasize slide elements during your live presentation.

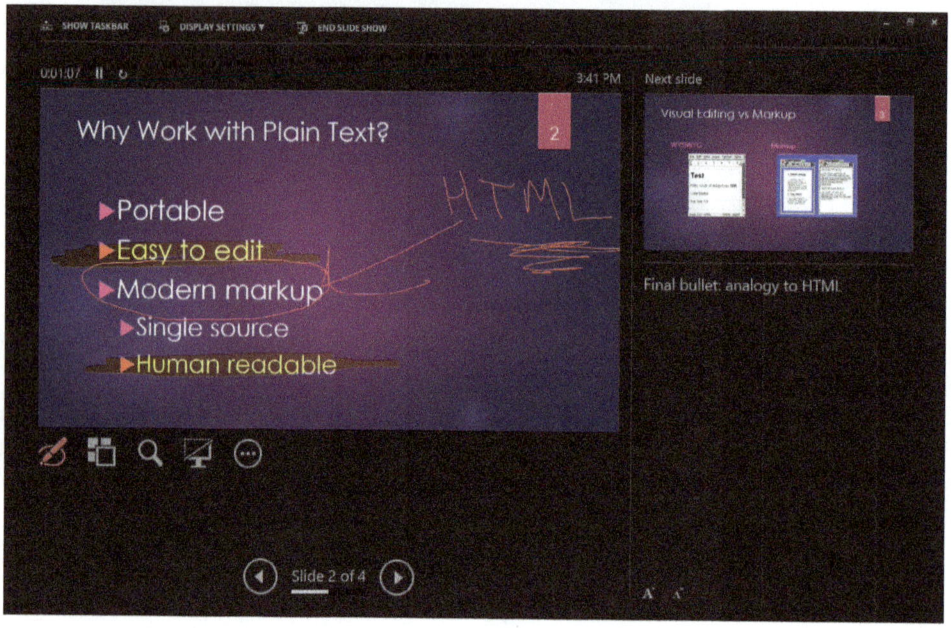


3 Click the **Zoom** tool and zoom in on one part of the slide, then move around the screen. The audience would see only the zoomed portion of the screen.

4 Finally, press **Escape** to leave Zoom mode, and then press **Escape** again to leave Presenter View. Click **Discard** to throw out your pen annotations.

## ANIMATING YOUR PRESENTATION

PowerPoint (PowerPoint's default behavior is to start new animations on mouse click; time-delayed animations require a little configuration.) slides don't need to be static cards; you can add visual emphasis by judiciously applying animations and transitions to slides and individual image/text objects. Remember: a little visual flair goes a long way. In this lesson, we'll emphasize bullet points and include flashy transitions, but we recommend using fewer visual effects when creating professional PowerPoint presentations.

**STEP BY STEP** **Animating your presentation**

1 Switch to slide 1 and open the Animations tab. Click in the subtitle, then in the Animation group, select the **Float In** animation from the Animation Styles gallery. As soon as this is selected, the slide will preview the animation assigned to the subtitle.

2 Press **F5** to start the Slide Show from the beginning. When you click to advance, the subtitle will drift onscreen. Your second click will move to slide 2.

3 Press **Escape** to return to editing slides and select slide 1. A box containing the numeral 1 appears next to the subtitle, indicating that it will animate on your first click to this slide.

4 Add the **Shape** animation to the subtitle (this is animation #2) using the Add Animation drop-down menu in the Advanced Animation group. Then click **Advanced Animation > Animation Pane**. In the Animation pane, switch the order of the two animations using the up or down arrow. You can press **F5** to run the beginning of the slide show again, to see how the animations add up. Remember to save your work afterward.

## Making the most of animations

The idea of animating every square inch of a slide is appealing. But some animations have more impact than others: revealing bullet points one by one, for instance, to focus attention on the current line, or fading in images. A couple of points in our miniature slide deck could profit from that kind of treatment.

**STEP BY STEP**

## Adding animations

1 Select slide 2. Click in the main text area, the bulleted list, and add the Fade animation. Note that the last three lines appear together as animation #3.

2 In the Animation pane, expand the list of events. Select the last entry in the list, and from the drop-down menu choose **Start on Click**. See Figure 1-12.

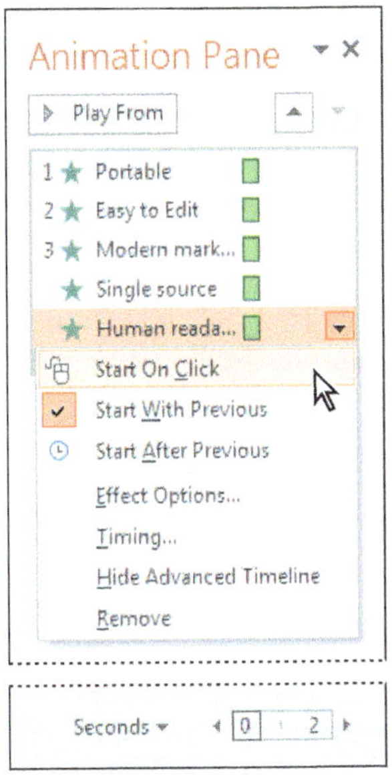


**Figure 1-12**

Configure the last entry in the Animation pane to Start on Click.

3 Repeat step 2 for the animation for Single source. All five lines now have separate click-triggered animations.

4 Press **Shift+F5** to start the slide show from slide 2, and click to advance through the bullets one by one. When you're finished, press **Escape** to return to editing mode.

5 Select slide 3. Shift+click the two headings (**WYSIWYG** and **Markup**) to select them both. Give them the **Bounce** entrance animation.

6 Shift+click to select the two images, and give them the **Fade** animation. Press **Shift+F5** to run the slide show from slide 3, clicking through the animations.

Revealing the images together (but separate from the headings) gives the slide a little drama, and the relative subtlety of the Fade animation is a nice contrast with the sillier Bounce animation. To close this part of the lesson, we'll add exit animations to take away the slide's visual elements before transitioning to the closing slide.

7 Select the two headings and two images, and give them the Fly Out **exit animation**. Preview the animations by running the slide show.

8 Choose **File > Save** or **Ctrl+S** to save your work.

**Take Note** You can tell Slide A to transition to Slide B automatically after displaying for a certain number of seconds (you could make a whole PowerPoint movie that way) but what if Slide A also includes animations? Happily, PowerPoint won't advance the slide to Slide B until Slide A's animations have played.

## Linking slides with transitions

**Transitions** work much like animations, but it's the entire slide that transforms. When you apply a transition to Slide B, Slides A and B are linked by a visual effect more complicated than the usual cut-on-click. Like animations, transitions can easily be abused; but a well-chosen transition can powerfully emphasize the relationship between the contents of two slides, or signal a shift in focus within the presentation.

We'll close the lesson by adding a couple of transitions, including sound effects. Then we will reorder the slides to alter the narrative flow of the presentation. In this task we'll make use of the Slide Sorter view, which offers a wide-angle look at the entire presentation, like a visual outline.

### STEP BY STEP Linking slides with transitions

1 Using the **Publishing-Markup** file, click the View tab and select **Slide Sorter** view. Beneath the slides that contain animations, a start icon is present; click each **star** to preview the animations.

2 Select slide 2. Open the Transitions tab and select the **Fly Through** transition. In the Timing group, check the **After**: check box, and set the After: value to **00:05.00**.

3 Add the Shape transition to slide 3 and the Ferris Wheel to slide 4. Adjust the look of the Ferris Wheel animation by clicking **Transitions > Effect Options** and choosing **From Left**.

4 Add sound to the slide 4 transition by selecting **Voltage** from the Transitions > Timing > Sound drop-down menu.

## Grouping and ordering slides in Slide Sorter

**Bottom Line**

**Slide Sorter** is useful after you've finished your individual slides and need to work on the overall architecture of your presentation. With the Home > Slides > Section tool, you can group slides logically into sections, which can help you think about the structure and pace of the slide show. (Sections are handy when you collaborate on a presentation too: Bob and Tim, clean up the 'Accounts' section, is clearer and less likely to suddenly make no sense during editing, than Bob and Tim, work on slides 53–70.

**STEP BY STEP** **Grouping and ordering slides in Slide Sorter**

1. Click slide **1** in the Slide Sorter, then click **Home > Slides > Section > Add Section**. Press **F2** or right-click **Untitled Section** to rename the section and type **Intro** and click **Rename** to commit the change and close the dialog box.
2. Select slides **2** and **3** by Shift+clicking, and add them to a new section called **Setup**.
3. Finally, make a section called **Synthesis** that includes only slide 4.

Right now we go straight to a bulleted list from our title slide. To add a bit of visual variety, we can move slide 3 to slide 2's spot.

4. Click and drag slide **3** to the left to switch the slide order within the Setup section. Finally, save your work. (See Figure 1-13.)

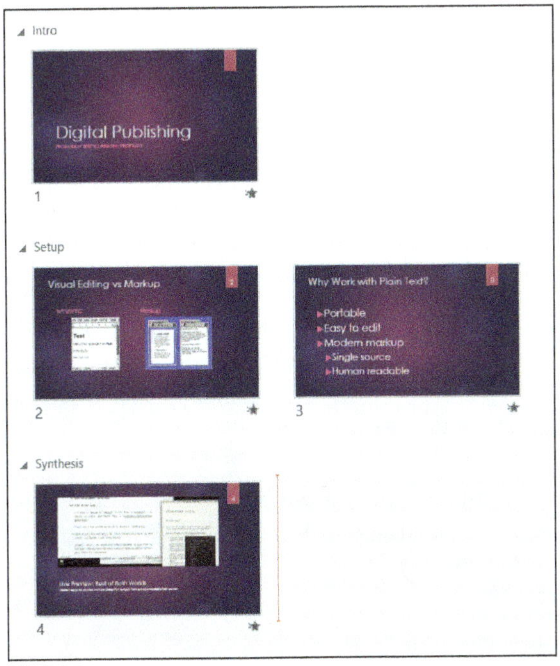


**Figure 1-13**
Shuffling the Slide Deck in the Sorter view.

5. Choose File > Save or press Ctrl+S to save your work.

## SETTING YOUR OVERALL LOOK WITH DOCUMENT THEMES

**Bottom Line**

The overall look and feel of a presentation is set with a Document Theme. Themes provide a matched set of fonts, colors, backgrounds, and visual effects, which can apply to any layout in a PowerPoint template. Indeed, themes can be used across Office 2013 applications to give a consistent visual identity to your work. In theory, a single click should switch your slide deck's theme with no additional work needed on your part; but if you've tweaked any document elements (such as an embedded image's layout) you may need to make further tweaks once you've applied the new theme.

We'll switch our presentation's theme to see what changes, and what needs changing afterward.

### STEP BY STEP Setting your overall theme

1. While in Slide Sorter view, open the Design tab. Select a handful of themes from the Themes gallery, one by one, to see what changes they make to your slide deck. (You may need to zoom out using the zoom slider on the taskbar to see the entire presentation at once.)
2. Select the **Parallax** theme found near the bottom of the Themes gallery. Then click each of the Variants, in the second gallery, to sample color choices. (Variants change only the theme's color scheme.) Choose the second variant, with the orange and grey stripes. Double-click slide 2 to switch to slide editing mode, then save your work.

What happened to our headings? As you recall, we manually altered the layout of this slide to line up the two images a little better relative to their headings in the Ion template. But headings and content have moved relative to each other in the switch to Parallax theme: now the images overlap the headings.

**Take Note** Blank slides handily illustrate the differences between themes. To see exactly what happened to slide 2 when we switched to Parallax, press Ctrl+M to add a blank slide (it will inherit slide 2's layout), then switch back and forth between the Parallax and Ion themes. The different aspect ratios and relative locations of the content areas account for the obscured headings

The easiest fix for the slide 2 layout is to move the images directly below the headers. You could also delete the images from the slide and place them again without tweaking their layout until after you've settled on a final theme. We'll manually position the images, and further balance the slide by making them both the same size.

3. Drag the right-hand image down below its heading. Align its left edge with the heading text, and place it vertically such that double-arrow spacing guides appear above and below the heading text. Repeat the process for the left-hand image.

4 Right click the left-hand image and select **Size and Position**. In the Format Picture pane, deselect **Lock Aspect Ratio** and set the width to **4.81"**. The result is shown in Figure 1-14.

**Figure 1-14**

Balanced image sizes make for more forgiving layouts.

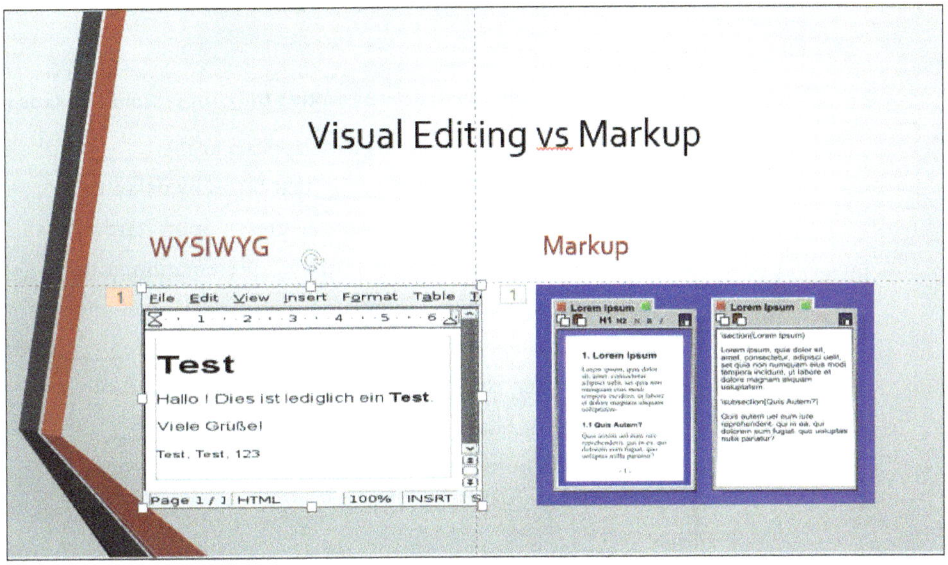


5 Choose **File > Save** and then **File > Close** to close the file.

## What you learned in this lesson:

- Selecting and Opening a Template
- Adding Slides
- Editing Slide Text
- Placing Images into Slides
- Adding Speaker Notes
- Adding Animations and Transitions
- Switching presentation Themes
- Presenting a Slide Show

# Knowledge Assessment

## Fill in the Blanks

**Complete the following sentences by writing the correct word or words in the blanks provided.**

1. By default, the Notes Pane appears at the _____ of the editing screen.
2. Title slides contain _____ text boxes by default.
3. Pressing _____ will run the presentation starting with the current slide.
4. To insert a new slide into your presentation, press _____.
5. Along with the Template Gallery, the launch screen shows a list of _____ documents.
6. Responsive guidelines are enabled with the _____ command.
7. Pointer, zoom, and annotation tools are available in the _____ View.
8. Theme variants differ in terms of their _____.
9. Slide numbers are inserted with the _____ command.
10. Empty text boxes display _____ which won't print on the final document output.

## True/False

**Circle T if the statement is true or F it the statement is false.**

T F 1. Widescreen slides are no longer supported in PowerPoint 2013.

T F 2. Selecting two images at once and applying an animation will animate first one, then the other.

T F 3. PowerPoint is a WYSIWYG document editor.

T F 4. The Change Case command increases or decreases the indent level of bulleted text.

T F 5. The Pictures content control brings up a text box for Bing image search.

T F 6. Most built-in PowerPoint templates open with a title slide.

T F 7. Presenter View is another name for Slide Show View.

T F 8. By default, animations begin five seconds after their slide displays.

T F 9. Transitions are actually specialized full-slide animations listed in the Animations Gallery.

T F 10. Grouped slides can be named for ease of editing and search, or assignment to collaborators.

# Competency Assessment

## Project 1-1: Using PowerPoint Templates

**Here you'll practice picking templates and switching themes.**

1. Launch Powerpoint. At the launch screen, click the search box and search for **business wireframe building**.
2. Select the template that appears in the gallery and create a new document with the template. The presentation template will download.
3. When the document opens, select slide 1. Change the words Title Layout to **First Presentation Project**.

   Note that the text is laid out in all caps no matter what capitalization you apply.

4. Change the subtitle to **Building Wireframe Template**.
5. Open the Themes gallery in the Design tab and mouse over several themes. Select one you like.

   Note that the wireframe template's theme is not available from the Themes gallery.
6. Click the **Undo** button or press **Ctrl+Z** until the building wireframe template is restored.
7. Press **Ctrl+W** to close the document. When prompted, save your file as **project_1-1_wireframe.**

### Project 1-2: Editing Slide Text

**In this exercise you'll add and edit some slide text.**

1. Open the project file **1-2-source**. Save your document as **project_1-2_text_edit**.
2. Select slide **2**. Click each text item in turn and change the slide's text to:

   **SAMPLE BULLETED LIST**

   **First claim**

   **Supporting evidence**

   **Second claim**
3. Click the second bullet point, then click **Home > Paragraph > Increase List Level** to indent it one level.

   The text of the "supporting evidence" line will resize to reflect its new list level.
4. Change slide 3's title to **Infographic**.
5. Reselect slide **2**. Click **Insert > Text Box** and click to place a text box in the lower right quadrant of the slide.
6. Type **Quotation or anecdote** in the text box and italicize the new text.
7. Save and close your document.

## Proficiency Assessment

### Project 1-3: Sorting and Presenting Slides

**Here you'll work on grouping slides in the Slide Sorter.**

1. Open the project file **1-3-source**. Save your document as **project_1-3_sorting**.
2. Open the Slide Sorter.
3. Select slides **7-11**, right click, and choose **Hide Slide**.
4. Select slides **1-3** and right click to create a new section. Then right click its section name and rename it **Main Content**.
5. Create two more sections: 4-6 (**Supporting**) and 7-11 (**Other**).
6. Collapse the section Other.
7. Press **F5** to run the presentation; click each slide to move through to the next. Note which slides are excluded.
8. Select the **Supporting** section and give it the Ion Boardroom theme, orange variant.
9. Save and close your document.

### Project 1-4: Adding and Styling Images

**This exercise focuses on image styles and visual effects.**

1. Open the project file **1-4-source**. Save your document as **project_1-4_images**.
2. Change slide 2's layout to **Two Content**.
3. Insert an online picture in the new content area: search for **action item** clip art (not Bing) and insert the resulting image.
4. Shift+drag the image straight upward until its top edge aligns with the top edge of the bulleted list content area – an alignment guide will appear.
5. Add the **Drop Shadow Rectangle Picture Style** to the image, and the **Watercolor Sponge Artistic Effect**.
6. Save and close your document.

## Mastery Assessment

### Project 1-5: Animations and Transitions

**Here you'll add animations and transitions to a presentation.**

1. Open the project file **1-5-source**. Save your document as **project_1-5_animations**.
2. Hide slides 4-6.
3. Add the **Shape** animation to the "Things to Do" image, and the **Fly Out** exit animation to the bulleted list.
4. Change the slide 2➔3 transition to **Random Bars** with a 5-second duration, and remove the slide 1➔2 transition entirely.
5. Run your presentation. Save and close your document and quit PowerPoint.

### Project 1-6: Creating an Animation...with Transitions

**In this final exercise you'll force PowerPoint to do something it wasn't designed for: create a short animation using slide transitions.**

1. Create a new blank file and save it as **project_1-6_animation**.
2. Find or create a series of photographs you'd like to "animate."
3. Add each image to a different slide in your deck and use slide transitions to quickly cycle through them without needing to click.
4. Search for a command to loop the presentation indefinitely, then run it full-screen to see your short animation.
5. Save and close your document.

# 2 Getting Started with PowerPoint 2013

## LESSON SKILL MATRIX

| In this lesson, you will learn the following skills: | |
|---|---|
| Navigating the PowerPoint UI | Inserting and Formatting Text and Images |
| Quickly Finding Design, Layout, Content, and Presentation Tools | Reordering Slides and Add Transitions |
| Choosing the Right Document View for a Task | Choosing and Customizing Themes |
| Building an Outline | |

## KEY TERMS

- Tab Bar
- Notes Page
- Animation

©MichaelDeLeon/iStockPhoto

©MichaelDeLeon/ iStockPhoto

Fabrikam's sales presentations are carefully targeted to individual investors and clients. Though much of their content is fixed, the presentations are edited up to the last minute to respond to new information. Knowing PowerPoint's interface and workflow are essential to this process of shaping and reshaping – when the basic material is nailed down, the sales folks are free to experiment, edit, and see how new or revised content affects the pitch.

## SOFTWARE ORIENTATION

This lesson helps you gain an understanding of outlining, along with the design, layout, and presentation tools. You'll reorder slides and customize themes.

**Figure 2-1**

Outline view and the Themes Gallery

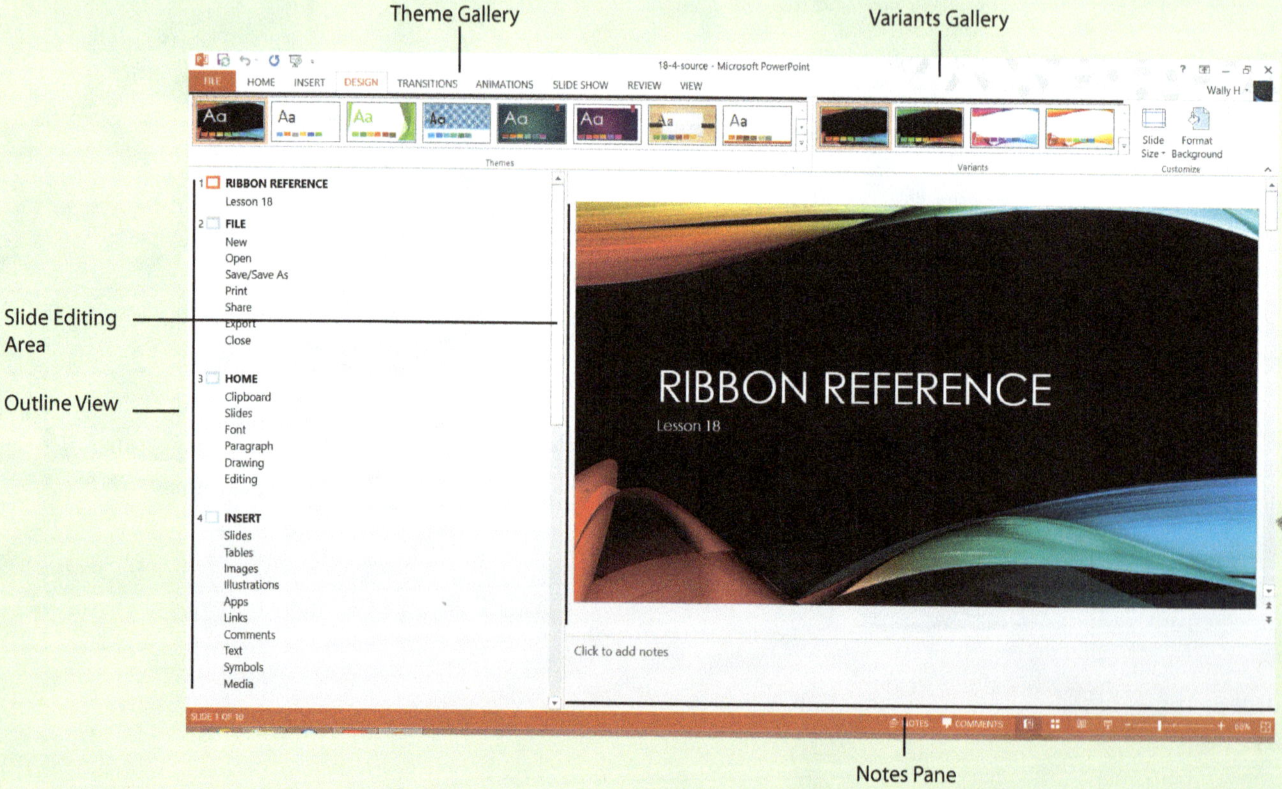

## STARTING UP

In this lesson, you'll work with several files from the PPT02lessons folder. Make sure that you have loaded the OfficeLessons folder onto your computer.

## YOUR WORKSPACE AND YOUR TOOLBOX

PowerPoint shares several features with the other Office 2013 apps, but it's purpose-built for a variety of specific tasks: writing, designing, and laying out slides; developing a presentation flow; generating handouts and presenter cues; refining and rehearsing the presentation; and sharing the presentation, whether live on stage or privately in a kiosk. Each task has an associated editing/viewing mode. Once you have a feel for your work environment and the tools it offers, you can focus all your attention on making useful content.

This lesson walks through the creation of a short presentation, focusing on the way the different features of PowerPoint work together. You won't present the slide show itself just yet; you will create it now and present the live act in a later lesson.

**Take Note** This lesson looks at PowerPoint's content creation and editing workflow; as such, it's divided into common tasks: outlining, writing, structuring, animating, and styling a presentation. Even leaving out custom slide layouts, presenter tools, and document sharing, this lesson contains a lot of information; it'll take several lessons to cover in depth all the material introduced here. We strongly suggest you take your time and stop as needed to explore the tools the lesson introduces.

To begin, launch PowerPoint and open the sample document for this lesson.

**STEP BY STEP** **Opening a PowerPoint document**

1 Launch PowerPoint 2013. From the Launch Screen, click **Open Other Presentations**, navigate to your PPT02lessons folder, and then select **pp02a.pptx**.

## POWERPOINT AND THE OFFICE 2013 USER INTERFACE

PowerPoint 2013 presents the basic Office 2013 user interface (UI) optimized for creating presentations of slide decks. In this section, we'll map out the various tools in the UI, and see how PowerPoint's tailored interface helps support a smooth workflow.

### The Ribbon and Backstage view

**Bottom Line**

The Ribbon, which appears by default atop the application screen, contains PowerPoint's many editing, viewing, and presenter tools. The Home tab, which is the default toolset, is where you can find the usual font/paragraph formatting tools (but no paragraph Styles; see below). In the Home tab, you can also find commands to add and edit slides, and quick shape-drawing tools. The Insert and Review tabs will be familiar to Office users, though PowerPoint is missing Word's Styles and Track Changes features. Several Ribbon tabs are shown in Figures 2-2, 2-3, and 2-4.

PowerPoint's file-management tools are found in the Backstage View (the File tab). The key PowerPoint-specific features are the theme variants for new documents, which let you preview different visual schemes for a given theme right in the New Document gallery, and the options for exporting your presentation as a video or web document (complete with animations, transitions, and audio).

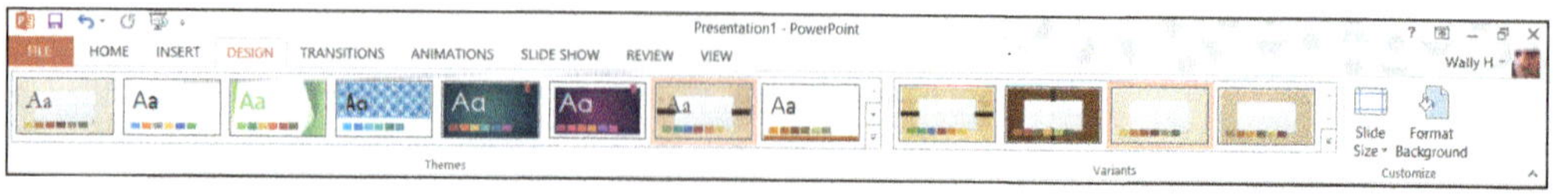


**Figure 2-2**

The Design tab houses the Themes gallery and slide design tools.

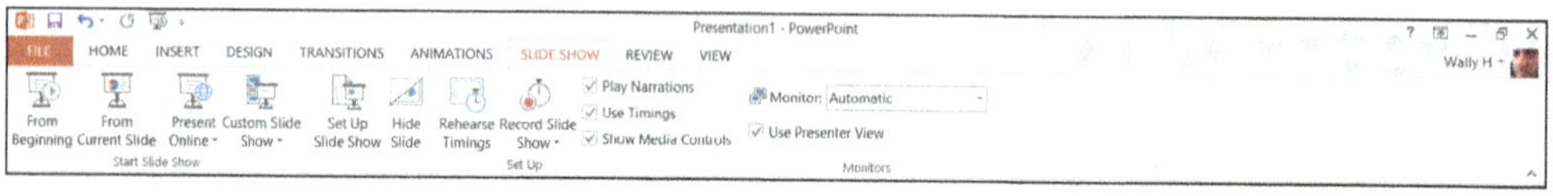


**Figure 2-3**

*Configure and run your presentation from the Slide Show tab.*

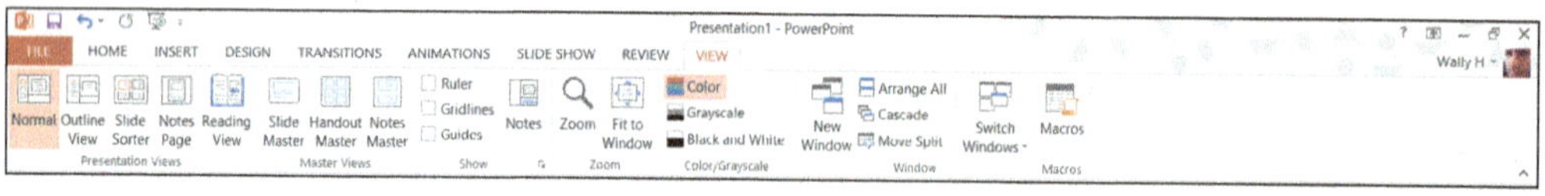


**Figure 2-4**

The View tab houses tools to customize your PowerPoint workspace.

**Take Note** PowerPoint's review/collaboration tools are minimal: you can't Track Changes within a document, though you can generate a set of changes by comparing two different versions of a slide show. Collaboration takes place in Comments, which are now threaded, just as in Word 2013

## Choosing a look with the Design tab

The Design tab illustrates a major conceptual difference between Word and PowerPoint. Word's Design tab lets you choose a theme, but hides the Themes gallery: you're expected to settle on one theme, then pick from its Style Sets to suit your taste. PowerPoint doesn't use Word's Styles; it has a simplified text style collection, which you edit with the Slide Master tools. The Design tab offers a Theme gallery and a second Variants gallery, which offers several color/background choices for each Theme.

**Take Note** A template includes a selection of slide designs and placeholders, along with default visuals: for instance, a calendar template might include Monthly Calendar and Weekly Appointment Book slides with dummy images where your preferred pictures would go. Themes set default text, image, background, and color options for the slide deck. You can choose from a variety of different themes for a given template. PowerPoint's built-in Themes generally include several Variants, providing several options for the same basic aesthetic.

## Moving from content to performance

Moving from left to right across PowerPoint's **tab bar**, you get a sense for the application workflow. First you generate your basic slide show content: the Home and Insert tabs support you in adding text, images, and data to your individual slides. Then comes aesthetics: you select a look and feel with the Design tools, link the slides into a series using the Transitions tools, and give individual slides some movement with Animations.

Transitions and Animations also help you think about your individual slides as tools for performance: as content is finalized, the workflow shifts from your slide deck to the slide show. In the Slide Show tab, you'll find controls for your presentation; crucially, this includes rehearsal and timing tools. The Review tools let colleagues respond to your work.

Finally, the View tab is a kind of master switch for shifting between different editing or viewing modes. The Master views let you set up document-wide formatting. The Slide Master sets default paragraph formatting values (font, color, emphasis), which propagate to all slide layouts; you can then customize each layout in turn. (The Slide Master is PowerPoint's rough equivalent to Word's Style Set.) Handout and Notes Masters determine the look for audience and speaker printouts, respectively.

Each of PowerPoint's Presentation Views is best suited to a specific part of the workflow:

- **Outline View:** quickly build a presentation skeleton
- **Normal View:** fill in individual slide content
- **Slide Sorter:** pull back to focus on overall flow
- **Notes Page:** turn slide deck into speaker script
- **Reading View:** review the slides as the audience would see it outside PowerPoint's interface

To see how the different parts of the PowerPoint workflow interact, we'll now quickly fill in our sample document, one viewing mode at a time.

## BUILDING YOUR PRESENTATION CONTENT

Just as is the case with Word, the fastest way to get started with PowerPoint presentations is to begin with an outline, flesh out each section, and only then work on style and visual presentation. We'll follow this pattern to turn our sample document skeleton into an internal marketing pitch.

### Building an outline

**Bottom Line**

Outline View shows the text content of your slides and nothing more: no images, no careful layout, and no design. PowerPoint presentation outlines work the same, in principle, as Word document outlines: top-level headings correspond to individual slides (rather than Word headings/sections), and each successive outline level maps to bulleted slide content. Since bulleted lists are the most common form of PowerPoint text content, drafting your presentation in Outline View is the fastest way to generate a lot of rough-and-ready slides.

We'll use Outline View to change our slide order and add a couple of new slides.

**STEP BY STEP** **Building an outline**

1 In the file pp02a.pptx, choose View > Presentation Views > Outline View.

2 Select slide 5 by clicking the white box next to its slide number, and drag it to its new position right after the title slide so it becomes slide 2, as in Figure 2-5.

**Figure 2-5**

Use the Outline View to move slide 5 under the title slide.

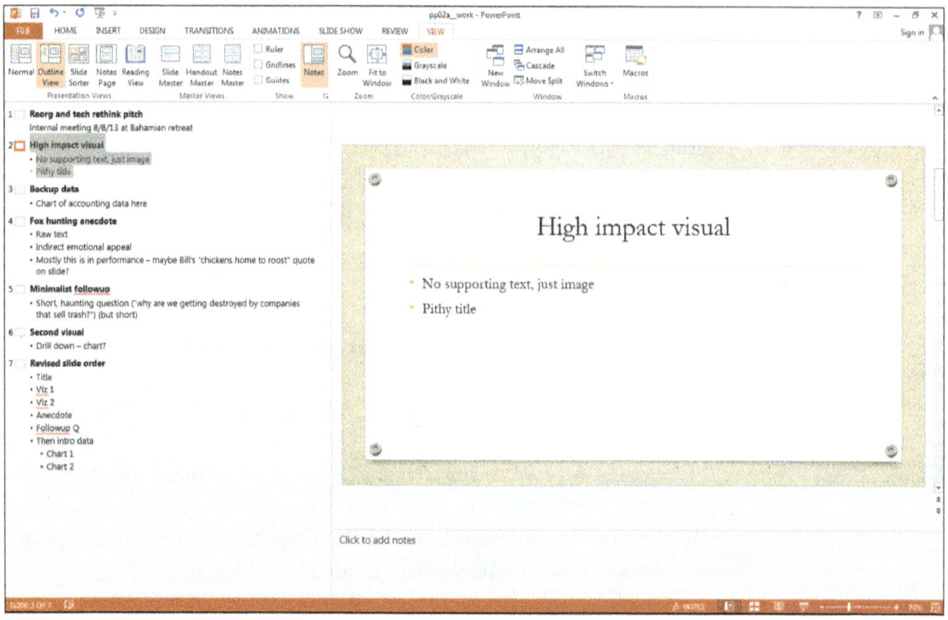


3 Select slide 6, Second visual, and press Ctrl+X to cut the entire slide. Place the cursor at the end of slide 2 in the outline and press Ctrl+V to insert the cut slide in its new position.

4 Resize the outline pane until it's about half the width of the screen to fit more slides onscreen at once by clicking and dragging the separating line to the right. Select View > Normal to flip back to slide editing mode, and then return to Outline View.

In Outline View, it makes sense to place the text content in the foreground by downsizing the slide visuals; after all, we haven't thought about layout and design, yet.

5 Finish reordering the existing slides according to the new order in slide 7 and then switch to Normal editing view.

6 Choose File > Save As. Navigate to the PPT02lessons folder and name this file **pp02a_work**.

## Editing slide content

**Bottom Line**

In Normal View, the content of individual slides is front and center. However, when editing slide content, you can temporarily shift from thinking of your presentation as a continuous narrative, and make each slide impactful in itself.

### STEP BY STEP Editing slide content

1 Select slide 1 and change the title and subtitle to **Reorienting Our IT Approach** and **A Modest Proposal**, respectively.

2 Delete the text content and title from slide 2. The controls to insert visuals appear. Right-click slide 2 in the slides pane, and choose Layout > Blank.

If you're switching to a blank slide layout, it's good to clear out all its text content first; otherwise it will carry over to the new layout, with text boxes appearing in odd places (and you'll have to delete the boxes themselves).

3 Still working on the now-blank slide 2, click **Insert > Online Pictures**. In the royalty-free clip art search box, search for **bad news**. From the gallery of results, choose the image of the woman frowning on the phone and click **Insert**.

4 Clear the title and content from slide 3 and change the layout to Blank. Click **Insert > Online Pictures** again, and in the clip art search box (not Bing), search for **charts and graphs**. Shift+click any two images and insert them both.

5 Finally, **Insert > Online Pictures** again and search office.com clip art for **graphs and charts**. Insert one more resulting image.

## SLIDES BACKGROUNDS AREN'T TEXT AREAS

PowerPoint differs from Word in several respects -- among them its assumption that slide content is always either background or <italic>floating elements</italic>. PowerPoint text always resides in a text box; there's no "text block" to act as a default location for text, as in Word.

### Formatting inserted images

**Bottom Line**

After inserting dramatic visuals in a blank slide, you can change their appearance and layout using the Format Picture pane.

**STEP BY STEP** **Formatting inserted images**

1 Right-click one of the inserted images and select **Format Picture**. Switch to its Size and Properties tab.

2 Under Size, make sure that **Lock aspect ratio** is checked (so images will keep the same proportions), then type **1.5** in the Height box and press **Return**. PowerPoint reads the unlabeled numeral as 1.5".

3 Do the same for the other two images. Then enable **View > Show > Guides**.

4 Drag one of the resized images to the very center of the slide. (With Guides turned on, it will stick when it's near the center.) Drag a second image to a spot directly to the right of the center image so that an orange span arrow appears between them. Drag the third image to the spot opposite the second, on the left side of the slide, as in Figure 2-6.

**Figure 2-6**

PowerPoint's drawing guides help you visually line up objects in the slide.

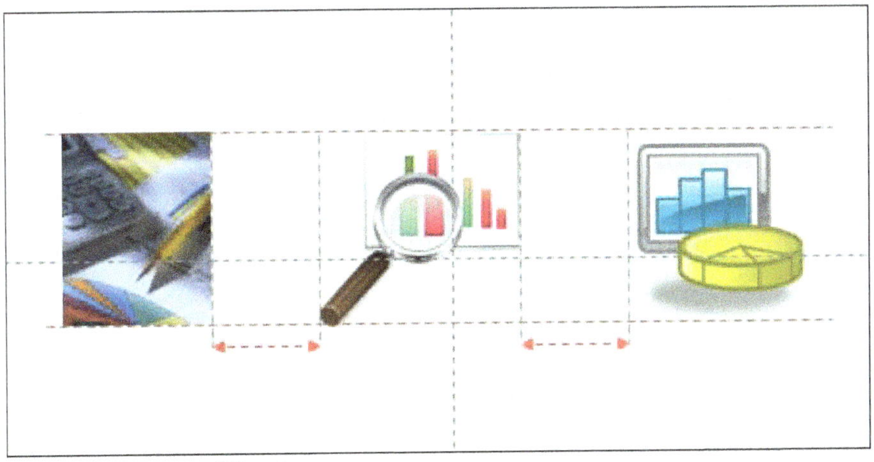

*Clip art used with permission of Microsoft*

5 If Notes are not already displayed, select **View > Show > Notes**.

The other commands in the Format Picture pane are reasonably self-explanatory; we'll return to them in a later lesson.

6 Edit the remaining slides as per these specifications:

- **Slide 2**: Add speaker note **Average IT response time: 4 years**
- **Slide 3**: Add speaker note **Move slowly through images – drama!**
- **Slide 4**: Set layout to Section Header, delete all text, change title to **"The chickens come home to roost...in the lion's den...among the eagles"** (including quotation marks)
- **Slide 5**: Set layout to Two content; change title to **Key Question**, and change slide content areas: **We trail ACME sales by 400%** (left) and **Why?** (right). No bullets in content area to the right (**Home > Paragraph > Bullets**)
- **Slide 6**: Set to Picture with caption layout, make title **Year-over-year numbers**. Text content: **$2B short of projections!**

We'll add a chart to slide 6 in a later section and make the visuals more interesting with animations and transitions.

7 Choose **File > Save** to save your work.

## Creating notes pages

**Bottom Line**

If you don't want to look at your screen while you deliver your presentation, you can print out **Notes Pages**, which let you control the layout of your speaker notes on a per-slide basis. This is handy if you want to alternate between improvisatory phrases or suggestions, and word-for-word reading of a complete slide script. We'll edit a single slide's notes to see how it works.

**STEP BY STEP** **Creating notes pages**

1 Switch to **View > Presentation Views > Notes Page**. Scroll through the presentation and select slide 6.

2 Navigate to your PPT02lessons folder and open **pp02b.docx**. Copy the text of the document, and then Paste it into the notes area of slide 6.

3 Resize the image of the slide on the notes page, making it much shorter, and then resize the text box to fill the remaining page space. Select all the text and set it to 16pt type in **Home > Font > Font Size**, as in Figure 2-7.

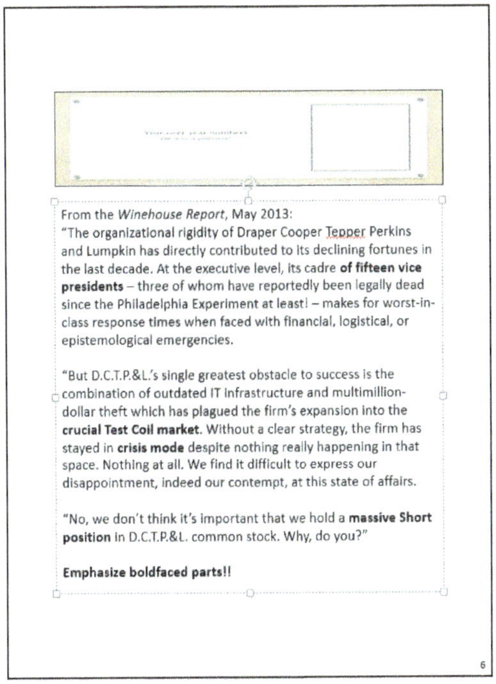


**Figure 2-7**

Notes Pages help place your written presentation in its performance context.

You can tailor the Notes Page for each slide in the same way: sometimes the most helpful visual aid is the slide itself; sometimes more textual detail is important.

## Reading view

Reading View, new in Office 2013, lets you view your presentation as a series of flat slides with no visual chrome (no animations or transitions, just single screens). Crucially, Reading View also hides the entire PowerPoint interface: there is nothing around the slides to distract you, not even presenter tools.

For a clean look at your presentation, click View > Reading View. Use the usual navigation controls: Space/Return/Right arrow to advance, left arrow to move back. When you've got a feel for the way the draft slides present visually, press Escape or navigate past the last slide to return to editing mode, then click Normal View.

# WORKING WITH TEXT, IMAGES, AND VISUAL EFFECTS

PowerPoint's text editing tools are more like Excel's than like Word's: simple, not meant to handle large-scale text pieces. (The general rule for slide text is: *Less Is More.*) Its image formatting tools are also streamlined. In this section, we'll briefly describe the different panes and toolbars.

## Simplified text handling

**Bottom Line**

PowerPoint uses a simplified Style model: you define a style by formatting the text on the Slide Master (for instance, declaring that all title boxes should default to boldface italic text); make changes to layouts using the Slide Layout (for example, no boldface title on a specific slide layout only); and then inherit that formatting when you fill in the slide itself. In complexity and flexibility, PowerPoint's editing tools are more similar to Excel's than to Word's.

Applying character and paragraph formatting works the same way in PowerPoint as it does anywhere else in Office. In this section, we'll make changes to the Slide Master and to individual slides using a variety of formatting tools.

**STEP BY STEP** **Simplified text handling**

1 Choose **View > Normal** and select slide **1**. Triple-click the subtitle and set the text color to red using the formatting popup.

2 Select slide **5**. Place the cursor at the end of the 400% line. Press **Return** to add a line. Press **Tab** to indent. Type **600% in fiscal Q4**. Add another line; press **Shift+Tab** to reduce indent. Type **...while winning customer satisfaction war**.

Tab and **Shift+Tab** work the same way as Word's bulleted lists or PowerPoint's outline mode.

3 Select the word ***Why?*** In the Home tab and set its font size to 96pt. Right-click ***Why?*** and select **Format Text Effects** to bring up the Format Shape pane.

4 Scroll down to 3D Rotation and select the **Parallel** preset, **Isometric Left Down**. Set the Z rotation to **15** degrees.

The Format Shape pane brings the various formatting tools together in a single toolbox; from there, you can alter the background, shape, line and fill colors, and texture of the text box, along with its contents.

5 Choose **File > Save** or press **Ctrl+S** to save your work.

## Inserting images

**Bottom Line**

Inserting images works consistently across Office apps. You can either click one of the controls in a content area, or use the tools in the Insert tab. We'll illustrate the principle by inserting a single piece of clip art from online.

1 Select slide **6**. Click in the image area, not on the Insert Image control, and then select **Insert > Online Pictures**.

2 Search the Office.com Clip Art collection for **magnifying glass bar graph**. Select the image that appears in the gallery, and click **Insert**.

**Take Note** You can reformat an image (apply visual effects, add or edit a border, change its size/location properties, and more) using the Picture Tools > Format menu, or the Format Picture command in the image's context menu. The picture formatting tools are self-explanatory and work the same way in PowerPoint as they do in Word; we encourage you to experiment with them. We'll provide more detailed treatment in a later lesson

## Adding and editing animations

**Bottom Line**

**Animations** apply to individual elements within a slide: images, boxes, even individual lines of text. The Animations tab contains the basic animation tools, whereas the Animation pane lets you organize the animations within a slide.

**Take Note** This lesson uses the Fade entry/exit animations exclusively: they're the most elegant of all, and altering the length of a fade won't make it look inane compared to a sped-up Fly In animation (for example). For sheer flexibility, the best option is the Custom Path animation, which lets you really animate an object by moving it around like a cartoon character.

## STEP BY STEP Adding Animation

1 In slide 5, click the word **ACME**. (Don't select the text, just place the cursor.) Open the Animations tab and apply the **Fade** animation. Then open the Animation pane. In that pane, click the double caret (⏬) to expand the animation list.

PowerPoint automatically animates the entire bulleted list: the first two lines appear on your first click, then the third line when you click again. We'll uncouple the first two lines, add a dramatic pause before the second, and draw out the animation on the third.

**Figure 2-8**

Animation order is indicated by numbered labels in the slide.

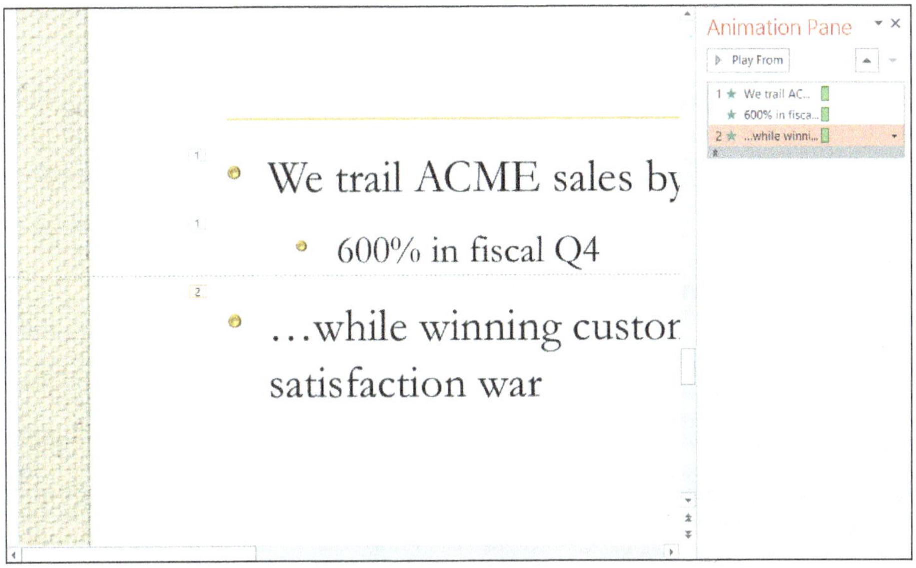


## STEP BY STEP Editing Animation

1 Select animation **#2** in the Animation pane (the *...while winning* bullet, marked in Figure 2-8). From its drop-down menu, make sure **Start After Previous** is selected. In the Timing group, set Delay to three seconds (type **3** in the entry box). Set the Duration to one second. What was animation #2 is now folded in to animation #1.

2 By Shift+clicking select both the title and the text box on the left. Click **Add Animation**, scroll down to the Exit Animations and choose **Fade**.

3 In the Animations pane, make sure animation #3 (the *...while winning* exit animation) is set to **Start with Previous**. The slide now contains three animation events on the slide, in two groups: (1) add top two bullets on click, then add third bullet three seconds later, (2) dismiss all text except *Why?* on click.

4 Click ***Why?*** and add the **Fade (entry)** animation. Make sure it is set it to **Start After Previous**, with a 4-second duration and 1-second delay.

5 Choose **File > Save** or press **Ctrl+S** to save your work.

Now preview your work by pressing **Shift+F5** to start the slide show from the current slide. The slide starts out displaying just the title, awaiting your input. Click through the various animations (remember to wait for the two delayed entrances) to see how a bit of customization can give a sequence of animations a slightly cinematic quality.

**Take Note** The hardest part of using time-delayed animations is setting the actual delay. Four seconds can feel like an eternity during a presentation. By cycling through edits and test runs, you can develop a flow for each slide that makes sense for your presentation style.

6 To close out this section, animate slide 3: fade in the image on the left 0.5 seconds after loading the slide, then load the other two images one by one.

The easiest way to apply the same animation to multiple objects is with the Animation Painter: after animating the first image, select the image, press Alt+Shift+C to copy its animation, and then click the next image to paint the animation onto it. Repeat this process for image #3.

## Transitions and slide sorter

**Bottom Line**

Adding a transition is like animating an entire slide. Think of it as a scene change in a movie: a transition tells the audience to prepare for a new context. The bigger the transition, the bigger the expected context change. This is why we don't recommend using splashy transitions for every single slide: they tire the audience out.

We'll add a couple of simple transitions to key points in the presentation and group slides to give us a sense of the presentation's proportions. For this task we want the Slide Sorter view, which affords a bird's eye view of the presentation. (In fact, you can't edit slide content in the Sorter.)

**STEP BY STEP** **Transitions and slide sorter**

1 Switch to Slide Sorter view. Right-click slide 4 and select **Add Section**. Do the same with slide 6 to make three sections in total.

Sections don't materially affect the presentation: unlike Word 2013, you can't reformat individual sections of a PowerPoint presentation. The purpose of sections is to aid with slide organization, for instance, when distributing the presentation to authors.

2 Click the **Default Section** heading and press **F2** to bring up the Rename Section dialog. Rename the first section **The Trailer**.

3 Rename the first Untitled Section **Make it personal**, and call the third **Hard data**.

The section divisions can be used to lay out the slides for printing later. Now let's focus on the movement of the presentation by adding a couple of slide transitions. The presentation starts jaunty and turns to finger-pointing later, so we'll start with some quick transition moves and give the last slide some melodrama with a long fade.

4 Select slide **2** and apply the **Push** transition (from the Transitions to This Slide gallery). Then apply the **Airplane** transition to slide 4, modifying it slightly by choosing Left **from the Effect Options** drop-down menu.

5 Select slide **6** and apply the **Fade** transition. Add the **Through Black** effect with the Effect Options tool, then set the transition duration to six seconds (type **6** in the Timing > Duration text box and press **Enter**).

6 Save your work, then press **F5** and walk through the presentation to see how the transitions and animations appear. Note that you can click to skip to the end of a lengthy transition.

The sprightly transitions in the early slides keep the tone light before slowing down on slide 5. Then the slow, dramatic crossfade divides the first section of the presentation, which builds to the question Why are we trailing ACME, from the data-driven second section.

The same basic steps apply to any transition: add the animation, tweak any effect settings, and alter timing if necessary.

## DESIGN TOOLS

You can find PowerPoint's design tools in the Design tab. To establish the look of a slide show, begin by choosing (or editing) a template, then apply a theme, and finally, make fine-grained edits to formatting.

### What's in a template?

**Bottom Line**

The easiest way to see how templates work is to open one up. The idea is the same as in any other Office 2013 app: a template is a skeleton that you fill in with your content. We'll peek inside a built-in template to see how much work a well-chosen template can save you.

**Take Note** Microsoft can always replace the template in this section with another, differently-named template; in such a case, follow along in this section using another calendar template from the Office template gallery.

**STEP BY STEP** **Customizing slide layouts**

1. Click **File > New**, and select **Suggested Searches: Calendars**.
2. From the template gallery, select **2013 Photo calendar (Sun-Sat)**. Click **Create**.

Looking at slide 1 (of 12) of the calendar template, you can see how this slide layout works: each calendar day is a content box waiting for text. The *Click to edit master styles* text is a dummy placeholder: when you click a day it disappears to make way for your own text.

A template can include custom slide layouts to avoid repeatedly and heavily editing the standard layouts; in a later lesson we'll create a custom Employee Bio layout to illustrate how this works.

3. In the Design tab's Themes Gallery, select **Ion**. Note that the slide layout doesn't change.
4. Switch to Slide Master view. Mouse over the current slide to see which layout is in use.

If you completed Lesson 1, you'll remember that switching themes altered the content layout, obscuring some heading text. The calendar's slide layout doesn't change when you change themes, though, because slide 1 uses a slide layout (see Figure 2-9) that's not overwritten by the Ion theme. We'll work more with the Slide Master view later.

**Figure 2-9**

Custom slide layouts in a monthly calendar template.

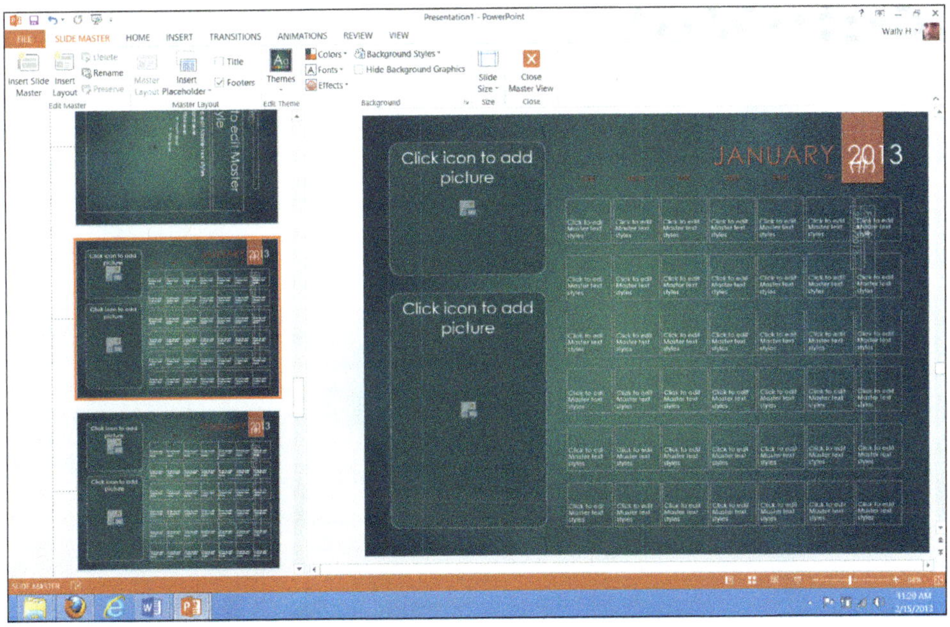

5 Close the calendar document without saving.

## Applying themes to a slide show

**Bottom Line**

The Design tab's main features are two galleries: Themes and Variants. A Theme is a slide deck's look, combining fonts, slide layouts, and theme colors into an aesthetically-pleasing overall design. Variants offer alternative color schemes for a given theme. Using standard slide layouts (as we are in this exercise) allows you to switch between themes without damaging your document layout.

We'll apply a theme to our slide show, tweak fonts and colors a bit, and then save our customizations.

### STEP BY STEP Applying a theme to a slide show

1 Return to your **pp02a_work.pptx** document.

2 In the Design tab's Themes Gallery, select the **Quotable** theme (they are listed alphabetically). Then choose the red color Variant.

**Take Note** We're trying to minimize our labor, so we're avoiding themes that format slide Titles in all caps. Why? Select slide 1 and preview the striking Integral theme: our presentation title includes the acronym IT, which reads as "it" when the whole title's in all caps. If you still prefer the Integral theme, try switching IT to red characters to set it off from the rest of the line.

## Customizing a theme in the Slide Master view

**Bottom Line**

Slide Master View is built for editing custom slide layouts, but it's also where you customize PowerPoint's themes. At a basic level, customizing a theme is as easy as selecting a new font, color scheme, and visual effect.

### STEP BY STEP Customizing a theme in the Slide Master view

1 Switch to Slide Master view.

2 In the Background group, change the color scheme to **Red Violet**; select **Garamond-TrebuchetMS** from the Fonts menu; and choose **Frosted Glass** from the Effects menu.

3 Click **Edit Theme > Themes > Save Current Theme**. Save your now-modified version of the Quotable theme as **Frosted Violet Quote**.

To build reusable frameworks for presentations (for example, a corporate visual identity and standard slide layout for in-house presentations) you would use these tools to create custom themes and slide layouts. We'll do so in a later lesson; for the moment, save your work and take this opportunity to further explore any of the editing tools covered in this lesson.

## What you learned in this lesson:

- Navigating the PowerPoint UI
- Quickly Finding Design, Layout, Content, and Presentation Tools
- Choosing the Right Document View for a Task
- Building an Outline
- Inserting and Formatting Text and Images

- Reordering Slides and Add Transitions
- Choosing and Customizing Themes

## Knowledge Assessment

### True/False

**Circle T if the statement is true or F it the statement is false.**

T F 1. The background of each PowerPoint slide is a text area, as on a Word 2013 page.

T F 2. PowerPoint themes are selected from the Layout tab.

T F 3. Normal View focuses attention on the content of an individual slide.

T F 4. The Format Picture pane is the central location for tools to fine-tune an inserted image's appearance.

T F 5. A Notes Page is a printed sheet that helps the audience follow along with a presentation on paper.

T F 6. PowerPoint uses the same Style Sets as Word.

T F 7. Animations can be triggered by mouse click, or activate after a specified period of time.

T F 8. Switching a presentation's Theme will erase any custom slide layouts you've created.

T F 9. Reading View provides quick access to all PowerPoint's document editing tools.

T F 10. In Outline View, each top-level heading corresponds to a new slide.

### Matching

**Match each term to its description or definition.**

1. Outline View
2. Slide Sorter
3. transition
4. title slide
5. Insert > Online Pictures
6. Notes Page
7. exit animation
8. Template Gallery
9. empty slide
10. Themes Gallery

a. presents collection of prebuilt document skeletons
b. despite open space, contains no text area as such
c. high-level view of presentation, for reordering and grouping slides
d. prompts, quotes, and directions for speaker, not audience
e. maps top-level headings onto slides
f. collects overall presentation aesthetics in Design tab
g. has boxes for title and subtitle only
h. "fly out" and other effects remove elements from slide
i. like an animation that turns one slide into another
j. takes search string, returns clip art/Bing image results

# Competency Assessment

## Project 2-1: Outlining

**In this exercise you'll create a reference of the various command groups in the Ribbon.**

1. Launch PowerPoint and create a new blank presentation.
2. Save your document as **project_2-1_outline.**
3. Open the outliner (**View > Outline View**) and click in the outline pane next to the orange box indicating slide 1.
4. Create an outline with each slide's title corresponding to a Ribbon tab.
5. For each slide, add bullets (one level down) for that tab's Ribbon command groups.
6. Insert a new title slide, and change the "File" slide's layout to **Title and Content**.
6. View the presentation in Normal and Slide Show views.
7. Save and close your document.

## Project 2-2: Visual Elements

**Here you'll alter several slide elements and add appropriate images.**

1. Open the project file **2-2-source**. Save your document as **project_2-2_visuals.**
2. Set the title of the presentation to **Ribbon Reference**, and its subtitle to **Lesson 2.**
3. Assign a document theme from the Themes gallery.
4. Change all non-title slides' layouts to **Content with Caption**.
5. Move each slide's caption text to the caption box beneath its title, rather than the main content box where it presently resides.
6. In each slide's content box, insert an image related to its Ribbon tab (e.g., a file cabinet for the File tab).
7. Save and close your document.

# Proficiency Assessment

## Project 2-3: Notes Pages

**In this exercise you'll create and format Notes Pages for a slide deck.**

1. Open the project file **2-3-source**. Save your document as **project_2-3_notes.**
2. Expand the Notes Pane at the bottom of the editing area, to make room for a few lines of typed notes.
3. On each slide, type a brief description of what the tools on that Ribbon tab do (in general; no need to go command-by-command).
4. Select **View > Notes Master**. Click **Check Out**.
5. **Select** the top-level notes text ("**Click to edit master text styles**") and change it to 20pt text in any font you like.
6. Click **Notes Master > Close Master View**, then select **Notes Page** view to see the new large notes page text.
7. Close and save your document.

### Project 2-4: The Presentation

**Here you'll run a slide show and experiment with the Presenter View interface.**

1. Open the project file 2-4-source. Save your document as **project_2-4_presentation**.
2. Add optional transitions between slides; use the delay/duration controls to alter the dynamics of the transitions.
3. Run the presentation in Presenter View (Alt+F5). Experiment with resizing panes and toggling screen elements like the Windows taskbar. Experiment too with ink annotations (the Pen tool); if you make pen marks on the slides, elect to keep them when you close your presentation.
4. Save and close your document, and quit PowerPoint.

## Mastery Assessment

### Project 2-5: Matching Interface to Workflow

**Here you'll use custom Ribbon tabs to streamline your PowerPoint workflow.**

1. Create a new blank document (no need to save).
2. Create a single custom Ribbon tab called Tweaks.
3. Add commands to the new tab to quickly do the following repetitive tasks:
   - Create a new file
   - Select a Theme
   - Modify the header
   - Add a new slide
   - Insert an online image
   - Run the slide show in Presenter View
   - Save the document
4. Close your document.

### Project 2-6: Putting It All Together

**The final exercise asks you to quickly assemble a presentation to order.**

1. Create a new blank presentation called **project_2-6_final**.
2. Craft a "marketing presentation" with four slides:
   - Title/creator/date, snazzy image
   - Good news re: recent sales
     - o add sales figure chart from online image search
     - o Fade transition to...
   - Future challenges
     - o animated bulleted list of new markets
     - o image that suggests "look out for challenges!"
   - Request for audience questions; speaker contact information
3. Run through the presentation in Presenter View and save your document.

# 3 Designing a Presentation

## LESSON SKILL MATRIX

| In this lesson, you will learn the following skills: | |
|---|---|
| Adding, Styling, and Filling Text Boxes | Creating Custom Layouts in the Slide Master |
| Using the Format Pane | Customizing Document Themes |
| Adding Styled Text with WordArt | |

## KEY TERMS

- Placeholder Text
- Title Slide
- Shape Style
- Format Pane
- Gradient
- WordArt
- Slide Master
- Slide Layout

©Anna Bryukhanova/iStockPhoto

©*Anna Bryukhanova/ iStockPhoto*

The PR team at Northwind Traders handed a hefty assignment to an intern: quickly make 25 poster designs for an upcoming in-store event series, each using a variant of the same basic design, with modified text and images on every poster. The intern hit on a clever response: build each poster as a PowerPoint slide, using the Slide Master and flexible, ready-to-fill custom layouts to generate the basic look and varying colors/effects from slide to slide. The work was done in no time flat.

## SOFTWARE ORIENTATION

This lesson helps you understand effective ways to create presentations using PowerPoint.

**Figure 3-1**

Parts of a PowerPoint presentation

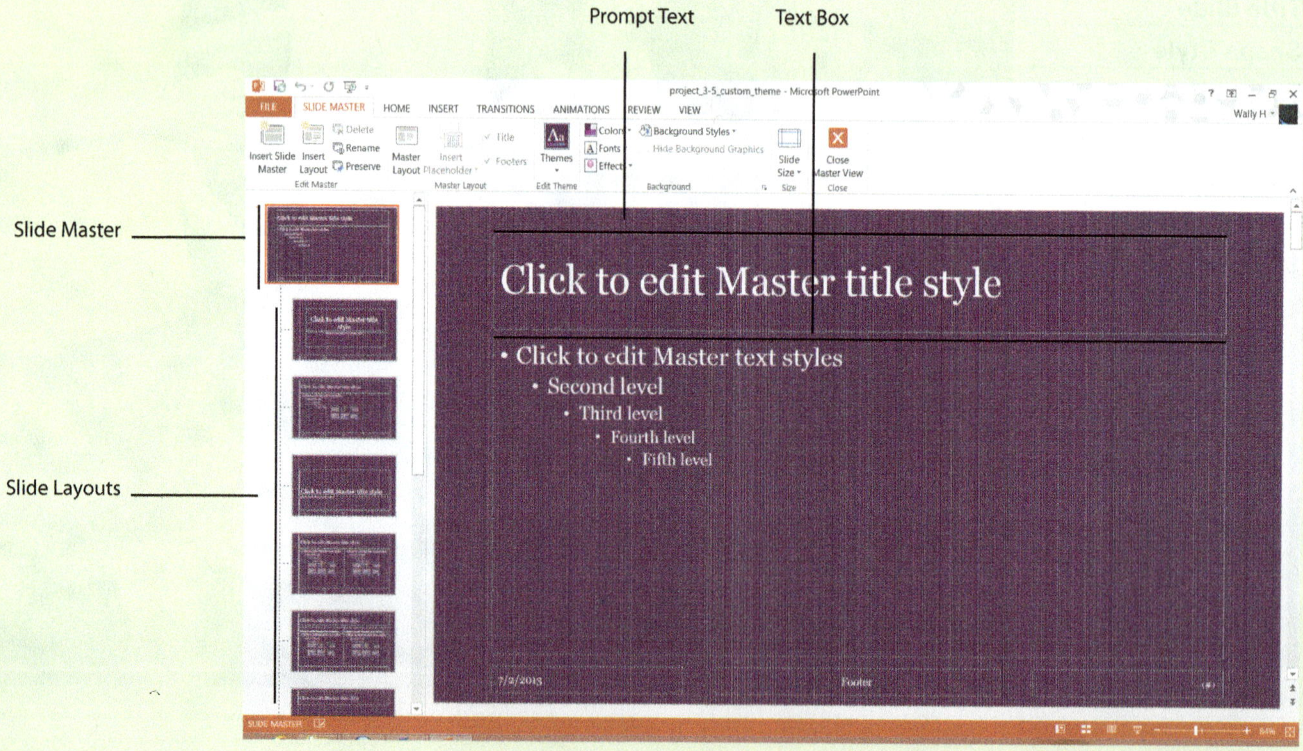

## STARTING UP

In this lesson, you'll work with several files from the PPT03lessons folder. Make sure that you have loaded the OfficeLessons folder onto your computer.

## BUILDING BETTER SLIDES

A good PowerPoint presentation isn't really about the slides; it's about a person communicating with an audience. A well-designed slide deck can illustrate a point that might be difficult to express in words, or subtly reinforce the speaker's message; it can flash hard data behind an impressionistic speech, or put mood lighting on a technical talk. It can even tell a story all by itself, not needing a speaker at all. Lots of presentations are boring; but they can also be beautiful.

The previous lesson explored PowerPoint's slide show creation workflow, from initial outline to final style touches. The next three lessons walk through specific aspects of slide building: text and layout, tabular data and SmartArt, and audiovisual elements. In this lesson, we'll discuss working with text, style and layout tools, and translating a presentation to print (as notes pages and audience handouts).

The finished project for this lesson, a short presented slide show, is saved as **pp03a-finished.pptx** in your PPT03lessons folder if you would like to take a look before getting started.

## WORKING WITH TEXT

The text handling tools available in PowerPoint are fairly simple. Whereas a middleweight layout program such as Word 2013 needs flexible paragraph- and character-level formatting tools, slide text is more constrained. The most common use for PowerPoint is to accompany a talk.

In the first part of the lesson, you'll build individual text-heavy slides, and then you will establish default formatting for your slides using the Slide Master tool. Our text-heavy sample document for this lesson is a rules and regulations talk for new interns.

### Filling in an existing text area

**Bottom Line**

Nearly every blank PowerPoint presentation starts with the same content: a blank Title Slide with two text areas for a title and subtitle, each with **placeholder text** (such as *Click to add title*). Within these text boxes, you can format your text much as you would in a Word 2013 text box (for example), applying character and paragraph formatting, but no Styles. You can also insert special dynamic text, such as the slide number or current date and time.

**STEP BY STEP** **Filling in an existing text area**

1 Launch PowerPoint 2013 and create a new Blank Presentation.

2 In the title box of slide 1, type **LSC Intern Orientation**. Right-click the new title text and choose **Font**. In Figure 3-2, note that instead of a font name, the Latin text font value is actually +Heading, which is inherited from the Theme. Click **Cancel**.

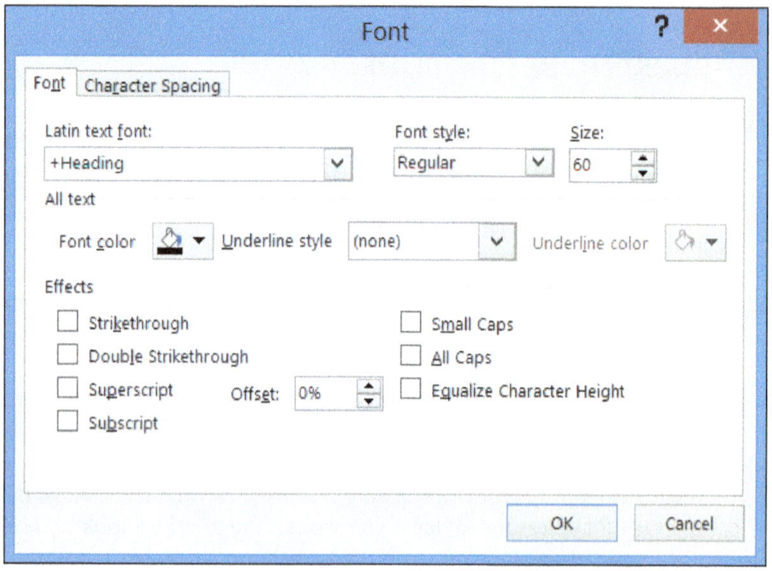


**Figure 3-2**

The Title Slide layout inherits the Theme's default Heading font.

3 Place the cursor in the subtitle text area. Type your name (for example, **John Q. Superuser**), press **Enter**, and then click **Insert > Text > Date & Time**. Make sure Update Automatically is selected and click **OK**.

4 Press **Ctrl+M** to add the next slide. Set slide 2's title to **Agenda** and add four bullet points: **Logistics**, **Housing**, **Lab practices**, and **Project schedule**.

5 Finally, click **Home > New Slide > Title Only** to add slide 3.

6 Choose **File > Save As** and navigate to the PPT03lesson folder. Name the new file **pp03a_work** and click **Save**.

The style and formatting for these slides came from the Document Theme, which bundles color scheme, default fonts, backgrounds, and slide layouts. **Title Slide** is a standard layout in Microsoft's built-in themes (see Figure 3-3), so by changing a theme, you'll automatically alter the slides' layouts (though the built-in themes make bigger changes to style than to layout).

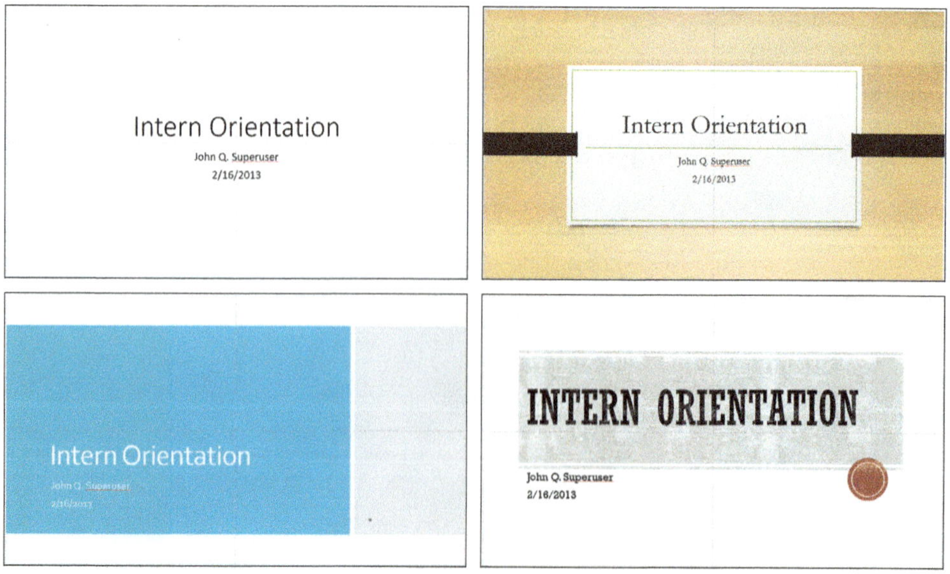


**Figure 3-3**

The layout and style of the title slide depend on the Theme you choose.

**Bottom Line**

## Adding and styling text boxes

The default Office theme, which the Blank Presentation template uses, includes the nine slide layouts found in the Home > Slides > Layout gallery (or the Slide Master view). In contrast, the Organic theme has 15 built-in layouts. On rare occasions, none of the included layouts will do, and you'll need to customize your own slide layout, with text boxes, images, and other content areas. For this, it's back to the Insert tab.

**STEP BY STEP** **Adding and styling text boxes**

1 Set slide 3's title to **Carpool Assignments**.

2 Click **Insert > Text > Text Box** to active the Text Box tool, then click somewhere just below the title. Enter four names, each on its own line: **Andy**, **Beth**, **Carlos**, **Dave**.

3 Insert two more text boxes in the slide, each with four names on four lines: **Ezra**, **Feliks**, **Gaffer**, **Hedges** and **Ibsen**, **Jake**, **Klaatu**, **Lopes**.

4 Click in the first box, and then open the Format tab. From the Shape Styles gallery, select **Colored Fill – Black, Dark 1**.

Note that when you mouse over an icon in the gallery, Office's Live Preview feature lets you see how your text box will look in that style. Applying a **Shape Style** to an object sets its line, fill, gradient, effects, and text formatting properties all at once. You can also set those properties one at a time. We'll change the look of one of our text boxes to show some favoritism:

5 Apply the Shape Styles Blue, Accent 1 and Orange, Accent 2 to the second and third text boxes respectively.

6 With the orange box selected, click the small icon in the bottom right corner of the Shape Styles group to open the Format Shape pane. Select its **Shape Options > Effects** tab and apply the following Shadow effect: **Offset Diagonal Top Right** preset, **120%** size, **20** pt. blur, **18 pt**. distance. See Figure 3-4. Then close the **Format Shape** pane.

**Figure 3-4**

The Format Shape pane is your primary tool for styling individual objects.

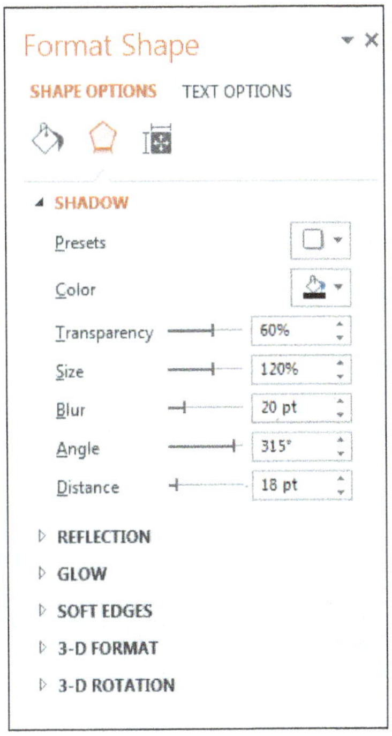

**Take Note** If you make changes to the placeholders on a slide, for example, move the title box, restyle an image placeholder, or delete a content area, you can revert to the default layout for that slide by clicking Home > Slides > Reset. Doing so won't affect the slide background or the elements you've added to the layout.

## The Format pane

**Bottom Line**

The **Format pane** is where you fine tune the appearance of slide elements such as text boxes, images, or the slide background. When you use it to style a text box, the Format Pane's tabs are grouped under two headings: Shape Options and Text Options, each with three tabs (fill and line, visual effects, and size/shape/margins/alignment). If you select nothing at all while the Format pane is open (for example, by clicking outside the slide or in an empty region of the slide), the Format pane will display formatting options for the background: solid color, a color **gradient**, an image (or texture made of tiled images), or a pattern.

## STEP BY STEP Formatting with the Format pane

1. Right-click in an empty region of slide 3 or right-click the margin. Select **Format Background** from the context menu.
2. Select **Gradient** fill from the menu, and then choose the Preset gradient **Top Spotlight – Accent 6**.
3. In the Gradient Stops slider, click to add a fourth gradient stop halfway between the second and third; set its color to **White**. This will give the slide a blown-out appearance as in Figure 3-5.

**Figure 3-5**

Add a green gradient fill background to slide 3.

The same principles apply to formatting text in boxes.

4 Select the entire heading. In the Format Shape pane, click **Text Options > Text Effects** in the Format pane. Apply the **Reflection Variation Half Reflection**, **4 pt**. offset, and the **Glow Preset Blue**, **8 pt. Glow**, **Accent color 5**.

5 Finally, Shift+click to select all three shaded text boxes (not the slide title, which is actually a text box, too). Turn on alignment guides (**View > Show > Guides**) and drag the text boxes to the center of the slide to give the vertically-extended heading text more room.

**Take Note** If you're in the habit of deselecting text after modifying it to get a clean look at the results, make sure you reselect the text before applying your next formatting change, or you may end up styling your slide background by mistake.

### Autofit and text boxes

You may have noticed, as you entered the carpool information, that the text boxes expand to fit the text inside them. Indeed, even if you draw a text box at the size you want, PowerPoint's default behavior is to collapse the text box around the text you're typing. This is Office's Autofit feature at work. The Format pane offers three options for Autofitting text in a text box: squeeze the text, stretch the box, or do nothing (spill over). Figure 3-6 compares the three.

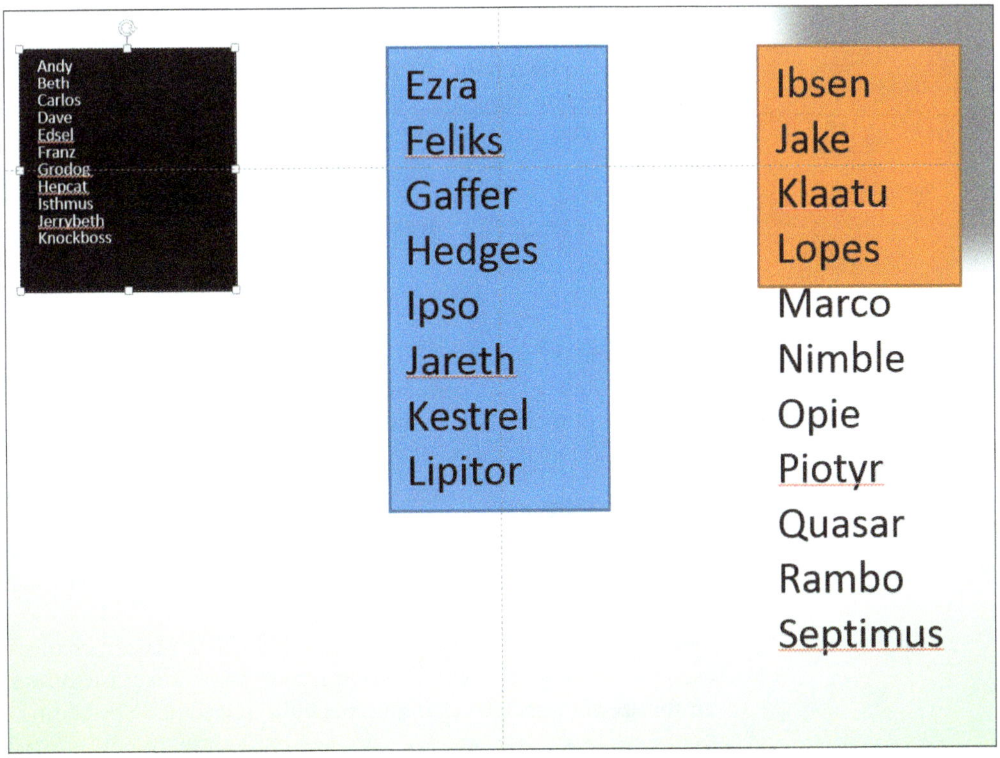


**Figure 3-6** Autofit options: Shrink Text (L), Resize Shape (C), Do Not Autofit (R).

## STYLING TEXT WITH WORDART

**Bottom Line** Adding complicated visual effects to a piece of text can be time consuming; PowerPoint speeds up the process with its **WordArt** feature, which bundles font, line, fill, shadow, and other effects into WordArt Styles that can be applied to text just as Paragraph Styles can be applied in Word.

You can use the WordArt tool in three ways: by selecting a piece of text and layering effects with the Format > WordArt Styles > Fill/Outline/Effects tools; selecting a ready made WordArt Style from the gallery; or choosing Insert > WordArt to add pre-styled dummy text to your slide. (By choosing the latter option with a piece of text selected, you will create a new text box that contains a copy of that text, but in the appropriate style.) The WordArt Styles group is an alternate front-end to the Format pane.

**STEP BY STEP** **Styling text with WordArt**

1. Add a new slide (slide 4) with layout Content with Caption. In the content area to the right, click the **Pictures** icon. Navigate to the PPT03lessons folder and select **pp03c.png** and click **Insert**.
2. Type **Dormitories** for the title. Navigate to the PPT03lessons folder and open **pp03b.docx**. Select the first paragraph and press **Ctrl+C** to copy the text. Switch back to **pp03a_work** and place the cursor in the text area below the title. Press **Ctrl+V** to paste.
3. Select the words, ***Aim for the oddly-shaped reflective tower***, in the text area. Use Live Preview to see how the various WordArt styles will look with this content. Choose the **Gradient Fill – Gray** WordArt Style from the Format > WordArt Styles gallery to apply it to the selected text.

Note the following about WordArt Styles: some apply their bundled formatting options to the entire paragraph, some only to the selected characters. Live Preview will help you see how your selected style will be applied.

## FORMATTING THE WHOLE PRESENTATION

Sometimes a project calls for slides that don't fit any of the built-in layouts. In that case, you'll have to design your own layout. If you need a single custom slide, start with a blank slide, or one that's close to what you want, and build from there: assemble your text and images, tables, charts, audio, or video. If you later need to reuse that layout, you can duplicate the slide and change the content.

If you know you will need multiple custom slides with the same design, you can save yourself time and effort by building a reusable layout in the Slide Master view. In this part of the lesson, we'll do just that.

### The Slide Master view

**Bottom Line**

The Slide Master View is where you set the visual standards for your entire presentation: the slide elements and formatting options that will be included on every slide. In the Slide Master View, you can edit two elements of your presentation:

The **Slide Master** itself is a template for every other layout in the deck; if you insert a background image or visual ornament, or alter the body or heading fonts, those changes will propagate to all the slides that inherit from the Slide Master (in other words, the whole deck).

The individual **Slide Layouts** build on the Slide Master; changes to one of a deck's layouts (for example, the Content with Caption layout) won't affect the others in the deck. You can further customize your deck by changing the built-in layouts or by adding one or more custom layouts.

If your presentation calls for multiple visual feels, you can insert multiple slide masters and assign each slide layout to a slide master depending on what visual feel it calls for.

### Editing the slide master

To quickly make the same visual edit to every slide, make changes directly on the slide master.

## STEP BY STEP Slide Master View

1 Open Slide Master View by selecting **View > Master Views > Slide Master**. In the left pane, scroll to the very top and select the **Office Theme Slide Master**.

2 Select the title text ***Click to edit Master title style***. Using the formatting pop-up menu or the Home > Font > Color tool, set its color to **Blue, Accent 1**.

As you can see from the tree diagram in the left pane (Figure 3-7), all the other layouts inherit formatting from the Slide Master; the change you've made to the Title style in the Slide Master affects all text formatted with that style in the whole deck. You can click the different layouts to see that all of them now include blue title text. This is the equivalent of editing the Title or Heading Style in Word 2013.

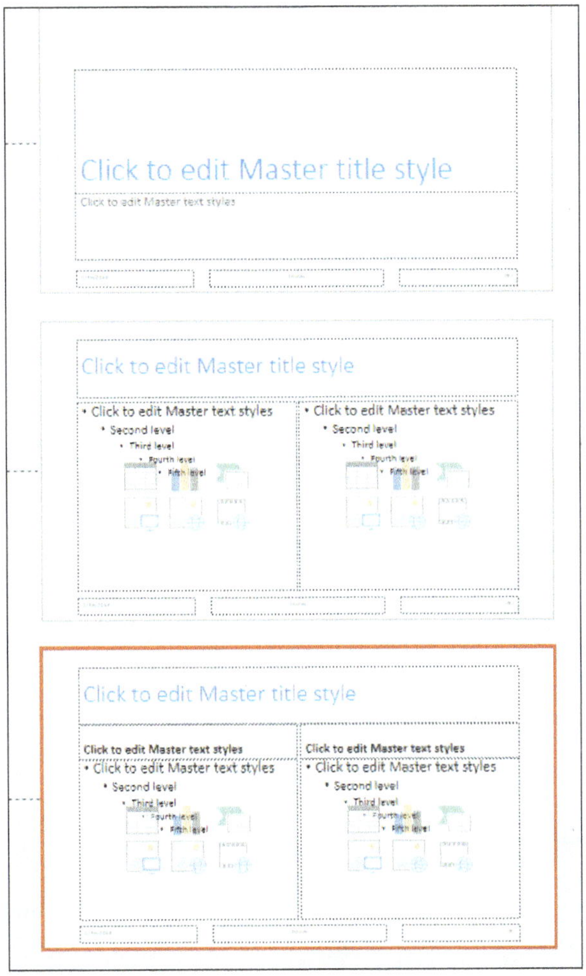


**Figure 3-7**
Formatting changes to the Slide Master are immediately reflected in all layouts.

If you scroll down to the Comparison layout in the left pane, you'll see that its subheadings haven't turned blue; you can right-click those subheadings and choose Font from the context menu to see that they're formatted with the +Body font, rather than +Heading.

Now let's add a small logo to the Slide Master at the bottom of the slide, but not strictly in the Footer text area.

**STEP BY STEP** **Editing the Slide Master**

1 Return to the Slide Master at the top of the left pane. Click **Insert > Illustrations > Shapes > Basic Shapes > Lightning Bolt**.

2 Shift+click+drag anywhere in the slide to place the image without modifying its proportions. (Note that it appears on every slide in the left pane.)

3 Drag the image to the bottom of the slide, over the footer area. Shift+drag one of its handles to resize the image to roughly the height of the footer. Place it at the bottom center of the slide; alignment guides will appear to help you place the image precisely. Save your work.

4 Now scroll down to the Title Slide layout and try to delete its lightning bolt logo; you will notice that you can't. It's part of the basic layout of the entire deck. Images and text placed in the Slide Master can't be edited on a per-slide basis; the Slide Master is for formatting, framing, and background; content should be edited in the slide layouts themselves.

## CREATING CUSTOM SLIDE LAYOUTS

Custom slide design helps your deck stand out from other nearly identical PowerPoint presentations that your colleagues will have seen prior to yours. You can add new layouts in the Slide Master View. Slide layouts include fixed and mutable elements:

- **Text** and **visuals** inserted into a layout appear in every slide using that layout and can't be edited.

- **Placeholders** are blank spaces set aside for content, and can be removed from any slide where they're not needed.

If you click in the Slide Master itself, you'll see that the Insert Placeholder command is greyed out. Adding and laying out content occurs in the slide layouts; the slide master is for formatting and ornamentation (borders, backgrounds, and so forth).

**Take Note** PowerPoint doesn't support field codes the way Word does; the only fields available are slide number and date/time. Expert users and programmers can get around this limitation with VBA code.

**Bottom Line**

### Adding a custom slide layout

Adding layouts is like adding slides, but instead of fixed content, you'll generally insert placeholders (where content will be added on the slides themselves). To demonstrate how they work, we'll make a reusable layout for tutor profiles with headshots and capsule biographies.

**STEP BY STEP** **Adding a custom slide layout**

1 Use the **Slide Master > Edit Master > Insert Layout** command to add a custom layout to your deck, and then use **Slide Master > Rename** to change its name to **Profile**.

2 Drag one of the handles on the right side of the Title box such that you resize the box to about half the width of the slide. Then change the title placeholder text to **Add tutor name here**.

Custom placeholder text is only visible while editing slides: the words, *Add tutor name here*, will prompt you for text, but won't appear on the final slides. Now add an image placeholder:

3 Click Master Layout > Insert Placeholder > Picture and Shift+click+drag to place a square image, roughly 2" high, in the upper-right corner of the slide. Click Format > Insert Shapes > Edit Shape > Change Shape to make the image placeholder an oval, then give it the Colored Outline – Blue, Accent 1 Shape Style from the gallery. Use the Shape Outline > Weight command to make the new circular border 4.5 pt. wide.

4 Make sure that View > Show > Guides is checked, and place the image so that its top edge aligns with the top of the Title box, and its right side with the right side of the right most footer. Then replace its prompt text with Tutor pic here as in Figure 3-8. Save your work.

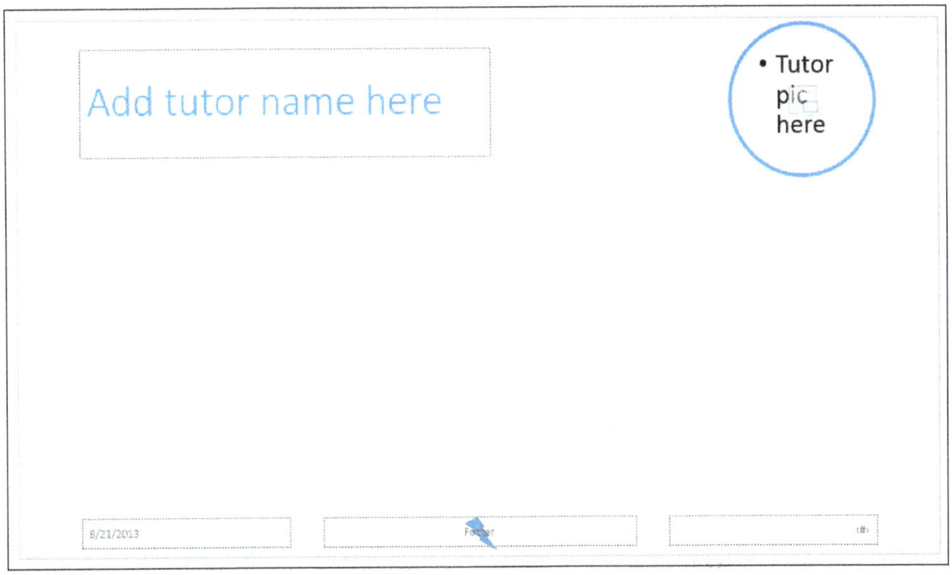


**Figure 3-8**
Adding an image placeholder to a custom slide layout.

At this point, you should take a look at your slide layout in progress.

5 Choose Slide Master > Close > Close Master View to close this view.

6 Insert a new slide and give it the new Profile layout. The main editing window shows your custom prompts, but only the image border appears on the final slide. Don't delete the new slide.

7 Choose File > Save to save your work.

## Completing the custom layout

You now have all the tools you need to finish the new Profile layout.

**STEP BY STEP** **Completing the custom layout**

1 Go back to the Slide Master view by choosing View > Master Views > Slide Master. Select the Profile layout.

2 Add a tall thin text placeholder below the image to hold a quote from each tutor. Format its top-level Master text style in 18 pt. italic blue-gray non-bulleted text. Change the top-level prompt text to Pithy quote here and delete the remaining placeholder text.

3 Fill the remaining slide space with a large text area, leaving the fonts unmodified. Set its top-level dummy text to Bulleted bio here. Align both new text boxes with the already-existing slide elements.

4 Right-click in an empty slide region, add a Pattern fill to the slide background, and select the 5% (dotted) pattern.

5 When you're finished adding slide elements, click **Slide Master > Close Master View** and return to editing your presentation.

6 Note that slide 5, the blank Profile slide, still uses the old layout: dummy text and background update, but new placeholders don't appear.

7 To refresh slide 5's layout layout, reapply the Profile layout (**Home > Slides > Layout > Profile**).

8 Add two slides to the end (slides 6 and 7), also with the new Profile layout

## Applying the custom layout

**Bottom Line**

Custom layouts behave exactly like built-in layouts. You're set to fill in three slides, each with a different tutor Profile. Now the custom placeholder text comes in handy: it'll help prevent clerical error when importing data into the slides.

**STEP BY STEP**

## Applying the custom layout

1 If it is not already open, reopen **pp03b.docx** and scroll down to the Tutor Profile Text.

2 Copy and paste the tutor profile text from **pp03b.docx** into the appropriate content areas on slides 5 to 7. Make sure not to insert a blank line at the end of the tutor name, or it'll alter the vertical alignment of the text.

3 For each profile's image, click the Insert Picture control in the profile slide's blue circular border, and then navigate to the PPT03lessons folder to select the image listed in the Tutor Profile Text.

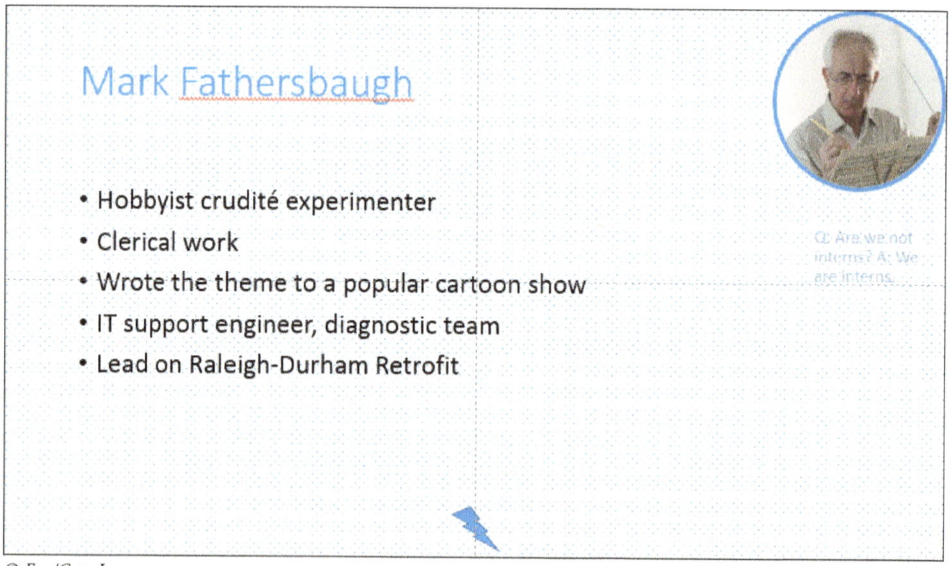


**Figure 3-9**

Slide 7 after inserting information into a Profile layout.

© *Fuse/Getty Images*

4 Save your work.

The picture placeholder seamlessly crops and styles the profile images as in Figure 3-9; no change is needed. You could generate this series of slides without using the Slide Master or creating custom layouts, but that's a poor long-term solution; next time you need something like this Profile layout, you'd be starting from scratch again. The power of custom layouts is their ability to scaffold your next several presentations.

## CUSTOMIZING A PRESENTATION THEME

If you want to edit the color scheme, font selection, background style, or visual effects for your whole presentation, you'll do so in the Slide Master View. The Slide Master > Background group contains tools to customize the various parts of your document's Theme. Once you've chosen a Theme, you have a collection of slide layouts and visual elements designed to work together, but small changes to color scheme or font pairing can personalize your presentation's look without compromising the structure of its slides.

Best of all, once you've worked out an overall visual scheme for your presentation, you can save it or share it, for instance, as a corporate visual identity. In this last part of the lesson, we'll apply a theme to the slide deck, make a couple of unobtrusive changes to its visual scheme, and export the theme for later use.

## CHANGING A THEME'S VISUAL SCHEME

**Bottom Line**

The difficulty with applying a theme to our document at this point in our slide deck design is that we've already styled several slides to taste; switching themes will change the way the slide elements work together, so it's good to watch out for oddities resulting from reskinning the presentation. You can preview the effects of a theme change by flipping to different slides in the deck and using Live Preview to see how the new background, layout, fonts, and color scheme affect the slides' look. The best slides for this purpose are custom slides, especially those dense with visual elements.

**STEP BY STEP** **Changing a theme**

1 Open the Design tab. Select slide 4, and then mouse over several themes in the gallery. Do the same with slides 3 and 5, which are already heavily visually customized.

As you change the theme, Take special note of the way the various elements in slide 5, which uses a custom layout, change appearance while holding position, and compare to what occurs in slide 4: the elements change size and switch places with the text column.

2 Select the **Wood Type** theme.

Several changes take effect: the logo disappears from the title slide; a circular red seal (meant to contain the slide number) appears in the lower right of each slide; the layout of slide 4 mirrors with the map moving left; the background on slide 3 takes on the Wood Type colors and a different gradient; and every slide's color/font settings are switched to the Wood Type settings. See Figure 3-10.

**Figure 3-10**

Wood theme applied to a Profile template slide.

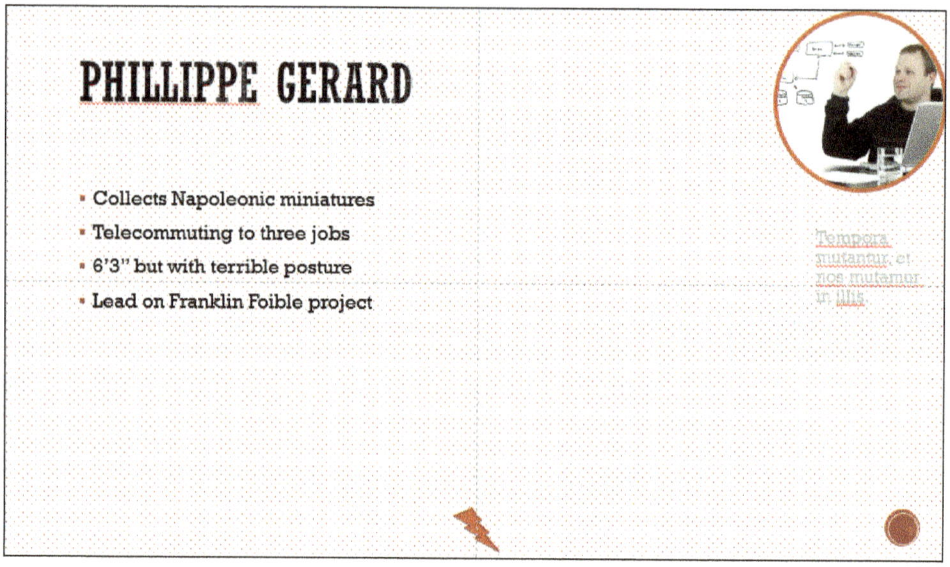


*Image used with permission of Microsoft.*

Experimenting with alternate color and font schemes is straightforward:

3 Open Slide Master View. Set Slide Master > Background > Colors to **Green Yellow**, and set Background > Fonts to **Tw Cen MT-Rockwell**.

4 Still in the Slide Master tab, select **Themes > Save Current Theme**. Assign to the modified theme the name **Intern Green Yellow**.

Your new Intern Green Yellow file includes not only the new color/font settings, but your new Profile slide layout, meaning you can send the exported theme to a colleague who might want to work with your overall aesthetic and your custom content.

5 Choose **File > Save** and then **File > Close**.

## What you learned in this lesson:

- Adding, Styling, and Filling Text Boxes
- Using the Format Pane
- Adding Styled Text with WordArt
- Creating Custom Layouts in the Slide Master
- Customizing Document Themes

# Knowledge Assessment

## Matching

**Match each term to its description or definition.**

1. WordArt
2. Format Pane
3. placeholder text
4. Slide Master
5. gradient
6. slide layout
7. text box
8. title slide
9. AutoFit
10. slide background

a. Floating slide element lacking image controls
b. Not a "page" in the Word 2013 sense; can't directly add text here
c. e.g., black fades to white from left to right in slide background
d. Default starting slide for most templates
e. Each template contains several of these; user can also custom design
f. Consolidates fine-grained formatting tools for slide elements
g. Sets visual basis for deck; slide layouts further specify
h. Squashes or stretches text boxes to fit contents
i. Appears in unfilled text box, e.g., as prompt or instructions
j. Complex text styles available regardless of theme

## Fill in the Blanks

**Complete the following sentences by writing the correct word or words in the blanks provided.**

1. To add a current Date field to a slide, use the _____ > Text > Date & Time command.
2. Adjust text/text box proportions automatically as you type with the _____ function.
3. PowerPoint lets the user set default +Heading and _____ fonts.
4. Slide _____ inherit background and placeholder information from the Slide _____.
5. To create a square (not just rectangular) content placeholder, hold down _____ while you drag to insert its border.
6. Complex fill/outline/effects combinations are achieved with one click in the _____ Styles menu.
7. To add the current date to a title slide along with the title itself, add it to the _____ text box.
8. Slide title boxes in the Slide Master contain the boilerplate text "Click to edit __________."
9. To leave a fillable box for an image in a slide layout, click Master Layout > _____ > Picture.
10. The Format > Insert Shapes > _____ > _____ command can be used to alter the shape of a slid element placeholder.

# Competency Assessment

## Project 3-1: Text Boxes

**This exercise involves creating a new document from a template and adding/editing several text boxes.**

1. Launch PowerPoint and create a new presentation using the Berlin template. Save your document as **project_3-1_textbox**.
2. Fill in **Text Box Test** (title) and **Lesson 3** (subtitle) on the title slide.
3. Add a blank slide, and add a text box to it. Add two paragraphs of text to the text box.
4. Experiment with resizing the text box to change the word wrapping. Open the Format Pane (right click text box) and adjust the AutoFit options in its Text Options > Text Box tab.
5. Experiment with multi-column text and turning off text wrap entirely (**Text Options > Text Box > Wrap text in shape**).

   Note the efficient use of space in a two-column format.
6. Experiment with adding text boxes in other shapes and proportions to the slide deck. Alter the backgrounds of your text boxes with **Format Shape > Shape Options > Fill commands**.
7. When you're comfortable with the text box editing controls, save and close your document.

## Project 3-2: WordArt and Text Style

**Here you'll try out several Style Options for newly-created WordArt.**

1. Open the project file **3-2-source**. Save your document as **project_3-2_wordart**.
2. Add a new slide with layout **Title and Content**, entitled **WordArt Samples**.
3. Add five lines of bulleted text (varying bullet levels) to slide 4's text area.
4. Select the final bulleted line and apply a WordArt Style (**Drawing Tools > Format > WordArt Styles gallery**) to the text. Try out several different WordArt Styles for the five lines of text.

   Note that WordArt Styles are character-level formatting – several styles can be applied to a single line of text.
5. Select the slide title and manually choose Text Fill, Text Outline, and Text Effects options (**Drawing Tools > Format**), along with a Shape Style for the slide title's text box.
6. Feel free to experiment further with these tools. When you're finished, save and close your document.

# Proficiency Assessment

## Project 3-3: The Format Pane

**In this exercise you'll tweak the formatting options in PowerPoint's Format Pane.**

1. Open the project file **3-3-source**. Save your document as **project_3-3_format_pane**.
2. Add a new slide. Open the Format Background Pane.
3. Switch to a Picture/Texture fill. Open the Picture Corrections tab of the Format Pane and choose the **Brightness -40%/Contrast +40%** preset.

4. Select the main content box on the slide and apply a **Top Spotlight – Accent 5** preset gradient fill.
5. In the main content box, do an Online Picture clip art search for **office stapler**, and insert one of the returned images.
6. Save and close the document.

### Project 3-4: Custom Slide Layouts

**This exercise challenges you to create a custom slide layout to spec.**

1. Create a new blank document. Save your document as **project_3-4_custom_layout**.
2. Follow the general outline of the instructions in this lesson to create a custom slide layout in the Slide Master. It should meet the following specifications: radial gradient background fill, one text box (besides title area), one circular image placeholder, two styled geometric shapes (not placeholders), one piece of WordArt (not a placeholder).
3. Add a slide using your custom slide layout and fill in the various content areas. (Pressing **Ctrl+A** while editing the new slide will highlight only editable content areas, leaving fixed (background) elements unselected.)
4. Save and close your document.

## Mastery Assessment

### Project 3-5: Customizing a Theme

**Here you'll customize a document theme to taste, and save it to your hard drive.**

1. Create a new blank document. Save your document as **project_3-5_custom_theme.**
2. Create a custom theme with the following features: subtle black/purple pattern in background, serif font, Milk Glass visual effects scheme.
3. Save your custom theme (**Slide Master > Edit Theme > Save Current Theme**) with the filename **project_3-5_blackpurple.**
4. Save your document and quit PowerPoint.

### Project 3-6: Custom Calendar Layout

**This exercise challenges you to create a complex custom slide layout.**

1. Create a new blank document and save it as **project_3-6_calendar**.
2. In the Slide Master, create a generic monthly calendar layout. It should contain five rows (for five weeks), a large space at the top for the name of the month, and placeholders for two images, one in a circular frame.
3. Use your new generic layout to create a 9- or 12-month calendar, with seasonally-appropriate images.
4. Save and close your document.

# 4 Using Tables, Charts, and SmartArt

## LESSON SKILL MATRIX

| In this lesson, you will learn the following skills: | |
|---|---|
| Transforming Bulleted Lists into SmartArt | Linking and Embedding Excel Worksheets |
| Visually Editing and Tweaking SmartArt | Creating Charts from Tabular Data |
| Styling SmartArt | Editing and Styling Charts |

## KEY TERMS

- SmartArt
- Infographic
- Text Pane (SmartArt)
- Bitmap
- Major Gridline

©mstay/iStockPhoto

At Northwind Traders, organizational information, sales data, process outlines, and marketing plans are shared between all the company's departments. Status updates need to be quick, plans need to be unambiguous, and org charts need to be crystal clear. To efficiently share all this information, Northwind's employees turn to infographics and other visuals, recasting complex data as memorable images. PowerPoint helps them turn out custom infographics quickly and easily.

## SOFTWARE ORIENTATION

In this lesson you will discover how to incorporate images, tables, and Smart Art in your PowerPoint presentations.

**Figure 4-1**

Smart Art tools and formatting functions

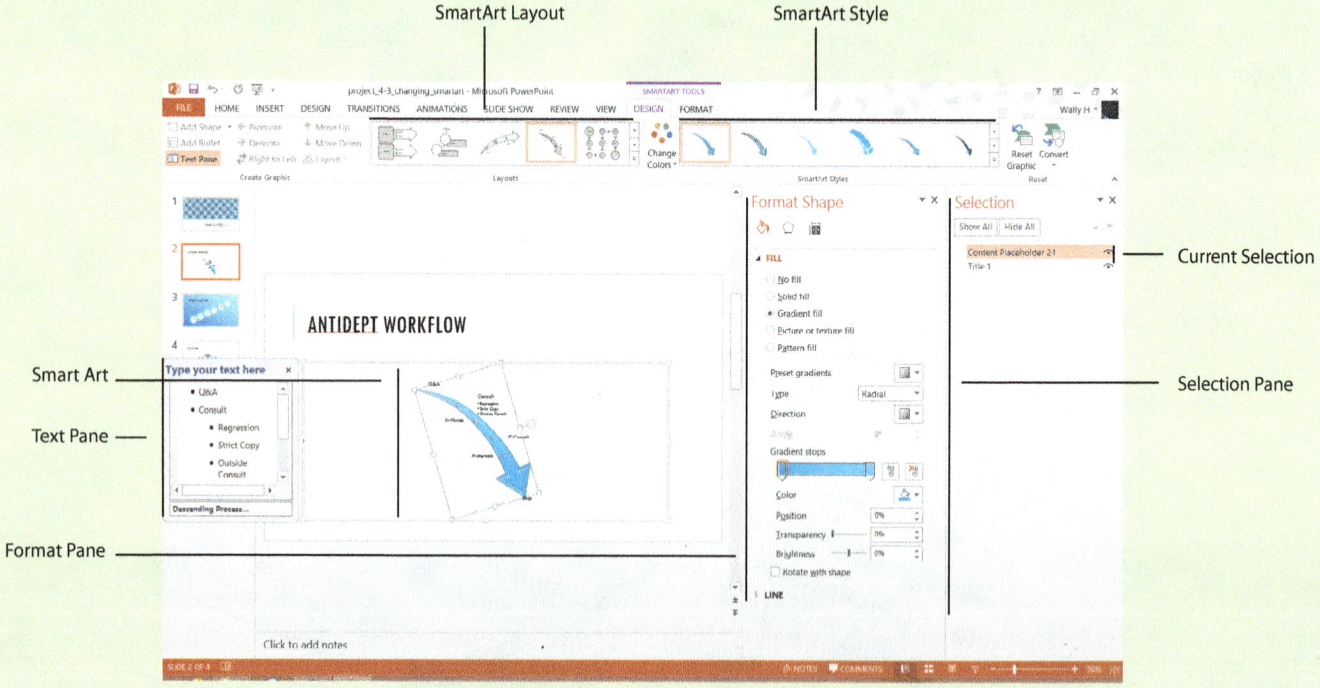

## STARTING UP

In this lesson, you'll work with several files from the PPT04lessons folder. Make sure that you have loaded the OfficeLessons folder onto your computer.

## GIVING STRUCTURE TO YOUR CONTENT

Tables, charts, and SmartArt occupy a middle ground between straight text and graphics: tables and SmartArt turn structured text content into styled visuals, while charts represent relationships between data points with shapes and colors. Tables can also be used to fit an entire slide's layout to a grid, turning cell text into a visual element.

In this lesson, you'll build slides around tabular data, format structured text as editable **SmartArt**, and transform spreadsheet data into graphs and charts. You'll also link a chart to an Excel document to include live external data in your slide.

## TRANSFORMING TEXT INTO SMARTART

The SmartArt feature available in Office lets you format lists as flowcharts, Venn diagrams, cycle diagrams, family trees, and other **infographics**. Moreover, if you build an organization chart from a bulleted list (for example), any later edits you make to the list will be reflected automatically in the diagram. And like other visual slide elements, SmartArt is easily styled using document themes.

1 Begin the lesson by launching PowerPoint 2013.

2 Open the document for this lesson, **pp04a.pptx**, located in the PPT04lessons folder. (For a look at its finished form, open **pp04a-finished.pptm**.)

**Take Note** For a Microsoft article that lists of all the SmartArt types, see the Descriptions of SmartArt graphics article in Microsoft's Support page at the following URL:

*http://office.microsoft.com/en-us/powerpoint-help/descriptions-of-smartart-graphics-HA010057065.aspx*

### Formatting lists as SmartArt

**Bottom Line**

Unsurprisingly, the most common text format in PowerPoint slides is used as the building block of PowerPoint SmartArt: the bulleted list. In this part of the lesson, we'll take a handful of lists and transform each into a different kind of diagram. (Note that lists needn't actually be bulleted to generate SmartArt, but bullets make a nice clear distinction between text levels 1 and 2.)

**STEP BY STEP** **Formatting lists as SmartArt**

1 In **pp04a.pptx**, select slide 2, ***Mamet Code Process Outline***.

2 Right-click the text of the bulleted list and select **Convert to SmartArt > More SmartArt Graphics**.

3 From the Cycle group, select the Cycle Matrix type near the bottom and click **OK**.

PowerPoint automatically styles top-level bullets as cycle elements and treats level 2 as text. The original list is preserved in the SmartArt's Text pane if it did not open automatically, from which you can directly edit the SmartArt's contents as well.

4 If the **Text pane** isn't already open, do so now: Click the cycle diagram, and then click the small arrow handle on the left edge of the selection box.

5 In the Text pane, change the Free heading to **Reset**.

Because the diagram and its source list remain linked (see Figure 4-2), editing either the Text pane or the image text will automatically update the other.

**Figure 4-2**

The Text pane offers a convenient editing interface to the SmartArt.

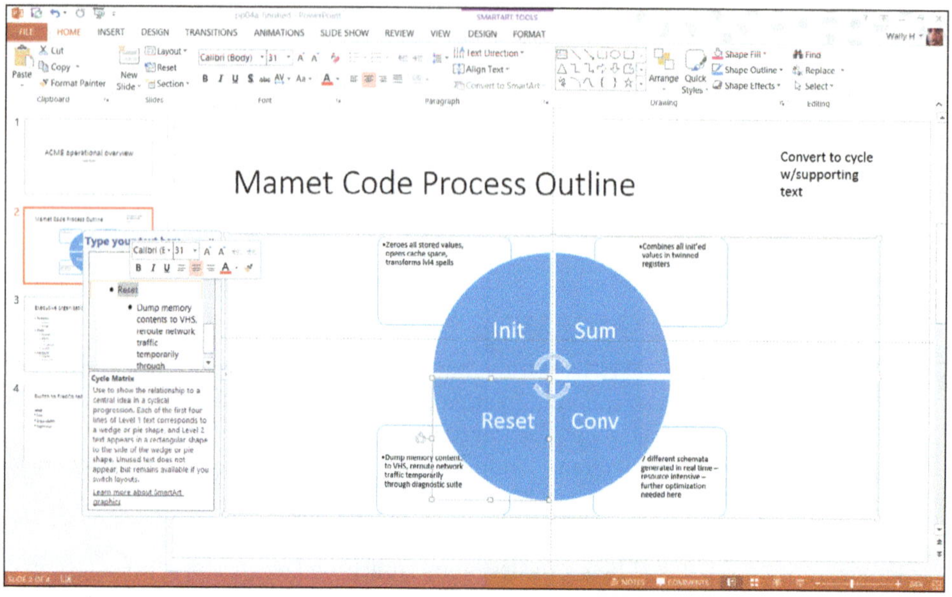


Note that the two lower level 2 text pieces are set too close to the cycle diagram. You can easily fix this, since the various components of a SmartArt diagram can be formatted just as any other floating slide element with the Format pane.

6 Right-click the SmartArt's lower-right label and choose **Size and Position** to open the Format Shape pane. In the Text Box section, set Vertical alignment (of the text) to Bottom; then click in the lower-left label and do the same to it.

7 Choose **File > Save As** and navigate to the PPT04lessons folder. Type **pp04a_work** in the File name text field and click **Save**.

## Visually editing a flowchart

**Bottom Line**

Slide 3 in the sample deck can be turned into a flowchart without making changes to it, but you can customize its content and visual style with the SmartArt Design and Format tabs.

**STEP BY STEP** **Visually editing a flowchart**

1 Advance to slide 3. Transform the list of names into an organization chart (**Home > Paragraph > Convert to SmartArt Graphic > Organization Chart**).

2 Click the Robeson box in the chart, and then click **SmartArt Tools > Design > Add Shape > Add Assistant** to insert an assistant box beneath it. Enter the name **Paul** in the new text box.

3 Right-click Pilfer and choose **Add Shape > Add Assistant** from the context menu. Enter **Drudge** in the text box.

4 Open the org chart's Text pane if it is not already opened. In the text pane, select **Atchison** and the lines below and press **Ctrl+X** to move them to the clipboard. Then Paste them between Paul and Pilfer in the Text pane by moving your cursor before Pilfer and pressing **Ctrl+V**. The entire Atchison branch of the chart moves to the center of the graphic.

5 Click **Atchison** in the SmartArt itself, and select **SmartArt > Design > Create Graphic > Layout > Right Hanging** to switch that branch to a narrower layout, as in Figure 4-3.

**Figure 4-3**

SmartArt layouts affect not just the look, but the meaning of your diagram.

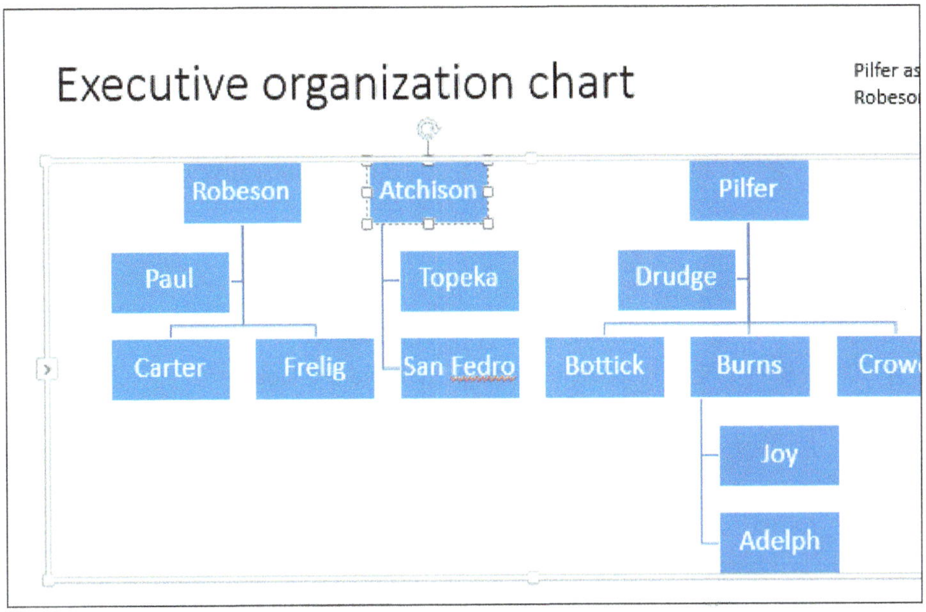


The other two branches in this SmartArt can't switch to the compact Right or Left Hanging layouts without confusing assistants with lower branches; not all layouts are created equal in terms of the information they format. That said, this new layout might not be the best choice: at present, it's reasonable to (incorrectly) read Topeka as Atchison's assistant. We may need a different visual scheme.

6 Click **Undo** in the Quick Access Toolbar to change the layout back.

## Styling a piece of SmartArt

**Bottom Line**

PowerPoint provides three sets of tools for altering the appearance of a piece of SmartArt. As usual, the document theme establishes the baseline appearance of your diagrams. The SmartArt Design tab lets you add structural elements (for example, additional nodes in an org chart), try out diagram variants, switch between sets of Theme Colors, and apply visual effects to the whole diagram with a SmartArt Style. Finally, the SmartArt Format tab provides access to the usual formatting tools for slide elements: lines, fills, colors, and so on.

We'll use each of these tools to give our org chart a coherent visual scheme; then we will discard the standard Org Chart format to make our organizational hierarchy clearer.

**STEP BY STEP** **Styling SmartArt**

1 Deselect the SmartArt and delete the small text box in the upper right of the slide. In the Design tab, apply the **Banded** theme (it has a white stripe through the middle) and select the third (charcoal/white) variant. All four slides take on the new look.

2 Reselect the **SmartArt**. In the SmartArt Design tab, change to the Hierarchy List layout found near the bottom. Then click **Change Colors > Colorful – Accent Colors**.

The available color schemes draw from the Theme Colors; you can further customize the SmartArt's coloration by going block by block through the chart, but that's not really a sustainable method.

3 Apply the **Brick Scene 3-D** SmartArt Style.

Note that Paul and Drudge, the assistants, have been dropped to the bottom of their respective branches; the Hierarchy List and Org Chart treat assistants differently. This works for our present purposes: we'll just individually style the assistant elements to show their special status.

4 Shift+click **Paul** and **Drudge**. Click **SmartArt > Format > Shapes > Smaller** five times. Then click **Shape Styles > Subtle Effect – Brown, Accent 6** to give the assistant nodes an appropriately modest look.

You can individually move and style the components of a piece of SmartArt, but the entire graphic appears as a single entry in the Selection pane. We'll use the pane to grab the whole SmartArt object at once.

5 Open the Selection pane (**Home > Editing > Select > Selection Pane**) and select the Content Placeholder entry, which refers to the SmartArt. Close the Selection pane and Format Shape pane to clear screen real estate, then drag the diagram to center it in the charcoal region of the slide. Figure 4-4 shows the result.

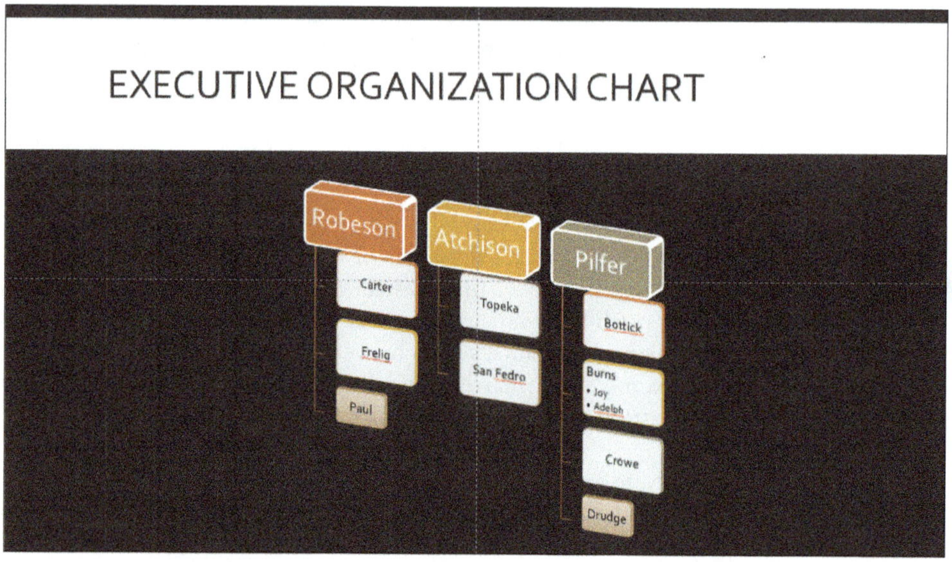


**Figure 4-4**
A more readable, less ambiguous org chart built from the same data.

6 Choose **File > Save** to save your work.

## Piecing together SmartArt

**Bottom Line**

Slide 4 of our test presentation requires some adjustments, mostly Cut and Paste, before you can transform it from text to SmartArt. To see what the slide will look like when you're done, see slide 4 of **pp04a-finished.pptm** in the PPT04lessons folder.

## STEP BY STEP Piecing together SmartArt

1 To start with, select the left bulleted list and convert it to the Balance SmartArt graphic (Home > Paragraph > Convert to SmartArt Graphic > More SmartArt Graphics > Relationship > Balance). With its Text pane open (see Figure 4-5), you can see what's happening: the Balance graphic takes two level 1 paragraphs (Fast and Dependable) to compare them and leaves out any other level 1 text.

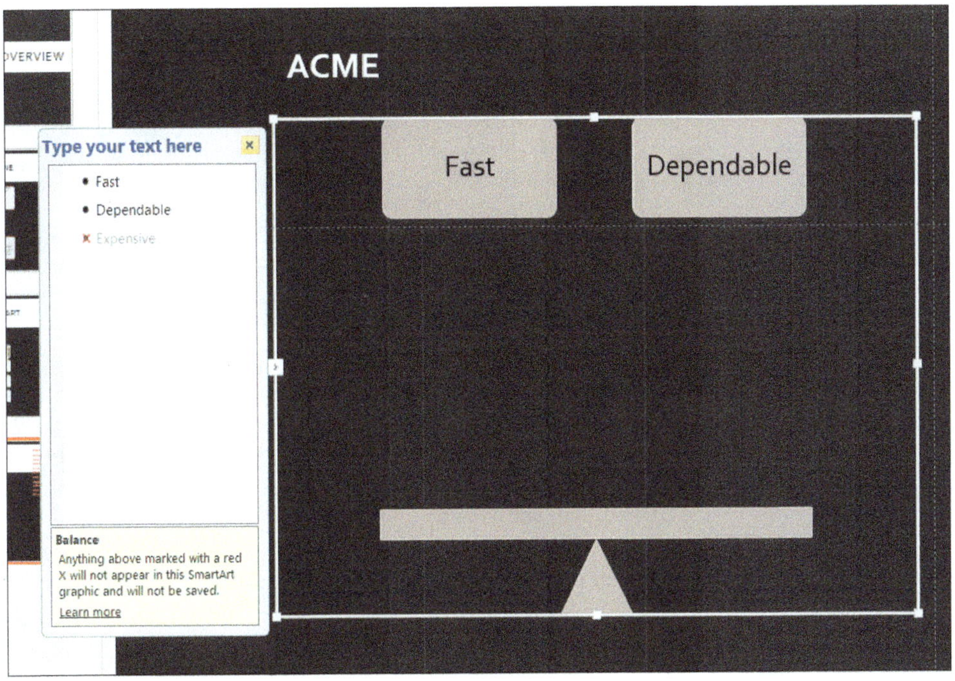


**Figure 4-5**

Studying the text pane provides insight into how to structure text for future SmartArt conversion.

To make this SmartArt graphic work, we'll need a bulleted list with two level 1 entries (ACME and FredCo), each with several pros/cons at level 2.

2 Right-click the bounding box of the SmartArt and choose Convert to Text to turn the SmartArt back into a bulleted list, then make the necessary changes to the list.

3 Cut and Paste the list to the right (FredCo) to the bottom of the ACME list. When you have a single list of seven lines, select all the text in the list and click Home > Paragraph > Increase List Level.

4 Insert the word ACME as a level 1 line at the top of the list, and insert FredCo at level 1 between Expensive and Sluggish.

5 Delete the ACME and FredCo headings above the two content areas, and then change the layout of slide 4 to Title and Content (Home > Slides > Layout > Title and Content).

6 Now place your cursor in the list and reapply the Balance SmartArt graphic (in the Relationships collection).

The balance tilts to the right, but the balance is dynamically set to tilt toward the side that has more level 2 text. Now let's make a frivolous change to the image and have *Future-proof* tip over and fall off the scale altogether.

7 Drag the Future-proof box a bit to the right, and use its rotate handle to tip it roughly 45 degrees clockwise, as in Figure 4-6. Then open the Text pane and change *Future-proof* to Open format.

8 To close, give the SmartArt a bit of panache by applying the **Intense Effect** SmartArt Style from the SmartArt Styles in the Design tab.

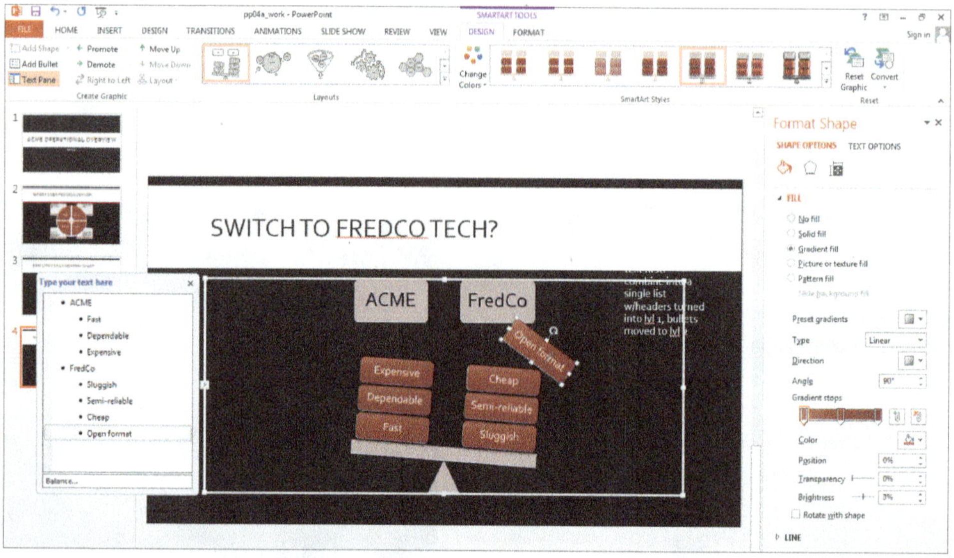


**Figure 4-6**

Apply the Intense Effect SmartArt Style.

As you can see, the *Open format* text box is still linked to its source list line despite having moved around; bullet order is unrelated to, and unaffected by, any graphical manipulations you might do. But deleting text (or a text box) from the graphic itself will still modify the bulleted list. In fact, if you delete the *Cheap* box from our teeter totter, the *Open format* box will snap into its place, and the balance will tilt back to the center.

To help you understand SmartArt better, think of it as unusually complicated text formatting, not as graphics with text labels.

## LINKING AND EMBEDDING EXTERNAL DATA

Because PowerPoint presentations are often used to show off other work, PowerPoint 2013 lets you link and embed external data in a presentation. A table in a slide can pull its contents from an Excel file, for instance, and automatically update when changes are made in Excel. You can even insert an entire Word 2013 document into a slide, which opens a copy of Word within PowerPoint, to bring the full power of Word's formatting and layout abilities to that slide.

**Take Note**

For step-by-step details of linking to external data, see the section on Embedding and Linking Objects in Word Lesson 6, "Beyond Word: Linking and Collaborating" in the first part of this book. This section will cover the Insert Object command, which lets you edit a slide element using applications such as Photoshop or MS Paint, while providing an alternate method to link to external data

In this part of the lesson, you'll use Excel, Word, and MS Paint to edit directly the contents of your presentation.

### Embedding an Excel worksheet as an object

**Bottom Line**

The Insert > Object command lets you create objects representing external data and add them to your presentation. An embedded object becomes part of the .pptx file itself (significantly increasing file size); double-clicking the object within the presentation launches the appropriate editing application. For instance, double-clicking an Excel worksheet embedded in a slide opens an instance of Excel 2013 right inside PowerPoint. If you embed an object created from an external file, changes to the original file won't affect the copy inside the presentation because the embedded version is a copy of the original.

A linked object, on the other hand, stays connected to its source data. If you create a link to an Excel spreadsheet in your slide deck, editing the object opens the original file (if it can still be found).

Embedding data as a slide object is as simple as inserting an image.

## STEP BY STEP Embedding an Excel worksheet as an object

1. Add a new slide, slide 5, to **pp04a_work.pptx**, with layout Title Only and title it **Stock Holdings**.
2. Select **Insert > Text > Object**. **Select Create** from file, and Browse to your PPT04lessons folder. Select **pp04b.xlsx** and click **OK**. Click **OK** again to insert the object.
3. Resize the object to fit in the content area and place it at the center of the slide.

Excel objects can be minimally formatted; if you click the embedded worksheet, the Drawing Tools > Format tab is mostly greyed out. However, the Shape Fill is still available.

4. Click **Format > Shape Styles > Shape Fill** and select **White**.

Notice in Figure 4-7 that the cells that fill in with white are the ones that haven't otherwise been colored in the original Excel document; this occurs because the unformatted cell are effectively transparent from PowerPoint's perspective.

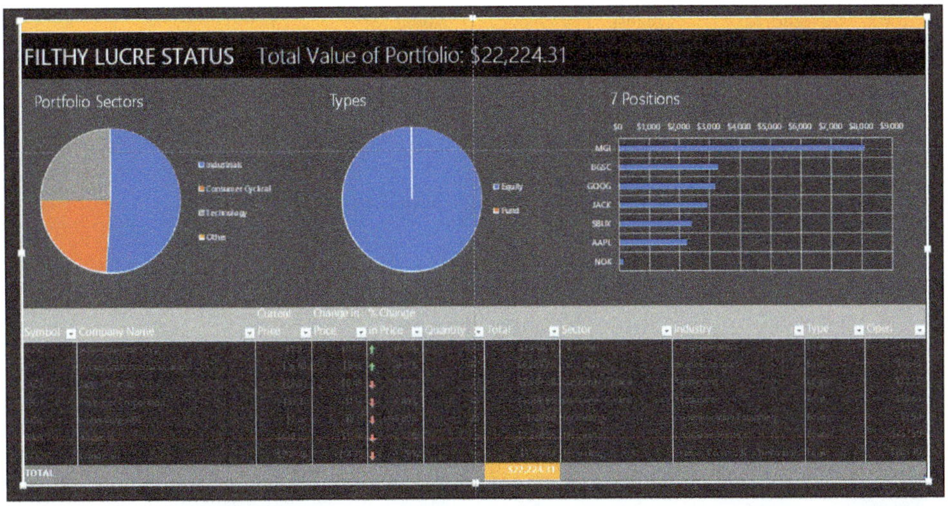


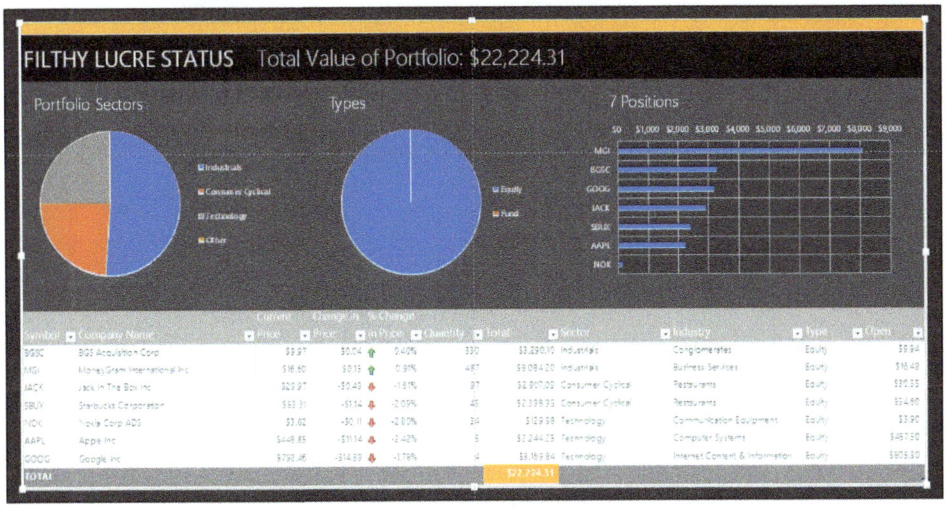


**Figure 4-7**

Unformatted cells in the original Excel file match the charcoal presentation background; white fill affects only those cells.

## Editing embedded objects

**Bottom Line**

To edit an embedded object, double-click it. If it's an Office document (in this case, an Excel worksheet), Windows launches an embedded version of the appropriate app within PowerPoint, as in Figure 4-8.

### STEP BY STEP Editing embedded objects

1 Double-click the portfolio spreadsheet object.

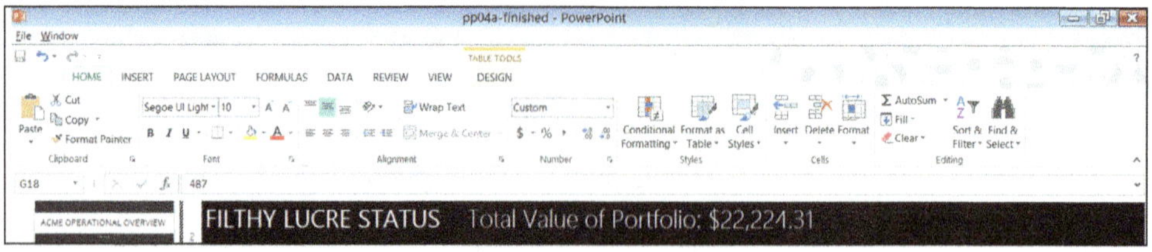


**Figure 4-8**

The File menu returns, along with a full Excel Ribbon, when you edit an Excel object within PowerPoint.

2 Click the word **FILTHY** (cell B2). Change the words FILTHY LUCRE STATUS to **CURRENT HOLDINGS**.

3 Press **Escape** to return to PowerPoint. The Excel object updates to reflect the new heading.

The editing interface for an embedded Excel worksheet can be a bit confusing: Excel's version of the Ribbon appears, but the File and Window menus float above it, and the PowerPoint application menu appears in the top left corner of the window. The PowerPoint Ribbon vanishes utterly; you can't change the enclosing presentation while you edit the embedded object. Remember that the Escape key functions literally here: pressing Escape pops you out of the embedded editor back to PowerPoint proper.

The same principles apply when you insert a Paint object, but to edit a **bitmap** image, Windows launches a full version of MS Paint.

### STEP BY STEP Editing a bitmap image

1 Select **Insert > Text > Object > Create new > Bitmap Image** and click **OK**. MS Paint launches.

2 Switch to a dark green color. Draw a picture of a dollar sign ($) in the white space provided.

3 Press Alt+F4 to close Paint and return to PowerPoint. Place the new image, resized to fit in the white band, in the upper-right corner.

You don't need to save your Paint document; you're not working on a separate Paint file as such, you're editing an object within your PowerPoint (.pptx) file using Paint as its borrowed editing interface (See Figure 4-9.) In fact, if you keep both PowerPoint and Paint visible at once while editing the bitmap, you'll see any changes you make in Paint reflected instantly in the slide.

**Figure 4-9**

An embedded object differs from a linked file in that its data exists only within the .pptx file

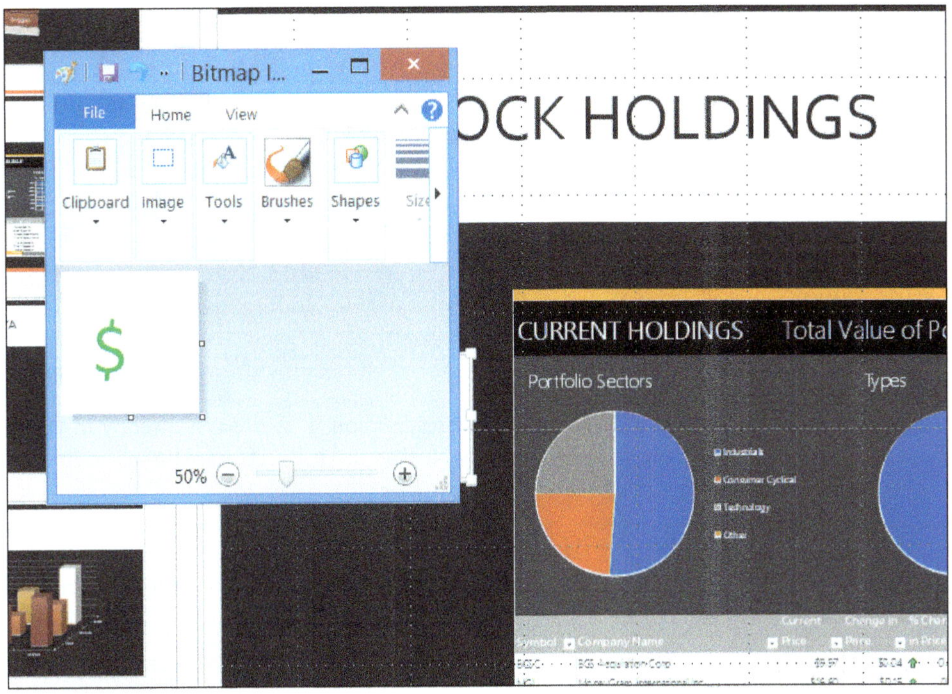


4 Choose File > Save to save your work.

## Creating a linked object

**Bottom Line**

Linked objects can be created using the Paste Special command to link to data on the clipboard, or with the Insert Object command. We'll use Insert Object in this section, building on the exercises you've just completed.

1 Add a new slide to your presentation with the title Expectations Management Plan.

2 Click Insert > Object. Select Create from file, and click Browse. Select pp04c.docx in your PPT04lessons folder, and click OK and click OK again.

PowerPoint takes a snapshot of the contents of the Word document and inserts it into the current slide, but leaves the data in the source file (keeping the presentation document itself slim). To edit, just double-click as usual; the original file opens in Word.

You can also choose to create a linked file, rather than an embedded one, when using the Insert Picture control in a slide: instead of clicking Insert after selecting your image, select Insert and Link, or Create a Link, from the Insert drop-down menu.

## CREATING A CHART FROM TABULAR DATA

Sometimes an audience wants to see raw data, but more often it wants a visual that highlights relationships between data: a graph or chart instead of a table (however cleverly designed). Excel offers a suite of powerful tools for representing data visually; PowerPoint borrows some of these tools to let you include charts and graphs in your slides.

**Take Note** Additional details on tables are found in Word Lesson 5, "Working with Tables," in the first part of this book. The commands for adding, navigating, styling, and editing tables are the same between Word and PowerPoint 2013; given the similarities between the two interfaces, you're encouraged to practice linking/embedding/drawing tables in both apps.

We'll add charts to our presentation in two ways: directly in PowerPoint (in an embedded Excel editing window), and by pasting in an Excel chart linked to its source data.

### Generating charts in PowerPoint

**Bottom Line** If you create a chart from scratch in PowerPoint, a mini Excel worksheet opens to let you enter data. This is a great way to quickly add simple info graphics to your slide show.

**STEP BY STEP** **Generating a chart in PowerPoint**

1. Add a new Title and Content slide (slide 7) to your open presentation, with layout Title and Content. Title it **Fall Semester Sales**.
2. Click **Insert Chart** in the content area. Select the **3-D Column** layout and click **OK**.
3. Insert the following data into the Excel sheet that appears:

| | CPU | Monitor | RAM |
|---|---|---|---|
| Wilson | 4.3 | 2.4 | 2 |
| Johnson | 2.5 | 4.4 | 2 |
| Clarkson | 3.5 | 1.8 | 3 |
| Wolfson | 4.5 | 2.8 | 5 |

4. Close the embedded Chart in the Microsoft PowerPoint window. Click the chart area, open the Chart Elements handle (+), and uncheck **Legend**.
5. Apply **Chart > Design > Quick Layout > Layout 7** and **Chart Style 11** to the chart.
6. Finally, right-click anywhere on the chart and select **Edit Data > Edit Data** to reopen the worksheet.

If you need the full features of Excel to edit your data, you can open Excel 2013 through the Edit Data mini-sheet or the Edit Data context command.

## Editing individual chart elements

Just as SmartArt pieces stay connected to elements in an underlying bulleted list, the individual pieces of PowerPoint charts (such as the red and orange bars in our sample chart) are linked to cell data in the associated table; you can tailor a chart's appearance and content by editing individual chart elements. To see how this works, let's give Wolfson and Johnson's RAM sales some extra emphasis:

**STEP BY STEP** **Editing chart elements**

1 If **pp04a_work.ppt** isn't open, open the file now. In the chart, click **Johnson's yellow RAM sales** bar in the back row; the entire RAM row is selected. (Hovering your mouse over the bar will bring up a tooltip identifying the bar and showing its source data.) Click the bar again to select the individual bar.

2 Click **Chart > Format > Shape Styles > Colored Outline – Orange, Accent 2** to format that individual bar.

3 Do the same with Wolfson's much larger RAM sales bar (Figure 4-10).

**Figure 4-10**

PowerPoint's chart tools offer fine-grained control over both aesthetics and content.

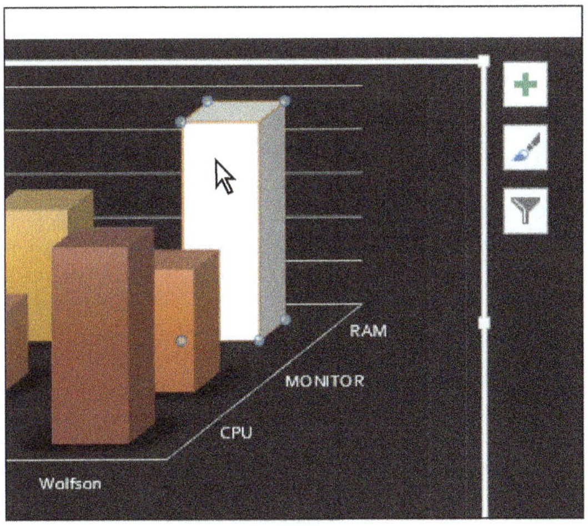


4 Close the worksheet.

Every element of the chart is equally customizable. Indeed, you can even right-click the tiny gridlines that run along the edges of the graph, and then open the Format pane (Format Gridlines) to change any of their visual parameters. Clicking through the various components of the graph with the Format pane open will show you how customizable your graph's visuals are. The Chart Design and Format tabs remain available, as they would for any floating slide element.

## Linking a chart to external Excel data

**Bottom Line**

Naturally, you can paste a chart directly from an existing Excel document, just as any other image. Since Excel charts are linked to the sheets that generate them, you can choose to maintain that link when you copy the chart into PowerPoint. Your presentation can then update to reflect changes to the underlying chart data.

STEP BY STEP **Linking a chart to external Excel data**

1 Add another slide (slide 8) to your presentation, entitled **Sales Comparison**.

2 Navigate to your PPT04lessons folder and open **pp04e.xlsx** in Excel 2013. Select the **Seasonal Beverage Sales** graph and press **Ctrl+C** to copy it. Make sure you're selecting the entire chart and not just one element; click in an empty region of the image to be sure.

3 In PowerPoint, click **Home > Paste > Use Destination Theme & Link Data**.

4 Place the chart near the lower left corner of the slide, then drag the upper right handle further up and to the right to fill the slide's content area.

5 Navigate back to **pp04e.xlsx** and change the PepDrink Spring sales value to **20**. Save the file as **pp04e_work** in the PPT04lessons folder and close Excel.

The data should automatically refresh, but in case it has failed to do so, we'll manually refresh the data in PowerPoint.

6 In PowerPoint, click the chart and choose **Chart Tools > Design > Data > Refresh Data**.

**Take Note** If you click Refresh Data with the Excel source file open, you may get an error message to indicate that the file is locked for editing by another user. In that case, Cancel the refresh and close the file in Excel. Note that a linked local file mirrored to SkyDrive may need to upload to the cloud before a data refresh will work.

## Styling charts and graphs

**Bottom Line**

As with a chart created directly in PowerPoint, double-clicking a chart linked to Excel opens the Format pane. From there you can make subtle or dramatic changes to your graphics' look.

STEP BY STEP **Styling charts and graphs**

1 Double-click the graph to open the Format pane. Select one of the gridlines; the Pane's heading changes to Format Major Gridlines.

2 In the Fill & Line subpane, click the Gradient line option button; PowerPoint recolors the gridlines along a gradient, using an accent color from the current theme.

3 With the gridlines still selected, click the drop-down menu beside the **Major Gridline** Options heading in the pane (see Figure 4-11). Select **Chart Area** from the drop-down menu.

**Figure 4-11**

From the Format pane, you can select any chart element for styling.

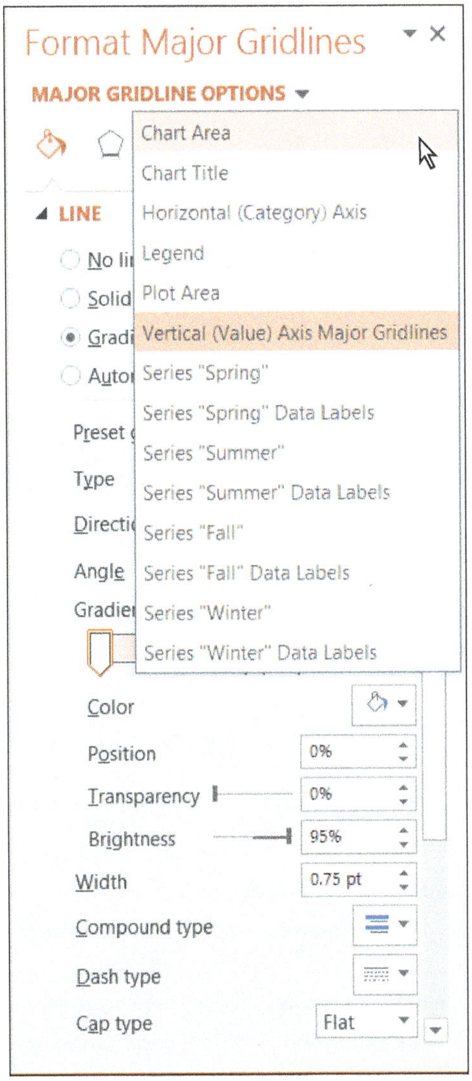


The Chart Options drop-down menu displays a list of every editable chart element so you don't have to search for half-hidden objects in the chart's back row. There's also space to translate your content for visually impaired audiences:

4 In the Chart Options > Size & Properties tab, edit the Alt Text: set the Title to **Seasonal Beverage Product Sales by Product** and the Description to **Breakdown of 5 soda product sales by season**.

As is the case with text and SmartArt, when you need to do fine-grained editing of floating slide elements such as charts and graphics (which you'll do in the next lesson), you'll spend a lot of time inside the Format pane. If you have the screen real estate, you could leave several editing/formatting panes open all the time, and switch back and forth between Normal Mode and Reading Mode to get a wide-angle look at your slides. As always, your location in PowerPoint's natural workflow will shape how you use the application's interface.

5 Choose **File > Save** to save your work.

## What you learned in this lesson:

- Transforming Bulleted Lists into SmartArt
- Visually Editing and Tweaking SmartArt
- Styling SmartArt
- Linking and Embedding Excel Worksheets
- Creating Charts from Tabular Data
- Editing and Styling Charts

# Knowledge Assessment

### Fill in the Blanks

**Complete the following sentences by writing the correct word or words in the blanks provided.**

1. To create a piece of SmartArt, begin with text in _____ form.
2. Double clicking a linked object in a slide allows the user to _____ the object.
3. The _____ popup lets you customize which components (gridlines, axis labels, etc.) are included in an infographic.
4. Chart elements like gridlines are styled in the _____ Pane.
5. Information in row/column form, such as a spreadsheet, is called _____ data.
6. The data behind a SmartArt infographic is accessible from the SmartArt's _____ Pane.
7. Inserting "live" data from an external file into a PowerPoint document is called _____ the data.
8. SmartArt Styles take their color choices first from the current document _____.
9. To show who works for whom within a corporation, use an infographic called an _____.
10. Clicking a piece of SmartArt adds the _____ and _____ tabs to the Ribbon.

### True/False

**Circle T if the statement is true or F it the statement is false.**

T F 1. Double clicking a piece of text in a SmartArt object brings up the Text Pane.

T F 2. The Paste Special command can be used to create a linked Excel spreadsheet within a presentation.

T F 3. Double clicking an embedded Excel file opens an Excel interface "inside" PowerPoint.

T F 4. Navigating PowerPoint tables works just the same as navigating Word tables.

T F 5. Photoshop files and MS Paint images can be embedded in PowerPoint slides.

T F 6. Editing embedded Office data in a PowerPoint document adds old-fashioned File and Window menus atop the PowerPoint window.

T F 7. Moving one shape within a piece of SmartArt "unlinks" the SmartArt from its source data.

T F 8. Linked data exists in a separate file, independent of the PowerPoint data itself.

T F 9. All SmartArt types can be made from bulleted lists of any length and depth.

T F 10. In an Office org chart, "child" means the same thing as "assistant."

# Competency Assessment

## Project 4-1: Adding SmartArt to a Slide

**In this exercise you'll insert SmartArt graphics into several presentation slides.**

1. Open the exercise file 4-1-source. Save your document as project_4-1_smartart.
2. Select slide 3 of the Northwind "Interoffice Mtg" presentation. Click somewhere in the bulleted list and choose Format > Paragraph > Convert to SmartArt. Select the org chart.
3. In the text pane, indent all the lines below "Cameo."

   The SmartArt automatically updates to reflect the new bulleted list structure.
4. Right click the flowchart on slide 2 and select Convert to Text.
5. Indent lines 3-5, then convert the list to Basic Timeline SmartArt.
6. Select several pieces of the SmartArt in turn – the blue dots, arrow, and text pieces – and move them around the screen.
7. Click SmartArt Tools > Design > Reset Graphic.
8. Save and close your document.

## Project 4-2: Changing SmartArt Layouts

**In this exercise you'll modify pieces of SmartArt in a presentation.**

1. Open the project file 4-2-source. Save your document as project_4-2_changing_smartart.
2. Select the SmartArt on slide 2. In the SmartArt Tools > Design tab, mouse over several entries in the Layouts gallery to see the changes the different layouts make to the chart's information.
3. Select the Circle Process layout.
4. Right click slide 2 in the slide selection pane and click Duplicate Slide. (The duplicate is now slide 3.)
5. On slide 3, select the SmartArt and in the SmartArt Design tools tab, click Reset > Convert > Convert to Shapes.
6. Rotate the new image 45 degrees counterclockwise.
7. Add a gradient fill to slide 3's background, Linear gradient, from bottom left to top right (like the image), color Orange – Accent 2.
8. Save and close the document.

## Proficiency Assessment

### Project 4-3: Styling SmartArt

**This exercise focuses on using SmartArt Styles and layouts.**

1. Open the project file **4-3-source.** Save your document as **project_4-3_styling_smartart**.
2. Switch to the Integral document theme.
3. Click the **SmartArt graphics** on slides 2 and 4 and experiment with different SmartArt Styles, Layouts, and color schemes in the Design tab.

   Note that the converted graphic on slide 3 can no longer be styled like SmartArt, though its fonts still update with any theme/font changes to the file.
4. Open the Format Pane and experiment with tweaking the appearance of individual pieces of the SmartArt graphics – the lines in the org chart, for instance. You can click **Reset Graphic** to return the SmartArt to its original appearance.
5. When you're finished experimenting, save and close your document.

### Project 4-4: Embedding Excel Data

**In this exercise you'll embed an Excel worksheet in a slide show.**

1. Create a new blank document. Save your document as **project_4-4_embedding**.
2. Look over project file **4-4-source.xlsx**.
3. Add a blank slide to the project file and use the **Insert Object** command with the **Create from File** option to embed the **4-4-source.xlsx** worksheet into your presentation.
4. Double click the embedded data to edit; choose **Home > Styles > Format as Table**, pick a table formatting style, and give the range **A3:C9** to change the appearance of the embedded data.
5. Update the "Books" data to **60** units for **200** total income, and format the column C data using the **Currency** number format.
6. Save and close your document.

# Mastery Assessment

## Project 4-5: Charts from Tabular Data

**In this exercise you'll generate a chart from new tabular data, right in PowerPoint.**

1. Create a new blank document. Save your document as **project_4-5_tabular**.
2. Add a pie chart to slide 2 entitled Percentage of Sector Profits, 2013, with the following data behind it:

| Company | Profit |
|---|---|
| Northwind | 3.3 |
| ProductCo | 4.1 |
| ObjectCo | 2.5 |
| FasterCo | 4.2 |
| FastestCo | 4.8 |

3. Delete the title placeholder from slide 2.
4. Save and close your document.

## Project 4-6: PowerPoint Genealogy

**In this exercise you'll build a family tree within PowerPoint.**

1. Create a new slide show and save it as **project_4-6_genealogy.**
2. Create a family tree on paper going back to your grandparents, then use SmartArt to turn that drawing into an infographic in PowerPoint.
3. Save and close your document and PowerPoint.

# 5 Adding Graphics and Multimedia to Your Presentation

## LESSON SKILL MATRIX

| In this lesson, you will learn the following skills: | |
|---|---|
| Recolor, Adjust, Crop, and Stack Images | Add Media Triggers to Slide Objects |
| Heighten Visual Impact with Animations | Embed Online and Local Video |
| Enrich Slides with Sound Effects and Background Sound | Use Grids and Guides to Lay Out Slides |

## KEY TERMS

- Crop
- Selection Pane
- Motion Path
- Codec
- Compress
- Alignment Guides

_human ©/iStockPhoto

_human ©/iStockPhoto

The sales and marketing team at Northwind Traders often needs to show their upcoming commercials and video presentations to stores that sell their products and other marketing partners. To easily share upcoming sales and marketing efforts, Northwind's communications and design teams integrate their multimedia content into dynamic and rich PowerPoint presentations. They can include sales data, planning information, and video all into a single PowerPoint file that is easy to share with their sales and marketing team.

## SOFTWARE ORIENTATION

This lesson helps you effectively incorporate graphics and multimedia into your PowerPoint presentations.

**Figure 5-1**

Animation and timing controls

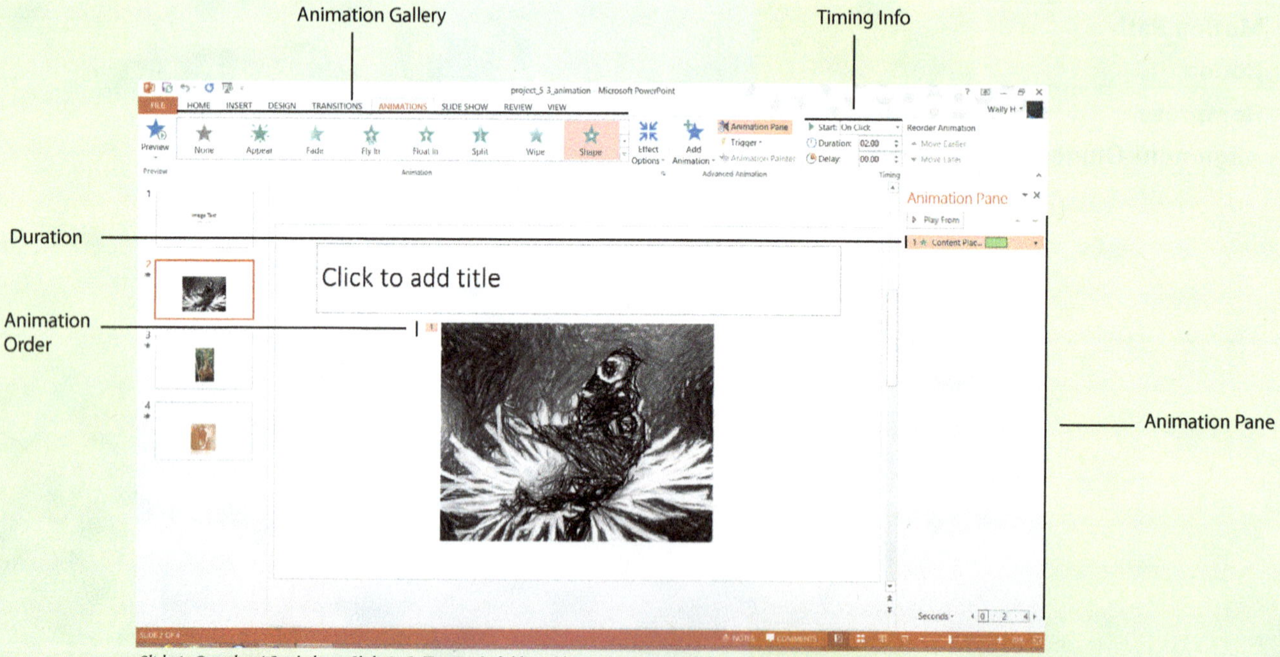


*Slide 1: © enduro/iStockphoto; Slide 2: © Tom Brakefield/Stockbyte/Getty Images; Slide 3: © Fuse/Getty Images*

## STARTING UP

In this lesson, you'll work with several files from the PPT05lessons folder. Make sure that you have loaded the OfficeLessons folder onto your computer.

## BEYOND BULLETED LISTS AND BAR GRAPHS

Now we come to the final elements of a slide builder's toolkit: graphics, sound, and video. PowerPoint handles images and video objects just as any other floating visual elements, with the standard Design and Format tools. Sound effects and music, much less common in presentations for a variety of reasons, work a little like animations or transitions: you can cue a sound up with a fixed time delay or start it with a mouse click.

In this lesson, you'll also explore PowerPoint's image-editing toolkit, which lets you make simple adjustments to images embedded in your slides. Finally, you'll add some custom animations to your slide elements, turning a single text block into a swirl of motion.

Your final product will look something like **pp05a-finished.pptx**; feel free to use it as a visual guide while you work through the exercises in this lesson. Read the comments in the sample file, which walk through the design choices behind the presentation.

### Recoloring and adjusting images

**Bottom Line**

The Picture Tools > Format tab in PowerPoint contains a collection of tools to set the layout, framing, size, and shape of an image; the same tools can be applied to clip art, SmartArt, and text boxes. But Word provides a set of tools to alter the content of an image (the Format tab's Adjust group), which you can use to obtain fine-grained control over the look of an image when attention to detail could have a huge impact on a slide's effectiveness.

Crucially, these are nondestructive editing tools: no matter how many edits you make to an embedded image, you can return to the original with a single click.

We'll use the image formatting tools available in Word to blend the image in slide 2 into the muted palette of the presentation.

**STEP BY STEP** **Recoloring and adjusting images**

1. Open the file called **pp05a.pptx** found in the PPT05lessons folder.
2. Choose **File > Save As** and navigate to the PPT05lessons folder. Name the file **pp05a_work** and click Save.
3. Select slide **2** in your presentation and click the blue image.

4 Click **Picture Tools > Format**. Recast the image in black and white by clicking **Adjust > Color > Grayscale** (Figure 5-2 shows the gallery of Color options.).

**Figure 5-2**

Choose Grayscale from the Color options.

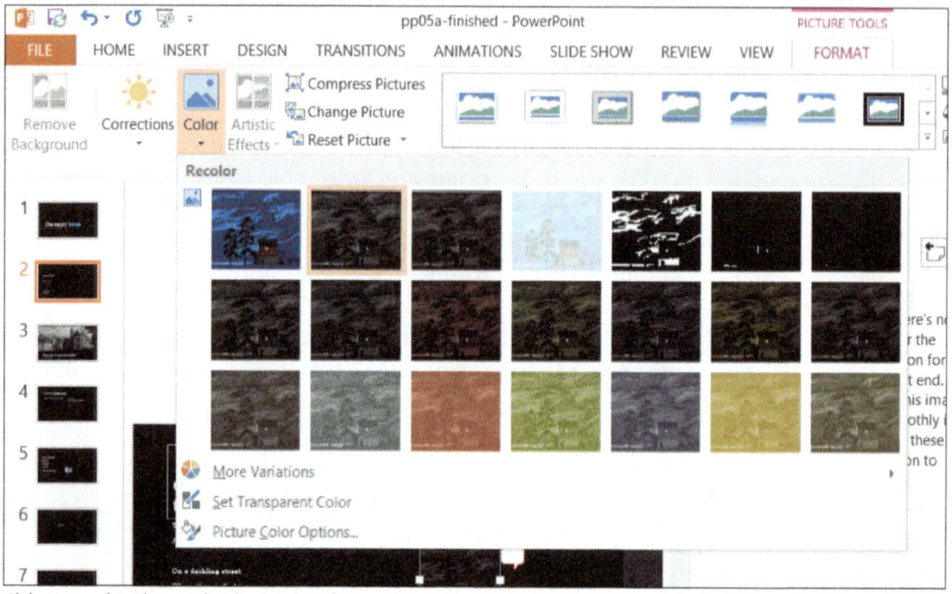


*Slides 2, 3, and 5: Photos used with permission of Microsoft*

5 Click **Adjust > Corrections > Brightness –20% Contrast –20%** to further mute the image.

6 Finally, click **Picture Styles > Picture Effects > Soft Edges > Soft Edges Options** to bring up the Format pane. Set the Soft Edges value to **17pt**.

The Format pane is your main tool for tweaking individual slide and floating element parameters.

7 Save your work, and then preview this slide only by pressing **Shift+F5** (then **Escape** when you're done).

**Take Note** At this level of blend, brightness, and contrast, the image is hard to make out, but in a dark room it will demand attention without stealing from the recurring blue text. Indeed, that's our main purpose in pulling the color out of the image in slide 2: it pulls focus into the slide while leaving the word *house* prominent.

**Bottom Line**

## Cropping an image

The Format tab includes a **Crop** tool for paring away unwanted parts of an image to keep viewer emphasis on the most important visual content. The image on slide 5 image stands out too much from its background; instead of blending it, we'll crop away the bright background.

**STEP BY STEP** **Cropping an image**

1 Select slide **5** and click the image of the keys.

2 Click **Format > Size > Crop > Crop to Shape > Oval** (in the Basic Shapes section).

3 Right-click the cropped image and choose **Format Picture**.

4 In the Size & Properties tab, deselect **Lock aspect ratio** and enter **1.25** for both width and height. Then go to the Effects tab and apply the Paint Strokes effect (shown in Figure 5-3) from the Artistic Effects gallery .

The Paint Strokes effect makes the image a little difficult to parse at first; this is not ideal for a conventional presentation, but it fits the visual tone of our narrative slide deck.

**Figure 5-3**

The image of the keys with cropping and effects applied.

*Photo used with permission of Microsoft*

5 Drag the resized image to center right, a little closer to the right edge of the slide. Save your work.

## Reordering images in the object stack

**Bottom Line**

At times, images and text will overlap, either because a slide is crowded or because you're using one element as background for another. You can alter the order of objects in the stack with the Format > Arrange tools, and use the **Selection pane** to grab an object hidden behind other slide elements.

**STEP BY STEP** **Reordering images in the object stack**

1 Select slide **3**. Click **Insert > Text > Text Box** and then click an empty region of the slide.

2 In the text box, type **It willed as it was**.

3 Click **Format > Arrange > Selection pane**. Click the eye icon next to Picture Placeholder 7 (to hide the image), then click to select the **TextBox 1** entry (Figure 5-4), and click again to edit its name. Rename TextBox 1 to **will-text**.

**Figure 5-4**

Toggling the visibility of slide elements in the Selection pane.

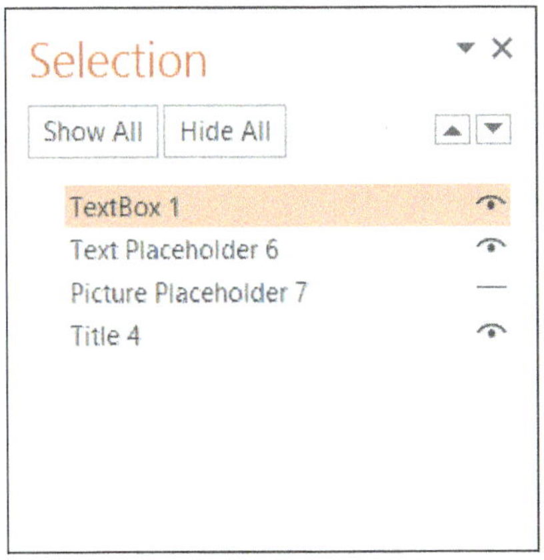


4 Rename Picture Placeholder 7 to **house-img**. Keep it invisible for the moment.

5 Position the new text box an inch below the midline of the slide, above *It breathes where it will*.

6 In the Selection pane, drag will-text to the bottom of the stack, then click to make house-img visible, obscuring the text box. Close the Selection pane, and then save your work.

The Selection pane works a little like a visual outline of the slide; just as is the case with outlines and text, the Selection pane lets you change the relative positions of objects without using the object's handles or selecting objects in the slide area itself. In this case, we're hiding the new text behind the image in order to reveal it later by fading the image out. We'll add that effect next.

## HEIGHTENING VISUAL IMPACT WITH ANIMATIONS

The basic commands for adding animations and transitions to a slide show were covered in Lesson 2, "Getting Started with PowerPoint 2013"; in this section, we'll add a single exit animation to generate a novel visual effect (revealing hidden text), then fill a slide with a complex jumble of animations using custom movement paths.

### Creating a crossfade effect with stacked slide elements

**Bottom Line**

First we'll finish slide 3 with a subtle animation effect. A "crossfade" is just a combination of two animations: one object fades out, another fades in, in its place.

**STEP BY STEP** **Creating a crossfade effect**

1 Click to select the **house** image in slide 3.

2 Open the Animations tab and scroll down the Animation gallery to apply the **Fade** exit animation.

3 In the Timing group, set the animation's duration to **3** (seconds). Save your work.

Preview the slide with Shift+F5. PowerPoint doesn't offer a crossfade animation equivalent to the Fade transition (which fades out one slide and fades in another), but this stack/fadeout combination accomplishes the same thing.

**Take Note** It's easy to add a sound to play along with an animation: just select Effect Options in the Animation pane and select the sound file. You can also play audio over a slide transition by selecting Transitions > Timing > Sound. Feel free to experiment with these commands on your own; you'll work with PowerPoint's audio tools in a later section of this lesson.

### Creating complex scenes by clustering animations

**Motion Paths** let you control the movement of an object around the space of the slide. Moving a single object draws attention to it; moving several objects simultaneously draws attention to the quality of the movement rather than any one moving part. The fifth slide of our storybook slide show offers an interesting opportunity to use a cluster of animations for dramatic purposes. (Important: This is a lengthy process; save your file often as you work through this section.)

**STEP BY STEP** **Creating complex scenes by clustering animations**

1 Select slide **5**. Click the title, ***Still it stands***. Apply the **Custom Path** animation (under Motion Paths in the gallery) in the Animations tab.

The mouse pointer now switches to a reticle. (On a touch device there's no pointer and the next step will be quite natural; this is another example of how touchscreens work great with PowerPoint 2013.)

2 Click and drag to draw a smooth arch shape from the current title's location to the lower-right corner of the slide. Press **Enter** when the line is drawn. Preview the new animation by pressing **Shift+F5**.

3 Now click the main text area located underneath the title, and then click **Advanced Animation > Add Animation > Custom Path**. Draw a wide flat loop that circles to the right, down a bit, then back to a spot just below its start. Press **Enter** when the arc is drawn, and then open the Animation pane in the Advanced Animation group.

**Figure 5-5**

PowerPoint animates a text block line by line.

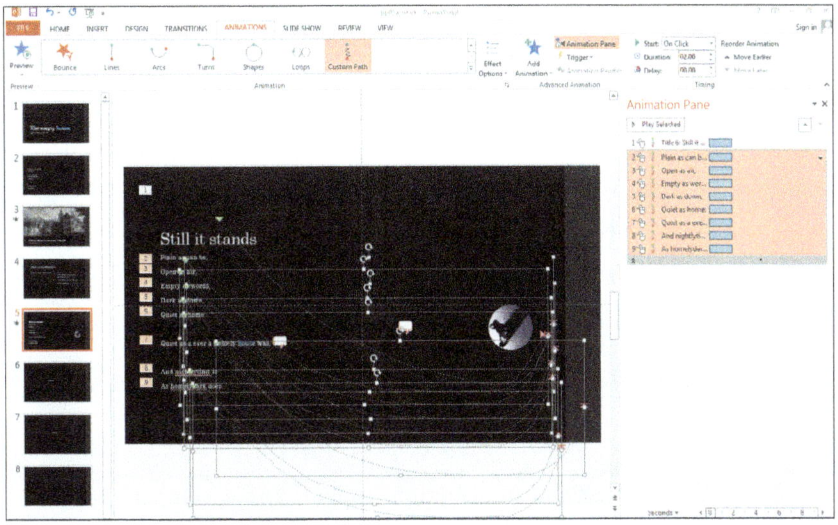


*Slides 2, 3, and 5: Photos used with permission of Microsoft*

As you can see in Figure 5-5, PowerPoint applies the animation to the entire contents of the text box, but by default, it splits the animation up by line. (You can customize this behavior under Effect Options > Sequence.) Our eight-line text box is now animated in eight separate steps, one line at a time. We're going for a different effect.

4 Click the double caret in the Animation pane to expand the animation list. The eight grouped animations are selected by default. Ctrl+click ***Plain as can be*** in the pane to deselect it, and then right-click and choose **Remove** to remove the remaining animations. Only two remain: the title and *Plain as can be*.

The rest of the work for this slide follows the same principle: animate the text block, then delete every new entry from the Animation pane except the line you want to apply the new animation to. Notice that these animations are pulling the short poem apart: for the purposes in this lesson, we'll sacrifice readability for the sake of visual drama.

**Take Note** PowerPoint can't animate a single word from a line of text; its chosen level of abstraction is the paragraph. If you need to animate one word from a text string, you'll have to do extra work: for instance, you might just animate a second text box with only that word in it, or with all the other text in the background color instead of the text color. Alternatively, you could download scripts online to split up a line of text into individual text boxes. As always, deciding in advance the kind of visual effect you want to generate can save you a lot of work when you start the actual animating.

5 Repeat steps 3 and 4 for four or five more lines of the main text block, drawing a motion path for the block and then deleting all the newly-added Animation pane entries except the one you want to keep.

**Take Note** Make sure to use Add Animation rather than the gallery when applying additional motion paths; otherwise, you'll replace the existing text animation instead of adding a second animation.

6 Select every animation in the Animation pane except the first two (title and first text line), right-click the selection, and choose **Start With Previous**. Save your work, then press **Shift+F5** to preview.

The slide animates in two parts: the title curves to bottom-right corner on your first click, and then the lines of text fly apart all at once on second click. Now we'll change the slide further, for drama's sake: we'll have these two effects occur without a click, as if the text were moving on its own.

**Take Note** To add more drama to our animation design, we might have moved each line of the text box just a handful of pixels very slowly, perhaps an inch over ten seconds. However, for the purposes of this exercise, it's more useful to see quick dramatic movement.

7 Click in the Animation pane to clear your selection. Then right-click entry **1** in the pane, and select **Start After Previous**. Set its Delay in the Timing group of the Animations tab to **2** seconds. Preview the slide with **Shift+F5**, and then save your work.

It takes a lot of work to generate this effect, but remember that PowerPoint isn't really an animation program. That said, it's a pleasantly odd visual effect that seems right for this particular slide deck.

After working on an appropriate set of visuals, we'll work on another of our audience's senses: hearing.

## ENRICHING SLIDES WITH SOUND EFFECTS

Most PowerPoint presentations support and accompany talks in front of audiences, and sound effects and music are generally a secondary concern at talks, if they're present at all. But a well-chosen musical transition or subtle background sound can have a big effect on an attentive crowd, or grab hold of an inattentive one.

PowerPoint 2013 offers basic support for including audio files in slide shows as both clickable objects and background sounds, and some basic editing commands (though nothing on the level of its image-editing commands). You can trim, fade, and trigger your sounds, but actual audio content editing has to be done in an external app; as a result, smart sound selection and pre-editing make a big difference to the effectiveness of your presentation audio.

In this section, you'll add both background and triggered sounds to your slide deck.

### Adding background sounds to a presentation

**Bottom Line** Adding background music or sound effects to an entire presentation is as simple as embedding an audio object in slide 1 (see Figure 5-6) and ordering it to play automatically on a loop.

**STEP BY STEP** **Adding background sounds to a presentation**

1 Select slide **1**. Click **Insert > Media > Audio > Audio on My PC**. Navigate to your PPT05lessons folder and select **pp05c.mp3**. Click **Insert**.

2 Drag the inserted speaker icon to the lower-right corner of the slide (just for convenience while editing). In the **Audio Tools > Playback** tab, select **Play in Background** and **Volume > Low**.

3 Set both the Fade In and Fade Out values to **2** seconds.

Now preview the presentation from the beginning by pressing **F5**. As you can see, selecting an Audio Style toggles several audio settings at once: the Play Across Slides and Loop until Stopped options are now selected, for instance, to keep the sound rolling through the entire presentation.

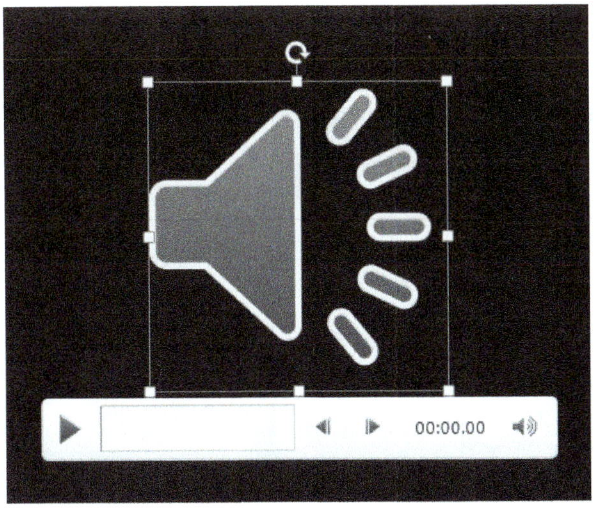


**Figure 5-6**

Editing playback parameters for embedded audio.

**Take Note** When choosing ambient background sounds, look for consistent volume levels; an unexpected, unwanted spike in volume can interrupt the momentum of a presentation.

## Trimming and triggering sound effects

**Bottom Line**

Sound effects in PowerPoint are triggered just as animations are: either cued up to begin after a delay, or set to play on a click. They can also be set to play along with animations or over slide transitions. We'll add an eerie heartbeat sound to one of our later slides, with a long fadeout. (Remember that the background sound will be playing quietly the whole time.)

The animation on slide 5 takes six or seven seconds from slide transition to final state; we'll trim our sound file to last just a bit longer than that, but instead of playing the sound automatically, we'll leave it to trigger when the user clicks the key image.

**Take Note** We've approached this slide show as a kind of storybook, for viewing on a computer or at a kiosk, but it could also work as an oddball public presentation. By triggering the sound on slide 5 to occur on a click rather than playing it automatically, we generate an interesting effect: a presenter can use the eerie sound to accentuate the animation or underscore additional narration; an onscreen reader exploring the slide would see the pointer change as it passed over the image, and get a strange surprised when she clicked.

**STEP BY STEP** **Trimming and triggering sound effects**

1. Select slide **5** and click **Insert > Media > Audio > Audio on My PC**. Select **pp05d.mp3**.
2. Move the audio icon to the corner of the slide as before. Select **Playback > Audio Options > Hide During Show** to make the icon invisible during the presentation.
3. Click **Editing > Trim Audio**. Set the clip's End Time to **10** (seconds) and click **OK** or press **Enter**. Then set the Fade Out value (in Playback > Editing) to **10**.

Neither of the edits in step 3 affects the original file; as with nondestructive image adjustments, you can always return to the unaltered original file. Now we'll customize the trigger, linking the sound to a click on the key image.

4 Open the Animation pane. Right-click the sound **pp05d** and select **Timing** (See Figure 5-7.).

5 In the Timing dialog, select **Start effect on click of Content Placeholder 9**. Click **OK** or press **Enter**. Save your work, and then preview the slide with **Shift+F5**.

**Figure 5-7**

Linking audio playback to a trigger object in the Animation pane.

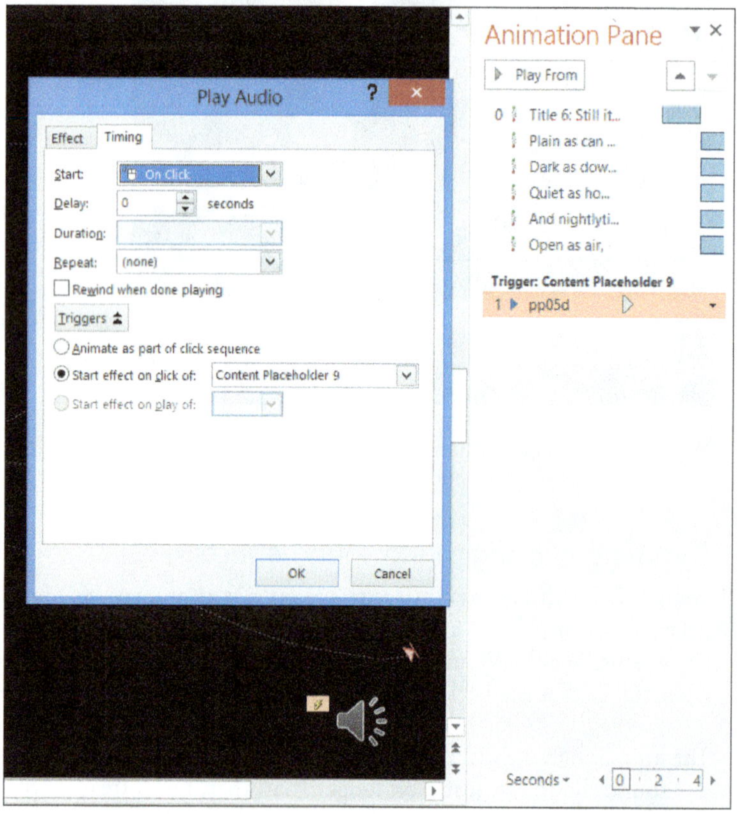


One nice side effect of linking the sound effect to a specific trigger object, rather than a click anywhere in the slide, is that the sound can play even while the text block animation is playing. This fits the off-kilter quality of the slide deck as a whole.

## Adding custom actions to slide objects

**Bottom Line**

In the previous section you linked audio playback to a click event. The process can also work in reverse: you can add an Action to a slide element, which triggers anything from a simple hyperlink to launching an external application. In this section, you'll add hyperlinks to the first and last slides by adding two invisible Shape objects and attaching a Hyperlink Action to each.

**Take Note**

PowerPoint does allow you to style your hyperlink text to an extent (by customizing font and color by modifying the Theme), but there's no option to turn off hyperlink underlines for text objects. This section shows you how to perform two effects: illustrate triggered actions, and generate non-underlined hyperlinks through a workaround.

**STEP BY STEP** **Adding custom actions to slide objects**

1 Select slide **1** and click **Insert > Illustrations > Shapes > Rectangle**. Draw a tight rectangle over the word *house*.

2 Click the rectangle and select **Insert > Links > Action**. Select **Hyperlink to: Last slide** as in Figure 5-8.

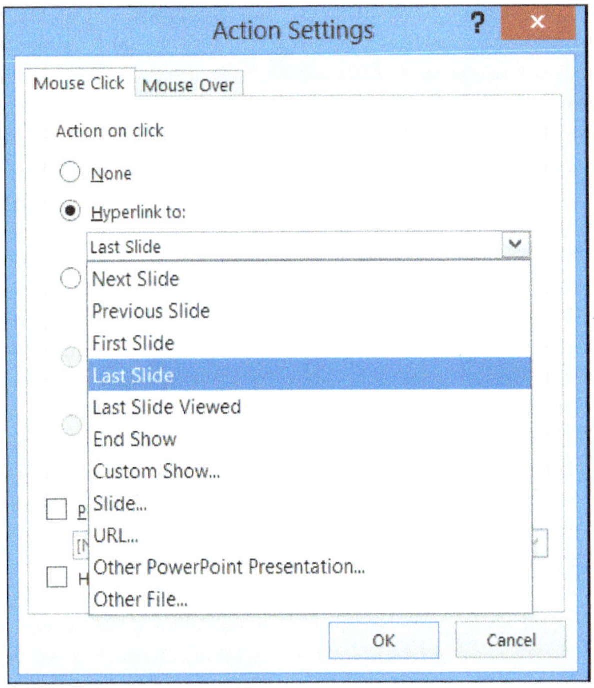


**Figure 5-8**

Associating a hyperlink action with a slide element.

3 Click **OK**. Select the new rectangle shape. In the Format tab, select **Shape Fill > No Fill** and **Shape Outline > No Outline**.

4 Repeat steps 1–3 to add a similar hyperlinked rectangle over the question mark in slide 8. Point the hyperlink toward the First Slide.

5 Save your work and test the links by previewing the slide show.

The Action Settings dialog box can also run macros (chains of actions), load external apps, or edit OLE objects (such as a linked Excel spreadsheet), either on mouse click or on mouse over. This lesson only scratches the surface of what a dedicated presentation designer could do in terms of interactivity, but the tools themselves don't get any more complex than what you've already seen.

## INTEGRATING VIDEO INTO A PRESENTATION

Fast processors, cheap bandwidth, big hard drives, and high-quality screens mean using video in a presentation is now neither a gimmick nor a hassle. Online media files (video, audio, images, templates) are easily incorporated into Office 2013 files, and adding a YouTube video into your presentation is no more complicated than embedding a local file.

In this final section, you'll embed, style, and trigger videos in your slide show.

### Embedding and formatting videos

**Bottom Line**

Microsoft's Bing video search is built into PowerPoint 2013, and YouTube can be added as an online video source. We'll use a video from Bing and another from a local file.

**Take Note** YouTube videos appear in Bing search (you'll find a YouTube video with Bing in this section), but you can also link your Live login to your YouTube account, if you have one, for access to account-specific information. Regardless, to add YouTube search to the Online Video screen in Office, click the Also Insert From YouTube icon in the Insert Video screen.

## STEP BY STEP Embedding and formatting a video

1. Add an empty slide to the end of the presentation. Click **Insert > Media > Video > Online Video**.
2. In the Bing Video Search box, type **house of leaves intro**. Select the first result (the minute-long YouTube video, House of Leaves – Intro) and click **Insert**.

PowerPoint embeds a single frame of the video, which serves as a preview image. Clicking the preview frame during the presentation brings up the YouTube player, which streams from *youtube.com*. We can skip the preview frame, however:

3. Select the image. Click **Video Tools > Playback > Start > Automatically**. The video won't play when the slide displays, but the preview image won't appear.
4. Click **Video Tools > Format > Video Styles > Slope Beveled Rectangle** in the Subtle categoryto add a border to the image, shown in Figure 5-9.
5. Save your work, then preview the slide.

When viewing the slide, click the embedded player to start the video, and press Escape to stop playback and clear the video frame.

**Figure 5-9**

PowerPoint treats video display and playback as animation events.

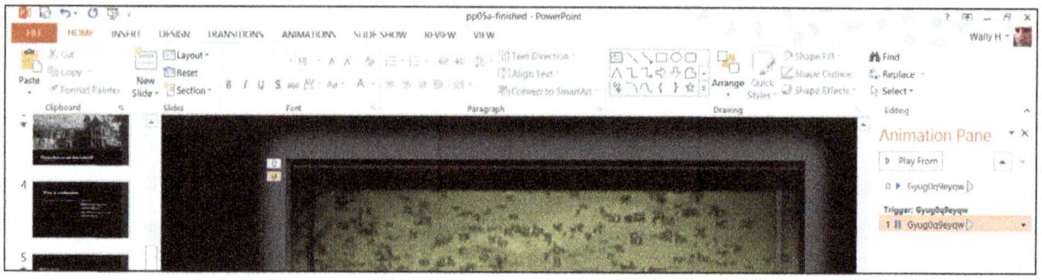


*Slides 2, 3, and 5: Photos used with permission of Microsoft*

PowerPoint has no control over the content of videos; you can alter the preview image with the standard image-adjustment tools (Video Tools > Format), but during playback, PowerPoint only draws the border and effects such as glow, shadow, and 3-D rotation. Note that the Trim Video command is greyed out.

## Considerations for embedding local video

Trimming and formatting local video works the same as for audio: select an embedded video clip, set playback options in Video Tools > Playback, adjust the frame and preview image in Video Tools > Format, and go. Unlike YouTube and other online videos, local video files can be altered to fit the needs of the presentation: Playback > Trim Video and the Fade tools become available, along with Bookmarks (which let you jump to specific spots in the Trim window) and Volume controls.

One extra consideration arises with local video: media format compatibility. PowerPoint 2013 works best with .mp4 video (H.264 **codec**) and .m4a (AAC) audio, but also supports the following video formats:

- **.avi, .wmv, and MPEG (.mpg/.mpeg):** common local video formats
- **.swf:** Flash video, intended for online streaming
- **.asf:** a multimedia streaming format for Windows

PowerPoint RT, on the Microsoft Surface, is less robust; Microsoft encourages Windows RT users to use .mp4 and .m4a media. PowerPoint 2013 can also play Apple's QuickTime video formats (.mov, .mp4, .qt) through the external QuickTime Player app.

As you can see, keeping up with video formats takes a bit of work; your best bet is to get your video file into exactly the shape you want using an external editor such as Premiere or Final Cut, then export to PowerPoint's preferred format.

## Media compression and compatibility

# Workplace Ready

**Bottom Line**

If disk space is at a premium (on a tablet or USB key, for instance), you could **compress** the audio and video in your slide show; doing so also makes for smoother playback on older machines. Since workplace ready embedded media are stored within the .pptx file itself, compressing your media will directly reduce the size of your presentation.

**Take Note** Comparing **pp05a.pptx** and **pp05a-finished.pptx** gives a sense of the relative size of embedded media files: the presentation with three small embedded images comes to less than 200KB the uncompressed final presentation adds another megabyte or so. Nearly the entire difference in size comes from a single audio file. Optimizing embedded media compatibility nearly doubles the file size, and compressing doesn't make any difference, since the media files are already in low-bitrate mp3 format. With larger, higher-quality media files, compression will be more useful.

Moreover, if you end up presenting your slide show using someone else's computer, media compatibility may become an issue. Fortunately, PowerPoint's File > Info tab includes tools to improve portability and performance. To see them in action, just open up the File tab:

**STEP BY STEP** **Media compression and compatibility**

1 If you haven't already done so, open your presentation and click the File tab to reach the Backstage View.

2 Click **Optimize Compatibility**. In the Media Size and Performance text below, note that embedded media files now measures 3MB.

3 Click **Compress Media > Presentation Quality** to eliminate wasted space in the file without obviously affecting playback quality. This saves 0.1MB. Save your work.

The more you compress the presentation, the more image and audio quality can degrade. Because you can undo a compression step, it's easy to e-mail a minimum-size presentation to a colleague for review, and burn the uncompressed file to disc (or upload it to the cloud) for actual presentation.

The other tools in the Info tab will come in handy in the next lesson, when you learn how to deliver your presentation.

## LAYING OUT SLIDE ELEMENTS

In earlier lessons, you learned about PowerPoint's alignment guides and layout tools. In this final section, you'll get a closer look at a crucial slide layout tool: PowerPoint's hidden grid, which guides object placement as gently or forcefully as you need. The grid and guides are shown in Figure 5-10.

Figure 5-10

Alignment guides and the slide grid are invaluable aids for relative positioning of slide elements

*Photos used with permission of Microsoft*

### Taking advantage of the grid

**Bottom Line**

Slide elements occupy space in a 1⁄12" grid, which can be made magnetic with the Snap to Grid setting. When Snap to Grid is enabled, objects in a slide will automatically stick to the nearest gridline rather than sliding pixel by pixel, making alignment and layout much less fiddly and a little less flexible. In this section, you'll vary PowerPoint's grid settings to see the kind of flexibility that they permit.

**STEP BY STEP** **Aligning items to the grid**

1 Add a new empty slide, slide 10. Use **Insert > Images > Pictures** to add three images to the new slide from your PPT05lessons folder: **pp05f.jpg**, **pp05g.jpg**, and **pp05h.jpg**.

2 Right-click an empty part of the slide and select **Grid and Guides**.

3 Select all the check boxes in the dialog box, and set the Spacing to **1/2"**. Click **OK**.

Open the View tab and notice that Show > Gridlines and Show > Guides are now enabled; they're equivalent to the Display grid and Display drawing guides toggles in the dialog box.

Now try dragging the images around the slide. There are two features to note here. The images stick instead of moving smoothly across the slide, naturally falling into grooves that are ½" apart from each other; when the centers or edges of the images are aligned, red **alignment guides** appear.

4 Set the grid back to 1⁄12". Place the smaller image near the center of the slide, and place one of the ghost images directly below it.

5 Shift+click to select both images, then click **Picture Tools > Format > Arrange > Align > Align Center** to align their centers vertically. Then drag to align the centers of the two images with the dotted vertical line down the middle of the slide, and place the small image dead center in the slide. (It will snap into place.)

6 Deselect the images and click only the lower large image. Shift+drag it vertically until its top edge is aligned with the bottom grid line on the slide as in Figure 5-11.

*Photos used with permission of Microsoft*

**Figure 5-11**

When two images' centers are horizontally aligned, they can move freely straight up and down without breaking the alignment.

When you press and hold Shift while moving a slide element, it sticks to one cardinal direction of movement: either straight up and down or right and left. This is handy when you've already lined up image centers or edges, and need to vary just one positional axis.

## Working with alignment guides

**Bottom Line**

PowerPoint's layout guides appear when the centers or edges of two objects are in alignment. They're sticky meaning objects will gravitate toward them,, though their effect is much less dramatic than a coarse grid. To see them at work, drag one image slowly past another:

STEP BY STEP **Using alignment guides**

1 Place the three images in a rough L-shape with roughly an inch between them and the small image at the joint of the L, as in Figure 5-12

**Figure 5-12**

For fine-grained object placement, make frequent use of the Zoom slider.

*Photos used with permission of Microsoft*

2 Align the left edges of the small image and the one below it. Then align the top edges of the small image and the one beside it, and place the side image roughly an inch away from the small image.

3 Shift+drag the lower image vertically until it's aligned with both of the other images.

With the image edges aligned, an off-kilter grid layout emerges. Image guides are more helpful when you place the three images in a line:

4 Zoom out. Drag the bottom image to the left side of the slide, positioned so all three top edges are aligned.

5 Shift+drag the smaller image to the right; when the three images are horizontally balanced, two equidistant markers will appear in the gaps between them.

6 Finally, select the current slide in the left pane of the screen and delete it from the presentation. (It doesn't quite fit the lonely house storybook theme.)

## What you learned in this lesson:

- Recolor, Adjust, Crop, and Stack Images
- Heighten Visual Impact with Animations
- Enrich Slides with Sound Effects and Background Sound
- Add Media Triggers to Slide Objects
- Embed Online and Local Video
- Use Grids and Guides to Lay Out Slides

# Knowledge Assessment

## Matching

**Match each term to its description or definition.**

1. Picture Tools > Format
2. crop
3. Artistic Effects
4. alignment guides
5. Custom Action
6. compression
7. View > Show
8. Animation Pane
9. trigger
10. Selection Pane

a. downsizing embedded media to keep .pptx file manageable
b. indicate even spacing/distribution of slide elements
c. toggles for positioning guides like ruler, gridlines
d. extract just one region of an image
e. lists animations in order w/sparklines indicating duration
f. lists objects in slide, front to back
g. Image adjustment, style, stacking tools
h. interaction (e.g., click) to set off effect (e.g., play audio)
i. run program, open hyperlink, play sound (etc.) on click
j. blur, glowing edges, pen strokes, etc.

## Fill in the Blanks

**Complete the following sentences by writing the correct word or words in the blanks provided.**

1. Shortening an audio file is called _____ the file.
2. An animated object's trajectory is called its _____.
3. To include only part of an embedded image, _____ the image to the desired dimensions.
4. The _____ Pane lets users move objects forward and backward in the object "stack."
5. The frame, color, and shape of an image are edited in the Picture Tools > _____ tab.
6. The _____ > _____ > _____ > Grayscale command converts a color image to black, white, and grey.
7. PowerPoint's favored video format is _____ files.
8. When images are evenly spaced across the slide while dragging, _____ will appear between them.
9. Toggle alignment guides and the grid in the _____ > _____ group.
10. Office's Online Video search command uses the _____ service by default, rather than searching (e.g.) YouTube directly.

# Competency Assessment

## Project 5-1: Adding Images to a Presentation

**In this exercise you will search for images online and insert them into a new slide show.**

1. Create a new blank presentation and save it as **project_5-1_images**.
2. Add the text **Image Test** (title) and **PPT Lesson 5** (subtitle) to slide 1.
3. Add a new slide (**Ctrl+M**) and in its content area click the **Online Pictures** control.
4. Do a **clip art** (not Bing image) search for **butterfly on flower**. Insert one of the resulting images.
5. Add a third slide with the same layout; insert online clip art using the search string **orangutan hanging**.
6. Add a new slide, slide 4, with the Blank layout. Click **Insert > Online Pictures** to add a piece of clip art using the search string **safari lion**.

   Note the way PowerPoint lays out the image on blank vs structured slides.
7. Save and close your document.

## Project 5-2: Styling and Cropping Images

**This exercise utilizes PowerPoint's image formatting and style tools.**

1. Open the exercise file **5-2-source** and save it as **project_5-2_crop**.
2. Select the image on slide 2.
3. Click **Picture Tools > Format > Artistic Effects > Pencil Grayscale**.
4. Select the image on slide 3.
5. Click **Format > Crop**.
6. Drag the sides and top of the cropping frame toward the orangutan in the image, to make a "tightly cropped," tall, thin frame.
7. When you have the crop you want, press **Escape**.
8. Crop the lion image on slide 4 to a tight 3.5"x3.5" square. Apply the **Orange, Accent color 2 Light** color correction and **Reflected Rounded Rectangle** Picture Style.
9. Save and close your document.

# Proficiency Assessment

## Project 5-3: Animating Slide Elements

**In this exercise you'll add a couple of animations to slide elements.**

1. Open the exercise file **5-3-source** and save it as **project_5-3_animation.**
2. Select the modified butterfly image on slide 2. Apply the **Shape** animation with the **Diamond** Effect Option.
3. Add a Fade transition from slide 2 to slide 3 with duration **3** seconds.
4. Select the slide 4 image and click the **Lines** motion path animation.
5. After the preview plays, drag the red destination dot to the upper right of the slide. Then press **Enter**.
6. Preview the slide 4 animation by clicking the **Play Animations** icon next to slide 4 in the slide selector pane.
7. Save and close your document.

### Project 5-4: Setting Transition Timing and Duration

**This exercise involves PowerPoint's slide transitions, including duration and delay parameters.**

1. Create a new blank presentation and save it as **project_5-4_pictureshow**.
2. Delete the title slide and add four (4) slides with Blank layouts. In the Design menu, change the slide size to 5"x5".
3. Insert an image into each slide.
4. Create a "photo montage" effect by applying Fade transitions into each slide, with 2 second duration, and Advance each Slide after 2 seconds.
5. Set up the slide show to loop continuously (**Slide Show > Set Up Slide Show**).
6. Save and close your document.

## Mastery Assessment

### Project 5-5: Triggering Media

**In this exercise you'll add custom actions to a button image in a slide.**

1. Create a new blank document and save it as **project_5-5_trigger**.
2. Insert a forward arrow icon on slide 1, and some image on slide 2.
3. Use the **Insert > Action** command to give the button special properties:

   On click, advance to slide 2

   Highlight on mouse over
4. Save and close your document.

(Note what happens if you add a transition into slide 2 – it will play whether you advance from 1 to 2 regularly or by clicking the button.)

### Project 5-6: Using Alignment Guides

**This exercise challenges you to use alignment guides and the Format Pane to precisely lay out a slide full of images.**

1. Open the project file **5-6-source** and save it as **project_5-6_alignment**.
2. Resize each image in your document to be 1"x1" square.
3. Turn on alignment guides and arrange the slide so each image is the corner of a square, with 1" separating each pair of images along the square's edge.

   You will need to use the Format Picture > Size & Position tools for this task along with the alignment guides.
4. Save and close your document.

# 6 Delivering Your Presentation

## LESSON SKILL MATRIX

| In this lesson, you will learn the following skills: | |
|---|---|
| Customizing Your Presentation Setup | Using the Laser Pointer, Highlighter, and Ink Annotations |
| Precisely Controlling Your Presentation | Rehearsing Timings and Recording Narration |
| Using Slide Show and Presenter Views | Delivering a Presentation Online |
| Creating Speaker Notes and Handouts | |

## KEY TERMS

- Kiosk
- Set Up Show
- Custom Slide Show
- Presenter View
- Slide Show view
- Notes Page
- Notes Master
- Handout Master
- Laser Pointer
- Ink Annotations
- Narration

©sturti/iStockPhoto

©sturti/iStockPhoto

Contoso internships end with a presentation to the project heads: "What I Accomplished This Summer." Impressing the heads isn't easy...especially when each talk is just 10 minutes long. There's no room for stumbling, being surprised by which slide is next, not being able to find a laser pointer, or not having printed notes to hand when a strong presentation might mean future employment. Fortunately, PowerPoint gives presenters control over even the finest details of their talks. "Are there any questions?"

## SOFTWARE ORIENTATION

This lesson helps you understand how to deliver effective presentations using PowerPoint.

**Figure 6-1**

The Presenter View collects PowerPoint's full suite of presenter tools in a clean multi-pane interface.

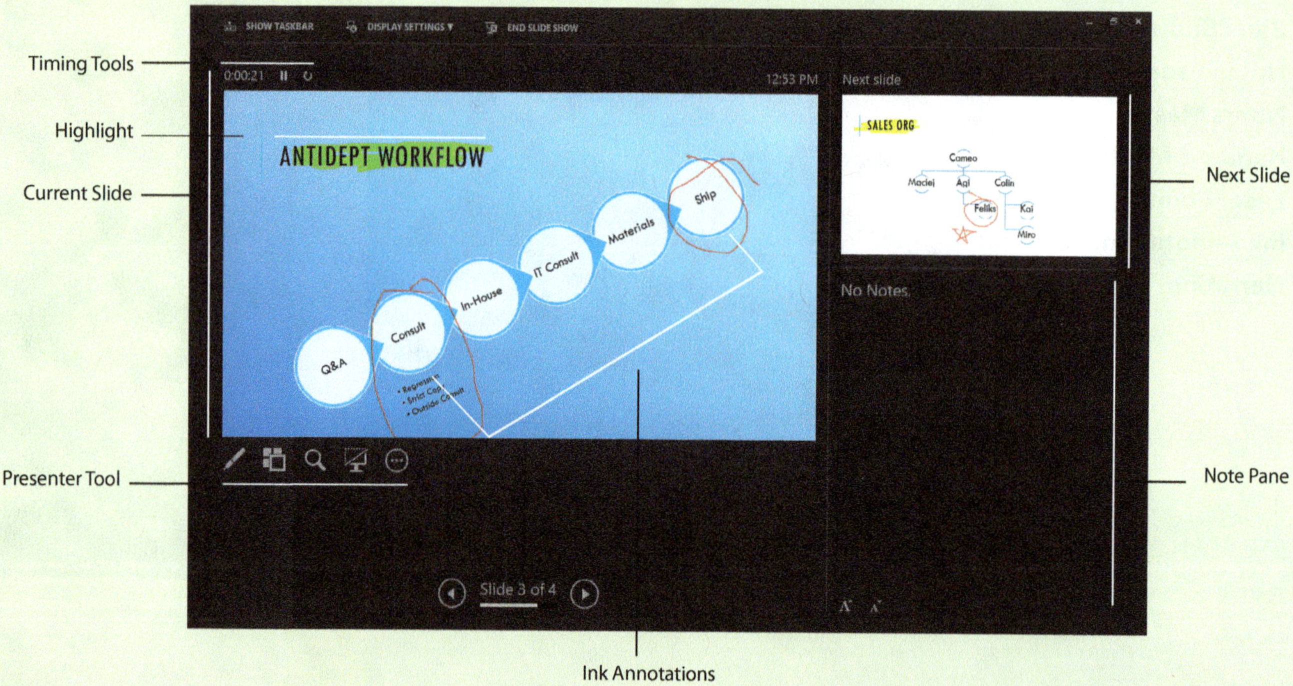

## STARTING UP

In this lesson, you'll work with several files from the PPT06lessons folder. Make sure that you have loaded the OfficeLessons folder onto your computer.

## PRESENTATIONS ARE PERFORMANCES

Presentations are meant to be *presented* your slides don't work unless they work for an audience. Regularly previewing and practicing your presentation while building your slide deck will give you a clear sense of whether the slides form an effective whole, and rehearsing will make for a much smoother and more confident presentation, too.

Your workflow should build toward an outstanding talk, not just perfect slides. Fortunately, PowerPoint 2013 offers a full suite of presentation tools to structure and improve the performance side of your slide show, including a totally redesigned Presenter View. In this lesson, you'll start from a finished slide deck, rehearse your presentation (and put your slide notes to use), pin down the timing of your talk, and use PowerPoint's pen tools and hand-drawn annotations to put audience focus right where it belongs. Then you'll learn to assemble multiple custom presentations from a single slide deck and shape your printed notes and audience handouts to your needs.

**Take Note** Most PowerPoint slide shows are used to accompany talks. Designing for a public kiosk is a separate but related concern, and this lesson gives an overview of kiosk aesthetics and usability. If you don't have access to a second screen or projector, you can go ahead and skip the material. Finally, the art of giving a strong presentation is rich enough to fill several books on its own; we will only cover the essentials in this one.

## PREPARING FOR YOUR PRESENTATION

Before you begin your talk, you need to configure your hardware (presenter console and display screen) and PowerPoint (the presentation app). As far as your hardware is concerned, the best advice we can give is to get to the room early and test out your projector because it rarely just works. Configuring the presentation itself is much more under your control.

### Setting up the slide show

**Bottom Line**

The Set Up Slide Show command (see Figure 6-2) offers several options to customize your slide deck and the dynamics of your presentation: looping, graphics settings, pen/pointer settings, slide controls, and monitor configuration will vary based on the type of slide show you're preparing:

- **Presented by a speaker (full screen)**: the standard big-slides-behind-the-speaker view, to accompany a talk.
- **Browsed by an individual (window)**: the full presentation running in a window with limited interactivity (for example, click to advance doesn't work); ideal for integrating presentations with work in other apps.
- **Browsed at a kiosk (full screen)**: an unattended presentation, minimally interactive, meant to transition automatically between slides and loop endlessly (for example, on a trade show floor or as advertising).

A **kiosk** presentation, for instance, always loops automatically, while a windowed screen slide show loops by default, but isn't required to; windowed presentations automatically display on your primary monitor; Presenter View is (naturally) disabled for kiosk and windowed slide shows; the laser pointer is available for kiosk/windowed shows, but the pen is disabled.

**Figure 6-2**

Configuring your slide deck for different presentation types.

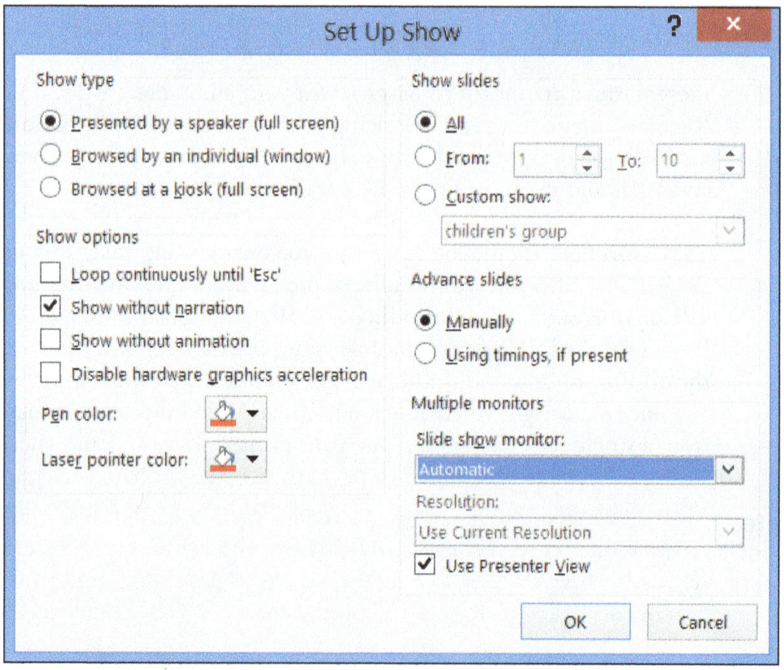


The **Set Up Show** dialog box offers a few additional options to customize your presentation. If you've recorded practice narration, or designed your slide deck for both unattended and live presentations, you can turn off the narration in the dialog box. You can also specify a subset of the deck to use in your presentation and disable automatic timings.

If you have multiple monitors connected (for instance, a laptop screen or tablet for the presenter and a projector facing the audience), you can also specify in this dialog box which screen will display which information.

## Controlling your presentation from the keyboard

**Bottom Line**

If you're using a Surface or other Windows tablet while presenting, touch commands will likely be the most convenient way to interact with your slide show; on a PC, however, the keyboard is probably your fastest input method. Rather than printing a complete list here, we'll mention the most common presentation commands, and refer you to the support pages at *office.microsoft.com* (from which this information is taken) for a full accounting:

Common presentation commands

| COMMAND | KEYBOARD SHORTCUT |
|---|---|
| **Next Trigger or Slide** | N, Enter, PgDown, Right Arrow, Down Arrow, Space |
| **Previous Trigger or Slide** | P, PgUp, Left Arrow, Up Arrow, Backspace |
| **Go to slide #** | Type #, press Enter |
| **Black screen** | B, period |
| **White screen** | W, comma |
| **Stop/restart** | S |
| **End** | Escape |
| **Pen** | Ctrl+P |
| **Arrow** | Ctrl+A |
| **Slide Sorter** | G |
| **Erase annotations** | E |

You can also get in and out of your slide show using only the keyboard: F5 starts your slide show from the beginning; Shift+F5 starts from the current slide; and Alt+F5 jumps right into Presenter View from the beginning.

Note that the only way to navigate directly between slides, skipping over triggered animations and effects, is by selecting a slide directly, either by typing its number or using the Slide Sorter.

## Creating custom slide shows

**Bottom Line**

Sometimes you'll want to give several different presentations using only parts of a single slide deck; for instance, you might give roughly the same talk to both a team of engineers and the middle managers who supervise them, and want to leave out your raw data in the nontechnical talk. PowerPoint offers the **Custom Slide Show** tool for just such situation.

**STEP BY STEP** **Creating a custom slide show**

1 Open **pp06a.pptx** located in the PPT06lessons folder. Click **Enable Content** to enable embedded media.

**Take Note** Slide shows that contain links to external media, such as YouTube videos, open in Protected mode by default. To automatically enable embedded media, make your file a Trusted Document.

2 Choose **File > Save As** and navigate to the PPT06lessons folder. Name the file **pp06a_work** and click **Save**.

3 Click **Slide Show > Custom Slide Show > Custom Shows**.

4 Click **New**. Enter **children's group** in the Slide show name text area (see Figure 6-3).

5 Select slides 1 through 3 and click Add.

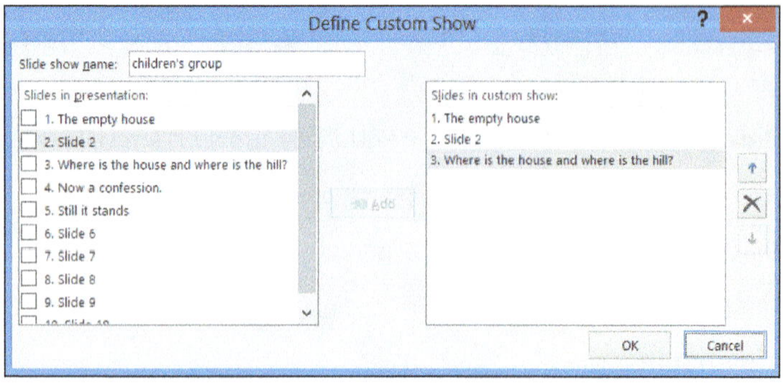


**Figure 6-3**
Custom Slide Shows include a subset of the full slide deck.

Now a children's group show appears in the list under Custom Slide Show, which cuts out the last three slides. You can create as many custom slide shows as you need; the slide list is simply saved in the .pptx file.

6 Click OK and then Close the Custom Shows dialog box.

**Take Note** If your slide deck contains a transition from slide 2 to slide 3, the transition will be included in any custom show that contains slide 3; transitions move into slides rather than out of them. A custom slide show that skips from slide 2 to slide 4 would include a transition only if slide 4 has a transition in. (Exit animations are contained within slides and aren't affected.)

Take careful note: custom slide shows renumber the individual slides. A custom show that skips slide 3 will renumber slide 4 as 3. If you've memorized specific slide numbers from your full deck, you may have to remember a whole new set of numbers for each custom show. When navigating a custom show, the Slide Sorter, with its slide thumbnails and section headings, becomes extremely helpful.

## PRESENTING IN SLIDE SHOW VIEW

**Bottom Line**

You've used the basic **Slide Show** command throughout this book's PowerPoint lessons. As you've seen, Slide Show gives you the audience's view of your presentation; it's especially well-suited to showing the slides in action during editing. If you give the same talk multiple times, you could find it easier to present straight from Slide Show mode; the stripped-down interface will minimize distraction.

The keyboard command and onscreen tools in the Slide Show are the same as for Presenter View; the difference is the amount of information on the screen. Crucially, Slide Show mode offers neither speaker notes nor a preview of the upcoming slide.

### STEP BY STEP Presenting in Slide Show view

1 Begin the Slide Show by pressing F5. Use any of the shortcut keys to advance to slide 3.

2 Press Ctrl+H to hide the pointer.

Oddly enough, Ctrl+H does not act as a toggle: pressing it twice won't make the pointer visible again. To do so, you have two options: switch to Pen mode and then back to arrow mode (press Ctrl+P twice), or right-click and select Pointer Options > Arrow Options > Visible from the context menu.

3 Press **Ctrl+P** to enter pen mode, circle the word ***house***, and then press **Escape** to switch the pointer to an arrow.

4 Press **Escape** again to end the Slide Show; Discard your ink annotations.

## MISSION CONTROL: POWERPOINT'S PRESENTER VIEW

**Bottom Line**

PowerPoint's standard Slide Show mode (invoked by pressing F5) shows you the presentation as the audience would see it: the current slide is displayed with no notes or additional information. Your Pen Tools are available in Slide Show mode, along with the Slide Sorter and Zoom tool, but the focus is on the slide and the audience experience.

In contrast, **Presenter View** is like Mission Control for presentations. It splits the screen to display slide notes, a preview of the next slide, and a handful of display options for your second (audience) screen. Your presenter tools are hidden from the audience unless you deliberately switch the Presenter and Audience screens. If you're giving the same presentation over and over (or prefer printed Notes pages) you may not need the full Presenter View, but for your early efforts at giving a talk, it's an essential tool.

**Take Note** PowerPoint 2013 launches Presenter View in a separate window from the Slide Show view, so you can press Alt+Tab to switch between the two views.

**Figure 6-4**

Presenter View gives you a big picture view of your presentation.

*Photos used with permission of Microsoft*

In this section, you'll quickly tour the Presenter View Interface , shown in Figure 6-4.

**STEP BY STEP** **Using PowerPoint's presenter view**

1 Activate Presenter View by pressing **Alt+F5**.

Note the large right and left arrows at the bottom of the screen. They do **not** let you skip from slide to slide without triggering animations. To move by the slide rather than interact with it by clicking, use the Slide Sorter. By default, Presenter View is split into three panes:

- a large display of the current slide with timing, annotation, and zoom tools nearby;
- a small preview of the next slide; and
- resizable speaker notes.

2 Drag the borders between the three panes to resize the current and next slides and the slide notes.

**Figure 6-5**

Resizing the Presenter View panes lets you focus on different aspects of your performance.

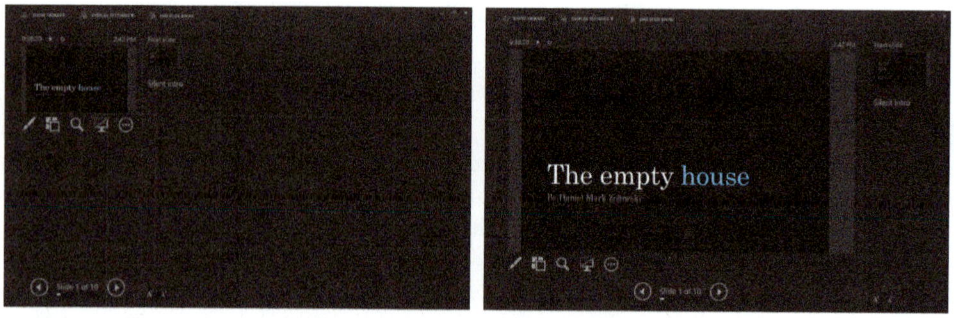


Moving the speaker notes and slide preview to the side (see Figure 6-5) can help you focus on tabular data or images; downsizing both slide images brings you speaker notes to the fore, which is important when you're reading lengthy or precisely worded text pieces.

## USING SPEAKER NOTES

**Bottom Line**

Speaker notes are easily overlooked during slide show construction. Even with animations and transitions, your slides are essentially static; slide-to-slide movement will come from you, the presenter, as you link presentation across slides and draw connections between ideas. The glue that holds your slide deck together (in other words, the logic that gets you from Slide A to Slide B) goes into your Speaker Notes.

**Take Note** One useful technique for building a presentation (or a piece of writing) is to outline its dynamic elements along with static content. Filling in a slide is often easier than figuring out how it transforms into the slide that follows: its implications, its relationship to the wider presentation. Including a single transition sentence between outline entries is extremely helpful when you need to flesh out your presentation. If you don't have time to rehearse, aiming for the transition sentence will make your improvisation a lot smoother.

In Presenter View, you can resize the text of your slide notes by clicking the two icons at the bottom of the Notes pane. If you don't want to be bound to a screen during your presentation, you can print out Notes Pages instead, which present a slide thumbnail with a large formatted notes pane. You can customize the look and layout of your notes pages with the Notes Master.

### How detailed should speaker notes be?

You can think of presentations as a form of theatrical performance: if you rely too heavily on your script, you could end up with a stiff performance. Obviously, you should tailor your notes to your personal taste and level of preparation, but ideally, by the time you reach the podium, your notes will be nothing more than prompts or reminders to help you move smoothly through natural, conversational spoken delivery.

For that reason, you should revise your speaker notes as you rehearse your presentation, refining scattered notes down to a telling word or phrase. If you're comfortable improvising or even memorizing, a written-out presentation can work too; but remember, you're writing a one-person stage performance, not a book report.

Incorporating direct quotes is another consideration. In general, long text passages fit awkwardly on slides. If you need to read verbatim text aloud, it's often best to leave a telling excerpt on the slide and leave the full text off to your speaker notes.

The most important guideline for speaker notes is this: *Focus on the talk, not the text.* Write only and exactly the notes that let you give the most fluid, memorable talk you can.

## FORMATTING AND PRINTING NOTES PAGES

**Bottom Line**

The notes pane in Presenter View can't be formatted like slide text; indeed, slide notes can only be formatted for the **Notes Page** view, and then only minimally (at the paragraph level). Such a limitation fits the approach suggested in this lesson: your speaker notes are notes, not a script, and great talks don't rely on notes for their impact; if you can wean yourself off speaker notes entirely, all the better.

That said, printed speaker notes can be of great benefit during a talk, freeing you from staring at your laptop or tablet screen. You can format your speaker notes (both the text itself and the layout of the printed notes page, including header and footer areas) in the **Notes Master** view.

### STEP BY STEP Formatting and printing notes pages

1. Select **View > Notes Master**.
2. Click in the Footer box at the bottom of the notes page and type **Not for distribution**.
3. Triple-click to select the entire first line in the notes pane (Click to edit…styles). Use the mini formatting pop-up menu (or the Home > Font group in the Ribbon) to format the line as 20pt boldfaced blue text.
4. Use the resizing handles to make the top content area (the slide image) about 2″ square, and drag the top of the notes text box upwards to fill the added space and give the text more breathing room. Click to select the notes content area itself and apply the **Colored Outline – Blue, Accent 1** style from the Drawing Tools > Format > Shape Styles gallery.
5. Click outside of the notes content area to deselect it. Finally, select **Notes Master > Close Master View** and save your work.

If you've worked through Lesson 3, "Designing a Presentation," this process will seem familiar; designing a notes page is exactly like making changes to a slide layout in the Slide Master. You can print your formatted notes page by selecting File > Print and selecting Notes Pages under Print > Settings; use the controls at the bottom of the screen (Figure 6-6) to flip through the slides in your deck. Note that Print Comments and Ink Markup is selected by default; this will insert separate pages containing only comments on each slide.

**Take Note** With the style options in the Notes Master > Background group, you can quickly change the overall look and feel of your notes page. Feel free to experiment with adjusting the look of your notes page using these commands, though you're more likely to need custom page formatting for printed handouts, instead.

**Figure 6-6**

Printing speaker with additional background formatting added to the Notes Master.

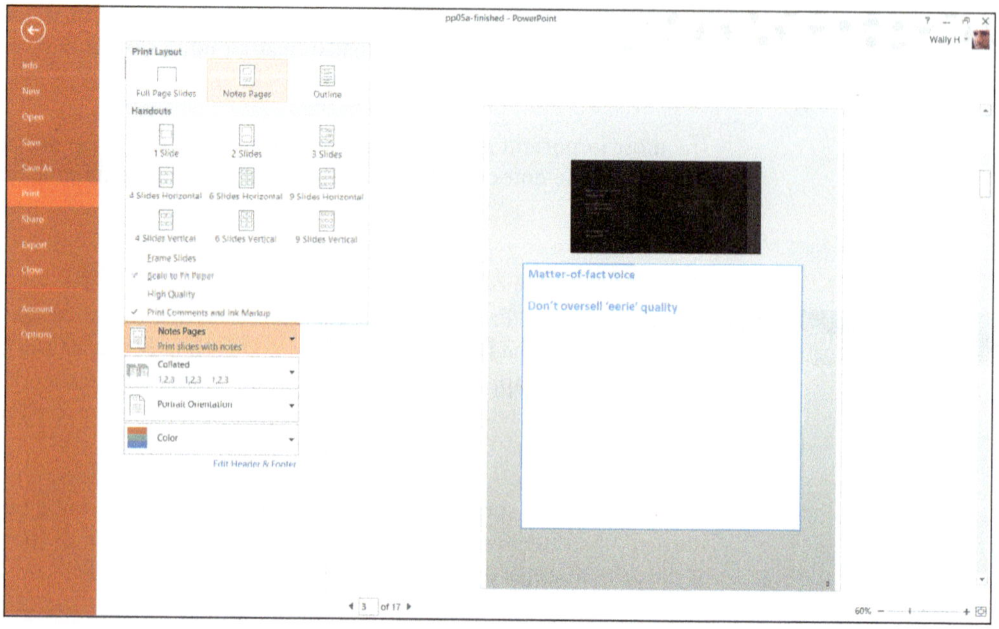


## DESIGNING A PRINTED HANDOUT

**Bottom Line**

Printed handouts are useful tools for presentation audiences as material for connecting their handwritten notes to slide content. But poorly formatted handouts (for example, many slides per page on an intrusively busy background), are worse than none at all. You can use the **Handout Master** to design a printout of your presentation for the audience to take away. The process is largely the same as for the Notes Master and printed notes page, except that the Handout Master > Page Setup group has a Slides Per Page button to set that crucial parameter. The layout for each Slides Per Page option is fixed, so handouts are less customizable than notes pages in that sense, but a subtle background or distinctive color scheme can make a printed handout more sticky in terms of audience retention.

**STEP BY STEP** **Designing a printed handout**

1. Select View > Handout Master to edit the handout's layout.
2. Establish the layout by choosing Handout Orientation > Landscape and Slides Per Page > 4 Slides.
3. Click Background Styles > Style 4, then close the Handout Master. Save your work.
4. Click File > Print. Select 4 Slides Horizontal from the third drop-down menu, and deselect Print Comment Slides and Ink Markup from the same menu.
5. Now preview the printed handout using the controls at the bottom of the screen. When you've done so, press Escape to cancel the print. (The black background uses a lot of ink.)

**Take Note** You can quickly generate a handout layout from the Print options screen.

### Navigating with the slide sorter

The Slide Sorter works the same in Presenter View as in editing mode: it shows thumbnails of your entire slide deck organized by section and navigable with the arrow keys. To invoke the Slide Sorter from Slide Show or Presenter modes, press G or click the See all slides icon. When the right slide is highlighted, press Enter to drop back into presenting.

Note that, as is the case with Presenter View, the Slide Sorter won't appear on the audience screen, just the presenter's.

**Take Note** When you compose and edit your slide show, sections are a handy organizational tool; especially if you're collaborating and wish to assign tasks to colleagues by section. During your presentation, sections are only relevant in the Slide Sorter.

### Going to a black or white screen

At times during a presentation, you'll want to clear the audience screen of content. PowerPoint provides commands to black out or white out the screen, rather than quitting the presentation entirely (popping back out to the edit window). This is extremely useful for the very end of your talk as a way of signaling to the audience that you're finished, without the awkward anticlimax of accidentally showing off your Windows desktop.

To black out the screen during a presentation, press B (or the period key); to white it out, press W or the comma. Press the same key to restore the slide content. The onscreen buttons to accomplish the same effects are shown in Figure 6-7

**Figure 6-7**

Black out your screen by clicking the highlighted icon beneath the slide; whiteout is only accessible from the keyboard.

## FOCUSING AUDIENCE ATTENTION WITH PEN TOOLS

No matter how much time you spend on slide design, there are plenty of uses for PowerPoint's pen tools during a presentation. A moving laser pointer can draw the audience's eyes to a specific region in a chart or a graph, or make the contour of a scatter plot clear. Ink circles can help listeners to later recall a specific fact. Subtle yellow highlights can make crucial words or phrases pop out of a paragraph or bulleted list. And you can save or print your pen annotations, making the live performance part of the written record of your talk.

Crucially, interacting with a slide can be an effective tool for you as the presenter; among other things, it lets you focus on specific physical action rather than staring over the heads of the crowd or fidgeting with papers at the podium. In this section, you'll mark up your presentation and save your pen annotations for later.

### Using the laser pointer and highlighter

**Bottom Line**

The **laser pointer** tool is available in both Slide Show and Presenter Views. It doesn't leave marks on the slide, just draws attention to a given slide element.

**STEP BY STEP** **Using the laser pointer and highlighter**

1. Press **F5** to enter the Slide Show.
2. Click the pen icon in the lower left of the screen, and then click **Laser Pointer**. Move the glowing red ring around on the screen to draw attention to features of the slide.
3. Press the right-arrow key to advance to the next slide. The laser pointer remains up.
4. Now press **Ctrl+P** to switch to Pen mode. Click and drag to circle the word ***house***. Then click the pen icon and select **Erase All Ink on Slide**. Press Ctrl+P to return to pointer mode. Advance to the next slide.

## Keeping ink annotations

**Bottom Line**

If you want to distribute a version of your slide show with live penstrokes included, choose to Keep **ink annotations** (and then save the file) when you finish marking up your slides.

1. Click the pen icon and select **Highlighter**. Highlight several words on the slide. Then switch to the pen tool (Ctrl+P) and handwrite **hotel** over the image.
2. Press **Escape** to return to pointer mode, then **Escape** again to exit your presentation. When asked to save your annotations, click **Keep**. Save your work.

The ink remains on the slide. This is an image object; indeed, when you select the lines you just drew in the editing window, an Ink Tools > Pens tab appears along with Drawing Tools > Format. Note that all the strokes you make on a single slide during a given presentation are combined into a single graphic object (See Figure 6-8.).

The easiest way to change the color of a pen stroke after the fact is with Drawing Tools > Format > Shape Outline; you can change the stroke weight with Ink Tools > Pens > Thickness.

Once you choose to keep your ink annotations from a given talk, the only way to remove them is in the editing window; the next time you run through the presentation, PowerPoint will treat them as part of the slide (in other words, the eraser tool won't alter pen strokes from previous run-throughs).

**Figure 6-8**

Saved ink annotations transform into graphic objects when you exit the Slide Show.

*Photo used with permission of Microsoft*

## REHEARSING YOUR PRESENTATION

Rehearsals are essential to the process of creating and shaping your talk and the slide deck itself. (After all, how can you know your slide show is working if you don't experience it in its proper context?) PowerPoint provides a suite of rehearsal tools to help you iron out the timing of your presentation and pre-record narration and pointer movements.

**Bottom Line**

## Recording slide and presentation timings

With the tools in the Slide Show > Set Up group, you can record your timings and spoken narrations, and play back the entire presentation with prerecorded narration, or just display slide timings while you run through the deck again. In this section, you'll start by recording timings; use the timings to run a hands-free slide show; and then record narration and laser pointer movements.

**STEP BY STEP** **Recording slide and presentation timings**

1. Click **Slide Show > Set Up > Rehearse Timings** to begin the slide show in practice mode. A small timer appears in the upper-left corner of the screen. Presenter View is unavailable in this mode.
2. Click through the presentation, taking five or so seconds per slide.
3. When the dialog box appears at the end of the slide show (Figure 6-9), click **Yes** to save your timings. Save your work.

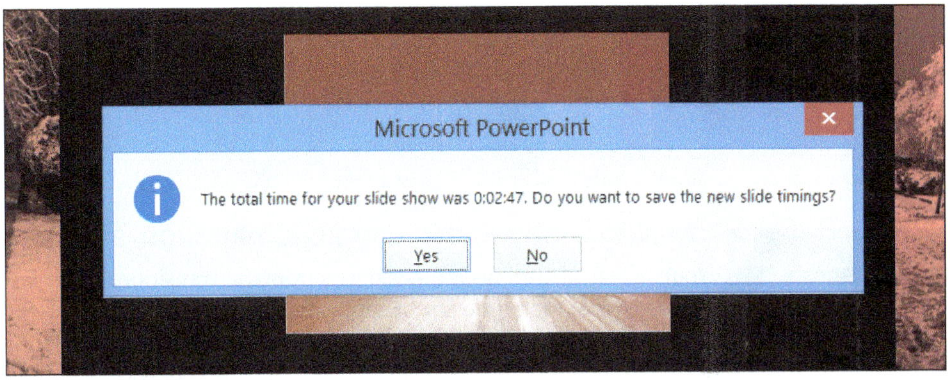


**Figure 6-9**
You can save one set of slide timings at a time.

*Photos used with permission of Microsoft*

After saving your timings, you can run through your presentation with the transitions playing automatically behind you. This is useful for rehearsing, but if you can give a smooth presentation without relying too much on the slides, you can also run the slide show at a fixed rate during the talk itself.

4. Now press **F5** to run your slide show again. Animations and transitions will run automatically at the previously recorded tempo. Press **Escape** when you're ready to move on.

**Bottom Line**

## Recording narration and pointer movements

Once you've fixed your slide timings to your satisfaction, you can record voice-over **narration** and pointer movements. This is an especially useful feature for kiosk slide shows, which can play like mini movies. But you can also use it to make recorded presentations for online distribution, or record a live presentation (for instance a team meeting) with listener feedback as a kind of audiovisual archive.

**Take Note** PowerPoint 2013 RT doesn't allow you to record narration. If you're working through this lesson on a Windows RT device such as a Surface, skip any steps that don't apply to your version of Office 2013. Surface Pro users have a full version of Office 2013 and should be able to follow the steps in this section.

**STEP BY STEP** **Recording narration and pointer movements**

1 Click **Slide Show > Record Slide Show**. In the dialog box, make sure only **Narrations and laser pointer** is checked. Click **Start Recording**. Speak some of the slide text aloud as you click through the presentation.

PowerPoint is now recording audio (from your system's default audio input; usually a built-in microphone), and will record any laser pointer movements you make.

2 Enable the laser pointer (using the button at the lower left of the screen) and move the pointer over some of the slides, holding still during others.

**Take Note** If you don't move the laser pointer at all during a slide, it won't be visible on playback, since only movements are recorded. Don't use the point if you don't need it.

3 When the slide show is finished, press **Escape** to quit.

4 Make sure **Play Narrations** and **Use Timings** are selected in Slide Show > Set Up. Then adjust your computer's volume to a comfortable level and press **F5** to play back the presentation.

The slide show plays back using your rehearsal timings (recorded earlier) and the narration and laser pointer moves you just recorded.

5 Choose **File > Save** or press **Ctrl+S** to save your work.

**Bottom Line**

## Tweaking and removing timings, narration, and laser pointer movements

Your rehearsal timings are saved as automatic transitions: look under Transitions > Timing and you'll see that each slide now has an Advance Slide After value. You can tweak these timings as you would any other transition. (If you only want to use recorded timings and don't want to be able to break them by skipping quickly through slides, deselect the On Mouse Click timing option.)

Recording rehearsal timings overwrites any Advance Slide After timings you might have already set. The only way to remove rehearsal timings is to delete them from the slides themselves. We'll do that now, to make the presentation timing more flexible.

**STEP BY STEP** **Tweaking and removing timings, narration, and laser pointer movements**

1 In the Normal edit view, select all the slides by clicking in the slide pane on the left and pressing **Ctrl+A**.

2 In the Transitions tab, deselect **Timing > Advance Slide After**. Save your work.

PowerPoint saves your narrations as audio objects, one per slide. If you don't need narration during a given presentation, you can always disable the narration in the Set Up Show dialog box; to reduce file size and speed up PowerPoint's performance, we'll remove the narration we've just recorded.

3 Click **Slide Show > Record Slide Show > Clear > Clear Narrations on All Slides**. Save your work.

## PRESENTING ONLINE

At times, you might need to present to someone across town or in a different time zone. Microsoft offers a couple of channels for online presentations:

- **Lync,** a paid groupware service offering integrated audio/video conferencing, instant messaging scheduling, and media sharing.
- **Office Presentation Service (OPS),** a free public service for making slide shows viewable in the PowerPoint Web.

From the speaker's standpoint, presenting online is similar to presenting in person. One key difference is that online viewers can flip back through the slide deck during the presentation without interrupting the presenter or anyone else in the audience. The potential downside to using OPS for presentations is that there's no speech integration: the audience gets the slide deck and embedded media, but your actual talk can only go out over an external service such as Skype and there's no built-in video presence. The Lync service provides these additional features.

You can also embed your slide show in a webpage using SkyDrive. This option gives you the least control over access or the viewer experience, but it's the easiest way to share your slide deck; you could use it to post a multimedia photo album to a blog, for example. An OPS presentation is only viewable as long as you're actually presenting (see Figure 6-10), and though it's theoretically open to the public, only invited viewers will be able to find it. Lync offers the most control over who can see your presentation and how.

### Delivering a presentation using Office Presentation service

You can present a slide show using OPS directly from the Slide Show tab.

**STEP BY STEP** **Delivering a presentation using Office Presentation service**

1. Click **Slide Show > Start Slide Show > Present Online > Office Presentation Service.**
2. Uncheck the option to make the slide deck downloadable (Enable remote viewers). Then click **Connect.**

The Enable remote viewers option does just what it says: if you leave it checked, your audience will be able to download the source file for your presentation.

The Optimize Media option appears because **pp06a_work.pptx** contains a link to a YouTube video, which might not display properly on older Flash-disabled computers. For our purposes, we needn't worry about it. PowerPoint now generates the online presentation. When it's finished, a Present Online pane appears.

3. Click **Copy Link**, then click **Start Presentation.**
4. Open a web browser, but don't stop the presentation by pressing Escape. Paste the URL into the location bar of the browser to view your presentation.
5. Return to your slide show in PowerPoint and advance to the next slide, and then switch back to your web browser; the presentation will have advanced there as well.

6 Return to PowerPoint and stop the presentation by pressing **Escape**. Select **Present Online > End Online Presentation**, then confirm your choice in the pop-up dialog box.

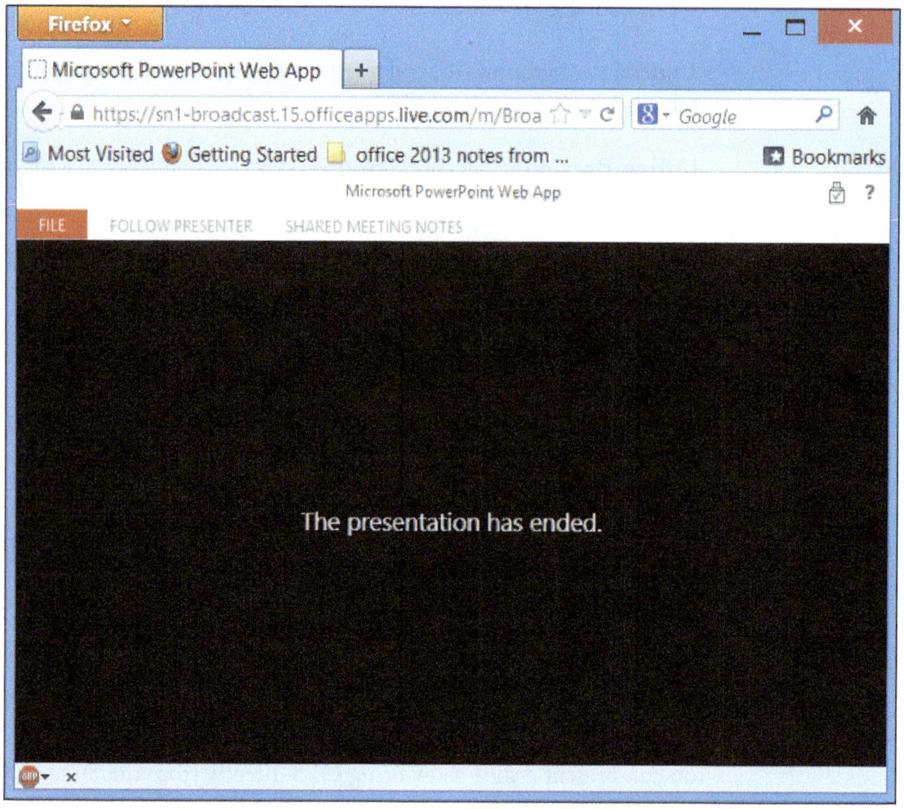


**Figure 6-10**

Your online presentation's URL expires as soon as you click End Online Presentation.

**Take Note** Your online audience might need to install or upgrade Silverlight or Flash in order to view a multimedia presentation. To ensure compatibility, follow the suggestions in Lesson 5, "Adding Graphics and Multimedia to Your Presentation."

**Bottom Line**

## Presenting in Lync

If you have a Lync account set up, the steps to present via Lync are much the same as the previous. Note that Lync sharing is not available on Windows RT devices, such as Microsoft Surface.

**STEP BY STEP** **Presenting in Lync**

1 Select **Slide Show > Present Online > Microsoft Lync**.

2 If you have a Lync meeting set up, select it from the list of scheduled meetings; otherwise, click Start a new Lync meeting and add invitees.

3 When the meeting is underway, begin the presentation as you normally would.

**Take Note** For more details on using Lync for online presentations, see the Lync documentation at onlinehelp.microsoft.com.

The important takeaway in this section is that the mechanics of presenting your slides are the same regardless of the physical or online venue.

## Embedding your slide show in a webpage

If you want to publish a standalone slide deck online, or let colleagues peruse your deck as a work in progress, you can embed your slide show in a webpage by sharing it directly from SkyDrive. (If you don't have a place to host your slideshow online, just read along, or skip to the next section.)

**STEP BY STEP** **Embedding your slide show in a webpage**

1 If you haven't already done so, save the practice presentation to your SkyDrive folder by doing one of the following:

Log in to *skydrive.com* in your web browser, click the **Upload** button in the SkyDrive screen, and navigate to the file; or

Use the desktop SkyDrive or SkyDrive Pro app to upload the file to your SkyDrive.

2 Open *skydrive.com* in your web browser and navigate to where your presentation is stored.

3 Right-click the presentation's icon in the browser, and select **Embed**.

4 SkyDrive will generate HTML to embed the presentation in a web page, along with a preview of the embedded slide show. Press **Ctrl+C** to copy the embed code.

5 Paste the HTML code into the blog editor of your choice; for instance, into a new Blog Post document in Word 2013. Then upload the file to your blog, and view the post in a web browser to see the embedded presentation.

If you want to share the original file via e-mail instead of embedding it on a webpage, follow steps 1 and 2 above, then choose Sharing in step 3 and e-mail a link to the original file instead. You can also open the file from your SkyDrive directory using the PowerPoint Web App, and selecting File > Sharing > Embed from the Web App to generate HTML embed code.

6 Choose **File > Save** and **File > Close**.

## GIVING EXCELLENT PRESENTATIONS

There's no single recipe for a great PowerPoint presentation except to practice, practice, practice. Of course you need to master the basics first. Speak to the audience, not the slide. Practice stringing multiple sentences together to avoid *um* and *uhh*. Spread text out over several sparse slides, rather than one crowded one. Pick a simple font/visual scheme and stick to it.

Once you have the basics down you start getting into style, where your presentations (ideally) begin to look less like everyone else's, because you're finding personal solutions to technical problems.

Great talks are always unique and personal. Some speakers put a single word on a slide; some do original art for every talk; and some rely entirely on infographics and speech. Great presenters never stick to the trusty title + bullet points + clip art scheme; there's always some twist, and the twist is what lets the talk hook into the audience's minds in the first place, and keeps it there long after you get to the end of your presentation.

That said, here are a few principles to keep in mind as you develop your first few presentations. Our hope is that this advice will scale up to stay relevant as your skill increases.

- **Slides aren't novels—they're paintings.** A slide crammed full of complete sentences is one of the classic PowerPoint blunders. If you're giving a talk, think of your slides as visuals competing with your speech for audience attention; if everyone's reading a well-crafted prose paragraph off the screen, they're not listening to your talk.

- **It's a visual medium—make sure the visuals are visible.** Use high-contrast colors, legible fonts (and not too many at once), and uncluttered layouts. The audience shouldn't have to figure out what you're saying.

- **Themes help you and your audience.** Every time you switch look and feel in the middle of a slide show, you impose a kind of cognitive tax on your audience as they adapt to change. Settling on a visual theme early lets you build text and images around the theme's layout library; designing your own theme gives you even more control, matching aesthetics and informational content. A theme isn't just a paint job; it's a tool for information design.

- **In general, use more images and less text per slide.** As text piles up, it loses immediate visual impact and gets harder to remember, but images can gain power in combination. Try splitting a slide into four quarters and filling each quarter, one by one, with images: you're building a collage, and the images talk to one another. Do the same with blocks of text, and you're just making a mess. If you need four blocks of text, use four slides.

- **Don't just read slides aloud.** Unless you must share a verbatim text passage, you should design your slides for visual impact and stickiness in memory and design your spoken lines for ease and fluency of speaking. Just talk to your audience; this generally involves looking at them.

- **A little flash goes a long way.** Every blinking doodad or complex animation draws attention from the content of the talk to the visual flash itself. Sometimes a slide needs an animated object or two; truly rare is the slide that needs any more than that.

- **Leave time for revision.** Your first idea is only special because it comes first, and you won't see the problems with your first draft until you get into your second. You'll often have an easier time revising a broken talk than starting from none at all, and revision takes time.

- **Leave time for rehearsal.** The first time you read through your slides, you'll notice weird juxtapositions, odd grammar, and plain old factual errors. You can do this in front of your audience if you insist, but the other way is better. Rehearsing out loud is part of the design process. The same goes for designing a kiosk presentation: if you haven't tested the talk at an actual kiosk, you won't know whether it'll work.

## What you learned in this lesson:

- Customizing Your Presentation Setup
- Precisely Controlling Your Presentation
- Using Slide Show and Presenter Views
- Creating Speaker Notes and Handouts
- Using the Laser Pointer, Highlighter, and Ink Annotations
- Rehearsing Timings and Recording Narration
- Delivering a Presentation Online

# Knowledge Assessment

## True/False

**Circle T if the statement is true or F it the statement is false.**

T F 1. Slide Show View provides a complex presenter-facing tools display.

T F 2. PowerPoint provides a single command to clear all rehearsal timings.

T F 3. Kiosk-mode presentations are designed to run automatically, without a human attendant.

T F 4. To move to the next slide, hit Enter, Space, right arrow, or down arrow (among others).

T F 5. To run the presentation, press F1 plus any desired modifier keys.

T F 6. The notes page's orientation can be set directly in the Notes Master tab.

T F 7. Notes pages can be styled all at once with document themes.

T F 8. Pressing G during a presentation brings up the Slide Sorter.

T F 9. Ink annotations are saved in a separate file, which can be layered on top of any presentation.

T F 10. Saved rehearsal timings are stored as Advance Slide After: data.

## Matching

**Match each term to its description or definition.**

1. ink annotation
2. narration
3. Notes Page
4. Notes Master
5. kiosk mode
6. laser pointer
7. Office Presentation Service
8. windowed presentation
9. Custom Slide Show
10. Slide Sorter

a. can add (e.g.) headers/footers to notes page
b. press G during show to display; allows quick selection of slides from any group
c. stored as audio files, one file per slide; can optionally play during presentation
d. hosts online slide shows; viewer join in from their browsers
e. includes a subset of slides from a deck; list resides in Slide Show tab
f. presentation loops automatically, keyboard/mouse not used except for hyperlinks
g. stored as graphic object in .pptx file, embedded in its slide
h. not intended for distribution; text styling/layout available from master
i. full presentation w/limited interactivity, keeping other apps available
j. this pen tool doesn't affect file, only draws attention during presentation

# Competency Assessment

## Project 6-1: Setting Up a Presentation

**In this exercise you will tailor slide show options for a specific venue using the Set Up Show dialog.**

1. Open the project file **6-x-source**.
2. Click **Slide Show > Set Up Slide Show** to open the Set Up Show dialog box.
3. Run the presentation first in regular full-screen mode, then windowed, and finally in kiosk mode.
4. Edit each slide to advance after two seconds, then run the presentation in kiosk mode again.

   Note that you can't interact with the presentation in kiosk mode at all.
5. Experiment, in the Set Up Show dialog, with using a subset of the slides, looping in speaker/individual modes, and altering pen/pointer colors.
6. When you're finished experimenting, close the file.

## Project 6-2: Custom Slide Shows

**This exercise reviews the Custom Slide Show command.**

1. Open the project file **6-x-source**. Save it to your project directory as **project_6-2_custom**.
2. Open the Slide Show tab and click **Slide Show > Custom Slide Show > Custom Shows...**
3. Create a new custom show called **Title/Org** containing slides 1 and 4 only. Click **OK**.
4. Select Title/Org from the Custom Slide Show dropdown menu in the Slide Show tab.
5. Create a second custom show called **Processes Only** including slides 2 and 3.
6. Save and close your document.

# Proficiency Assessment

## Project 6-3: Presentation Views

**In this exercise you'll explore the different presentation viewing modes in PowerPoint 2013.**

1. Open the project file **6-x-source**.
2. Run the slide show from the beginning (F5).
3. Select slide **3**. Run the presentation from there, stopping it on slide 4 (Escape). Enable looping in the Set Up Show dialog and loop through the presentation a few times.
4. Press **Alt+F5** to run the slide show in Presenter View. Experiment with resizing the notes pane and current/next slides in Presenter View.
5. While in Presenter View, press **Alt+Tab** to switch between all three PowerPoint windows – Presenter View, Slide Show View, and the main editing window.
6. While in Presenter View, click the **...** button to invoke a custom slide show.
7. When you're finished experimenting, close the file.

### Project 6-4: Adding Ink Annotations to a Presentation

**In this exercise you'll add ink annotations to a presentation and save them to the .pptx file.**

1. Open the project file **6-x-source** and save it to your working directory as **project_6-4_ink**.
2. Run the presentation in Slide Show or Presenter View.
3. In slides 2 and 3, circle the **Consult and Ship** steps using the pen tool.
4. On the final slide, circle **Feliks** and place a star next to his name. Keep the annotations when prompted.
5. Rerun the presentation and highlight the title of each slide except the first. Again, keep the annotations when prompted.

   Note that slide annotations are additive – the second round won't replace the first.
6. Close and save your document.

## Mastery Assessment

### Project 6-5: Rehearsal Timings

**In this exercise you'll use saved rehearsal timings to nail down your presentation delivery.**

1. Open the project file **6-x-source** and save it to your working directory as **project_6-5_timings**.
2. Use the **Slide Show > Rehearse Timings** command to add slide timings (a few seconds per slide) to the file.
3. When prompted, keep the timings.
4. Run the presentation, making sure Slide Show > Use Timings is selected.
5. If you have a microphone, rerun the slide show, recording both narration and ink/laser pen marks. Keep your narration and markup.
6. Save and close your document.

### Project 6-6: Presenting Online

**In this exercise you'll deliver a brief presentation using the Office Presentation Service.**

1. Open the project file **6-x-source**. Save it as **project_6-6_online**.
2. Add a slide with your name and image, and save the document.
3. Set up an online presentation using the Office Presentation Service. Set it up so that remote viewers can download the presentation.
4. Deliver the presentation to your instructor online. When you're finished, close the file.

# Microsoft Access 2013

# 1 Introduction to Microsoft Access 2013

## LESSON SKILL MATRIX

**In this lesson, you will learn the following skills:**

| | |
|---|---|
| What is Access? | Getting Help |
| Ways to use Access | Ending An Access Session |
| Database basics | |
| Exploring a database | |
| Working with records | |
| Customizing the Quick Access Toolbar | |

## KEY TERMS

- **Database**
- **Relational database**
- **Table**
- **Query**
- **Form**
- **Report**
- **Field**
- **Record**

©Squaredpixels/iStockPhoto

©Squaredpixels/ iStockPhoto

Tina owns a small boutique and would like to create a database of information regarding her customers. She wants to use Microsoft Access and have the database track information like customer addresses, favorite products, order dates, and products ordered. She needs to learn to use Microsoft Access and then create her database in the software.

## SOFTWARE ORIENTATION

This lesson helps you understand database essentials and introduces you to Microsoft Access 2013.

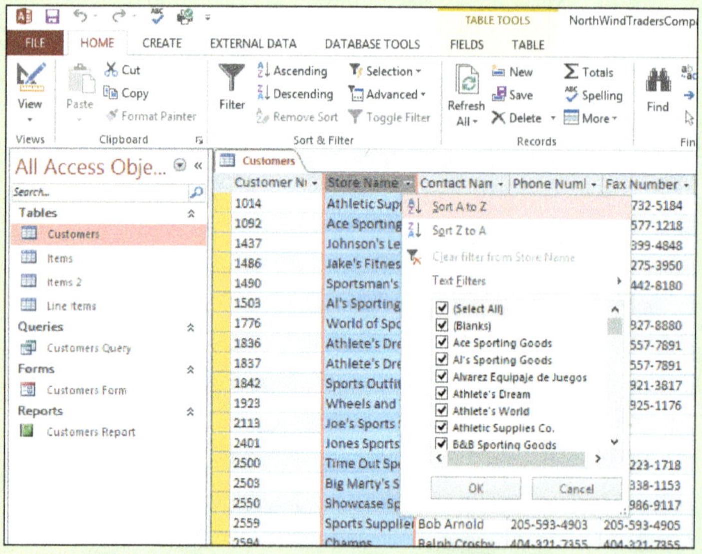


**Figure 1-1**

Access is a database for storing and managing records.

## STARTING UP

In this lesson, you'll work with several files from the Access01lessons folder. Make sure that you have loaded the OfficeLessons folder onto your computer.

## WHAT IS ACCESS?

Access is a **database** program that allows you to store and organize your data in useful ways through reports, forms, and webpages. It is available in certain editions of Microsoft Office, but you can also purchase it separately.

Access is a **relational database** program that uses related tables to store, organize, and retrieve data. You can use Access locally on your computer or through the Internet. Access is used by small and large companies throughout the world to store their data and make it accessible in useful ways.

## WAYS TO USE ACCESS

You can use Access to create, modify, and manage databases through any of the following tasks:

- Creating a new database from scratch or based on a template.
- Establishing relationships between types of information.
- Adding data to a database through a table or through a form.
- Designing forms for data entry or viewing information.
- Importing data into Access from other programs or linking to external data sources.
- Running filters and queries on the database to extract relevant data.
- Generating reports to emphasize and present different portions of your data.

## DATABASE BASICS

Access 2013 is a software database program that allows you to organize a collection of data. This includes the data's storage, query, retrieval, and maintenance of information. Databases are used to organize data from company customer addresses and phone numbers to company products and parts.

Databases and spreadsheets serve similar purposes; however, they are also different. If your data can be easily entered, stored, viewed, extracted, and managed within a spreadsheet, it is best to keep the information within Microsoft Excel. An example would be a small staff directory that includes items such as Last Name, First Name, Office, Phone Number, Department, and Start Date. However, when your data becomes more complicated, Access might be a better tool for managing the data.

### Basic database terminology

The terms described in this section are frequently used when discussing databases, and it's useful to understand them before starting to work with an Access database.

Databases are made up of objects. With these objects, you can perform specific tasks. Below is a list of the main objects available in Access:

- **Table:** the most important and foundational object in an Access database. Tables store data in records and fields, which correspond to rows and columns, respectively. The data is usually about a particular category of things, such as employees or orders.

- **Query:** a question that you ask about the data stored in a table. Queries can also make a request of the data or perform an action such as a filter on the data. A query can bring data together from multiple tables to serve as the source of data for a form or report.

- **Form:** an object where you place controls for taking actions or for entering, displaying, and editing data in fields. Access objects resemble online forms. They are primarily used for viewing information from database tables and also for entering data into tables.

- **Report:** a printout of your database information that's formatted and organized according to your specifications. Examples of reports are sales summaries, phone lists, and mailing labels.

Tables are the most important object in your database because this where all the information in your database is stored. The other database objects access the tables to organize, report, and perform different actions to the information contained therein. This is why a solid understanding of tables is critical to using Access and understanding how the other database objects work in conjunction to the tables.

Below are two important terms you need to understand about database tables:

- **Field:** a table column or category. For example, a FirstName field would likely be found in an Employees table.

- **Record:** a set of fields containing data for a single entry and appearing in one row of a database table.

## Database design tips

Database design can be complex and require a high degree of advanced designing skills and background that can take a great deal of time and training to obtain. However, for basic database design, you can start with the following tips:

- Plan, plan, plan! You should never rush into creating the components of a database. We highly recommend that you gather as much information as possible from individuals who will be using the database. Examples of important components to plan are: the types of tables that are needed, the table fields, how the tables are related, etc.

- Create a sketch of the database tables on a piece of paper, and use lines and arrows to show how they're related.

- Each table should have only one purpose; for example, one table will be used to keep track of orders, another to keep track of customers, yet another to keep track of employees, etc.

- Avoid duplication of data; for example, don't add Customer fields to the Orders table. Redundant data increases the size and complexity of your database, increases the likelihood of data entry or retrieval errors, and slows the speed of the database.

## QUICK TOUR OF ACCESS 2013

Understanding the capabilities of Access helps you understand and use the program more effectively. Before you start using a database, you need to either open an existing one or create a new blank database. You will create a new blank database, so that you can overview database's user interface in the next section.

**STEP BY STEP** **Opening an Access 2013 file**

1 To open Access, choose **Start > Programs > Microsoft Office > Microsoft Access 2013**.

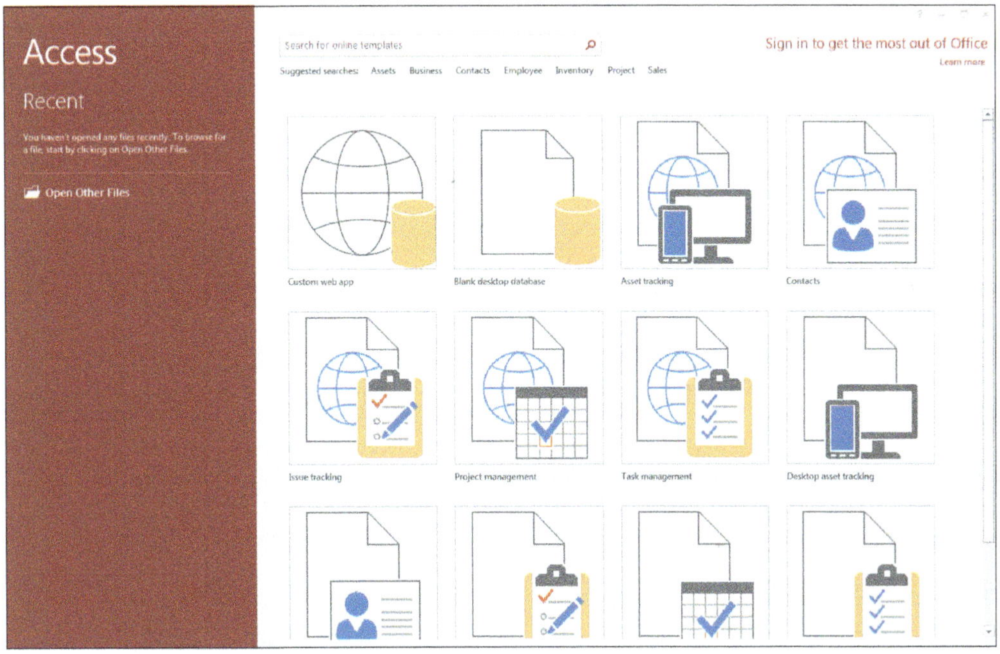


**Figure 1-2**
Backstage view of Access 2013.

Access 2013 opens in Backstage view, where you can create a new database, open an existing database, and view featured content from *Office.com*. Backstage view is described in more detail in the next section.

You can always access Backstage view, even when working in a database, by clicking the File tab.

2 At the bottom left of the Access opening screen, click **Open Other Files**.

3 From the Open screen, click **Computer > Browse** to the Access01lesson folder, and Open **NorthWindTradersCompanyDatabase**.

**Take Note** You can get out of the Backstage view by pressing ESC on your keyboard or by clicking the Back button (the circle button with the left facing arrow in it at the top of the Backstage menu.)

### Access 2013 components

The Access 2013 interface has the following main components:

- **The Ribbon**: this bar across the top of the interface contains several tabs, which in turn contain groups of commands that are visible on all tabs, except File.
- **Backstage view**: this view appears by default when you launch Access 2013; it's comprised by the group of commands available on the Ribbon's File tab.

**Take Note** The File tab always has a colored background, even when it is not the active tab. You can identify the active tab by the borders on either side of it.

- **The Navigation pane**: the area on the left side of the interface that displays lists of database objects when a database is open. You can use it to open and organize database objects.

**Figure 1-3**

NorthWindTradersCompany-Database, showing an open Navigation pane.

Let's examine these components in more detail.

## The Ribbon

The Ribbon is divided into tabs, and within each tab there are groups of commands. The Ribbon replaces the traditional menus that existed across the top of the screen and the toolbars that were found in older versions of Microsoft Office. The primary Ribbon tabs for Access 2013 are File, Home, Create, External Data, and Database Tools.

**Figure 1- 4**

The Access 2013 ribbon is divided into tabs.

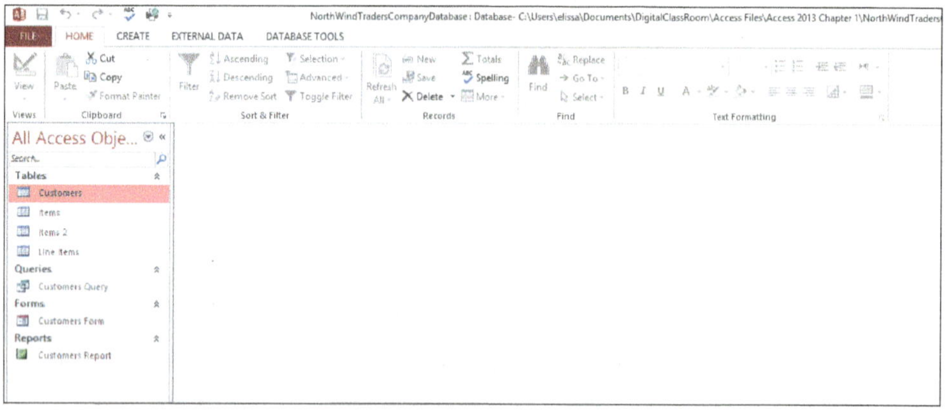


There are times when different Ribbons open in Access depending on your current task in the software. These are called Context Ribbon tabs. The Table Tools and Fields and Tables are Context Ribbon tabs that only open when you are adding or editing records in an Access table. When you close the Access table or switch to a different view, the Fields and Tables Ribbon tabs turn off.

You can also hide and show the Ribbon by double-clicking the active command tab, making it easy to maximize your workspace as needed.

**STEP BY STEP** **Showing the Ribbon**

1 Notice the Ribbon and its tabs divided into groups of commands.

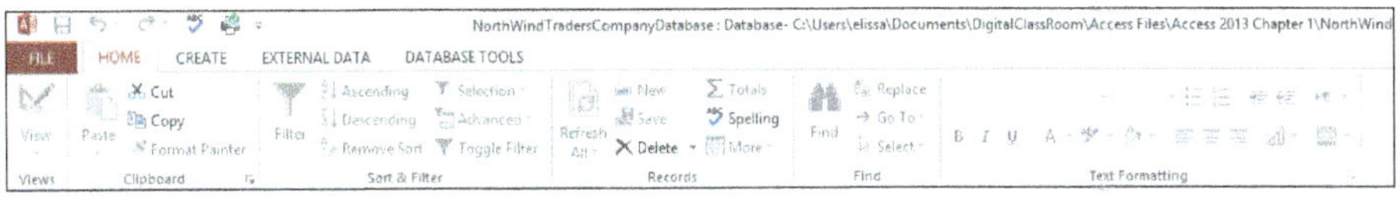


**Figure 1-5**

The Ribbon in full view, showing groups of commands.

2 Hide the Ribbon by double-clicking the **Home** tab.

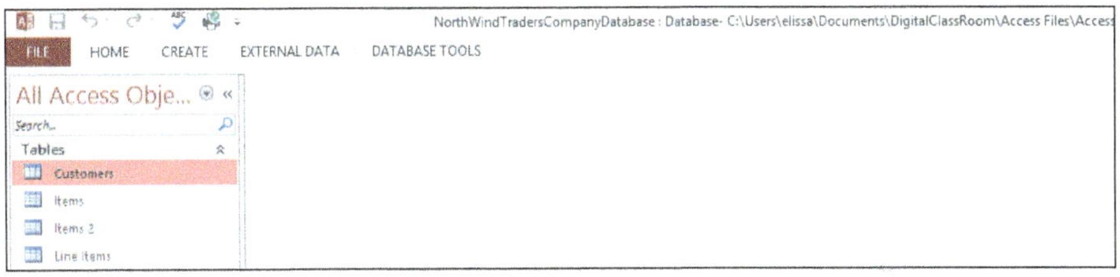


**Figure 1- 6**

The Ribbon with its command groups hidden.

3 Show the Ribbon by clicking the **Home** tab again.

You have successfully toggled the Ribbon by clicking the active tab. You can also toggle the Ribbon by clicking the Minimize/Expand arrow button in the upper-right corner.

## Backstage view

Backstage view is the first view you see after you launch Access 2013. It contains information and commands that affect an entire database, such as the following: opening and saving a database; a list of recently opened databases; tabs for database information, recent databases, and database creation. You can also launch the help system and manage options in Backstage view.

## Navigation pane

The Navigation pane, which replaces the Database window of some older versions of Access, is located on the left side of the Access 2013 interface when a database is open.

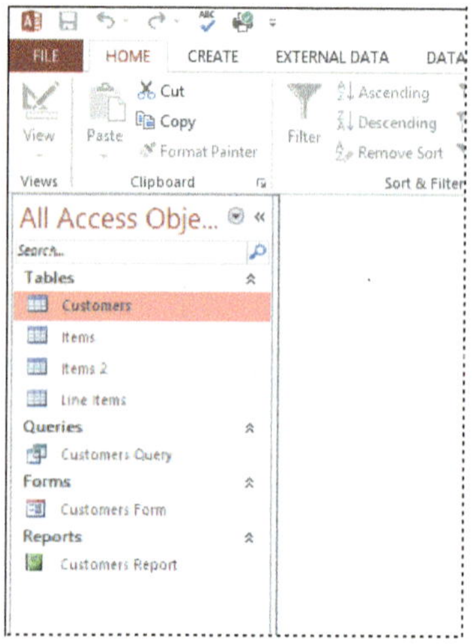


**Figure 1-7**

The Navigation pane allows you to view and manage the database's objects, and is customizable.

**Take Note** A database's objects include items such as tables, queries, forms, and reports.

You can toggle the Navigation pane just as you did with the Ribbon. Although the result is the same, the procedure is slightly different. You'll toggle and examine the Navigation pane in more detail after you've opened a database that contains some actual data.

Choose File > Close to close this file.

## EXPLORING A DATABASE

Now that we've covered some introductory information, we'll examine a database and discover how it works.

## STEP BY STEP Opening a sample template

1. Click the File tab to get back into Backstage view.
2. From Backstage view, select **New**, and then click the **Contacts** category located next to the Suggested Searches.

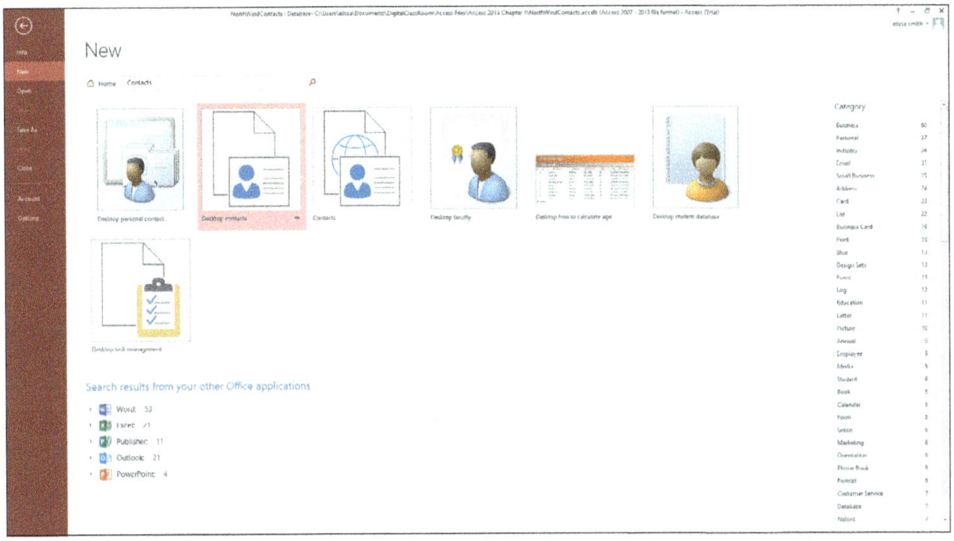


**Figure 1-8**
Choose the Desktop contacts template.

3. Select Desktop contacts. Then, in the Desktop contact box, type **CustomerContacts** for the File Name. Click the small folder icon, browse to the Access01lessons folder and click **OK**. (You need to save the new database with a file name before you can start using it.)
4. Click **Create**. If the tutorial box Getting Started with Contacts opens up, click the **Close** button in the top-right corner. The database opens and the Home Ribbon tab is currently open.

**Take Note** You might see a Security Warning at the top of the screen. If so, click **Enable Content**.

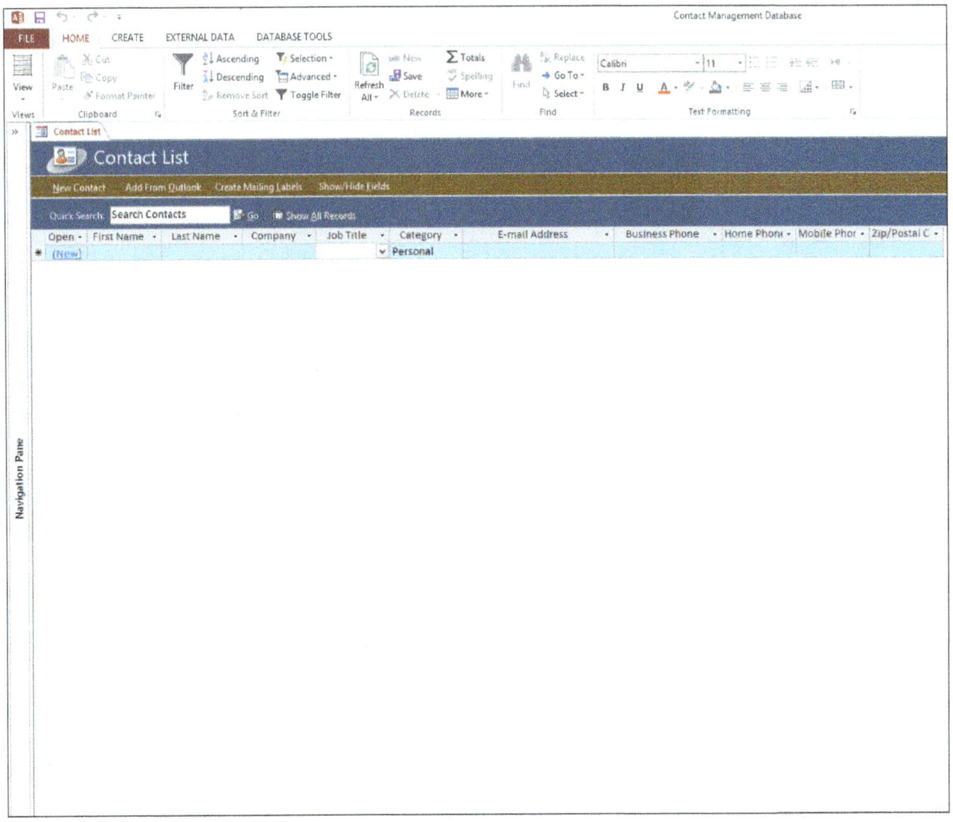


**Figure 1-9**
The contacts database, showing a collapsed Navigation pane on the left side.

Let's explore the Navigation pane. Just as is the case with the Ribbon, you can show or hide the Navigation pane to get more or less room to view individual database objects.

## STEP BY STEP Showing and hiding the Navigation pane

1 If the Navigation pane is closed, click the **Open/Close** button («) in the upper-right corner to view the contents.

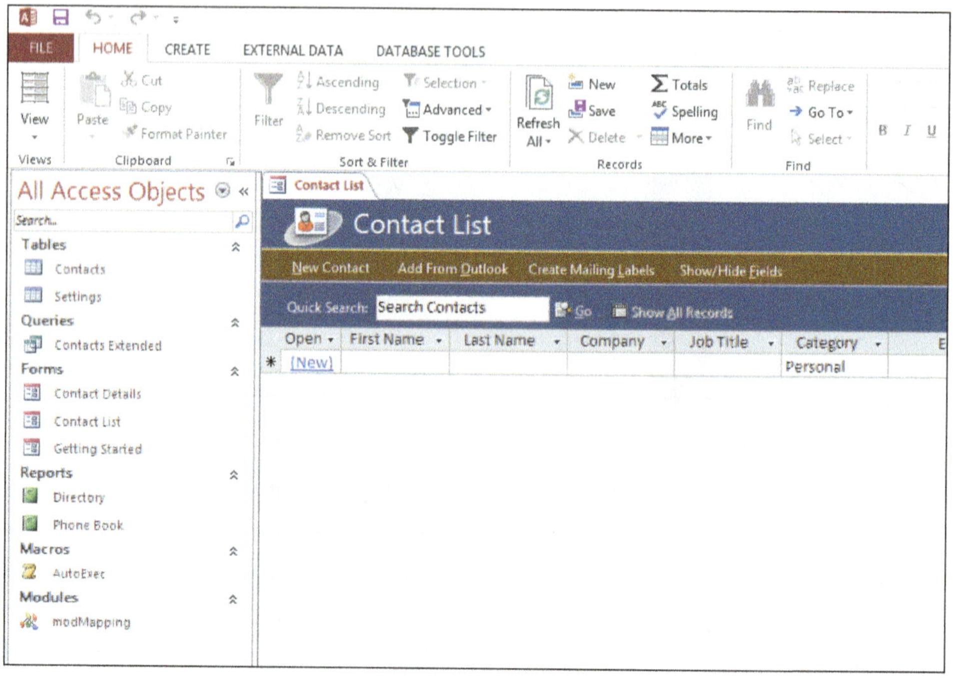


**Figure 1-10**

Click the Open/Close button to expand or collapse the Navigation pane.

2 Click the **Open/Close** button a second time to close the Navigation pane. It doesn't quite disappear, but it collapses to show only the title bar of the pane.

3 Click the **Open/Close** button again to restore the Navigation pane.

**Take Note** You can alter the Navigation pane's width by clicking and dragging its right border.

The Navigation pane displays the database's objects. The default view shows all the main categories, which are Tables, Queries, Forms, Reports, Macros, and Modules. The database's different objects are listed under their appropriate headings. Your database can contain as many objects as necessary to manage your information.

You will use the Search text box at the top of the Navigation pane to search for a specific object.

## STEP BY STEP Searching for an object using the Navigation pane

1 On each heading in the Navigation pane, click the **down-arrow** to show objects. You will need to scroll down to access all the headings.

2 Type **contact list** in the Search text box.

As you type, objects that contain this text begin to appear in the Navigation pane below, until only objects containing the exact same spelling remain.

**Figure 1-11**

The Search engine will instantly finds objects that match the text you type.

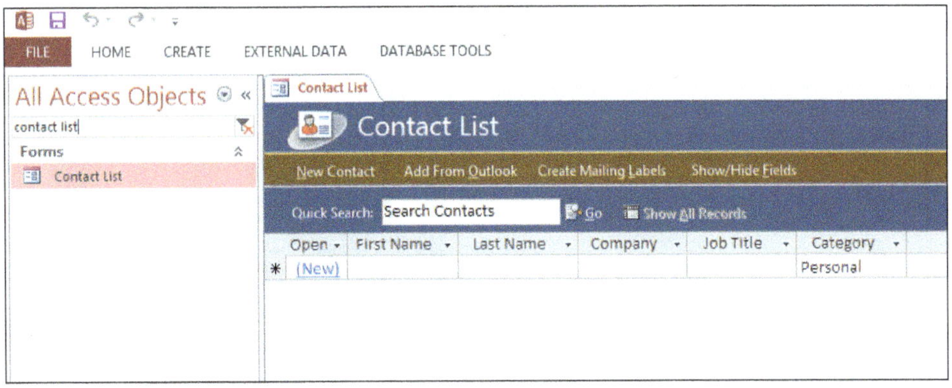


3 Delete the text in the Search text box, either by clicking the **Clear Search String** icon ( ) to the right of the Search text box, or by pressing the **Delete** or **backspace** key on your keyboard. This will turn the Navigation pane back to showing all your database objects.

There may be times when you only want to change the view in the Navigation pane or only view one specific category of object to arrange the appearance of the objects in the Navigation pane.

## STEP BY STEP Changing the view in the Navigation pane

1 Click the **down-arrow** button in the upper-right corner of the Navigation pane.

The Navigation pane shows that the Object Type and All Access Objects are checked. This means that all the database's objects are currently showing in the Navigation pane.

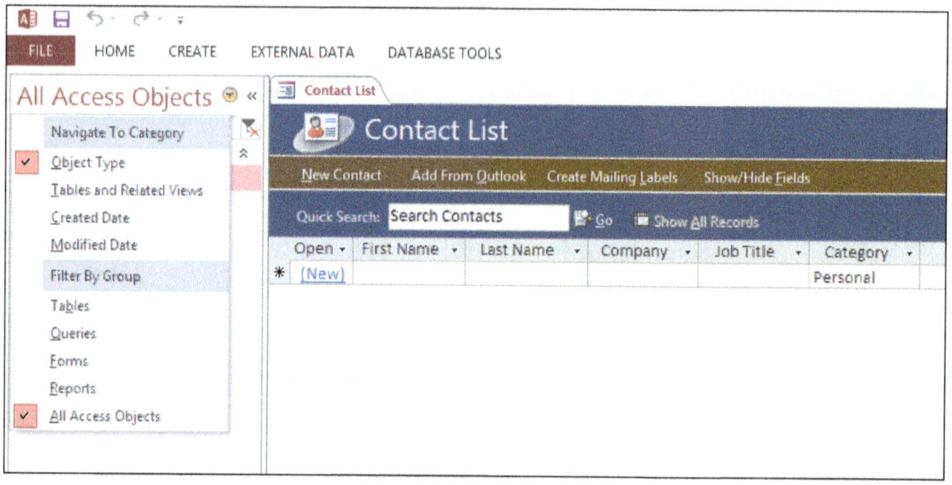


**Figure 1-12**

Use the Navigation pane to choose how objects are displayed and organized.

2 Change the Navigation pane to show tables by clicking **Tables** in this drop-down menu. Only Table database objects appear in the Navigation pane.

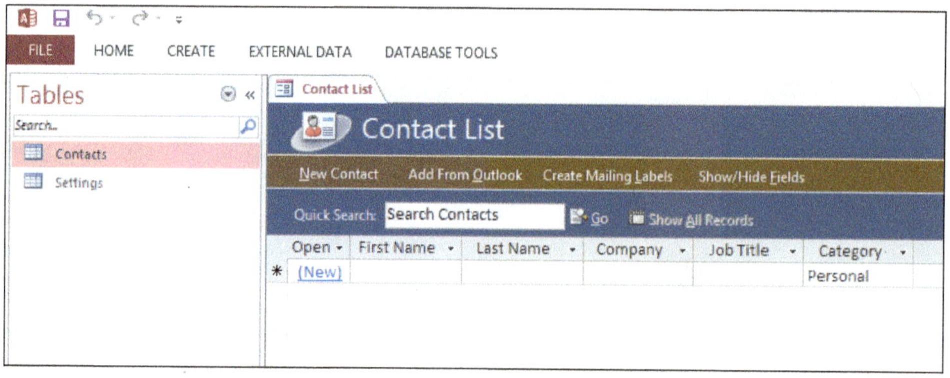


**Figure 1-13**

The Navigation pane configured to display only Tables.

3 Click the **down-arrow** button again and change the display settings back to **All Access Objects**. The Navigation pane will again show all the categories of database objects.

Double-click an object to open it or access more options by right-clicking an object.

To manage objects in the Navigation pane follow these steps:

## STEP BY STEP Managing objects in the Navigation pane

1 Right-click an object, such as *Contacts*, to open a context menu.

The menu lists several options, depending on the object. For a table, these options include such items as Open, Design View, Import, and Export. (For more details about Importing, see Lesson 2, "Getting Started with Microsoft Access 2013.") The important thing to remember is that you can right-click objects to perform actions or to view information.

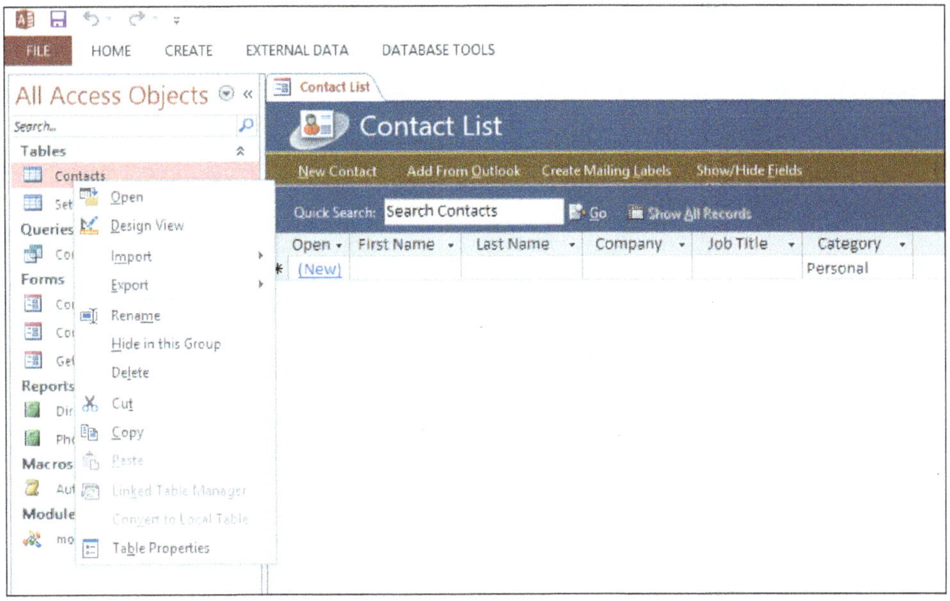


**Figure 1-14**

The context menu lists many options for managing items in the Navigation pane.

2 Choose **File > Close** to close this file.

Access is made up of database objects. The foundational object is the database table. All database objects can be viewed, opened, and even renamed from the Navigation Pane. The Ribbon tabs replace tool bars from past versions of Access and the Backstage view provides users with database management tools like saving, printing, and opening existing databases.

## WORKING WITH RECORDS

Now that you've become familiar with basic database components, you can begin working with database tables. We'll use the Customers table in the **NorthwindTradersCompanyDatabase** database to search for, sort, add, and delete a record.

### Searching for a record

There will be times when you need to locate a specific record in a table, and it can become especially critical if your table contains thousands of records.

## STEP BY STEP Searching a table for a record

1 Choose **File > Open** and navigate to the Access01lessons folder. Double-click **NorthwindTradersCompanyDatabase** to open the file.

2 Double-click the Customers table listed in Navigation pane, or right-click the Customers table and select **Open**. The Customers Table opens in the middle of your screen and looks like a table or spreadsheet with rows and columns.

3 With the Customer table opened, press **Ctrl+F** or click the **Find** button () in the Home tab Ribbon (Editing group). The Find and Replace dialog box appears.

4 In the Find What text box, type **Chris Long**.

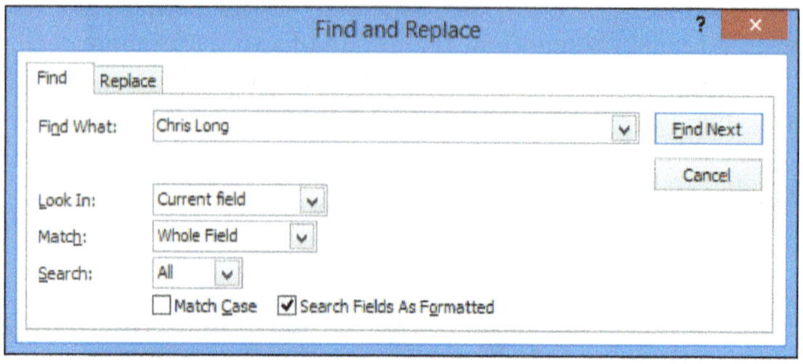


**Figure 1-15**

The Find and Replace window appears.

5 From the Look In drop-down menu, select **Current** document.

6 Click the **Find Next** button on the right side of the box.

Access highlights the record and the specific cell containing the name Chris Long. If you press the **Find Next** button again, a dialog box appears telling you that no more search items were found. There is only one occurrence of the name Chris Long in the Customers table. Click **OK** to close the box.

7 When you are finished using Find and Replace, click **Cancel** to close it.

## Sorting records

Notice that the Customers table is sorted in order by the Customer Number field, which is the first field on the far left side of the table. You can choose to sort by other fields in the table.

**STEP BY STEP** **Sorting records**

1 Click the drop-down arrow on the right side of the Store Name column heading.

2 From the drop-down list that appears, select **Sort A to Z**.

The records are now sorted by StoreName, not by ID.

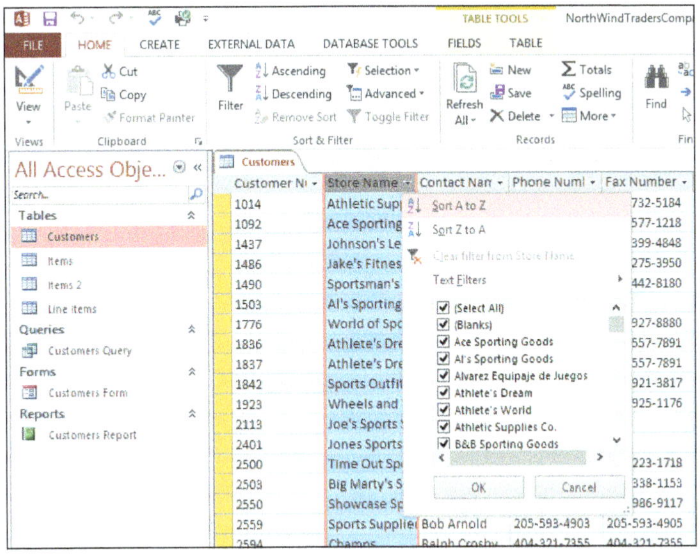


**Figure 1-16**

Sort Records in Store Name column in Ascending Order.

## Adding and deleting records

There are times when you might need to add or delete records from a database table, and this section explains how.

## Adding a record

There are a few different ways to add new records to a table. The first is to click in the very last row of the table, where there will be a star to indicate that the row is blank (note that you might need to scroll down to find it if your table has a lot of records). To add a new record, just start typing in this blank row.

If you don't want to scroll to the very bottom of the table, which might be particularly inconvenient if the table has numerous records, you can add a new record by right-clicking any row.

## STEP BY STEP Adding a record by right-clicking

1 Right-click the **Record Selector** (the leftmost square) of any row.

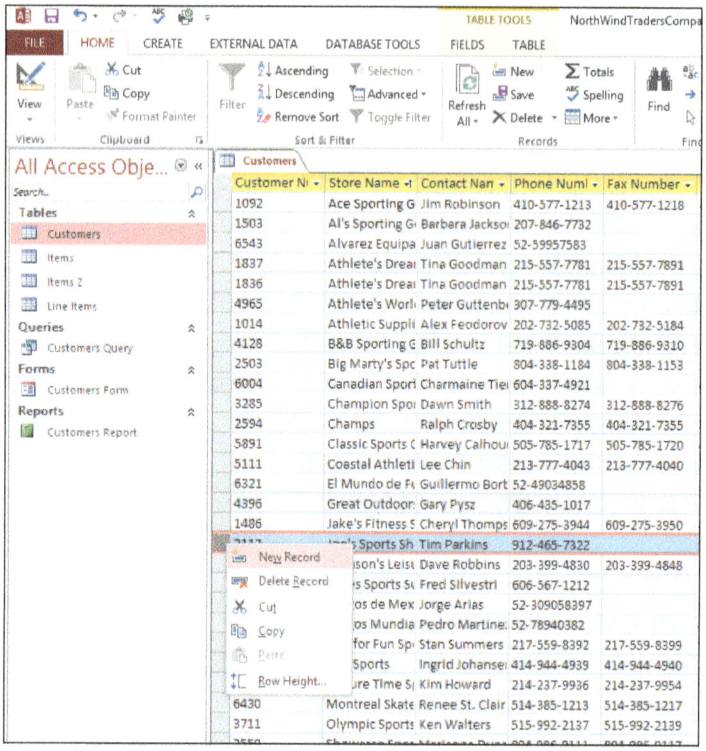


**Figure 1-17**

Add a record regardless of your present location in a table.

2 From the context menu that appears, choose **New Record**. This will automatically move your mouse cursor down to the bottom row of the table. Note that the mouse cursor is blinking in the Customer Number field of the last row.

**Take Note** You can move to the next field by clicking in it with your mouse, or pressing **tab**, **enter**, or the right arrow key on your keyboard.

3 Add three records with the following Customer Numbers:
**7001**
**7002**
**7003**

**STEP BY STEP** **Deleting a record**

1 Right-click the **Record Selector** (the leftmost square) of the record that you want to delete. (For practice, choose one of the records that you added in the previous exercise.)

2 Click **Delete Record**. A Warning box appears asking whether you are sure you want to delete the record, since the activity can't be undone. (This means that you Undo button will not work after the record is deleted.) Click **Yes** to delete.

**Take Note** When an Access table is open, records can be added, deleted, and edited in the table. When a record is deleted, it is a permanent deletion. Undo will not bring it back.

## CUSTOMIZING THE QUICK ACCESS TOOLBAR

The Quick Access Toolbar provides convenient, one-click access to your favorite tools. Initially, the toolbar in the document displays the Save, Redo, and Undo options, and the Customize Quick Access Toolbar button.

You will customize the toolbar to include the Quick Print and Spell Check buttons. If you have completed some of our other Microsoft Office lessons, you will already be familiar with this process.

**Figure 1-18**
The Quick Access Toolbar.

To customize the Quick Access Toolbar to include the Quick Print and Spelling commands:

**STEP BY STEP** **Customizing the quick Access Toolbar**

1 Click the **Customize Quick Access Toolbar** button and from the drop-down menu, choose **Spelling**.

The Quick Access Toolbar now contains the Quick Print and Spelling commands.

**Figure 1-19**
The new command is now added to the Quick Access Toolbar.

2 To remove a command, right-click it, and then choose **Remove from Quick Access Toolbar**.

## GETTING HELP

Microsoft Access contains a Help system designed to help you quickly get answers to questions regarding your Access database.

**STEP BY STEP** **Using the Help System**

1 Press the **F1** key or click the **Help** button (?) in the top-right corner of the Access screen. The Help System appears.

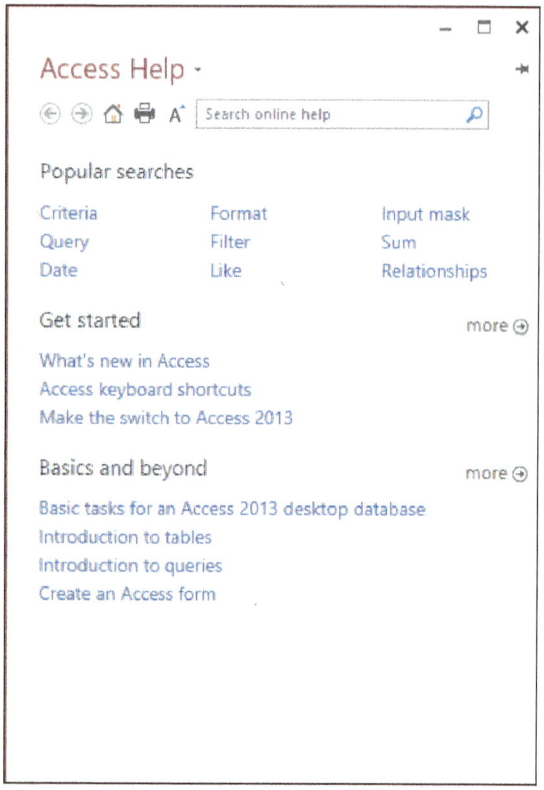


**Figure 1-20**
Get help by pressing F1 or clicking the Help button.

2 To close the Help box, click the **X** button (☒) in the top-right corner.

## ENDING AN ACCESS SESSION

You can quickly end a Microsoft Access session by following these steps.

**STEP BY STEP** **Ending a session**

1 Click the **File** tab and then **Save**.

2 Click the **Close** button (☒) located in the upper-right corner of the program.

## What you learned in this lesson:

- What is Access?
- Ways to use Access
- Database basics
- Exploring a database
- Working with records
- Customizing the Quick Access Toolbar
- Getting Help
- Ending an Access Session

# Knowledge Assessment

## True False

**Circle T if the statement is true or F it the statement is false.**

T F 1. Microsoft Access allows you to store and organize your data through the use of graphics.

T F 2. Databases and spreadsheets have many similar functions.

T F 3. When data becomes too complicated to manage in a spreadsheet, a database is often a very useful tool for begin managing the data.

T F 4. Microsoft Access is made up objects.

T F 5. The most important object in an Access database is a Form.

T F 6. In an Access database a table column is called a Category.

T F 7. The Navigation Pane located on left hand side of the Access interface allows you to open, close, and organize database objects.

T F 8. If you hit Ctrl + F on the keyboard while in a Table, you will open the Spell Check.

T F 9. If you delete a record in an open Table, Undo will bring it back.

T F 10. One method for inserting a new record into an open Table is to right-click the Record Selector next to an existing record and then select New Record in the context menu.

## Multiple Choice

**Select the best response for the following statements.**

1. Why are tables considered the most important object in an Access database:
   a. They allow users to print data in useful ways.
   b. They allow data to be filtered and categorized in new ways.
   c. They allow users to more easily enter data into the database.
   d. They allow data to be stored in rows and columns and manipulated in other database objects.
2. What is the main purpose of a data base Forms?
   a. Creating a pleasing print out of database information.
   b. To allow for easy filtering and sorting of large database tables.
   c. To allow for easy data-entry, editing, and display of data stored in Tables.
   d. To allow for easy viewing of data in an internet browser.
3. What are some important points to consider before creating database?
   a. Plan carefully, each table should have only one main purpose, and avoid duplication in your data.
   b. Planning isn't critical. You will need most of your time for data-entry.
   c. Ensure your forms have carefully planned out layouts to create excellent visual impact and clarity.
   d. Spent the bulk of your time considering what size paper your reports will need to print on to fit all the information.
4. What screen does Microsoft Access open when you first enter the program?
   a. The Save screen.
   b. The Backstage view.
   c. The Options box.
   d. The Navigation Pane.

5. What are the main (default) categories of the Navigation Pane?
   a. Tables, Queries, Forms, Reports, Macros, and Modules
   b. Forms only
   c. Reports and Queries
   d. The database by itself
6. To sort records in an Access table, you
   a. Click on the Create Ribbon tab. and select Sort
   b. Right-click on the field heading and select Sort A to Z or Sort Z to A
   c. Use the navigation area at the bottom of the table
   d. Go to the Backstage view
7. What two methods will open the Help in Access?
   a. Right-click anywhere on the screen and select Help or type Help in a table cell
   b. Hit the F1 key on the keyboard or click the Help button in the top right hand corner the Access window
   c. Select Help from the Backstage view or click the Help button on the bottom of the screen.
   d. Click the Help button on the Quick Access Toolbar or click the Help button on the Home Ribbon tab.
8. Why do different Ribbon tabs open in Access depending on what you are doing in your database?
   a. Depending on your task in the database, different Ribbon tabs called Context Ribbons may open to help you complete your task.
   b. If different Ribbon tabs open, it means you need to save your database.
   c. Different Ribbon tabs may open when a database table becomes too large.
   d. Different Ribbon tabs never open in Access.
9. What is the difference between a record and a field in a database?
   a. A record is can only be viewed in a form
   b. A field only allows for numerical information to be stored in it; while a record can hold any type of information
   c. There are no differences between fields and records, the two terms can be used interchangeably
   d. Records are rows in a database table and fields are columns.
10. Where can you add your favorite database shortcuts?
   a. Shortcut buttons can placed on the Quick Access Toolbar
   b. Add favorite shortcuts to any Ribbon tab by customizing it
   c. Add shortcuts to the bottom of the Access window
   d. Add shortcuts to the Navigation Pane

## Competency Assessment

### Project 1-1: Creating and editing a new database using a template

**Create a new database based on a Microsoft Template and edit an existing table in the database to track information regarding your company's inventory.**

1. Click **File**. From the Backstage view, click **New**.
2. In the New area, click **Desktop asset tracking**.
3. Browse to the Access01lessons folder.
4. In the File name box, type **Northwind Traders Products** and click **Create**.
5. The Navigation pane will open with many database objects already created. Expand and collapse the Navigation pane.
6. From the Navigation pane, double-click on the **Assets** table to open it.
7. Double-click the **Contacts** table and open it up.
8. Minimize the Ribbon tabs.
9. Enter a record of your choosing into the top row of the table.
10. Click the **File** Ribbon tab and in the Backstage view, click **Close**.

### Project 1-2: Creating a new database

**Create a new database from scratch.**

1. Click **File** and from the Backstage view, click **New**.
2. Click **Blank desktop database**.
3. Type the File name: **HR Management**.
4. The new database will open with one table. The new table will be open and is called, Table 1.
5. Collapse the Navigation pane.
6. Click on the **Customize Quick Access Toolbar** arrow and add three new short-cut buttons to the Quick Access toolbar of your choosing.
7. Minimize the Ribbon tabs.
8. Maximize the Ribbon tabs.
9. With the Table1 open, notice the Context ribbon tabs that are open.
10. Click on the **Table Tools, Field Ribbon** tab and explore some of its buttons.
11. Click on the **Table Tools, Table Ribbon** tab and explore some of its buttons.
12. Click **File** and **Close** to close the database.

# Proficiency Assessment

## Project 1-3: Creating a customer database using a template

**You are working for a company that has been tracking their customer contacts in an Excel spreadsheet. However, you need a more powerful contact management tool and want to see what Access has to offer. You will open a new database based on a contact management template available from Microsoft and explore it.**

1. From New in Backstage view, click the **Contacts** category in the templates categories.
2. Click the **Desktop** contacts template.
3. Name the database, **Customer Contacts** and create the database.
4. If a tutorial box titled, Getting Started with Contacts opens, close the box.
5. From the Navigation pane, open the Contacts table.
6. Type three new records into the table using information of your choosing but applicable to the table. (Hint: Don't worry about typing anything in the ID field; Access will automatically fill in this field for you.)
7. Right-click on one of your records and delete.
8. Type a new record to replace the deleted one.
9. Save and then close the table.

## Project 1-4: Creating a new database and adding tables

**You need to create a new database to track information regarding a new project. The database will need to have three tables. It will be created from scratch because none of the Microsoft Access templates are applicable to your information.**

1. From New in Backstage view, click **Blank desktop database**.
2. Name the database, **Project X** and click **Create**.
3. When the database opens, it will contain one blank table.
4. Click the **Create Ribbon** tab and click the **Tables** button in the Tables group. A second blank table called Table 2 will open.
5. Click the **Create Ribbon** tab again and create a third blank table. It will be called Table 3.
6. In the Navigation pane, filter the Navigation pane list to only display tables.
7. Return the Navigation pane to display all objects.
8. In the Search box, above the Navigation pane, type **Table2** and hit enter.
9. Notice even though it is opened, it will become the active table in the middle of your screen.
10. Click **File > Save** and then **File > close** to close the database.

# Mastery Assessment

## Project 1-5: Selecting the best template for a project

**You have just started working for a small business that currently maintains all its HR data in a spreadsheet. The HR manager would like to begin managing this data in an Access database. After meeting with the HR manager, you decide to create your database based on an Access template.**

1. Select the best Access template for managing HR data from the templates available with Microsoft Access.
2. Explore the tables that are created with the template and make note of which tables in the template will be most useful to your company's needs in regards to this project.
3. Select a table in your new database and enter 10 records into your new database using applicable company information (that you create). Then perform a **Find and Sort** on the new records to show your HR manager how the data can be managed from the database tables.
4. Save your file as **Project1-5_done**.

## Project 1-6: Finding and editing data

**You need to locate specific data in a database and make some changes to it.**

1. Reopen the database used at the beginning of this lesson called **NorthWindTradersCompanyDatabase**. Save this database as **Project1-6_done**.
2. In the Customers table, delete three records with following Customer Numbers: **3711**, **3285**, and **3504**.
3. Sort the Customers table by the Store Name field in ascending order.
4. In the Items2 table, sort the Product Description field by ascending order.
5. Close both the tables and the database.

# 2 Getting Started with Microsoft Access 2013

## LESSON SKILL MATRIX

| In this lesson, you will learn the following skills: |
|---|
| Access 2013 database types |
| Tables, views, and data types |
| Importing data from a Microsoft Excel spreadsheet |
| Renaming a New Table from an Excel spreadsheet |

## KEY TERMS

- **Desktop (standard) Database**
- **Web app database**
- **Datasheet view**
- **Design view**
- **Primary Key**
- **Data type**

Javier owns a company that manufactures custom clocks. He has always kept track of his inventory and products in an Excel spreadsheet. However, he wants to be able to create reports and forms to make it easier to track his clock inventory using a database program like Microsoft Access. He has a basic understanding of Access, and he is now ready to create tables for an inventory database and also import some of the data from his Excel spreadsheets into his Access database.

## SOFTWARE ORIENTATION

This lesson helps you to work with creating databases and importing data into a database using Microsoft Access 2013

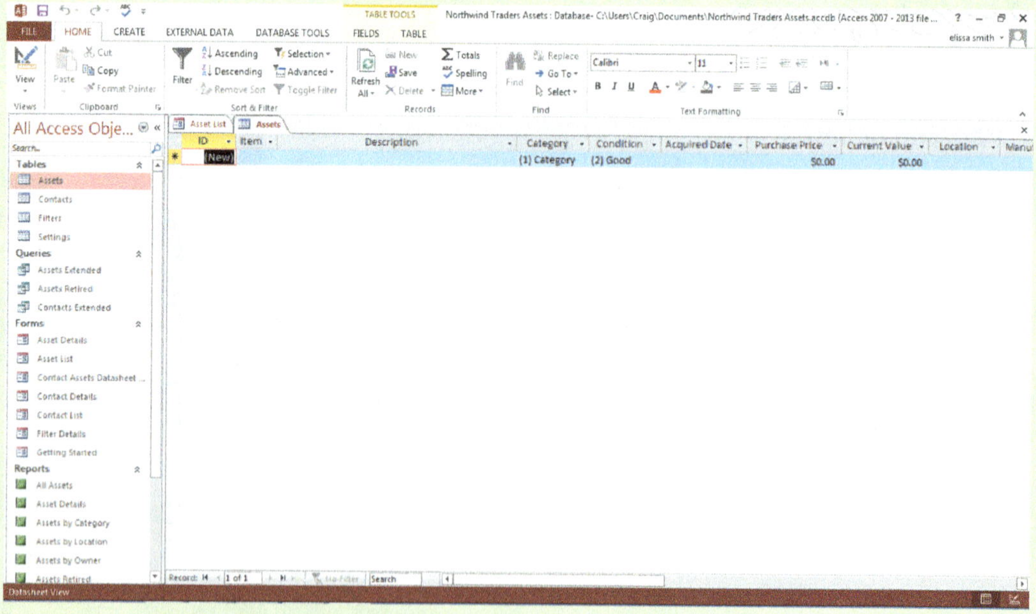


**Figure 2-1**

Microsoft Access database interface

## STARTING UP

In this lesson, you'll work with several files from the Access02lessons folder. Make sure that you have loaded the OfficeLessons folder onto your computer.

## ACCESS 2013 DATABASE TYPES

Access 2013 has two types of databases:

**Desktop (standard) database**, which is stored on your computer, a network, or another computer storage location and run directly from the location on your computer. The exercises in this lesson involve the desktop database type.

An **Access web app**, which was introduced with Access 2013. This new type of database can be built from Access, and then used and shared with others as a SharePoint app in a web browser. You create the app by selecting the type of data you want to track (contacts, tasks, projects, and so on), and Access makes the database structure, complete with views that let you add and edit data.

### Creating a simple database

In Lesson 1, you explored a database. Now you will create one. Access 2013 has two methods for creating a database.

The first method is to use the templates provided with Access 2013. A template is a database created for a specific type of task that contains several pre-made database objects. When using a template to create a database, all you need to do is add your own data to the tables, and customize the template as needed.

When you use templates to create databases, you're not limited to using the objects as they come with the templates; you can customize the objects and adapt them to fit your needs. For example, if you have a better design for a form, you need a different field name for a table, or you need a new table, you can customize these objects. You can also add your own database objects to the ones that already exist in the template.

The second option for creating a database is to create a new and empty database from scratch. Many people use this option when the database they need to create is too complicated and they cannot locate a suitable template.

## Workplace Ready

It's also very common for Access users to work with existing databases. You will probably enter information into the database, create new database objects, and edit existing data.

### Creating a database using a template

**STEP BY STEP** **Creating a database using a template**

1 Open Access if it is not already opened and open the Backstage view. Select the **New** command.

The New area displays several categories of templates. In the Search for Online Templates box, you can search for online templates from the Office.com site. There are also suggested search topics listed under the search box, such as Assets, Business Contacts, Inventory, Project, Sales, and more.

Workplace Ready: Microsoft Access templates are created to fit the needs of many broad business uses. If you are needing to create a database, be sure to carefully look over the Access templates, one of them may fit your needs.

The next area includes different templates that appear as thumbnails. These templates are available for you to select directly from the New area of the Backstage view, and they are either Access apps or Desktop Access databases. Below is a list of these templates:

- Custom web app: Access app made for you to customize from scratch
- Blank desktop database: creates a new blank database
- Desktop contacts
- Asset Tracking
- Contacts
- Issue tracking
- Project management:
- Desktop asset tracking
- Desktop issue Tracking
- Desktop project management
- Desktop task management

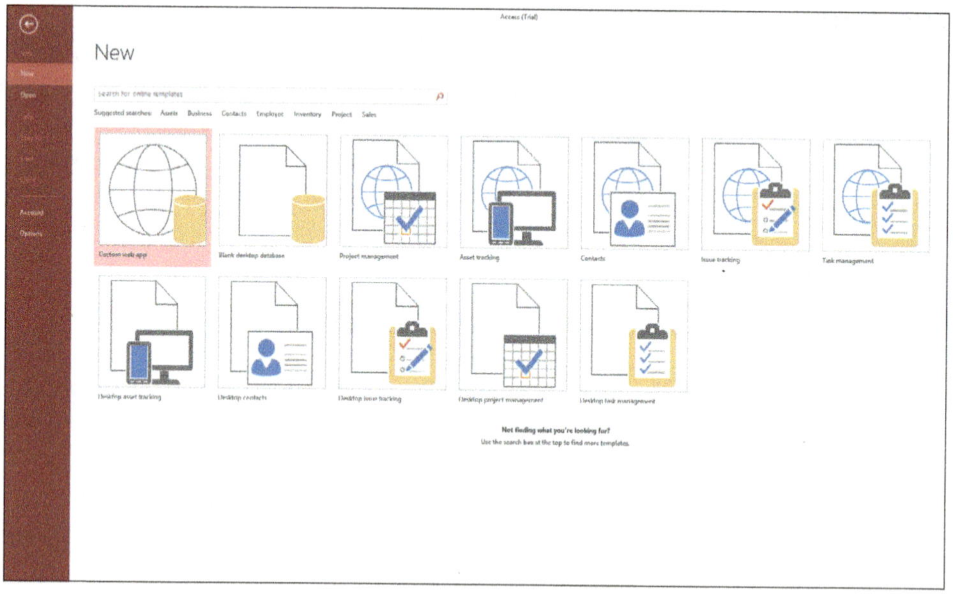


**Figure 2-2**
The Backstage view appears with the New tab selected.

2 From the second row, select the ***Desktop asset tracking*** template. The Desktop asset tracking information box opens.

**Figure 2-3**

Desktop asset tracking information dialog box.

3 In the File Name box, type the File Name **NorthWind Traders Assets**. Click **browse**, navigate to the Access02lessons folder, and click **OK**. Now click **Create**.

When the database opens, you may see a warning about disabled content. Click **Enable Content**. You may then see a message box labeled *Getting Started with Assets*. You can close it by clicking the **Close** button in the top-right corner.

Look at the Navigation bar. Notice the different objects that are automatically created because your database is based on a template.

4 In the Navigation pane, under the Tables Object category, double-click the table called ***Assets***.

When the table opens, notice that there are no records in it. However, all the fields (columns) are set up and prepared for you to enter information into the table.

5 Click the File Ribbon tab and select **Close**. This closes the database, but leaves Access running.

**Take Note** You can have multiple databases open simultaneously, but closing unused databases frees up your computer's resources and speeds up processes in the database that you are working with.

## STEP BY STEP Creating a database from scratch

1. Click **File** to enter the Backstage view, and then select **New**.
2. From the first row, select ***Blank desktop database***. The Blank desktop database box opens.
3. In the File Name text box, type **SCRATCH**, browse to the Access02lessons folder, and click **OK**. Click **Create** and notice that only one object is created for this database: Table1.

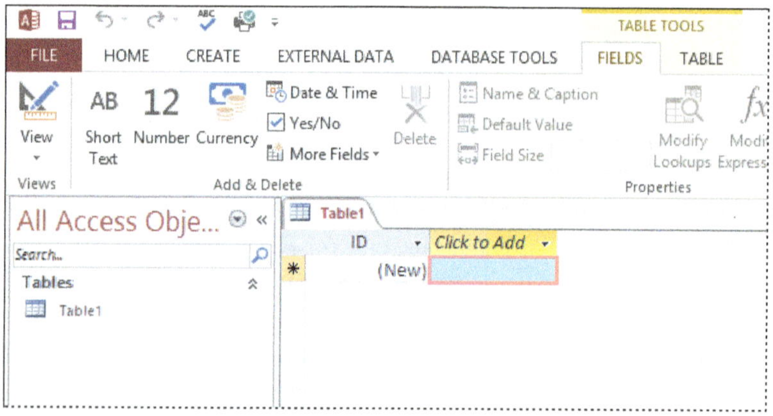


**Figure 2-4**
The SCRATCH database opens with the Table1 object open and ready for data entry. It is the only object that is created when you make a new blank database.

### Saving a new table

Now that your new database is open, and you have one new table created, you need to give your table a name.

## STEP BY STEP Saving a new table

1. In the Quick Access Toolbar, click the **Save** icon ( ) or choose **File > Save**. The Save As dialog box appears.
2. In the Table Name text box, type **Assets**. Press **Enter** or click **OK**.

## TABLES, VIEWS, AND DATA TYPES

Tables are crucial to Access databases and form the framework of relational databases. Next, you will investigate various ways to view tables, and how to prepare them for the data they will hold.

- You can view tables in Access 2013 in one of two ways: Datasheet view and Design view.
- **Datasheet view** is designed for data entry and viewing records. You can add, delete, edit, sort, filter, and print records from this view. You can also insert, delete, categorize new fields, and change their order.

- **Design view** is where the table's design is the focus. It lists all the fields with their data types and descriptions. In this view, you do not see the actual records.

## Creating a table in Datasheet view

Datasheet view allows you to add tables and fields to your database. It resembles a spreadsheet, such as you would find in Excel.

### STEP BY STEP Creating a table in Datasheet view

1. Using the **SCRATCH** database that you created in the previous section, click the **Create** tab.
2. From the Tables group (second group of commands from the left), select the **Table** command. *Table1* appears in Datasheet view.
3. To rename Table1, click the **Save** button in the Quick Access Toolbar. When the Save As dialog box appears, type **Products** in the text box, and then press **Enter**.

In Datasheet view, you can examine the table more closely and notice the following:

- The words Datasheet View are displayed in the lower-left corner of the Status Bar. (The status bar is located at the bottom of the Access window.)
- The Datasheet view icon ( ) is active in the lower-right corner of the Status Bar; the Design View icon ( ) is inactive.

In the Views group of Home tab, the Design View command appears in color. When you click the down-arrow, you can see in the menu that the Datasheet view option is active, but the Design view option is inactive. The Design View icon is the one that appears in the View group because it's the option that you can toggle to when you are in the Datasheet view.

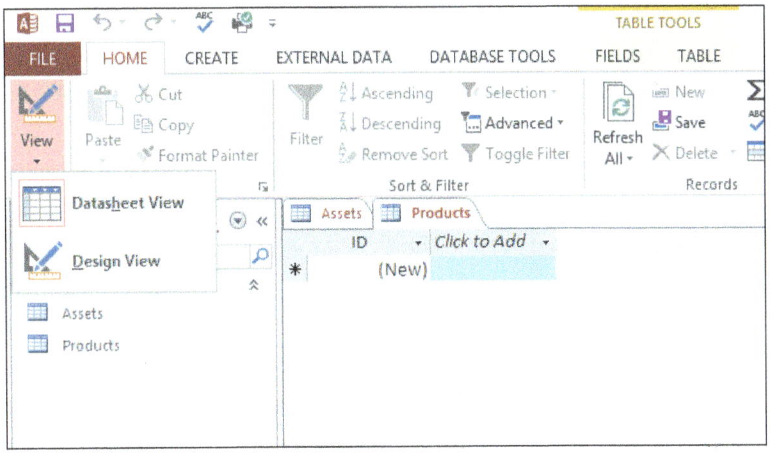


**Figure 2-5**

Datasheet View button active on Home tab after clicking the Design View command.

**Take Note** Although the Design View command is in color in the Views group of the Home tab, Access is currently in Datasheet view.

Next, you'll spend some time examining the table's Datasheet view. When you create a new table, Access automatically creates a field (first column) in the new table. This field is called ID and Access assigns it to be a Primary Key. (A Primary Key is a unique record identifier for a table.)

The second column is ready for you to assign it a field data type.

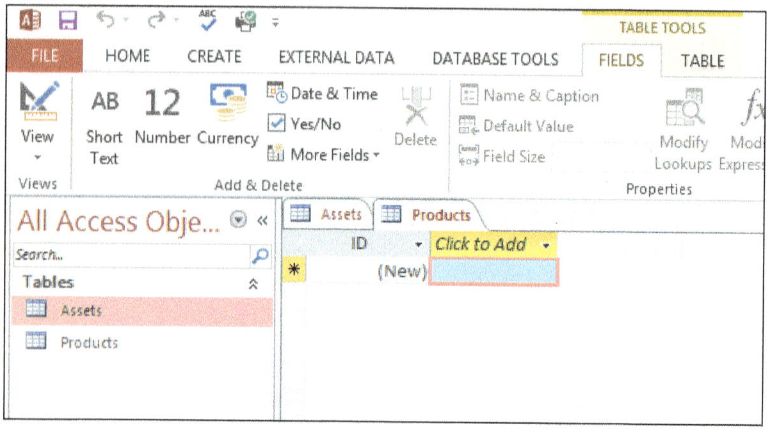


**Figure 2-6**

The highlight on the first cell under the ID field heading indicates that it is ready for data entry.

## Adding fields to an Access table

There are multiple ways to add fields to a datasheet. One way is to assign the **data type** and then enter the name of the field. A field's data type determines the type of information that can be stored in that column of your table, and the type of information that *cannot* be stored in the column. For example, if you have a Funds field of data type Currency, you couldn't enter letters or characters such as A, B, C; you also could enter letters into a Birthday field with a Date/Time data type.

There are ten basic data types available in an Access table:

- **Short Text** (*formerly called* **Text**): alphanumeric data (names, titles, etc.). The maximum length allowed is 255 characters.
- **Long Text** (*formerly called* **Memo**): large amounts of alphanumeric data, for example, sentences and paragraphs. The maximum number of characters allowed is up to about 1 gigabyte (GB), but controls to display long text are limited to the first 64,000 characters.
- **Number:** numeric data.
- **Date/Time:** dates and times.
- **Currency:** monetary data, stored with four decimal places of precision.
- **AutoNumber:** unique value generated by Access for each new record; often a primary key field that Access automatically generates in new Access tables.
- **Yes/No:** Boolean (true/false) data. Access stores the numeric value zero (0) for false, and -1 for true.
- **OLE Object:** pictures, graphs, or other ActiveX objects from another Windows-based application.
- **Hyperlink:** a link address to a document or file on the Internet, on an intranet, on a local area network (LAN), or on your local computer.

- **Attachment:** files such as pictures, documents, spreadsheets, or charts that you can attach to a field. Each Attachment field can contain an unlimited number of attachments per record, up to the storage limit of the size of a database file.

- **Calculated:** an expression that uses data from one or more fields. You can designate different result data types from the expression. Dependent on the data type of the Result Type property. Short Text data type results can be up to 243 characters long. Long Text, Number, Yes/No, and Date/Time should match their respective data types.

- **Lookup Wizard**: the Lookup Wizard entry in the Data Type column in Design view is not actually a data type. When you choose this entry, a wizard starts to help you define either a simple or complex lookup field. A simple lookup field uses the contents of another table or a value list to validate the contents of a single value per row. A complex lookup field allows you to store multiple values of the same data type in each row. Dependent on the data type of the lookup field.

The most common data type is Short Text.

Data types can have some unexpected properties. For example, the Text field can contain numbers, and numbers can have a data type such as Text, Number, and Currency.

For this next exercise, you will add these three fields to the Products table you created in the previous exercise: Product Name, Product Number, and Order Date.

## STEP BY STEP Adding fields to an Access table

1. In the second column heading, click the **Click to Add** down-arrow, and then select ***Short Text***. The words Click to Add are replaced with Field1.
2. Rename the heading Field1 by typing **Product Name**, and then press **Enter**.
3. Repeat steps 1 and 2 for the third column heading. Choose **Number** for the Data Type field and rename the heading to **Product Number**.
4. Repeat steps 1 and 2 for the fourth column heading. Choose **Date/Time** for the Data Type field and rename the heading to **Order Date**.

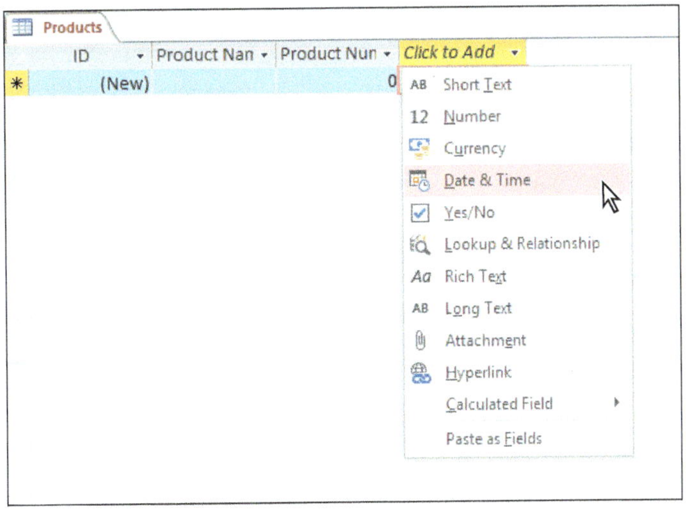


**Figure 2-7**

Creating a Date/Time field called Order Date in the Products Table.

5. Save the Product table, but don't close it. You will use it in the next section.

## Creating a table in Design view

You can use Design view to add tables and fields to your database. Design view offers more control over field structure and properties than Datasheet view. Design view is also well-suited for controlling field data types and descriptions.

When creating a table using Design view, you begin by creating the table structure in Design view; you then switch to Datasheet view to enter or import data.

**STEP BY STEP** **Adding a table to a database using Design view**

1 Using the **SCRATCH** database you used in the previous exercises, click the **Create** tab, and then select the **Table Design** command from the Tables group.

The new table appears as a separate tab and is open in Design view. Look at the status bar at the bottom of the window. The words *Design View* appear on the left side of the status bar, and the Design View icon ( ) is active on the right side.

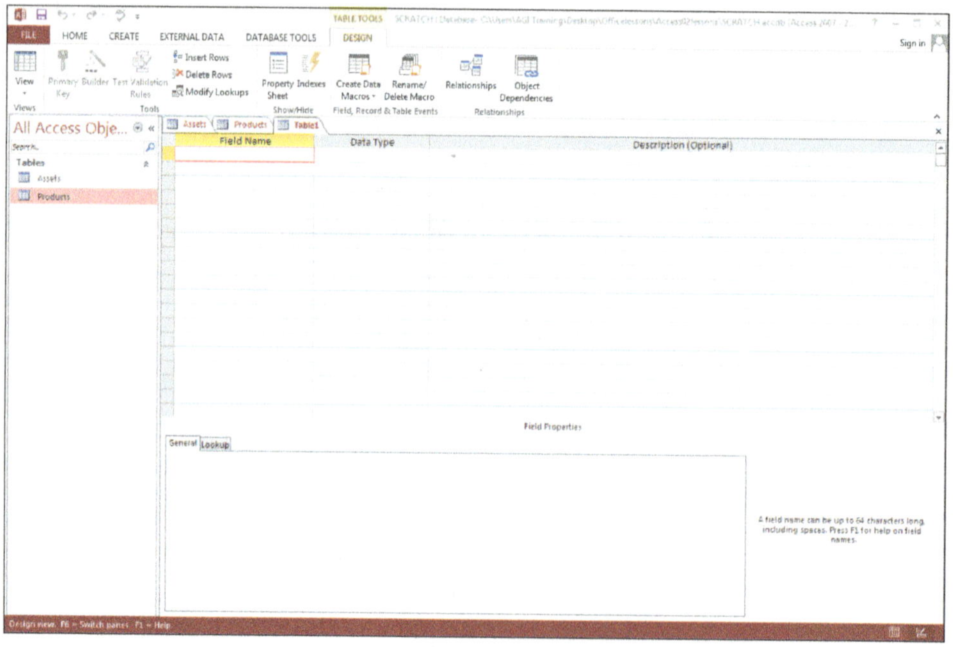


**Figure 2-8**

The Status bar shows the Design view icon. The new Table opens in Design View.

## Adding fields to a table

Many database tables require a unique field (column) or set of fields that uniquely identify each record stored in the table. This field is called the **primary key field**. The selection of a primary key is one of the most critical decisions you'll make in the design of a new table.

Primary key fields cannot be memo fields, OLE fields. A primary key field is often a unique number or combination or letters and numbers that make each record unique. You will now add fields to the table you just created in Design view.

## STEP BY STEP Adding fields to a table

1 Add the following information in each of the columns:

| FIELD NAME | DATA TYPE | DESCRIPTION |
|---|---|---|
| Vendor Number | Short Text | Vendor Identification Number |
| Vendor Address | Long Text | Vendor Address |
| Vendor Contact Name | Short Text | Contact Person's Phone Number |
| Current | Yes/No | Active Vendor |

**Figure 2-9**

Creating a Yes/No field in Design View.

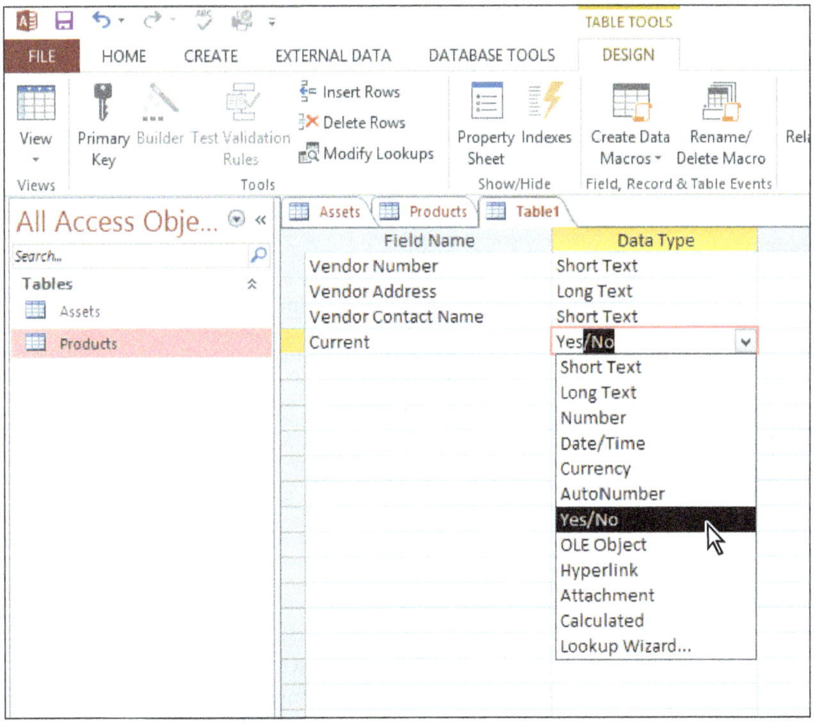


For many fields, a description might seem unnecessary, but you should enter a description for any field that might have an unclear name. The description appears in that table's status bar when the field is selected using Datasheet view; this is helpful to others when entering data.

2 From the Field Name column, select the **Vendor Number** cell.

3 From the Table Tools > Design context Ribbon tab, click the **Primary Key** button ( ). A small gold key appears to the left of the Vendor Number cell representing that this field has now become the primary key for this table. It will allow each row to be uniquely identified and assist in sorting, filtering, and table relationships.

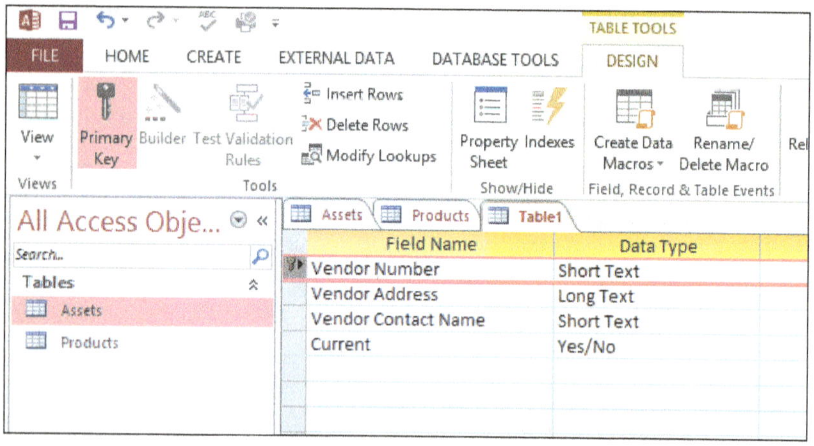


**Figure 2-10**

Selecting the Primary Key.

4 Right-click the **Table1** tab and choose **Save** from the context menu. The Save As dialog box appears.

5 In the Table Name text box, type **Vendor Info**. Then click **OK**.

6 Now, the table is ready for data-entry from the Datasheet view. To change views, right-click the tab of the Vendor Info table and select **Datasheet view** from the context menu.

**Bottom Line**

Access tables can be create in two views. These views are the Table View and the Design View. A critical component in Table Design is field data types. Data types determine what types of data can be entered into Access tables.

## IMPORTING DATA FROM A MICROSOFT EXCEL SPREADSHEET

Spreadsheets can store data, but databases are more powerful, expandable, and often easier when managing large amounts of data. You can import data from external sources, such as text files, XML files, other database types, and spreadsheets into your Access 2013 databases. In this next exercise, you will use the Import Spreadsheet Wizard to import data from an Excel spreadsheet into your table.

### Workplace Ready

Many businesses utilize Microsoft Excel spreadsheets to track business information. As time passes, they realize they need more tools for reporting and tracking information and Access provides that tools. Importing Excel spreadsheet into Access is an easy process and allows Excel information to be made into an Access database.

**STEP BY STEP** **Importing data from a Microsoft Excel spreadsheet**

1 Open the program Microsoft Excel and choose **File > Open**. Navigate to the Access02lessons folder and double-click **Orders** to open the spreadsheet.

When the Orders spreadsheet opens in Microsoft Excel, notice that each column has a column heading (name) and that each row underneath is continual with no blank rows between.

This spreadsheets looks very much like an Access table. When the spreadsheet is formatted like this, it makes it easy to import it into Access as table.

2 Switch back to Access where your **SCRATCH** database is still active by clicking the **Access** icon found on the Task bar along the bottom of your screen.

3 In Access, select the **External Data** tab. From the Import & Link group, click **Excel**.

4 In the Get External Data window, click **Browse**, navigate to the **Orders** Excel file in the Access02lessons folder, and select it. Click **Open**. The path and file name of the **Orders** Excel file appears in the File name text field.

5 The option Import the source data into a new table in the current database is selected by default. Don't change this selection.

6 Click **OK**. The Import Spreadsheet Wizard opens. Click **Next**; the first row of your Excel spreadsheet already contains column headings.

7 Click **Finish**, and then click **Close**.

8 In the Navigation pane, double-click the new table called **Sheet1** to open it and see the imported data.

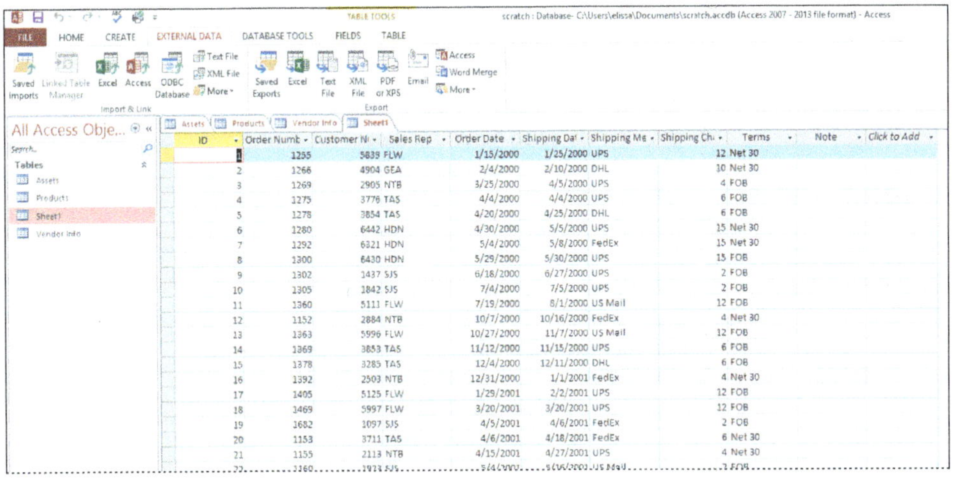

**Figure 2-11**

The data has been imported from the Excel spreadsheet into your Access table.

## TO RENAME A NEW SHEET

**STEP BY STEP** **Renaming a new sheet**

1 Right-click the **Sheet1** table Tab, and select **Close** from the context menu.

2 In the Navigation pane, right-click the **Sheet1** Table. A context menu appears.

3 From the context menu, choose **Rename**. The Sheet1 name appears highlighted.

4 Type **Orders** to replace the highlighted text, and then press **Enter**.

**Take Note** Data can be imported into Access from various program including Microsoft Excel. The Spreadsheet Import Wizard is a tool designed specifically for this purpose.

### What you learned in this lesson:

- Access 2013 database types
- Tables, views, and data types
- Importing data from a Microsoft Excel spreadsheet
- Renaming a New Table from an Excel spreadsheet

# Knowledge Assessment

## True/ False

**Circle T if the statement is true or F it the statement is false.**

T F 1. Microsoft Access 2013 provides users with three types of databases: desktop, web app, and mobile.

T F 2. There are two methods for creating a new database: creating an empty database from scratch or creating a database based on a template.

T F 3. It is very common to Access users to work in existing databases by updating data, creating new objects, and entering new data into the existing database.

T F 4. When creating a database based on a template, it isn't necessary to provide a file name before the template can be used.

T F 5. Access 2013 will only allow you to have one database open at a time.

T F 6. Access tables have two views that are called the Datasheet View and the Design View.

T F 7. The Table Design View is created for data-entry and viewing records.

T F 8. When you create a new table in Access, the first column in the table is called ID and is a Primary Key field that acts as a unique identifier for information in the table.

T F 9. There are twelve basic data types (field types) available in Access tables.

T F 10. Primary key fields cannot be memo fields, OLE fields, or Memo fields.

## Multiple Choice

**Select the best response for the following statements.**

1. What is the most common data type in Access?
   a. AutoNumber
   b. Short Text
   c. Date/Time
   d. Currency
2. Why is the data type of a field so critical to a table's design?
   a. Data type will determine the type of information that can be stored or not stored in that field (column) of your Access table.
   b. Data type's password protect specific table fields, and only those with the password can enter data into those columns.
   c. Data type is only critical if the table is being imported from another program like Excel.
   d. Data types determine how many records an Access table can hold.
3. An AutoNumber data type is created by Access and has what specific characteristics?
   a. AutoNumber fields can only hold text.
   b. AutoNumber fields must be blank.
   c. AutoNumber fields contain a unique value and often act as a primary key.
   d. AutoNumber fields allow users to link images to their Access tables.
4. When importing spreadsheet information from Excel into access, what tool is used?
   a. The Table Wizard
   b. The Query Wizard
   c. The Table Design Wizard
   d. The Import Spreadsheet Wizard

5. You can easily rename a table in Access by:
   a. Closing the table and opening it again in Design View
   b. Closing the table, right-clicking on it in the Navigation Pane, and selecting Rename
   c. Creating a query with the new table name
   d. Printing all the records in the table
6. What makes the web app database type different from the desktop database type?
   a. The Web app database can be used and shared with others as a SharePoint app in a web browser; while a desktop database will only work if the user has Access installed on their computer.
   b. The web app database will only run on a computer with an Apple operating system, and the desktop database will only run on a computer with a windows operating system.
   c. The web app will only run in Internet Explorer and the desktop database type will only open databases in Firefox.
   d. None of the Above.
7. From the Access Datasheet view, you can:
   a. Set specific properties on your table data types
   b. control how many records are entered into your table
   c. Create new data types
   d. add, delete, edit, sort, filter, and print table records
8. How many characters can a Short Text field hold?
   a. 105
   b. 255
   c. 305
   d. 105
9. If you need to create a field to hold monetary information, what should the data type be?
   a. Date/Time
   b. Yes/No
   c. Currency
   d. AutoNumber
10. When creating a table in Design view, you first focus on:
   a. Creating the table's design, data types, and properties
   b. Entering data
   c. Printing data
   d. Creating new database objects

# Competency Assessment

## Project 2-1: Creating a new table in Design view

**You will open the Northwind Traders Tables database and create a new table in the Design view and set table properties in the table.**

1. Click **File**. From the Backstage view, click **Open** and navigate to your student drive.
2. Open the file **Northwind Traders Tables**. Save the file as **Project2-1_done**.
3. Click the **Create Ribbon** tab. From the Tables group, click **Table Design**.
4. Your new blank table will open in the Table Design view.
5. Your cursor will be blinking in the Field Name column. Type **Manager Name** in the Field Name text field.
6. In the Data Type column, type **Short Text**.
7. In the Description column, type **Full Manager Name**.
8. From the following table, enter the following field names:

| Field Name | Data Type | Description |
|---|---|---|
| **Department** | **Short Text** | **Department Name** |
| **Department Description** | **Long Text** | **Department Description** |
| **Department Code** | **Number** | **Department Numeric Code** |

   Right-click on the new table tab and choose **Datasheet** view.
9. Name the new table, **Managers**. Don't set a primary key, when it prompts to do this.
10. Close the database.

## Project 2-2: Editing a table in Datasheet view

**Edit an existing table in the Datasheet view by editing data types and also inserting some new columns into the table.**

1. From Open in the Backstage view, navigate to the Acces02lessons folder and open the **Northwind Traders Tables** database. Save the file as **Project2-2_done**. From the Navigation pane, open the Customers table in the Datasheet view.
2. Right-click on the **Customers** table tab and click **Design view**.
3. In the Description field, for Customer Number, add the following, **Each Number should contain the prefix CU#**.
4. Scroll down in the field names list and under the last field, Contract Date, add an Email field.
5. Set the data type to **Hyperlink**.
6. Close the database.

# Proficiency Assessment

## Project 2-3: Creating a new database from a template

**You will create a new database based on a template from the Business category of Microsoft Access templates.**

1. From the File Ribbon tab, select New.
2. Under New, search the Business category of templates.
3. Select the Desktop customer service template.
4. Name the template, Northwind Traders Customer Service.
5. Make sure the Navigation pane is open and is sorted by Object Type.
6. Open the Customers table.
7. Enter three new records into the Customers table.
8. Switch and view the table in the Design View.
9. Close the database.

## Project 2-4: Importing Excel data into a database

**You need to open an existing database and import some data from an Excel spreadsheet into the database.**

1. From the Access02lessons folder, open the file, Northwind Traders Import.
2. From the lesson folder, open the Excel file, Northwind Traders Employee List. Take a look at the information in this spreadsheet. It contains an employee list that you want to be part of your Northwind Traders Import database. You will import this spreadsheet into the Northwind Traders Import database. Close Excel.
3. Return to Access and click the External Data Ribbon tab.
4. In the Import & Link group, click Excel. The Get External Data dialog box will open.
5. Browse to the lesson folder and select the Northwind Traders Employee List. Keep the top option, Import the source data into a new table in the current database, selected. Click OK.
6. The Import Spreadsheet Wizard will open.
7. Click Finish and Close in the Import Spreadsheet Wizard.
8. Open the new table. It will be called Employees.
9. Close the database.

# Mastery Assessment

## Project 2-5: Choosing an appropriate template for a project

**Your company needs an inventory tracking database. You will find a template to create the database from and create a new table in the database with specific fields.**

1. Create a new database based on the template, Desktop Product Inventory. Name the new database **Northwind Traders Inventory**.
2. Create a new table in the database with the following Fields and data types:

| Field Name | Data Type |
|---|---|
| **Inventory Number** | **Number** |
| **Inventory Category** | **Short Text** |
| **Inventory Description** | **Long Text** |
| **Date Established** | **Date/Time** |
| **Currently in Stock** | **Yes/No** |

3. Enter three records of your choice into the table.

## Project 2-6: Importing and editing Excel data in a database

**You need to import an Excel spreadsheet into an existing database and also edit the data once it is imported into Access.**

1. From the Access02lessons folder, open the file, **Northwind Traders Fields**. Save the database as **Project2-6_done**.
2. Using the External Data Ribbon tab, import the spreadsheet titled, **Northwind Traders Quarterly Sales** into your database. You will need to import the data from the sheet titled, Qtr 1.
3. After the Qtr 1 sheet data is imported into Access, open the new table and delete the heading rows containing the spreadsheet's titles, rename the fields (columns), and set some data types where appropriate in the Access table.
4. Close the table and database.

# NOTES

Printed in the USA
K065473SCI092517 01S29053000000002280

# NOTES